SIXTH EDITION

The Process of Management

Strategy, Action, Results

William H. Newman
Columbia Graduate School of Business

E. Kirby Warren
Columbia Graduate School of Business

Andrew R. McGill
University of Michigan

Prentice-Hall, Inc., Englewood Cliffs, New Jersey 07632

Library of Congress Cataloging-in-Publication Data

Newman, William Herman (date)
  The process of management.

  Includes bibliographies and index.
    1. Industrial management. I. Warren, E. Kirby.
II. McGill, Andrew R. III. Title.
HD31.N484 1987   658.4   86-18707
ISBN 0-13-723602-6

Editorial/production supervision: Marjorie Borden
Interior design: Judith A. Matz-Coniglio
Cover design: Jules Perlmutter
Manufacturing buyer: Ed O'Dougherty/Barbara Kittle
Photo research: Chris Carey
Cover photo: Michael Melford/Peter Arnold, Inc.

Printed in the United States of America

10 9 8 7 6 5 4 3 2 1

ISBN 0-13-723602-6 01

Prentice-Hall International (UK) Limited, *London*
Prentice-Hall of Australia Pty. Limited, *Sydney*
Prentice-Hall Canada Inc., *Toronto*
Prentice-Hall Hispanoamericana, S.A., *Mexico*
Prentice-Hall of India Private Limited, *New Delhi*
Prentice-Hall of Japan, Inc., *Tokyo*
Prentice-Hall of Southeast Asia Pte. Ltd., *Singapore*
Editora Prentice-Hall do Brasil, Ltda., *Rio de Janeiro*
Prentice-Hall, Inc., *Englewood Cliffs, New Jersey*

Contents

PART II Planning

PART VI Managing in Diverse Settings

24 Managing Service Businesses 593

Index 617

Preface

U.S. managers are on trial. Slow economic growth, foreign competition, and industry restructuring have put an end to complacency about our managerial supremacy. The mood is now sober; managers must increase productivity if the country is to retain its leadership role. Fortunately, we know how to manage much better than we are doing; our crucial task is putting that knowledge to work.

Currently, managers face a mixed future. New technologies—electronics, CAD/CAM manufacturing, dazzling communications, and transportation—offer exciting opportunities. At the same time, there is strong competitive pressure for zero defects, customer service, on-time delivery, and lower costs. This combination of opportunity and pressure calls for tough, well-prepared management—a clear shift "back to basics."

Mission of This Book

This book focuses on educating present and future managers to meet the challenges emphasized above. We assume that most students using this book expect to be managers for most of their careers. Thus their primary interest will be concepts that they can apply as professional managers.

To serve this audience most effectively, the book must do more than describe organizations and managerial problems. Concepts that are presented should meet an additional test: Can they be applied to improve productivity?

In both business firms and business schools, core management concepts—ideas that have been widely tested in actual practice—are receiving renewed emphasis. The rise of foreign competitors prods us to be more diligent in using our strengths. Just as basic skills in English and math are back on center stage in elementary education, the fundamental ideas of planning, organizing, leading, and controlling again are central to management education.

Focusing on management fundamentals has a double benefit. In addition to building a solid foundation for action on today's problems, mastery of fundamentals provides a base for dealing with *future* unexpected situations. Future managers surely will face an array of new issues (as outlined in Chap. 3); adapting management structures to these changes will be crucial. During this adjusting process, slips or oversights are likely unless the managers involved are aware of the complete management cycle. They need a way of acting—a model—that leads to desired results even when the specific facts change rapidly.

Each of the authors of this book is actively engaged in front-line research and in experimenting with management design and development. For example, McGill—our new co-author—is an experienced news media executive who is just completing a Ph.D. in organization behavior at The University of Michigan. Appropriately, these research exposures are embedded in concepts presented in the book. However, our major aim is to help students grasp accepted fundamentals of managing. New frontiers can be confronted most effectively with this underpinning.

So, *management fundamentals for the future* is the dominant theme. We are deeply concerned that today's and tomorrow's managers master the underlying management concepts—not just know the terminology, but be skilled in applying the ideas in business firms. We hope that you share this concern.

Distinctive Features of the Book

1. Our *target audience* is managers—present and future managers. We want them to be more effective as a result of studying this book.

    Each chapter draws substantially on research findings. However, we have reorganized and restated this material into operational terms—issues that managers confront, and approaches that they can use. This reformulation helps practicing managers build bridges between the actual problems they face and the more abstract research concepts. Also, the operational view is much more appealing to professionally oriented students who conceive of themselves in managerial roles.

2. Two sets of cases are provided. To our knowledge, no other text provides both kinds of cases.

    Each chapter has a *Management-in-Action* case. These are short, fast-reading accounts of some action taken by an identified, well-known company. Their primary purpose is to stimulate interest in the subject discussed in the accompanying chapter, and to help students sense real-life problems encountered by managers.

    Managerial Decision cases are placed at the end of each Part of the book. These are much longer than the Management-in-Action cases; they present multi-dimensional situations that call for careful diagnosis and balanced judgment. Such cases help students develop skill in applying managerial concepts, and also to see the interdependence of the sub-processes of managing.

3. The book *combines the time-tested "management process" framework with insights emerging from behavioral research.* The process framework is operational for professional managers, as its widespread use throughout the Western world attests. By linking behavioral concepts to this process framework, the behavioral ideas also become applicable by managers.

4. The management ideas presented can be readily *applied to a wide range of businesses:* large and small, manufacturing and service, local and international. Not all the considerations and constraints are discussed, of course, but the framework relates to managing in general. Text examples, a diversity of cases, and especially the three chapters in Part VI all develop the theme that the core elements of managing are similar, even though specific action is contingent upon each local setting.

5. The issue of *improving productivity* receives repeated emphasis. Future managers will not have the luxury of being casual about productivity. Survival in the competition for resources will require high output. Consequently, one vital consideration in all managerial actions should be the impact of such action on the quality and volume of output. We systematically remind the reader of this "fact of life" throughout the book.

What's New in This Edition

The present edition of this book is a substantial revision of its predecessors.

1. Three of the six Parts have been recast beyond recognition. These are Part I—The Current Challenge to Managers; Part IV—Leading; and Part VI—Managing in Diverse Settings.

2. The following chapters have been newly written: Chapter 2—Evolution of Management Thought; Chapter 3—Environmental Pressures; Chapter 8—Managerial Decision Making; Chapter 22—Managing Multinational Organizations; Chapter 23—Small Business Management and Entrepreneurship; Chapter 24—Managing Service Businesses. Other chapters were heavily revised, and all were updated.

3. All of the Management-in-Action cases are new, and half of the managerial decision cases are being published here for the first time.

4. A concluding note on the "Impact on Productivity" has been added to each chapter as a recurring theme about the importance of attaining increases in actual results.

5. To make room for this new material, the continuing chapters have been tightened up and rearranged.

6. The net effect is a book more sharply focused on the mission outlined at the beginning of this preface.

Teaching Aids

This book provides opportunities for diverse mixes of text and cases. Each of the fourteen managerial decision cases can be used with several parts to provide integration. Also, each case has questions keyed to individual chapters. Some professors will prefer to use the cases to open up issues; others will use them for practice in application of concepts.

Each chapter has discussion questions and annotated suggestions for further reading. Students with managerial experience will, of course, fit their personal cases into the analytical framework.

Some choices in what to feature must be made because the total possibilities exceed the time available for a single course.

Acknowledgments

Helpful comments and suggestions have come from many professors, students, and managers using the previous editions of this book. To track these inputs through three authors and numerous drafts would defy the most sophisticated mapping technique. We are keenly aware that the cumulative influence has been substantial, and wish to acknowledge here our debt to this ambiguous social network.

More clear-cut is the incisive help of reviewers of the manuscript for this edition, especially the suggestions of Professor A. Aish of California State University, Los Angeles, Professor Ralph Katz of The Massachusetts Institute of Technology, and Professor Michael H. Korzenoiwski of La Salle College. For this we are grateful.

The inputs of two other persons are even sharper. Professor Narendra C. Bhandari of Pace University drew on his extensive contacts with small business to write Chapter 23. Our former co-author, Dr. Jerome E. Schnee, now vice president of Research-Cottrell, deserted academia to practice what he preached, but his insights and fine editorial hand persist throughout Parts II–V.

Professor Charles E. Summer of the University of Washington in Seattle has graciously permitted us to include two now-classic cases that he wrote for early editions of this book: Dayton Metal Works and Norman Manufacturing Company. We can only hope that the new Managerial Decision Case Studies in the present edition will raise management issues as well as these pillars do.

Our gratitude also goes to Camilla Koch of Columbia University, who ministered to literally thousands of pages—from deciphering abstruse handwritten notes to meticulous reading of proof.

At Prentice-Hall, we wish to thank Alison Reeves, Business editor; Marjorie Borden, production editor; Nancy Morgan Andreola, copy editor; and Judith A. Matz-Coniglio, designer.

The Samuel Bronfman Foundation, through its support of the Management Institute at Columbia Graduate School of Business, has nurtured this book through all its editions. We hope the Foundation is as enthusiastic as we are about the timely shift in focus of the present edition.

1

The Changing Role of Managers

LEARNING OBJECTIVES

After completing this chapter, you should be able to

1. Understand the significance of the role managers play in our society.
2. Describe major shifts that are enlarging the role of managers.
3. Explain why public opinion now stresses managers' ability to improve productivity.
4. Understand the management process framework and its use as the basis for the design of this book.
5. List and describe the major management processes.

Survival in today's world calls for the organized cooperation of many groups of people. Our capacity to rebuild the slums, eliminate pollution, give individuals an opportunity for self-expression, raise the standard of living, and achieve many other social objectives rests on joint activity. If individuals or even whole tribes attempt to be independently self-sufficient—producing their own food, clothing, and shelter—subsistence is meager at best. But when people join together in various enterprises, pooling their resources and exchanging their outputs, they grasp the means to flourish.

Managers are vital to such cooperative enterprises. They conceive of the service an enterprise can render, mobilize the necessary means of production, coordinate activities both within the enterprise and with the outside world, and inspire people associated with the enterprise to work toward common objectives. *Managers are the activating element.*

Management concepts are being vigorously applied in private firms, but the need for effective managers is just as pressing in nonprofit enterprises such as hospitals, training centers, space agencies, urban transport, and wildlife refuges. Whatever the end product or service, managers are essential to guide our efforts.

Briefly, then, *managing is the guidance, leadership, and control of the efforts of a group of individuals toward some common goal.* It is a special kind of activity, distinct from actual performance of the work. Clarifying the group's goals, coordinating members' efforts, allocating scarce resources, representing the group in negotiations with other groups, making tough decisions so that group activities may proceed, inspiring cooperative action, exercising discipline when a member is lazy or goes off on a tangent—all are necessary for effective and efficient group action to achieve desired results. Without managers to perform these activities, the group's output would be inadequate indeed.

Broadening Scope

The role of managers is becoming more challenging, tougher. Managers today are expected to do more and have more skills than they did a generation ago. Four ways that the emphasis is shifting, highlighted in Figure 1–1, call for special attention.

1. **Things → people.** When management concepts were being formulated early in the century, the focus was on things—on mining coal, building roads, making automobiles, selling clothes and soap. A company that manufactured physical products was the dominant organization around which concepts for managing developed. And for making and moving things, an *engineering* viewpoint was the most relevant. Indeed, it is

no accident that early management consultants were called management engineers.[1]

Today, however, more and more attention is being given to people rather than to things. We now speak of converting engineers into managers, which implies that human issues often pose more difficulties for managers than do physical problems. The guidance and motivation of workers, for instance, is an ever-present task in our turbulent society. Building teamwork calls for skills quite different from those needed for designing a plant (although the physical layout may affect team behavior). In managing almost any activity, the people involved—their values and their behavior—are very important.

Note that this shift in emphasis from things to people does not suggest that managers can skip over problems of equipment, materials, computers, and other physical things. These continue to be essential. Rather, the people aspects must *also* be managed. Which equipment people select and what they do with it often is the key to successful results. So managing people must be accomplished *in addition* to managing things. And people are often more difficult to control. They change their minds and talk back; machines don't.

2. **Reactor → innovator.** For many years managers were widely regarded as individuals who merely adapted to their situation. If demand for products fell off, they cut back production; if a new source of low-cost raw materials opened up, they switched suppliers; if labor became scarce, they raised wage rates to get the workers they needed. According to this conception, managers performed an essential function—responding to changing conditions—but their actions were dictated by forces beyond their control. The early economists clearly held this view; consequently, they gave scant attention to the problems of management, and that blind spot permeates much of economic literature to this day.

Actually, modern managers go well beyond adapting; they must be *proactive* as well as *reactive* and exercise a positive influence to make things happen. When they anticipate that the need for their product will drop off, managers seek new products or services in order to maintain employment of the resources they have mobilized; they take the initiative in looking for cheaper sources of energy and promoting their development; they sponsor research for more economical methods of production; they try to anticipate manpower needs and train people to fill them. In short, they are a dynamic, innovating force.[2]

This self-confident, aggressive attitude reflects a deep-seated sense of obligation, or mission. Managers are not complete masters of their activi-

[1] A leading trade association of management consultants is still named Association of Consulting Management Engineers (ACME).

[2] S. Ramo, *The Management of Innovative Technological Corporations* (New York: John Wiley, 1980).

ties, of course; indeed, they must be highly sensitive to a wide range of pressures and restrictions. But managers do more than simply adjust passively. They *initiate* changes in their operating situation and *follow through* with action that, to some extent, makes dreams come true.

The pressure for managers to innovate is increasing. Unemployment remains at unacceptable levels; foreign imports—from autos to zippers—are replacing domestic products; college students want exciting jobs combined with free, long weekends; and the list goes on. Because our society relies on free enterprise, and within an enterprise it is the managers who initiate change, managers are on the spot. They are expected to innovate.

3. **Internal director → public executor.**   During their early development, management concepts dealt primarily with internal operations of a company or department. The task was "to get our house in order," by clarifying jobs and relationships, establishing dependable procedures, and the like. Indeed, in the early part of the century, each department was like a little fiefdom with its own way of working, and little outside interference was permitted. Improvements in management were usually made within separate departments, one at a time. The walls around these separate estates were high, and a department manager was judged largely on what occurred within those walls. When, following World War II, it became more common to study the management of a total company, attention still centered on internal direction.

No longer is this inward focus adequate. The fiefdoms and dukedoms must increasingly operate as parts of a total nation. Not only is it more efficient that way—avoiding the reinvention of the wheel—but it is also essential, because all sorts of government regulations constrain what managers can do today. Fair employment laws affect who can be hired or promoted. Laws regarding publicly traded corporations affect accounting and financing practices. The Food and Drug Administration (FDA) regulates what medicines can be sold and what claims are made about them. Disposing of factory wastes may determine what can be manufactured. In these and a myriad of other ways, managers must adapt their internal operations to external guidelines.

Figure 1.1   Enlargement of the role of managers.

Restraints are only the tip of the iceberg. Managers are expected to take the lead, at least to some extent, in helping to meet a diverse set of social goals. These goals include

1. *Racial equality and urban renewal.* Society must make racial equality meaningful; interwoven with this is urban renewal.
2. *Pollution control.* Our material achievements are fast overtaking the finite capacity of our natural environment, as is painfully evidenced by air and water pollution.
3. *Health, education, and welfare.* An ever-increasing share of our natural resources is being directed into such things as medical care, education, public recreation, pensions.
4. *Guns and butter.* Our combined space and military expenditures are already on a scale that challenges our ability to have both guns and butter.
5. *Inflation.* Overriding this array of social aims is control of the crippling effects of inflation.

These new priorities, and others that will undoubtedly emerge, are *additions* to the long-standing goals of a rising standard of living, full employment, national security, and so on; they are not replacements. We want the new benefits without sacrificing any of the old ones.

It is unclear how much initiative managers should take with respect to such problems. Moreover, new social goals tend to be vague. No agreement exists as to how much, by what date, and at what cost the new goals are to be achieved. In fact, it is managers who are dealing with specific operations that force realism into the lofty objectives. Managers of necessity confront social reform at the level of concrete action.

Although the degree to which managers should become involved with social reform is debatable, these issues cannot be brushed aside. At a minimum, managers must consider the indirect effect on such issues as they make decisions regarding internal operations.

4. **ROI → "productivity."** A reasonable return on investment (ROI) is vital for the survival of any company. Managers dare not overlook this requirement for continuing health. However, the measurement of "return," or profit, is so surrounded with traditions and safeguards that it is a crude standard. Also, it is an abstraction removed from *how* the company operates, much in the same way that the score at a football game reveals little about how well the teams actually played.

Consequently, managers need a standard that tells them more than the ROI does about the underlying strength of their enterprise. *Productivity* is such a concept. It relates the attractiveness and quantity of company output to the various costs of creating that output.

In this book, the term *productivity* is used broadly. Both the output and the costs have many elements. The *output* of goods or services must be desired by customers: The product must fill a market need. A total package of attributes is involved: function, quality, durability, repair service, availability and delivery, financing, instructions for use, and other features insofar as they are valued by the consumer.

On the *cost* side, productivity is concerned with direct expenses, dependable and continuing flow of material and labor inputs, modern technology, effective use of production capacity, low pollution and other side effects that are acceptable to the community, and other arrangements that utilize resources in an optimum way. The aim, of course, is to create packages of output that have a value that exceeds the full array of costs.

With such a definition, when we say that the productivity of a United States automobile plant—to cite a much debated case—should exceed the productivity of a Japanese plant, the challenge to managers is broad.

A business with good productivity will normally enjoy an attractive ROI—assuming a sound financial structure. But switching the emphasis to productivity from ROI raises many more operating and long-range implications. With the accent on productivity, managing has to be more than a numbers game.

NEED FOR BASIC MANAGEMENT APPROACH

The role of managers is expanding, as is indicated by the rise in relative importance of people, innovation, public sector activities, and productivity just described. Some managers might prefer to stick with traditional things, reacting, internal direction, and ROI; these all continue to be necessary, and less initiative and risk is required in dealing with them. But society is demanding more of managers. In short, managers have been given power over the use of critical resources, and they can't sidestep the broader challenge.

Fortunately, a valuable body of management concepts now exists. Some concepts are supported by scholarly research; many more are distilled from the experiences of thousands of managers. The practical problem—and the mission of this book—is to select and organize these ideas into a framework that will help present and future managers deal with their shifting roles.

Designing such a framework is not easy. Because management concepts have been developed in different settings, and because observers stress different viewpoints, the concepts are far from a neat set of rules. Actually, the field is very dynamic. Needs change, as already noted; actors change; new models—such as matrix management or Japanese quality circles—appear frequently; new technology—computers, for instance—becomes available. Current ideas will be refined and elaborated in the future, as is true of knowledge in all fields.

As a result of all this turbulence, too many recent books on management deal only with the latest fashion or focus on some one point of view. In contrast, most potential managers need a basic approach that combines and integrates the various one-sided treatments.

The *management process approach* is best suited to this back-to-basics need. It deals with the underlying activities of managers in a way that managers find applies to their day-to-day actions. At the same time, the management process approach is general enough to be applicable to all sorts of organizations and sizes of companies. It is by far the analytical framework most widely used by practicing managers to think through their managerial problems.

This approach divides the total task of managing into four subprocesses: planning, organizing, leading, and controlling. Each of these subprocesses is a crucial part of the work of managers at all levels, from supervisor to the chief executive. Because these four elements serve as the framework of this book, an overview is presented here.

Planning

Speaking generally, *planning* is deciding in advance what is to be done; that is, a plan is a projected course of action. Considered in this light, planning is a widespread human behavior: The venture capitalist plans a new enterprise, a marketing vice president plans a sales campaign, the lawyer plans the presentation of the next case, a social worker plans relief for an unemployed woman, a parent plans lunch, the carpenter plans the repair of a screen door.

Managers make many judgments that are not plans. For instance, a manager may decide that Zip Zilch is honest, that wholesale prices will probably rise this year, that existing wage data are an adequate sample of the market. Such judgments are often necessary in *arriving* at plans, but they are *not* plans because they do not stipulate action to be taken.

To sharpen the focus, managers must distinguish between various kinds of plans. For instance, more and more companies are using *strategy* as their dominant, overriding plan. Strategy defines the scope of activities, selects a basis for excellence, sets targets, and chooses key moves to reach those targets. This central plan then guides more detailed planning.

Specific planning is a crucial step in executing any strategy. Managers consulting with each other and with the people who will carry out the plans set *goals* for each subdivision. They establish *policies* and *standard methods* to guide those who do the work, and they develop *schedules* to keep the work moving toward the objectives. Then they readjust these plans periodically in light of new information and changes in operating conditions.

Planning can be improved if the basic stages in making a rational decision are understood: diagnosing the problem, finding good alternative solutions, projecting the results of each alternative, and, finally, selecting the course of action. The means by which decisions are made within an organization deserve special attention.

Organizing

Once the work of an enterprise grows beyond what a single craftsperson can do, *organization* becomes necessary. The various tasks must be assigned to different people, and their efforts must be coordinated. As the enterprise expands, this process leads to departments and divisions, each of which has its particular mission. One way to think about the resulting organization is as a complex machine—say, an airplane designed for transatlantic passenger service. Each part of a plane performs a necessary function—supplying power, pressure, heat, steering, communication, and so forth—*and* the different parts are so carefully balanced and fitted together that changing any one of them often calls for an adjustment in most others.

In addition to dividing the necessary work into departments, sections, and individual jobs, each manager has to decide how much freedom of action each subordinate will be allowed. At a television station, for instance, the advertising manager may have a great deal of flexibility in deciding where to solicit advertisements, whereas the announcer must stick closely to a prepared script.

A manager must also view the organization as a social arrangement, because it is composed of people rather than physical objects. The people who are assigned tasks are independent, self-respecting individuals with a variety of motives; informal groups influence the way people respond to managerial action; and the attitudes of all these people are continually shifting and evolving. In organizing, then, managers must seek ways of getting the necessary work done while building a social structure that helps meet the needs of the people doing the work.

Leading

Planning and organizing set the stage. Then *leading* triggers action. This "make happen" phase of managing calls for motivating people through personal leadership. All sorts of issues are involved; including individual needs, group behavior, informal organization, conflict, internal politics, and communications, just to name a few. These forces may either support or work against company plans.

Managers must deal effectively on a person-to-person basis in order to activate plans. Selecting a suitable leadership style, communicating, and giving orders require skills that differ significantly from planning skills.

Controlling

For a ship to reach its destination without sailing far off course, the captain must regularly "take his bearings." Managers likewise must measure their progress if they are to reach their objectives. And when they discover that operations are not proceeding according to plan, they take corrective action to get things back on course; or, if this is not feasible, they readjust their plans. This process of measuring progress, comparing it with plans, and taking corrective action is called *control*.

Control is not a simple matter. Measuring intangibles such as customer goodwill or executive morale poses difficulties, and devising corrective action that both overcomes the immediate difficulty and creates a favorable climate for future performance calls for ingenuity. Moreover, the dispersal of activities that results from organization creates problems of just who should control what.

Integrating the Concepts

Now a word of caution. The study of any complex subject like management must be divided into parts, and each must be examined carefully. This is the pattern we will follow in this book, with separate Parts devoted to planning, organizing, leading, and controlling. *All the while, the reader must keep in mind that the subprocesses are interdependent.* For instance, managers cannot expect to maintain control over their departments unless they also follow sound practices in their other duties. A well-conceived program, workable policies, well-understood organization, empathetic leadership—all contribute to obtaining the desired results. The more effectively these tasks are carried out, the easier will be control.

Like the nervous system in the human body, control is only one of the vital subprocesses in effective management. Planning, organizing, and leading are also essential. If we change one, we may need to redesign the others (see Figure 1-2). Fortunately, this interaction is a potential source of strength. By designing an organization that is suited to company plans and reinforcing both with compatible leadership and controls, a manager can generate high synergistic force.

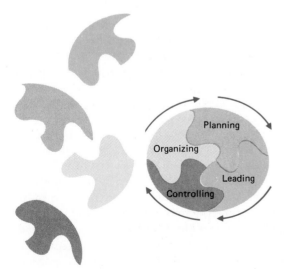

Figure 1.2 Management is so complicated a process that separation of its subprocesses is necessary for full understanding, but we should never lose sight of the way the processes fit together to form the whole.

LEARNING FROM THIS BOOK

This book provides you with two main sorts of learning aids: text and cases. They can be studied separately, or in various combinations.

Text Focuses on Managerial Processes

The text is organized around the four fundamental management processes of planning, organizing, leading, and controlling. Inputs from the other approaches to general management are woven into this process framework.

Thinking of management as a process has great advantages. The process approach is (1) *operational,* because it expresses ideas in terms of actions a manager must take; (2) *comprehensive,* embracing the major tasks of managing; (3) *universal,* in that all managers should give some attention to each part of the process; and (4) a *key for harnessing* executive action to the mission of managers as discussed in the beginning of this chapter.

A Framework for Managerial Thinking

After the introduction, a separate Part of the book examines each of the four elements—planning, organizing, leading, and controlling—with four or five chapters in each Part. The chapters deal with even narrower subprocesses.

Such a systematic view of management provides a convenient device for (1) diagnosing complex management problems and (2) working on improvements at one stage without losing sight of other stages.

But a framework that helps us think in an orderly fashion is not necessarily a step-by-step procedure that must be followed. Actually, when dealing with a concrete management problem, the available information is not neatly classified and labeled; instead, a great array of facts hits at once, while some data remain stubbornly hidden. In response to such confusion, a manager's thoughts tend to flit first to one subject and then to another. So the chief purpose of a conceptual framework, such as the systematic examination of the management process in this book, is to help people quickly place diverse ideas in a useful order.

The framework is more than a series of pigeonholes to tuck ideas into, however, for among the pigeonholes there is a rational relationship that is known in advance. Thus, when mentally classifying a new bit of information as bearing on the long-range objectives of Department A, we can immediately relate it to a host of other ideas we have stored in our minds; the piece of information then takes on relative meaning because it contributes to our comprehension of the total situation. Humans have advanced from a primitive state largely by developing orderly ways of thinking about problems; in proposing a systematic approach to management, then, managers are simply following this time-proven method.

In the final summarizing part of this book, the management process viewpoint serves as a tool for analyzing three types of companies that will become even more important in the years ahead: international organizations, small businesses, and service businesses.

One further introductory note: Because people with diverse backgrounds talk about management, words are used in different ways. Since this is so, we should clarify our terminology. For ease of discussion, we shall use *manager, executive,* and *administrator* synonymously. And when we deal with person-to-person relationships, we may use *supervisor* or even *boss* to designate the manager who sits *immediately* above a subordinate in the organizational hierarchy. For these terms, this approach simply follows common usage. Other words, which have more precise meanings, will be defined as they are encountered.

Impact on Productivity

Productivity, as described earlier, is a good way to think about how well a company is contributing to social needs. It stresses both the output of needed goods and services and the total cost of creating that output. So a pertinent question about any management practice is, "How will this practice affect productivity?"[3]

To keep that key question before readers, the conclusion of each chapter in this book will include a paragraph or two on *Impact on Productivity*. These brief sections will repeatedly underscore the fact that effective management can and should make significant social contributions.

Cases for Learning to Apply Concepts

Cases offer an opportunity to start applying general concepts to specific situations, and discussing proposed solutions with other people will give you some check on how well you are able to apply the concepts. At best, these cases can offer only a beginning in the practice that is necessary for developing managerial proficiency. But this beginning is important, for it *builds a bridge* between general concepts and concrete situations; and we hope it will establish a pattern for the use of such concepts in real life.

You will find two sorts of cases in this book.

Management-in-Action cases.   At the end of each chapter is a short case called "Management in Action." Each of these describes an incident or action in a well-known company that is related to the subject of the chapter. You can speculate about why the managers acted as they did. Was it wise behavior? Should other comparable companies do likewise? What can I learn from this?

Such cases make the ideas in the chapter more *meaningful*. Sometimes an idea may appear rather simple—even obvious—as explained in

[3]For a summary of several current approaches to improving productivity, see *Special Issue: Productivity,* the May 1985 issue of *Interfaces.* Also, see J. M. McInnes, "Corporate Management of Productivity: An Empirical Study," *Strategic Management Journal,* Oct. 1984.

the text, and only when applied to a real problem will its full and complex meaning begin to unfold. Applying concepts helps to clarify and reinforce their meaning.

Managerial decision cases. The cases at the close of each Part are longer and more complicated. Here you will be asked, among other questions, what action the local manager should take.

These longer cases help overcome the unrealistic separations that are inevitable in any analytical treatment of an interdependent phenomenon. For example, we shall discuss planning, organizing, and leading separately. In actuality, the plans and policies of a company (Part II) are partly determined by the organizational structure (Part III), and vice versa. And the leadership style of an executive (Part IV) is somewhat influenced by the organizational structure. Thus, a manager must solve planning and leadership problems *along with* organization problems.

Most of these cases present a whole situation; that is, they do not merely illustrate the issues in any one chapter. Instead, they provide a way of viewing the interrelated application of various concepts from all chapters in a realistic, whole-problem sense. They provide a sense of the *system,* while the chapters enable concentration on the parts.

Moreover, these cases help show that we do not always have facts and concepts that cover all aspects of a complex management problem. As in medicine, management problems often include variables that theory does not explain; each situation has unique elements. At times, then, all the answers needed to solve a case *neatly* will not be found in the book. This can be frustrating. Nevertheless, it is a difficulty that has been faced by leaders through the ages. Actually, it is precisely this need to blend general concepts with the stubborn facts of a practical situation that makes management challenging and fascinating.

Because these managerial decision cases include confidential, often highly personal information, the actual names of companies and individuals have been disguised.

FOR FURTHER DISCUSSION

1. Using the items listed in Figure 1.1, compare the tasks of managers in a 1900 river ferryboat company with the tasks of managers in a 1990 passenger airline. In which organization would you prefer to work?

2. "In capitalistic countries each company must earn a profit to survive. In the final analysis, it's the bottom line that counts." Do you agree? Is profit a better measure of the effectiveness of managers than productivity? Explain.

3. "All we needed were tough times to bring us back to basics. Now that we are slipping behind other nations, we can expect much greater emphasis on productivity instead of all that behavioral and systems mumbo-jumbo." Comment.

4. "The primary function of any business is to offer products and/or services to those who can afford them and to do so in a way that is profitable to the firm. Thus the basic goal of a business is profit, its source is in the market, and its components are revenue and cost. The science of economics, which has for hundreds of years been devoted to studying these phenomena, is the major discipline for a business manager to draw on. Everything else should be viewed in the context of the economics approach." Do you agree? Explain your position.

5. Use the family household in which you spent most of your life to illustrate (a) planning, (b) organizing, (c) leading, and (d) controlling.

6. In what ways do you feel that the process of managing a large private corporation (a) differs from and (b) is similar to the process of managing equally large or larger public or nonprofit organizations, such as hospitals, universities, or government agencies?

7. Which of the four elements of management is likely to be most important in a small new business? A large mature business? Discuss.

8. The basic framework of this book is built around management processes—planning, organizing, leading, and controlling. An alternative framework would be to study the various disciplines that a manager draws on, such as economics, the behavioral sciences, operations research, and so on. What are the advantages of the "process" approach over the "discipline" approach? What are the limitations of each?

FOR FURTHER READING

Hirschhorn, L., *Beyond Mechanization*. Cambridge: MIT Press, 1984. Describes current shift in technology from simple mechanization to "flexible automation," then focuses on the impact of this shift on worker-machine relationships and on management. A short book, but not light reading.

Kantor, R. M., *The Change Masters: Innovation for Productivity in the American Corporation*. New York: Simon & Schuster, 1983. Penetrating sociological study of the conditions necessary to secure innovation in United States companies. Readable and challenging, but does assume background knowledge about life in a large corporation.

Newman, W. H. (ed.), *Managers for the Year 2000*. Englewood Cliffs, N.J.: Prentice-Hall, 1978. Report of a symposium that previews the year 2000 and the qualities managers will need in order to cope with future responsibilities.

Shetty, Y. K., "Management's Role in Declining Productivity," *California Management Review,* 25:1, Fall 1982. Builds a case for believing that management's preoccupation with growth, diversification, mergers, and short-run results has injured productivity.

Young, J. A., "Global Competition: The New Reality," *California Management Review,* Spring 1985. Summarizes findings of the President's Commission on Industrial Competitiveness, of which Young was chairman.

MANAGEMENT IN ACTION CASE 1
Helping Feed the Poor

For years, American corporations have been major contributors of dollars and time in efforts to solve some of the world's most pressing problems: hunger, poverty, and disease.

Corporations were called upon again in 1984 and 1985, when thousands of Ethiopians were dying of starvation. Many responded, but some companies complained that short-term reactions didn't encourage serious consideration of longer-term solutions.

One company, Computerland Corporation of Hayward, California, went to great lengths to express its controversial views. In a full-page advertisement in *The Wall Street Journal,* the company boldly told readers why it decided not to send money to help the hungry in Ethiopia.

Computerland said that the effort to gather money for starving Ethiopians

will not supply the long-term solution to the causes of hunger, which continue to devastate Sub-Saharan Africa and many other regions of the globe.

We at Computerland believe it is time for the brightest, most powerful minds in corporate America to develop the long-range programs that can eliminate world hunger permanently, before the end of this century.

Computerland argued that several studies had shown that enough food was available to feed the earth, and that the starvation dilemma was not one of food, but of distribution, resources, and logistics. To help underdeveloped countries address those problems, Computerland said, United States corporations should offer their "problem-solving abilities, management skills, business systems and . . . goal-oriented philosophy."

To channel those skills, Computerland said it had created a department to provide interested parties with information about programs, private relief agencies, and government organizations.

The company appealed to the corporations' business motives, arguing that revitalized economies in underdeveloped areas would lead to new markets, improved worker skills, enhanced international trade, and a stronger global financial system.

"But besides these business benefits, we ask you to consider the other, more personal benefits you will reap," Computerland said in its advertisement. "For when your actions as a business executive help improve the lives of others, you have successfully integrated your professional skills with your values as a human being."

Questions

1. Do you think that the managerial and technical skills of Computerland can be of help to the starving people in Sub-Saharan Africa? Explain how.
2. Should Computerland confine its contributions to this kind of aid?

For more information, see *The Wall Street Journal,* May 28, 1985.

APPLICATION CASES

To develop a sense of the array of issues facing managers in a business enterprise and to relate the concepts discussed in this chapter to concrete managerial situations, see the following managerial decision cases. The case questions particularly relevant to this chapter are listed by number after each case name.

2

Evolution of Management Thought

LEARNING OBJECTIVES

After completing this chapter you should be able to

1. Explain how management concepts have expanded in scope and dimension during the last century.
2. Describe the major turning points in the development of current management concepts.
3. Identify five broad stages in the evolution of management thought, and place at least ten more specific viewpoints or approaches (such as budgeting) within these stages.
4. Describe the need for an integrating framework that pulls the diverse approaches into understandable relationships.
5. Note the acceleration of change in systematic management thought.
6. List a dozen individuals whose names are often used to identify a particular management concept or approach.

The careful study of "managing" is a recent activity. In contrast to philosophy, language, or physics, management is just emerging as an academic field. Indeed, 1986 was the 100th birthday of the first *scientific* study of managing—by Frederick W. Taylor and his colleagues in mechanical engineering—and the 50th birthday of the Academy of Management, the leading association of professors interested in the process of managing. And both these births involved only a few individuals. It is only within the last thirty years that professional management has become a major worldwide movement.

The novelty of the study of management makes the field dynamic, a bit raw, challenging. Fresh ideas are being tried. Research evidence on which practices work well in what circumstances—and why—is still being accumulated.

To help you appreciate where management concepts come from and the emphasis and bias they inevitably contain, this chapter traces the evolution of present management thought. This review will show how recent many of the ideas are. You can also note how the concepts are being enriched, perhaps complicated, by new perspectives.

Multiple Influences

Tracing the development of management concepts is strongly affected by three factors:

1. Managing is an activity that is as old as civilization. Whenever people start working together to reach common goals, managing their efforts becomes necessary. The builder of the Egyptian pyramids, the captain of the first sailing ship, the leader of an army brigade—all were involved in elementary managing. We have inherited useful ideas from these *centuries of experience*. However, the task of managing has changed markedly—in size, complexity, use of specialists, attitudes of workers, available technology, and societal expectations. Managing in this new setting calls for an array of new techniques. And it is this new mode of managing that must be the center of our attention.

2. The idea that managing can, and should, be studied as a *distinct social process* is actually a twentieth-century concept. Formerly, how a person managed was usually largely determined by that person's personality. Historians focused on unusual leaders. Physical processes, such as making steel or sailing by the stars, were studied and written down. But social processes, including management, received scant attention. Universities were among the laggards. Economics was as close to management as university professors came, and the economists of the last century buried management beneath their convenient assumptions.

Figure 2.1
Construction of the
ancient Egyptian
pyramids required
complex managerial
skills.

3. After the dam was broken and management was recognized as a vital activity, specialists moved in with their own particular views of life. First came the mechanical engineers, then the accountants, soon to be followed by vocational psychologists, lawyers, managerial economists, institutionalists, historians, group psychologists, sociologists, and industrial anthropologists. Each provided analytical techniques and some insights. But these contributions have been *one-sided viewpoints*—only part of the picture. Now the main task is to weave these partial insights into an integrated framework.

Because managing is so old, but has been carefully studied only recently and is now being approached from many viewpoints, the history of management thought does not consist of a series of clear-cut steps. Instead, this development is as complex as that of all the countries of the world and their distinct histories and heritage.

In this chapter, rather than listing names of the many diverse contributors, a broader view of the mainstreams of ideas is presented. Awareness of these primary sources will help today's managers fit fresh ideas into their broad understanding of the total management process. As new ideas are proposed—in an article, speech, or conversation—managers (and aspiring managers) can place this new thought into context with accumulated knowledge from the past. The aim is to build an integrated grasp of management, not just a storehouse of miscellaneous facts.

The wellsprings of ideas about managing include

1. Early glimmerings
2. Scientific management
3. Cost and efficiency
4. Basic management processes
5. Behavioral research
6. Strategy and values

EARLY GLIMMERINGS

Jethro's Counsel to Moses

One of the earliest bits of advice on how to manage is found in the Bible, in the book of Exodus. When Moses was leading the Israelites on the long, hot trek out of Egypt, he tried to be a one-man manager. Fortunately, his father-in-law, Jethro—the first management consultant on record—came for a visit.

> Moses sat to judge the people; and the people stood about Moses from the morning unto the evening. And when Moses' father-in-law saw all that he did . . . he said unto him: "The thing that thou doest is not good. Thou wilt surely wear away, both thou and this people with thee; for the thing is too heavy for thee—thou are not able to perform it thyself alone.
>
> "Hearken now unto my voice . . . Be thou for the people Godward, and bring thou the cases unto God. [Then] thou shalt teach [the people] the statutes and the laws, and shalt show them the way wherein they must walk, and the work that they must do.
>
> "Moreover thou shalt provide out of all the people able men, such as fear God, men of truth, hating unjust gain; and place such over them, to be rulers of thousands, rulers of hundreds, rulers of fifties, and rulers of tens; and let them judge the people at all seasons. And it shall be that every great matter they shall bring unto thee, but every small matter they shall judge themselves. So shall it be easier for thyself, and they shall bear the burden with thee. If thou shalt do this thing . . . then thou shalt be able to endure, and all this people shall go to their place in peace."
>
> So . . . Moses chose able men out of all Israel, and made them heads over the people, rulers of thousands, rulers of hundreds, rulers of fifties, and rulers of tens. And they judged the people at all seasons; the hard cases they brought unto Moses, but every small matter they judged themselves.

Note that Jethro dealt with three elements in managing. (1) *Planning:* With God's help, Moses was to develop what we now call policies and procedures, and then teach these behavioral guides to his followers. (2)

Organization: Then Moses was to decentralize, creating a managerial hierarchy ranging in today's terminology from vice presidents to first-line supervisors. Authority to decide daily matters was to be delegated far down this line. (3) *Leadership Qualifications:* There were no management training courses in those days, but Jethro did stress basic ability and character, which still apply in the twentieth century—"able men, such as fear God, men of truth, hating unjust gain."

Decentralized Management of Cyrus the Great

Cyrus the Great of Persia provides another ancient example of managerial insight. In the sixth century B.C., Cyrus decided to expand his kingdom into an empire composed of many kingdoms. He then faced a managerial problem similar to running a modern conglomerate with many subsidiaries. Each kingdom had its own needs and traditions, and local management was better suited to deal with these.

Nevertheless, some kind of unifying direction and control was necessary to hold the Persian empire together. For this purpose Cyrus relied on three devices—power, finance, and information. Lacking the convenience today's chief executive officer (CEO) has of an accepted legal system and stockholders' meetings, Cyrus retained power by centralizing command of the army. No local kingdom had its own army; instead, each depended on "headquarters" for this service. A second centrally controlled function was tax collection and the reallocation of those funds as Cyrus saw fit. Today, the central control of the flow of funds is a primary method that large corporations use to guide the actions of their subsidiaries. Third, Cyrus sent to each kingdom a loyal observer who reported regularly on how well the local management was handling the local activities and needs of that country. Home rule (decentralization) was encouraged *provided* the nation continued to be economically sound, socially stable, and loyal. But Cyrus needed what we now call a *management information system* to be sure that localized managers were in fact effective.

Incidentally, the Romans, some five centuries later, adopted a very different management approach than that used in the Persian empire. The Romans tried to convert any conquered territory to the Roman way of life; language, government, architecture, entertainment—all were Romanized. A counterpart today of the Roman approach is the way IBM follows common practices worldwide.

Managerial Responses to the Industrial Revolution

The Industrial Revolution, starting in the eighteenth century, brought about a drastic technological shift in the production and distribution of goods. This shift created the need for a new kind of business organization—the forerunners of business firms that we know today. But for these early enterprises to grow, they had to devise a managerial system that suited the new technology.

One development during the Industrial Revolution was increased *di-*

vision of labor, in which each worker performs the same limited task over and over. This forerunner of the automobile assembly line was strongly advocated by Charles Babbage in the early 1800s because the time required for a worker to learn his or her factory job could be lowered significantly. Such concentration on worker efficiency—which Babbage, a mathematics professor, typifies—set the stage for Scientific Management, the founding approach to modern management.

Also during the early 1800s, Robert Owen, a manager of cotton mills in Scotland, experimented with increasing worker productivity by improving working conditions. He cut the working day from 13 hours to 10½ hours, built better housing for workers, and operated a company store where necessities of life could be purchased at low prices. Although Owen advocated such reforms on humanitarian grounds, he also argued that the reforms would increase profits because of improved health and morale of the workers. As we shall note frequently throughout this book, at the close of the twentieth century, managers continue to seek ways to improve worker morale even though working conditions have vastly improved. Owen was right in his basic premise: Conditions of work, employee morale, and productivity are indeed interrelated.

Clearly, the techniques of managing have been evolving for a long, long time, as the bits of history just discussed show. Until very recently, however, this learning from experience was never summarized and integrated.

SCIENTIFIC MANAGEMENT

The first systematic study of management in the United States was conducted by production engineers. Frederick W. Taylor and his associates shifted an interest in production bonuses to a focus on management, and thus launched what became known in 1910 as *Scientific Management.*[1]

Before bonuses could be set, Taylor insisted, the best conditions and manner of doing a job must be determined.

1. First Taylor analyzed in detail the method for doing each task, seeking simplified motions and newly designed equipment that would reduce human effort and speed output. He then set the "one best way" to perform each task.
2. To ensure that machines operated properly, he insisted on preventive maintenance and on keeping properly sharpened tools in a central toolroom.

[1]See F. W. Taylor, *Shop Management,* first published in 1903 and republished in his book, *Principles of Scientific Management* in 1911 by Harper and Brothers. Also see E. A. Locke, "The Ideas of Fredrick W. Taylor: An Evaluation," *Academy of Management Review,* January 1982.

3. For these methods to work, raw materials could not vary, so he set up raw-material specifications and quality-control checks.

4. Also, to prevent delays due to time lost in giving workers new assignments, careful production scheduling, dispatching, and internal-transport systems were established.

5. Finally, workers suited to the newly designed jobs had to be selected and trained.

Only when all of these conditions were met was Taylor ready to use time study to determine a standard day's work.

This sort of approach creates a minor revolution in a shop or hospital that has operated in a haphazard, traditional manner—a revolution in the method of work, in planning and control by management, and in productivity. Nevertheless, these basic concepts, nurtured in a machine shop, have been adapted to all sorts of production operations in plants throughout the world.

Scientific Management caught the public imagination, much as computers have done more recently, and hundreds of articles were written and speeches made on the new way of managing. Unfortunately, when the movement became popular during and after World War I, managers were often unwilling to support the long and careful studies that are necessary, and incompetent consultants made ghastly mistakes. In spite of these difficulties, though, techniques born of Scientific Management have become an integral part of modern management.

The founders of Scientific Management made two great contributions. First, they invented and developed an array of techniques that vastly improves productivity in a shop. The United States could never have developed into the leading industrial nation of the world without these concepts. Second, and more important, they fundamentally altered the way we think about management problems. Instead of relying on tradition and personal intuition, students of management now believe that any management problem should be subjected to the same kind of critical analysis, inventive experimentation, and objective evaluation that Taylor applied in his machine shop. Although Taylor himself did not apply his ideas outside of production operations, he did insist that his essential contribution was "an attitude of mind" that could be applied to any management problem.

COST AND EFFICIENCY

The period between the world wars saw widespread interest in "rationalizing" the major departments within a company. This included an array of systems and techniques that increased efficiency in each functional department. In many respects such rationalization was an application of the "attitude of mind" recommended by Taylor.

Most of these new systems, such as the layout of sales territories, could be used only in the specialized departments for which they were designed. However, several of the techniques that started within a single department have found widespread application. For instance, approaches to personnel management (now often called "human resources management") have become tools for managers everywhere. Financial and other quantitative tools are now also important parts of a modern manager's kit.

Personnel Management

A variety of activities were merged into personnel management in the 1920s. Safety work, corporate training schools (originally founded to prepare immigrants to pass citizenship tests), central hiring (using psychological tests developed during World War I), welfare activities such as lunchrooms, athletic teams, and perhaps company housing, and union relations—all become part of new departments charged with recruiting and maintaining a competent work force. Personnel departments have since become a major staff service to help companies deal with their ever-changing human resource needs. And skills in selecting, training, and motivating subordinates are now recognized as an essential part of every manager's job.

The many technical aspects of personnel work need not be addressed here. This surge of attention to the personnel aspects of company operations does impact general management, however. For example, job definitions—used for recruiting, promoting, training, evaluating, and setting pay scales—encourage managers to sharply define their organizations. Long-range personnel development makes sense only when it can be tied directly into company planning. Company policies regarding compensation, employee services, communication, and discipline all affect which leadership style will be most effective. Thus, general management draws heavily on the more detailed work of personnel management.

Budgeting

Financial budgets are among the oldest means we have for controlling operations. Governments started using rudimentary budgets about two centuries ago; their aim was to secure a balance between tax income and operating expenditures, a problem that continues to haunt public administrators. In business, full-scale budgeting was not undertaken until the 1920s, but since that time it has become widely accepted as a basic management tool.[2]

Business managers soon discovered that using this control device forced them to improve their planning. They could not prepare standards of performance months in advance without giving some thought to objectives, operating conditions, and an acceptable manner of working. Today,

---

[2]J. O. McKinsey, *Budgetary Control* (New York: The Ronald Press Co. 1922) was the first book ever published on the subject of business budgeting.

in fact, many executives find that the planning necessary for the preparation of budgets is as valuable as the subsequent measurement and control. In some companies, too, budgets are an important means for coordinating related activities such as hiring, purchasing, production, storage, and sales. As is the case with any control system, the secret of success lies in stimulating preventive action so that little corrective action is necessary. The evaluation of performance against standard becomes routine if work prior to the evaluation has been well executed.

Alternative budgets—or at least those parts of a budget that are relative to a specific problem—are often used in the allocation of resources. By comparing the profit yield from alternative uses of capital (or any other scarce resource), that resource can be placed where it will be most productive.

Cost Analysis

Like budgeting, cost analysis is useful in both planning and control. Cost estimates, based on careful analysis of required activities, help managers make any choices that are necessary to develop plans. Moreover, records of actual costs compared with previous estimates are essential parts of control systems.

Interestingly, the early development of cost analysis occurred in the shop, alongside the growth of Scientific Management. Much later, "cost finding" was merged with financial accounting, forming the field of cost accounting. Many refinements have since been made, and the concepts of cost analysis and cost control are now applied to all phases of business operations.

Operations Research

The central concept of operations research was developed during World War II. A group of pure scientists who were asked to study military operations from a fresh viewpoint came up with some helpful suggestions on such problems as air reconnaissance for submarines. The general way in which these scientists framed their problems has since been adapted to many business situations.

In current practice, operations research is not so much a search for new knowledge as it is a technique for selecting a course of action. Three key features distinguish it from less formal decision making. (1) Problems are stated in mathematical symbols. Thus, problem statements are concise and can be easily manipulated by a mathematician. (2) A set of equations, or "model," is designed for each problem. This model shows the various factors that should be considered and the relationships among them. The model presumably presents an orderly picture of the total problem that otherwise would be dealt with unsystematically in the mind of an executive. (3) Quantitative data must be provided for each of the variables and their weights. Achieving this quantification requires an extensive fact search and the expression of subjective judgments and values in numerical terms. If the data is then inserted into the model, a highly rational decision can, in theory, be made.

Obviously, the operations research technique is particularly well suited to problems that are complex, yet have known characteristics that can be quantitatively measured. Prime examples are the scheduling of an oil refinery or inventory management for a company that has many products in many warehouses.

Operations research, then, is a useful tool for finding answers to particular types of problems. But, like many other management techniques, its indirect contributions may be more valuable than its specific application. Operations research encourages managers to clearly define, and think more sharply about, all problems, including those that cannot be quantified or are not important enough to justify the expense of a complete quantitative analysis. But operations research must be kept in perspective: Operations research deals with the decision-making aspect of planning, and its unique contribution lies more in analysis and choice than in the diagnosis and identification of alternatives.

Systems Analysis

The whole is greater than the sum of its parts—especially when we are thinking about a total system. Just as a television set differs from a collection of parts, managing is more than an assembly of plans and reports. The pieces must fit together into a workable system.

Just as a physician must think of the total body, or a telephone engineer must think of all the parts of a communications system, anyone dealing with a complex system must study it completely; this study is the field of systems analysis. Systems theory applies to many complex situations, ranging from nursery schools to space exploration. Most formal systems analysis relies heavily on symbolic models and mathematics, however, as does operations research.

The management of a company can be viewed as a system.[3] The various moves that executives make—borrowing capital, controlling quality, hiring executives—do indeed interact. By relating all these moves in terms of an overall management system, we can create a much stronger, coordinated force.

This book repeatedly stresses the benefit of thinking about managing as a total system. But a systems view is only one dimension. Before considering such action, we must know the nature of the pieces, what purposes they serve, the conditions under which they work well, and their cost. We need to know about the environmental resources and requirements.

In summary, all these approaches to management—from Scientific Management to systems analysis—continue to be useful to managers. But each gives only a partial picture—one hue in a multicolored landscape.

[3]R. H. Miles, *Macro Organizational Behavior* (Santa Monica, Calif.: Goodyear, 1980), Ch. 9. Also P. P. Schoderbek, et al., *Management Systems: Conceptual Considerations,* 3d ed. (Plano, Tex.: Business Publications, Inc., 1985).

Managers need a framework that (1) draws together these diverse approaches, (2) has practical application to real-life problems, and (3) applies anywhere in a company, including to the company as a whole.

BASIC MANAGEMENT PROCESSES

The *management process* approach provides this needed integration. Starting in the early 1950s, the basic process approach quickly gained such wide acceptance among practicing managers and management scholars that it is often called the *classical approach.*[4] Actually, the management process approach draws many of its ideas from the streams of thought already discussed, as shown in Figure 2.2.

[4]W. H. Newman, *Administrative Action*, 1st ed. (Englewood Cliffs, N.J.: Prentice-Hall, 1951) was the first book to set forth basic management processes for business settings. Others soon followed. The General Electric Company formulated a similar framework based on extensive study of its successful managers. See "The Work of a Professional Manager," *Professional Management in the General Electric Company*, Vol. 3 (New York: General Electric Company, 1954).

Figure 2.2 Expansion of Management Concepts. Dates shown suggest when a concept was making its greatest impact on the development of management thought. For each approach there were earlier roots, and each approach continues to have significant influence today.

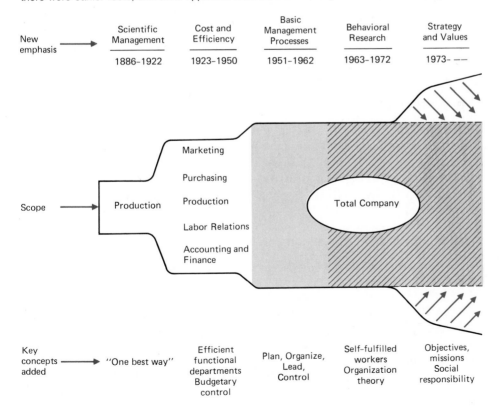

Viewing management as a social process.　　The key to the power of this fresh approach to management was the concept of universal social processes. Instead of focusing on ways to deal with particular types of problems, such as production scheduling or employee retirement plans, the process approach says that a number of underlying steps, or phases, are always needed. These involve the behavior of individuals and groups.

Social processes, of which management is one, are common in civilized society. People worship together, play group games, stand in line to wait for buses, negotiate contracts, and try other people for murder. In each case, with an established pattern of what we should do and what we expect others to do, we can achieve a result that would not otherwise be feasible. The particulars of a process may, of course, be changed from time to time. A major college football game has rituals for spectators and players that are quite different from those of the old-fashioned jousting match, and a modern murder trial has changed considerably since legal proceedings were conducted in the days of Henry VIII. But to understand what is happening in any social activity—including the management of an enterprise—and, especially, to ensure that what we want to happen does happen, we need a keen appreciation of the *social process* involved.

Management Process Framework

When this social process viewpoint was applied to managing, four subprocesses were identified by several independent analysts:

1. Planning
2. Organizing (including the mobilizing of resources)
3. Leading
4. Controlling

These four elements, which were described in the preceding chapter, are vital to the success of managers at all levels, from first-line supervisors to presidents. And planning, organizing, leading, and controlling are essential to the management of every kind of enterprise—small and large, manufacturing and selling, partnership and corporation, profit and nonprofit.

Forerunners of the Four-dimension Framework

As is the case with most powerful concepts, the management process approach had several roots.

A French mining engineer, Henri Fayol, set forth a similar framework in 1916. Unfortunately, it was not translated into English until 1927, and even then it received little attention in the United States for another two decades. Fayol's primary influence in this country was probably through a public administration scholar, Luther Gulick. While serving on the President's Committee on Administrative Management in 1936, Gulick wrote a background paper that said government administration could be analyzed in terms of planning, organizing, staffing, directing, coordinating, reporting, and budgeting (POSDCORB).[5] The POSDCORB framework became widely known among public administrators working on World War II problems.

Another forerunner was the Taylor Society and production management professors who believed that the Scientific Management concepts could be applied to all parts of a company. Professor Ralph C. Davis especially promoted this view, and he was the leading figure in the founding of the U.S. Academy of Management.

Formulating and Spreading the Gospel

By 1950, many companies were eager to improve the skill and versatility of their managers. World War II had forced numerous people into unfamiliar jobs and thus demonstrated that many features of managing were transferable to new situations. A framework was needed to identify and organize these transferable features.

So when Newman's 1951 book titled *Administrative Action* laid out a process approach to company management, it, and digests of it, quickly became the basis of many management development courses. Within a few years, other management books adopted a similar structure. The General Electric Company, on the basis of its own internal studies, designed a comparable four-part framework (planning, organizing, integrating, and measuring). General Electric then launched an intensive management education program that not only spread the ideas internally, but also attracted nationwide attention.

Meanwhile, university business schools were exploring the idea that managing is a basic social process. Existing courses in production management and business policy often expanded their scope to embrace a general management viewpoint. Here again, the management process framework was usually, though not always, used.

Within the decade of the 1950s, then, the concept that managing is an identifiable, widespread, social process had become almost commonplace. Both business companies and university faculties had learned that this framework was a powerful tool for improving the capabilities of managers.

BEHAVIORAL RESEARCH

Behavioral scientists have added new insights to the management processes just described. Based on objective *research* on how individuals and groups behave in work situations, these scientists often challenge some of

[5]The committee was appointed by President Franklin D. Roosevelt to recommend improvements in the executive division of the United States government. Gulick's paper appears in L. Gulick and L. Urwick, eds., *Papers on the Science of Administration* (New York: Columbia University Press, 1937).

the assumptions made by those who design management systems. Motivations, values, group processes, and communication are examples of subjects often studied by behavioral scientists.

Early Studies

Pioneering management studies were conducted long ago. For instance, at the Western Electric Company from 1927 to 1932, Elton Mayo and Fritz Roethlisberger found that workers responded as much to social relationships and personal recognition as they did to the physical conditions of work.[6] Much earlier, a German sociologist, Max Weber, developed a theory about the way bureaucracies function in governments and churches.[7] But these studies had little impact on the streams of thought discussed so far.

A different sort of pioneer was Chester I. Barnard, for many years president of New Jersey Bell Telephone Company. In his private life, Barnard read such writers as the Italian sociologist Pareto, and from this broad perspective developed his own theories about managing. His book *Functions of the Executive* (1938) provides insights about managerial authority, internal communications, problem solving, and the like.[8] These ideas were expressed in theoretical terms and in recent years have inspired an array of empirical studies by behavioral scientists. Probably because Barnard's writings were so abstract, a generation passed before many of his ideas were incorporated into the mainstreams of management thought.

The Boom in Behavioral Studies

Not until the rapid expansion of business school faculties in the 1960s did many behavioral scientists address problems of business managers. Even then, relations were strained. Young professors trained in psychology, sociology, or cultural anthropology were attracted by the salaries offered by the business schools. Like the Puritan settlers of New England, they arrived with convictions. They had unquestioning faith that their particular brand of scholarly research was the only road to salvation. Fortunately, the business terrain (along with medical institutions and government agencies) provided rich research sites, and soon a wide variety of research papers began to flow forth. Professional societies were formed, journals mushroomed, and independence from other disciplines was encouraged.

This behavioral research touches on a very wide range of human experience. *Individuals* are the primary unit of analysis. Their perceptions,

---

[6]E. Mayo, *The Human Problems of an Industrial Civilization* (Boston: Graduate School of Business Administration, Harvard University, 1946), and F. J. Roethlisberger and W. J. Dickson, *Management and the Worker* (Cambridge: Harvard University Press, 1939).

[7]Although originally published in German in 1922, Max Weber's *Theory of Social and Economic Organization* had minor influence on management thought until after an English translation was first published in the United States in 1949 by the Oxford University Press.

[8]C. I. Barnard, *The Functions of the Executive* (Cambridge: Harvard University Press, 1938).

beliefs, motivations, cognition (problem solving), responses to frustration, values, skills, and similar characteristics all may affect their behavior in work situations. *Interactions between two people* raise a second set of issues. Communication, influence, power, authority, motivation and manipulation are all important in relationships within an organization, especially between a boss and subordinate. *Small group behavior* has been the subject of much research. Here, team effort, conflict between groups, social conformity, group loyalty, communication patterns, representation and "gate keepers," leadership, and even how-to-run-a-meeting are topics that relate to managing. *Organization theory* focuses more on large groups of people. The design of formal organizations, social structure, relationships of organizations with their environments, stability and change, technology, and work satisfaction are examples of important research topics.

An issue remained. How could this behavioral research be related to the concrete, multifaceted problems facing managers? The problem is similar to that encountered when an attempt is made to use the results of biological research carried out in medical schools. Research findings need to be translated into useful guides for the practitioner, whether the family doctor or the manager. For the practitioner, it is the actual problem—often poorly defined and overlapping—that determines which ideas are relevant, not the refinement of some theory.

Most of the behavioral research lacked this applied focus. It was also scattered among questions about personal and group reactions, and each piece was confined to a single theoretical view. So for managers to grasp meaning from the research, a marriage of the behavioral research and the management process approach described earlier was needed. Thus, *instead of replacing the management process concepts that grew out of years of practical experience, behavioral research findings are being used primarily to confirm, expand, and enrich that lore.*

This merging of behavioral science findings and guidelines for management is still going on. Some of the linkages have not yet been developed and, more important, a wide array of behavioral studies are currently under way.

STRATEGY AND SOCIAL VALUES

The purposes and values of managers further influence "how to manage wisely." Until recently, managing was considered to be similar to driving an automobile. There is a skill in driving; this skill can be studied and improved without discussing where one might be going. We often just refer to a person as a good driver or a poor driver; the destination doesn't matter.

Likewise with managing. Much can be learned about managing—for example, to plan, organize, lead, and control—that is useful anywhere. The knowledge can be applied in a hospital, an advertising agency, or an airplane plant. Of course, these management concepts will be adapted to the

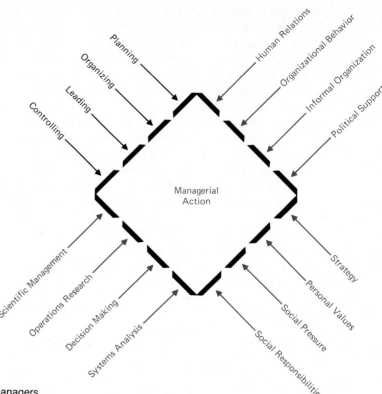

Figure 2.3 Multiple views of the work of managers

particular situation, just as an automobile driver adapts to the traffic. That's part of the skill.

However, running an organization efficiently is not enough. The significance of the output must also be considered. A manager must not only do things right, but also do the right things. In recent years these questions about goals and the value of company outputs have focused on two issues: company strategy and social responsibility.

Company Strategy

Within the last twenty years, *strategy* has become a major management concept. Unfortunately, the word has become so fashionable that people use it loosely to cover almost any kind of plan—one can even have a strategy for crossing the street. When properly applied to a company, however, strategy can be a powerful expression of where a company is headed, of what it wants to accomplish. Company strategy defines the range of products and services that the organization will produce and the way the company will build a competitive advantage. In other words, strategy tells what a particular enterprise will do to justify its continuing existence.

Two management consultants played leading roles in developing the strategy concept for businesses. James O. McKinsey laid the foundations back in the 1930s. Wide acceptance of strategy as a managerial tool, however, awaited the work of Bruce Henderson and his associates in The Boston Consulting Group in the 1960s and 1970s. Since then, both academicians and business people have greatly refined and enlarged the concept.[9]

Company strategy is directly and profoundly tied to planning, organizing, leading, and controlling—managerial tools that were already well understood when strategy moved to center stage. The management structure of a company should be specifically designed to carry out its strategy. For instance, when General Motors Corporation made the strategic move of entering the aerospace technology industry through its acquisition of Hughes Aircraft Company, it had to modify its organization significantly. Similarly, if your college decided to offer vocational training for astronauts, it would have to revise its organization and controls would be necessary.

The linkage of strategy with other aspects of managing is so important that in this book we start the Part on planning with Chapter 4 on strategy, and repeatedly throughout the book return to strategy as the overriding and guiding objective of a business.

Social Responsibility

Company strategy deals with mission and target results from a company viewpoint. A broader issue is how well each company is serving society.

Impressive as our achievements in living standards, education, individual liberty, and so on may be, much remains to be done. In the longer run, no company will be allowed to use scarce resources unless it makes a net contribution to these social needs. Of course, each company provides some employment and a market for the outputs of other employers, pays taxes, supplies goods and services, and rewards the providers of capital. Nevertheless, questions remain. (1) What about the quality of these outputs? For instance, fair employment, product safety, and industrial accidents leave room for improvement. (2) Who deals with side effects like air pollution, toxic waste, technological unemployment, and other unintended social costs? (3) What aid can and should a company provide to urban renewal, crime reduction, military defense, better government, and other needs that are only indirectly related to its primary mission?[10]

The responsibility of managers to confront such problems is much debated. Yet because business enterprises play such an influential role in

[9]McKinsey's approach to what is now called business strategy was developed as the central feature of a "general survey" of a company. The consulting firm that bears his name refined the approach over the years following his death in 1938. See W. H. Newman, *Business Policies and Management* (Cincinnati: South-Western Publishing Co., 1940) for an early statement of the approach. Henderson's approach to a strategic portfolio, including the popular four-cell matrix, appears in *Perspectives on Experience* (Boston: The Boston Consulting Group, several dates in the 1960s.)

[10]M. Ashen, *Corporate Strategies for Social Performance* (New York: Macmillan, Inc., 1980). Also H. Mintzberg, "The Case for Corporate Social Responsibility," *Journal of Business Strategy,* Fall 1983.

modern society, many people are demanding that executives include action on these fronts as part of their objectives. They say, "With power goes responsibility."

To date, social responsibility has not been widely incorporated into management theory. It is an unresolved frontier issue.

This much is clear. Ideas of *how* to manage—the subjects dealt with through most of this chapter—will continue to be useful. The social responsibility issue, like strategy, deals primarily with *what* outputs managers should seek. Modern methods of managing are sufficiently flexible to serve modified objectives if society is willing, somehow, to pay the associated costs.

CONCLUSION

Insights and ideas about managing have a very long history—more than twenty-five centuries. Systematic study of managing is only about one century old, however; even within this span the interest started with a small number of engineers and only recently took off on amazing exponential growth.

One consequence of this burst of attention in a relatively short time is that ideas about managing are still being fitted together. A neat package of "truth" has not yet emerged. Instead, students of management should be aware of different viewpoints and be versatile in deciding which one to apply to each situation.

The historical review in this chapter revealed two major breakthroughs in thinking about managing. The first was Frederick W. Taylor's insistence that management could be *systematically analyzed,* like an engineering problem, and an optimum method designed for each situation. Taylor himself studied factory production in this way, and Scientific Management was born. More important, the analytical view that Taylor recommended was subsequently applied to many other functions of business, resulting in marked improvement in the cost and efficiency of these activities.

The second major breakthrough was the treatment of managing as a vital *social process,* a process that is found in any purposeful venture in which several people are involved. This approach enables us to transfer insights about managing—and its subprocesses of planning, organizing, leading, and controlling—to a total company and to all sorts of other organizations. The process viewpoint also lends itself to behavioral research, which has enriched our grasp of basic concepts. Furthermore, the process approach links neatly with clarification of company strategy and other mission statements.

Fortunately, these various approaches to managing do not conflict with one another, except in minor ways. Rather, one builds on the others, adding new perspectives, as suggested schematically in Figure 2.3. Of course, considering several viewpoints does complicate the way a manager has to think through the problems he or she faces; by considering several viewpoints, however, a manager is likely to improve the wisdom of the action taken.

This historical sketch of the development of management concepts indicates that

1. We now have a substantial body of knowledge about ways to manage wisely.
2. This knowledge comes from so many viewpoints that one integrating framework is needed, and the process approach is best suited to be such an integrating framework.
3. The rapidity with which management ideas have advanced in recent years clearly suggests that we should expect further refinements in the years ahead.

Impact on Productivity

The managerial concepts developed since Frederick W. Taylor commenced analyzing managerial practice have greatly increased the productivity of business enterprises, especially in the United States. Other factors, such as larger investment and improved technology, also contributed. But adaptive management was crucial if these other inputs were to be taken advantage of. The overall growth is unmatched in human history.

Less clear is our ability to maintain the momentum. The complexities of managing increase almost daily, as was noted in Chapter 1. Perhaps the most encouraging development is the merging of strategic direction with the enriched management process approach. Strategy aids the *effectiveness* of company actions by seeking a closer fit with the external environment, while managers' skills to plan, organize, lead, and control aid in more *efficiently* moving toward the selected objectives. Taken together, these approaches help managers to *both* do the right things and do those things right.

FOR FURTHER DISCUSSION

1. Do you think Scientific Management, which was developed in factories, can be applied in hospital operating rooms? In hospital kitchens?

2. Select a behavioral research finding that you learned about in a psychology or sociology course and explain how this finding can be used to refine management concepts dealing with planning, organizing, leading, or controlling.

3. The evolution of management thought shows that an increasing range of considerations are being woven into guidelines for managers. Does this increase, or enrichment, make the job of managing easier or harder?

4. One of the scarce resources in many developing nations is trained managers. Suppose you were responsible for setting up a management course in such a country. Someone else will develop courses in finance, marketing, and accounting. Which of the approaches to management would you draw on in your course, and why?

5. Could Moses have deliberately used the concepts of planning, organizing, leading, and controlling, which are discussed in the latter part of Chapter 1? Why or why not?

6. How will the entrance of more well-educated women into managerial positions affect corporate responses to social responsibility?

7. Five stages in the development of management concepts are shown in Figure 2.2. Illustrate how ideas from each stage could be used (a) by the manager of your college bookstore, and (b) by the manager of a professional basketball team.

8. "The study of management history is just entertainment. It satisfies our curiosity, and it makes us feel good when we see improvements over the past. But the future will be very different from the past. For useful principles about managing in the future, we have to start with the best we know now and concentrate on how that can be adapted to tomorrow's problems. Don't waste time on history; history is obsolete." Do you agree with this statement?

FOR FURTHER READING

Bolman, L. G. and T. E. Deal, *Modern Approaches to Understanding and Managing Organizations.* San Francisco: Jossey-Bass, 1984. Summarizes concepts about managing under four frameworks: structural, human relations, political, cultural.

Koontz, H., "The Management Theory Jungle," *Academy of Management Journal,* October 1961; and "The Management Theory Jungle Revisited," *Academy of Management Review,* April 1980. Compared with the broad perspectives sketched in the foregoing chapter, these articles try to map the forest while standing among the trees. They stress the need to bring the diverse approaches to management into a more integrated framework.

McGuire, J. W. ed., *Contemporary Management:* *Issues and Viewpoints.* Englewood Cliffs, N.J.: Prentice-Hall, 1974. A valuable set of papers describing schools of management thought, current management thinking, and likely future directions.

Taylor, F. W., *Shop Management.* New York: Harper and Brothers, 1911. Few people who talk about Taylor's ideas have actually read his books. This one puts you in direct touch with Taylor's recommendations to managers.

Worthy, J. C., *Shaping an American Institution: Robert E. Wood and Sears, Roebuck.* Champaign, Ill.: University of Illinois Press, 1984. A remarkable biography that reveals the evolution of management practice during the twentieth century.

MANAGEMENT IN ACTION CASE 2
Putting Theory to Work

In the early 1970s, many manufacturing operations around the world were beset with problems. Productivity was declining. Absenteeism was on the rise. Workers were demanding huge wage increases. And, worst of all in the eyes of some managers, those same workers wanted a voice in what they would do and not do—something that became known across Europe as *codetermination.*

As social scientists had long demonstrated, workers would ultimately become frustrated if they were perceived as machine-like parts of the assembly process, without pride or feeling. And, while many corporations fought such humanistic notions, a few did something about them.

In retrospect, the most successful effort took place at Volvo, the Swedish automaker. In the early 1970s, Volvo was a rare but respected auto nameplate in the United States. The company sold under 20,000 cars a year in this country. But the Volvo name had long been synonymous with quality. And the Scandinavian approach to social welfare made Volvo not only the ideal place for a test case, but also the ideal society in which to make humanistic ideas lead to success.

After careful study, Volvo abolished the assembly line. It was replaced by groups of six to twelve workers, depending on the job being done, who would work in teams. Subassemblies of cars would move from station to station, as assembly was completed. There were no fixed times of component movement, unlike the days of assembly lines that would move at specified rates, day in and day out.

At Volvo, this flexibility allowed workers to manage their own time and, more important, the quality of their own work. Thus, it was no secret that through the 1980s, Volvo quality had become so much better than most of its competitors that its cars placed high in most surveys. And, even more important from a business standpoint, sales grew five-fold—to over 100,000 units in the United States by 1985.

Along the way, the Volvo workers learned how to rotate jobs, manage their own arrival and departure times, and meet production targets within such "flex-time" systems.

In reality, productivity increased only slightly. But quality of work improved tremendously. And, maybe most important of all, the morale of workers, who determined within teams their own priorities and work assignments, improved substantially. Rather than do one job for years at a time, no matter what the job in the auto-assembly process, workers learned several and moved among them according to team desires. They set the work pace. They set quality norms, which turned out to be higher than Volvo's overall standard. And they helped determine what would be done when.

In so doing, the findings of social science were melded with reality: Workers like to be involved in decisions about themselves, they do better when their jobs are dynamic rather than static, and they need to feel important, if not *vital,* as human beings. What Volvo did accomplished that. And it transferred directly to the Swedish automaker's bottom line.

Questions

1. Why do you think Volvo workers increased quality rather than volume of output?
2. In light of Volvo's experience, should General Motors change its assembly lines in its Chevrolet plants to small teams as Volvo has done?

3

Environmental Pressures

LEARNING OBJECTIVES

After completing this chapter you should be able to

1. Understand the dynamic environmental conditions under which business managers operate.

2. Evaluate technological, economic, political, and social changes and how they influence—or are likely to influence—an organization.

3. See how changes in each of the environmental aspects influence an organization's mix of planning, organizing, leading, and controlling.

4. Realize that alternatives in organizational or management design can be used to respond to changes in an organization's external environment.

5. Understand the relationship between the social responsibility of managers and the notion that organizations must behave in a socially responsible way to function effectively in their "exchange process" with each other and with the external environment.

THE THEATER OF ACTION

An effective manager must have a keen sense of the setting in which management takes place. When Henry Ford introduced his first assembly line, he faced a very different setting than did Lee Iacocca when he authorized production of the first Chrysler minivan. Company size, technology, worker attitude and experience, and many other factors affected the way the two situations were managed.

Even if a company is creating essentially the same product—say, a life insurance policy—in the same office, the management task will be very different today than it was in 1970 (and probably will be in 2000). Both the technology and the people have changed a great deal.

This chapter discusses a set of basic changes in our environment that affect the job of managing. Some of these changes make the job easier; many make it harder. But the most critical is awareness that environmental shifts such as those discussed do call for modifications in the way managers plan, organize, lead, and control. A useful framework for identifying these pressures is to think about the impact of major changes in technology, economics, political and legal settings, and social patterns.

TECHNOLOGICAL CHANGE

The attitudes and atmosphere within a company are often shaped by its technology. Dramatic new technology, such as satellite communication, is associated with growth, different jobs, fresh opportunities. In contrast, obsolete technology leads to cost cutting and perhaps plant closings.

Technologies Spurring Growth

The world has new technology for pole vaulting, retailing, cooking hamburgers, and many other activities. Those attracting the most attention are both amazing, almost miraculous, and widely useful. Here are some examples.

Electronic computers. The rapid development of computers has become the classic example of a new generation of technology. Computer capabilities have been increasing tenfold every three or four years. Meanwhile the minimum size has dropped from that of a freight car to a wristwatch. The physical capabilities have clearly outrun human knowledge of how to use this electronic wonder.

The new uses that will have the most influence on business operations still lie in the future. Banks, for example, may maintain a whole set of books for depositors, pay their bills, and provide subtotals for use on annual income tax returns. And these changes may contribute to a rearrangement of financial institutions. Medical diagnosis, traffic control, and chemical analysis may experience similar dramatic changes. The postal clerk sorting mail may eventually be as obsolete as a telegraph operator sending messages over the wireless.

Manipulative biology. Potentially more dramatic than electronic advances are the technological advances in biology. By tinkering with the DNA structure of a reproductive cell, new living forms can be created. One hopeful prospect is the transfer of genetic information among species of plants, enabling the design of hardy plants that have high protein contents. Such plants could substantially improve the world food supply, especially for countries where the present diet is deficient in protein.

A related technique is *cloning*—producing identical copies. Thus, a prizewinning bull or cow might be duplicated over and over again. This process, coupled with the use of surrogate mothers, could quickly change animal husbandry throughout the world.

One disturbing aspect of manipulative biology is the possibility of applying such techniques to human beings. Even the idea of being able to predetermine the sex of a new baby has caused intense debate. So, as often happens, technological developments become entwined with social and political pressures.

Energy and resources. The difficulty of maintaining a balance between the accelerating use and the supply of natural resources is illustrated by basic energy. American society's insatiable appetite for electrical energy may outstrip the supply that can be economically produced. For Europe and Japan especially, the uncertain supply of oil from the Middle East has stepped up construction of nuclear power plants. The United States can postpone heavy reliance on nuclear plants by turning back to coal. But the required investment in any shift away from oil is tremendous. As a result, the manufacturing of products requiring high-energy inputs is moving out of traditional U.S. industrial centers.

Perhaps the supply of fresh pure water, rather than energy, will become the bottleneck on expansion. Most large metropolitan areas in the United States face serious water shortages, and the decline in water tables suggests that the problem may be more than lack of adequate facilities. Clearly, new technologies will be needed if water is to be used more effectively.

One of the greatest related potential resources is the ocean. It contains vast mineral supplies and has a virtually untapped capacity to support both animal and plant life.

Managing new technologies calls for a great deal of movement and training. The growth of most of these operations calls for additional personnel. Process refinements lead to the frequent restructuring of jobs. New skills may be needed. More on-the-spot changes are inevitable, and controls will have to be loosened. For people who like change, this is the place to be.

Obsolescence in Smokestack Industries

Unfortunately, frontier technology of the sort just discussed does not prevail in much of American business. Instead, compared to the world generally, the U.S. lead is eroding.[1]

Many American steel mills, world leaders for decades, are now obsolete; their high costs invite imports of cheaper products from abroad. Capacity is being reduced and employment is dropping. This situation is further complicated by high wage rates, even by American standards, and by new pollution control requirements, which demand substantial investment without increasing output or lowering costs.

The plight of the automobile industry has been compared to the dominance and then decline of dinosaurs. For over fifty years, automobile production and related activities were a major force in the country's growth. Management techniques of the big auto companies were held up as models for others to follow. But with OPEC's success in skyrocketing petroleum prices, imports of small foreign cars captured a significant and growing share of the total market. First the German Volkswagen, followed by several Japanese lines and then even Korean and Yugoslavian models, demonstrated that United States quality standards were lax and prices were high.

Part of the weakness has been product design. Japanese automobile engineers were somehow able to achieve quality *and* low cost, while Detroit's experts settled for quality *or* low cost. In the process, American management technology lost its luster. Japanese techniques such as "quality circles," "just-in-time inventory," production-engineering coordination, greater worker participation, and progressive automation enabled their companies to produce automobiles at significantly lower cost—even with allowances for differences in wage rates and the trading value of currencies.

General Motors Corporation and other U.S. companies are diverting huge resources to regain technological leadership. For instance, instead of closing down the Buick plant in Flint, Michigan, General Motors is investing $300 million in a completely reengineered assembly plant for a new front-wheel-drive car model. Meanwhile the city is also undergoing a major $2 billion renovation. These giant steps are an indication of the degree to which American industries have failed to keep production capabilities in top form.[2]

The auto and steel industries are by no means alone. The tire industry, to cite another example, has much obsolete equipment and chronic overcapacity. It too faces a need for basic renovation. Other industries or companies within industries that once enjoyed leadership positions have rested on their laurels too long.

---

[1]J. Dutton and A. Thomas, "Managing Organizational Productivity," *Journal of Business Strategy,* 3:1, Summer 1982.

[2]S. Wheelwright, "Restoring the Competitive Edge in U.S. Manufacturing," *California Management Review,* 27:3, Spring 1985.

Reluctance to Reinvest

The U.S. slippage in technological leadership has at least two causes. One is complacency. Having been a leader, Americans underestimated the ability of competitors to devise even better ways to serve new needs.

A second contributor is the financial criterion used for reinvestment decisions. The widespread use of the discounted cash flow method with a high hurdle rate for returns on investment discourages maintenance of technological leadership. While logically sound, the inputs into the equation too often lack long-run perspective. Typically, the planning horizon is only ten years or less, and the estimated net (differential) incomes are based on past competitive conditions. The question "What will happen if we don't keep up?" may not be addressed at all. The method favors patching up the old plant rather than bold investment in the future.[3]

This reluctance to reinvest shows up in a decline in the ratio of long-term assets per worker. When adjustment is made for the rising prices of machinery, many companies are not maintaining their "capital intensive" policy. A more pertinent measure, however, would include investment in research and development, in production know-how, and in employee training—in addition to physical assets that are reported on a balance sheet. The U.S. slippage in technology arises in these intangible areas as much as it does in machinery.

ECONOMIC PRESSURES

Managers must also contend with shifting economic pressures. Both the sources and nature of competition are in a state of flux for many industries.

International Competition

Improvements in satellite communication and air transportation make possible worldwide trade in an increasing number of products. Grapes from Chile and fashion clothing from Hong Kong are now common in the shops of, say, Omaha, Nebraska. Consumers benefit. But domestic producers and their employees are likely to suffer.

The shoe industry illustrates the problem many U.S. managers are facing. Although Americans purchase one billion pairs of shoes each year, there are now only half as many manufacturing plants operating in the United States as there were fifteen years ago, and employment has shrunk even more. Imports from Italy and Far Eastern countries are rapidly increasing their share of the market, as Figure 3.1 shows. Imports can underprice domestic producers; and with modern communication and trans-

---

[3]R. H. Hayes and D. A. Garvin, "Managing as if Tomorrow Mattered," *Harvard Business Review,* 60:3, May 1982.

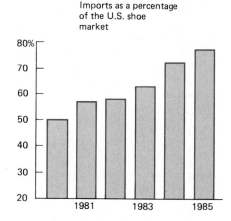

Figure 3.1
Competition in the U.S. Shoe Industry

Source: Footwear Industries of America Inc., Arlington, Va.

portation, desired styles can be delivered from abroad almost as fast as from local plants.

Foreign competition affects many industries, although not all. The range is from basic materials, such as copper and steel, to sophisticated products like television sets and computer chips. These products may be able to enter our markets for diverse reasons: a technological lead, low value of the local currency relative to the U.S. dollar, low labor costs, high dependence on a natural resource such as copper ore for foreign exchange, and the like.[4]

To respond effectively, managers must understand both the specific advantages foreign producers possess and their vulnerabilities.

Maturing Industries

Part of the economic problem is just the aging process. New products or production technologies often grow rapidly in their youth; then after the formerly untapped market is supplied, growth switches to more stable demand. For example, after most households get an electric refrigerator and a doorbell, demand tapers off—maturity sets in. As already noted, managing a company in a mature industry is quite different from managing in a booming one.

Whole nations and their economies mature. England is a favorite example, and there is much debate as to whether the United States has reached that stage too. When this occurs, do Americans "get old gracefully," or do they try to recapture their youth with a new set of goals and technologies and risks?

New Sources of Competition

Pressure on existing companies may come from outside their traditional industry boundaries. The possibility of rising foreign competition already has been noted. In addition, firms in related businesses may jump their

[4]J. A. Young, "Global Competition: The New Reality," *California Management Review,* 27:30, Spring 1985.

traditional industry boundaries. Philip Morris, for example, took its cigarette marketing skill and its dollars into the beer business and raised
Miller Beer into second place in that industry. RCA tried, unsuccessfully,
to enter the computer business and was eventually taken over by another
boundary jumper, General Electric. Often the *fence jumpers* are firms in
mature industries that seek greener pastures.[5]

The financial services industry is as unsettled as any. Insurance companies are going into the stockbrokerage business. Stockbrokers are offering checking accounts. Commercial banks are selling insurance and underwriting municipal bonds. Investment bankers are becoming more active in
large real estate transactions. And these are only a few examples. In fact,
a basic *restructuring of the industry* is occurring, the outcome of which is
far from clear. Meanwhile, competition is arising from unexpected sources,
and new or repackaged services are aggressively promoted.

Competition from *young upstarts* may add fuel to the flames. People
Express, with its no-frill airplane service, cut into the business of the major carriers. In the same industry, a little-known Texas company is reshaping two much larger lines, Continental and TWA. In the academic arena,
institutions that were formerly vocational business schools are now accred-
ited and compete with older universities for graduate students; for instance, Pace University in New York, for years a vocational business
school, now offers a doctoral degree as well as a variety of majors in its
graduate business administration program.

Because of this industry restructuring, fence jumping, and invasion
by upstarts, company managers can no longer watch only their well-rec-
ognized competitors. A stranger may have moved into the backyard.

Growth in Services versus Manufacturing

Optimism or pessimism about the economic outlook depends upon which
business sector is being discussed. We traditionally think in terms of manufacturing, which is no longer the mainstay of our economy. Since the end
of World War II, the United States has moved steadily from an industrial
economy based on physical resources to a diversified economy based
largely on human resources.

Today service industries employ three out of every four working
Americans and generate two-thirds of the U.S. gross national product
(GNP), as Figure 3.2 shows. "Services" involve more than barbershops and
restaurants. Also included are banking, insurance, telecommunications,
retail distribution, public relations, engineering and legal services, medical care, and data processing. Private services account for about 57 percent
of GNP, while government service adds another 11 percent.

Services have provided dynamic growth. Over 95 percent of the 25
million new jobs created since 1970 were in the service sector. Since 1945
the service sector has created an average of fifteen new jobs for each one
new manufacturing job.

[5]G. C. Anderson, "Planning for Restructured Competition," *Long Range Planning,* 18:1, February 1985.

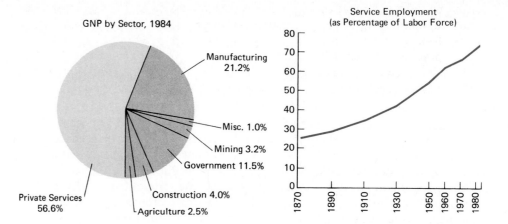

GNP by Sector, 1984

Manufacturing 21.2%

Misc. 1.0%

Mining 3.2%

Government 11.5%

Construction 4.0%

Agriculture 2.5%

Private Services 56.6%

Service Employment (as Percentage of Labor Force)

Figure 3.2 The Importance of the Service Sector in the United States

The increasing importance of service activities has, of course, affected the occupations of workers. The occupational data, which cuts across the industry data, shows a substantial increase in the number of white-collar workers and a drop in blue-collar workers between 1930 and 1980, as shown in Table 3.1. Also striking is a reduction in farm labor, especially since farm output almost tripled during the same period—an extraordinary technological achievement.

It is by no means clear that service activities can continue to surge. The economist Lester Thurow points out, for instance, that 37 percent of the new service workers between 1977 and 1982 went into health care, a trend American consumers may not be willing to sustain. Another 33 percent went into business and legal services. Thurow observes, "Suing each other is good clean fun and it generates a lot of jobs, but it is not productive."[6]

In summary, these economic trends pose major challenges to American managers. Competition will demand improved productivity. If our country is to maintain its position in the world of nations, managers must find ways to create goods and services in abundance. And this outpouring

Table 3.1 SHIFTS IN OCCUPATIONS OF U.S. EMPLOYED WORKERS

	1930	1980
White collar	29%	52%
Blue collar	40	32
Services	10	13
Farm managers & workers	21	3
	100%	100%

[6]"Revitalizing American Industry: Managing in a Competitive World Economy," *California Management Review,* 27:1, Fall 1984, p. 13.

must be achieved even though (1) large segments of the U.S. economy are mature, and (2) significant shares of domestic dollars go toward consumption of such items as legal services and military weapons, which do not build productive capability. Because the United States has already moved so far from manufacturing to producing services, much of this increased productivity must come in the service industries.[7]

POLITICAL AND LEGAL ENVIRONMENT

Free enterprise is a relative term. While our government does not establish plans for each company, it does set up the rules of the game. If managers choose to engage in various activities, they then devise a corresponding set of rules within which they must operate. Such rules are likely to be diverse, changing, and important.[8]

Rules of the Game

There are a number of important laws and regulations affecting managers in business firms. The aim in this section is to illustrate government constraints and conditions of competition to which managers must adjust—unless they can modify those conditions. Some managers spend a large part of their time negotiating in and around these rules of the game, and all managers are affected by them.

Labor relations. Suppose that you are president of the local bank and have just decided that someone would make a better janitor than the one you now have. You can't simply put the new person to work cleaning the ceiling. Uncle Sam has set some *conditions of employment.* There are rules to provide fair employment opportunities to women, minorities, even old people. Safety and health conditions must be met. Minimum wages are required, and they may amount to more than you think the new guy is worth.

Provisions for retirement—through *Social Security*—must be met. And if the person holds the job for a few months, there will be some unemployment compensation if you decide to lay him off. Moreover, he* may join a union. If there are enough janitors to get certified, you will have to bargain with their representative about wages, hours, and working conditions.

---

[7]D. A. Collier, "The Service Sector Revolution: The Automation of Services," *Long Range Planning,* 16:6, Dec. 1983.

[8]J. E. Post, "Business, Society, and the Reagan Revolution," *Sloan Management Review,* Winter 1983.

*Repeated use of the expressions "he or she" and "his or her" is awkward and sometimes confusing. Therefore, we shall use "he" and "she" as synonyms, except in specific cases where consistency in gender helps to identify the person referred to.

All these provisions and an array of related matters are designed to provide equity and to prevent exploitation of workers by employers. These regulations of labor relations have become very technical and complex in some industries.

Environmental and consumer protection.   Another set of laws are framed to protect particular groups or particular resources. For example, the Pure Food and Drug Act has protected consumers for years against potentially dangerous drugs and foods. Safety standards (often state regulations) also apply to fire hazards, explosives, and numerous other products. Furthermore, companies may be required in their advertising and packaging to advise users about safe use of their products. Indeed, the pendulum is swinging from the old "let the buyer beware" to a new burden of responsibility—"let the producer beware." Cigarette manufacturers, for instance, must place warnings about the dangers of smoking right on the packages. For a manager, the extent to which this new viewpoint must be taken is far from clear.

Environmental protection is even more ambiguous. In the case of air pollution, for instance, the sources of objectionable elements may be difficult to identify, and what degree of contamination over what period will cause how much damage are usually debatable questions. This uncertainty naturally creates friction between those who focus only on the long-term risk and those who must pay the cost of proposed remedies. Similar quandaries arise in the control of water pollution. Extreme abuse is clear-cut; the debate centers on where to draw the line.

Atomic energy is a tender subject—and an emotional one. Aroused by the arguments about atomic weapons, the safety of atomic energy plants has become a subject of great public concern in the United States, especially after a nuclear power plant accident in the Soviet Union in 1986. As safety requirements have escalated and been made retroactive, the costs of building and operating an atomic energy plant in the United States have more than quadrupled. Very large sums are involved, and several public utility companies will probably go bankrupt before the financial dust settles.

Taxes.   For a corporation, taxes are more certain than death. Company treasurers, like all the rest of us, will have to pay some share of government expenses. They may try to predict fiscal and monetary policy, and the resulting total tax bill, but these are issues on which their influence will be negligible.

The critical problem for company managers is that taxes are often used by the government as incentives or as penalties. For example, tax reductions may be granted to encourage innovative research, to stimulate training of teenagers, to attract plants to Oshkosh, or for many other special purposes. Less common but still possible are tax penalties for late payments or failure to meet some reserve requirements.

The potential to lower or raise the actual cash paid out for taxes can have direct impact on actions that a company takes. An entire modernization program may hinge on its short-run tax consequences. Thus the search for a tax break is more than an entertaining puzzle. Moreover, managers may well spend time in legislative halls trying to protect, or get enacted, tax incentives favorable to a program they wish to pursue.

"Deregulation" of competition.   Government regulation of competitive practice is a long-established part of the "rules of the game." The antitrust laws start with an underlying premise—basically that several competing suppliers should exist in each market. However, overlaid on top of this base are many federal and state exceptions. Monopolies, with accompanying regulation, are granted to companies supplying electricity, water, gas, telephone connections, and other "utilities." In addition, the supplying companies in selected industries are chartered (licensed) and regulated; such regulation of competition occurs in banking, insurance, transportation, radio and television broadcasting, hospital care, and to lesser degrees in many other industries. Thus, in fact, there is much regulation in the free enterprise system.

Such regulation of competition almost inevitably becomes more complicated as the years go by. Bureaucratic judgment replaces competitive forces. To counter this bureaucratic encroachment, however, the Ford, Carter, and Reagan administrations launched "deregulation" campaigns. Airlines, trucking, banking are examples of industries in which deregulation has occurred. Important subjects such as the entry of new competitors, pricing, and geographic scope of activities have been returned (at least partially) to competitive forces.

"Deregulation" opens new possibilities for company managers—and for competitors. Restraints are removed and risks are increased. No one can be sure where the new freedom will lead. But managers know that they cannot escape a new jockeying for favorable positions.

The Right to Sue and Be Sued

The political issues just sketched—labor relations, environmental and consumer protection, taxes, "deregulation"—all deal with interactions between company managers and some arm of the government. There is another legal arena with a voracious appetite for managers' time—suing one another in the legal courts.

Part of this game deals with the past—suing for damages suffered because of the illegal act of the defendant. Since both the law and the facts are open to various interpretations, such suits can drag on for years and be costly in both time and expenses. Nevertheless, the volume of such wrangling is on the rise.

The second part of the game seeks to stop the defendant from taking a future action. For instance, the court may be asked to stop a merger.

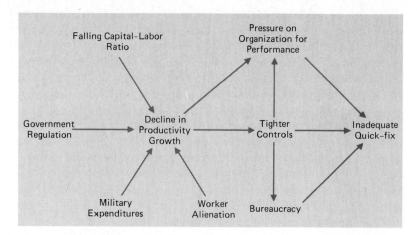

Figure 3.3 Productivity Growth Rate. In this diagram, Charles Fombrun pictures a combination of forces conspiring to block improvements in productivity.

Source: C. Fombrun, "Productivity Growth Rate," reprinted with permission from *Journal of Business Strategy*, Summer 1982, vol. 3, no. 1; copyright © 1982 Warren, Gorham & Lamont, Inc., 210 South St., Boston MA 02111. All rights reserved.

This sort of maneuver is typically short-run and tactical. The volume here is also on the rise. One effect of the current popularity of suing and being sued is that litigation is becoming more important to business success and is absorbing more of a manager's limited time.

Compounding effect of government regulation.   The "rules of the game" established by the political and legal system often have a marked impact on the ways a company can operate. As noted, these rules regulate, in varying degrees, how managers can work with labor, consumers, environmental groups, competitors, and other key actors. Tax incentives and penalties further shape managerial action. Litigation adds still another dimension. Managers must learn to anticipate changes in the rules and act accordingly.

This government regulation often has a depressing effect on productivity, as suggested in Figure 3.3.

SOCIAL TRENDS

Each of the three broad influences on the work of managers already reviewed—technology, economics, and politics—creates new demands on the people filling managerial jobs. This section will focus on the people who must deal with these demands. What is the nature of the human resource pool from which managers of the future and their associates will be recruited?

The Size and Sex of the Work Force

Between 1930 and 1980 the number of people in the work force more than doubled, growing from 50 million to 107 million.[9] This large increase oc-

[9]Statistical data in this section are drawn primarily from E. Ginzberg and G. Vojta, *Beyond Human Scale: The Large Corporation at Risk* (New York: Basic Books, 1985), Ch. 5.

curred in spite of (1) young people remaining in school longer, and (2) older people retiring earlier, largely on their Social Security and other retirement income. What happened was that a substantially higher percentage of middle-aged adults sought employment—almost two-thirds by 1980.

The revolutionary change was the increase in the number of women in the work world. Women accounted for 60 percent of all new job holders in the post-World War II period. In a shift from the prewar era, most of these working women were married and often had small children at home. The experience of holding important jobs during the war, coupled with a fundamental shift in social attitudes about the role of women, made working socially acceptable. The Women's Movement took a giant step forward.

Rising Educational Level

The present work force is not only larger, it is also better prepared for the white-collar jobs that are increasingly available. Between 1940 and 1980, the number of adults who were high school graduates increased from about 25 percent to about 70 percent, as Table 3.2 shows. Those graduating from college increased from about 5 percent to close to 17 percent. In the years since 1980, these ratios have continued to rise significantly.

This higher level of education has several effects:

1. It provides the graduates with at least some knowledge and skills that will be useful on their jobs; especially, it prepares individuals to learn more quickly the specific on-the-job knowledge they will need.
2. College graduation raises expectations. A widespread belief in American culture is that education is a magic pathway to more interesting, well-paying jobs. If such work is not forthcoming, the graduate is likely to feel cheated, or like a failure, or both.
3. College graduates are typically mobile. They are psychologically ready to move, and are likely to do so if their current situation is unfulfilling.

Clearly, problems of balance will arise if the trend toward more education continues. The number of attractive jobs may not match the larger flow of graduates. Moreover, graduates may overestimate their qualifications and be unwilling to continue their self-development only to take unglamorous work.

Table 3–2 **CHANGES IN EDUCATION ACHIEVEMENT**

	Total U.S. Adults (25 years of age or older) 1940	1980
High school graduates	1 of 4	7 of 10
College graduates	1 of 20	1 of 6

Professional education for business is also flourishing. In 1950, only 4,335 Master of Business Administration (MBA) degrees were awarded in the United States. The number had increased tenfold to 44,300 by 1980, and estimates for current output approximate 60,000 a year. About one-third of this current crop are women. In addition, professional education for experienced managers, sponsored by companies and trade associations, is growing.

This movement toward making management a profession fits well with the idea that management skills are applicable to all sorts of organizations—large and small, profit and not-for-profit, national and global. However, some critics doubt that entrepreneurship—the opportunity-sensing, risk-taking, enthusiasm-generating function—can be turned over to trained professionals. If professional managers can't be trained to be entrepreneurs, it may be necessary to discover how to train entrepreneurs to be good managers.

Life-styles and Values

The rising tide of prospective managers and workers just identified have a life-style that differs from that of their parents. For example, the nature and role of the family is being transformed. This shift grows out of a more permissive attitude about sex, later marriages, fewer children, and the pursuit of careers by both spouses. Home-sweet-home is not the dominant social unit it once was.

A strong sense of national affiliation is also eroding. Instead, people are becoming more involved with particular groups. Such groups may focus around ethnic background, athletic or cultural interest, religion, occupation, physical handicap, or even old age. Improved communication and ease of travel enable dispersed people to form these social bonds. These groups often want special services or products, and thereby become differentiated markets. Some groups will advocate a particular cause—like antiapartheid, preservation of snail darters, or bilingual schools—so strongly that they complicate political processes. This drift toward special groups means that close-knit neighborhoods, like large families, are dwindling.

With the shifting about of personal ties, widely held sets of values are now hard to find. A manager can no longer assume that a graduate of, say, Georgia Tech who then served in the Navy will have a predictable set of values. Nevertheless, there is substantial agreement that the following generalizations do apply to the values of a large portion of men and women just entering the work force.

1. Condemnation of "the establishment" (government, big business, and the like), which was popular in the late 1960s, has now been replaced by a strong interest in self-fulfillment. A somewhat cynical "me generation" currently prevails.
2. Even committed workers and managers feel that personal interests are entitled to considerable chunks of one's time and effort.

3. Jobs should provide not only economic rewards and long-term material benefits but also opportunities to use one's competence, to compete for advancement, to be judged on the basis of performance, and to add to one's knowledge and skills.[10]

4. Companies as such are not entitled to much loyalty. Rather, they should continue to earn workers' and managers' support by providing the kinds of jobs just described. If and when such conditions are not met, an employee should feel free to seek employment elsewhere.

5. If a worker or manager does elect to stay with a company, however, the company has a moral obligation to provide uninterrupted, attractive employment for that person if at all possible. Loyalty should flow from company to worker.

If these observations about the values of the people moving into key jobs are correct, then managers of the future face yet another challenge. How can the new breed of workers and managers be motivated? How can the numerous pressures outlined earlier be dealt with while simultaneously meeting the expectations of the highly educated, self-centered, ambitious, and mobile new cohort of workers?

PRECEPTS FOR MANAGEMENT DESIGN

The technological, economic, political, and social trends discussed in this chapter are only a small sample of the many developments that are interacting in our exciting world. A few that are sure to impinge on managers and management during the next decade have been singled out. The particular trends will be among the compelling features of the environment.

Throughout the book, as we explore planning, organizing, leading, and controlling, these environmental pressures will continue to surface.[11] They help shape the problems that must be considered, and any conclusions will be uncertain if those problems are ignored.

While the main purpose of this chapter is to provide this environmental backdrop for all of the following discussion, a few precepts for management design already stand out.

1. The previous discussion indicates that the situations facing different managers are likely to have very different characteristics. For instance, sometimes an aggressive program into a new technology will be needed; in another setting, steady perseverance with existing resources may be the wise course. The *management design*—the plans, organization, leadership, and control—should be *tailored to fit the specific need.* No single structure suits all situations.

[10]Ginzberg and Vojta, *Beyond Human Scale*, p. 232.
[11]R. D. Zentner, "How to Evaluate the Present and Future Corporate Environment," *Journal of Business Strategy,* 1:4, Spring 1981.

2. Competition is increasing from so many directions that close attention to *improving productivity* is essential. (Recall from Chapter 1 that *productivity* includes finding a desired mix of product and services, as well as creating that package with dependability, quality, and efficiency.) Because of the rising importance of services, much of the productivity improvement will have to come from increased productivity of *people*.

3. A particular challenge is finding ways to motivate the new breed of workers and managers. Somehow *their values and improved productivity must be melded* together. This means that steps taken to achieve productivity must at the same time provide the self-achievement that these individuals are seeking.

We shall refer back frequently to these precepts while progressing through the book.

A fourth issue, which also permeates the whole discussion of management design, could be added to this list. That issue is the *social responsibility* of companies and their managers. Effective management and socially responsible action are intimately related. Social responsibility, like the three precepts just listed, should be made an inherent aspect of good management design.

Because we wish to treat social responsibility of managers as a pervasive theme, this issue will be outlined in the final section of this chapter.

SOCIAL RESPONSIBILITY OF MANAGERS[12]

The social responsibility of a business manager is far from clear. Some idealists would like to include every reform that is socially desirable. But business executives have neither the competence nor the means to undertake improvements in prisons, churches, classrooms, and other areas remote from their normal activity. So, to give practical meaning to the idea of social responsibility, we need an approach for business managers that relates to those actions and outcomes directly affected by managerial decisions.

A useful approach is to think of a manager as a *resource converter*. From the viewpoint of society, an enterprise justifies its existence by converting resources into desired outputs. The resource inputs of labor, materials, ideas, government support, capital, and the like are converted by the firm into outputs of goods, services, employment, stimulating experiences, markets, and other things desired by those who provide the inputs. The job of a manager is to design and maintain a converting mechanism that will generate a continuous flow of these inputs and outputs.

[12]This section is adapted from W. H. Newman, J. P. Logan, and W. H. Hegarty, *Strategy, Policy, and Central Management*, 9th ed. (Cincinnati: South-Western Publishing Co., 1985), Ch. 1.

Building continuing exchange flows with resource suppliers. The relationship with each resource supplier always involves an exchange. Figure 3.4 shows these flows for six typical outside groups. For a specific company there will be a wider variety of subgroups, but the underlying concept is the same. Each group of contributors provides a needed resource and receives in exchange part of the outflow of the enterprise.

Much more than money is involved. An array of conditions usually provides the basis for continuing cooperation. Employees, for instance, are concerned about meaningful work, stability of employment, reasonable supervision, future opportunities, and a whole array of fringe benefits in addition to their paychecks. Suppliers of materials want a continuing market, sure and prompt payment, convenient delivery times, quality standards suited to their facilities, minimum returns, and the like. Investors are concerned about uncertainty of repayment, security, negotiability of their claims, veto of major changes, and perhaps some share in the decision-making process. For each resource contributor, mutual agreement about the conditions under which the exchange will continue is subject to evolution and periodic renegotiation.[13]

[13]J. J. Chrisman and J. B. Carroll, "Corporate Responsibility: Reconciling Economics and Social Goals," *Sloan Management Review,* Winter 1984.

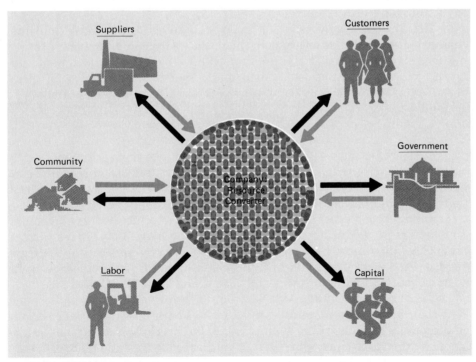

Figure 3.4 Resource Converter Model

→ Resource inputs

→ Need satisfaction outputs

The real core of social responsibility of a business executive is the maintenance of resource flows on mutually acceptable terms. And this is a very difficult assignment in times of rapidly changing values and expectations, as the succession of labor disputes and energy supply crises illustrates. But note that social responsibility is not something that has been newly tacked onto an executive's job. Rather, it is reflected in the recognition of shifting social needs and the approach an executive takes in adapting to them.

Designing an internal conversion technology.   Each enterprise, large or small, must maintain a balance between the outputs it generates and the satisfaction it has agreed to provide to its resource suppliers. For instance, promises of stable employment must be compatible with protection promised to suppliers of capital. Such ability to make ends meet depends partly on the skill of executives in devising a *conversion technology* suited to their particular company. The way the resources are converted strongly affects the outputs available. So, in addition to negotiating agreements that ensure the continuing availability of resources, central managers must design internal systems to effectively utilize the resources.

Every enterprise has its technology for converting resources into outputs. For example, a school has its teaching technology, an insurance company has its technology for policy risks, and a beauty shop has its technology for shaping unruly hair.

This internal conversion technology involves much more than mechanical efficiency. The desired outputs, as already noted, include interesting jobs, low capital risks, minimum pollution of the environment, improved job opportunities for women and minorities, and a host of other features. Consequently, devising a good internal conversion technology is a complex task.

Integrating and balancing the external and internal flows.   As important as attracting resources and designing conversion technologies may be, it is the *combination* of (1) responding to new "needs" of resource contributors and (2) restricting total responses to what total output permits that poses the final challenge to management. Socially responsible executives must respond quickly enough to the ever-changing desires of resource contributors to maintain a continuing flow of needed resources; at the same time, they must keep their enterprises alive by generating the right quantity and mix of outputs to fulfill commitments. If they do not, some key resource will be withdrawn and the enterprise will collapse.

Community hospitals, to cite a not-for-profit service example, must keep their technology up to date; this includes both putting patient records on computers and installing sophisticated diagnostic and treatment equipment. At the same time, employees want higher wages and shorter hours. The main squeeze, however, arises from a reduction in the average number of days patients are staying in hospitals; patients want excellent service, but less of it, so hospital income is not keeping pace with the cost of improved technology and higher wages. Somehow, hospital central managers must reconcile these *combined* pressures.

Considering a company as a resource converter uses a broad social viewpoint. This is a better way to conceive of "the purpose of a company" than the more common cliché "to make a profit." Indeed, every successful resource converter must make a profit in order to continue to attract capital. But this is a narrow oversimplification. To survive, a company must also provide attractive employment, be a good customer, earn continuing support of governments and the community, and serve customers well. The task for management is to find a way to do all these things simultaneously while keeping abreast of changes in each field.

CONCLUSION

The quick review of the environmental pressures on management in this chapter points to both broad and more specific needs—needs (opportunities) that will be explored throughout the rest of the book. The broad needs include the following:

1. A contingency approach to managing—in other words, a recognition that managers should fit their management design to the size, stability, freedom of action, risk, and other factors of the specific situation they face.
2. A recognition that technological, economic, political, and social aspects should all be weighed in describing such a managerial situation.
3. A skill in advancing from the descriptive analysis, called for in needs 1 and 2, to managerial action—which requires a careful mix of planning, organizing, leading, and controlling.
4. A concern about managing in a socially responsible way.
5. A commitment to improving productivity, which is necessary if the social obligations, noted in need 4, are to be possible.

Impact on Productivity

The specific needs flagged by this review of environmental pressures on management include the following:

1. Learning to apply known technology more adroitly, as well as searching for dramatic new techniques.
2. Increasing economic flexibility so as to promptly confront new competition. This involves adopting longer-term objectives and overcoming inertia.
3. Attaining better balance in the "rules of the game," instead of narrow and often conflicting laws, each focused on a particular political goal.

4. Finding practical ways to motivate the new breed of workers and managers.

Achievement of these last four targets would contribute substantially to higher productivity.

FOR FURTHER DISCUSSION

1. (a) Do you agree with the description of the "new breed of worker" presented in this chapter? Does the description fit you and your friends? (b) For people who fit this description (or a revision that you believe is more appropriate), do you honestly believe that company managers can organize work so as to meet your desires? (c) If some, or many, companies cannot provide these conditions of work, are those companies doomed to fail in increasing their "productivity"?

2. "Automated bank tellers" are machines that enable you to withdraw cash from your bank account any time during the day or night; you can also charge retail purchases to your account or pay other bills. Banks can install these machines in department stores, airports, office buildings, even college dorms. (a) Give your impression of how this new technology will affect the organization of a commercial bank, and of the bank's control system. (b) What may the technology do to competition faced by small local banks?

3. Do you think that "deregulation" of the airline industry in the 1980s simplified or complicated the tasks of managers in the industry?

4. Farming has an outstanding record for increases in productivity. How do you explain so much more improvement in this area than in, say, the steel industry? More capital investment? Better-educated managers (or better motivation)? New technology? Government price supports?

5. Companies facing increased global competition—such as textile manufacturers, investment bankers, and producers of electronic equipment—have several options: improve their domestic productivity, transfer all or part of their operations abroad, seek a niche sheltered from foreign competition, or ask the government for tariff and related protection. Briefly indicate how each of these four alternatives complicates or simplifies the job of managing a company that adopts it.

6. Assume that new technology makes practical two-way interaction on cable television connections to homes. Subscribers will be able to talk back to announcers and/or sponsors; they can also initiate the connection and request information. What changes in programs and other services using the cable connections do you think would result from such a change? If these changes do occur, would a change in the management of cable networks be desirable?

7. Again assume, as suggested in question 6, that two-way cable television is practical and that your predicted changes in services take place. Are new competitors likely to enter the industry? Who will they be? What is likely to happen to the structure of the industry?

8. Our discussion of social responsibility suggested that managers of companies should seek continuing long-run cooperation of stakeholders. Among other things, this implies steady employment for people working in the company. If such steady employment is socially desirable, why not have the federal government pass a law requiring companies to provide it?

9. Describe five environmental pressures that will have important effects on the future of the school (or department) in which you are studying. Be sure to consider the implications of technologic, economic, political, and social changes. Should the "management" of the school take any action to deal with these pressures?

FOR FURTHER READING

Drucker, P. F., *Managing in Turbulent Times.* New York: Harper & Row, 1980. Section Three focuses on environmental factors that are causing turbulence and conflict.

Hagedorn, H. J., "The Factory of the Future:

What About the People," *Journal of Business Strategy,* 5:1, Summer 1984. Outlines personnel and management changes that new production technology will require.

Mintzberg, H., "The Case for Corporate Social Responsibility," *Journal of Business Strategy,* 4:2, Fall 1983. Reviews debate about social responsibility of companies and concludes that, in spite of the difficulties, managers must accept this obligation if the business system is to survive.

Porter, M. E., *Competitive Strategy: Techniques for Analyzing Industries and Competitors.* New York: The Free Press, 1980, Chs. 1, 7, and 8. Excellent guide for analyzing likely future competition in an industry.

Roehrich, R. L., "The Relationship Between Technological and Business Innovation," *Journal of Business Strategy,* 5:2, Fall 1984. Shows why technological innovation calls for closely related changes in industry and management structures.

Taylor, B. and L. Ferro, "Key Social Issues for European Business," *Long Range Planning,* 16:1, Feb. 1983. Social problems facing European business managers often foretell similar issues in the United States.

Thurow, L., "Revitalizing American Industry: Managing in a Competitive World Economy," *California Management Review,* 27:1, Fall 1984. A challenge to management to step up productivity, written by a well-known economist.

MANAGEMENT IN ACTION: CASE 3
The Tobacco Industry Adjusts

When the Surgeon General and the general public thumbed their noses at cigarette smoking in the late 1970s, things looked bad for the U.S. tobacco industry. Sales fell swiftly as thousands of smokers quit the habit and young people chose not to pick it up.

At Philip Morris, Chairman Hamish Maxwell didn't panic, but neither did he sit back and wait for the ax to fall. He adapted to the changing external environment. Although Philip Morris had diversified twice in the past, with acquisitions of Miller Brewing Co., the nation's No. 2 beer maker, and Seven-Up, a leading soft drink manufacturer, the company was still heavily dependent on the tobacco business, which was providing 90 percent of Philip Morris' profit in 1985. With that industry facing seemingly inevitable decline, it was clearly time to diversify again.

Maxwell considered an alternative strategy—buying back Philip Morris shares—but ultimately rejected it because, for one thing, such a move could demoralize employees accustomed to a growth-oriented environment and, for another, it would do nothing to lessen Philip Morris' dependence on tobacco.

After studying potential acquisitions for nine months, Philip Morris lighted on General Foods Corp., the huge, diversified consumer products concern. Maxwell said General Foods "has a diversified product line, and it has available all forms of distribution. It's a company other products of acquisitions can be added to. I think it's a great way to start." On Friday, 27 September 1985, Philip Morris agreed to buy General Foods for $5.75 billion, or $120 a share.

Some could have argued that Philip Morris, until then the least diversified tobacco company, didn't need to diversify in such grand fashion. While unit sales of U.S. cigarettes dropped about 5 percent from 1982 to 1985, Philip Morris increased its unit sales by 6 percent. Philip Morris passed R. J. Reynolds to become the nation's largest cigarette company, and by 1984 had 35 percent of the U.S. market, more than any other firm since American Tobacco in the 1940s. Too, the company's other major acquisitions in beer and soft drinks were contributing little to sales and earnings.

But Maxwell was convinced that Philip Morris could not risk being victimized by further contraction in the tobacco business, a strong likelihood in the changing national political environment involving cigarettes.

"This company has been animated by growth," he said. "You have to make people feel they're in a dynamic environment with job opportunities opening up." In any case, the merger of Philip Morris and General Foods gave both firms greater muscle to withstand downturns in any industry—including tobacco—in the future.

Question

Does Philip Morris' acquisition of General Foods appear wise to you in terms of *your* forecast of trends in the cigarette industry and the nationally advertised food industry?

For more information, see *The Wall Street Journal*, 30 September 1985

APPLICATION CASES

To develop a sense of the array of issues facing managers in a business enterprise, and to relate the concepts discussed in this chapter to concrete managerial situations, see the following managerial decision cases. The case questions particularly relevant to this chapter are listed by number after each case name.

Grant Chemical Corporation (p. 59) 2
Fyler International (p. 68) 5
Consolidated Instruments (p. 189) 1
GAIN Software (p. 303) 2, 10
Clifford Nelson (p. 308) 1

PART I MANAGERIAL DECISION CASE STUDIES

"I have little use for all this current preoccupation with elaborate write-ups of strategy and corporate culture," said William Lee, President of Grant Chemical Corporation.

"It's not that they are unimportant," he added. "Quite the contrary: Clear strategic direction consistent with the culture or values of a company are extremely important. It is the preoccupation with form, with words rather than with substance and example, that bugs me. I was brought in seven years ago to take over a dying business. It had lost money for five years in a row and the banks were ready to close it down and sell the plumbing.

"The company had a full-blown corporate creed, a fancy strategic planning process, and a fixation on continuing to build on its 'cultural roots.' Horsefeathers! They were all fancy words with no real clear sense of direction or purpose."

Lee went on to point out that during his first years as president, he had two primary objectives:

1. Reduce the size and scope of the company to concentrate on those product/market segments where the company might enjoy competitive advantages.
2. Identify internally and recruit externally key people to fill top divisional and corporate jobs.

During this period, he reduced Grant's volume from $350 million to under $200 million. He eliminated many products from the company's line and concentrated 85 percent of their sales in the six states of Oklahoma, Texas, Arkansas, Louisiana, Kansas, and Missouri.

By its third year under his direction, the company showed a small profit; by the end of his seventh year, sales approached $400 million, and return on sales and investment ranked with or higher than those of the industry giants.

"It has not been easy," Lee said. "But we did it by getting back to fundamentals. When you are as small as we are you can't survive by challenging the huge chemical and petrochemical companies. We have to pick our spots very carefully and remain alert and agile. There is plenty of room to maneuver among the elephants' feet. Just be careful to avoid getting stepped on or 'romanced' by them."

Lee focused on products where economies of scale could be reached at low volumes and where technology and capital investment outlays could be managed by a company Grant's size.

"Even so," he pointed out, "we can't survive trying to underprice the big outfits on the basis of lower cost. Neither can we match their top-quality items or overall service on a continuing basis. The best we can do is stay close enough in these areas and really excel where the giants either can't or more likely don't choose to put their emphasis. For the most part, we get our business through *reliability*. We have to be very careful to select customers who need what we have to offer. We can't offer the fastest delivery or the highest quality but we can and have offered the most reliability possible in these two areas. We also try never to get so big or important in any one market that we tempt one of those elephants to charge.

"The key is accountability. We have set up profit centers for each of our major product groups to emphasize commitment to results. We also have a number of small corporate staff departments to advise me and create the checks and balances needed to deal with our greatest threats: (1) complacency, (2) forgetting who we are and how we got there, and (3) putting undue emphasis on short-term profit center results."

The company has three major operating divisions: the Industrial Chemicals Division, the Plastics Division, and a small Agricultural Chemicals Division. Each division has its own manufacturing, developmental research, and marketing operations, and each is operated as a profit center. The division presidents report to Lee and are paid a salary, plus a bonus based on divisional profits. In good years, their bonuses may amount to 40 or 50 percent of their base salaries.

Under such an organizational arrangement, Lee feels he can leave most of the divisional operating decisions to the division presidents. To assist him in his review of divisional plans and performance, he has created corporate staff groups in such areas as marketing, production, research, and human resources. With the exception of research, and a materials management staff group disbanded last year, these staff groups are relatively small, typically having only one or two technicians assisting each staff vice president. According to Lee:

"I don't want big staff groups that are likely to start masterminding things. Each division has its own support departments and they should be able to help their presidents in their functional specialties. I've picked my corporate staff people with an eye toward finding the most knowledgeable person in each functional area. My vice president of marketing knows as much about the markets for our products and ways of identifying them as anybody in the company. He and my other staff vice presidents have three major responsibilities. They are

1. To keep me and my advisory committee informed as to the major market and technological factors affecting our business. With this background, we can then develop the broad, longer-range strategies and parameters, which I ask the divisions to implement.
2. To help me evaluate and decide on the one- and five-year plans submitted to us by the divisions and to review their performance. They give me the expertise to evaluate the specifics of both where the divisions are headed as well as how they are doing.

3. Whenever they can be helpful, to assist the division general managers and their divisional staff counterparts to keep on top of fast-moving changes in their fields of specialization."

Until recently, one of the best examples of how these corporate staffs could be of help to both the division presidents and to Lee was the corporate production staff. Harry Young, vice president of the production staff, is clearly one of the most knowledgeable people in the company in production and processing. He rose from the production ranks of the industrial chemical division to plant superintendent and has broadened his background in plastics and agricultural chemicals. Five years ago, he worked with Norman Allison, who was then president of the plastics division, in the design, purchase, and layout of production equipment for the company's redesigned plastics plant. When Allison moved over to become general manager of the larger industrial chemicals division two years later, Young continued to work closely with his successor, Frank Sommers, who was promoted from plant superintendent to general manager.

Young has continued to advise Sommers on major production questions but recently has worked more directly with Jack Parks, the new plant superintendent, and Peg Mathis, divisional staff director of production and traffic. Young, Parks, and Mathis have worked together quite well in this period. Recently, however, a rather serious dispute has arisen between Young and Sommers.

As is the company's practice, Sommers recently presented copies of his annual and five-year plans to the several corporate staff groups. After they complete their review of the plans, the staff groups are supposed to confer with the division presidents and their key staff members to seek amplification and/or modification before the plans are presented to the advisory committee for review and approval. The corporate staffs then sit with Lee to help him interpret and question the divisional proposals. Although this arrangement has generally worked quite smoothly, Sommers and Young have reached a stalemate in their disagreement on a key part of the plastic division's production plan.

Sommers has requested $800,000 in next year's budget for capital investment to replace process equipment used in the production of plastics. Sommers maintains that he must order the new equipment immediately to avoid costly overhaul of present equipment and to get the additional capacity to meet an expected sales increase.

Young feels that the purchase of new equipment should be delayed at least 18 months. He explained:

"In looking ahead at what's being done in the design of the kind of equipment Frank [Sommers] wants, I am virtually certain that we will see a major breakthrough in 18 months. Two of the manufacturers of this equipment are making good progress, and within a year and a half one of them should have something that will cost about the same and give us from 10 percent to 20 percent more output than with the stuff Frank wants to buy. It also looks as if the new equipment, because of design modification, will save us maintenance cost. In addition to productivity increases, I think we may benefit from greater quality control and suffer less down-time."

Sommers disagrees.

"Harry may know equipment, but he has been out of line responsibility for so long he has lost touch with the more practical application questions. The equipment that he says will be ready in 18 months will more than likely take closer to three years to be perfected. We considered it and have reflected the cost of waiting that long in our request for the investment. As we see it, and I have talked with my superintendent and staff people, waiting three years will cost us too much to overhaul and maintain present equipment over the next two or three years.

"In addition, if we use present equipment to meet our present market plan for the next three years, we will have to go to a three-shift operation for four months each year to avoid stockouts. According to my production people, going from our standard two shifts to three shifts will cost us premium pay and additional operating costs. Overall, I feel that to wait three years may cost us between $125,000 and $130,000 more than replacing right now.

"Even if Harry's estimates on the newer equipment are valid, it may take five or six years from the time we get it to cover the cost of making do with what we have while we wait. As far as his views on quality control and down-time, I feel much safer with replacement of equipment we have years of experience with."

Young feels that Sommers has taken a most pessimistic view of the picture.

"I've worked with his people (Parks and Mathis) enough to know that it won't cost nearly as much to make do with what he has. In the first place, I'm quite sure it will only be 18 months, not three years, before the newer equipment is ready. Secondly, I don't think it will cost him anywhere near what he now estimates as cost to patch up what he has. I talked with Parks and Mathis when the matter first came up three months ago, and I helped them work out maintenance costs. Admittedly, we didn't go into a lot of details but I still have the rough estimates we worked up at the time. I don't know what kind of juggling has gone on since then, but I'm sure that Sommers has padded the overhaul estimate. Thirdly, I'm sure that he won't need more than two months of three-shift operations to meet his expected volume.

"By the way, I think he is being very optimistic about sales—further exaggerating his overtime estimates, but the marketing staff has not supported his forecasts."

"What really disturbs me," Young explained, "is that when I went to Jack Parks and Peg Mathis to discuss the differences in our estimates, both of them refused to go over the details with me. They told me that they had given this material to Sommers, and that he had told them not to discuss the matter further with me. They said Sommers wants me to see

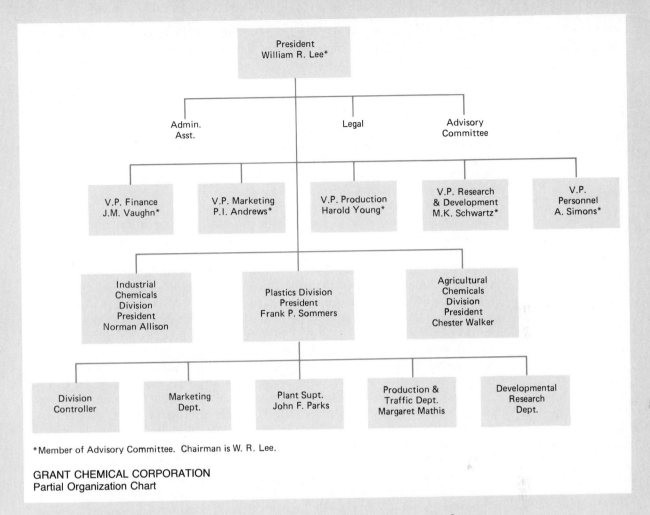

President
William R. Lee*

Admin. Asst.

Legal

Advisory Committee

V.P. Finance
J.M. Vaughn*

V.P. Marketing
P.I. Andrews*

V.P. Production
Harold Young*

V.P. Research & Development
M.K. Schwartz*

V.P. Personnel
A. Simons*

Industrial Chemicals Division President
Norman Allison

Plastics Division President
Frank P. Sommers

Agricultural Chemicals Division President
Chester Walker

Division Controller

Marketing Dept.

Plant Supt.
John F. Parks

Production & Traffic Dept.
Margaret Mathis

Developmental Research Dept.

*Member of Advisory Committee. Chairman is W. R. Lee.

GRANT CHEMICAL CORPORATION
Partial Organization Chart

him, not them, from now on when I want to get information or make suggestions about his division. I talked with Frank yesterday but he sticks to his assumptions, and says the details will bear them out if I challenge him before the advisory committee. He has never tried to stonewall me before.

"Frankly, while I don't want to see them go after new equipment too soon and lose some sizable longer-run savings, I would hate to push him if it meant destroying the good working relationships I have at present with his production people. At this point, I don't know what course to follow when this comes before the advisory committee."

GRANT CHEMICAL CORPORATION—PART B

After giving much thought to what to do next, Harold Young took several steps. First, he visited the vendor most likely to have the newer equipment ready in 18 months. While the people Young talked with remained optimistic about the new equipment, they seemed much less interested than they had formerly been in enlisting Young's help to convince Sommers to wait.

Young then spoke with Norman Allison, president of the Industrial Chemicals Division, and formerly president of the Plastics Division.

"I thought Norm might help me understand why Frank is being so mulish on this one and I hoped he might be willing to help me convince Frank to go over the details with me. Norm was very busy, however, as he was finalizing his plan, readying it to present to us next week. He said he was sorry but couldn't help."

"I told Harry not to make a federal case out of this," said Allison. "I don't know why Frank is taking the position he is and I'm not about to meddle. Near as I can tell, it won't affect my division so I'd rather stay clear. Frank used to work for me, you know. He's a proud person and I know he wouldn't appreciate my second-guessing him. I recommended him to succeed me when I moved over to Industrial and he will probably do it again here when I retire in three years.

"I'm sure he knows what he is doing and probably just wants to keep Harry out of his hair."

Young's next step was to visit Sommers again. "I all but brought him myrrh and frankincense," said Young. "I told him that if he felt I was out of line working with Parks and Mathis, I was sorry, and explained that I was only trying to help. I told him that unless I got into the plants and got close to the action, I would lose touch and be unable to do my job. I reassured him that if he would simply give me his files on the project, and a few hours in the plant, that I could be back to him in 24 hours, and in all likelihood we could iron everything out.

"The son-of-a-gun just sat there shaking his head. 'We've wasted enough time on this one already, Harold.' He always calls me Harold when he's acting like a know-it-all. 'Just let it be!' he said.

"I'll be darned if I'll let it be. After all, it's my job to review these kinds of things and I am not about to have him tell me what I can go over and what I can't!

"If I have to, I will see Lee about this one."

When asked why he hesitated to see Lee, Young said, "If I told the old man what was going on he would be furious. He wouldn't tolerate Frank stonewalling me. But he wouldn't be happy with me either. After he got done dressing down Frank, he'd let me have it for not figuring out a way to avoid a spat.

"Lee is funny that way. He tells us (staff VPs) how we are his 'watchdogs,' but he doesn't want us to bite, doesn't like it if we bark too often, and won't tolerate it if we whine. Most of us would rather try and 'settle out of court' than take a big issue to Lee to decide."

Sommers feels that Young would be foolish to see Lee on this matter. "Bill has more important things to do than waste his time arbitrating an issue that should be settled by us. The difference in our numbers just is not great.

"I feel sorry for Harry. He's probably feeling bored and out of the mainstream, but I'm not going to have him wasting my time or my people's, either. Heck, if he wants to be helpful, let him do some long-range study or something we don't have time or budget for."

GRANT CHEMICAL CORPORATION—PART C

The day following their second meeting on the equipment issue, Young saw Sommers for the third time and handed him a draft of a memorandum.

```
From:     H. Young
To:       F. Sommers
Subject:  Decision not to seek new technology
Dear Frank:
    I am distressed that the pressures of the moment
have made it difficult for your people to find time
to provide me with information critical to a thorough
evaluation of this major capital project.
    Obviously you do not want this project considered
until review is complete. Since it is a key element
in your division's plan, you will need a delay in
presenting your plan to the advisory committee and
Mr. Lee. Please let me know how long it will take for
your people to provide me with the worksheets, tests,
and detailed information you must have developed to
come to your current recommendation.
    I will then seek an appropriate delay in committee
review of your division plan.
    Please give me a ring as soon as you can.
                          Sincerely,

                          H. Young

CC:  W. R. Lee
     J. M. Vaughn
     P. I. Andrews
     M. K. Schwartz
     A. Simons
```

"Do you want me to send this, Frank?" Young asked.

Frank read the draft memo and said, "You're bluffing, Harold. You know what this means. Bill can't stand these sleazy bureaucratic butt-protecting memos. Who do you think you're dealing with—one of my plant people who you can impress with your scrapbook?"

"That does it, Frank," said Young. "I've had enough of your patronizing crap. We have been friends for a long time, and even if you weren't a great plant manager, you know I respect the way you took charge of this division. But you're getting too big for your britches. Whether you think I can help or not is immaterial. If I ever do get out of touch, it will be because I let you think you can dictate how I do my job. Now you either let me go over this one in detail or I send this memo this morning."

"Calm down, Harry," Sommers said. "We have been through enough together not to let our tempers box us in. I do not believe there is anything to be gained by going over stuff that my people have already been through carefully in the last month. But if it will make you happy, okay. I'll get you the files and let's settle this by Thursday or Friday at the latest."

After a careful review of the files, and a two-hour meeting on Friday, Sommers and Young agreed to disagree. The gap in their positions, if anything, widened based on three or four highly technical and quite judgmental differences of opinion.

When Lee received a copy of the Plastics Division plan the following week, much to his surprise he found a major supplement from Sommers supporting his recommendation on the new equipment. Even more surprising was a second supplement from Young, which went into even greater detail on why the proposed purchase should be delayed for at least one year.

Lee, a chemical engineer by training, said, "I was intrigued by these supplements but soon found myself lost. What did I hope to find, anyway? If my two experts couldn't agree, I certainly wasn't in a position to resolve their judgmental differences. Since we had never had a major flap like this in the three years-plus that our current structure has been in place, I did a little investigating and learned from Allison about the 'huffing and puffing' that preceded these reports.

"I'm tempted to call them in and bang their heads together. I'm not sure what makes me madder—the fact that they can't achieve consensus, or that they didn't come to me earlier and ask for clarification as to what I expect by way of checks and balances. Frankly, I'm not going to do anything until I cool off. In a way maybe I'm to blame. Perhaps we can use this issue to discuss how to improve the way I want our system to work. I might just allocate some time after our planning sessions and get the advisory committee and division presidents to talk this kind of problem through with me."

Part I

1. What appear to be the most significant elements in Grant's strategy?

2. How much attention does Lee appear to pay to changing forces in the external environment relative to the attention he gives to Grant's existing or potential internal strengths and weaknesses?

3. What key operating decisions should be shaped significantly by Grant's master strategy?

4. In what ways does Grant's strategy affect the roles played by Mr. Sommers? Mr. Young?

5. What are the greatest threats to Grant's success given its current strategy?

6. *Summary Report Question for Part I*. In what way do the structure and job definitions created by Lee attempt to deal with threats to Grant's current strategic efforts? Please relate your answers to questions 2, 4, and 5.

Part II

7. Given Grant's current strategy, what are two or three areas requiring very clear, high-level standing plans? Why?

8. How would Harold Young's definition of his problem differ with Frank Sommers' definition?

9. In what ways does the present staff-line relationship balance short- and long-term goals of the divisions and the company? How might staff-line relations be improved?

Part III

10. What are the strong points of the present organizational structure? What are its major weaknesses? How, within the framework of the present organization, might the weaknesses be minimized?

11. Is Sommers justified in refusing to allow Young to talk with Parks and Mathis? As president, would you support Sommers on this or overrule him and let Young talk directly to Parks and Mathis? What factors would you as president consider in making your decision?

12. How sound are Lee's definitions of the roles of corporate staff? What kinds of conflicts might arise from the three types of tasks they are assigned?

Part IV

13. What form of leadership should Lee employ to resolve the Young/Sommers conflict? To avoid it in the future?

14. Is the current conflict between Young and Sommers healthy or not? Explain.

15. What roles should staff play in effecting change in Grant Chemical?

16. To what extent might the Young/Sommers conflict stem from poor communication? How should any serious communication problems be corrected?

Part V

17. How should Lee measure and control the longer-range elements of divisional performance?

18. What are the roles of staff in measurement and control?

19. In what ways will Young's efforts to meet his responsibilities reduce Sommers' accountability for divisional results? How would you deal with these potential impacts?

Summary Report Questions for Solution of Case as a Whole

20. What are the basic causes of the conflict? Is there any way to resolve them short of action by the president?

21. Write a report advising Mr. Lee on what action he should take. Assume that Young is able to cast considerable doubt on Sommers' figures but that it is uncertain who is right.

Decision Case I–2
FYLER INTERNATIONAL

In the years since the break-up of the Bell System, Fyler International has grown from a small, highly regarded supplier of devices used in the telecommunications industry to an international firm. Sales last year approached $400 million and profits as a percent of investment placed Fyler in the top three of this fast-changing industry.

Joan Fyler, daughter of founders Helen and William Fyler, credits the company's recent success to strict adherence to what she calls the company's "Guidelines for Growth."

"We have always been known for having ingenious, high-quality products," Joan said. "Even before the Bell break-up, we sold a number of components that were rated superior to Bell's. Most of these were products we developed in our own labs. While our R&D budget was a tiny fraction of what Bell Labs spent each year, we came up with a number of superior devices. Mom was the 'scientist,' having taught electrical engineering and physics at Columbia University for years before Poppa and she started the business. Poppa worked for Bell Labs as well as Western Electric, and while he didn't have my mother's research skills he was an extremely creative development and design person.

"They were in their fifties when they decided to start the company. At first, they limited the scope of our operations to inventing new devices or improving on existing devices. Then they either sold their patents or licensed them to one of the 'biggies.'

"Several years before the break-up of Bell, a senior executive with GT&E and two of his associates convinced my parents to incorporate and retain sales rights to more of their products. These three people played key roles in building the business. Virtually all production was subcontracted to a number of small but high-standard producers. We did some final assembly and production of key parts but kept very close control over the quality of everything we bought. We still follow much the same approach, although we now do some production and most testing and final assembly of large subsystems.

"I came into the business soon after and took charge of all contracts, licenses, and other legal matters. I have a law degree and worked for almost ten years for a large investment banking firm."

When her mother died several years ago, Joan Fyler took on responsibility for all financial and treasury functions and looked after the firm's fast-growing international sales. Not long after this, with other key retirements, Joan became president and chief executive officer.

"Poppa is chairman and still the largest shareholder, but he is not really interested in the business aspects of the company. He spends most of his time in the lab 'tinkering,' as he calls it.

"Well, last year he 'tinkered' two new devices that will be used for monitoring transmission signals. Each promises to add another $10 million to $20 million in sales over the next five years."

While the company's sales and license revenues have grown each year, it still has fewer than 400 full-time employees. Several larger firms have offered to merge with or purchase Fyler but were turned down by Fyler's board.

"If their stock wasn't so tightly controlled, they would have been bought out or taken over by now," said an industry analyst. "They are very undervalued in the market because they are so conservative. With their patents and reputation they could increase sales and profits two or three times."

"Why sell?" Joan Fyler asked. "We can take pride in what we do and make more money than any of us ever expected to have. We pay a good dividend and those outside the family who own our stock know what to expect from us and what we expect from them. I am not smug, since we could be in real trouble in ten years. Many of our patents are running out. While Poppa and his people in the labs are amazing, they are really adapters, not inventors or scientists. We still can't begin to afford the sums it would take to compete with the research major firms do. Mother was the scientific genius. She not only did major research but attracted a number of brilliant young scientists who wanted to work with her. Most are gone now, attracted by bigger money or more exciting colleagues. Poppa could take Mother's ideas and create products, but he hasn't her scientific ability or her interest and skill in attracting outstanding young scientists.

"In all likelihood, we will have to sell out someday as our stream of patents and new devices dry up. But, it won't be while Poppa and his friends are still alive and active. We will probably be offered less later but we would have nothing without what they created.

"In the meanwhile, we will run a first-rate operation and stick to our 'Guidelines for Growth.' "

The Guidelines for Growth to which Joan Fyler refers evolved over the years from practices followed by her parents and other key executives. They were codified shortly after Joan Fyler became president and distributed to all personnel.

Exhibit 1: Guidelines For Growth

Growth will be best attained and most rewarding if we follow a few key guidelines. It is our belief that these guidelines make economic sense but, more importantly, represent the way we choose to direct this enterprise. There certainly are *other* ways; there may be *better* ways, but these are *our* ways.

None are etched in granite; all may be subject to change. Well-reasoned debate is invited. Carefully considered arguments for change or exceptions will be given quick attention. So will questions of interpretation. Unless written change or exception is given, however, these principles will guide our growth.

1. Never take or authorize an action you would not be prepared to explain on the 10 P.M. news in your hometown.
2. We do not have personnel, only people working with us. Following a three-month period for testing compatibility, a person becomes a "member of the family."
3. Fixed investments limit not only flexibility but creativity. Keep fixed investments (including our people) to a minimum in number and the absolute best in quality. Only make fixed investments that you must have *now* and plan to live with for a long time.
4. Seek the greatest degree of "leverage" from ideas. If you have a good idea, find ways to get it to the market as fast as possible, letting others do the production and distribution or low-value added work for us.
5. Pay well for services we need but don't wish to provide because of their low value added and tendency to create fixed investments. Never try to "squeeze" a key partner who does the work we chose not to do.
6. Never compromise on any standard once set. Therefore, be realistic. We have strict standards for products, vendors, and licensees. If you cannot measure and reach standards you feel to be realistic, forget the project until you can.
7. Don't be greedy. Lots of good, safe, small deals are better than risking all at one game of pitch and toss.

"Many non-company people read these and smile knowingly at what they consider another list of corporate clichés," Joan Fyler said. "Those who have been with us for a time know differently. Each of these seven guides help our people make the most important decisions they face. They know as well that calling people *people*—not personnel—translates into not only our practices, but is not inconsistent with considering people who are with us more than three months a fixed investment."

She went on to add: "Poppa and I *are* open to debate on most if not all of these guides. We rewrote Number 3 ('Fixed investments limit not only flexibility . . .') quite recently. It used to read: 'If you can rent it don't buy it; if you can borrow or barter, don't rent; if you can do without don't borrow or barter.' Some people took that one too literally or found it incompatible with guide Number 6 ('Never compromise on any standards . . .').

"We had some heated debate over this change, but now we have a better guide and, through debate, a clearer sense of what it means."

Fyler's International Operation

Sales and license revenue outside the United States has grown steadily in recent years and now represents 20 percent of the company's total. Return on investment of $20 million is a bit lower than the company's very fine return domestically, but overseas volume helps the company domestically.

"We have been careful with overseas capital given our attitude toward fixed investment," said Roger Black, Fyler's director of international operations.[1] "There are two explanations," he added. "*First,* we only put fixed capital in very low-risk areas where we can get high productivity and advantageous transportation. In fact, several or our facilities ship a large percentage of their products to the U.S. for domestic sales. We pro-rate the investment to reflect this so that my international operation doesn't suffer by comparison.

"*Second,* our insistence on quality and reliability makes it necessary for us to invest in some areas to assure our standards are met. We only do so, however, where a facility has a large served market, very low risk, and a sufficient number of highly trained people to staff the facility."

Most products sold outside the United States come from either the United States or vendors located outside the United States whose products serve American markets. The company licenses or sells through franchises in some countries but usually finds it more profitable to set up its own sales and service operation.

"We operate in different ways and with very different volumes in more than thirty countries," Black said. "More than half of our $80 million comes from five or six countries. In a few we have very small operations. Normally we look for our overseas sales to help us achieve volume domestically. We do not do research or product design for non-U.S. markets. We just aren't big enough. Instead we look for foreign markets that have sufficiently compatible technology to use products we sell in the U.S. Apart from our license deals, most overseas sales add to total volume to allow us lower cost to develop, make, or buy devices for the U.S. market.

"This may seem old-fashioned, but it helps a small company like us get the volume we need to stay profitable in the States. Since our fixed

[1]Black, an attorney, is also in charge of all contracts, licenses, and legal matters.

investment is very low and in safe spots, every dollar we earn is low-risk gravy.

"We still must be careful not to spread ourselves too thin. Every so often we reevaluate each non-U.S. operation against our Guidelines for Growth."

Fyler's operation in Brazil is currently under such a reevaluation. Fyler's sales there have over the past three years dropped gradually from $400,000 to $300,000,[2] despite an increase in the market for comparable products. Fyler's market share has dropped from roughly 22 percent to under 10 percent during this period.

"I asked Ruy Gerias, who heads our Brazilian operation, for an explanation and recommendations," Black said.

"Gerias has been with us more than seven years, so he is 'family.' If we were to fold our operation there, we would offer him work elsewhere. He is outstanding at recruiting and training our sales representatives. Perhaps he is too good. Our turnover of sales reps has been over 200 percent the last eighteen months. Even though our pay, bonus, and benefits are well above the average, we are losing our reps to other importers and domestic producers."

Black explained that all products sold in Brazil are imported. About 30 percent are considered "standard" products with some competition from domestic producers. The balance represents "high tech" products that have no real domestic competitors but varying amounts of competition from dozens of other importers.

Black feels it is best to concentrate on these high-tech items not just because of better margins but also because most are bought by only a small number of customer companies. These companies, while concentrated in five large cities, are geographically quite distant.

"Gerias claims we should have at least ten reps to cover these customers and sell our standard products," said Black. "But he currently can't even hold on to the six he is authorized to hire."

Technically, the six authorized representatives, while hired, trained, and supervised by Gerias, are not employed by Fyler since Fyler has not incorporated in Brazil. The reps are paid through the two distributors who warehouse and distribute all Fyler products in Brazil. Funds are channeled through the distributors, and a small fee is paid to them for handling the necessary paperwork.

When asked to explain recent declines and suggest remedies, Gerias blamed lack of inventory, the insufficient number of authorized sales representatives, and lack of any Brazilian manufacturing as the major causes. His recommendations were to

1. Authorize hiring, training, and salary benefits for ten representatives.
2. Permit him to supplement the "inadequate" warehouse space provided by the

---

[2]All figures are adjusted for inflation.

two distributors by purchasing two small satellite warehouses in Sao Paulo and Belo Horizonte.

3. Enter into a joint venture agreement with a local manufacturer to produce at least one-half of the company's standard products sold in Brazil.

4. Begin negotiations and accept low margins with all of the major state telephone companies to ensure further domestic production in return for large contracts and the prestige of such contracts.

Black's reaction to Gerias' report was more sad than angry. "I'm afraid Gerias is ill," he said. "He has done a fine job for us in the past, slowly building volume until recently. He already has more than $280,000 in receivables and inventories, and while we have gotten our profits out at acceptable indexed levels, this is a lot of money to tie up in an ever-promising but troubled giant.

"To add five more people means a minimum of $100,000 a year. If he keeps them, at current sales levels they'll only generate $60,000 in volume each, and that's not enough. Of course, he promises to increase sales to $4 million in two years with ten people and his other requests.

"The warehouse space would mean another $200,000 in fixed expenses and more to operate them. The joint venture he has outlined requires a $1 million investment by us over five years. I haven't even pressed him for details since the scheme is so far out of line. I have sent one of my people to see him, more to check on his health than on his figures."

QUESTIONS

1. Founders of corporations have historically had difficulty meeting the changing challenges of management as their businesses grow. How effective do you feel the Fyler family has been in overcoming these difficulties? What actions can you cite as examples?

2. How good a job has been done at Fyler in defining the company's overall mission? What are strong and weak points in their definition?

3. How sound do you feel Fyler's international strategy is? What are its strong and weak points?

4. How well does Fyler's international strategy fit its overall mission?

5. Which environmental factors need to be monitored most carefully, given potential impact on Fyler's strategy? By whom and how should this monitoring take place?

6. *Summary Report Question for Part I*. What steps should Joan Fyler take over the next year to prepare for the possibility that she will have to either sell out to a larger company or see her company fail as their patent stream dries up?

Part II

7. How useful do you feel Fyler's "Guidelines for Growth" are to key managers in the United States? Overseas? Explain.

8. Develop a thorough diagnosis of Fyler's problems in Brazil, taking at least one problem to root cause.

9. Analyze Ruy Gerias' recommendations in the light of Fyler's international strategy.

Part III

10. In staffing positions in countries such as Brazil, what are the advantages and limitations of using either (a) Brazilian nationals, (b) people who have worked for Fyler in other countries but are neither U.S. nor Brazilian citizens, or (c) U.S. citizens trained and experienced in U.S. operations?

11. In what ways do Fyler's "Guidelines for Growth" facilitate effective delegation?

12. How, if at all, might a small staff group located in the United States help Roger Black deal with problems such as those he faces in Brazil?

Part IV

13. Does the high turnover of sales representatives in Brazil indicate that Gerias is a poor leader?

14. What might he do to motivate his representatives to stay with Fyler?

15. In what ways may the current difficulties in Brazil be caused by communication problems?

Part V

16. How do Fyler's "Guidelines for Growth" affect the company's potential for establishing good control systems domestically? Internationally?

17. What control systems might help Black better pinpoint the cause of Gerias' problems in Brazil?

18. In what ways is the establishment of a control system for a foreign operation and its integration with other management processes more complicated than within domestic operations?

Summary Report Question for Solution of Case as a Whole

19. Prepare a report to Black in which you analyze the total situation regarding the Brazilian operation. Include what you believe to be the best course of action for Fyler to pursue and indicate in sufficient detail *how* your recommendations should be implemented.

4

Strategy: Defining the Mission

LEARNING OBJECTIVES

After completing this chapter, you should be able to

1. Explain the importance of an organization's strategy.
2. Understand how systematic analysis at the industry, company, and key-actor level can reduce the risks involved in strategy setting.
3. Discuss a four-part formula for strategy setting based on domain, differential advantage, strategic thrusts, and target results.
4. Explain the differences between business-unit, corporate, and functional strategies.
5. Illustrate how strategy affects the productivity of a business firm.

SCOPE OF PART II: MANAGERIAL PLANNING

Planning is an essential management task, one that has a major place in the overall division of managerial work—along with organizing, leading and controlling. In every enterprise, managers plan a wide variety of actions: what markets to enter or leave; what prices to charge; what salaries to pay; how to deal with governments and outside pressure groups: plus a host of other issues. The skill with which these plans are made makes or breaks an organization.

Whenever several people work together to reach a goal, planning becomes complicated. Because several people are taking part in the decision making, ways must be introduced to secure consistency in actions, coordination of various planning units, and economy in planning efforts. The five chapters of Part II look at various types of plans—or planning instruments—used to obtain such consistency, coordination, and economy.

Our analysis of planning takes a managerial point of view. Starting with the establishment of a mission or purpose, a manager can then move on to more specific goals for departments, sections, and specific individuals. With the goals known, guidelines for repetitive work can be established and programs for single tasks laid out. Of course, at each step in this planning, managers must make many specific decisions. So, at the close of this Part we will review ways that managers can improve their skill in action-oriented decision making.

CONCEPT OF BUSINESS STRATEGY

A business firm, like any organized group, needs some central purpose—a reason for existing. Outsiders may think of the firm as, say, a low-priced fast-food outlet or a sporting goods store. For employees, the organization's purpose guides all sorts of decisions. The question "What business are you in?" is central to everything that managers intentionally do.

Therefore, any effort at examining management processes must begin with a discussion of the selection of a concrete purpose for an organization. That selection of purpose is the first step in building a *strategy*.

In practice, the wise selection of strategy is often difficult as well as crucial. Rapid external changes, summarized in the preceding chapter, are requiring basic shifts in the way many companies operate. Converting a going business to a new strategy is proving to be much more difficult than managers had expected. To make a strategy realistic and practicable, the *major moves in attaining the selected purpose must be included*. Like landing a man on the moon, the goal may be clear, but getting from here to there is the real managerial challenge.

To provide a base for this execution-of-strategy theme, this chapter analyzes the nature of business strategy. Just what is business strategy? How is it determined? What are the main levels of strategy?

Broadly speaking, a business strategy is the *choice* of (1) the key services
that an organization will perform and (2) the primary bases of distinctiveness in creating and delivering such services, which will (3) enable that
organization to obtain a continuing flow of necessary resources.

Here are three illustrations of strategy in quite different fields.

Digital Equipment Corporation (DEC) established itself in the computer industry by being different. At a time when almost all computer
companies were increasing the size and complexity of their products,
DEC's strategy was to concentrate on small, simple "minicomputers." Also
contrary to industry practice, its early strategy was to provide a minimum
of service and to lower its prices repeatedly as experience and redesign
permitted. These decisions enabled DEC to become the leader in a niche of
the market that was growing faster than the total market; each was based
on a belief that the company could best succeed by being distinct from
competitors. As the organization expanded its customer focus from scientific users to business firms, it had to add more service. Nevertheless, its
internal structure continues to feature low expense. The strategy of consistently focusing on minicomputers for relatively simple uses, on frequent
redesign, and on lowering prices to discourage competition, has spurred
DEC into becoming a profitable $5 billion enterprise.

Avis follows a very different strategy. It competes head-on with the
leader in the car-rental industry—Hertz. It offers the same kind of service,
at about the same price, in most of the same locations. The "We try
harder" slogan (Figure 4.1) is the key to Avis' survival. Avis seeks to differentiate itself by more pleasant and adaptable relations with customers,
and by internal efficiency. By building a competitive enthusiasm based on
the idea that the underdog can take on the big boy, Avis makes a me-too
strategy work.

Strategy is also needed by not-for-profit enterprises. For example, Pa-
cific Hospital[1] is located in an area with an increasing population of retired
people. Consequently, the hospital administrator is pushing a strategy of
service to the elderly. This strategy involves discontinuing the maternity
and pediatric sections while expanding both staff and facilities for heart
problems and geriatric care. Out-patient service is stressed, and a free bus
makes daily trips around the community. The administrator faces resis-

[1]Disguised name.

Figure 4.1 The Avis "We try harder"
slogan has been instrumental in the
company's success.

tance by some personnel who contend that a hospital should be prepared to care for all medical needs; however, the strategy of focused service makes possible better care at less cost for the narrower market.

Common Characteristics of Strategy

Four characteristics of strategy stand out in each of the examples cited. These qualities characterize the strategy of almost any successful enterprise.

1. The strategy guides the enterprise over a period of years. Time is needed to build momentum; once built, it is hard to change in major ways.
2. The strategy is quite selective in the points it emphasizes. It focuses on key features that are to be important and continuing bases of distinctiveness.
3. The strategy is the dominant guide to action. It provides the overriding operating goals. Ideally, the strategy permeates the entire organization with a sense of mission.
4. The strategy guides the relationship of the enterprise to both its external environment and its internal activities.

These characteristics also suggest what a strategy is *not*. It does not include short-run, tactical moves or the large volume of short-range plans necessary to carry out strategy; it is not comprehensive, covering all external relations and all internal operations; it does not include all the goals and values endorsed by the company; it does not always focus on the same group of stakeholders or on the same internal department.

Strategy is valuable as a managerial tool because it is selective, enduring, and priority-setting. It provides a beacon light for the many other essential managerial decisions that must be made. Managers devote most of their effort to carrying out strategy and to related activities. As Figure 4.2 suggests, by separating out strategy for special attention, managers get two benefits: (1) they reduce the risk that clear thinking about strategy will be swamped by short-run, expedient action; (2) they can more easily

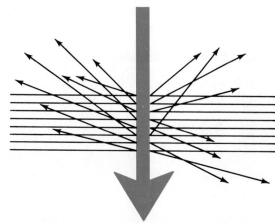

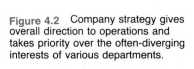

Figure 4.2 Company strategy gives overall direction to operations and takes priority over the often-diverging interests of various departments.

tie the many diverse activities to strategy in a consistent, synergistic manner.

HOW STRATEGY IS DETERMINED

Informal, Emerging Consensus

An enterprise can have a strategy even though no one ever systematically set one forth. For instance, strategy may grow out of a series of decisions regarding immediate problems; similarities in these decisions are gradually identified and accepted as norms that employees are expected to follow. If such emerging norms deal with strategic matters, then the enterprise does, in fact, have a strategy that almost everyone follows.[2]

A small liberal arts college in Ohio—which we'll call Midwest College—had such a strategy. Founded by a church denomination, Midwest always thought of itself as a "Christian" liberal arts school. Each year the faculty considered changes in courses to be offered, and from these discussions came a strong tradition that Midwest would not offer professional training (except the minimum of education courses necessary to teach in high school and a few music courses). As other denominational schools closed their doors and state-supported universities grew, Midwest increasingly emphasized liberal arts and Christian education in recruiting students and raising funds.

Located in the suburbs of a medium-size city, Midwest students often found part-time jobs. Then the college added an employment director, and provision for part-time work became an integral feature of the schedule. As a result, Midwest tended to attract students who could not afford to attend the big-name colleges. A related aspect was the prevailing seriousness and Protestant work ethic among students; Midwest did not cater to the playboy type. Tuition was kept somewhat lower than what was charged by other private colleges. Few experimental courses were offered, and academic standards were at least as high as those of the state university. (Midwest faculty believes they are higher.)

Clearly, Midwest College has a strategy. It caters to a particular segment of the college market. It has developed distinctive appeals, and its teaching technology is adjusted to the special needs of its clientele. The strategy just grew incrementally, but commitment to it is strong.

Strategy in some profit-seeking companies evolves in much the same way as it did in Midwest College.

Intuitive Decision by Powerful Individual

Henry Ford is a classic example of a domineering entrepreneur who personally set the strategy for his company.[3] High volume/low price, mass

---

[2]J. B. Quinn, *Strategies for Change: Logical Incrementalism* (Homewood, Ill.: Richard D. Irwin, 1980).

[3]For a portrait of Henry Ford and other outstanding American entrepreneurs, see H. C. Livesy, *American Dream* (Boston: Little, Brown, 1980).

production, and standardized products were pillars of the strategy that led to early success. Ford tolerated no deviations. For him, these (and related concepts) were *the* right way. And he had the power to insist that his strategy be followed. Henry Luce, the founder of Time, Inc., played a similar role in the early days of *Time* magazine, and to a lesser extent, at *Fortune* and *Life*.

Such a strong leader does not usually explore alternatives. Perhaps the directions chosen are merely personal preferences that luckily suit the conditions of the time. Often, though, the leader is an astute observer and has a sense of what will, and will not, succeed. The process of picking strategic elements is intuitive, however; and if early hunches result in success, the confirmed belief becomes "truth."

Reliance on intuition is risky. Only through experience can managers tell whether strategy based on intuition is well suited to the prevailing environment. And such past experience is a shaky foundation for further action in a dynamic setting. Few managers in the automobile or magazine industries today are willing to risk their careers on the intuition of some new Ford or Luce.

Likewise, to hope that a good strategy for the future will somehow grow out of focusing on daily problems is hazardous. Change lurks everywhere. New political and social alignments upset economic trends. Technology based on the computer invades working habits. So, special attention is needed to ensure that today's actions prepare for tomorrow's world.

Systematic Analysis

Systematic analysis helps to reduce strategy risks. One well-tested approach involves three sets of data and estimates.[4]

1. *Industry outlook.* By focusing on a single industry, the numerous changes in the world at large can be sorted; only those shifts believed to have a major impact on the industry need be studied in detail. The sales volume and profit outlook depend on (1) demand for the services of the industry, (2) supply of these services, and (3) competitive conditions. (*Service* is used here to include both physical products and/or intangible values provided by an enterprise.) A further breakdown of factors to consider is laid out in Table 4.1.

   The purpose of the industry analysis is to predict future volume and profitability for the entire industry. In addition, *key factors for success* should be identified. These are vital guideposts in designing a company strategy.[5]

[4]For a discussion of the approach outlined in Tables 4.1, 4.2, and 4.3, see W. H. Newman, J. P. Logan, and W. H. Hegarty, *Strategy, Policy, and Central Management,* 9th ed. (Cincinnati: South-Western Publishing Co., 1985), Chs. 3, 4, and 5.

[5]C. R. Christensen, K. R. Andrews, and J. L. Bower, *Business Policy,* 5th ed. (Homewood, Ill.: Richard D. Irwin, 1982).

Table 4.1 INDUSTRY OUTLOOK

81

Strategy: Defining the
Mission

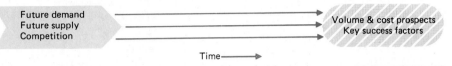

Future demand
Future supply
Competition

Volume & cost prospects
Key success factors

Time⟶

(Use judgment to select factors important to specific industry)

1. Future demand for service of the industry:

Long-run growth or decline	Consumer direct need vs. derived demand? Dependent on what life-style or technology? Specialized vs. varied uses?
Stability of demand	Substitutes available? Durable vs. consumed when used? Necessity vs. luxury? Government vs. cyclical? Number and size of buyers?
Stage in product life cycle	Still experimental? New, high potential? Mature? Dying?
Segments of market	Geography, usage, customer type, associated services, quality level?

2. Future supply of such services:

Capacity of industry	Present capacity vs. demand? Ease of entry? Speed of exit? Sunk vs. variable costs?
Availability of needed resources	Trained labor? New materials? Energy? Specialized equipment? Number and reliability of sources? Potential substitutes?
Volatility of technology	Frequency and degree of product improvement? Of process improvement? Competitive emphasis on R&D? Availability to latecomers?
Social constraints	Environmental protection? Product safety? Worker welfare?
Inflation vulnerability	For costs vs. selling prices. Flexibility up? Down? Timing of changes? Use of replacement costs?

3. Competitive conditions in industry:

Structure of industry	Dominance of few competitors? Strong trade association? Cutthroat tradition?
Government support and regulation	Subsidies, tariffs and other protections? Restraints on competition? Monopoly regulations? Tax target?

Conclusions:

Prospects for volume and profits	Total industry vs. segments? Degree of risk and uncertainty?
Key factors for success in industry	Total industry vs. segments?

Table 4.2 COMPANY STRENGTHS AND LIMITATIONS

Market position
Supply position   ⟶   Strengths & Weaknesses
Special strengths   vs.
                             Key success factors

Time ⟶

(Use judgment to select factors important to specific company)

1. **Market position of company:**

   Relation of company sales to total industry and to leading competitors

   Past trends? Reasons for change? Opportunities to increase share?

   Relative appeal of company services

   Quality as seen by customer? Product/service leadership? Relative prices? Synergy of marketing mix?

   Relative strength of major markets

   End-use markets? Geographic markets? Relative strength of distribution system?

2. **Supply position of company:**

   Comparative access to resources (availability and price)

   Material? Energy? Labor relations? Capital? Government aid? Overall resource costs?

   Unique productivity advantages

   Relative position on learning curve? Location advantage? New vs. old plant? Key patent? Optimum size?

   Comparative R&D strengths

   Creativity tradition? Own work vs. joint ventures? Areas of leadership? "Critical mass"? Capacity to switch emphasis?

3. **Special competitive considerations:**

   Relative financial strength

   Current and future cash flow? Relative ability to borrow? To sell equity? Vulnerability to cash squeeze? Future cash commitments?

   Community and government relations

   Reputation in community? Likely target? Ties to government programs? Skill with regulators?

   Abilities and values of managers

   Age/energy? Risk-takers? Adaptability? Demonstrated skills? Dependence on few key people? Doctrinaire?

Conclusions:

Summary of strengths and weakness of company relative to major competitors—in terms of key success factors identified in industry outlook.

Table 4.3 KEY ACTOR ANALYSIS

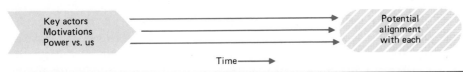

(Significance of each point varies widely, depending on particular situation)

1. **Who will be key actors?**

Vital resource suppliers	Banker? Key material supplier? Large customer? Union leader? Patent owner?
Aggressive competitors	Competitors for key resources? Competitors for customers?
Regulators	National or local commissions? Permit (license) grantors? Law administrator? Special-interest spokespersons?

2. **Motivations and likely responses of each key actor:**

Objectives—driving aims	Status? Growth in selected area? Political power? Security? Reform mission?
Patterns of behavior	Established methods and responses? Sources of new information and ideas? Past action leading to success?
Other commitments for use of resources	Announced programs? New opportunities? Pressures on resources?

3. **Power relative to use of each key actor:**

Actor's ability to withhold what we need	His alternatives? His ease of contraction? Impact on others?
Your alternative sources	Other customers? Other suppliers? Substitutes? Contraction?
Your power over the actor	Dependence on you? Consistent treatment with his competitors?
Willingness to use power	Future retaliation? Carryover to other cooperators? Reserve for future use?

4. **Potential alignment with each key actor:**

One-to-one relationship	Cooperate? Dictate? Accommodate? Fight?
Degrees of collaboration	Informal aid? Formal agreements? Joint ventures? Merger?
Coalitions	Scope of activities? Members? Common interests? Payoff for each member?

2. *Company strengths and limitations.* Each company (or division) has a history and momentum. It already possesses some strengths, and inevitably will have some weaknesses *relative to its major competition.* Also, it may be in either a weak or strong position to attract further resources. Naturally, a company will look for a strategy that utilizes its strengths and bypasses its limitations. Important dimensions of a company include (1) its market position, (2) its supply strengths, and (3) its financial and managerial resources.[6] See Table 4.2 for factors to consider in each of these categories.

3. *Key actor analysis.* Specific organizations with which the company must deal (suppliers, bankers, customers, regulators, and so on) will have their own programs and idiosyncrasies; individuals in those organizations will have their personal ambitions and values. Any new strategy will require that at least a few of these persons and organizations adjust their behavior to suit your company. Those whose response is crucial become *key actors.*

   When studying key actors, it is important to predict (1) who will be key actors, (2) their motivations and likely reactions, (3) the power each one has relative to you, and (4) what kinds of alignments are feasible. Information of this sort throws light on the specific help or hindrance that can be expected of other people active in your area. Table 4.3 outlines such an analysis.

Armed with predictions about the industry, company, and key actors, a manager can evaluate strategic proposals. The feasibility of pushing in particular directions can be assessed and the probable results predicted.

Systematic strategy analysis, along the lines just sketched, is a common practice in many leading companies. Its chief drawback is that it requires hard work. And when a manager is considering possible thrusts in several different industries, a separate study of each industry is necessary. Nevertheless, objectivity is introduced and risk reduced. Company experience and personal intuition can still be considered, but these inputs are cross-checked and weighed in light of the best analytical data that can be mustered.

CORPORATE, BUSINESS-UNIT, AND FUNCTIONAL STRATEGIES

Too often, strategy remains just a broadly stated objective. The linking of strategy to actual operations requires explicit and continuing attention. A crucial aid to this linking is to state strategy in operational terms.[7]

[6]M. E. Porter, *Competitive Strategy: Techniques for Analyzing Industries and Competitors* (New York: Free Press, 1980), Ch. 7. See also P. Shrivastava, "Integrating Strategy Formulation with Organizational Culture," *Journal of Business Strategy,* Winter 1985.

[7]J. M. Hobbs and D. F. Heany, "Coupling Strategy to Operating Plans," *Harvard Business Review,* 55:3, May–June 1977.

Especially useful is to distinguish strategy for three organizational levels: top management of a diversified corporation; business unit or company; and functional departments within a business unit.[8] Business units are the primary centers for initiating strategic action. Business-unit strategy will thus be addressed first, and then the discussion will move up to corporate strategy and down to functional strategy.

Business-Unit Strategy

A business unit in its simpler form is an independent, single-product-line company such as a bakery, coal mine, or shoe manufacturer. The enterprise could be nonprofit—a drug rehabilitation center, for example. Or it might deal only in services, such as a public accounting firm. Each of these business units has a homogeneous product line, serves a defined group of customers, and manages most of the resources necessary to create its services. Consequently, it can devise a coordinated strategy for its total business.

As a business unit grows, it may add sales outlets or production plants, but it can still be managed with one central strategy. If a firm diversifies into several different kinds of business, however, it becomes a "diversified *corporation*" and should treat each of its self-contained product divisions as a separate business unit. For instance, the typewriter division of IBM is a business unit even though it is legally in the same organization as computers. If the shoe manufacturer adds a line of luggage, the corporation would then have two business units. Incidentally, for ease in reading, in this book we will use the terms *company* or *enterprise* as synonyms for *business unit*.

Four-Part Business-Unit Strategy

A business unit, then, is a particular kind of organization. Because it has a distinctive character, a manager can be more specific about the elements in a good strategy for it.

As Figure 4.3 shows, a business-unit strategy should indicate the following:

1. *Domain sought.* What products or intangible services will the business unit sell to what group of customers? Answering this question requires selection of an industry, and one or more related niches within that industry, in which to operate.[9]

2. *Differential advantages in serving that domain.* On what basis—for example, access to raw materials, better personnel, new technology,

---

[8]P. Lorange, *Corporate Planning: An Executive Viewpoint* (Englewood Cliffs, N.J.: Prentice-Hall, 1980), Ch. 2.

[9]D. F. Abell, *Defining the Business: The Starting Point of Strategic Planning* (Englewood Cliffs, N.J.: Prentice-Hall, 1980).

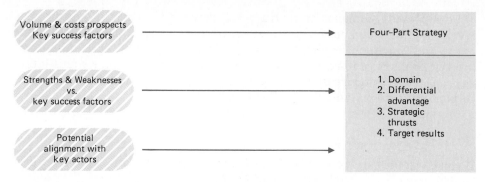

Figure 4.3 Designing a Business-Unit Strategy

or low costs and prices—will the business unit seek an advantage over competitors in providing its products or services?[10]

3. *Strategic thrusts necessary and their approximate timing.* To move from where the business unit is now to where it wants to be, what strategic moves will be made immediately and what can be deferred?

4. *Target results expected.* What financial and other criteria will the business unit use to measure its success, and what levels of achievement are expected? These are the agreed-upon objectives. Theoretically, the objectives could be listed first instead of last, but rarely can the objectives be sharply defined until the modus operandi just outlined is settled. For operational purposes, specific targets agreed to by key resource contributors are very useful.

These four dimensions of business-unit strategy are clearly illustrated in the Crown Cork & Seal Company. The tin can division of Crown Cork has a remarkable record of growth and profits in spite of maturity and sharp competition in the can industry. Selection of domain is vital. Crown Cork's niche is cans for hard-to-hold products—beer, carbonated beverages, aerosol sprays. Twenty-five years ago, it withdrew from making ordinary cans, and it has stayed out of bottles, paper, and plastic containers. Within its niche, however, it is the leading producer, with sales well over $1 billion.

Crown Cork seeks a differential advantage over competitors by giving fast, personal service that its less specialized competitors can't match, and by keeping expenses low. Its tough, no-frill operation results in selling and administrative expenses that are less than 4 percent of sales—significantly lower than competitors.

When Kaiser Aluminum Company introduced an attractive two-piece aluminum can, Crown Cork's leadership was threatened. This led to two strategic thrusts—development (with steel industry R & D) of the technology to make two-piece steel cans, and rapid investment in equipment to

[10]S. E. South, "Competitive Advantage: The Cornerstone of Strategic Thinking," *Journal of Business Strategy,* Spring 1981.

manufacture such cans. The risks were large, the timing crucial; only a sharp drop in the price of aluminum prevented Crown Cork from enlarging its market share even further.

Target results—sales growth of about 15 percent a year while maintaining past profit margins—reflect the values of Crown Cork's president. Incidentally, no dividends have been paid for over twenty-five years. . . . An outsider may consider Crown Cork's strategy narrow and risky, but the course the company has set for itself is crystal clear.

Statements of strategy too often deal with only a single dimension. A new market or a desired financial return on investment, for instance, may be labeled as "our company strategy." By its narrowness, such a goal robs strategy of a needed, balanced operational quality. To achieve this balance, all four of the elements just listed should be carefully considered. The resulting strategy will then be an *integrated,* forward-looking plan.

The multidimensions of strategy—domain sought, differential advantage, strategic thrusts, and target results—do not require that a strategy be detailed and comprehensive. Rather, strategy should concentrate on *key* factors necessary for success and on *major* moves to be taken by the particular organization at the current stage in its development. The selectivity of key points, and by implication its designation of others as supportive, gives strategy much of its value as a planning device.

Corporate Strategy

Successful business units often outgrow their original mission. Their market may have matured; they may have strengths that can be applied to related businesses; a broader base may be needed to match competition or spread risk; or assurance of supplies may become critical. For reasons such as these, many companies find themselves engaged in several different businesses. Potentially, the federation of units will be stronger than the sum of each business operating independently, but this does not happen automatically. A corporate strategy is needed to yield the benefits of union.

Corporate strategy is primarily concerned with building an effective collection of business units. This requires thoughtful investment (allocation) of resources. Some units will be built up, others liquidated; perhaps new units will be acquired. Because this allocation process is similar to the process by which financial investment managers change the composition of securities in their portfolios, the term *portfolio problem* is widely used to identify the distinctive aspects of managing a diversified corporation.

The main elements in a corporate strategy, then, include the following:[11]

1. The desired portfolio of business units five to ten years hence.
2. Major moves (thrusts) to get from the present situation to the holdings desired in (1). Three sub-elements should always be covered:

[11]B. Yavitz and W. H. Newman, *Strategy in Action* (New York: Free Press, 1982), Chs. 3 and 4.

a. a "charter" for each business unit to be retained, indicating the domain of the unit, expected results, and resources that the corporation will make available; within these limits, each unit will develop its own business-unit strategy as outlined in the previous section;

b. changes in the portfolio, including desired acquisitions and any sale or liquidation of existing units;

c. consolidated plans for the mobilization and allocation of corporate capital, key personnel, and other resources.

3. Target results.

Such a corporate strategy relies on the business units to be the active, competitive centers. They are the dynamic building blocks. The main role of the corporation is to help its operating units be effective and to shift resources to areas where service and result opportunities are the highest.

A successful research-based firm, Coated Optics, Inc., recently faced a corporate-strategy problem. Their main business involves depositing an extremely thin layer of molecules on telescope lenses, radar receivers, and the like. Most orders are small and often require pioneering technology. A few of the company executives now want to use their existing know-how in mass production. One suggestion is to produce fiber optics for use in the next wave of office copier machines ("the successor to Xerox"). However, volume production would require mechanization, automated quality control, new marketing and financial arrangements, and so on. The scientist-engineers who now dominate the firm have no interest in such "factory" work.

Coated Optics, Inc. has therefore created a separate business unit to develop large-volume orders, and the original work has been split between a government division and civilian products division. Each division has its own shop, gets its own business, and is accountable for its results. Thus, the domains are defined. Technical personnel have been assigned. Targets are set. The new fiber optics division is still tooling-up, and is not scheduled to make a profit for three years. During that period, the corporate officers may shift the strategy, expanding or contracting any of the divisions, or perhaps entering still another area.

Functional Strategy

Functional strategy is useful for departments that operate right below the business-unit level.[12] Marketing, for instance, may select a few key approaches that become its persisting, overriding tenets. Human resources, finance, production, or another function that is a major contributor to a particular business may have its strategy. Of course, such strategy should be compatible with and reinforce the broader business-unit strategy.

---

[12]For a comprehensive discussion of functional strategies and policies, see W. H. Newman, J. P. Logan, and W. H. Hegarty, *Strategy, Policy, and Central Management,* 9th ed. (Cincinnati: South-Western Publishing Co., 1985), Part 2.

1. assigned mission or role within the business unit;
2. kinds of excellence to be stressed;
3. major moves or "initiatives" to be started in the near future;
4. target results.

A book-publishing firm, for example, needs personnel for its expanding output, but in its location, skilled workers who do quality work are scarce. One hope is the increasing number of homemakers or hobbyists who want part-time employment. So the firm is trying a personnel strategy of a work week of 20 to 40 hours, scheduled largely at an employee's convenience. The plan will be tried first in the editorial sections, and if scheduling and workplace arrangements can be developed there, the plan may be extended to accounting and shipping. The targets are a 50 percent increase in output with no increase in turnover rates, and better quality with a stable real cost per unit. Results to date show that some very able people are attracted to the firm, but problems of supervision are rising exponentially.

Nestlé, S. A. (a world-renowned Swiss chocolate firm), to cite another example in marketing, sells in many countries a scientifically prepared infant food that can be used as a supplement to mothers' milk. This product became the target of a worldwide boycott because of the way it was promoted in developing countries. After several years of heated publicity (often exaggerated), Nestlé modified its marketing strategy. Now, instead of using newspaper advertisements and direct contacts of its representatives with new mothers, Nestlé promotes the product only through contacts with medical personnel. The aim of the new marketing strategy is to avoid unfavorable publicity that might hurt sales of other Nestlé products, while retaining at least some volume of sales of the infant food.

Note that in both the Nestlé and the book-publishing examples, functional strategy is a prime continuing force, but it is subordinate to broader business-unit strategy.

CONCLUSION

Every enterprise needs a mission—a specific purpose. Survival depends on it. However, that purpose must be realistic in terms of the desires of society, resources available, competition, and technology. There must be a practical fitting together of hopes and things that work.

Strategy is the best tool yet devised to clarify such a mission and to harness human effort for the achievement of that mission. A well-developed business strategy defines its domain, flags differential advantages sought, lists strategic thrusts, and specifies target results. Once understood, such a strategy provides the focus for joint endeavor. Corporate,

Table 4.4 **THREE LEVELS OF STRATEGY**

	Corporate Strategy	*Business-unit Strategy*	*Functional Strategy*
Scope	Desired portfolio	Domain: industry and niche	Assigned mission
Sources of Distinction	Charters for desired business units	Differential advantage	Kinds of excellence
Initiatives	Changes in portfolio Resource plans	Strategic thrusts	Major moves
Objectives/ Expected Results	Target results	Target results	Target results

business-unit, and functional strategy (see Table 4.4) serve a similar purpose for broader and narrower organization units.

For managers and other employees, strategy is an ever-present, potent force. The examples of Avis and Crown Cork illustrate how strategies are translated down to the operating level. Materials are bought and customers served in a way that is consistent with an overall explicit strategy. Good strategy leads to action.

Because strategy has an unusual power to unify action, the concept has been introduced early in this book. In following sections we will note how other managerial tools (1) are guided by strategy and (2) can be used to execute strategy. Thus, we are using strategy as an entering wedge into the interdependent, dynamic mechanisms of the total management process.

Impact on Productivity

The dominating influence of strategy, as just noted, has a company-wide impact on productivity. Strategy helps to make "productive" both the services rendered and the way those services are created.

For instance, (1) a clear strategy is the best mechanism for starting fundamental changes *promptly*. As the environment shifts, changes to meet new customer needs or changes to lower costs may be possible. Good strategic planning identifies these opportunities early.

(2) A clear strategy *centers company-wide attention* on the same mission, thereby reducing conflicting efforts that undermine productivity.

(3) If the "four-part strategy" concept is used, a *bridge is built* between broad objectives and managerial action. A mere statement of financial goals or desired market often produces more talk than action. Productivity is aided only when well-selected objectives are translated into operating results—and that is why all four parts of a well-developed strategy are stressed.

1. (a) Compare what you consider to be the key success factors in the following industries: atomic energy, computer software, cosmetics, hospitals, ski resorts. (b) In which industry would you prefer to build your career?

2. (a) The number of farmers in the United States continues to decline (31 million in 1940, 16 million in 1960, 8 million in 1980). Does this mean that there are no attractive niches in the farm industry? (b) Briefly outline what you believe would be a successful strategy for a farmer in your home state.

3. A Grand Rapids firm that supplies the auto industry wants to expand, either at its present location or with a branch plant in northeastern Indiana. In Indiana, the local bank would help with a low mortgage; to discourage unionization, wage rates would be above local rates but below those in Michigan; a site next door to a retirement home is available if zoning can be altered. Who are the key actors in this situation? How is each likely to respond to a branch move?

4. "Our 'strategy' is to watch what the giants in our industry are doing and then look for crumbs they drop or markets too small for them to bother with." Comment on this statement by the president of a $100 million company in an industry dominated by three $1 billion companies. Contrast his views to those illustrated by the actions of Crown Cork.

5. A large stockholder in Neptune Pharmaceuticals says, "Fundamentally, our strategic objective should be to maximize the return on investment in the long run." Is this a good way for managers of Neptune to state their strategic target?

6. Can—or should—a non-profit organization attempt to develop a long-term strategy when it must seek funding on an annual basis? (Assume that the organization has little in the way of endowments or long-term financial commitments.)

7. Use the four parts of a business-unit strategy suggested in this chapter to outline a career plan that you are seriously considering.

8. Three levels of strategy are illustrated in recent actions of the Singer Company. (a) In the United States, production and sale of domestic sewing machines are being phased out; instead, emphasis on defense products is to be increased. (b) The main target for the remaining U.S. sewing machine activities is to generate cash, not long-run profit. (c) Marketing through Singer retail stores is to be liquidated. Can you suggest other examples of business-unit and functional department strategy, in addition to (b) and (c), that are likely to result from the new corporate strategy noted in (a)?

Donaldson, G. and J. W. Lorsch, *Decision Making at the Top: The Shaping of Strategic Decisions.* New York: Basic Books, 1983. In-depth study of how strategic decisions are actually made in large operations; considers balancing of financial and noneconomic objectives.

Linneman, R. E., *Shirt-Sleeve Approach to Long-Range Planning.* Englewood Cliffs, N.J.: Prentice-Hall, 1980. Practical advice on the development of strategy in the smaller, growing corporation.

Makrides, S. and S. Wheelwright, eds., *The Handbook of Forecasting.* New York: Wiley Interscience, 1982. Presents wide range of forecasting techniques available to business planning specialists.

Newman, W. H., J. P. Logan, and W. H. Hegarty, *Strategy, Policy, and Central Management,* 9th ed. Cincinnati: South-Western Publishing Co., 1985. Business-unit strategy (Part 1); policies needed to support strategy (Part 2); corporate strategy (Part 3); organizing and executing strategy (Parts 4 and 5).

Porter, M. E., *Competitive Advantage.* New York: Free Press, 1985, Chs. 2–6. Primary focus on techniques for finding potential "differential advantage." This book is a sequel to Porter's *Competitive Strategy,* which deals primarily with "domain."

Schendel, D. and C. Hofer, eds., *Strategic Management: A New View on Business Policy and Planning.* Boston: Little, Brown, 1979. Good review of major research developments in strategy and planning systems.

Yavitz, B. and W. H. Newman, *Strategy in Action: The Execution, Politics, and Payoff of Business Planning.* New York: Free Press, 1982. Targeted for business managers; Part 1 focuses on strategy formulation.

As the 1980s approached, the nation's largest banks—Citibank and Chase Manhattan of New York, Bank of America of San Francisco, and a half dozen others—prepared for the biggest change in banking in a half century. With the anticipated end to federal laws limiting interstate banking, all the big banks were jockeying for position in the national consumer banking market. Some estimated that as much as $600 billion in new money in the consumer business was waiting to be attracted by the big banks.

Citibank, long recognized as the most aggressive and risk-taking institution in an industry that rarely rewarded such behavior, decided not to wait for its competitors. Its leaders knew the potential of the consumer business. And Citibank executives knew that if they could get their Visa credit cards in the hands of consumers across the country—even before the interstate banking laws were changed—it would provide Citibank with a distinct advantage in approaching these new prospective customers.

With the strategy clear, during a few months of 1979 Citibank mailed out more than 10 million Visa cards to people living in postal zip code regions inhabited by those of upper and upper-middle incomes across the United States. During the next two years, some industry estimates show, Citibank lost as much as $200 million in its credit card business, largely because of transaction costs and defaults on credit card purchases. But the mastermind of the credit card strategy had anticipated those losses. And John S. Reed, who later became Citicorp chairman because of his successes in consumer banking, knew it would only be a short time until Citibank could charge an annual fee for each Visa card it had in use. While many cards were returned by customers when the $20-a-year fee was added in 1982, millions were kept.

Those fees produced enough additional revenue—about $500 million a year—that the Citibank Visa business moved from a big loser in its early years to a big winner. In the mid-1980s, Citibank was making between $250 million and $400 million a year in the business—about one-quarter of its total worldwide profit. Even more important in the long term, Citibank was putting itself and its name in front of consumers from across the country who also would come to the bank with money market accounts, savings certificates, and certificates of deposits, and even to obtain loans. And as it became legal, there was the promise of Citibank's winning still more business from across-the-country consumers first attracted to Citibank by the Visa card mailing.

It was a risky strategy, but one that was well thought out. And it appeared to be successful.

Questions

1. If you had a Citibank Visa card, would *you* also turn to that bank for a money market account, savings certificate, or certificate of deposit?

2. In view of the recent aggressive promotion by many other banks of their own Visa cards, do you believe that Citibank's early and costly promotion of its cards was a wise strategy?

For more information, see "Citicorp's Atypical Leader: John Shepard Reed," *The New York Times*, 21 June 1984, p. 31.

APPLICATION CASES

For practice in applying concepts covered in this chapter to managerial situations, see the following managerial decision cases. The case questions particularly relevant to this chapter are listed by number after each case name.

Grant Chemical Corporation (p.59) 1, 5
Fyler International (p. 68) 2, 6
GAIN Software (p. 303) 3, 4
Peter Jeffries (p. 428) 6
Unisa Sound (p. 530) 3

5

Sharpening Goals and Operating Objectives

LEARNING OBJECTIVES

After completing this chapter, you should be able to

1. Develop a hierarchy of operating objectives that is consistent with the organization's strategy for an organization you know.
2. Tell the difference between meaningful objectives and mere hopes that are beyond reasonable expectations.
3. See how short-term objectives fit in with long-term goals.
4. Know the four key elements and five main benefits of Management by Objectives (MBO) programs.
5. Understand General Electric Company's eight key-results areas for the management of a business unit and how they tie in with limitations on the number of objectives that can be handled by a single individual.

Bridges must be built between organizational strategy and specific activities that must be carried out as workers go about their everyday jobs. Once the broader strategy has been established, operating objectives can be formulated for various organization members operating at various organizational levels. Strategy can be translated into effective action only when sharply defined goals have been understood and accepted by each member of the organization.

Three kinds of issues arise as operating objectives are molded into the driving force toward some master strategy. First comes the translation—or "spelling out"—of broad goals into smaller and more specific assignments for each part of the organization. Next, these specific objectives become a vital focus in the local managing process; there are a variety of methods for accomplishing this, although Management by Objectives (MBO) is the most thorough and proven technique. Finally, problems that result from the melding and adjusting of operating objectives must be resolved.

Hierarchy of Plans

Strategy already contains two leads into shorter-range plans. First, strategic thrusts call for a series of actions, such as opening an office in Sao Paulo or selling a public issue of company stock. Each thrust can be subdivided into steps and substeps that are assigned to individuals. This breakdown is continued until, to extend the Sao Paulo office example, one person finds the site, another determines the equipment and layout, and a third hires personnel. Note that a hierarchy of assignments emerges with the specific, immediate steps contributing to an intermediate objective, while the intermediate objectives build toward the broader strategic goal, as suggested in Figure 5.1.

Second, the target results component of strategy is the source of a

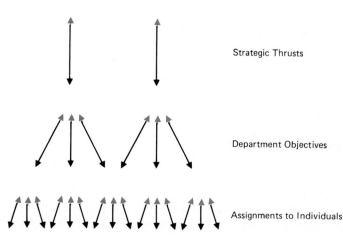

Figure 5.1 Hierarchy of Objectives. Broad objectives are achieved by dividing the total task into pieces, or steps. The black arrows indicate this successive division into practical assignments. The points show how the local, immediate objectives contribute to the broad goals.

Strategic Thrusts

Department Objectives

Assignments to Individuals

series of moves necessary to achieve the target. These moves are further divided until tasks of a size suitable to a single person are reached. Again, there is a hierarchy, with each task finding its justification as a contributor to a broader objective.

Much planning effort is necessary to develop operating objectives from strategy. Strategy is selective in the subjects it covers; in contrast, operating objectives should be comprehensive. Current operations as well as strategic changes should be covered. Monthly or even weekly progress, and the development and use of resources, should be spelled out. Because these operating objectives are so crucial to achieving results, we need to look at them more closely.

Operating Objectives

For managerial purposes, it is useful to think of objectives as the results we want to achieve. The words *goal, aim,* and *purpose* also have much the same meaning, because they, too, imply effort directed toward a preselected result.

In this book, the word *objectives* is used broadly. It covers long-range company aims, more specific department goals, and even individual assignments. Thus, objectives may pertain to a wide or narrow part of an enterprise, and they may be either long- or short-range. A salesperson may have an immediate objective of clearing up a misunderstanding with a customer, and she may have a five-year objective of cultivating a territory to provide $25,000 in sales each month. Similarly, a company may have a short-term objective of providing stable employment during the next summer and a long-range objective of being a product leader in its industry. These are all results to be achieved.

Objectives of a particular nature are often given special names—equal-opportunity quotas, expense ratios, budgets, absentee rates, or market positions are examples. The use of such descriptive terms does not remove them from the broad category of objectives.

Meaningful Objectives for Each Job

Company objectives are always broad and inclusive. Thus, the president of Crown Cork & Seal Company speaks of "$2 billion in sales within five years." Or, an R & D vice-president wants specifications for a low-cost solar water-heater in two years. Such targets are too vague to provide a guide to action for most members of the company. What bearing specific decisions have on the objective is often indirect, and particular activities tend to lose their significance when they are merged into a large, total result. Perception of the broad picture, desirable as it is, does not replace the need for more specific goals for each job. In fact, it is entirely possible for an effective worker to be dedicated to doing his job well and at the same time be indifferent to the broad company objectives.

One task of every manager, then, is to help clarify intermediate objectives for each subordinate. A subgoal may be to achieve a dominant

market position in a particular city, to attain leadership in salary administration, to keep abreast of new techniques in the industry, or to maintain
well-kept grounds around the plant. This is the kind of goal a subordinate
executive or operator can go to work on.

Care and ingenuity are needed in refining these subobjectives. A total
system is involved, as Figure 5.2 shows for an urban-development project.
All of the contributions to a broad objective—not just one or two—must be
assigned to somebody. These contributions often interact—as in the urban
development case—so that if we change Irene's subgoal, it may upset
Bob's. Moreover, such jobs always have several subgoals—various aspects
of one end result (quantity, quality, cost, and so on). Tinkering with one of
these subgoals may complicate another. Actually, this multidimensional
interrelatedness creates so much inertia that it is difficult to adjust operating objectives to support shifts in strategy.

Clarifying objectives and subobjectives is a continuing task. Some
people often like to think that objectives are fixed, but this is only partially
true. We shift company strategy to seize a new opportunity; and because
the specific objectives assigned to individuals are derived from the broad
company goals, a change in strategy is likely to require adjustments in the
objectives of several supervisors and operators. In fact, little effective
change will occur until assignments down the line are revised. Clearly,
defining objectives is neither static nor automatic.

Hopes versus Expectations

An objective may be optimistic, in that the results hoped for will occur if
everything works just right—like par on the golf course. Or it may be realistic, a statement of what we actually expect to accomplish—like par
plus our handicap. Both types of goals have their uses, but it is important
to distinguish between them.

Advocates of optimistic objectives believe that a person will accomplish more with sights set high. If we have the courage to dream great
dreams, then we can bend our efforts to make them come true.[1]

Everyone knows of examples of such determination succeeding. The
largest transatlantic air-cargo line would never have been more than a
small charter carrier without the high objectives of its president. The company spent years obtaining government permission to operate scheduled
flights. In the midst of these negotiations, a decision to place a multimillion-dollar order for new jets was made. In this instance, acting on hope
rather than on "sound" expectation led to significantly better results.

In all such cases, the aimed-at results are at least possible, with supreme effort, good luck, and favorable operating conditions. Occasionally,
even objectives known to be unattainable are used—this, for example:
"Give every employee the maximum opportunity to reach his highest po-

---

[1]E. A. Locke and G. P. Latham, *Goal Setting: A Motivational Technique that Works!* (Englewood Cliffs, N.J.: Prentice-Hall, 1984).

Figure 5.2 In dealing with so vast an undertaking as an urban-renewal project, it is necessary to break down the project into a series of subobjectives—financing, excavation, construction, and selection of tenants. This practice can be useful on a smaller scale as well.

tential." This an an ideal to strive for. It provides direction, as stars do for sailors, but it is never reached.

In contrast, a manager may choose to state objectives in realistic terms, seeking levels that can be achieved without superhuman effort and uncanny luck. Thus, reasonable sales quotas can be filled by most sales representatives; with normal diligence, expense ratios can be met by good managers; personnel programs can come up with able workers, if not geniuses; profit targets will bear some resemblance to last year's results. These are goals that management expects to be met. In some areas, performance may surpass the objectives, and this good fortune may help offset lagging performance in other areas.

In business planning, emphasis is generally on tough, but achievable, objectives. There are two reasons for this preference. (1) Frustration or indifference is apt to develop if stated goals are rarely, if ever, achieved. (2) Objectives are used for planning and coordination as well as for motivation, so related activities may go awry if management tries to synchronize them with an objective that proves to be more hope than reasonable prediction.

Short-run Objectives as Steps Toward Long-run Goals

A major task becomes more manageable when it is divided into small pieces. This analytical concept is, of course, employed in setting up hierarchies of objectives and in organizing work by departments. Another breakdown is by steps or results to be achieved within a given period of time. This method is commonly used in personal career decisions. For instance, suppose Joan Casey wants to become an executive in a local publishing firm (long-run objective). She may decide that a business education (intermediate objective) will help her achieve this goal. So she takes a course in management as one of several steps toward a formal business education.

A step-by-step breakdown is particularly valuable in complicated business projects. The use of satellites in telephonic and television communication, for example, is a vast and complex undertaking. Receiving and broadcasting stations have to be located on the basis of technical, economic, and political considerations; equipment has to be designed and built, personnel trained, satellites launched, users of the service educated, rates set, and a staggering amount of capital acquired. A job of this sort becomes manageable only when it is broken down into a series of steps. In fact, each major step will be divided and subdivided.

Even relatively simple assignments, such as a political campaign for U.S. senator, may well be divided up into small work units.

The creation of such short-run objectives has several advantages.[2]

1. *They help make objectives tangible and meaningful.* We all find it easy to project ourselves into the immediate future, whereas the more dis-

[2]J. B. Quinn, *Strategies for Change* (Homewood, Ill.: Dow Jones-Irwin, 1981).

tant future is filled with uncertainties; besides, we have no compelling reasons to face remote problems now.

2. *Short-run objectives provide a hope-expectation bridge.* It is entirely possible to have optimistic long-run goals and at the same time be quite realistic about the immediate steps to be taken toward these ends. Working on a tangible, immediate project tends to relieve the frustration that can arise from the magnitude and difficulty of a major objective. This tendency is an asset, provided a manager himself does not become so engrossed with a short-run objective that he loses sight of the existence and nature of the long-run objective.

3. *Short-run objectives provide short-run benchmarks.* These interim measures provide a great aid in motivation and control. When workers see that they are making progress, they get a sense of accomplishment, even when the job is not yet finished; they also build confidence to tackle the work still ahead.

MANAGEMENT BY OBJECTIVES

Once operating objectives are specified, how are executives and workers induced to accomplish them? This is largely a matter of motivation and leadership—the subject of Part IV. However, one approach—Management by Objectives (MBO)—is so widespread and so intimately related to the setting of objectives that it should be briefly explained now.[3]

Elements of MBO

MBO represents a whole cluster of management techniques. It combines selected aspects of planning, organizing, leading, and controlling. Having become a fashionable term, different meanings are attributed to MBO by different writers. Nevertheless, virtually all the definitions stress the following elements, as depicted in Figure 5.3:

1. *Agreement.* At regular intervals, a manager and each subordinate agree on the *results* (objectives) that the subordinate will try to achieve during the next period (quarter, half-year, or year). The subordinate *participates* actively in spelling out the meaning and feasibility of the assignment he accepts. The broad purpose and the organizational constraints, however, are dictated by the strategy of the enterprise and the mission of the supervisor. Both the subordinate and supervisor will understand and feel committed to this statement of what will constitute good performance.

[3]G. S. Ordiorne, *The Change Resisters: How They Prevent Progress and What Managers Can Do About Them* (Englewood Cliffs, N.J.: Prentice-Hall, 1981); and S. J. Carroll and H. L. Tosi, *Management by Objectives: Applications and Research* (New York: Macmillan, 1973).

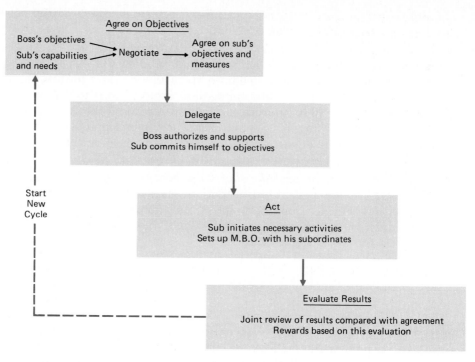

Figure 5.3   Steps in Management by Objectives (MBO).

2. *Delegation.* The supervisor then delegates activities to the subordinate. During this period, the main role of the supervisor is to *assist*
the subordinate in fulfilling the agreement. As part of the agreement,
the supervisor may be committed to provide certain help, and the subordinate may call for more. But the subordinate is expected to take
whatever initiative is necessary to achieve the agreed-upon results.

3. *Evaluation of results.* At the end of the period actual results are measured, and the supervisor and subordinate discuss reasons for success
and failure. This evaluation becomes the basis for making another
agreement (perhaps at a later meeting) for the next period. And so
the cycle continues.

4. *Associated activities.* The evaluation of results often serves as the basis of setting salaries and bonuses and of planning personal development. Also, the negotiation of agreements may lead to modifications
in organization, procedures, policies, and controls. But these associated activities are not essential parts of MBO.

Main Benefits of MBO

Personal motivation.   The potential benefits of MBO are impressive.
Foremost is the greater *personal motivation* of the people who commit
themselves to achieve a set of results. Through participation in setting

meaningful and realistic targets, and the accompanying delegation of initiative, many individuals internalize their role in meeting company objectives.[4]

A sense of accomplishment—of meeting objectives—is a universal desire. The captain of a ship takes pride in keeping his vessel on schedule; a telephone lineman wants to keep the circuits open; a chief engineer works overtime to make sure that a newly designed product will not break down under operating conditions. Without a recognized objective, none of these people would put forth such effort.

Clarification.   A second benefit of MBO is a *clarification* of the results that will best serve the enterprise. Especially in large organizations, the mission of a particular section often becomes distorted. And as strategy changes over time, the desired results may be blurred even more.

A situation that illustrates unclear objectives arose in the training section of an urban-renewal center. The training director was pushing hard to increase the number of people trained and placed in regular jobs. Consequently, he encouraged registration and gave first attention to highly competent people who could be placed quickly. However, these were not the people who needed help the most. Welfare workers in the area reported that as far as they could detect, the training center was not relieving economic distress. Welfare workers encouraged their clients to sign up for training, but few stayed more than a couple of days, and most said there was no point in going there. Only after the objective of the training center was redefined and understood did the coordination between the center and the welfare workers improve.

Focus of thought and effort on results.   This is a third benefit. All too often, mere activity is treated as a goal. Under MBO, the activity "call on new customers" is unsatisfactory; instead, a result is stated, such as "firm orders from eight new customers each month." Similarly, "monitor smoke-stack emissions" is unsatisfactory; "hourly stack emissions always within federal standards, and temporary excess never more than five minutes in any hour" is better. The supporting activity may well be necessary, but management's attention is on results.

Personnel evaluation reflects this same emphasis on results. Under MBO, instead of relying on personality traits, people are assessed in terms of the results they produce. And fresh data are available at the close of each period. Perhaps some personality analysis will help explain good or bad performance, but it is better to start from the more objective and clearly pertinent comparison of actual results with planned results.

Better response to controls.   This is the fourth benefit of MBO. Both the control standards—the objectives for the period—and the way perfor-

[4]M. Evez and I. Zidon, "Effect of Goal Acceptance on the Relationship of Goal Difficulty to Performance," *Journal of Applied Psychology*; Mar-Apr., 1984: 69–78.

mance will be measured are part of the agreement between the manager and the subordinate. So the subordinate usually regards the controls as being fair—they are not unexpected or arbitrary. Moreover, with the subordinate personally desiring the objectives, control feedback is helping to achieve personal goals as well as company goals. As Chapter 20, "Behavioral Responses to Control," will show, such understanding and acceptance alter one's feeling about controls; they become like the gas gauge on a car—an aid in reaching a destination instead of an instrument of repression.[5]

Finally, MBO has a synergistic effect. The delegation is feasible because of the agreement on objectives; the participation in setting the objectives adds to motivation, as does delegation, and the evaluation based on these same objectives reinforces their significance. Furthermore, in the broader scope, the forward planning for the specific job is consistent with the job duties laid out by organization design; this job mission has significance and value because its contribution to broader company objectives can be easily traced. The objectivity and impersonality arising from the stress on agreed-upon results reduces feelings of personal dominance and increases the sense of joint endeavor. Each of these features builds upon and reinforces the others, and because they are combined together under the banner of MBO, the psychological effect is synergistic.

Establishing MBO

Because MBO embraces a cluster of management techniques, it requires hard work to establish. Organizing is involved. Job duties and delegation must be carefully developed, keeping in mind the factors that will be discussed in Part III. Communication and leadership style are also essential aspects; the options and issues in this area are examined in Part IV. Controlling, the third phase of the MBO cycle, has its own set of problems, as will be seen in Part V. And objectives, the take-off pad for MBO, should reflect a rational selection process, as outlined in the remainder of this Part. Of course, in a successful *going* enterprise, most of the necessary managerial system will already be operating. So installing MBO calls only for adjustments and refinements. Nevertheless, any needed changes should be made only after a review of the total situation; MBO provides no easy shortcut.

Defining the operating objectives for each job included in the MBO system is by no means simple. In addition to specific substantive questions, the issue of multiple objectives keeps reappearing.

---

[5]E. A. Locke et al., "Goal Setting and Task Performance: 1969–1980," *Psychological Bulletin,* Fall 1981: 125–52.

Never does a job, department, or company have a single objective. It may have a dominant mission, but other goals will also demand recognition.

The manager of an airport, for instance, may be charged with making it easy to move planes, people, and freight in and out of the facility. But, among other things, the manager will also be expected to keep operating costs low, use only as much capital for equipment and inventory as is necessary, maintain an efficient work force, and develop employees for promotion to key jobs. Thus he is confronted with diverse, and perhaps competing, goals.

Multiple Objectives of a Company

The belief that "the purpose of a business firm is to make a profit" is part of American folklore. It probably started as an *assumption* made to simplify economic theory. Being a half-truth, it proved to be an easy way for even business executives to talk about a complex problem. Then when public accounting made the profit-and-loss statement one of the few universal measures of business performance, the notion became ingrained.

But the suggestion that profits are the sole objective of a company is *misleading*. Obviously a company must earn a profit if it is to continue in existence; earnings are necessary to attract additional capital and to provide a cushion for meeting the risks inherent in business activity. But, for survival, it is also essential that a company produce goods or services customers want, that its conditions of employment continue to attract competent employees, that it be a desirable customer to the people who supply raw materials, and that it be an acceptable corporate citizen in the community in which it operates. Remove any one of these essentials, and the enterprise might collapse. To argue that profit is the supreme objective is like saying that blood circulation is more important to survival than breathing, digestion, or proper functioning of the nervous system.

Suitable measurement of profit poses an additional drawback. Profit figures reported by existing accounting systems are based on past costs. A new system that attempts to be a common denominator for setting and measuring all company objectives would have to deal with the present worth of past and future values. This would call for estimates of future conditions, of present values of past investments, and of the influence of intangibles such as morale and customer goodwill; comparability from year to year and between companies would be desirable. The theoretical and practical difficulties in designing such a system are overwhelming.

In discussing strategy, the need for multiple criteria for overall company targets was pointed out. Now, in seeking ways to state objectives that have operational relevance, the principle of multiple objectives takes on added significance. For the manager, no enterprise—public or private—has a single objective.[6]

To assist the managers of the enterprise in setting objectives, the General Electric Company has singled out eight "key-result areas."

1. Profitability—in both percentage of sales and return on investment.
2. Market position.
3. Productivity—improving costs as well as sales.
4. Leadership in technological research.
5. Development of future employees, both technical or functional and managerial.
6. Employee attitudes and relations.
7. Public attitudes.
8. Balance of long-range and short-range objectives.

Several other companies use variations of this format. Note that the list identifies only areas; each firm must fill in specific subjects and levels of achievement that fit its circumstances at a particular time.

Service enterprises likewise should determine their key-result areas. Here is such a list for a public library: circulation (loans and in-library), reference questions answered, cooperation with schools and other libraries, percentage of population using the library, contribution to community cohesiveness, collection of books and reference materials, personnel development, operation within financial budget. As soon as we start dealing with objectives that can readily be translated into action, we are faced with multiple goals.

Each of the objectives of the enterprise will, of course, call forth an array of more specific operating goals, and this fanning out continues through to the detailed objectives for each person in the organization.

Number of Objectives for Each Person

Having too many objectives can be troublesome, as Figure 5.4 shows for the case of a jet pilot. When a company's multiple objectives are subdivided and elaborated into an array of specific, short-term objectives, the work is split up among various people. Nevertheless, one manager may be confronted with thirty or forty identified results that he is expected to achieve—quality output, meeting deadlines, overtime pay, self-development, training of others, aid to other departments, plans for next year, budgeted expense, customer service, and so on.

Such a large array of objectives tends to disperse attention and fails to provide clear direction of effort. Consequently, the number of objectives upon which anyone is expected to focus should be limited. Some executives

---

[6]P. F. Drucker, *Management: Tasks, Responsibilities, Practices* (New York: Harper & Row, 1974) 95–102.

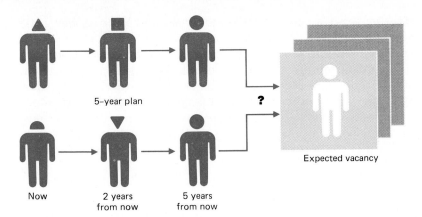

5-year plan

?

Now · 2 years from now · 5 years from now

Expected vacancy

Figure 5.4 Too many objectives for one person can be hazardous. In a conventional aircraft, the pilot must contend with a bewildering variety of informational devices. New instruments, such as the contact analog (left), condense information about the plane's movement and position and present it to the pilot in forms that can easily be grasped. Deviations from the intended course are thus instantly revealed. Matters related to course—speed, position, and so on—can be ignored until deviation is indicated. The analog demonstrates two ways of reducing the problem of multiple objectives: (1) integrating a variety of elements under a few headings and (2) adopting the "exception principle" of ignoring any given factor as long as it is in a satisfactory range.

feel the number should be narrowed to the range of two to five, thereby ensuring concentrated attention; this is in keeping with the finding in psychological research that the short-term memory is capable of simultaneously dealing with approximately seven items.[7] However, some executives maintain that a person can keep up to a dozen objectives in mind. In either case, agreement exists that motivation is improved by reducing the number of objectives to a manageable limit.

Two methods are used to narrow the number of objectives for an individual. First, a distinction is drawn between what Herbert Simon calls *satisficing* and *maximizing*.[8] This notion—which Simon termed "bounded rationality" and won the Nobel Prize for explaining—describes how individuals, for a variety of reasons, simply try to achieve a satisfactory standard using *heuristics,* or decision shortcuts, based on previous experiences. Only when events fall outside these experiences, or require optimum attention to detail, do individuals give them maximum attention. Otherwise, people often use what experts call "mindless" behavior in life's most prevalent situations.[9] In a sense, such routine objectives are passive, at least for the moment, while objectives requiring maximization are the stimulants to action, and they are fewer in number.

[7]G. A. Miller, "The magical number seven, plus or minus two: Some limits on our capacity for processing information," *Psychological Review*, 63, 1956: 81–97.

[8]H. A. Simon, *Administrative Behavior,* 3d ed. (New York: The Free Press, 1976).

[9]E. J. Langer, "The Illusion of Incompetence," in L. C. Perlmutter and R. A. Monty, *Choice and Perceived Control,* (Hillsdale, N.J.: Erlbaum, 1979).

Consolidating several objectives that are means to some higher goals is a second way of limiting the number of key objectives for a job. For example, a manager might say that the head of the Atlanta office of an accounting firm should obtain ten new accounts next year; embraced in this objective are subgoals regarding speeches, public-service activities, contacts with bankers and other influential people, and visits with potential clients. To be sure, most of the subgoals have to be met if the accountant is to get ten new clients. Yet focusing on the one net result is easier to deal with, and it encourages delegation of the problem of how to achieve results.

Adjusting Short-Run Emphasis

Even half a dozen objectives create difficulties, for emphasis on any one goal tends to reduce attention given to others. The welfare worker urged to process more cases gives less consideration to each problem.

Everyone, in planning their personal work or in correcting that of others, likes to assume that they can give more effort to some goal that is pressing at the moment *without* slackening off on other work. Sometimes they can. Sooner or later, however, a point is reached when attention and effort are simply diverted from one activity to another. More time on football or campus politics means less with the books, and vice versa.

Keeping diverse objectives in balance is hard. A common difficulty is that the tangible, *measurable ends receive undue attention*. It would be easy for a professor to stress the appearance of a report rather than the learning that went into its preparation, simply because the paper itself is so much easier to see. Similarly, in business, those results that show up directly in accounting reports often command priority; thus avoiding overtime expense may be preferred to maintaining quality in advertising copy.

Furthermore, *immediate problems tend to take precedence* over long-run issues. The dilemma of choosing recurs time and again in engineering departments. Customers' orders for immediate delivery have a "here-and-now" quality about them. If they are not careful, engineers will find themselves simply going from one order to the next, always leaving for tomorrow the design of a new product.

The case of *one's own work versus teamwork* may also pose a balancing problem. We all know friendly individuals who are so ready to help with another person's problems that they have difficulty getting their own work done on time. But a self-centered view may also cause trouble. Some results for the company can be created only by teamwork; the task cannot be divided into parts and accountability assigned to separate jobs. Task teams, described in Chapter 9, and the combined work of line and staff are of this nature. Several people are thus jointly accountable; the manager should measure the result of their combined effort and give each of them credit for the success or failure. But then the problem is this: Smith is a member of a team and also has several individual objectives. Does she give priority to those results for which she alone is accountable, and let team-work slide? Or does she stress the team project even though other results that are more clearly hers may suffer?

According to rational decision theory, people should pursue each of their diverse objectives to the point at which added increments of achievement have equal value. Actually, behavioral research suggests, most people first attend to one objective and then turn to another, the sequence and direction of effort being determined largely by momentary social pressures.

The desirable balance among objectives shifts over time. With success or failure and with external changes, the incremental values also change. So the wise manager must reappraise preferences. This job is like that of the captain of a large ship who is continually changing speed and direction in relation to the ship's present position, tides, winds, and other conditions.

A regional sales manager of a well-known computer company uses MBO for such a reappraisal on a systematic basis. He sits down every month with each branch manager to review past performance; together they agree on three, four, or at most five goals that will be emphasized during the next month. This list may include any of several desirable aims: calling on new customers, pushing the sale of a particular product, recruiting additional salespeople, clearing up customer complaints, or reducing expenses. The same item may appear on the list for several months. It is generally understood that the branch managers will not completely neglect items missing from the list, but special emphasis will be given to only a few goals. The manager contends that he gets better results by *highlighting* a few items than by talking about many. He is able to maintain an overall balance by the frequent reviews and by shifting from one objective to another as necessary.

The details of this technique are not important here. But several of its desirable features should be noted: (1) Any misunderstanding about the quality, timing, or costs of a specific objective can be cleared up at the monthly discussions. (2) Plans are adjusted in light of progress already being made. This practice permits comparison of incremental values. (3) New information and new pressure from headquarters can be promptly incorporated into the action taken at each branch—thus giving recognition to the problems and needs of the many branches, instead of blithely following blanket orders from headquarters. (4) Broad objectives are translated into meaningful and immediately applicable terms for each branch manager.

CONCLUSION

Business strategy deals with the company as a whole. It stakes out the role in society that the enterprise wishes to play. Functional strategies likewise set broad guidelines. But these strategies can be achieved only if they have an impact on the behavior of people working in the company.

Consequently, a manager must give close attention to fashioning objectives and subobjectives that are understandable and significant to the executives and other workers affected by them.

These operating objectives are tied to jobs and thus to individual managers and operators who hold these jobs. In terms of "decision making within organizations," this goal structure is the starting point for diagnosis. Each responsible person predicts potential gaps between objectives and actual results, and these gaps become the focus of search, decision, and action.

In the hurly-burly of organization life, everyone is bombarded by all sorts of information and influences; thus, operating objectives serve the important role of leading to purposeful, consistent action. MBO especially builds this focus; it also encourages commitment and enthusiasm for accomplishing the objectives.

In practice, the definition of clear-cut objectives for each job is far from simple. To make operating objectives a vital, energizing managerial tool, a manager must deal with the following: distinguishing between hopes and expectations, setting short-run objectives as steps toward long-run goals, recognizing the presence of multiple objectives, and adjusting the short-run emphasis on various objectives. Once objectives have been clarified, they provide the guiding, unifying core of company planning.

Impact on Productivity

This sharpening of operating objectives helps a company perform its particular, distinctive role in our economic system. Each company and, in turn, each department and each operator, makes some small input into the overall structure. In terms of national productivity, it is important that each task be (1) on target (in other words, what is needed) and (2) done well.

Operating objectives are the concrete, down-to-earth definitions of what those inputs should be.

In addition to helping to keep individual efforts on target, operating objectives aid in coordinating such efforts. To be fully productive, everyone relies on other people to do predictable tasks, such as provide information, deliver quality parts on time, fill the car's gasoline tank. Operating objectives create this mosaic of reasonable expectations. Of course, as conditions change, the objectives are revised; coordinated change is a vital aspect of productivity.

FOR FURTHER DISCUSSION

1. (a) At school, do you get a reasonable balance among your various personal objectives, such as good grades, a good time, preparations for a future job, convenience and effort, low cost? Do you "satisfice"? Do you change the balance each term? (b) When you take a full-time job, who is going to decide what the balance should be among your various job objectives? Will you continue to be free to make the kinds of choices you make now?

2. Should a standard or objective that is given to a person be the most reasonable guess about what can be attained? Or should it always be beyond what might be considered the most reasonable expectation? Discuss both sides of the question and indicate its implications on coordination and subsequent control.

3. The discussion early in the chapter about the hierarchy of plans implies that objectives for, say, your specific job should be derived from higher-level goals. How do you reconcile this concept with MBO, in which you presumably negotiate job objectives with your boss?

4. The importance of periodically adjusting objectives is stressed in this chapter. List ways in which a superior may judge whether a subordinate's requests for frequent changes in longer-term objectives are the result of good or poor planning by the subordinate.

5. In what ways might the demand for clarity and quantification of objectives lead to difficulties when seeking to balance long- and short-run objectives? If long-run objectives are left somewhat vague and tentative, will not the more quantitative short-run goals be given too much attention?

6. "Whenever I set joint goals with my subordinates, I begin by stating clearly my expectations and invite them to change my mind. If they know where I stand, it avoids a lot of game-playing." What do you think of this approach to joint goal setting?

7. Select any one enterprise with which you are familiar—perhaps a restaurant, bus company, sports team, or parents' business—and explain how you would (a) state and (b) measure the target achievement of each of the "key result areas" listed by General Electric: profitability, market position, productivity, leadership in research, human resources development, employee attitudes and relations, public attitudes, and the balance of short- and long-run objectives.

8. For each of the eight areas covered in your answer to Question 7, *who* should set the level of achievement? Should MBO be used for this purpose?

FOR FURTHER READING

Guth, W. D., *Handbook of Business Strategy,* Boston: Warren, Gorham & Lamont, 1985. Excellent applied articles on how managers can set goals and implement strategy.

Locke, E. A. and G. P. Latham, *Goal Setting for Individuals, Groups, and Organizations.* Chicago: Science Research Associates, 1984. Concise, clear distillation of studies on setting goals in a way that creates motivation. This 34 page module summarizes the authors' book *Goal Setting: A Motivational Technique That Works!* Englewood Cliffs, N.J.: Prentice-Hall, 1984.

Richards, M. D., *Readings in Management,* 7th ed. Cincinnati: South-Western Publishing Co., 1986, Ch. 6. Useful articles on the role of goals and objectives in the management process.

Simon, H. A., *Administrative Behavior,* 3rd ed. New York: The Free Press, 1976, Ch. 12. Theoretical discussion of multiple organizational goals and of the way they are resolved into useful operational goals for personal action.

"The Focused Web: Goal Setting in the MBO Process," *The Classic Reprint Series,* New York: American Management Association, 1985. When MBO has failed, a prime reason has been difficulties in setting objectives.

MANAGEMENT IN ACTION CASE 5
Tom Monaghan's Pizza Goal—Speed

Thomas S. Monaghan's story doesn't sound like the thing from which success is made. He spent his early childhood in an orphanage. He was booted out of the seminary for mischievous behavior. He didn't have enough money to finish college. And in 1970, his pizza company was $1.5 million in debt and flirting with bankruptcy.

But Tom Monaghan had one important thing going for him: a sharply focused goal. It sounded simple, but no one had been able to do it before him. Monaghan figured that if he could promise delivery of a pizza within 30 minutes of the time it was ordered, he could make a killing.

He was right. And from that goal, 15 years later, Monaghan was sitting pretty—at the top of Domino's Pizza, America's second-largest pizza chain, with 2,600 stores. The baby-faced pizza magnate was spending $130 million to build an office complex that would be the new home of his company. He was shopping for an island in the Florida Keys, spending $2 million to triple the size of his home, buying an old Deusenberg at auction for $1 million, and helicoptering to Detroit's Tiger Stadium to watch the Detroit Tiger baseball team he bought in 1984 for $53 million.

Although he took more than a decade to achieve such remarkable success, the rise of Monaghan was really a race against a 30-minute clock. The foundation of Domino's growth was Monaghan's promise that every Domino's pizza would be delivered to customers' doorsteps in under 30 minutes.

While his competitors were touting crusts and toppings, Monaghan was making sure he could deliver on his 30-minute vow. At first, it won him loyal followings in college towns—such as Ann Arbor, Michigan, home of the University of Michigan and Domino's—and in areas neighboring military bases. By the early 1980s, though, Domino's stores were opening everywhere. In 1985, the company adopted the slogan, "One-point-five in '85," as Monaghan aimed to more than double sales to over $1.5 billion.

Like many entrepreneurs, Monaghan was a workaholic who knew his business from top to bottom. He had tossed pizzas himself in the first store he opened with $900 in the 1960s. Guiding Domino's explosive growth in the late '70s and early '80s, Monaghan demonstrated commitment to inspiring his people by instituting generous incentives, including bonuses, trips to Hawaii and excursions on the company yacht.

Through all the success, he retained his innocent schoolboy charm, a trait that endeared him to Michiganians—and probably won him more than a few customers.

"I still make pizzas in my sleep," he said in 1981. "I always find myself in the middle of a rush and I can't ever seem to get caught up." By 1985, though, it seemed Tom Monaghan could make money in his sleep.

Question

How does this case illustrate Herbert Simon's "satisficing" concept?

For more information, see *The New York Times*, 6 June 1984.

For practice in applying concepts covered in this chapter to managerial situations, see the following managerial decision cases. The case questions particularly relevant to this chapter are listed by number after each case name.

Grant Chemical Corporation (p, 59) 9
Heartland Union Bank (HUB) (p. 183) 4
Consolidated Instruments (p. 189) 3, 6, 9, 10
Graham, Smith, & Bendel, Inc. (p. 442) 4
Norman Manufacturing Company (p. 538) 14

6

Planning for Stabilized Action

LEARNING OBJECTIVES

After completing this chapter, you should be able to

1. Explain the difference between policies, standard methods, and standard operating procedures.
2. Differentiate between standing plans as guides and standing plans as rules.
3. Develop some basic plans for stabilized action for an organization with which you are familiar.
4. Give an example of a situation requiring strict plans for stabilized action, as well as an example of a situation in which such plans can be more flexible.
5. List three principles that should be considered in restraining the use of rules within an organization.
6. Give six good reasons for using standing plans.

CONSISTENT AND ENDURING BEHAVIOR PATTERNS

Objectives, however soundly conceived and clearly communicated, provide only part of the guidance essential to united effort. Even the most highly motivated people need some plan of action, as has become painfully clear in several minority small-business development programs where the absence of customary patterns for joint effort has thwarted lofty aims.

Basically, management uses two kinds of plans to direct activities toward established goals: *single-use* plans and *standing* plans. Single-use plans include programs, schedules, and special methods designed for a unique set of circumstances; these plans will be examined in the next chapter. This chapter considers standing plans, a group that includes policies, standard methods, and standard operating procedures, all of which are designed to deal with recurring problems. Each time a particular, but familiar, problem arises, a standing plan provides a ready guide to action.

Need for Standing Plans

A wildlife magazine ran into serious difficulties with three firms that bought considerable advertising space in the publication. These firms objected to articles on conservation appearing in the magazine. The editor contended that he was serving readers by reporting on critical conservation issues. The advertising manager argued that there were two sides to every question and that the magazine did not have to join the popular clamor for more regulation. The problem arose because the magazine lacked a clear, well-known editorial policy.

In this instance the editor won. The policy became "Challenging, informative articles that would excite the interest of readers." With this new policy firmly established, the advertising manager had to shift his approach to advertisers; he now says, "You may not like our editorial policy but it builds an audience you would like to reach." The new policy has removed internal conflict; it enables all magazine personnel to work in a consistent direction.

Moreover, procedures have to be adjusted to support policies. This became dramatically evident when the City University of New York adopted an "open-admission" policy. The number of entering freshmen jumped fifty percent, and their academic preparation varied drastically. This change had been anticipated—it was the aim of the new admission policy. But the procedures for registering this heterogeneous group and assigning members to appropriate classes were grossly inadequate. For weeks, students shifted from class to class, and no one was sure who should report where.

If a group of people are to live or work together, they must be able to anticipate one another's actions. There must be some consistency or pattern of behavior. The more interdependent the activities, the more important the ability to anticipate; this is especially true in a football play, as Figure 6.1 indicates. Without this ability, individuals cannot know what they should do; they are doubtful about what they can depend on from

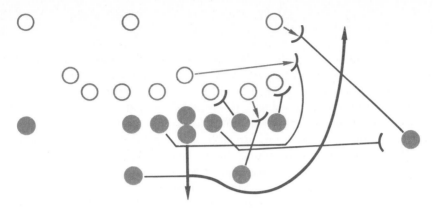

Figure 6.1 Plans should be clearly plotted in advance, as they have been for this football play. But they should also be flexible enough to allow for necessary adjustments in the field of action.

others; and they are unsure whether their own efforts will be helpful or harmful. This is true for a symphony orchestra, a sports team, a diplomatic corps, a ship's crew, a bank, a coffee plantation, or any other working group.

Standing plans are an important means of building predictable patterns of behavior in an organization. They are especially valuable in the execution of strategy, when managers rely on work being done consistently. In addition, outsiders do business with a firm because of its reliability. Thus, policies and other standing plans buttress strategy by inducing sustained, dependable actions.[1]

TYPES OF STANDING PLANS

Within the broad category of standing plans, a manager has a choice of several—notably policies, standard methods, and standard operating procedures. Like formations for a football team, one type of plan may be more useful than another in a certain situation. So a manager needs to know the characteristics of the tools he has to work with if he is to be effective in achieving balanced results. Here are some characteristics of the principal types of standing plans.

Policies

A policy is a general guide to action; it does not tell a person exactly what to do, but it does identify direction. Familiar policies are summed up in these statements: "We sell only for cash." "We lease, rather than buy, office space." "We insure all property worth more than $10,000 against fire

[1]D. Hampton, C. E. Summer, and R. Webber, *Organizational Behavior and the Practice of Management,* 4th ed. (Glenview, Ill.: Scott, Foresman, 1983). This book provides an interesting account of the development and evolution of standing plans at Xerox.

loss." In each instance, an important aspect of a recurring problem has been singled out, and a guide established for dealing with it. When establishing policy, the manager must give considerable attention to these questions: Should a policy give explicit guidance or merely set limits? What kinds of problems should be covered?

Some policies provide only broad guidance. For example, "Our policy is to make college education available to all students graduating from an in-state high school" leaves much leeway as to what is done about classroom space and about keeping up with standards. Similarly, a statement that "Preference will be given to goods made by union labor" indicates intent but leaves the purchasing agent free to decide whether the preference comes first or only when all other considerations are equal.

But policies can be much more specific. An investment-banking firm makes this statement on length of vacation:

Employees shall normally be entitled to vacations according to the following schedule:

1. On payroll six to twelve months prior to March 1—one week.
2. On payroll thirteen months to three years prior to March 1—two weeks.
3. On payroll three to five years prior to March 1—three weeks.
4. On payroll over five years prior to March 1—four weeks.

What subjects policies should cover and what they should say depends entirely on what will be helpful in solving specific problems. Take customer policies. Many companies believe it wise to establish lower, and perhaps upper, limits on the financial or consumption size of the customers they want; location limits are also common. These guides are useful not only to the selling organization, but also to people who must plan production scheduling, warehousing, and shipping. Establishing a policy covering the quality characteristics of customers is more difficult. Credit rating, stability of demand, desire for special service, history on cancellation of orders—all contribute to a definition of "a good firm to do business with." Few companies, however, attempt to incorporate these considerations in a policy, because most customers are strong in some respects and weak in others; thus a general guide applicable to many situations is hard to formulate. For guidance on this aspect of selecting customers, certain companies have a policy that simply lists all factors that must be considered in arriving at a decision.

Even when most aspects of a problem do not lend themselves to policy guidance, perhaps one or two aspects do. The complex problem of selecting suppliers of raw materials and parts is a good example. Purchasing agents must make a separate analysis of possible suppliers for each item they buy. Nevertheless, most companies do have a few policies to guide this selection. It may be a policy to buy no more than 75 percent of any one product from a single supplier to avoid being dependent on a single source.

It may be a policy to secure bids from at least three sources to encourage competition for the company's business. Note that such policies deal only with the number of suppliers, leaving open the selection of specific firms.

A policy, then, may (1) be specific or general in its instruction, (2) deal with one, or many, aspects of a problem, (3) place limits within which action is to be taken, or (4) specify the steps in making a decision. The skill of a manager in using policies lies in how he decides just *what kind of guidance* will be helpful.

For easy reference, policies are often classified by subject, such as sales, production, purchasing, human resources, or finance.[2] Or they may be referred to as *general* policies and *departmental* policies, depending on the scope of activities to which they apply.

Standard Methods

The distinction between a standard method and a policy is one of degree, because both provide guidance about how a problem should be handled. The chief differences relate to viewpoint, completeness, and the attempt to control operating conditions.

Viewpoint. A standard method deals with detailed activities, whereas a policy is a general guide. But what is general and what is detailed? The answer depends on your point of view. For example, a vice-president in charge of human resources would probably say that a general rule to pay wages comparable to those prevailing in the local community is a policy, whereas job evaluation is simply a method for carrying out this policy. But the chief of the wage-and-salary division would look on a decision to use job evaluation in establishing pay rates as a major policy covering her work; she would consider a particular way of relating one job to another— say, factor comparison—a standard method. What about still a third person, a job analyst who works for the wage-and-salary chief? He, too, has his own point of view. He thinks the choice of factor comparison is a policy decision; for him, methods are such things as determining whom to contact and how to conduct interviews in analyzing each job. Clearly, then, whether a particular guide to action is called a policy or a standard method depends on the perspective of the person who is talking.

Still, even such a slippery distinction as this is useful. In planning the work of each job, at whatever level, executives should think of both the broad framework in which they operate and the more detailed methods they will use. Good policy requires both viewpoints, and terms must distinguish between them.

Completeness. Standard methods never cover every aspect of an activity, although they do provide fuller guidance than a policy because standard methods apply to a narrower scope of activities. Therefore, it is easier

[2]W. H. Newman, J. P. Logan, and W. H. Hegarty, *Strategy, Policy, and Central Management,* 9th ed. (Cincinnati: South-Western Publishing Co., 1985), Part 2.

to find general guides that fit most cases. Besides, thanks to Frederick W. Taylor's attempt to plan everything in detail, such as how coal should ideally be shoveled,[3] tradition favors developing detailed methods on the assumption that the more completely a method is planned, the more efficient it will be.

Control of environment.   The pioneers of Scientific Management— Frank Gilbreth, Taylor, and others—quickly discovered that the conditions surrounding a job often had more influence on output than the performance of the person holding the job.[4] The successful use of standard methods called for standard conditions for such brawn-type jobs.

The scientific managers therefore set about to control raw materials, machine maintenance, work flow, tools, training, and other factors that affect output. After such work conditions were controlled, it became reasonable to expect an individual to follow a standard method of work and to achieve a standard output.

Today we can see many applications of this basic idea of controlling conditions in routine, mechanical work so that standard methods will be applicable. An automobile assembly plant is perhaps the most widely known example. In this case, standardized parts reach the assembly line precisely on schedule. Necessary tools are placed within easy reach of the worker. Special instructions for auxiliary equipment are readily available. In fact, management has gone to great lengths to make sure that standard methods are applicable to car after car. Although most industries do not go to this extreme, attempts to maintain uniform and effective working conditions are common.

Standard methods are essential in the use of computer programs that make routine automated decisions. Such methods are employed today even in medical diagnosis or in tracing legal case histories and precedents. Several conditions are necessary for a computer to "decide"—that is, issue instructions to another machine or to a person about action to be taken: (1) The significant variables in the situation must be measured and this information fed into the machine. (The rest of the environment is assumed to be constant.) (2) Any deviation from acceptable performance flashes a specific cue. (3) Each cue trips a "programmed" response—a standard method for dealing with the situation. All three conditions call for intense standardization. It is clear that unless an operating situation lends itself to a very high use of standard methods, automation is not applicable.

One drawback of developing standard methods and standard working conditions is the cost. Industrial engineers may spend months developing the one best way to perform a single operation. In a large plant, thousands of studies may be needed. Even then, the engineers may be unable to discover a feasible way to control one or two factors. This planning is expen-

[3]F. W. Taylor, *Scientific Management* (New York: Harper & Row, 1947).

[4]H. Mintzberg, *The Structuring of Organizations* (Englewood Cliffs, N.J.: Prentice-Hall, 1982).

sive, and the resulting standard method must apply to a large enough volume of work so that the cost can be recovered through greater efficiency.

A shortcut is to standardize a method already in use, probably the method of the best workers.[5] This approach enables a company to predict processing costs and delivery times. Careful analysis, however, usually reveals places where methods that have simply evolved over the years can be improved. If a company is going to adopt a standard method at all, it pays to adopt a good one.

Standing plans are not always consciously and deliberately established. Some are like common law; they are practices that just grow, become accepted behavior, and are then enforced by those in official positions.

There is no sharp line that divides a company's traditions and customs from its standing plans. From a manager's point of view, we might say that a custom becomes a standing plan when (1) it is sufficiently recognized so that those it affects can describe it, and (2) individuals would be subject to criticism if they disregarded it merely on their own initiative. Other customs and traditions undoubtedly influence behavior, but they can scarcely be considered a part of the planning structure, because they are not sharply enough defined to be enforced.

Standard methods are more difficult to apply to sales and other client contacts than they are to jobs within a plant-like environment. These activities are varied, and the diversity of individual behavior is often an important consideration. Consequently, two approaches already mentioned in connection with policies are often used. First, certain parts of the total activity can be standardized—for instance, in sales work, the presenting of merchandise and the writing of sales orders; in a hospital, the handling of admissions, routine tests, and accounting. Second, for some activities a series of steps can be specified, as in conducting an interview or reconciling a bank statement. An executive or operator can use these standard parts in whatever combination seems appropriate for a day's work. This practice permits flexibility while still achieving some of the benefits of standard methods.

Standard Operating Procedures

A procedure details the *sequence of steps* several individuals must take to achieve a specific purpose. When a procedure for dealing with recurring problems becomes formalized, it is called a *standard operating procedure.*

Company action on even relatively small matters usually requires the work of several individuals. A procedure helps to integrate their bits of work into a meaningful whole. Consider the standard operating procedure set by an insurance company for the employment of exempt personnel (that is, employees not subject to wage-and-hour regulations):

---

[5]C. F. Vough, *Productivity* (New York: AMACOM). Chs. 4–5 show the importance of work simplification in improving productivity at IBM.

1. A supervisor decides he needs an additional person to help with technical problems.

2. The budget officer must approve the addition unless the supervisor's existing budget has funds available for this purpose (which is unlikely).

3. The supervisor advises the human resources director by phone or in writing of his new need.

4. The human resources director sends a job analyst to the supervisor; the analyst writes a description of job duties and qualifications of the person needed to fill the job, and gets the supervisor's approval.

5. This job description is reviewed by the wage-and-salary administrator, who classifies the job and thereby sets the salary range for the new job.

6. The employment manager looks for candidates who have the qualifications stated in the job description. She first checks present employees who might be qualified and interested. If necessary, she turns to outside sources. She then picks the two or three most promising candidates.

7. The supervisor interviews the candidates sent to him by the employment manager; he selects the one he prefers or asks for more candidates.

8. The employment manager checks the references and tries to uncover other pertinent information about the leading candidate.

9. The candidate is called back for a second interview with the supervisor. They try to reach a tentative understanding about the job duties, salary range, and other matters.

10. The supervisor's boss interviews the candidate.

11. If everything is in order, the supervisor makes a firm offer.

12. The candidate reports to the office of the employment manager, fills in company forms, benefits instructions, and so on. The employment manager gives him background information on the company and its personnel policies.

13. The person takes a medical examination from the company physician.

14. He reports for duty.

15. The employment manager sends instructions to the payroll clerk about starting date, rate of pay, deductions, and so forth.

Most companies have literally hundreds of such procedures—for grievances, capital expenditures, arranging to use a company car—and most are essential for smooth operation. Picture the confusion if there were no standard procedure for customers' orders. Somehow each order must get immediately from the sales representative to the shipping clerk, the credit manager, and the accounts-receivable clerk; later the persons responsible for billing, inventory records, sales analysis, and sales compensation must be advised. Without a regular routine for handling such matters, customer service would be poor, salespeople would be angry, bills would have errors and become troublesome to collect, and inventory controls would collapse.

Most standard operating procedures apply to the flow of business papers—orders, bills, requests, reports, applications, and so forth. The papers are simply vehicles for information and ideas. But there can be standard procedures with no papers at all; for example, when an exception to a normal price is at issue, the three or four people involved may have a well-established understanding about the steps necessary in making a decision.

Although standard forms are not an essential part of a standard operating procedure, they can be very helpful for a large volume of routine transactions. A well-designed form with space for all essential information aids accuracy of communication, permits rapid handling, and serves as a convenient record.

Relation to organization.   Formal organization divides the total work of a company into parts, thus permitting concentrated and specialized attention where necessary. Procedures help tie all the parts together. Like an automatic shuttle on a loom passing back and forth through the warp threads, the procedures weave woof threads that bind a firm fabric. Some of the weaving must be done by hand, as explained in the next chapter, but a large part of it must become routine and standardized. This is the role of the standard operating procedure.

Clearly, the way a company is organized affects the number and sequence of steps in any procedure.[6] For instance, if each supervisor in the life-insurance company recruited his own technical personnel (as is the case in some companies), at least Steps 6, 8, and 10 of the procedure just listed would be changed. Fifty years ago, when there would have been no central human resources department, a supervisor might well have done all the work himself, except for Steps 2, 10, and 15. But if the company had more personnel specialists, the procedure might well be more elaborate—as anyone who has been recruited into the Armed Forces can testify.

Keeping procedures simple.   Standard operating procedures tend to become complex and rigid for several reasons. Each unit takes jurisdictional pride in performing its part accurately. Control points are added to avoid difficulties that are often temporary, and these controls then survive like the proverbial cat with nine lives.[7] Executives habitually look for information at certain spots, not realizing that it might be more simply compiled elsewhere. Standard forms acquire a sanctity that few dare challenge.

Avoiding the choking effect of overelaborate procedures is a continu-

---

[6]A. Jay, *Management and Machiavelli*, (New York: Holt, Rinehart & Winston, 1967) pp. 61–62.

[7]I. Mitroff and R. Kilmann, *Corporate Tragedies* (New York: Praeger, 1985).

ing task for a manager.[8] A variety of techniques are open to him. He may hire a special procedures-analyst for assistance in this area alone. Among the many possibilities for simplification are mechanical devices for communication and duplication. Perhaps a procedure can be revised so that some steps are taken concurrently. One company found that checking all invoices from vendors was unnecessary; by concentrating on those for over $100, 74 percent of the invoices could be handled more promptly, with a likely annual loss of only $200; furthermore, the work of two clerks was eliminated.

In appraising a standard procedure, a manager wants to ensure that (1) the action each person must take is clear, (2) the information each person requires is provided, (3) the work proceeds promptly, (4) economies are obtained where feasible, (5) control checks are made at critical points, and (6) necessary records are kept. Meeting these tests and also keeping procedures simple often calls for keen resourcefulness.

HOW STRICT SHOULD PLANS BE?

There is much double talk about the flexibility of standing plans. An executive may spend ten minutes emphasizing the need for a policy, standard method, or standard operating procedure, and then finish by saying, "Of course, we want to keep it flexible." In a single breath, she has cast out her whole point. How flexible? Flexible in what way? The catch is that the executive has several available courses of action.

One approach is to change standing plans frequently: a policy, method, or procedure remains in effect until a new guide is established, but such revisions are made promptly whenever operating conditions warrant. Unfortunately, this approach has serious limitations. Many of the advantages of dependability, habitual behavior, customary social relations, and predictable results are lost. Communication about changes in standing plans is difficult, especially if a large number of people are involved; the reasons for the new plan and its full meaning become confused, and loyalty to informal groups encourages resistance to new alignments. Therefore, using frequent change to secure flexibility in standing plans needs to be confined to a few issues—such as a special procedure to handle a holiday rush—and preferably applied to a small group that understands why the change is necessary.

Another approach to flexibility is to state a standing plan generally, or loosely, in order to permit a wide range of variation within the plan; Figure 6.2 shows the variety of jobs in which different limits apply to standing plans. Still another approach is to list many exceptions to which the plan does not apply. In effect, this simply restricts the scope of the plan; flexibility is achieved by not giving full power to the plan.

Still a third way is to think of standing plans partly as guides and

---

[8]R. Townsend, *Up the Organization* (New York: Fawcett World Library, 1970) p. 129.

Laimute E. Druskis/Taurus Photos

Figure 6.2 For each position, these questions arise: What aspects of the job should be covered by standing plans? In how much detail? Should these plans be guides or rules?

partly as rules. If this distinction can be drawn clearly, the usefulness of standing plans can be greatly extended. This approach merits more comprehensive exploration.

Guides versus Rules

Some policies are intended to be definite rules having no exceptions. For example, a large pharmaceutical manufacturer has this policy: "All company products, whether prescription or nonprescription drugs, will only be sold in retail pharmacies." This does not mean that the company prefers to distribute only to pharmacies or that only the distribution manager may authorize exceptions; it means just what is says. The company does not want its products carried in nonpharmacy outlets, such as supermarkets or discount stores. By restricting distribution to pharmacies, the company believes that its professional image among physicians and pharmacists is enhanced. The policy is also designed to build strong company loyalty among retail pharmacies. Hence the policy is rigidly enforced.

Contrast the distribution policy of the drug firm with the employment policy of a large data processing department in an insurance company: "Individuals added to the computer programming staff should receive a grade of B or better on the programming aptitude test administered by an outside psychological consulting firm." This policy was instituted to ensure that the department's heavy investment in training new programmers was spent wisely. Experience in the insurance company, as well as in other data processing settings, indicated that new hires with a test grade of B or better were very likely to become successful programmers. An analysis of the department after the policy had been in effect for several years showed that 32 percent of the staff had been employed without having taken the programming aptitude test or with a test grade lower than B. What good, then, was the policy? Managers in the insurance company insisted that the policy was very helpful. "It is a distillation of our experience. It reminds us that any time we ignore the test results, we are asking for trouble. However, there are several other factors involved in a selection decision and it has become extremely difficult to hire staff in this field. Consequently, we do not believe that we should be bound by this single consideration. Because of the policy, we are doubly careful when the test results do not measure up." In short, this policy served as a guide, but not as a rule that could not be overriden even in exceptional circumstances.

Variations in strictness of application will also be found among standard methods. Even a Fuller Brush representative's sales pitch and a Disney World tour guide's script are only suggested; good representatives adapt their sales presentation to individual customers or circumstances. On the other hand, the methods for running a test in a medical laboratory are usually precisely followed so that the results will be reliable.

Because standard operating procedures always involve several people, less freedom is possible than with standard methods. Each person relies on the other links in the chain. When exceptions to a usual routine are necessary, everyone affected should be notified, for the very existence of the standard procedure creates a presumption that everyone will follow the customary path. Sometimes there is even a standard procedure for making an exception to a standard procedure! Handling rush orders at a plant or registering a special student at a university, for instance, may call for such refinement.

Restrained Use of Rules

Variation in strictness can cause confusion, however. In some cases, the reliability of a standing plan is its virtue. In other instances, rigidity is anything but a virtue. This dilemma can be recognized and dealt with in the following ways.

Make intentions clear.   An executive who had built his company from scratch had a large rubber stamp that read, "And this time I mean it." When he wanted his orders followed precisely, he used the stamp on any documents involved. Modern executives who are otherwise fond of "flexible policies" might well adopt a similar device. Subordinates are often uncertain whether a standing plan is a guide or a rule. Simply making clear how much flexibility is intended will remove much of the confusion.

Establish rules only for compelling reasons.   When a manager sets up a policy, method, or procedure, she often has a strong conviction about the soundness of that plan, and believes others should follow it to the letter. Her natural tendency is to state it as though it should be strictly observed. But she should remember that a standing plan may remain in effect for a long time. Circumstances may change. Those who apply the plan later may be in a better position to judge its fitness. If they are permitted to treat the policy or method as "recommended practice," they profit by the guidance but are not pushed into an action that fails to accomplish major objectives. Consequently the manager should have compelling reasons for insisting on strict observance, especially when the policies involved are aging and possibly outmoded.

Strong reasons for strict observance may indeed exist. *Consistency of action* by several people may be necessary, as in pricing to avoid illegal discrimination or communication of proprietary "inside" information. Or, *consistency over time* may be desirable; for instance, accounting reports should be comparable from one year to the next. *Dependability* may be crucial if several people must rely on knowing what others will do, as when a plane lands on an aircraft carrier. *Doers may clearly lack judgment* on the subject covered by a standing plan; most operators of electronic computers do not know enough about the inner mechanism to deviate from standard instructions, nor does the student who is selling magazines to get through college have enough background to adjust subscription rates. In circumstances such as these, standing plans should be strictly observed.

Use the exception principle.   The so-called exception principle simply refers to an understanding between an executive and his subordinates that as long as operations are proceeding as planned, the subordinates should not bother him; when exceptions arise, however, they should consult him. The principle applies to standard plans in this way: Subordinates are expected to abide by policies, standard methods, and standard procedures in most instances, but if an unusual condition arises in which a standard plan does not seem suitable, they turn the matter over to a higher authority, who decides whether an exception should be made. Perhaps the "higher authority" will be the executive who established the standing plan in the first place; at other times, permission to make exceptions may be assigned to lower-level executives. Note that in this setup, the standing plans are strict *rules* for operating people, but they are only *guides* for the executives who handle the exceptional cases. Of course, successful operation of the scheme requires that operating people be able to recognize when a situation may merit an exception and demand the attention of the "higher authority."

WHAT TO COVER AND IN HOW MUCH DETAIL

For what activities should standing plans be established? More specifically: What aspects of such activities? With what type of standing plan—policy, standard method, or standard procedure? In how much detail?

Reasons for Standing Plans

Because the ways of using standing plans and the extent to which they are applied always depend upon specific situations, a manager cannot avoid the continuing task of deciding when to add or drop policies, procedures, or standard methods. Here are several reasons why a standing plan may be introduced.

1. The need for *consistency* and close *coordination* of work, as we have noted, affects the desirability of detailed planning. Where consistency is crucial, as in accounting, pricing, hiring and promoting, wages, vacations, and the like, the pressure for detailed plans is strong. Where adjustment to local conditions is paramount, detailed plans are apt to get in the way. Similarly, if the activities of several persons must interlock (in timing or quality), detailed planning may be necessary. To the extent that work is independent, or coordination is easy to achieve through personal contact, a compelling reason for detailed planning may be lacking.

2. Higher executives may lighten their work load by using standing plans. Once a policy, method, or procedure is developed, an *executive can delegate* to subordinates the job of applying the plan to specific cases. This delegation relieves her of the need to become personally familiar with each case, while still enabling her to be confident that work will proceed according to her wishes. One decision—like a pattern or computer program—can shape the output of many workers.

3. The *quality* of operating decisions may be improved. Because a standing plan is followed repeatedly, a manager can afford to give careful thought to the formation of the plan. A policy is one means of transmitting the company's heritage of knowledge to many people. The painstaking analysis upon which a standard method is based will benefit many operators when they follow "the one best way."

4. If it uses standing plans extensively, an organization may find that it can employ people with less experience or ability to do certain jobs

because individual flexibility is limited. If so, *payroll economies* should result.

5. Standing plans also lay the *groundwork for control*. By setting up limits within which activities take place, and perhaps by specifying how those activities are to be performed, it is easier to predict results. These predictions can then be translated into control standards. In fact, establishing detailed plans encourages tight supervision and control, which may or may not be desirable.

6. A manager should also take heed of the people who do the work, as well as of the work itself, in deciding how detailed the plans must be. The greater the dependency of subordinates, the greater the need for detailed plans. Dependent subordinates want guidance, and they feel ill at ease without it. But if subordinates are highly self-assertive and informed, general rather than detailed plans will be more applicable. Ability also plays a part in deciding on degree of detail. The greater the decision-making talent of most subordinates, and the greater their knowledge about the business, the less detail in standing plans is necessary.

Drawbacks to Standing Plans

A manager must remember, however, that these potential benefits are offset by several inherent limitations; the more detailed the planning, the greater the drawbacks. Standing plans introduce *rigidity*.[9] Indeed, the *purpose* of plans is to limit and direct action in a prescribed manner, and such plans become ingrained attitudes and habitual behavior. If plans are written down, they tend to be followed until new plans are written and approved. Naturally enough, the executives who develop such plans are inclined to defend them. Thus, it will be hard to change standing plans once they are well accepted. In dynamic situations, where frequent change is desirable, such rigidity is a drawback.

Planning also involves *expense*. Fully as important as direct outlays for industrial engineering and management research is the time that operating executives devote to analysis, discussion, and decision. Teaching people to understand and follow a new plan also takes effort. Unless particular kinds of problems keep recurring, there is no point in even considering standing plans. The more the repetition, either inherent or contrived, the more useful standing plans will be. But as planning is extended to more areas of an organization and is increasingly detailed, a point will be reached at which the improvements in results do not justify the cost of further planning.

Time taken in preparing and installing standing plans—time to analyze, to secure approvals, to develop understanding and skill in their use—may also have strategic value. A customer may want prompt delivery, or the board of directors may want a report next week. In such situations,

[9]Hampton et al., *Organizational Behavior*.

immediate action may be more important than taking time to discover the best possible method.

Clearly, then, the choice of what a standing plan should cover and how detailed it should be is strongly influenced by the particular work and people involved.[10] Essentially, it is the operating situation, not the personal preference of the manager, that dictates a specific structure of planning. The manager's task is to identify the salient features of each situation.

CONCLUSION

Freedom versus Regulation

Standing plans are a significant part of a company environment in which workers (managers and operators) make decisions. Policies, standard methods, and standard operating procedures provide decision makers with limits, alternatives, and other premises. These premises have a double effect: they simplify the task of deciding how a specific problem is to be resolved, and they ensure a degree of consistency, dependability, and quality of decision throughout the organization.

Nevertheless, the further standing plans are extended, the more pressing becomes the dilemma of freedom versus regulation. This is an age-old conflict that people have faced as long as they have participated in joint activities. But urban living and working together in specialized, purposeful organizations accentuates the problem. How much regulation of individual action is desirable? The question takes many forms.

In political philosophy, the conflict is between authority and freedom. Every law limits someone's freedom. Yet society must have laws when people live together, so that the actions of one person will not unduly infringe on the rights of others. In psychology and sociology, the conflict is between individual self-expression, initiative, and creativity, and group norms, rules, and customs. Every time a social group derives a customary way of thinking or acting, someone's independence is circumscribed. Yet without such customs, the group would disintegrate. In ethics, the conflict is between individual dignity and the common good; and in law, it is a major issue in rendering justice. Finally, in business management, the conflict is expressed as the problem of making plans that coordinate the action of people and regulate their job activities and their communications, but at the same time do not stifle the creativeness and energies of people who are contributing to the group effort.

Unfortunately, no plan is perfect for resolving the conflict between freedom and coordination. Several key factors to be considered in resolving these issues have been discussed, but the manager's final array of standing plans can be established only on the basis of the specific needs within the organization.

[10]R. Shrank, "Are Unions an Anachronism?" *Harvard Business Review*, Sept.–Oct. 1979, pp. 107–15.

A change in strategy always requires a modification in at least some of the existing standing plans; since the present policies and procedures were designed to carry out the old strategy, they will not fully support a revision of that strategy. In fact, the difficulty of changing established practices is one common reason why new strategies fail. Once established, policies, procedures, and methods become habits; they provide employees with a comfortable feeling of familiarity and security; people develop personal skills—even careers—around them. Consequently, they cannot be changed simply by a memo from the president. Just try, for example, converting a college cafeteria into a gourmet restaurant!

This reluctance to change means that a new strategy takes time and effort to implement. Careful thought must be given to which standing plans will serve the new strategy well and which should be altered. Detailed studies may be required to find the best new patterns, then training and revised rewards are necessary. Experience shows that a strategic change in, say, selling stereo equipment directly to retailers instead of through distributors takes at least two years to complete. Automating a large office may take even longer. And more complex alterations—such as the U.S. auto industry's responding to the Japanese dominance of the small-car market—can take a decade or more.

The great virtues of stability and predictability that prevailing standing plans provide also retard change. However, this inertia can be redirected, like a gyroscope. If effort is devoted to creating new patterns of behavior—which support a new strategy—then a continuing driving force bolsters the revised strategy.

Impact on Productivity

Productivity, as noted in Chapter 1, involves both (1) creating goods and services that society needs, and (2) using resources effectively in this process. Standing plans are intimately tied to both of these prongs of productivity. By shaping the customary patterns of behavior within a company, the policies and procedures will affect what is produced and, even more, the way resources are used.

Because well-chosen standing plans can fashion a behavioral base for productivity, managers should be alert to any need to curtail, extend, or revise prevailing policies, methods, and procedures.

FOR FURTHER DISCUSSION

1. Should your university have a policy covering special treatment for outstanding athletes—for example, financial aid, campus jobs, rescheduling exams, coaching for exams, course exemptions, and so forth? How detailed should it be? What about similar special treatment for outstanding scholars?

2. For the regulation of driving an automobile on the highway, each state and most cities have laws and customs. How *strictly* should these laws be enforced? If not strictly enforced, should they be repealed? In an organization, how strict should enforcement be of (a) policies and procedures covering

consumer credit? (b) policies and procedures covering "equal opportunity" for women and for racial minorities?

3. "People like firm, clear rules that let them know what is expected and guide them to better performance. Vague guides are worse than no guides at all." Comment.

4. "Standing plans are really substitutes for thinking. They are organizational habits formalized to make sure that no one uses his head as long as he can remember what page in the manual the answer is on." Comment on this position.

5. To what extent, if any, should a university have policies and procedures covering the selection of new faculty members? How about a professional baseball club selecting new players?

6. Custom and tradition provide a great deal of guidance in the operation of a small company. Under what circumstances does it become desirable to formalize this guidance into written policies and procedures?

7. "We have a policy that says no employee shall be required to work overtime for more than twelve hours per month, and then only if given one week's notice of need. Yet our supervisors often ask us to put in more than twelve hours and seldom give us more than a day's notice. That has been going on for years. I wish they would either change the policy or follow it." Comment on this statement by a worker in a large electronics plant.

8. Consider a fairly significant change in policy that you would like to see implemented in your organization (business, school, class). (a) List other policies affected by this change. (b) List and discuss changes in procedures and methods that would be needed if the policy were implemented.

FOR FURTHER READING

Feldman, D. C., "The Development and Enforcement of Group Norms," *Academy of Management Review*, January 1984. Identification of the kinds of behavioral norms that are supported by group pressure.

Lawler, E. E. and J. G. Rhode, *Information and Control in Organizations*. Santa Monica, Calif.: Goodyear, 1976, Ch. 6. Incisive discussion of the dysfunctional effects of planning and control systems.

Moore, F. G., ed., *Management of Operations*. New York: John Wiley, 1983. Discussion of the design and integration of the entire operating structure of a manufacturing firm.

Newman, W. H., J. P. Logan, and W. H. Hegarty, *Strategy, Policy, and Central Management*, 9th ed. Cincinnati: South-Western Publishing Co., 1985, Part 2. Extensive coverage of the development and use of policies for each major functional area within an enterprise.

Tushman, M. L., W. H. Newman, and E. Romanelli, "Keeping Structure Dovetailed with Strategy: Congruence and Upheaval," *California Management Review*, Fall 1986. Research shows why stabilized company structures tend to persist, and why major changes—when they do occur—are usually revolutionary in character.

Yavitz, B. and W. H. Newman, *Strategy in Action*. New York: The Free Press, 1982. Ch. 8 provides a discussion of the building of revised patterns of behavior in an organization.

MANAGEMENT IN ACTION CASE 6
McDonald's Masters Consistency

In a McDonald's franchise in tiny Warrendale, Pa., a 21-year-old college student munching two Quarter Pounders utters what could be the slogan for McDonald's management style:

"You know what you're getting when you come to McDonald's," Bruce Lewis says.

Indeed, McDonald's forte as the nation's largest fast-food feeding trough has been in giving its customers what they expect when they expect it. McDonald's may not deliver the best burgers or the crispiest french fries in the land, but a customer who orders a Big Mac knows precisely what he'll get—whether he's ordering in Fairbanks, Alaska, or the Ginza in Tokyo, or in Fairfield, Connecticut. And he knows he'll get it fast.

Such predictability is the result of exhaustive planning for stabilized and uniform action in McDonald's thousands of franchises, complemented by rigorous corporate training. It also results from the disciplined, assembly-line style with which McDonald's youthful crews prepare Big Macs, Quarter-Pounders, fries, and other edibles. In that respect, it's awfully hard to tell one McDonald's franchise from another.

All of them strive to achieve a single goal, however: To serve the customer within 60 seconds of the placing of an order. That requires crews to work together in machine-like precision, following a raft of specific preparation rules designed to keep the process moving, such as leaving a batch of fries in the warming bin no longer than seven minutes.

McDonald's brainwashes its franchisees on such discipline at its Hamburger "U" training center at company headquarters in Oak Brook, Ill. Franchisees graduate to operate outlets in far-flung regions with a singular purpose—give the customer "quality, service, cleanliness and value"—and the corporate-honed tools to uphold it.

The formula works. By the end of 1983, McDonald's was serving more than 11 million customers a day and had sold more than 45 billion burgers since founder Ray Kroc opened his first burger stand in Des Plaines, Ill., in 1955.

Question

To what extent do you think McDonald's emphasis on standing plans should be applied to (a) branches of commercial banks?; (b) barber shops and hair stylists?

For more information, see *U.S. News & World Report*, 21 November 1983.

APPLICATION CASES

For practice in applying concepts covered in this chapter to managerial situations, see the following managerial decision cases. The case questions particularly relevant to this chapter are listed by number after each case name.

Grant Chemical Corporation (p. 59) 7
Fyler International (p. 68) 7
Heartland Union Bank (HUB) (p. 183) 4, 5
Dayton Metal (p. 198) 4, 5
GAIN Software (p. 303) 5
Delphi Insurance (p. 316) 4

7

Programming

LEARNING OBJECTIVES

After completing this chapter, you should be able to

1. Understand when single-use plans are more desirable than standing plans.
2. Explain the six basic steps in programming.
3. Develop an adaptive program.
4. Differentiate static and adaptive programs.
5. Appreciate the importance of timing in any kind of programming.
6. Understand the basics of PERT and critical path programming techniques.

The previous chapters have examined two broad types of plans: strategy and objectives, which focus on desired results, and standing plans, which establish customary rules of behavior for achieving those results. Both types of plans are highly useful for managerial decision making in recurring circumstances, but they do not exhaust the arsenal of weapons a manager can use in attacking problems.

A third type of plan deals with single, rather than repetitive, situations. In such cases, a manager decides in advance what action to take within a given period or how to respond to a particular problem or opportunity. Once the time has passed or the problem has been dealt with, a new plan is devised for the next problem. These are called single-use plans, so named because they are unique to the situation encountered.

Programming

The basic characteristics of single-use plans can best be explained in terms of programs; a program lays out the principal steps for accomplishing a mission and sets an approximate time for carrying out each step, as Figure 7.1 shows. Elements of the program, such as schedules and projects, evolve later, and they can be viewed as particular types of subprograms. After examining several types of programs and subprograms, this chapter turns to the more uncertain and complicated problems of adjusting programs to a dynamic and uncertain environment.

A change in strategy always calls for a program to shift from the old to the new. For instance, when General Foods Corporation withdrew from the fast-food business, it needed a program for selling off its Burger Chef outlets, dismissing employees, terminating contracts for materials, and recording liquidation losses. Many locations and people were affected, so subprograms focusing on the various facets (such as the sale of real estate) were drawn up.

The sequence and timing of major moves is often so important that they are included as a component of a new strategy—as suggested in

Figure 7.1 Programming can be used at any level, for large or small clusters of activities.

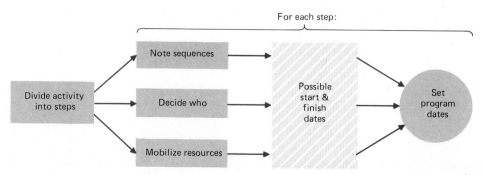

Chapter 4. Each of these moves highlighted in the strategy requires a more detailed program of the steps necessary to advance from the present situation to the target. In addition, getting things done under an established strategy often calls for a program.

Good programming is crucial to smooth and efficient operations. Consider, for instance, the problem faced by an airline in introducing a new type of plane, such as the Boeing 747 or the Concorde supersonic jet. Flight crews and ground personnel—literally thousands of people—have to learn new skills. To postpone a reeducation program until the planes are delivered would result in chaos. Instead, a company must anticipate by two years the need for competent maintenance people, experienced flight crews, different weather information, and solutions to other new problems. Some personnel need classes of only a few hours; others must spend several months learning complex theories and skills. All this training has to be carried on while regular operations with older planes are maintained.

Only through careful programming can an airline (1) anticipate possible crises and make provisions for them, (2) review the subprograms to be sure that they fit together into a consistent whole, (3) avoid stop-gap decisions in favor of taking sound, reasoned, and economical steps, and (4) use its limited (and expensive) training facilities most effectively.

Skill in programming is a major asset for any operating executive. A human resources director, for instance, needs a program for recruiting more blacks; a treasurer is concerned with a program for selling new bonds; an executive vice-president works out a program for introducing a new product. Programs, in fact, are useful at all levels in a firm: The president may develop a program for merging two companies, and a first-line supervisor may have a program for training Sally to take over Joseph's job.

BASIC STEPS IN PROGRAMMING

Many programming problems can be solved by following six basic steps.[1]

1. Divide into steps.   Dividing work into steps is useful for planning, organizing, and controlling. Planning is improved because concentrated attention can be given to one step at a time. Organizing is facilitated because the steps or projects can be assigned to different persons to effect speedier or more efficient action. Controlling is also enhanced because an executive can watch each step and determine whether progress is satisfactory while work is actually being done, instead of waiting for final results. If the division into parts is to be effective, the purpose of each step should be clearly defined, indicating the kind of work, the quality, and the quantity expected.

[1]W. H. Newman, J. P. Logan, and W. H. Hegarty, *Strategy, Policy, and Central Management,* 9th ed. (Cincinnati: South-Western Publishing Co., 1985), Ch. 20.

2. Note relationships. Note the relationships among steps, especially any necessary sequences. Usually the parts of a program are closely dependent on one another. The amount of work, the specifications, and the time for each step often affect the ease or difficulty of taking the next. Unless these relationships are closely watched, the very process of subdividing the work may cause more inefficiency than it eliminates.

Necessary sequences are particularly significant relationships. In a drug-addiction program, for example, local counseling centers must be set up and staffed before general publicity is released; otherwise, early interest turns into frustration, and the entire effort is regarded as a sham. Necessary sequences have an important bearing on scheduling because they tend to lengthen the overall time required for an operation; since a shorter cycle gives an organization more flexibility, the need for delaying one action until another is completed should be carefully checked.

3. Who is responsible? Decide who is to be responsible for doing each step. In programming a company's normal operation, the existing organizational structure will already have determined who is to perform each activity. But if the program covers an unusual event—merging with another company, for instance—careful attention must be given to deciding who is accountable for each step. These special assignments may create a temporary set of authorizations and obligations. A special team may be formed to carry out the program.

4. Resources needed. For realistic programming, the need for facilities, materials and supplies, and human and financial resources must be recognized. The availability of these necessary resources must be appraised. If any one of them is not available, another project should be set up to obtain this resource. For example, if a company is short on qualified personnel, it should make plans for hiring and training new employees. Many a program breaks down because the executive who prepares it does not realistically understand what resources will be required.

5. Estimate time. Estimate the time required for each step. This act has two aspects: (1) the date when a step can begin and (2) the time required to complete an operation once it is started. Starting time, of course, depends on the availability of the necessary resources: how soon key personnel can be transferred to a new assignment; what work is already scheduled for a machine; the likelihood of getting delivery of materials from suppliers; the possibility of subcontracting part of the work—all have an effect on when each step may begin.

Processing time, once the activity has begun, is usually estimated on the basis of past experience. In addition, for detailed production operations, time-study data may permit tight scheduling. But for a great many operations, more time is consumed in securing approvals, conveying instructions, and getting people to work than is required for doing the work itself. Unless this "nonproductive time" can be eliminated, however, we should include it as part of the estimated time.

6. Assign dates. An overall schedule is, of course, based on the sequences noted under Step 2 and the timing information assembled under Step 5. The resulting schedule should show both the starting date and the completion date for each part of the program.

A good deal of adjustment may be necessary to make a final schedule realistic, however. A useful procedure is to try working backward and forward from some fixed controlling date. Availability of materials or facilities may set the time around which the rest of the schedule pivots. In sales, a particular selling season, such as Christmas or Easter, may be the fixed point. A manager must, of course, dovetail any one program with other company commitments. He must also make some allowance for delay. Allowances all along the line are not desirable, because they would encourage inefficient performance, but a few safety allowances are wise so that an unavoidable delay at one point will not throw off an entire schedule.

In summary, a well-conceived program covers all actions necessary to achieve a mission, and indicates who should do what when. Note how all the programming elements arise even in the simple example shown in Figure 7.2. The controller of a pharmaceutical company decided to install a large Xerox duplicating machine to make multiple copies of the many re-

Figure 7.2 A program for installing a new duplicating machine in the controller's office. Starting and completion dates for each step are indicated here by the colored bars. The moving of partitions was delayed so that the office would not be torn up at the end of the month. Training included a visit to see a similar machine in operation in another company. Supplies could be obtained quickly from local jobbers.

When

Sequence	Steps	Who	Jan. 6	13	20	27	Feb. 3	10	17	24
1	Plan new procedures	Office Manager	██							
2	Explain change to office personnel	Office Manager	■		■		■		■	
3	Obtain OK for investment	Treasurer		██						
4	Order new machine	Purchasing Agent			■					
5	Move partition, install shelves, etc.	Engineer			▭▭▭▭			██		
6	Train operator and supervisor to use new machine	Office Manager							██	
7	Obtain new supplies needed	Purchasing Agent						██		
8	Install new machine	Vendor							■	
9	Record investment and expense in accounts	Accountant								■

ports his office issued. The Xerox salesperson said, "All you have to do is plug in the machine." But the controller realized that a shift in the office routine was more complicated than that. After some thought, he developed the program summarized in Figure 7.2. With this plan, he was able not only to specify when he wanted the machine delivered but also to prepare both the physical setup and his personnel for the change. He avoided having the office torn up when people were busy with month-end closing, and he had a plan that could easily serve as a control as the work progressed. Most programs are more complicated than this, of course, but their essential nature is the same.

Wide Use of Programming

Hierarchy of programs.   For some firms, a major program encompasses a large part of company activity. This situation is true in the automobile industry, where annual model changes pace the work of all major engineering and manufacturing departments, usually for years in advance of the model change. Lead times are long, because there is a necessary sequence between market and environmental research, functional design, engineering, tooling, and actual production and sales. In fact, in any one year a company must do preparatory work for models that will be sold two, three, and four years later.

Such programming of major steps must necessarily lump together large amounts of work. But each step, in turn, has a program of its own. The stage of providing necessary facilities may thus be divided into a more detailed schedule showing when building construction and machine purchase must be started and completed. Again, building construction will have its own program, including such steps as defining requirements, selecting a site, getting architectural plans, gaining community approval, completing engineering plans, selecting a chief contractor, and so on. The executive charged with finding a site will probably establish an even more detailed program for his own chore.

Detailed programs are not necessarily connected to successively broader programs; any executive may use them by himself if he wishes. Nevertheless, when the programming approach permeates managerial thinking at all levels, it sets a tone and a pace for the entire organization.

Projects.   A single step in a program is often set up as a "project." Actually, a project is simply a cluster of activities that is relatively separate and clearcut. Building a hospital, designing a new package, and soliciting gifts of $500,000 for a college dormitory are examples. A project typically has a distinct mission and a clear termination point—the achievement of the mission.

The task of management is eased when work can be set up in projects.[2] The assignment of duties is sharpened, control is simplified, and the

[2]B. V. Dean, ed., *Project Management: Methods and Studies* (New York: Elsevier–North Holland, 1985).

people who do the work can sense their accomplishment. Calling a cluster of work a project does not, of course, change its nature. It may still be part of a broader program, and programming the project itself may be desirable. The chief virtue of a project lies in identifying a nice, neat work package within a bewildering array of objectives, alternatives, and activities.

Schedules.   A schedule specifies the time when each of a series of actions should take place. It is one aspect of a program, as we are using that term. When, as a result of standing plans, the tasks to be done and the persons who must do them are clear, then scheduling may be the only element that needs management's attention. This would be the case, for example, in a frozen food plant where the line is all set to go, as soon as the manager decides when to start and how many of each size package to produce. Under some conditions, then, planning is simplified by focusing separately on scheduling. In thinking about management broadly, however, the more inclusive concept of programming has wider usefulness.

STATIC VERSUS ADAPTIVE PROGRAMMING

This discussion of programming has been based on two assumptions that are realistic only part of the time: (1) That most of the actions necessary to achieve an objective are subject to direction and manipulation by management, and (2) that management can forecast the time factors—both availability and elapsed time—with considerable accuracy. For a good many problems, notably those that occur chiefly *within* organization offices and plants, these assumptions are usually correct.

But when the timing of several important steps is outside management's control and is uncertain, the character of programming changes. Social attitudes, competition, business cycles, and market conditions are indeed independent variables. When such events do not conform to an organization's master strategy, the organization needs more adaptability, more resourcefulness, and more hedges and retreats. A manager must still think in terms of major steps, sequences, and timing and duration of each step, but under such circumstances he must do so creatively rather than perfunctorily, as though he were dealing with a routine engineering problem.

Contingency Programs

Typically a manager draws up a single program; it is the best way to get from the present position to a stipulated objective. However, he must be aware that external events may not occur as predicted and that the results of his actions may not turn out as anticipated. These unknowns may be serious—perhaps catastrophic. If the manager sticks to his original program, he may get into deep trouble.

The most elaborate way to plan for such uncertain events is to prepare contingency programs. Here managers develop a set of programs in advance. Each is ready to use if a particular circumstance arises. In planning flights to the moon, for instance, a whole array of contingency programs are developed in detail. On the Apollo 13 moon shot, such a contingency plan permitted partial completion of the mission and probably saved the lives of the crew. Contingency planning is also common in military operations, and has been evident in the boom of mergers and hostile takeovers in the business world.

In contrast, little contingency planning is done under normal conditions by most enterprises.[3] Aside from limited plans for action in the event of fire, managers prefer to focus on the success of a single program. Is this disregard of admitted unknowns wise?

The reasons for shunning contingency programs are plain. (1) The effort and expense of preparing such programs is large. Contingencies are many, so the number of programs could quickly multiply. To keep the programs viable, necessary preparations have to be put into effect. (2) Contingency programs are disconcerting. A manager tries hard to develop enthusiastic, committed effort behind the preferred program. Discussing and preparing for a lot of "ifs" adds confusion and distraction. (3) Postponement of planning until the contingency arrives (or can be more reliably forecast) *usually* permits a manager to get by without very serious losses.

The prudent manager, however, should identify those contingencies whose risks are so large that special programs are justified, and he should ensure that sequential adjustments are promptly made.

Sequential Adjustments

An alternative to setting up contingency programs is making successive modifications in a program as unpredicted (or unassumed) conditions develop.

Anticipating that feedback data will lead to revisions.   One way to deal with unpredictable and uncontrollable conditions is to ensure a flow of current information as work progresses and to adjust the program when necessary. A surgeon has a general plan of action before an operation starts; a football coach should have a game plan in mind before the kickoff. But each of these specialists expects to be guided more by current developments than by prediction. An executive-development program is similar—a company may have a tentative ten-year plan for the progression of its outstanding young employees, but everyone expects that the actual performance of these people and the needs of the company will lead to drastic modifications long before the ten years are up.[4]

[3]W. E. Rothschild, *Putting It All Together: A Guide to Strategic Thinking* (New York: AMACOM, 1976); and J. B. Quinn, *Strategies for Change: Logical Incrementation* (Homewood, Ill.: Richard D. Irwin, 1980). In strategic planning, more firms are likely to develop contingency programs.

[4]W. H. Newman, *Constructive Control* (Englewood Cliffs, N.J.: Prentice-Hall, 1975), Ch. 8.

On the matter of revising plans, the key distinction between static and adaptive programming lies in executive attitude toward change. When a program is regarded as a blueprint, executives are heavily motivated to make the plan work; changes, they feel, are a confession of partial defeat. But under the adaptive approach, managers consider some change normal and respond readily when reasons appear for modifying plans.

Long-range programs, used to round out a company's strategy, are almost always revised. This is a prime example of how feedback data lead to revision of the program. In other programs, the feedback and revision cycle occurs more frequently, perhaps monthly, or when key steps are completed—for example, after test marketing, or when the quantity of available funds is firmly established.

Restricting scheduling to the near future.   When a pharmaceutical company put a new tranquilizer on the market, all executives were confident of a rapid growth in sales; there was talk of enlarging the plant, opening new branch offices, and using profits for additional research. Until the hoped-for sales volume actually developed, however, specific programming was confined to promoting the new product. Timing and determining the magnitude of other moves were held in abeyance until sales prospects became more certain.

A manufacturer of women's shoes got into trouble for not following a similar course. The firm opened a new plant in the South; it borrowed money and changed executive personnel on the assumption that most of its production could be transferred to the new plant within two years. Actually, the company had great difficulty in securing quality production from its new plant, and training expenses and spoilage made costs even higher than at the old plant. Consequently, the company was forced to postpone the move and found itself in serious financial difficulty. Had this firm merely scheduled the opening of the new plant, while leaving the time of closing the old factory unspecified, it might have avoided the crisis.

These devices for flexibility—anticipating changes and deferring program commitments except for the near future—sacrifice some of the benefits of a clear, direct program. But preparing for the future is more difficult, and some economies may be lost as a result; these drawbacks are simply the price paid for a somewhat cautious approach to an unpredictable future.

Adjusting to leads and lags in the flow of goods.   A program for a continuing flow of goods and services differs in important respects from a program for a single event. Producers and distributors of goods, such as gasoline or aspirin, must think in terms of a *rate* of output for a week or month. Such companies may be affected by seasonal fluctuations in consumption and by the buildup or cutback of inventory in the hands of distributors and perhaps consumers. Production must thus precede seasonal peaks in demand, and if a stable level of operations is desired, a firm must build inventories.

Programs that deal with the flow of goods rarely provide exactly the rate of activity that proves to be needed. The rates of flow must be adjusted, a little here and a little there, as one adjusts the hot and cold water in a shower. When a variety of products is involved, this adjusting process becomes complex. Most organizations have operating programs for some months ahead but revise them at least monthly on the basis of feedback information. The U.S. automobile industry, for instance, watches 10-day sales reports and 30-day inventory figures; production decisions are adjusted accordingly. For perishable products, like bread, adjustments may be made daily.

A program, then, must be suited to the operations it covers, but its essentials remain the same. By anticipating the what, who, how and when, it enables a manager to prepare systematically and carefully for difficulties.

IMPORTANCE OF TIMING

Timing deserves special emphasis. Many a strategic program, sound in all other respects, has failed in application because action was taken at the wrong time. Figure 7.3 underscores the importance of timing in critical project decisions.

A shipping company built a large dock on Lake Erie, anticipating the movement of ocean freight through the St. Lawrence Seaway. The volume of business has been so slow in developing that the dock is now closed down. Perhaps ten years hence the necessary traffic *will* develop, but clearly the construction was premature. On the other hand, many a product has reached its market after the demand has waned—witness the multimillion-dollar loss on the oversized Edsel automobile. There are better and poorer times to ask the boss for a raise, to buy raw materials, to float a bond issue.

Two major sources of timing errors are economic shifts and the moods of key people. Programs inevitably rest on forecasts (or unstated assumptions) about *when* economic and social conditions will be attractive. If the forecast is early or late, the program suffers.

Adjusting to Economic Conditions

One strength a company may have, in contrast to an individual decision maker, is its own economic forecasting staff. These experts gather data from many sources and make predictions about factors that directly affect company planning.[5] Although forecasters undoubtedly provide useful insights on questions of timing, their occasional errors are conspicuous. The public knows, for instance, that when Dacron fiber was first introduced to the market, du Pont built production facilities that far exceeded the de-

[5]S. C. Wheelright and S. Makridakis, *Forecasting Methods for Management,* 3d ed. (New York: John Wiley, 1980).

Tom McHugh/Photo Researchers

Figure 7.3 The speed with which an atomic energy plant can be built, for example, requires careful balancing of the need for electricity, construction costs, alternative fuel supplies (notably crude oil), popular safety concerns, and conditions in the capital markets.

mand. As a result, a new $18 million plant was idle for more than two years. The demand eventually developed, but the mistake lay in the estimate of how fast demand would grow and, more important, the decision to invest its capital based on such a guess.

Objective appraisal. A review of a variety of examples of poor timing[6] suggests that executive attitude is more likely to be faulty than the forecasting and programming techniques. As already noted, executives become strongly committed to programs; they believe in them, and desperately want them to succeed. Because of this feeling, it is only natural for them to underrate information that might hint at a need for modification. An executive's unwillingness to face clear trends in the wallpaper industry, for instance, led one company to postpone closing an old and inefficient plant; this decision prevented the company from taking the necessary steps to pull itself out of serious debt.

Prudence requires an objective appraisal. Somehow, either through checking with outsiders or through self-discipline, executives must try to make a detached forecast of when key events will occur. Moreover, as Part

[6]I. Mitroff and R. Kilmann, *Corporate Tragedies* (New York: Praeger, 1985).

V on controlling will detail, key planning assumptions should be monitored as a program gets underway. Objective appraisal will not ensure perfect timing in our fast-moving world, but it will avoid the significant number of problems that can be attributed to rigidity of executive attitude.

Keeping flexible. When forecasts are not fully reliable—and few are—a wise executive seeks to *avoid making commitments until necessary.* He tries to distinguish between a bear-by-the-tail situation and one that consists of independent steps. In a marketing program, for example, one move, such as national advertising, may necessitate a string of accompanying moves. As in passing a car on a crowded two-lane country road, once we start we have to follow through. But in many research projects, a process may be halted at the end of any of several steps and then begun again without major loss. In the latter situation, because the key people are not yet committed to subsequent steps, new timing is possible.

A related way to retain flexibility in timing is to *keep two or more alternatives open.* At one stage in its development, Boeing Aircraft had a large military contract that would eventually necessitate a new plant. The time arrived when the firm had to acquire a plant site and begin engineering work if the terms of the military contract were to be met; yet there was sharp disagreement among several parties about the location of the plant. To avoid being caught later in a time squeeze, the company took options on land in both Seattle and San Francisco and hired engineers to make detailed plans for plants in both localities. More than a year later, but before any building contracts were let, the Seattle location was selected. The company kept two alternatives open until it became clear which one should be followed. Of course, substantial costs were involved in obtaining this flexibility. Boeing had to pay for two land options and two sets of engineering plans, though it knew that only one would eventually be used. Flexibility can often be achieved only at a price.

Anticipating Reactions of Key People

Among the many forecasts needed for good timing of executive action is a prediction of how key people will react to parts of a program. Temptation is always strong to concentrate on tangible, quantitative elements and slide over the more nebulous human factors. Yet the responses of people may make or break a program. A proposed action often calls for a major effort or readjustment on the part of several individuals or groups, for their behavior patterns, beliefs, and values may be involved. Perhaps political behavior (to be explored in Chapter 16) will also be involved.[7] In timing, managers have to judge when the situation is ripe for a new move.

For years, a leading Midwestern department store had no blacks in sales positions. The human resources director believed this tradition

---

[7]J. P. Kotter, *Power and Influence: Beyond Formal Authority* (New York: Free Press, 1985), pp. 19–21.

should be changed, but he anticipated resistance from supervisors and salesclerks. So he waited until there was a shortage of well-qualified sales-people and then hired two blacks, placing them under supervisors who were sympathetic to the change. Actually, these two were noticeably better qualified than most of the whites who could have been employed at the time. Word got around that they were unusually competent, and soon several other supervisors were asking for similar help. Had this change been introduced when well-qualified white applicants were in ample supply and were being turned down, the response might have been quite different.

A large bank installed a long-needed job-evaluation system. Officers and supervisors were pleased with the way the system was working, and the vice-president was anxious to move on to a training program that was also badly needed. The president turned down the proposal, explaining that job evaluation had not yet become normal behavior. To introduce a second change on the heels of the first "might give us indigestion." This was the president's judgment on how fast his group could comfortably adapt to a new human resources practice. Not until a year and a half later did he launch the training program.

An executive with a good feel for timing must be socially perceptive, as with this bank president. He must know enough about people's needs, hopes, and fears to be able to anticipate their reaction to a proposed plan.

ADAPTIVE PROGRAMMING TECHNIQUES: PERT

PERT is a special technique for scheduling and controlling large, complex programs.[8] Originally developed as a planning aid for the design and production of Polaris missiles, PERT (Program Evaluation and Review Technique) has been adapted to a wide variety of undertakings, including new product introductions and the construction of the World Trade Center in New York City.

The design and the production of Polaris missiles involved a staggering number of steps. Specification for thousands of minute parts had to be prepared, the parts had to be manufactured to exact tolerances, and then the entire system had to be assembled into a successful operating weapon. And time was of the essence. The basic steps in programming discussed in the preceding pages were applicable; but the complexity of the project (and the fact that many different subcontractors were involved) called for significant elaboration in the programs.

Recording the Network

As with any programming problem, PERT begins with a plan of action. Suppose the goal is to launch a new product or place a communications

---

[8]J. D. Wiest and F. K. Levy, *A Management Guide to PERT/CPM: With GERT/PDM/DCPM and Other Networks,* 2d ed. (Englewood Cliffs, N.J.: Prentice-Hall, 1977).

satellite in orbit. The managers must determine the actions that will be necessary to achieve their goal. The first phase of a PERT analysis is to note carefully each of these steps, the sequence in which they must be performed, and the time required for each. This information is recorded in the form of a network—usually on a chart such as the one shown in Figure 7.4.

The chart is highly simplified so that readers can easily grasp its main features. It shows the main steps that an American auto-equipment manufacturer would have to follow to market a new antismog muffler. The manufacturer has purchased a tested European patent so that engineering to domestic requirements is simple; furthermore, the firm already has a well-organized plant and distribution setup. Arrows on the chart indicate the sequence of steps that must be followed to get the new product on the market; the numbers on the arrows show the required time for each step.

Essentially, the network is one highly structured approach to recording a "program." This list of events, the sequences, and the elapsed times, are all the data necessary for program planning. The network does not show the resources needed for each step, but an understanding of human resources, machines, and money underlies the estimated time for each step. The chief advantage of expressing a program as a network is its emphasis on sequences and interrelationships.

The Critical Path

Because the focus here is on *time,* the managers wish to know where delay, should it occur, would be most serious. The network is very helpful for this purpose. By tracing each necessary sequence and adding the time estimates for each step, the manager can identify which sequence will require the most time. This is the "critical path." Other sequences will take less time and hence are less critical.

The critical path is especially important in planning and control. Any delay along this path will postpone the completion date of the entire pro-

Figure 7.4   A simplified PERT chart. Events—that is, the start or completion of a step—are indicated by circles. Arrows show the sequence between events. The time (in days) required to move from one event to another appears on each arrow. The critical path—the longest sequence—is shown in color.

EVENTS

(A) Decision to add product

(B) Engineering work completed

(C) Financing arranged

(D) Material purchase orders placed

(E) Production started

(F) Sales campaign arranged

(G) Initial orders received

(H) Initial orders shipped

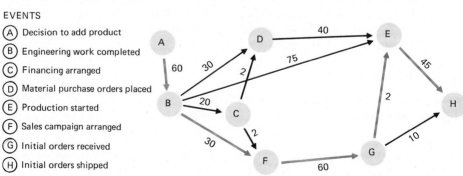

ject. On the other hand, by knowing in advance which series of steps are critical, the manager might be able to replan (allocate more resources, perform part of the work simultaneously, and so on) in order to shorten the total time. In other words, (1) the manager must focus control where it is most essential; (2) be in a good position to spot potential trouble early; and (3) avoid emphasizing activities that will do little to hasten completion.

Moreover, as work progresses, reports on activities that are ahead of, or behind, schedule will enable the manager to reexamine the timing. Perhaps an unexpected delay has created a new critical path. (For example, if "tooling up"—B to E in Figure 7.4—required an additional thirty days, a new critical path would be created.) Then corrective action can be shifted to this new sequence in which no slack time exists. In this way PERT becomes a strong control, as well as scheduling, technique.

Uses of PERT

PERT is typically applied to a much more complicated network than the illustration just used; in practice, each of the major steps would be programmed in more detail. The preparation of the sales campaign, for instance, would involve packaging, pricing, sales brochures, installation manuals, training of sales people, placing of advertisements, and the like; and each of these activities should be shown separately in the network. Such delineation improves the chance of catching delays early, and it also spells out the need for coordination at numerous points.

For a complex project, such as the construction of a large plant, the network becomes complicated indeed. A network with 137 events is shown in Figure 7.5. PERT is especially suited to large "single-use" programs having clear-cut steps and measurable output. The concepts of an event network and the critical path can be applied to many kinds of situations in which managers are interested in getting a job done on time.

Figure 7.5 PERT in an actual situation.

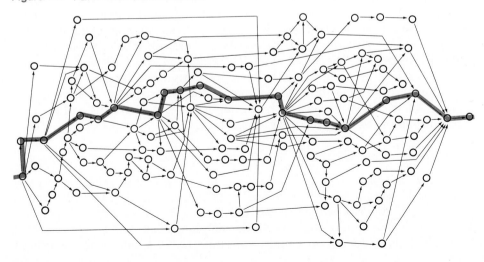

Having just reviewed in the preceding chapters a whole array of planning methods and problems, we notice that the complexity of the process stands out. The power and benefits tend to be forgotten. Actually, as experience aptly demonstrates, using the resources of an organization to do the planning has many potential strengths. The task of managers is to use this potential skillfully.

To take advantage of the specialized knowledge, ideas, and energies of the various members of an organization, managers divide the planning work (as they do other kinds of work) into bits and pieces. Planning in organizations requires many people and much time. This gives numerous inputs, but the manager must develop ways to fit all these pieces together and to ensure that the far-flung planning team is pulling in the same direction.

The best-known mechanisms for achieving such integrated planning have been discussed in the last three chapters. *Strategy* sets the mission. *Operating objectives* spell out the goals for each executive and serve as company values in making short-run choices. The strategy and objectives together provide the coordinated direction so essential to purposeful endeavor.

Then, to simplify planning while taking advantage of accumulated wisdom, managers create standard patterns—*policies, methods, procedures*—for dealing with recurring problems. Added benefits of this established social behavior are a dependable flow of information and an ability to predict and depend upon the actions of others. And by no means the least of the planning instruments are various programming techniques that tell scattered people how to fit their actions into a united effort.

A recurring theme in planning is that of freedom versus the regulation of individual behavior. Managers want unified effort *and* individual initiative, commitment to enterprise objectives *and* fulfillment of personal needs, use of expert judgment *and* creative imagination, coordinated action *and* individual resourcefulness. Fortunately, wise management can provide for both. Fortunately, human needs and organizational needs are not mutually exclusive. We have explicitly indicated the factors a manager should weigh in deciding when the benefits of giving individuals discretion counterbalance—or even improve upon—the advantages of regulation. Making such choices wisely is essential in view of changing values and expectations in the contemporary work force.

Impact on Productivity

Programs, the focus of this chapter, aid productivity by tying nonrepetitive—single action—activities to the work targets discussed in Chapter 4. Programs (1) identify what actions and resources are needed, (2) as a by-product, raise questions about activities not so needed, and (3) set dates on which each step should start and end. Thus they set both a direction and a tempo for work that is geared to productivity. The deadlines force a review of the results achieved. Well-programmed operations don't just drift.

FOR FURTHER DISCUSSION

1. "If overall strategies are well conceived and communicated, and good standing plans created, adaptive programming becomes a simple, mechanistic series of steps that could probably be developed by a computer, trained apes, or some combination of the two." Comment.

2. How far ahead—and with respect to what aspects—should you plan your career? How far ahead—and with respect to what aspects—should a business firm program its human resources development activities? Why the difference between the two, if any?

3. Which of the six basic steps in programming is most important in developing a plan for closing down one of a company's thirty-seven manufacturing plants? Which step would be least important? Which would be most difficult?

4. The Bluegrass Auto Insurance Company wants to move from its offices in downtown Louisville to a new building in the suburbs. Such a move should be made when business is good, when protests from downtown retailers will be ineffective, when most employees will be willing to move, and so on. Forecasts on such matters are unclear. How should Bluegrass proceed with its programming, if at all, in the face of such circumstances?

5. How should a manager determine when to develop a contingency program rather than write a more flexible plan that allows those who must implement it to make on-the-spot adjustments if circumstances warrant?

6. Assume that a local bank in your hometown has just decided to enter the real estate business. It intends to have a department that performs all the functions of a local real estate firm. First, make a list of the various steps necessary to get the new department in operation. Then, explain how the "critical path" concept could be applied to the task of getting the department going.

7. "Since all good programs must sooner or later be stated in budget terms, the controller's office should have primary responsibility for determining the form of the program and overseeing its development." What do you think of this suggestion from the controller of a large multinational company?

8. Television national news "programs" obviously have to decide what to broadcast on very short notice. What sort of planning makes this possible (objectives, policies, standard methods, programming, and so forth)?

FOR FURTHER READING

Camillus, J. C. and J. H. Grant, "Operational Planning: The Integration of Programming and Budgeting," *Academy of Management Review,* July 1980. The authors recommend a process for getting better linkages between strategy, programs, and budgets.

Dean, B. V., ed., *Project Management: Methods and Studies.* New York: Elsevier-North Holland, 1985. Articles by experts on the actual use of project management and its relation to other sorts of programs.

Levin, R., *The Executive's Illustrated Primer of Long Range Planning.* Englewood Cliffs, N.J.: Prentice-Hall, 1983. A popularized introduction to long-range planning.

Lorange, P., *Corporate Planning: An Executive Viewpoint.* Englewood Cliffs, N.J.: Prentice-Hall, 1980. Ch. 4–5 discuss problems of implementing programs and the ties between programming and other phases of planning.

Stonich, P. J., "How to Use Strategic Funds Programming," *Journal of Business Strategy,* Fall 1980. Outlines a seven-step process for linking strategy formulation and resource allocation.

Yavitz, B. and W. H. Newman, *Strategy in Action.* New York: Free Press, 1982, Ch. 7. Deals with too much versus too little programming.

The business associate brought chilling news.

"You're not going to believe this," he said.

Two people were dead and another was dying. They had taken capsules of Extra-Strength Tylenol to get well. Instead they were casualties of a mysterious and frightening cyanide poisoning that panicked the country for more than a week.

It was a Thursday morning, September 30, 1982, when an associate of Johnson & Johnson Chairman James E. Burke brought word of the nightmare involving J&J's Tylenol product.

"Somebody had chosen our product for a murder weapon and we didn't know why," Burke said.

But Burke didn't waste any time trying to find out why. Instead he saw the impending crisis for what it was—a unique situation requiring a unique response. Johnson & Johnson had never faced such a problem, so Burke had no precedents to follow.

Johnson & Johnson moved quickly to get Tylenol off store shelves and out of customers' hands, implementing an unprecedented recall that might have cost as much as $100 million. But this was a case where money was no object. The key was safety and responsibility—getting the potentially dangerous product off store shelves and then working just as hard to get consumers to buy the popular painkiller again after the problem was solved.

While police scrambled to find the Tylenol killer, Johnson & Johnson answered thousands of news media queries, recalled millions of bottles of capsules, halted Tylenol advertising, set up special consumer phone lines, and sent 450,000 electronic alerts to the medical community and drug distributors across America.

The company also began polling consumers to determine what they knew about the deaths and whether they thought Johnson & Johnson was to blame.

Before the poisonings, Tylenol had been on a market rise. With 100 million users in the United States, the drug claimed a 35 percent share of the $1.3 billion over-the-counter painkiller market. After the poisonings, Tylenol's market share plunged to 8 percent. Industry analysts predicted the end of the painkiller.

But the product's death notices were premature. Mere weeks after the deaths, market surveys indicated consumers would support the drug's return. On November 9, Johnson & Johnson salespeople, rallied by Burke, gathered to kick off a new sales campaign. By December, fresh bottles of Tylenol were on the shelves of U.S. supermarkets and drug stores. The company courted its old customers with the offer of a $2.50 coupon—the average retail price of a bottle of Tylenol.

In a year, Tylenol had regained most of the market share it had lost, claiming 29 percent of the market. Burke bragged that the biggest consumer complaint the company was receiving was that Tylenol's new, tamper-resistant packaging was "too tough to get into."

The chairman praised government agencies, law enforcement organizations, and the media, but he was especially pleased with the performance of his people. "We can't get over how smoothly this occurred," he said. "There were literally dozens of persons making hundreds of decisions, any one of which could have blown us out of the water."

In 1986 disaster struck again. Another person died because someone had put poison into a Tylenol capsule. This time Johnson & Johnson quickly thought of the possibility that the way a dose of Tylenol was enveloped—in a capsule, not in a pill—permitted a clever person to alter the contents. So in 1986, after another massive recall of Tylenol capsules, the company announced that Tylenol would never again be sold in capsules, but would continue to be offered in pill form, and that dramatic act saved the product's market position for yet a second time.

Question

Contrast the programming problem Johnson & Johnson faced in 1986 with that in 1982.

APPLICATION CASES

For practice in applying concepts covered in this chapter to managerial situations, see the following managerial decision cases. The case questions particularly relevant to this chapter are listed by number after each case name.

Fyler International (p. 68) 6
Heartland Union Bank (HUB) (p. 183) 9
Dayton Metal Works (p. 198) 5
Delphi Insurance (p. 316) 22

8

Managerial Decision Making

LEARNING OBJECTIVES

After completing this chapter, you should be able to

1. Explain some of the complexities that can influence the decision-making process.
2. Make a decision using the four-step rational approach.
3. Discuss the differences between decisions under conditions of certainty, decisions under risk, and decisions under uncertainty.
4. Explain how a person's previous experiences and beliefs can affect the decisions he or she makes.
5. Understand the benefits—and risks—of group decision making.
6. Help a group avoid the dangers of groupthink.
7. Know the eight steps that a manager can take to avoid the dangers of a risky decision.
8. Conduct a basic quantitative decision analysis.

Strategy, operating targets, policies, and programs combine to form a road map on how to get to a desired goal. They chart a course. Nevertheless, managers must make many critical decisions as they steer along that course, seeking to avoid unforeseen dangerous obstacles while exploiting opportunities along the way. What should they do? When should they do it? These and a host of other questions must be answered along the way.

Strategy and its supporting plans must guide the choices made by managers. But within those limits, alternatives must be found and costs and benefits compared for specific situations. In fact, even the choice about which strategy to pursue calls for all the decision-making skill an organization can muster—so much so that some experts believe that decision making is the most important thing a manager does, because a manager won't be able to organize, control, or lead well if he is not a competent decision maker.

Rational Decision Making

In Western society, with its emphasis on the scientific technique, it has long been argued that decision making should be rational. Plans can be selected by intuition, precedent, voting, or divine guidance, but in a goal-oriented organization such as a business firm, the *rational decision* is widely believed to be the best.[1]

The problem is that so-called rational decision making is difficult because of the large volume of information that must be considered and the shortcuts people develop to get around those taxing demands on time and memory—what Herbert Simon calls "boundedly rational" behavior.[2] Since this rational approach makes such enormous demands on decision makers, it is used in practice only for the most important decisions. And even this limited use requires considerable effort and concentration.

The rational approach.   Fundamentally, rational decision making is quite simple. The four essential phases are (1) diagnosing the problem, (2) searching for the most promising alternative solutions, (3) analyzing and comparing these alternatives, and (4) selecting the best alternative as a plan for action.

A physician follows all four parts of this procedure in examining a patient and in prescribing a course of action. In practice, making the diagnosis may not be easy, because some of the same symptoms can result from a number of causes. Clearly, if the wrong cause is assumed—such as appendicitis instead of gallstones—treatment will be ineffective, and possibly disastrous. Many advances in the last decade have improved medical

---

[1]E. F. Harrison, *The Managerial Decision-Making Process.* (Boston: Houghton Mifflin, 1975), Ch. 2.

[2]H. A. Simon, *Administrative Behavior,* 3d ed. (New York: Free Press, 1976).

decision making. The use of diagnostic computers, for example, has limited variability among physicians, or even for the same physician at different times.

Having made a sound diagnosis, the physician then considers possible remedies, such as changes in diet or life-style, medication or surgery. Some remedies will be standard practice, but if the patient has limitations—a weak heart or allergies, for instance—other alternatives must be considered. The physician must next weigh the advantages and disadvantages of each alternative for each specific case. How long will the patient be incapacitated? Are the necessary resources—professional aid, equipment, money—available?

Finally, the physician uses his judgment and selects the best plan or prescription. He considers the probability of success and the risks of complications, usually employing simple-remedy alternatives before moving on to more drastic ones. He may do nothing. Or he may call an ambulance and rush the patient to the hospital. Every good physician follows this rational approach: diagnosis, review of possible remedies, analysis of probable results, and prescription.

To be sure, the decision-making process becomes less clear when tackling organizational problems. The manager must obtain agreement on diagnosis, define alternatives, gather reliable information from specialists on the existing situation, forecast what will happen, and win enough support to justify positive action. Successfully completing all of these tasks, especially in an uncertain environment, is by no means simple.

THE CRITICAL ROLE OF DIAGNOSIS

Diagnosis is the critical first step in organizational life, as it was for the physician. Unless the diagnosis is accurate, subsequent planning will be misdirected and wasteful.[3]

The love of quick action, and perhaps an illusion of omniscience, makes some managers impatient with careful diagnosis and detailed planning. The basic issue, too often forgotten, is that quick action is not nearly so important as the *right* action.

In pursuing sound diagnosis, the following questions should be addressed:

1. Just what gaps exist between the desired results and the existing or predicted state of affairs?
2. What are the direct root causes and the intermediate causes of the gaps?
3. Does examination of the problem in the context of higher-level goals place limits on the range of satisfactory solutions?

[3]W. F. Pounds, "The Process of Problem Finding," *Industrial Management Review,* Fall 1969, pp. 1–19.

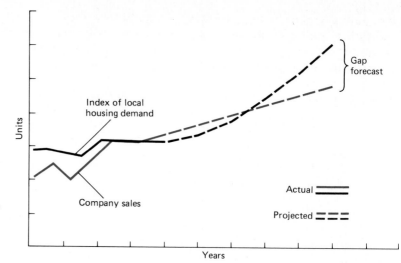

Figure 8.1 A gap may exist between forecasts of future conditions and present company plans, as shown in this five-year projection of a mobile-housing contractor.

Such questions must be taken into account in considering the plan shown in Figure 8.1. In addition, some situation-specific questions must be addressed: Is the manager operating in the same old world, with which she is very familiar? Or have fundamental changes occurred, forcing an alteration in how the situation is perceived? Should the manager isolate interdependent pieces of a problem to diagnose them independently? Or should she link independent pieces to assess their chain effects?

Managers' answers to such questions determine what they are likely to find. For instance, Charles Perrow's study of the nuclear power plant accident at Three Mile Island discovered numerous flaws in the linking of subsystems that were initially designed to stand alone, aggravating conditions and leading to major and potentially deadly delays in the detection of critical irregularities within the nuclear facility. Perrow calls such problems "normal accidents" because they were unforeseen by designers who combined the systems and because they are increasingly likely as society becomes more complex.[4]

Similarly, a two-part business classic[5] analyzing varying production quality on four different auto-panel assembly lines shows how focusing on the wrong narrow issues in problem diagnosis can lead to big mistakes. A team of managers was convinced that quality problems were deliberately caused by rebellious workers after a co-worker was dismissed; this was in keeping with the managers' general mistrust of the unionized workers, their motives, and their commitment to quality. But a thorough analysis found that, quite to the contrary, the problem was not worker-based. It

[4]C. Perrow, *Normal Accidents: Living With High-Risk Technologies* (New York: Basic Books, 1984).

[5]P. Stryker, "Can You Analyze This Problem?" *Harvard Business Review,* May–Jun. 1965; and "How to Analyze That Problem," *July–Aug. 1965.*

was caused by a new supplier using a new type of steel to which the work process had not been adjusted. As in the medical example, this underscores the importance of accurate diagnosis. Many managers are simply reluctant to entertain new ideas that challenge their beliefs.[6]

The Individual and the Decision

As hard as decision theorists have tried over the years to streamline decision processes, the individual decision maker remains a key variable. People vary in their experiences, tolerance for taking chances, desire for security, and socialization. They process information to be used in decision making in the context of those underpinnings. If a person has a world view, or "mental model of the world," in which only cheaters win, he will probably resign himself to a life of cheating—or a life of losing. If someone experiences repeated frustration in trying to do something—even a simple task—a condition known as "learned helplessness" can develop,[7] rendering that person ineffective in that situation.

All too often in organizations, disgruntled managers, whose earlier recommendations for change have been spurned, sit back and sulk. They decide to conform to the noncreative preferences of their superiors and never again submit that idea—or maybe any other creative idea. Asking such an individual to take on a decision task requiring novel solutions later may only rekindle the helplessness they experienced earlier, and may not lead to very creative problem solving or decision making for the organization, even though times have changed and the organization desperately needs it.

The mental models, or "schemas," of individuals provide structures with which they assimilate information from the world around them. Those structures are a product of an individual's entire life experiences. The more active a person's mental models and the more information a person gathers and evaluates before diagnosing a situation, the greater that person's level of cognitive complexity. The manager with high cognitive complexity is processing more information than the less complex manager. The high-complexity manager is also more likely to view situations in a more creative and open manner than will the low-complexity manager wedded to the traditions of a few old mental models.[8] A number of modern testing procedures that are far more focused than general personality assessments can measure cognitive complexity and preference for many or few mental models, as well as comfort with much or relatively little information in decision making.

---

[6]C. Argyris, *Strategy, Change and Defensive Routines* (Boston: Pitman, 1985).

[7]M. E. P. Seligman, *Helplessness* (San Francisco: W. H. Freeman, 1975); J. Garber and M. E. P. Seligman, *Human Helplessness* (New York: Academic Press, 1980).

[8]M. J. Driver, "A Human Resource Data-Based Approach to Organizational Design," *Human Resource Planning*, Spring 1983, pp. 169–82.

Cultural Blocks

Just as diagnosis can be limited by an individual's experiences, so can it be hampered by cultural blocks. These blocks develop because society pushes its members toward conformity and strongly influences their thinking, often rewarding them when they conform and punishing them when they don't. Almost everyone, consciously or unconsciously, tends to conform to the attitudes and modes of living of their associates. Minor exceptions may be acceptable or even desirable, but it is a daring employee who wears pantaloons or goes barefoot in the office.

This same tendency to follow the crowd—this unwillingness to be different—affects people's imaginations as well as their actions. And until they are ready to break with current fashions of thought—in a department, in a company, or in a society—truly creative ideas will be scarce.

In addition to the barriers that arise from social background, people often have difficulty with new ideas simply because of the way they perceive things. Psychologists have devised many experiments that demonstrate the importance of perception. In one of the simplest, six matchsticks are placed in front of a person and he is asked to make four triangles with the sticks touching each other at the ends. Most people have trouble, and may even give up, because they think only of arranging the matches on a flat surface. Once they conceive of the task as a three-dimensional problem, they quickly form a pyramid. Similar conceptual blocks are shown in Figure 8.2.

Transferring habits is probably the biggest cause of perceptual blocks. The mechanics who built the first automobiles, for instance, were in the habit of thinking of carriages. It was only natural that their early designs for the "horseless carriage" merely substituted a motor for a horse. It took a half century before rear-engine cars became commonplace. Similarly, in a company in which engineering has always been physically and organizationally part of the plant production department, executives have a hard time devising a new organization that ties engineering closely to marketing. That transfer of past habits to new situations may block out a fresh perception of alternatives.

Figure 8.2 Our perceptions can be an obstacle to creativity, preventing us from seeing the wholeness or diversity of situations, or even permitting us to see "impossible" objects. Does the silhouette show two profiles or a vase? How many stacked cubes do you count? Why is the third object called "irrational"? New perspectives are often required to enable us to break through our perceptual blocks.

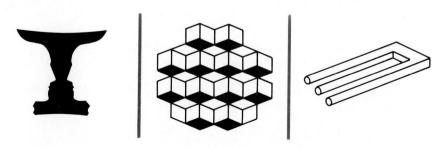

An additional source of difficulty is that people too readily approach a problem as an "either-or" dilemma and examine only two courses of action. For example, when one medium-size manufacturing concern found its plant running to capacity, its executives wrestled for several weeks with the choice between trying to attract extra capital for building an addition to its plant or giving up plans for future expansion in volume. But these were not the only available alternatives. A third possibility involved subcontracting some of the work, and a fourth one, which the company actually adopted, was the arranging of a "sale and lease-back" deal whereby the company sold its old plant and the new addition to an investor and then leased them back for a long period.

SEARCH FOR ALTERNATIVES

Group Creativity

One approach that is sometimes effective in overcoming individual limitations and life-experience burdens in making decisions is to employ a creative group approach. Under favorable conditions, groups produce more creative ideas than do individuals—as long as groupthink does not develop.

Groupthink[9] can result when people are involved in a cohesive group in which members' striving for unanimity overrides their motivation to realistically appraise unpopular alternatives. A number of crises—such as the ignoring of numerous reports that Japan might bomb Pearl Harbor in late 1941, the Bay of Pigs fiasco in Cuba, and the Watergate coverup—can be traced at least in part to groupthink at its worst. Groupthink can be avoided, however, if these caveats are followed:

1. Members must place a high priority on airing objections and doubts.
2. Group assignments should be given impartially, rather than being tainted with suggestions of management's preferences or expectations.
3. Several independent groups should work simultaneously on the same question under different leaders.
4. Each member of the group should periodically discuss the group's deliberations with trusted associates away from the group.
5. Outside experts or colleagues should be invited to each group meeting on a staggered basis to candidly challenge the views expressed.
6. Group members should be assigned, on a rotating basis, the role of devil's advocate.
7. Extensive time should be spent surveying warning signals from a rival and constructing alternative scenarios of a rival's intentions.

[9] I. L. Janis, *Groupthink,* 2d ed. (Boston: Houghton Mifflin, 1982).

8. After reaching a tentative policy decision, group members must be given time to sleep on the decision, and then a "second-chance" meeting should be held to make certain that group members still support the action.

Once inoculated against groupthink, a group may use several techniques to make the most of its creativity. One of the most popular methods is known as *brainstorming*. Perhaps you have been involved in a group making up a skit to mimic your professors; but even in a more formal group—perhaps a hospital board thinking about ways to gain public support for a new building—the flow of ideas might be similar: One person tosses out an offbeat idea that is quickly topped by another. While chuckling over the suggestions, a third person chimes in with something that sounds ridiculous, but can partly be salvaged to improve on the other ideas. The animated spirit of the group is contagious. No one cares whether each idea is practical; just thinking them up is good fun. Out of such sessions, an ingenious plan that no group member alone would have thought of is likely to emerge.

When confronted with a problem requiring an original solution, Osborn suggests presenting the problem to a group and asking them to come up with as many solutions as possible.[10] The following are Osborn's important rules for group procedure:

1. Rule out making quick judgments. Criticism of ideas must be withheld until later.
2. Welcome freewheeling. The wilder the idea, the better; it is easier to tame down than to think up.
3. Solicit many ideas. The greater the number, the more likely one will be a winner.
4. Seek combinations and improvements. In addition to contributing ideas of their own, participants should suggest how ideas of others can be sharpened or how two or more ideas can be joined.

Executives have used this technique on a wide variety of problems, including how to find new uses for glass in autos, how to improve a company's in-house newspaper, how to design a new tire-making machine, how to improve highway signs, and how to cut down on absenteeism. An hour session is likely to produce from 60 to 150 ideas. And a few may be worthy of serious consideration.

Brainstorming works best when the problem is simple and specific. In more complex settings, discussions tend to lose their spontaneity. But this risk to brainstorming can be dealt with by dividing a complex issue into many parts and developing brainstorming teams to deal critically with the parts.

---

[10]A. F. Osborn, *Applied Imagination* (New York: Scribner's, 1960).

Sometimes acceptable alternatives emerge during the diagnostic stage. Some experts know what other firms are doing; outside consultants may be more likely to keep their hands on the pulse of an industry. In fact, the cue that triggered the recognition of a problem may have been an action taken by someone else, such as a supplier or customer.

Once a search for new ideas has been undertaken, the next problem becomes when to end the search. Sooner or later, continuing the search for additional alternatives is not worth the trouble or cost involved. Yet to avoid falling into the trap of quitting too early, some wise managers insist on the consideration of at least four alternatives. Such a rule of thumb does not guarantee a careful search, but it does avoid the tempting simplicity of an either-A-or-B formulation.

Another tack is to invite suggestions from all key people who would be affected by the contemplated change. One case in which that didn't happen, and dire consequences resulted, involved a major metropolitan newspaper trying to cut operating costs in a recession. Senior managers determined that $45,000 a year could be saved and one press crew fired if two rather than three presses were used to print the early-evening edition. Of course, the two presses would have to start earlier and run for a longer time than if three were operating, but that didn't trouble the senior managers. Had they taken the time to invite suggestions from affected parties, such as the financial editor, the senior managers would have discovered that the New York Stock Exchange was about to extend its operating hours. The managers didn't check, but pushed ahead with their cost-cutting plan. A year later, circulation of that edition had fallen by 25 percent, or 15,000 papers a day—largely because so much stock market news, a very popular feature, was lost from the edition. Worse still, the cost savings never took place; while $45,000 was saved in the pressroom, an additional $50,000 in composing room costs was added to deal with the later stock market reports.

This is an example of what can happen when managers aren't given the opportunity to respond to proposed changes—or when changes are proposed that do little more than divert costs, making one manager look good politically in the short run, and making the manager who picked up the unexpected cost burden in another subunit look equally bad. Also, senior managers must pay attention to the feedback they receive from affected parties. Too often the process of asking them to react to contemplated changes is little more than an early move to prepare them for imminent change, and submitted proposals are brushed aside by senior managers as biased or as ploys to avoid the inevitable. If these internal hurdles can be overcome, several fairly workable alternatives can often be assembled with the help of key people who are close to the problem.

Separate Creative Units

What happens when no acceptable alternative bubbles to the surface in the normal organizational process? For many reasons—political, social, and environmental—major changes may require a firm to organize to get fresh ideas. Product or process research in the pharmaceutical industry is an example. Specialists are hired and laboratories built to create a flow of new, useful drugs. Advertising agencies similarly hire specialists to create new themes, as do politicians.

One drawback to relying on specialists is that they may differ sharply in attitude; battles between production and marketing people are legendary, for instance. That same conflict is often found between "creative people" and "tough operators." The imaginative person who is ready to entertain all sorts of fanciful notions has a very different outlook from the operator who carefully distinguishes between fact and fiction, right and wrong, and established practicality and daydreaming. Because of this contrasting orientation, managers must anticipate friction when two such people are asked to collaborate. To minimize this difficulty, physical separation and relatively few interactions are probably desirable.

EVALUATING ALTERNATIVES

As soon as most, or all, of the possible alternative solutions to a problem have been identified, managers start to compare them. "What will happen if we do X? Is that clearly better than Y? Might costly side effects arise? Does the proposed action really solve our problem, or will it be only a first step?" All sorts of estimates and forecasts have to be made in this process of evaluation.

As an old saying suggests, time is money. And it is especially true for managers. Since time and energy are limited, a manager can expedite the consideration of alternatives by (1) accepting constraints on alternatives and (2) grouping similar alternatives. Once this is done, the manager can proceed to analyze the consequences of the alternatives being considered.

To fully anticipate such consequences, managers must be thoroughly acquainted with an operation, and their imaginations must be tempered by realism. For instance, the sales manager of a manufacturer of power lawn mowers and related equipment recommended that his company establish an assembly shop on the West Coast. He said that this move would lower costs and improve customer service, thereby enabling the company to meet competition from West Coast manufacturers. At the time, the company had only a sales office and a warehouse for finished products in California. Among the questions to which the company sought answers were the following:

1. What will be the difference in cost between shipping parts and shipping assembled products?

2. How much will we have to pay for direct labor in the California plant? How much for indirect labor, such as maintenance, janitors, and so on? What reduction, if any, in labor costs will there be at the main plant?

3. How much additional overhead will the California shop require? This includes rent (or, if we own the plant, taxes, depreciation, maintenance, and interest), power, heat, and light. How many clerks and supervisors, at what salaries, will we need for assembly work? Will there be any offsetting reduction in overhead at the main plant?

4. How much additional capital will we have to tie up in West Coast operations if the new shop is opened? This includes capital for equipment, office furniture, and other fixed assets; additional inventory; moving and setup costs; and operating losses during the period when the shop is getting under way.

5. Will the new shop be flexible enough to adjust to seasonal changes in volume of business? What minimum staff will have to be retained during low periods? Would there be greater flexibility at the main plant than at the new shop?

6. Will manufacturing in California subject the company to special state taxes or added liability insurance? Will it be advantageous to establish a separate corporation?

7. Just what will be the improvement in service to customers? How will local assembly ensure speedier deliveries than warehousing finished products? Will local repair and troubleshooting be feasible, and how much weight will this carry with customers? Will delivery of repair parts be improved?

8. In addition to actual improvement in customer service, will the "local industry" appeal have a significant effect on sales volume?

9. Will the quality of the product be as well controlled in California as in the main plant?

10. Will the union at the main plant object to transferring work to another location? Might jurisdictional problems arise if a different union organizes the West Coast operations?

11. Should the West Coast shop be under the direction of a West Coast sales manager? What responsibility, if any, will the production manager have for West Coast operations? How will accounting and human resources be coordinated with the main plant?

12. How much additional sales volume can be anticipated as a result of establishing a West Coast assembly shop? How much will company profit be increased as a result of this additional volume?

Only after checking into all of these questions was the president of the mower company prepared to make a decision on the proposed West Coast assembly shop.

Making the Choice

That which emerges from a comparison of alternatives does not constitute a decision. Someone has to decide which predicted outcomes are best. To do that, the decision maker must apply values.

A college student, in picking an elective course, makes a value judgment. Suppose she has narrowed the choice to either History of the Soviet Union or Computer Programming. Investigation indicated the first course would be fun—an interesting professor, an air-conditioned room, lively discussions of current events, and a useful background for the years ahead. The second course would require much more work, but it would offer a large practical payoff given the importance of computers in society. Tuition and course credit can be disregarded because they are the same for each course. The student's projections of the alternatives help her see the implications of each, but she still has to make a final decision based on personal, subjective values. Business decisions, although they can involve more quantifiable values, ultimately place large demands on the decision maker to similarly understand and assign weights to subjective preferences.

Is the Choice Correct?

As a manager moves toward a preferred alternative, how can she determine whether it is the correct choice? There is no sure way. Decisions are ultimately risky, but the risks can be minimized if different methods are employed to test the soundness of a decision, as Figure 8.3 shows. Managers should be familiar with the techniques so that they can pick those appropriate to a specific decision.

An open mind is essential at this stage. Challenges should be carefully considered. For centuries the Roman Catholic Church has used the institution of the *devil's advocate* to test decisions, especially those relating to the canonization of new saints. A person is assigned the task of pointing out weaknesses and errors in proposed actions. He assembles the best negative arguments he can. If a proposal cannot withstand such an attack, action is postponed. This is the same role addressed earlier as critical to the avoidance of groupthink.

The devil's advocate is apt to be unpopular, especially when critical decisions are involved, so the senior manager should be sure that everyone recognizes that the devil's advocate is not passing judgment on a matter, but simply ensuring that all negative points have been duly considered. A

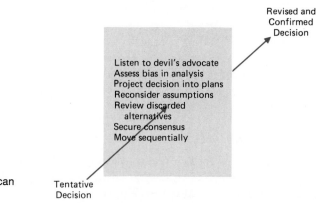

Figure 8.3 Ways a manager can test a tentative decision.

decision may be challenged on the basis of evidence, logic, values, or other grounds. During cross-examination by a devil's advocate, all sorts of embarrassing questions can be raised. For example:

"If officers need the proposed five-week vacation, why not all employees?"

"True, our annual reports do show a high correlation between sales volume and advertising expense, but does that mean more ads will increase sales?"

Or, acknowledging that determining causation is tricky:

"Remember that the United States leads India in heart attacks and baths per capita. But does it follow that baths cause heart attacks, or vice versa?"

Understanding Bias

Any decision is predicated on some estimate of the future. Are such estimates reliable? Are they optimistic or pessimistic? Bias is almost inevitable in such projections, and it can be helpful to know some common forms of such bias. Here are four common reasons why projections may be off base:

1. Differences in the perception of objectives. Managers who are making decisions may have different objectives from the people who are giving them advice.[11] This is most likely when the advisers have strong, professional indoctrination, as in, for example, accounting, law, social work, and, to a lesser extent, engineering. The advice and help such people provide may be strongly influenced by what they believe to be important. If a decision maker is trying to achieve different objectives, the sympathetic help she is expecting may turn out to be suggestions that lead off on a tangent. The help may still be of some value, but she has to make allowances for its source.

Difference in objectives was found to be an important factor in a study of seventy-four companies' decisions on the use of outside contractors for maintenance work. The study showed that senior executives place high value on stable union relations, whereas maintenance superintendents give greater weight to keeping their costs low and to the number of their employees who might be laid off. Managers cannot tell from the available information which objectives deserve priority, but the difference in objectives clearly affects the way in which the two leadership groups respond to this problem.

[11]A. D. Szilagyi and M. J. Wallace, Jr., *Organizational Behavior and Performance* (Santa Monica, Calif.: Goodyear, 1980), pp. 72–77.

2. The "persuasive" adviser.   People vary in their persuasive ability, and it is entirely possible that a person who is making a projection will be unduly swayed by the counsel he receives from an impressive adviser. A review of the role of business economists in twenty firms revealed that the use made of economic forecasts was significantly influenced by personal feeling toward the company economist and by how well he "sold" his conclusions.

Status and company politics are factors here, as is manner of speech. The treasurer of a food chain served as chairman of its capital-expenditures committee, and his views carried heavy weight in decisions on which division received the largest share of capital for expansion. Partly because of his "power," his recommendations on other matters were seldom challenged. Such influence, again, makes it difficult to reach completely objective decisions.[12]

3. Special pressure.   Informal groups have a strong influence on the values, beliefs, and socially acceptable actions of their members. All people are members of several such groups and take part of their counsel from these unofficial sources as well as from the advisers and information centers provided in the formal organization. Informal groups, particularly among executives, may strongly support official company objectives and plans—but not necessarily. When managers base their planning on numerous personal interchanges, they must be prepared for this reality: Social relations cannot be prescribed by an organization manual.

4. Personal needs.   The aspirations and beliefs, as well as the sweet or bitter experience, of a person making a projection affect her response to the array of help provided by an organization. To be sure, supervisory review keeps reminding the adviser of company objectives and other basic "premises." Nevertheless, there is still room for personal bias to affect the predictions the adviser makes. The fallibility of human nature is simply another source of conflict to bear in mind as the organization as a machine for making plans is contemplated.

Project Decision into Plans

Another way to detect flaws in a decision is to spell out its consequences in more detail. A large manufacturing company, for example, tested its tentative decision to decentralize into product divisions by projecting the consequences of such a move. It allocated customers, outlined a proposed divisional organization, devised a tentative realignment of executives, and estimated the administrative cost of the new setup. The analysis uncovered so many weaknesses and difficulties that the original decentralization plan was abandoned. Not until a year later was a substantially modified reorganization put into effect.

[12]R. Miles, *Macro Organizational Behavior* (Santa Monica, Calif.: Goodyear, 1980), pp. 132–34.

Reconsider Assumptions

Virtually every decision is based on a critical series of assumptions. On closer examination, these assumptions may be supported by sketchy data about future demand for products, the availability of raw materials, attitudes and future behavior of employees, or even values that are undergoing change. In finalizing a decision, it is useful for a manager to ask which assumptions are crucial to the success of a proposed action and to try to get further clarification of those pivotal points. All premises cannot be verified. Managers must resign themselves to contending with incomplete data, errors in perception of facts, and distortion in communication. But the risks that are critical to an undertaking should at least be reconsidered so that managers understand the risks they are taking, and are not proceeding naively.

Review Discarded Alternatives

Too often an otherwise excellent alternative is discarded because it has a single drawback or because it was initially bypassed as being unthinkable. In such cases, it is wise to determine whether that drawback is insurmountable, and whether its being discarded was appropriate. As will be described later, in this chapter's "Management in Action" case, in the mid-1970s a nationwide swine flu inoculation program was undertaken because decision makers concluded that if the program were not undertaken, an epidemic would result. President Ford, bowing to pressure from within his own cabinet and health bureaucracy, endorsed the program. More than 40 million people were immunized within ten weeks, a feat never before accomplished in history. But many died in the process—a risk that had been overlooked in the decision process. As for the swine flu, it never came, and, in retrospect, it never posed a serious health threat in the United States. An analysis of the problem by a political scientist and physician[13] concludes that if the alternative "do nothing" had been reconsidered—rather than discarded early and forgotten—the fiasco might have been avoided. Thus, rejected alternatives should always be reconsidered; critical drawbacks might be removed or removable. And if an alternative is rejected on further consideration, at least the manager has done his best to openly test alternatives.

Securing Consensus

A director of Exxon Corporation has observed, "When a proposal comes before our Board for decision, there is rarely sharp difference of opinion. We try to anticipate problems, and then we discuss possible solutions with everyone directly affected and those who might have useful views. These discussions often seem slow, but by the time we are ready to act, a clear

---

[13]R. E. Neustadt and H. Fineberg, *The Epidemic That Never Was: Policy-Making and the Swine Flu Affair* (New York: Vintage Books, 1983).

consensus backing the proposal has usually developed."[14] Most people and organizations use similar techniques, making a tentative decision and then seeking support from trusted associates. In seeking such advice, however, it is important that neither polite agreement, nor logrolling politics, nor cavalier advice be tolerated.

Pilot Runs

The surest way to test a decision is to try it out. A test won't tell if another decision would work better, but it will tell whether a proposed plan is at least promising. Sometimes a new product or process can be tried out on a limited scale with custom-made models or equipment. Road tests are extensive in the automobile industry—so much so that engineers are working five to seven years ahead on some models. Pilot operations have their limitations, of course. They are costly. They may consume valuable time. And they may not be feasible for some actions, such as testing a market's reaction to one alternative or another. Although analysts and customers can indicate how they might respond, a manager can take to the bank only that which they actually *do*.

Sequential Decisions

Occasionally, managers have the good fortune of being able to test a decision by implementing it one part at a time. If the first part works, the manager can go ahead with the second part. If the first part doesn't work, the manager can reconsider the first part or kill the entire project. In so doing, a manager makes a series of decisions to solve one main problem.

This type of decision is often used in executive promotions. Suppose, for instance, a company president has his eye on a salesperson, Linda Watson, as a likely replacement for a sales manager who will retire in three years. The president's first step might be to bring Ms. Watson into the home office as sales promotion director. If she does well, Ms. Watson might be put in charge of sales planning. And if her work continues to be good, she may be named assistant sales manager six months before moving up to the big job. These successive assignments serve a double purpose: They give Ms. Watson experience and a chance to learn about home-office operations, and the company can make a series of appraisals on her capability to be sales manager. The results of each step provide data that can be used in deciding what the next step should be.

QUANTITATIVE ANALYSIS IN DECISION MAKING

Before a final decision is reached, a comprehensive quantitative analysis of the decision alternatives often takes place. This allows an executive to

---

[14]P. F. Drucker, "What We Can Learn from Japanese Management," *Harvard Business Review,* Mar.–Apr. 1971, pp. 110–22.

weigh many pertinent factors while at the same time reducing the complexity of the issues. It also introduces a major risk: Because quantitative concerns are easier to grasp than subjective factors, and because their mathematical roots make them seem more reliable, managers, to their own peril, often become dependent on such numbers. These tools, while powerful, should always be regarded as additional pieces of the pie that, while cut with precision, do not substitute for immeasurable logic and good-sense concerns.

The elusive numbers.   Quantification of economic factors depends on a manager's ability to use accounting data developed for tax or financial purposes and statistical data derived from experience to identify those elements of income, expense, or investment that actually change with the alternatives considered.

One overriding rule is to always remember where the numbers came from and what the charter was of the unit producing them. For instance, one large media company developed a so-called market research department to produce selected and slanted "data" to make the company look ideal for whatever advertisers it was trying to attract. Although morally questionable, it was a standard practice in the industry. The real problem developed, however, when the company forgot the propaganda base of the department, and senior executives began to take its numbers as gospel. This led to making strategic decisions on the basis of poor and slanted data used to attract customers, which ultimately contributed to the company's being taken over after a hostile stock fight by outsiders who were more in tune with the marketplace.

Adjustments for uncertainty and risk.   Another major consideration in choosing among alternatives is the unpredictability of environments. Business cycles, weather, wars, competition, inventions, new laws, and a host of other dynamic situations and events make for a less-than-certain future. Within an organization, machine breakdown, irregularity in human performance, and failure to maintain standard operating procedures increase a manager's quandary. But managers must be willing to make decisions even when they lack complete certainty.

Three Levels of Doubt

Decision theorists note that managers can make decisions under three possible conditions—certainty, risk, and uncertainty. Conditions of *certainty,* in which managers have enough information to know the outcome of their decisions with perfect accuracy, are rare. *Risk* refers to situations in which a manager knows the likelihood of various possible outcomes associated with a decision. And complete *uncertainty* exists when managers can't predict various outcomes associated with a decision.

Actually, most managerial decisions lie between clearly known risk and complete uncertainty. In order to use quantitative analysis, it is convenient to condense the uncertainties and to make judgments or assumptions so that the final choice among alternatives is based on "risk." The following discussion will demonstrate how useful this translation of uncertainty into assumed risk can be.

Decision Making Under Risk

For some events, a manager may possess enough statistical data to compute the chances that an event will occur. Life insurance provides the classic example. The insurers know that fewer than 1 percent of twenty-year-old men will die during the next five years, whereas about 5 percent of fifty-year-old men will die in the same period. The companies charge insurance premiums that allow these probabilities to fit their business. Thus, if an insurance executive were drawing up five-year contracts for twenty-year-olds and fifty-year-olds, he knows he should get five times as much for the latter policy as for the former in order to make the two comparable. Because mortality statistics enable the insurance executive to accurately estimate the probability of each occurrence, he is making his decision under risk.

Similarly, if a manager had an investment opportunity with a 50 percent chance of returning $100,000, a 40 percent chance of only a $20,000 return, and a 10 percent chance of losing $50,000, she could weigh these payoffs by their respective probabilities and develop an "expected value for the alternative"—in this case, $53,000—that is, ($100,000 × .5) + ($20,000 × .4) − ($50,000 × .1). The expected-value technique is the principal approach for adjusting alternatives to account for risk. But statisticians are quick to warn that rarely does an organization experience the same kinds of events frequently enough—as the insurance company does—that the losses or gains work out to the most probable result. They will almost always deviate.

Use of Subjective Probabilities

In practice, managers do have *feelings* about what is likely to happen in the future, and about whether such outcomes are attractive or unattractive. If these judgments (guesses) can be quantified into probabilities, then the convenient risk calculations can be utilized. Such judgments are called *subjective probabilities*.

For instance, a company with annual earnings before taxes of $750,000 was rapidly approaching a stalemate in union negotiations. Workers wanted a large wage increase that management was not willing to grant. After a long conference with key executives, the president concluded, "I think there is a 25 percent chance of a serious strike. If it comes, our earnings will probably drop $300,000."

The controller responded, "Then in comparing costs of various alternatives, we should figure the risk of a strike as a $75,000 cost ($300,000 × .25)."

After more discussion, the president and controller worked out a probability chart that is informative because it shows the likelihood of earnings losses ranging from 0 to $800,000 (Figure 8.4). It also indicates that when a full range of possible consequences is included, the seriousness of a strike threat is worse than the company first thought.

Figure 8.4

Possible Length of Strike	Estimated Loss of Earnings	Subjective Probability	Loss × Probability
0 days	0	35%	0
3–5 days	$ 50,000	40	$ 20,000
3 weeks	200,000	15	30,000
6 weeks	400,000	7	28,000
10 weeks	800,000	3	24,000
		100%	
		Loss adjusted for probability	$102,000

A similar analysis would be helpful to that president of the power mower company who was considering a new West Coast assembly shop. Estimates indicate that $19,000 would be lost if the proposed shop handles only the current volume of business in that territory, whereas a net gain of $59,000 would be realized if a local assembly plant doubles sales, as the sales manager predicts. The chief unknown is the sales volume. The president feels that the sales manager is excessively optimistic but grants that some increase in volume is likely. The president believes that the chance that the $400,000 volume will be achieved within a few years is small. Figure 8.5 sharpens these judgments and relates them to estimates of gain for different sales levels.

Figure 8.5

Possible Sales Volume (Annual)	Estimated Net Gain	Probability Inferred by President	Net Gain × Probability
$200,000	$-19,000	0	0
250,000	600	50%	$ 300
300,000	20,100	30	6,030
350,000	39,700	15	5,955
400,000	59,300	5	2,965
		100%	
		Net gain adjusted for probability	$15,250

Rate of return on initial investment of
$55,000: 28% (i.e., $15,250 ÷ $55,000)

The president's informed guess is that sales volume will be between $250,000 and $400,000 a year, with the lower volume much more likely. When he adjusts the net-gain estimate by subjective probabilities, the final value he assigns to the new shop is about $15,000 a year. Although this figure is not very enticing compared with what the sales manager fore-casted, it still represents an attractive 28 percent return on added investment in West Coast operations.

Unfortunately, these final figures, "adjusted for probability"—the $15,250 in the power mower illustration and the $102,000 in the strike example—are quite elastic. If a manager wants a single value, they are the best he can do. But to act on such information involves some chance that cannot be avoided.

Decision Trees

Managerial decisions are often much more complicated than the preceding example. In fact, a whole series of interrelated decisions may be involved. When faced with such complexities, managers may find that *decision trees* provide considerable help.

Take this example: Exports from Organic Fibers Inc. to Australia have been expanding, and the local sales agent is now insisting that he be given a ten-year contract. But Organic Fibers' overseas manager recommends opening a sales office there as a first step toward building a plant in Australia in three or four years. Decision A is the choice between the sales agent or the sales office. Decision B, to build a plant, will be made only after sales growth has been demonstrated. An alternative to Organic Fibers building its own plant is to subcontract. In fact, if a sales office is opened and growth is slow, subcontracting would still be an alternative to exporting from the United States; that would be Decision C.

To clarify (1) the decisions to be made, (2) the probabilities of key events, and (3) the estimated yields, the decision tree shown in Figure 8.6 was prepared. Laying out on a chart the alternative sequences of events, along with estimates of probabilities and estimated net profit, is a very helpful device. To further sharpen that choice, the manager should calculate the "position value" of an established sales office. This can be done by rolling back the expected values as follows:

1. On the basis of the manager's best estimates *Decision B will be to subcontract*. The difference in expected return from the plant and sub-contracting ($300,000 − $210,000 = $90,000) is not large enough to justify the difference in additional investment ($1,200,000 − $200,000 = $1,000,000). So we assume that the outcome of Decision B will be an expected yield of $210,000 and an investment of $200,000.

2. *Decision C will also be to subcontract.* The difference in expected return between subcontracting and exporting ($140,000 − $37,500 = $102,500) is large enough to justify the additional investment of $200,000. So we assume the outcome of Decision C will be an expected yield of $140,000 and an investment of $200,000.

3. Using the probabilities of high and low demand, which dictate whether we will be faced with Decision B or C, the manager can com-

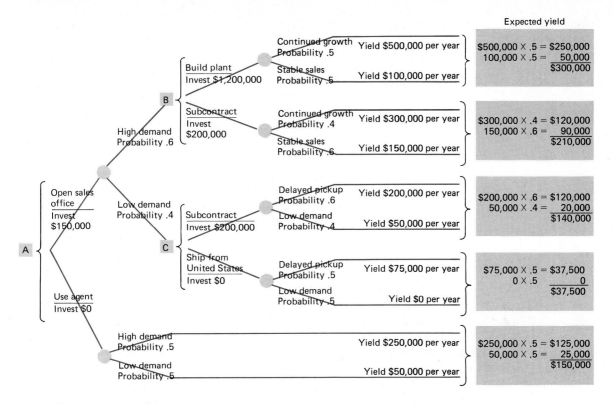

Figure 8.6 A decision tree for projected Australian expansion. The probabilities and amounts of investments and yields as shown represent management's best estimates on the basis of present knowledge.

pare the two alternatives at decision point A. If the company opens the sales office, the expected yield from Decision B is $126,000 ($210,000 × .6), while the yield from Decision C is $56,000 ($140,000 × .4). The total expected yield from opening the sales office is therefore $182,000 ($126,000 + $56,000) on a total investment of $350,000 ($150,000 to open the sales office and $200,000 to subcontract). On the other hand, if the company uses a sales agent, the total yield that can be expected is $150,000, without any initial investment.

4. *Decision A will be to use the agent.* The difference in expected yield from opening a sales office or using the agent ($182,000 − $150,000 = $32,000) is not large enough to justify the initial investment in the sales office plus the investment necessary to subcontract in Australia ($150,000 + $200,000 = $350,000).

Decision trees can be drawn to fit all sorts of situations, but they can grow to dozens of branches representing the alternatives being analyzed. Trees can quickly become very complex.

Computer Simulations

One way to deal with more elaborate and complex pictures is through com-
puter-generated simulations. With this technique, a model—admittedly
incomplete, but the best the manager can design—is used to project possible results from various alternatives under various assumptions. Such a
model enables a decision maker to test all sorts of contingencies—tight
money, high demand, production lags, and so on—and construct various
actions to combat those situations. It is like running through football plays
on a practice field: One knows that actual conditions will be more complicated, but nonetheless one gets some indication of how things will go under
such conditions.

This sort of "what if" analysis of complex situations is feasible under
most business conditions only on computers.

Matrix Summaries of Intangibles

In addition to decision trees and computer simulations, a *matrix* is another
device for reducing uncertainties into a concise quantitative form. Figure
8.7 presents an example. The president of a large paper company had to
choose a new mill location. She narrowed the choice to four sites and consolidated as well as she could the dollar benefits of each into an estimated
return on incremental investment. She then identified five other factors
that, while partially reflected in the dollar figures, had additional intangible implications. For each intangible, the president faced two questions:

1. What degree of satisfaction may I expect for each intangible at each
   mill site?
2. How important is each intangible to me, in the range being considered?

Because the president could not avoid answering these two questions,
at least subjectively, she went one step further and translated her feelings
into numbers. She ranked each alternative on a scale from zero to ten for
each question, with low ranking reflecting low satisfaction or low importance. These evaluations of the intangibles are summarized on the matrix
shown in Figure 8.7. To arrive at a rough indication of the relative significance of intangibles for each site, the degree of satisfaction (in color) in
each cell of the matrix has been multiplied by the relative importance (in
black). The resulting numbers are a rough index of the relative degree of
importance of each intangible for all four sites.

To summarize, the index numbers have been added to show a combined score for each site. The total score had significance only for comparing alternative sites. Nevertheless, it did help the president make a choice.
By concentrating on the last two columns of the matrix, she quickly decided that Site 2 was preferable to Site 1: The score for the intangibles was
about the same, and Site 2 had a decided edge in rate of return. After

Alternative Sites	Predicted Availability of Desired Labor/Skill Mix	Predicted Favorable Union Relations	Predicted Favorable Local Legislation and Taxes	Predicted Ability to Hold Capable Mill Managers in This Location	Predicted Unlikelihood of Competitors Moving Nearby	Weighted Total Score for Intangibles	Estimated Incremental Return on Investment Compared with Doing Nothing
Site 1	6 × 9 = 54	5 × 8 = 40	6 × 9 = 54	9 × 9 = 81	4 × 3 = 12	241	12.1%
Site 2	5 × 6 = 30	8 × 8 = 64	6 × 9 = 54	9 × 9 = 81	3 × 3 = 9	238	14.7
Site 3	5 × 6 = 30	1 × 8 = 8	8 × 9 = 72	5 × 9 = 45	4 × 3 = 12	167	16.1
Site 4	10 × 6 = 60	6 × 8 = 48	8 × 9 = 72	8 × 9 = 72	5 × 3 = 15	267	10.8

Figure 8.7 A matrix for choosing mill locations, showing the president's subjective evaluation of intangibles. Sites below minimum acceptable level on any factor have already been eliminated. The company can easily finance the dollar investment required at any of these locations with an 8 percent bond issue. Quantity and quality of output will not be affected by the choice of site. Key: colored numbers = degree factor is achieved at each site; black numbers = relative importance of a factor; colored underscore = weighted score.

thinking about it, the president decided that Site 3 was preferable to Site 4: The significant intangible advantage of Site 4 simply could not offset a 50 percent higher rate of return at Site 3. That decision left a final choice between Sites 2 and 3.

Were the intangible advantages of Site 2 worth sacrificing an estimated 1.4 percentage point difference in rate of return? Looking at the cells in the matrix, the president could see that the chief difference in intangibles was in the favorability of predicted union relations; after further reflection, she decided to sacrifice rate of return rather than build a plant where union relations might be troublesome. Although the matrix did not give the president an automatic answer, it did two things: (1) It forced her to clarify her judgments about intangibles, and (2) it provided a mechanism by which she could balance them in her mind. Crude though the weights were, the matrix helped integrate the implications of each alternative into a final choice.

All sorts of matrices are possible. Verbal statements can replace numeric data. Probability estimates may be added. Predictions based on flimsy evidence can be flagged. Basically, these techniques, when coupled with the other methods explored in this chapter, can help managers get a handle on complex decisions so that they can proceed in a more rational manner.

Managers' need for a wide array of information has been stressed throughout this chapter. At each stage—diagnosing, finding alternatives, projecting consequences, and making the choice—both hard data and subjective opinions should be considered.

If managers had to start fresh in gathering such data, the process would be both time consuming and expensive. Actually, every established organization has accumulated much of the needed information—in its records and in the heads of its employees. The organization will also have people who are skilled in getting additional data and judgments from outside sources. But simply having the data available is not enough. A vital further step is to bring together the relevant information at the right place and the right time.

Management information system is the term used to describe the way in which information that is needed by managers flows within organizations. To the extent that decision problems can be anticipated, it is possible to plan this information flow. Designing such a system involves (1) identifying the kinds of information that will be needed, (2) establishing sources and storage points to collect and refine the information, (3) assessing who will need what data at what time, and (4) communicating the information in a timely and reliable manner to the decision makers.

A company's management information system will, of course, be strongly influenced by its organization, because the organization influences both who the decision makers are and who should collect information on particular topics. Organization is the subject of the next Part of this book. In addition, leading—the subject of Part IV—requires a great deal of person-to-person communication, which is involved in the management information system. Furthermore, useful data are often generated in the controlling process—to be considered in Part V.

Consequently, many of the issues yet to be discussed have a direct bearing on management information systems. Thinking about such systems forces consideration of the interrelationship of the total management process.

Clearly, companies with well-developed management information systems should be able to make decisions faster and better.

CONCLUSION

Making decisions may be the manager's single most important task. Strategy, plans, results—all flow from the quality of managerial decision making.

Theoretically, the so-called rational approach is best, for it applies techniques steeped in scientific rigor and prescribes four critical steps: (1) diagnosing the problem, (2) searching for promising alternatives, (3) analyzing and comparing possible alternatives, and (4) selecting the best choice from the alternatives under consideration.

Of course, a number of real-world variables influence how such rational choices are actually made. Differences among individuals can limit how thoroughly alternatives are explored. Social conformity and weddedness to certain narrow models of the world can restrict both how much information a manager gathers and weighs and how that information is assimilated.

Groups can help overcome such obstacles because they involve a number of people with a number of backgrounds; yet they are not without risk, either. The dangerous phenomenon of groupthink is always possible, although smart and able managers can protect against it. Other methods of developing creative alternatives include using creative units or consultants and soliciting the opinions of workers close to the problem. The latter method is commonly used in Japan, where workers close to problems are thought to have the best ideas of how to solve them; asking such workers how a prospective change might influence them has the additional benefit of potentially protecting a company from implementing a poor decision.

When the time comes to make the final decision, a large volume of numbers will often have been generated as conditions are quantified for comparison's sake. These numbers can be especially useful when past experiences and probabilities can be used to generate expected-value statistics for the various alternatives under consideration. Decision trees and computer simulations that map out and help to test various assumptions may also be helpful.

Underlying all these systematic approaches to business decision making are the values of the decision maker, the organization's values, or some combination of the two. Such values can sometimes be far from what the organization needs at a given time.

To minimize the potential for a serious mistake, a decision maker should do as many of the following as possible: (1) listen to the devil's advocate, (2) understand whatever biases may have influenced information used in the decision-making process, (3) project the prospective decision into plans and test how they hold up, (4) reconsider basic assumptions used in generating alternatives and making choices, (5) review discarded alternatives—which might end up being better than first thought, (6) try to secure honest consensus from respected associates, (7) use pilot runs to test the effect of a proposed decision, and (8) make the decision in sequences so that losses can be cut early if things don't turn out as expected.

Impact on Productivity

Decision-making skill is crucial to improvements in productivity. Both deciding what products or services will be needed in the future and deciding how an organization can improve its efficiency in producing these products or services are critical.

The decision to transfer resources—engineers and equipment—from paper to plastic wrapping material enabled an Italian-food processor to expand into an international market. In another setting, a pharmaceutical manufacturer recognized that satellite television would change the demand for medicines in remote areas and is thus changing its distribution channels. Examples of this sort suggest that creativity in defining the problem and in thinking of nontraditional alternatives is vital to some decisions. Long-run productivity is at stake.

Decisions that increase efficiency are also involved in productivity. For example, the *Wall Street Journal* has decided to print its daily paper in a half-dozen locations throughout the country, using a single editorial office and transmitting preset copy via satellite for electronic composing at each printing plant. This cuts printing and distribution costs substantially and also speeds delivery. A decision to close down a high-cost copper mine may be disheartening, but it may nonetheless be necessary if productivity is to be improved.

Wise managerial decisions are crucial in the chain of events that leads to higher productivity.

FOR FURTHER DISCUSSION

1. The mid-1980s decision to change the formula of Coke was a multimillion dollar one. If you had to make that decision, how would you have checked the wisdom of your choice?

2. Describe a great creative idea for which you were primarily responsible; it should be both original and practical. (a) Where did the idea come from? (b) Did you have any difficulty getting the idea put to use?

3. Four steps are commonly recommended for problem solving by an *individual:* (a) diagnosing, (b) finding good alternatives, (c) projecting the possible consequences of each alternative, and (d) making a choice for action. Explain how each of these steps should be taken in a *company,* not by a single person.

4. Outside experts often have the greatest "feel" for the occurrence of certain events, but they lack the perspective to evaluate the broader implications of alternatives. How should specialized expertise be utilized in choosing among alternatives?

5. Although a "devil's advocate" may be vital for testing decisions, the unpopularity of people in this role renders them an endangered species in many organizations. How should this dilemma be dealt with?

6. "Any decision that can be made by a computer does not require line management attention. Staff technicians who can identify the factors to be processed by the computer are all that is needed." Do you agree? Discuss your answer.

7. Can a computer develop creative alternatives to a problem? What are the similarities in the way a computer and the human mind operate in searching for a new idea? What are the differences?

8. How will the large increase in the number of women entering middle and upper management affect organizational decision making?

9. How may the existence of many detailed standing plans affect decision making in an enterprise?

10. Should those individuals most closely involved in the diagnosis stage of a decision be expected to play significant roles in the search for alternatives? Should the same people who have developed alternatives play a major role in choosing among them?

FOR FURTHER READING

Adams, J. L., *Conceptual Blockbusting,* 2d ed. San Francisco: W. H. Freeman & Co., 1980. A short book on creativity; identifies various mental blocks and suggests an array of ways to overcome them.

Allison, G. T., *Essence of Decision: Explaining the Cuban Missile Crisis*. Boston: Little, Brown, 1971. Already a classic, this book describes three views of decision making in organizations—rational, bureaucratic, and political—and applies these models to the ways in which decisions were made during the Cuban missile crisis.

Bass, B. M., *Organizational Decision Making*. Homewood, Ill.: Richard D. Irwin, 1983. A concise summary of behavioral issues and concepts about decision making in organizations.

Narayanan, V. K. and L. Fahey, "The Micro-Politics of Strategy Formulation," *Academy of Management Review*, January 1982. Explores politics versus rationality in the choice of company strategy.

Nutt, P. C., "Hybrid Planning Methods," *Academy of Management Review*, July 1982.

Quinn, J. B., *Strategic Change: Logical Incrementalism*. Homewood, Ill.: Richard D. Irwin, 1980. Contends that most companies do not rely on the rational decision model to make strategic decisions; instead, they try out incremental moves.

Rowe, A. J., J. D. Boulgarides, and M. C. McGrath, *Managerial Decision Making*. Chicago: Science Research Associates, 1984. Clear, concise, insightful description of managerial decision making; useful for self-study.

MANAGEMENT IN ACTION CASE 8
The Swine Flu Decision

In March 1976, the United States government launched the most massive immunization program in history—to guard against a feared epidemic of something called "swine flu." More than 40 million people were inoculated in a short ten-week period at a cost upwards of $135 million. In the process, several people died as a result of the shots—although determining the exact number is difficult.

The swine flu outbreak never came.

And that begs the question: How could the medical minds behind the immunization program have been so wrong?

The answers touch some of the fundamental issues surrounding decision making as it occurs in the real world—an underside not often exposed for clear view.

In this case, there were political desires on several levels. President Gerald R. Ford was facing a tough election campaign that year and some advisers thought this government program would help establish Ford as a leader who cared about people and their health.

Little did Ford know that his top medical advisers had agendas of their own—to try a mass inoculation program just to see if it could be done on such a large scale. It was that bias that caused the President's medical advisers to push ahead with their full plan—avoiding critics, sharing little information with the public where it could have been analyzed independently, planning for few contingencies. In short, the advisers encouraged a full and complete program without providing opportunities for later updates, changes, or reconsiderations.

The program's prime backers wanted to immunize 95 percent of the American people. And, in retrospect, it seemed that no amount of data was going to stand in their way. Two students of the swine flu decision-making process, conducting a study for the government, concluded that there were seven mistakes that led to flawed decision making by President Ford's medical advisers:

1. Overconfidence in theories spun from meager evidence.
2. Conviction fueled by some preexisting personal agendas.
3. Zeal by health professionals to make their lay superiors "do right."
4. Premature commitment to deciding more than had to be decided.
5. Failure to address uncertainties in a way that would have left the door open to reconsidering going forward with the program.
6. Insufficient questioning of scientific logic and of implementation prospects.
7. Insensitivity to media relations and the long-term credibility of institutions.

Looking back, it would have made far more sense to prepare the swine flu vaccine—so it would be ready just in case—but not begin the mass inoculations until sufficient numbers of people with the flu disease were found in the country.

But, as this example shows, decision making can become less than rational when people's individual agendas cloud their assessment of the information confronting them.

Question

Do you think President Ford would have made the same decision if he had used the test listed in Figure 8.3?

For more information, see R. E. Neustadt and H. Fineberg, *The Epidemic That Never Was: Policy-Making and the Swine Flu Affair* (New York: Vintage, 1983).

APPLICATION CASES

For practice in applying concepts covered in this chapter to managerial situations, see the following managerial decision cases. The case questions particularly relevant to this chapter are listed by number after each case name.

Grant Chemical Corporation (p. 59) 8
Fyler International (p. 68) 8, 9
Consolidated Instruments–B (p. 189) 4, 5
Delphi Insurance (p. 316) 6, 7

PART II MANAGERIAL DECISION CASE STUDIES

The Heartland Union Bank (HUB) is a successful regional bank located in a large midwestern city. Despite lower earnings in recent years as a result of major changes in the financial services industry, HUB remains a profitable and growing organization.

One of the most profitable portions of the bank is the Trust Division, headed by J. Woodward Hazen. Hazen, known throughout the bank as "Woody," is highly regarded by employees at all levels. Although a member of a prominent family in the area, Woody was regarded as a down-to-earth individual with a genuine interest in the people who worked for and with him. However, he also has a deserved reputation for being an extremely demanding superior who can be as impatient and harsh in penalizing failure as he is patient and generous in rewarding progress.

"You have to get to know Woody to really see that even at his toughest he still cares about people," said a subordinate of his. "He doesn't hesitate to blast you if he thinks you are wrong, but usually it's when you are not only wrong but stubborn or unwilling to admit it, or change. He has little patience with failure but even less with excuses and unwillingness to listen to new ideas."

Hazen has been in charge of the Trust Division for seven years. When he took over, he was instructed by the chairman of the bank to either make it profitable or get rid of it.

"Justin [the chairman] felt that we spent far too much money in the Trust department," Woody said, "in an attempt to appeal to the vanity of our large trust customers. Our offices were filled with antiques—both furnishings and staff. Entertainment expenses were more than twice as high than they are now for less than half the number of accounts and one-fifth the assets.

"Plans and budgets were ignored, and the attitude was 'when in doubt, spend more.' We had three professors receiving high retainers and fees to create econometric models and act as members of our trust investment board. Despite all the money we spent, our return to our clients was less than our competitors' and our service, while extremely lavish, was slow and often antiquated.

"While the chairman probably hoped I would sell it or close it down, I took it as a challenge and through discipline, good planning, and tight controls, we have turned things around. I really enjoyed it. My only regret is that things now run so smoothly I'm not sure how much they need me. I have asked the chairman to keep me in mind for a new and challenging assignment but I'm not sure he took me seriously. He said something like, 'Sure, if we get another impossible situation to turn around I'll be sure and offer it to you.' Frankly, I'd like to have at least one more tough one before I retire."

At least one of HUB's competitors shares Woody's assessment of both before and after conditions and gives virtually all the credit to Hazen.

Judd Stewart, head of the trust department of a major money-center bank in Pittsburgh, said, "We knew they were having trouble seven years ago and offered to 'buy' the department. Woody turned me down so I decided to 'recruit' his key people. We set up shop right next door and in four months took three of his most senior trust people, five key support staff, his 'professors,' and almost half of his big accounts.

"I was sure he would unload the rest at a bargain price, but I was wrong. I found out later that what I had gotten were a group of over-paid, under-talented, or, at best, spoiled professionals and a lot of headaches. Woody used our 'raid,' as he called it, to create a tremendous underdog spirit and rebuilt his group in his image. He isn't the most creative guy in the world but he sure knows how to pull his people together and get them to take pride in superb execution of basics."

Hazen concentrated on the disciplined use of plans, budgets, and systems thinking. While some of the remaining staff objected to the imposition of tight budgets, procedures, and standing plans, most agreed that they succeeded in reducing costs and improving service.

One who disagreed left the bank and complained, "Hazen took the soul out of trust work. The man has no class. His single-minded focus on 'the best way' ignores the fact that building relationships and mixing with the right people in the right places is still the key to trust work. Most of our good clients couldn't care less if they earned a bit more on their holdings. In fact, they hardly knew what they had.

"Breeding, family ties, a sense of gentility still matter to wealthy clients. Taking them to luncheon at the right restaurant, advising them on wines, and checking on prospective sons- or daughters-in-law meant more than making a few extra dollars by shifting into or out of zero-coupon bonds.

"Because the wealthiest or at least more prominent families were our trust clients, many of the nouveau riche came to us for class by association. Hazen hasn't the foggiest notion of what class is. I'm sure his father, rest his soul, is spinning in his grave. Woody is nothing like his father. No creativity, and all the flair of a diesel engine. I'm surprised he has lasted as long as he has. He no longer can claim the most prominent families as his clients, and the mob he now counts on for his margins will leave as fast as they came when some other bank installs a better 'assembly line' than his and promises them a bit more money and *two* electric can openers."

When told of this statement, Hazen's response was a hyphenated expletive. "I think I know who said that," he said, "but it could be any one of several people I let go because they couldn't cope with modern banking.

Our actions not only cut costs but provided much better service not only to our individual trust accounts but to our corporate clients. The corporations, small and big, who come to us with their pension and benefit programs want sound, safe, low-cost service. They aren't interested in gimmicks or lots of razzle-dazzle 'relationship' stuff. They want programs that are proven, and quick, fair service. We provide this and at a cost that makes it profitable for us and our clients. We don't have to sell our corporate clients; our programs and reputation over the last five years almost sell themselves. In fact, I reduced sales effort by 40 percent in three years and volume went up every year. We place our emphasis on delivering what we promise and being a phone call away with fast, fair service when we are needed."

While individual trust business became less important under Hazen, corporate trust accounts increased greatly. Elaine Wallace, Vice-President of Employee Benefits, explains, "When Woody rebuilt, he asked me to go after the biggest and best corporate accounts in the area. He told me to promise them the best returns and services on their pension and benefits programs and then fight for what it took to keep the promises.

"I'm basically a conservative woman and I know how tough Woody can be if you don't keep a promise, so I started slowly—more slowly than he wanted—but it paid off. Our corporate business now represents 60 percent of our assets and over 70 percent of our profit. Woody agrees but needles me because I'm even more 'buttoned down' than he is. To me, a promise is kept; no excuses. You make a plan, you set a budget, you meet it. If you are off one place, make it up in another. My people know that I do not accept excuses. I push, I stretch them, but not too far because they must believe they can achieve what they promise.

"One of the advantages of offering fewer, standardized but high-quality programs is that we can manage them at a low cost to us, and to our customers. We have hundreds of standards, procedures, methods, but every one was discussed, understood, and agreed to before it was instituted, and we review them regularly to see if they need to be changed, dropped, or added to.

"This department runs like a clock and it has paid off. Our corporate clients know what to expect from us, and while we give them a minimum of bells and whistles and less variety than our competitors offer, we are *sound!*"

In recent years, a series of events have caused HUB to reexamine some of its markets. Changes in banking laws and moves by giant banks and financial service institutions have led to intense competition. Many of HUB's former competitors have merged or been acquired. Others have consolidated and closed down or sold off parts of their operations.

Justin Purdy, Chairman of HUB, feels his bank is well positioned to meet these challenges and related changes but expressed concern that the bank needs more creative thinking in coming years.

"We survived the first shake-out by becoming more efficient. I'm sure our success in the next few years will come from being more imaginative.

In the past, an entrepreneurial banker was about as welcome out here as a creative parachute-packer. Now we must engender more entrepreneurial or—what's that new word?—intrapreneurial spirit.

"Consider Woody Hazen, for example. He took our Trust Division and made it profitable by developing a lean, well-organized staff. He changed the very culture of the division. His people have policies and procedures on how to change their desk calendars and they have made us money. With more and more pressure from the big banks and others, however, being efficient and reliable soon may not be enough.

"I had two young MBAs working for us this summer looking for new business opportunities. I really didn't think we would get any great ideas, but for less than $10,000, I had two bright youngsters scampering around the bank making a few waves and helping me recruit, if not them, good people from their business school. While I haven't seen it, I hear on the grapevine that they came in with a proposal to go after several good-sized chunks of new employee-benefit business."

Liz Winters and Will Kirkby will begin the second year of their MBA work in two weeks. They have developed a proposal while working as special projects staff to the chairman.

"Will and I feel," Liz said, "that the rash of mergers, takeovers, and downsizing of companies represents a real opportunity for creative employee-benefit work. Every time one company gobbles up another, all the benefits programs have to be looked at and quite possibly modified, if not scrapped."

"In addition," Will said, "dozens of companies in our market area are reorganizing or downsizing in order to increase their productivity. They need new, creative, flexible benefit packages. Many of the old packages were designed to lock people into the so-called golden handcuffs. Now companies want handcuffs for few, windows for many, and parachutes for others. They need flexible, creative pension, stock option, deferred compensation, and other benefit programs."

Both Liz and Will feel that HUB could not only generate a great deal of additional business but also convert existing employee-benefit business to new, more creative, and more profitable business.

"Woody Hazen read our preliminary report and told us he liked it," Will said. "He cleared us to get more details from Mrs. Wallace.

"She has been incredibly cooperative," Liz added. "We were worried that she would consider our ideas as too radical, but she was even more excited than Woody, I think. She kept telling us how interesting our ideas were even though she felt we might not fully appreciate some of their legal and actuarial implications."

The two have finished their analysis and framed their recommendations on the broad characteristics of what "products" would appeal to companies involved in mergers, takeovers, or significant restructuring.

"We would like to give Mr. Purdy a copy of our detailed recommendations," Will said, "but Mrs. Wallace feels that it would be unwise to do so at this point. She asked us to let her set up a meeting with Woody and invited us to develop a presentation for him and his key associates. She volunteered to get us help with slides and transparencies and to host a luncheon after the presentation."

Liz suggested that they might invite Mr. Purdy since he seemed so interested in their work, but Mrs. Wallace vetoed the idea.

"Let's keep it in the family until we have more of the bugs worked out," she said, "You and Will have done a magnificent job of giving us food for thought. I will have two of my key people come. Mr. Hazen will be there and will bring his top legal, actuarial, and information systems people as well. After we have time to sort out and follow up with more precise programs we can brief Mr. Purdy. He won't be a problem. He has enormous respect for Mr. Hazen and if Mr. Hazen says go, he will support him all the way. But we have to think this through. What you propose could add another 15 to 20 percent to our employee-benefit business, but it will require considerable work to make sure it doesn't adversely affect our ability to deliver on our core business.

"I will also draft a memo for Mr. Hazen to send to Mr. Purdy describing your project and complimenting you on outstanding staff work.

"While I don't want to go off half-cocked on these proposals, I want Mr. Purdy to know the general nature of your ideas and that you deserve full credit for getting this project rolling."

Liz and Will were pleased with Mrs. Wallace's enthusiasm and offers to help. Both were disappointed, however, that they wouldn't get a chance to present their work to the Chairman.

"I'm not sure," Liz said, "that Mrs. Wallace really appreciates how different the programs we are talking about will be from the traditional benefit programs we are offering now. Ours need lots of custom-tailoring. Really working with companies to develop the variety of benefit packages they need to offer takes a lot of flexible sales effort as well as legal and actuarial soundness."

"We will both be back in school before Mrs. Wallace or Woody takes action on our suggestions," Will said. "Neither of us wants to rush too fast but we are both a little uneasy. I don't think that it is just a matter of being impatient or wanting recognition. We are kind of worried that things may get bogged down or overly structured once we leave."

QUESTIONS

Part I

1. Is there any substance to the remarks made by Hazen's critic that in changing the character of the Trust department he "took the soul out of trust work"? Is what this critic suggests solely a voice from the past, or does his criticism have any value as a warning to Hazen of how to monitor environmental change?

2. Under Hazen's new strategy, what are the most important changes in the roles of key managers from their roles in the past?

Part II

3. List significant potential problems with the master strategy that may arise if Liz and Will's proposal were to be implemented.

4. What are the most significant attributes of the planning system Hazen created to reshape the Trust department when he took it over?

5. List and discuss the most important changes in operating plans that Liz and Will's project would necessitate. Will there be more or fewer standing plans, for example?

6. What are the key factors Hazen should consider in deciding whether to support Liz and Will's proposal and how far and how fast to implement it?

7. Would implementation of the new proposal increase or decrease the need for contingency planning?

8. Would Hazen's views on the disciplined use of plans and systems be helpful in introducing Liz and Will's proposal?

9. *Summary Report Question for Part II*. Develop a step-by-step plan for what Liz and Will can do to increase the likelihood that their proposal is implemented. Who should they see? What should they do? How should they do it? Discuss both the strengths and potential pitfalls of your proposed plan.

Part III

10. Would the implementation of Liz and Will's proposal require more or less delegation than currently is practiced in the Trust department?

11. How might key staff selected for the new project be similar to or different from the kinds of people staffing the existing Trust department?

12. What are the benefits and possible drawbacks of having someone like Elaine Wallace as the "champion" of the new proposal?

Part IV

13. How might motivation of personnel chosen for the new project differ from techniques utilized to motivate key people in the current Trust department?

14. Will clear, two-way communication be more or less important to the success of the new project than it currently is in producing beneficial results in the existing Trust department?

15. What do you think of Hazen's leadership style? How would you characterize it?

16. Since Hazen effected significant change once in the Trust department, do you feel he can lead the group to make the changes necessary for the new project's success?

17. Would you require more or fewer budgetary controls to be applied to Liz and Will's project (if approved) than to existing business?

18. How would you develop controls for the new project that would increase the likelihood of creativity within the group working to implement it?

19. Will measurement of results of the new project be easier or more difficult than it is for the existing trust business?

Summary Report Question for Solution of Case as a Whole

20. Assume Hazen and the chairman accept Liz and Will's proposal. Develop a detailed plan for implementing it within the existing department. What are the key first steps? What kind of people should lead it, staff it, and so on?

Decision Case II–2
CONSOLIDATED INSTRUMENTS[1]

Consolidated Instruments (CI) began as a producer of precision control devices for the petroleum industry. During World War II its president, Homer Peake, successfully developed several important control devices used in aircraft; by 1980, through internal developments and acquisitions, Peake and his successor, David Myers, had broadened CI's market still further. With its most recent acquisition of the PCD (Pollution Control Devices) Company, CI found itself listed in *Fortune* magazine's list of the five hundred largest corporations in the United States. The company now designs and produces control devices and markets them not only to the oil and chemical industries, but also to the food processing, aircraft, space, and missile industries.

The newly acquired PCD Company differs from other parts of CI in that it is the only business that manufactures the end-products in which control devices are used. When acquired, there was considerable debate as to how PCD should be integrated into the existing organization, and it was finally decided to permit it to remain a separate division reporting directly to the president. Given its sales of only $28,000,000 PCD might more properly have been made a part of one of the three existing divisions (see Exhibit 1).

There was a double reason for maintaining PCD's separate identity. First, although PCD sold products in all the markets served by the other divisions, none of the existing divisional general managers wanted to take on the responsibility for the PCD business. Each argued that PCD fit bet-

[1]This is more formally known as Consolidated Instruments–B Case.

ter in another's division. Underlying this disinterest were the low margins and high risks associated with work in the pollution-control area. Many companies in recent years had sought to establish themselves in the pollution abatement market, but despite growing concern over pollution by industry and government alike, very few companies were able to earn a profit in this market. When acquired, PCD had shown a $2,000,000 loss on $28,000,000 sales in its last fiscal year.

President Myers' second reason for keeping the PCD company intact as a separate division reporting to him was to facilitate its sale if in five years the division failed to satisfy him that it could meet at least minimum profit standards as well as contribute to technology in other divisions. "I'm eager to do my part to deal with our ecological problems," he told his Board, "and we will not expect any miracles from PCD, but within five years it will either be in the black or on the block."

He assigned several capable executives from other divisions of CI to key posts in PCD but kept Joseph MacAllister, PCD's founder and president, as president of the new division. Myers stated:

> MacAllister knows the business. He is only fifty-one and although he may be a little too much of the Tom Swift inventor-type, he is an adequate coordinator. By backing him up with a new man in the top engineering post, a new controller, and two of our good marketing service people, I think we have the makings of a good team. Because MacAllister took most of his equity in PCD in the form of CI stock and options, I'm sure he is as anxious as we to see things work out.

> Finally, we have assigned one of our best personnel people, James Dickenson, as his new director of personnel. Jim will see to it that we bring their salary and benefit programs into line with ours as smoothly as possible, and more important, he will get them working with our management by objectives and related programs.

The new division director of engineering is Paul Horn. He is fifty-six years old and has been with CI for over twenty years. Before moving to the PCD division in Pittsburgh, Horn held several key posts in other parts of CI. Trained initially as a mechanical engineer, Horn gained both bachelor's and master's degrees in electrical engineering by attending night school for eleven years. After holding the second highest engineering post in first the oil and chemical and then the food processing divisions, he served as the director of engineering estimates and then divisional director of the government products division. A drop in government sales led to a reorganization of that division, and for sixteen months Horn served as manager of the corporate engineering review department and reported to the corporate vice-president of engineering.

Horn at first resisted the move to PCD, but he was eventually persuaded that he was needed there to put the new division on the road to profitable operations.

Myers himself spoke with Horn, telling him, "I would not ask this of you, Paul, if I didn't think it important. We need your experience, good

Myers himself spoke with Horn, telling him, "I would not ask this of you, Paul, if I didn't think it important. We need your experience, good business sense, and knowledge of our practices to help get them out of the red."

Myers informed the casewriter that

> Horn had some fool notion that we were unhappy with him for being a little hard-nosed in his corporate review job. Heck, that's why I wanted him in that post—to help Shel Thayler (vice-president of engineering) sift through requests for new projects and get rid of the old ones that hadn't worked out. Paul Horn may not be the easiest man to work with, but technically he is first-rate and he's experienced enough and energetic enough to take on a tough assignment like this.

Horn accepted the new post, but he made it abundantly clear to Jim Dickenson, PCD's new personnel director, that he had a different understanding about the reasons behind his transfer.

> I know why I'm here, Jim, regardless of what Myers and Thayler say. They are all excited about your human relations ideas and these new organization development concepts. I've done a lot of tough jobs for this company over the years when we didn't have the time or resources to pussyfoot around. But times change; nowadays maybe the people-problems are more important than the technical ones. I've still got what I hope are eight to ten good years to go before retirement and I found when they sent me off to the six-week management course[2] that I adapted to, and handled, the new material and cases as well as men twenty years my junior.
>
> Although I was plenty upset about this transfer at first, I don't intend to go around sulking for the next ten years. Neither do I intend to make the same mistakes I've made before. If it's "develop people" and a "healthy climate" that they want, whatever that means, then I'll develop people and climate. But I'm going to need your help, Jim.

Dickenson explained to the casewriter that he had been pleasantly surprised by Horn's words. "I had expected that Paul would be something of a problem," Dickenson said, "I had heard that he was upset about the move and I had him down as a potential trouble spot in installing our management-by-objectives program in PCD. But he seems genuinely interested in working with me and proving that he can be more than a hard-boiled engineering manager."

The MBO program that both Myers and Dickenson spoke of involved working with all key managers to develop new techniques for dealing with their subordinates in the planning, decision-making, and review phases of their work. Dickenson explained the program further:

> It is difficult to summarize the MBO approach because it deals with intangibles like climate as well as specific procedures. In essence, a manager sits down with each of his key subordinates and they establish a few key objec-

[2]Horn attended a six-week management seminar at a leading eastern university.

tives, which then serve as targets. Most of the targets will be for a six- to twelve-month period but some will be longer-range. There are four main points to keep in mind during the target, or objective-setting, stage:

1. Regardless of who initiates the objectives, the manager and the subordinate should discuss them until they are jointly satisfied that they can be reached.

2. Wherever possible, objectives should be formulated in measurable terms.

3. Where objectives might take a year or more to achieve, measurable checkpoints should be agreed to.

4. The objectives, wherever possible, should be few and on the broad, integrated, end-result level. The department managers should not get into the numerous procedural steps to accomplish end-result objectives; these will be worked out by their subordinates. If managers interfere, they will remove much of the challenge and commitment the subordinate should feel for the objective.

Periodically, these objectives should be reviewed as results come in and are updated or revised as required. Unless significant failures to achieve key objectives take place, or appear imminent, the superior should not involve himself in the means by which his subordinates seek to accomplish their objectives.

This approach involves an entire network of corollary systems. In order to make it work, you have to build recruiting, training, career development, and compensation programs that reinforce the MBO approach. Communications, including management information systems, budgetary systems, and planning procedures have to fit too, and a climate of mutual respect and trust must be built. The total system, which is designed to more fully tap human resources by meshing individual and organizational goals, is often called OD, or Organizational Development.

The casewriter asked Dickenson whether he felt Horn was sincere and if so, would he be able to learn and use these concepts. Dickenson's response was:

I think he is sincere, and despite his history of being a driver, I think he can learn. You know, the only time when you can't teach an old dog new tricks is when the dog thinks he is too old to learn. Paul can learn but is likely to be impatient with himself as well as with the system. One thing that will help is that he will be managing quite a few departments headed by people who are far more knowledgeable than he is in the specific areas in which they work. At least, I think this will help. His inability to plunge in with both feet and show them a "better way" may force him to learn how to manage a process rather than make a series of technical decisions.

Horn, in fact, seemed anxious to get started when interviewed by the casewriter just after his appointment was announced.

There are some people in this company who think I can't adjust to new management techniques. At first, I was angry about this move, but now I see it as a good opportunity to try something new.

Two years ago, when they first asked me to install the MBO program in my corporate engineering review department, I talked Dickenson's former superior out of it. I explained that mine was an unusual department with a very tough, dirty job to do at that time and that it would be better to leave us alone for awhile. That was a mistake on my part. I am sure that it is one of the reasons why I am in Pittsburgh now. At that time, I was more interested in immediate results than in trying to understand and institute what seemed like the latest in an unending stream of management fads.

Furthermore, many of my friends at division level who were trying to install MBO didn't like it one bit. They complained that it often left them with an uneasy feeling that they were losing control of the work they supervised and that by focusing on results they were overly dependent on their subordinates. Fred Biggs, whom I worked with in Houston, said, "Paul, this is the gol-dangest approach I ever saw. It's like playing poker. Only now my subordi-nates play all the hands—with my money—and according to the rules they don't even have to show me their cards. They just call me up twice a month and tell me how much they won or we lost."

I guess my biggest objection, though, was that instituting a new system like MBO takes time and I wasn't prepared to invest it. Judging by what hap-pened, I made a poor decision. I won't make the same mistakes twice, though!

For the next six weeks Horn spent almost all of his time trying to familiarize himself with the work done by the four departments under his control and the people who managed them.

I found [Horn said] that I was really in over my head on much of the work they are doing. With all of my experience, I know very little about the tech-nical aspects of their work. Only in production estimating do I have a good feel, and this is based on my knowledge of good procedures and practices. This knowledge helps some in the technical service group but as far as the design and development departments, it would take me at least a year to feel qualified to make technical judgments in those areas. As I understand this MBO approach, I shouldn't be terribly concerned about this.

At the end of the first six weeks, Horn requested that each of his department managers develop a plan for the next twelve months showing how they would increase their efficiency by at least 10 percent during that period. Horn did not give them any specifics on how this was to be accom-plished but indicated that this efficiency must be achieved without deteri-oration of service or cutbacks in development of key personnel.

I told them that it was up to them to show the initiative and imagination required to give as good or better service for less money. I don't know enough about their work to know how they can do it, and I might interfere with their personal development if I did know enough to try. The one thing I do know, after more than twenty years' experience, is that there are almost always ways of improving efficiency. What you need are good men and a little pres-sure from above.

A month after making his request, Horn set up a meeting with each of his subordinates. He spent less than an hour alone with each man in the morning and then at a general meeting in the afternoon he allocated one hour for each man to present his plan to the others.

The tone of the meeting was described by one of the department managers as "firm but friendly." Andy Drechsel, manager of the technical service group, said:

> I explained to Mr. Horn that it was difficult for me to forecast cost or efficiency, because so much of our work was tied to requests from the marketing people. We have several measures of productivity that we use, but they are rough and involve a number of intangibles. I tried to explain some of these to Mr. Horn, but he indicated that he didn't feel he should get into them. He asked me to give him my honest estimates of how much I could do to meet his 10 percent increased efficiency goal.
>
> Frankly, I came into the meeting prepared to hedge a bit and give him something a little more conservative, by way of targets, but he made me feel that he was counting on me and that I owed myself as well as him the best I could do. I ended up by giving him rather optimistic estimates and I am going to work like the devil to meet them. Judging from the afternoon meeting, my overall target of 18 percent increase in efficiency is the highest, but we can make it if Mr. Horn helps when marketing puts too much pressure on.

Edward Deeb, manager of production estimating, agreed with Drechsel that his meeting with Horn had been friendly.

> Even though he understands my department better than the others [Deeb said], he made no attempt to get into the details I worked out to support our annual plan. All he wanted to know was, could I do it? I came away feeling that he didn't really want to know how I would make my objectives. He didn't even keep a copy of my department plan; just a one-page summary of our overall budget. I promised him the 10 percent he wants and I think we can do it.

Sam Elster and Charles Graf, managers of the design and the development departments, respectively, were more mixed in their reactions to the day's meeting.

> I spent a full month with my people [Elster said] working up a very detailed plan. It is difficult to be precise about cost and efficiency in our design work but we tried. We made the best estimates we could of what kinds of things would come out of development and production and how we would tackle them. I developed several PERT diagrams to work out schedules and costs, but as near as I can tell, Mr. Horn never even looked at them.
>
> When I asked him this morning what he thought of our plans he said, "We're not here today to talk plans, Sam; we have to agree on targets—objectives. I'll leave the plans to you. All I want to know is what objectives we can set down now and count on your reaching by next year."
>
> When it became clear that he was not going to let me go into any detail on the many imponderables that I had to face in my plan, I was glad I had been a little cautious with my summary targets for departmental operations. If I thought he would be willing to dig in with me to understand why I may or may not succeed, then I might have revised my targets upward a little. Overall, I showed what amounts to a 7.5 percent improvement in efficiency. Mr. Horn went over the six key targets that will be the basis of this improvement and tried to get me to increase them to bring the total up to 10 percent, but I stood fast. I said, "Mr. Horn, if you want me to change the totals then you have to show me where we disagree in my plans." He laughed and said,

"Sam, you know I don't know enough about the operation of your department to win a debate with you. I'm sure you can figure out how to get to 10 percent. Everybody else has."

Elster maintained, however, that he had given Horn the most accurate and aggressive objectives he could and Horn begrudgingly accepted them. On several occasions during the afternoon session, however, Horn made reference to the lower than 10 percent target for the design department.

Charles Graf, or "Doc" as he was known in his department, was a brilliant engineer himself and had built a very strong group of development people. His department was highly regarded for the quality and dependability of its work, but it also exceeded budget more frequently and by larger amounts than the other three. Graf gave his reaction to what had happened at the meeting.

I feel like the man who had a magician pull a tablecloth off the table without disturbing the food. I came in this morning with a plan that I felt supported my claim that it was impossible for our department to show any tangible evidence of improved efficiency, and I left agreeing to a 15 percent improvement. The nature of development work and its heavy dependence on inputs from research and production make planning virtually impossible. We must be able to do creative work under time pressure and do it well. If I get everyone overly budget conscious, I will lose more than I gain.

I told Horn this from the first day he arrived and I told him again this morning. I tried to show him why we should be evaluated in a different way. He had leafed through my plan but apparently only in search of budget or output summaries. When it became apparent that I wasn't getting anywhere, I decided it would be wiser to go along with him. We went over the four major elements of cost in my department and for each of my targets he would ask, "How about it Doc, can't we tighten up a little here?" Before I knew it, we had "agreed" to objectives that show me improving overall efficiency by 15 percent.

It wasn't until this afternoon, when I had to present my "revised" plans to the others, that I realized what I had agreed to. Well, Mr. Horn made it clear that we would review our progress each month, and so now I have to figure out how I can gradually move his expectations back to a more realistic level.

Paul Horn was pleased with the meetings and told Jim Dickenson so the next day.

Jim, you have no idea how much I appreciate your help on this management by objectives approach. I have just gotten my people to agree on some good, ambitious objectives for the year and I think I can bring in a much better cost-effectiveness ratio as a result.

By staying away from details with them, Jim, I not only kept them from getting me to make the tough decisions for them, but I'm in a much better position to hold them fully accountable for results. The ones who deliver will be rewarded and if anyone doesn't, I'll have more time to help them out. I doubt that we will reach all our targets this year but it is healthy to try. Three of my men will probably come very close. There is only one about whom I am worried, but I will leave him alone for at least six months and give him a chance to prove me wrong.

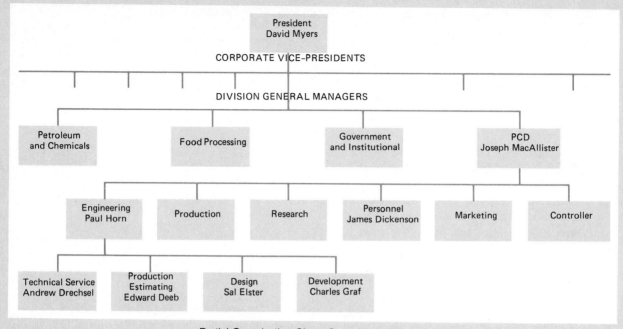

Partial Organization Chart, Consolidated Instruments

Finally, Jim, by staying out of details, I will have time to work more closely with production, marketing, and research and better coordinate our overall efforts.

Dickenson was somewhat taken aback by Horn's comments and a little concerned.

I think Paul is sincere but I'm not sure he is fully aware of what it takes to make a management by objectives system work. I had no idea he would move this quickly, because I thought he would take a few more months to get a feel for operations. As a result, I haven't worked very closely with him on some of the wrinkles that have to be ironed out of this approach.

QUESTIONS

Part I

1. How do you feel about Myers' statement, "I'm eager to do my part to deal with ecological problems." What are the best things that people in positions like Myers can do? How may this role have changed over the past 50 years?

Part II

2. What are the strategic roles the PCD division is being asked to play?

3. What effect on creativity, at the level of Horn's subordinates, is his approach to MBO likely to have?

4. Comment on the process of reaching decisions on key goals. How rational was the choice process?

5. How do you feel Horn's approach with his subordinates will influence the nature, degree, and level of uncertainty absorption that takes place in future planning sessions?

6. What effect is the MBO approach taken by Horn likely to have on the long-range planning needs of the division?

7. What are the potential strengths and weaknesses of a well-designed and well-implemented MBO program?

8. How appropriate are the three objectives Horn has set with his people as guides to their future action?

9. Myers discusses three or four key expectations he has for PCD. What are they? How will Horn's objectives serve as means to Myers' ends?

10. *Summary Report Question for Part II.* What specific changes should Horn make in his approach to MBO to (a) create a greater likelihood of improvement in engineering services and (b) contribute more directly to Myers' strategic reasons for acquiring PCD?

Part III

11. With which of Horn's subordinates (Drechsel, Deeb, Elster, or Graf) do you think he is most likely to become embroiled in serious conflict? In your opinion, what will cause this conflict?

12. Was Paul Horn a good person for the job assigned him? Does he appear to have the right technical and other qualifications?

13. Did Myers make a wise decision in having the president of the PCD division report directly to him? What factors should he have considered in determining how to deal with the questions of basic departmentation and balance in the overall structure?

14. Discuss what else James Dickenson might do as a staff person to help Paul Horn develop a better grasp of MBO.

Part IV

15. How well do you feel this new job meets Paul Horn's needs at the present stage of his life?

16. How would you rate the communication between Horn and each of his subordinates? Discuss both strong and weak points of the direction he has given them.

17. Do you believe Horn will be able to change his leadership style? What are the major factors affecting his chances for successful change?

Part V

18. How well will Horn be able to determine what constitutes appropriate

corrective action if results in any of his four departments differ significantly from the objectives that he will use as control standards?

19. It is clear from the case that Myers expects to see the PCD division become profitable but realizes this may take several years. Because the basis for moving to a sound future profit will require many less tangible results in the short run, how should Myers determine whether the division is making satisfactory progress? What kinds of intermediate control points should he set and how should he measure and control them?

20. How successful do you feel Paul Horn will be in controlling the overall results of his department if he continues to follow the approach to MBO indicated in the case? Explain.

Summary Report Question for Solution of Case as a Whole

21. Based on your answers to questions 10, 17, and 20, what would you recommend that Myers and MacAllister do with regard to Paul Horn?

Decision Case II–3
DAYTON METAL WORKS

The Dayton Metal Works is owned and managed by James E. Foote. He went to work for one of the automobile companies in Detroit immediately after graduating from high school at the age of 18. He began as an apprentice working on a punch press and, over a period of years, progressed to jobs of machinist, master mechanic, and finally foreman of one of the company's largest machine shop installations. He had experience on almost all of the machines in a large shop (single-purpose, multi-purpose, and fully automatic), and he had six years' experience in managing the entire shop operation. Although he had never served in the so-called staff positions of the shop (inspection, scheduling, routing, inventory control, and so on), James Foote became acquainted with these functions while he was foreman.

After 20 years in Detroit, Mr. Foote received an offer from his father-in-law, P.M. Brown, to become part owner in the Dayton Metal Works, a small machine shop in Dayton, Ohio, with the stipulation that Brown would retire in three years and sell the remaining part of the business to Foote.

When Mr. Foote took over the business from Mr. Brown eight years ago, he continued to operate it very much as his father-in-law had. The company's products were fairly simple—stamped metal parts and custommade valves for liquid and steam pipelines. In addition, the company did a fairly large business in repairing valves from steam generating companies and chemical manufacturers.

The machine shop consisted of twelve single-purpose machines—grinding, cutting, milling, and threading machines, punch presses, and so on. Plant space came to a total of 11,000 square feet, with machines spaced in two lines on either side of a 30-foot middle aisle. Eighteen machinists and helpers were employed, all of whom had been with the company for over ten years, a fact that Foote recognized as remarkable for a small firm located among larger companies such as Frigidaire and NCR Corporation. This loyalty he attributed to the company's high wage policy, and to Brown's habit of spending a good deal of time with the machinists on the job, not only in watching and advising on their work, but also in helping them learn and in rotating them among jobs. Foote says that each employee not only was expert in his present job, but also knew a great deal about all others in the shop. Although customers ordered job lots, Dayton Metal Works had supplied all the customers for a number of years, so the company had considerable experience in producing all the items ordered. The Ohio Paint Company, for instance, ordered certain standardized containers two or three times each year. Each month the Dayton Power Company sent over large batches of valves of the same type to be ground and repaired.

During his first two years in charge, Foote continued to deal with the customers developed by Brown. He visited their engineers and production and purchasing people frequently. Gross sales remained approximately the same over this period, at about $490,000.

Expansion Over a Six-Year Period

After his first two years with DMW, Foote began to travel to other cities to seek business for the company; Cleveland and Pittsburgh yielded a good bit of business both in the valve and the metal product lines, and he added customers from Columbus and, later, as far away as Indianapolis.

Of considerable importance in the growth of the business was a developing demand for "specialized" metal products which, once designed, could be sold to other companies in the same lines of business. Foote found that after producing these in large quantity for one account, he could sell them to other customers in other cities. Demand eventually rose to the point at which the company now carries an inventory and mass-produces these products. Volume has also necessitated renting another Dayton shop of 8,000 square feet with seven machines, eight machinists, and seven helpers, plus two combination service-maintenance people. One salesman is employed exclusively in this product, known in the company as "the conveyor line." The conveyor shop is located eight blocks from the main shop.

Quite by accident, at a meeting of the National Association of Manufacturers, Foote became interested in the possibility of securing government contracts for Dayton Metal Works. Through an attorney whom he retained, and some hard work on his own, he succeeded in obtaining a government contract for a very large quantity of high-quality, precision hydraulic valves used in aircraft. In fact, this contract alone has yielded $750,000 in sales annually and is expected to continue for at least five more years.

Foote himself has handled all negotiations with the government, with the aid of a lawyer and an outside accountant who provide technical information on cost allowances, government procurement regulations, price redetermination, and so forth. He has rented an old warehouse next door and set up a special production line for hydraulic valves. This facility contains six machines in an area of 6,000 square feet. Twenty-two employees in two shifts are currently engaged in the production of hydraulic valves.

At present, eight years after Foote's takeover, the company has annual gross sales of $2.5 million. This represents an increase of roughly $2 million in six years.

Profit Picture

The company was unusually profitable under Brown and during the first two years of Foote's ownership. Net profit to sales averaged 19 percent. During the last six years, while total profits have increased, they now represent only 12 percent of sales. Although general business conditions have been partly responsible, both Foote and his auditor recognize that part of the decrease has resulted from an increase in the overhead burden. Overhead costs have climbed from 13 percent to 20 percent of total costs. This has been especially disappointing to Foote in view of the remarkable increase in sales.

Problems in Government Contracts

The government-contract business is judged by Foote to be well worth his efforts and those of his other personnel, even though there has been a lower profit ratio in this line, and even though government work has caused many problems.

First, there have been financial troubles. Two years ago, John M. Freeman, a certified public accountant (CPA) was employed to head the accounting and clerical function of the business. Freeman is thirty-six years old, had four years' experience with a public accounting firm and ten years' experience with a larger machine shop in Columbus. Since Freeman has a wide knowledge of machine-shop operations and substantial experience in government contracts and taxation, Foote feels fortunate in having hired him. A graduate of Ohio State, Freeman has technical competence as well as a personality that all the employees seem to like.

Government work calls for accurate accounting records that are especially set up for proving to the government what expenses were allocable to the contract. The company has also been subject to price redetermination by the General Accounting Office (GAO). On two contracts, the GAO has disallowed certain expenses, amounting to a total of $18,000. Foote is sure that these expenses were recorded improperly by Freeman's department at the time the money was paid out, and that profit on the contract would have been shown as lower had they not been. Furthermore, when prices were redetermined on the basis of the profit (figured without these expenses), the company was penalized by having the price, and therefore its revenue, cut.

Foote reports that since he has had more dealings with the government than anyone else, and since he has studied procurement regulations and been exposed to more "education" by his lawyer and outside accountant, he spends about six hours each week reviewing expense allocation accounts from the controller's department. He also spends about six to eight days each quarter attending meetings of industry groups in order to learn more about government procurement regulations. He has also studied a great deal, and he makes two or three trips to New York to consult with the Eastern Air Procurement District headquarters.

Freeman says that he welcomes the frequent advice he receives from his boss, especially since the subject is so complicated and since there is a fairly high degree of risk if a mistake is made.

In addition to the financial problems, there has also been some trouble in quality control of the hydraulic valves produced for the Air Force. Threading has been the greatest cause of rejection at receiving points. When returned, these valves have been suitable for reworking, but Freeman compiled figures to show that they have cost the company approximately $29,000 in the last four months. This is in addition to a $17,800 loss due to other defects in the same period.

A. M. Fowler, foreman of the general (main) shop, is responsible for inspection and quality control at both the main shop and the hydraulic shop. Since new customers have increasingly ordered custom-made parts, he has spent most of his inspection efforts in the main shop, because the many and varied items produced there are especially susceptible to deviations in quality. Actually, quality standards for finished hydraulic valves were set by Foote and Fowler jointly, according to government specifications. All personnel understand them. No systematic check points in the production process itself (until valves are finished) have been set up. Both feel that a system is unnecessary since Fowler makes continuous rounds of informal observation. On all days that he is in the plant, Foote also drops in to the hydraulic shop and checks the newly finished work on various machines.

In view of this seemingly effective arrangement, Foote is puzzled by just what the cause of quality deviations might be. He has confided in his master machinist on the dual buffing machine, Clyde Noble. Noble not only functions as machinist on the key machine operation, which is the end of the hydraulic production line, but also serves as foreman of the hydraulic shop. Because of the repetitiveness of this process and the small number of personnel, Noble is able to shift work to his helper and also to train and supervise other personnel in the shop.

There has been some friction between Noble and Fowler, particularly when Fowler makes suggestions to Noble about maintaining machines or utilizing personnel in the hydraulic shop. Another conflict occurs periodically over the shipping operation. The carters, who transport finished parts from both production lines to the shipping room and loading platform, report to Fowler. When there is a peak load of work in the main shop, Fowler sometimes removes the carters from the hydraulic shop in order to keep up with movements in the main shop. This results in congestion at the end of the hydraulic line and has actually stopped production there on several occasions. Foote must spend a great deal of time in settling these disputes. But he feels that both men are so valuable that he must live with this kind of trouble. He once attempted to resolve the shipping problem by writing a procedure for handling carting loads in the main shop, but Fowler forcefully objected to having his operation "strapped down" because he needed the flexibility of calling on carters when he needs them. Foote has noted that Fowler also resents having him (Foote) come in and ask that the carters be sent to the hydraulic shop in order to remove congestion there. At one point, Foote discovered that a rule specifying that the hydraulic carters could be reassigned for a maximum of two hours on any one day would prevent actual stoppages on the hydraulic line. It would also allow Fowler flexibility in the main shop. Noble agreed to this, but Fowler again made it clear that he would resent this intrusion on his prerogative of managing his people.

Personnel Matters

Foote says that he is the only person in the company who has had extensive experience in supervising, hiring, and training a large number of personnel. In addition, he has studied labor relations, training programs, how to interview job applicants, and setting wage rates. This study has been accomplished "on my own, with a lot of hard night work," and "in some pretty good training programs conducted by the company while I was in Detroit."

Hiring.   Foote has employed an assistant, Herbert Rowzee, who is in charge of personnel problems and also spends about one-half of his time in Freeman's department keeping the books on maintenance cost and equipment depreciation. Rowzee is primarily an accountant, but he had formerly hired and trained office personnel. All requests for jobs are generally channeled to Rowzee. He interviews applicants and, if they appear qualified, arranges for them to see the boss. Foote has been so successful in picking good people that he judges it a waste of company time, and a creation of needless red tape for those under him, to hire someone to draw up forms, standards for selection, or procedures for hiring. This custom has also been most acceptable to his foremen, who do not want unnecessary procedures. However, Fowler, in his own words, has "had a rough time getting along with two of the people Mr. Foote hired."

Employee regulations.   The company has never had a "book of rules." Mr. Foote has said that, "This is one competitive advantage we have over NCR and other big companies that we compete with in the labor market. People like to work in a place where they get treated separately; line managers don't like to be told how to run their shows either." Employees are granted days off for personal business as they need it, and Christmas bonuses are granted on merit and individual need, not on specific wage scales.

Next to scheduling, Foote spends more time dealing with his people than on any other task. Some occasionally charge that he has not been fair; for example, Will Jarvis, a machinist in the metal plant, told his foreman that Foote didn't give him as much paid time off when his son was born as he gave Chapman in the hydraulic shop. Foote once wrote up a procedure to be applied to time off, so that he could point to it and explain that for everybody's good he had to have a rule. He abandoned this for several reasons. "First I can, if I listen patiently and make just decisions, settle things for the good of everybody. Everybody's good can also be served by deciding each case on its merits. We have customs and can treat everyone fairly over the long haul. Secondly, when I asked the foreman about this, not only Fowler, but on this point Noble and Richards, pleaded not to start laying down rules. Richards said, 'We just can't do our job, Mr. Foote, if we get tied up in rules. You yourself have told me many times about how we have a better shop here than them big shops in Detroit.'"

These examples give some picture of the entire range of employee relations. While there are some difficulties, a personnel officer from a larger company advised Foote that he had far fewer problems than most companies. The only rules that exist and are known by everyone are the base rates paid on each job. Thus, there is no question about what a helper will get per hour; it has not been put in writing, but it is well known. Consequently, no one complains that rules are being made or that one person is getting more than another.

James Foote's Personal Status

At 48, Foote appears to be in robust health and extremely interested in his work. Although owning his own business has been troublesome in many respects, he declares that he has never regretted leaving the automobile company. Two business associates mentioned that Foote is known in Dayton as a person who is respected by other business leaders and by his employees. In a conversation with a partner in the auditing firm retained by his company, Foote said:

> Actually, I get a little worried at times about the way things are going. I'm not particularly "old," but I surely haven't got the energy I used to have. The Washington trips take time, and there is an endless bunch of problems with customers. Employees at the shop think we have a fine place to work, but there are times when petty differences get out of hand. What happens is ei-

ther I go nuts listening and worrying about problems, or I make quick judgments and settle them—sometimes wrong, and sometimes making people mad.

My wife has been complaining that I spend too much time at the plant. We have always intended that I would slow down when I got to be over 45. I want to, but I just can't. I know of many close calls that the business has had even with my staying as many hours as I do.

A Problem in Production Scheduling

Foote says that production scheduling can be described quite simply:

It means taking the customer orders that we receive, seeing which of our products has to be produced, translating the finished product into the various machining operations it has to go through in process, figuring how much time must be spent on each machine for the particular volume requested by the customer, assigning machines that are available, then sending this information to the first-line supervisors. There are lots of automated and computerized ways of doing this but I don't feel our volumes justify such investments or dependence on service bureaus.

In order to help with this process, Mr. Brown, the previous president, employed two clerks. One of these clerks has been with the company ten years now, the other twelve years. Since the company used to produce a more or less stable, repetitive group of products for essentially the same customers, these clerks were familiar, as a result of doing the same task over and over, with the customers, the products they usually ordered, and the appropriate machines on which each order should be run.

The clerks drew up simple work orders to instruct machinists on which operations to perform on each customer order. Routing sheets from machinist to machinist were simple: They showed the various machines on which raw metal had to be processed for each customer order. Both clerks and machinists knew the approximate time that would be required on each machine. The clerks looked at the size of the order, estimated the time, and fitted the whole shop each Monday morning into what they called the "jigsaw." Foote studied this on Monday, and since he had an intimate knowledge of about how long each operation would take, he sometimes adjusted the time spent on each machine and the schedule from machine to machine. He says that by applying his more expert planning ability, he could eliminate some of the time "padding" that the clerks left in the schedule. The result of this padding is that machines and personnel sometimes remain idle.

One of the clerks maintained a perpetual inventory of materials, such as tin plate and castings for valve parts. She knew from experience what twelve or thirteen major materials items had to be kept at certain levels, and she adjusted these levels for the number of sales orders she saw come in. Tool control was no problem since thirty to forty tools were all that were required. Foote inspected these tools fairly frequently to see whether new ones should be ordered.

During the recent years of company growth, Foote reveals, certain orders have frequently been delayed because the clerks either got mixed up and scheduled the same machine for two different products or customer orders, or because some machines were left idle when there was a heavy backlog of work to be done.

Foote has found that one of the schedulers works all right as long as he is scheduling orders for the same kinds of valves that he has always worked with. But he takes an unusually long time to schedule machine times, work routings, and materials requisitions on products that are slightly different from the usual, or on those for new customers that require unusual specifications. Foote has spoken to this scheduler "for six months, but when that did not work, I began to watch his work even more carefully. He gets along with the machinists fine, but he has created more bottlenecks than the other two schedulers put together."

A third scheduler has been added, and all three work closely with Foote. Also, certain changes have been made in procedures. All weekly orders for each product are now usually totaled by an accounting clerk and forwarded to Foote on Friday. Foote looks at each product and makes out a routing sheet (called "the machine list") that shows which operations— grinding, cutting, threading, polishing—must be performed on raw metal in order to produce the finished product. Foote then passes this routing sheet to any one of the schedulers who doesn't seem to have a full week's work ahead. The scheduler looks at the volume of the order, figures out the time that needs to be spent on each machine, and assigns specific machines. This is where machinists, schedulers, and Foote have all complained about the present system.

The problem is to consider all available machines in the plant and find a time when each order can be run, without either leaving machines idle or having two orders that call for punch presses arrive at the punch press machines at the same time. For example, one order for 20 large gate valves required a sequence of grinding (ten hours), threading (six hours), and drilling (five hours). A second order, for another type of valve, which was processed by another clerk, required grinding (eight hours), threading (eight hours), and polishing (five hours). Since there are only two grinding machines of sufficient size to handle both orders, the first order would take five hours to run on grinding, and the second order would take four hours. The mistake on these orders was that the first order arrived at the grinding machines at 11 AM Monday, and the second order arrived at the same machines at 1 PM the same day. The second order was put aside while the first was run. The threading machines thus stood idle Tuesday morning because the second order, which had been scheduled to arrive at the polishing machines early Tuesday afternoon, did not even arrive for the threading operation until late Tuesday afternoon.

These problems are supposed to be settled by informal communications among the schedulers. Watching the three of them at work, one sees them frequently asking among themselves, for instance, "Does anybody have punch press Number 2 busy on Thursday morning?" or "I've got both threading machines tied up all day Wednesday." In addition, Foote catches about two or three mistakes every Monday when he goes over the "jigsaw."

Foote complains that the workers make entirely too many mistakes, and that too much of his time is taken up in checking on this every Monday and in going out on the plant floor to make on-the-spot arrangements when there is an actual bottleneck. The schedulers, on the other hand, complain that Foote himself has made some mistakes in readjusting their scheduling. "After all, he is so busy that he just tears through our schedule, making adjustments."

One scheduler also complains that the other two are not careful about listening to what she says and taking it into account in their own work. For instance, "The jam that occurred on the gate valves the other day wouldn't have occurred if Jack had remembered that I told him that I was tying up the large grinders starting at 11 AM on Monday. Besides, that jam was partly Foote's fault, since he is the one whose job it is to catch the errors we're naturally bound to make operating this way."

QUESTIONS

Parts I and II

1. Does Dayton Metal Works appear to have a strategy, a clear mission? What elements can you find? Can you suggest useful portions of a strategy to James Foote?

2. From evidence in the case, state what appear to be the objectives of this company as revealed in current operations and the actions of managers. Then criticize these objectives, specifying (a) which are desirable and why, and (b) which should be modified and why.

3. Make a list of the eight or ten most important points at which policies might be established to improve operations and administration in this company. For each point, state as specifically as possible (and give an example of) the type of policy you recommend. Then describe both the potential advantages and any drawbacks of each policy.

4. Assume that Foote has asked you to draw up a list of major changes that must be made in the company over the next three years. Give him your recommendations for the major steps in such a program, together with the time of accomplishment of each step and any strategies that you feel are important.

5. Take the two most important policy statements that you think should be formulated in this company and describe how participation might be used to improve the quality of these decisions. State also any other benefits the company might derive from participation in these two decisions. Be as specific as possible, citing effects on operations and people in the case.

6. *Summary Report Question for Part II*. After thinking about the preceding questions, write a report in which you (a) state the principal problems

this company faces in planning and programming, (b) trace the basic causes of these problems and give examples, and (c) recommend the courses of action you would take to overcome the problems.

Part III

7. Suppose that you are given the job of dividing up the managerial function of the Dayton Metal Works. Take the position of president, and the positions occupied by Fowler, Noble, and Richards, and list the important decisions that each should make. Then state the factors that indicate why each decision should be made at that point. Be as specific as possible in your reasoning by citing evidence from the case.

8. Considering the Dayton Metal Works as a whole, what are the major problems the company faces in its formal organizational structure? Cite evidence from the case. What recommendations would you make to help solve each of these problems? Be sure to cover the division of operations and managerial work and any other problems of coordination and balance.

9. What do you feel to be the major obstacles facing Foote if he decides he must delegate more?

10. Does Foote need any staff support? What kind? Why?

Part IV

11. As you see it, why has Foote been somewhat unsuccessful in getting Fowler to accept certain of his suggestions for changing Fowler's operations? Cite specific examples of basic causes. What do you recommend to overcome this problem in the future?

12. What do you think of Foote's personal handling of the production scheduling problems? What could he do to help solve this problem?

13. What leadership actions is Freeman taking? What do these actions mean in terms of the organizational structure?

Part V

14. After thoroughly studying the case, list the major control points that might be established to enable Foote to delegate more decision making to others and yet retain some control himself. Give specific examples of what activity or objective is to be measured.

15. Do you recommend that Mr. Foote install a detailed budgetary control system?

16. How will Foote's efforts to delegate increase or decrease his ability to establish clear controls?

Summary Report Question for Solution of Case as a Whole

17. After considering the preceding questions and your own knowledge and experience, write a report in which you (a) state the central problems

in the operation of the Dayton Metal Works and the important strong points of the company; (b) Give examples of these problems from the facts in the case and trace basic causes; (c) Recommend courses of action that, while capitalizing on the company's strong points, might help to overcome these problems and to prevent their recurrence.

9

Strategy and Structure: Designing Operating Units

LEARNING OBJECTIVES

After completing this chapter, you should be able to

1. Better understand how organizational structure flows from organizational strategy.
2. Give examples of situations that ideally should have (a) very broad and (b) very narrow job scopes.
3. Explain how to strike a balance between job specialization and integration of diverse tasks.
4. Know the key elements of effective work groups.
5. Understand how to structure departments, and the five basic approaches that can be emphasized in that structuring.
6. Discuss the key factors in departmentalization.

PART III—FROM PLANNING TO ORGANIZING

Planning tells *what* should be done; organizing tells *who* should do it. So, this Part of the book covers the inevitable issue of who does what.

Whether its members are few or thousands, every effective enterprise requires a well-designed organizational system. This is as true for a football team as it is for a government agency, a hospital, or a large corporation.

Individual jobs have to be clustered together to promote teamwork, as will be discussed in this chapter. Then the ever-present questions of decentralization and of taking advantage of expert knowledge via staff or matrix structures will be considered. Finally, in the fourth chapter of Part III, the selection of specific individuals to fill prescribed jobs will be explored.

To a large extent, such organizing will be based on the tasks that are necessary to carry out the company plans (discussed in Part II). Closer examination will reveal, however, that planning does not always precede organizing. The way managers organize has a strong influence on future decisions and plans that will be proposed. Moreover, leading and controlling—to be examined in Parts IV and V—also feed back into planning and organizing.

Like an architect who must consider convenience, strength, beauty, and cost of a new building, the manager also faces a mixture of considerations. Nevertheless, also like an architect, the manager must periodically focus on each aspect *separately*. None of us can give attention to everything at once. In this Part of the book we shall stress organizing, knowing all the while that organizing is only one of the subprocesses of managing.

STRATEGY-STRUCTURE LINK

The tie between corporate strategy and organizational structure has long been recognized as a cornerstone of management theory. Three decades ago, Alfred D. Chandler traced the impact of strategy on the structure of General Motors, duPont, Exxon, Sears, and other large firms.[1] Chandler told of how GM patriarch Alfred P. Sloan, Jr., called in sick for thirty straight days just so he could stay home and rationalize the proper structure to match GM's strategy. There just wasn't enough time to do the necessary thinking in the midst of a busy workday.

On an organization-wide level, the linkage between strategy and structure is well understood. Within smaller business units, however, this interdependence of strategy and structure becomes more murky and less well understood. The growth of conglomerates and the waves of business consolidations since the 1960s make these business-unit operations critical to future managerial success and provide the means and opportunity for

---

[1]A. D. Chandler, *Strategy and Structure* (Cambridge: The M.I.T. Press, 1962).

potential productivity improvements if these business units can be managed well.

In each business unit, the strategy and its supporting plans call for action of many sorts. People don't run machines, sell, and devise computer programs just to look busy; each task arises because it contributes directly or indirectly to the company mission. Questions of emphasis, priority, and coordination are always present, and strategy and its supporting plans provide the basis for official answers. Organizing deals with the way numerous activities are combined into jobs and departments; it combines activities into a team effort.

Organizing is a creative process. The form that any particular organization takes depends on the kinds of activities involved, and on the results called for in the specific strategy. The emerging organization is a tailor-made instrument designed for a specific situation and purpose.[2] When the situation or purpose changes, the organization should also be changed.

Harnessing Specialized Effort

Organizing starts when basic operations—such as baking bread or teaching class—are assigned to different individuals. Then, to aid in coordinating this work, several of these jobs are combined into sections, sections into departments, and so on until all operations of the enterprise are covered. Organization designers may choose to add a variety of advisers and helpers, but it is the operating work that generates the actual flow of services to consumers.

This grouping of operating activities into jobs, sections, and departments—*departmentation* in technical jargon—should be done carefully. For example, the kind of service customers get in a department store or medical office depends greatly on how work is divided. Or to cite production examples, the effectiveness of textile mills in India and electronic plants in the United States has been sharply improved by changing the basis for *combining* operations into sections and departments.

The way work is structured also affects the kinds of people who are qualified to be hired and promoted. After a job is established, employees often guard their roles jealously; in fact, companies and even whole industries have been shut down by jurisdictional disputes.

SCOPE OF INDIVIDUAL JOBS

How many jobs can a single person do well? The key to the answer is the word *well*. There are numerous examples—especially in modern team manufacturing operations, where workers routinely switch jobs—of workers doing many jobs adequately, and a few excellently. In many manufac-

[2]D. J. Hall and M. A. Saias ("Strategy Follows Structure," *Strategic Management Journal,* April 1980) contend, however, that there can be a reverse flow when structure constrains strategy, or at least contributes to its shaping.

turing research studies, the novelty of such independent work units and the fact that workers were being treated as human beings after decades of being viewed as little more than extensions of machines have led to improved quality, productivity, and worker attitudes. But to encourage managers to give many people many different jobs on the basis of these research findings would go too far. To ignore the skills that flow from specialization would be a mistake, especially since American society becomes increasingly specialized as the years go on.

How Much Division of Labor?

Consider a sport such as football. In the 1950s, it was the norm in college football for the same players to stay in a game from start to finish, playing both offense and defense. A placekicker or punter might well be a running back or end on offense and a defensive back on defense. Few athletes did well at all jobs, although most were acceptable at all and did very well at one or two. Contrast this with today's game, in which some players do only placekicking, others specialize on short-yardage offense, and still others work only on special teams. The overall quality is no doubt improved today, as a result of matching individuals and specialized jobs.

The same is true in the work world. Consider the bush pilot who flys a small plane in Alaska. The pilot fuels, loads, navigates, communicates with the ground, calms his passengers, and makes minor repairs. But in the operation of a 747 jet, these tasks are divided among dozens of people, each of whom has a limited number of clearly specified things to do. Why the difference?

The explanation lies partly in the volume of work required to operate a 747 jet. Also, each person must be highly skilled in a particular task. Moreover, the larger passenger payload can financially support the expense of a multiple crew. Hence, in this situation a greater division of labor is both desirable and affordable.

So it is in other fields as well. In banking, managers who learned their business when it operated in a risk-averse climate with government-issued franchises and little competition are now being forced to compete in a deregulated world with the likes of Sears, American Express, Merrill Lynch, and others.[3] Clearly, the skills that allowed a person to succeed in the regulated banking business might be quite different from what it takes to win out in a highly competitive consumer-oriented context. So people must be assigned and reassigned with their skills in mind, to take advantage of their special abilities.

In medicine, too, general practitioners are now scarce. Physicians are becoming much more specialized, and even the general practitioner of a few years ago is now a more specially trained family practitioner. The move toward specialization means that patients spend much more time

---

[3]A. R. McGill and N. M. Tichy, "Operationalizing a Strategic Organizational Transformation: The Chase Manhattan Bank," Part I, in press.

reaching the particular physician who deals with a specific ailment, but it also increases the likelihood that the ailment will be properly and expertly treated when the patient finally gets to the specialist. Again, benefits are associated with a high degree of skill and knowledge.

But should this approach extend to other fields, such as, advertising, as shown in Figure 9.1, or insurance sales? Should an insurance sales force be specialized—one staff member for annuities, another for individual retirement account programs, separate people for fire and casualty insurance, still others for life insurance? And should such specialists be allowed to sell mutual funds and NOW checking accounts, generate loans, and perform a variety of other services? Several companies initially concluded that such specialization was unwarranted and that a single relationship with each customer provided coordinated service at less expense, benefits that often offset the gains from high specialization. But this issue will no doubt come up again and again, with different answers at each reemergence, as more and more financial offerings bulge the briefcases of insurance representatives.

College-level teaching is an area in which high division of labor along functional lines has been resisted. The tasks of course design, instruction, and testing could be allocated to separate specialists. However, most college professors resent any interference with "their" courses. In fact, professors are urged to do research and still perform the whole gamut of teaching tasks. The rationale for such a broad job scope includes the ease of coordinating the various phases of teaching and a belief that a professor cannot be effective at one teaching task without being proficient in all the others.

The question of job *scope*—the number of different tasks one is expected to carry out—arises in every walk of life. Because of the way jobs are structured, people quit jobs, professions are built, unions call jurisdictional strikes, psychological security is found and lost, companies prosper or languish.

Striking a Balance

As the preceding examples show, effective job structure requires a careful assessment of what the physical circumstances permit and of the primary benefits sought. Factors that usually deserve attention include the following:

Benefits of functional specialization. By narrowing the scope of a job, full utilization can be made of any distinctive skill an individual possesses.[4] As workers concentrate on a limited range of duties, they can learn these very well and give them full attention. Wage economies may also arise; instead of paying a premium for a versatile "triple-threat person" for all positions, the more routine tasks can often be assigned to less experienced and less expensive employees. Furthermore, whenever a sufficient volume of routine work is isolated, mechanization becomes a possibility; use of computers for office work is an example.

[4]F. W. Taylor, *The Principles of Scientific Management* (New York: Harper & Row, 1947).

Bill Anderson / Monkmeyer Press

Figure 9.1 Division of labor in an advertising agency.

Karen R. Preuss / Taurus Photos

Cliff Moore / Taurus Photos

Michael Hayman / Photo Researchers

Richard Wood / Taurus Photos

Need for coordination.   Often several tasks should be closely synchronized or coordinated—as in labor negotiations—and one person can do this more easily than several. When information about a specific situation has to be pooled in a single spot, the difficulty of communicating bits of information from person to person may more than offset the benefits of specialization. Relevant here is the rule that tasks should be separated only where there is a clean break.

Morale of the operator.   A worker's feelings about the scope of her job may be vital.[5] Pride in work and work suited to professional dignity are positive factors. On the other hand, monotony is depressing for most people. Monotony can sometimes be partially relieved by rotating workers from job to job or by allowing them to deviate from set routines. If a *wide variety* of choices must be made, however, some workers feel that the job is unreasonably complex.

Rarely will any single job design be all good or all bad. Some potential benefits of specialization may have to be sacrificed for better coordination and employee morale, or vice versa. That choice depends primarily on values derived from the strategy of the enterprise.

Three restraints on designing individual jobs should not be overlooked. (1) The volume of work always places a limit on the division of labor. A specialist should not sit around most of the day waiting to do his part. (2) One technology may be so superior for some kinds of work that the managers have little choice in job design. Operating a taxicab, playing first violin in a symphony orchestra, and removing bark by means of a hydraulic machine in a lumber mill are situations of this type. (3) It takes effort not only to design a sophisticated system of work but also to have the workers adopt it as a normal way of doing things. Such investment is warranted only when the system will have repeated use.

EFFECTIVE WORK GROUPS

It is not sufficient to design jobs well. Too often in the past, workers were viewed as cogs in a wheel—one could be replaced by another without incident, or so some believed. Modern research and the complexities of modern production have caused major changes on this point. Increasingly, effective work is seen as resulting from a combined effort by a variety of people who work effectively together.

After tasks are grouped into jobs, the next step is to combine the jobs into work groups. These work groups are the sets of people who see each other on the job almost all day, every day. While their work may be independent in some respects, it is primarily interdependent, and the output is viewed by outsiders as a single achievement. How should such groups be structured?

[5]J. R. Hackman and G. R. Oldham, *Work Redesign* (Reading, Mass.: Addison-Wesley, 1980).

Combining Interdependent Tasks

It is sometimes appropriate to form teams of workers to deal with such interdependent tasks. When General Foods was opening a dog food plant in Topeka, Kansas, several years ago, it developed such a group system to overcome problems of worker competition that had been prevalent and antiproductive at a similar plant in Illinois.[6] Other efforts at teamwork have been seen in the tire industry, cardboard-box manufacturing, and even in the auto industry, where workers are grouped and even have their names printed on the tires, boxes, or cars built by the group as a symbol of their involvement.

In terms of organizational structure, then, whenever several similar jobs exist, they can be grouped *functionally* into the same section, as suggested in the upper portion of Figure 9.2. On the other hand, when several different skills are needed to complete a block of work, jobs can be grouped as indicated in the lower part of the diagram. For example, a salesperson, repairperson, and bookkeeper could be placed together in the branch office of an office-equipment company, in what is known as a *compound* design.

Benefits of Compound Groups

Under some circumstances, the use of compound groups permits managers to take advantage of a combination of several benefits that are sought in the design of jobs. Individual members of the group can be specialists in different fields, and coordination is achieved by interaction within the group. Furthermore, close personal relationships and a sense of group achievement contribute to morale. Small branches of a bank, a 747 airplane crew, and other geographically separated units often have these characteristics. Compound work groups may also be formed around a product or service, such as a maternity ward in a hospital.

[6] R. E. Walton, "*Teaching an Old Dog Food New Tricks,*" *Wharton Magazine,* Winter 1978.

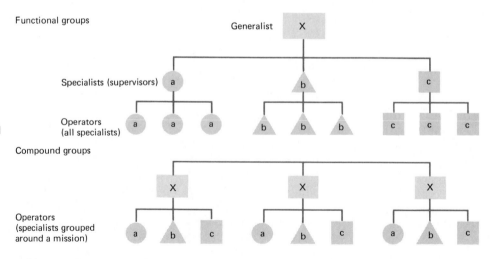

Figure 9.2 In functional groups, operators perform the same kind of work, and their supervisor is a specialist in that field. In compound groups, operators perform different but related work, and their supervisor is more of a generalist concerned with coordination.

A crew of workers operating a highly automated chemical plant or power station is usually a compound group of specialists. In fact, the operators on a single assembly line can be viewed as a compound group, although here the design and pace of the equipment carry most of the burden of coordination.

Compound groups should be used when local coordination is vital.[7] An industrial-equipment company, for instance, might combine sales, repair service, and parts warehousing in each of its local offices in an effort to provide distinctive customer service. Local coordination is even more vital for a surgical team composed of a surgeon, assisting doctor, anesthesiologist, and nurses (Figure 9.3). Here, as in the previous examples, a clear-cut block of work calls for the effort of several specialists.

Reasons for Functional Grouping

Attractive though compound groups may be, functional grouping of operations is actually more prevalent.

Functional grouping usually makes full-time jobs easier to arrange. While a compound group may consist of six sales representatives, two repairpersons, and one accountant, it cannot readily be made up of six sales representatives, one and two-thirds repairpersons, and five-sixths of an accountant. With the latter workload, the spare time of the repairperson and the accountant is usually lost. Also, the need for different specialists in

[7]A. H. Van de Ven, A. L. Delbecq, and R. Koenig, "Determinants of Coordination Modes Within Organizations," *American Sociological Review,* 41, 1976, pp. 334–35.

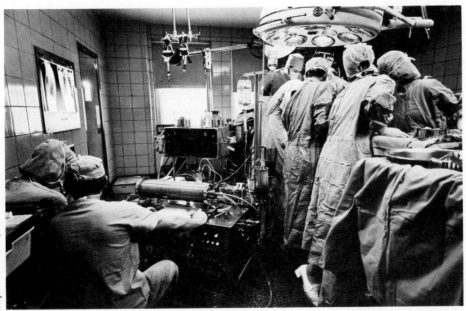

Stephen I. Feldman, Photo Researchers

Figure 9.3 A surgical team illustrates (1) clear division of labor within the group and (2) responsive interaction of the group to achieve a coordinated result.

any one compound group may be high today and low tomorrow. Functional grouping, with interchangeable people in the same group, allows a manager to balance these partial and irregular workloads more efficiently.

When each specialist requires high-cost equipment, the expenses of idle time are even greater. The operator of a multimillion-dollar wind tunnel used in aircraft engineering is an extreme example, but even the office space and company car of a field investigator can be expensive.

Technical supervision is often desirable. Unless the operators themselves possess high professional competence, their manager will normally need substantial technical knowledge. Even when plans are made centrally, the supervisor must interpret policies, resolve on-the-spot problems, coach new employees, and relay to his bosses the information they need. This kind of supervisory work can be done with greater expertise within a functional group. A supervisor need not be the only source of technical guidance as will be covered more thoroughly in Chapter 11, on staff-line roles. Nevertheless, the supervisor's expert understanding of the work is essential.

Compatibility within a group and with the supervisor is more likely to exist in a functional group than in a compound group. Such feelings of compatibility with fellow workers rests heavily on similar attitudes and values—for example, attitudes toward risk taking, meeting deadlines, short-run versus long-run achievements, and the importance of people versus things. In these terms, greater compatibility can be achieved by putting caseworkers together, researchers together, accountants together, and so forth. It is true that the members of such a group tend to reinforce each other's biases and as a result may be less cooperative with other functional groups. But the social satisfactions they derive from their work will also be enhanced.

The design of work groups, then, involves, at least broadly, a set of considerations similar to those used in the formation of individual jobs; benefits of specialization, need for coordination, effect on operators' morale, and expense repeatedly claim attention.

As Part IV will emphasize, work groups tend to become close-knit social groups. Once jelled, they tend to resist change. They can be a great source of strength for an enterprise or a seriously retarding influence; they should be composed with care.

SHAPING MAJOR DEPARTMENTS

To achieve unified action, work groups must be combined into departments. At this level, organization designers shift attention from an array of very specific operations to a broad grouping of activities that will facilitate central management. The work groups become building blocks to be arranged so that the major missions of the enterprise receive proper emphasis, while the various operating groups are supported in performing their respective tasks. As the enterprise adjusts to its changing environment, the shape of these major departments may have to be altered.[8]

Growth forced a small manufacturer of instruments to recast its basic organization structure. A resourceful instrument maker and a chemistry instructor had teamed up to make high-quality instruments for laboratories, and the business grew around specially designed equipment. The organization consisted of a production shop, a sales manager, and an office that handled all finance and clerical work. Then the company designed a machine for testing water pollution and found a potential market for hundreds of identical instruments. Sales jumped, and the shop was swamped with work.

The new business called for a major reorganization. Instead of merely expanding the three existing departments, the company established a separate department for each product line. While overhead expense is higher in the new setup, the prospect for preserving the strength of a close-knit, responsive laboratory-instrument business while opening the way for unfettered growth in the pollution-control field offsets this extra cost. Note that the choice of departmentation in this example depends on where coordination and specialized attention are most needed, and on the impact of technology.

The Basis of Departmentation

Jobs or work groups cannot be effectively designed without taking the major departments into consideration. Contrariwise, the scope of departments depends partly on what makes a good work group. Design choices are interdependent. A final decision at one level is held back until thought has been given to its impact elsewhere in the structure.

The principal options for organizing work in a major department include groupings by *function, product, process, territory, and customer.*

Function.   Under this arrangement, operations are divided into major functions. For example, firms concentrating on automobile insurance usually have departments for sales, underwriting, claims, finance, investment, and legal. A stereo equipment manufacturer will probably have research and development, production, marketing, and finance as basic departments. As noted in the previous section, such functional departments become expert in their particular area, give adequate attention to an activity that otherwise might receive hurried treatment, and act consistently on matters that require uniform, organization-wide treatment.

Product.   The work of a purchasing department is often divided by products—permitting each buyer to become expert in dealings with certain supplying industries and companies. In department-store merchandising,

[8]H. Mintzberg, *Structure in Fives: Designing Effective Organizations* (Englewood Cliffs, N.J.: Prentice-Hall, 1983).

specialized knowledge about product lines such as hosiery, jewelry, furniture, and women's suits is essential in selecting goods to sell, in pricing, and in sales promotion. Product subunits are often introduced within an engineering department to help acquire detailed knowledge about the diverse aspects of a product.

Such product subdivisions are used when the products handled differ significantly from each other, and when those differences are important in gaining a relative advantage over competitors.

Process. Manufacturers—and government offices—often perform several distinct processes that may serve as the basis for organization within a production department. In steel production, separate shops for coke ovens, blast furnaces, open-hearth furnaces, hot-rolling mills, cold-rolling mills, and the like are usually found. Each process is performed in a separate location and involves a distinct technology.

The grouping of activities by process tends to promote efficiency through specialization. All the key people in each unit become expert in dealing with their aspect of the business. On the other hand, process classification increases problems of coordination. Scheduling the movement of work from unit to unit becomes somewhat complex; and since no unit has full responsibility for a customer's order, a process unit may not be as diligent in meeting time requirements and other specifications as a group of people who think in terms of the total finished product and their customers.

The conflict between the desire to increase skill in performance through specialization and mechanization, and the need for coordination to secure balanced effort, recurs time and again in organization studies. Insurance companies, hospitals, and even consulting firms face the same issue.

Territory. Companies with salespeople who travel over a large area almost always use territorial organization within their sales departments. Large companies will have several regions, each subdivided into districts, with a further breakdown of territories for individual sales representatives. Airlines, finance companies with local offices, and motel chains all have widely dispersed activities and consequently use territorial organization to some degree.

The primary issues with territorial organization are three.

1. What related activity should be physically dispersed along with those that, by their nature, are local? For example, should a company with a national salesforce also have local warehousing, assembling, advertising, credit and accounting, and human resources? And how far should the dispersion occur—to the regional level or to the district level? Typically, whenever such related activities are dispersed, they are all combined into a territorial organization unit.

2. How much authority to make decisions should be decentralized to these various territorial units? In other words, how much of the planning and control work should go along with the actual performance?

3. What will be the relationship between the home-office service and staff units, and these various territorial divisions?

The major advantage of territorial organization is that it provides supervision near the point of performance. Local conditions vary and emergencies do arise. People distantly located will have difficulty grasping the true nature of a situation, and valuable time is often lost before an adjustment can be made. Consequently, when adjustment to local conditions and quick decisions are important, territorial organization is desirable. On the other hand, if many local units are established, some of the benefits of a large-scale operation may be lost. The local unit will probably be comparatively small; consequently, the degree of specialization and mechanization will likewise be limited.

Customer.   A company that sells to customers of distinctly different types may establish a separate unit of organization for selling to, and serving, each. A manufacturer of men's shoes, for instance, sells to both independent retail stores and chain stores. The chain-store buyers are very sophisticated and may prepare their own specifications; consequently, any salespeople calling on them must have an intimate knowledge of shoe construction and of the capacity of their company's plant. In contrast, sales representatives who call on retailers must be able to think in terms of retailing problems and be able to show how their products will fit into the customer's business. Few sales representatives can work effectively with both; thus, the shoe manufacturer has a separate division in its sales organization for each group.

Commercial banks, to cite another example, often have lending officers for different types of customers—aerospace companies, manufacturing concerns, stockbrokers, consumer loans, and the like. These people recognize the needs of their own group of customers, and are in a good position to appraise their credit worthiness.

Ordinarily, customer groups include only selling and direct-service activities. Anyone who has been shunted around to five or six offices trying to get an adjustment on a bill or a promise on a delivery will appreciate the satisfaction of dealing with one person who understands the problem and knows how to get action within the company. On the other hand, this form of organization may be expensive, and a customer-oriented employee may commit the company to actions that other departments find hard to carry out.

This description of functional, product, process, territory, and customer departmentation indicates that many variations are possible when organizing within a major department.

Key Factors in Departmentation

Several key factors are found in almost every departmentation problem, regardless of level, so an optimum arrangement of the various factors is usually sought instead of reliance on a single consideration. Here is a useful listing of factors already noted and some new dimensions of several of them. They are summarized in Figure 9.4.

Take advantage of specialization.   A division of labor that permits specialization in certain kinds of work should be considered. Such concentration enables employees to become experts and, assuming appropriate placement of personnel, allows a company to make full use of the distinctive abilities of its operators.

Specialization is usually thought of by function, but the possibility that an employee may become an expert on a product or on a particular type of customer should not be overlooked. In other words, "What is the focus on the person's specialty?" The question forces consideration of whether a particular body of knowledge and skill is important for getting a job done. The more crucial such knowledge and skill is to the success of the enterprise, the stronger will be the pull to set up a division or a job built on that specialty.

Aid coordination.   Even though certain activities are dissimilar, they may be put under a single executive because they need close coordination.[9]

[9]P. R. Lawrence and J. W. Lorsch, *Organization and Environment* (Boston: Harvard Business School, 1967).

When grouping and reassigning activities
into administrative units,
seek the optimum combination of the following benefits:

1. Take advantage of specialization
     Functional specialists
     Other kinds of specialists
     Special equipment
2. Aid in coordination
     Interrelated activities
     Common objectives
     Most-use criterion
3. Facilitate control
     Independent check
     Deadly parallel
     Clean break
     Ease of supervision
4. Secure adequate attention
5. Reduce expenses
6. Recognize human considerations
     Available personnel
     Informal groups
     Full-time jobs

The importance of each point must be determined for
the specific situation at the given time.

Figure 9.4 Basic factors in departmentation.

Buying and selling women's dresses in a department store, for example, may be the responsibility of a single executive because she can sense style trends and customer reactions and can time changes accordingly.

A clearly recognized *common objective* is important in securing coordination. The type of decentralization stressed by duPont, General Electric, and many other companies splits up engineering, production, and marketing among product divisions. This arrangement enables the management of each division to coordinate these diverse functions because the dominant objective of each unit is to make a success of its particular product line.

Coordination may be a factor when placing miscellaneous activities, as well as when grouping major functions. In any organization, there are a number of "orphan operations"—receptionists, chauffeurs, telephone operators—and no compelling reason may exist for putting them in a particular place. They can be assigned to the department that makes the *most use* of their work. This solution at least simplifies coordination between a service and its major use.

Facilitate control.   The way activities are apportioned has a marked effect on control in an organization. Clearly, if one activity is to serve as an *independent check* on another—as accounting on disbursement of cash or inspection on quality of production—the activities should be separated.

Departmentation, which makes it easier for management to measure performance and to hold people accountable for results, is a real aid to control. Thus it is desirable to make a *clean break* between the duties of one department and those of another. Oil companies, for example, often place all the work done by a refinery under a single manager because the line between what is inside and what is outside the refinery is a fairly clear one and also because all work within the refinery is so interrelated that a neat separation into two or more divisions would be difficult to establish.

Those companies whose volume and technology justify two or more operating units may use the *deadly parallel* as an aid to control. This means that operating units are made as nearly identical as possible so that their respective expenses and productivity can be directly compared. Chain stores, telephone companies, government bureaus, and even schools find that the deadly parallel provides performance standards that bring inefficient operations into sharp focus.

Control of actual operations is always simplified if an *immediate supervisor is on the spot* where he can see what goes on and can talk to workers frequently during the day. For this reason, a firm may place final assembly operations in a branch warehouse under the control of the sales department, even though the work logically seems part of production.

Secure adequate attention.   A principal reason for placing an activity high up in an organization structure is to ensure that this operation receives full consideration from top administrators. Similarly, auxiliary services are sometimes separate from primary operations in order to obtain adequate attention for all phases of work that should be done.

"Adequate attention," however, is a difficult guide to use in departmentation. Executives who pay heed to all demands for attention may be inclined to break up an otherwise neat pattern that works well most of the time. An executive must therefore decide not only how important an activity is at a given moment but also how important it will be in the future.

Reduce expenses.   The pattern of departmentation may directly affect expenses in two ways. First, a new unit—say, a purchasing department or a central training service—may require additional executives. These new executives will add to salaries, traveling expenses, secretarial work, telephone, and other services. In addition to these identifiable costs, the people in a new unit inevitably use up some of the time of other executives by talking with them and writing memoranda that have to be read and answered. Perhaps the addition of a single person will make no marked difference, but if an array of specialists all press for attention from busy line managers, the total burden on the line managers can become quite heavy.

A second expense consideration is the rate of pay needed for different kinds of jobs. An industrial sales department, for instance, might require that all sales representatives have engineering training plus five years' experience with company products. But another organization might reserve such high-paid positions only for special assignments, using lower-paid people for routine sales work. Obviously, no company will want to incur additional payroll expense unless it will benefit significantly from improved effectiveness by doing so.

Recognize human considerations.   Part IV will give careful attention to the human aspects of organization structure. There are a number of reasons that the coldly logical and emotionally detached organization plans discussed here must be modified once those elements are considered. Among the reasons are availability of personnel, the existence of informal groups, traditions within an enterprise, and prevailing attitudes toward different forms of organization.[10] These points are mentioned here simply as a reminder that human factors must be brought into consideration before a final decision is reached.

CONCLUSION

This chapter has been concerned with the way operating activities are assigned to people. The grouping of operating work has been analyzed by using a bottom-up approach that consists of three phases: (1) the grouping

[10]P. Nystrom and W. Starbuck, *Handbook of Organizational Design (New York: Oxford University Press, 1981).*

of operating tasks into individual jobs; (2) the combining of jobs into effective work groups; and (3) the combining of work groups into departments.

The overriding consideration at each of the three levels of organization design is strategy, and the plans that elaborate that strategy. These plans determine the nature of the work to be done; organization then translates the work into jobs, groups, and major departments.

In choosing a basis for departmentation, managers attempt to do six things: (1) take advantage of specialization, (2) aid coordination, (3) facilitate control, (4) secure adequate attention, (5) reduce expenses, and (6) recognize human considerations. No single organization design provides the desired level of each of these six features. In essence, departmentation is the subtle task of selecting the proper compromise among the features.

Organizational structure should contribute to the stability of working relationships. It enables all employees to know the particular part they are expected to play in the total activities of the company. And from it, employees also learn what they can expect others to do. For these reasons, duties should not be shuffled among people each time a new idea strikes. On the other hand, dynamic pressures in society and within a company require the modern manager to be constantly alert to the need for readjusting the way work has been divided among subordinates. In most enterprises, *thoughtful* changes in departmentation are made too infrequently rather than too often.

Impact on Productivity

The way operating units are structured affects productivity in terms of both efficiency and effectiveness. (1) Some forms of organization promote efficiency; for instance, a division devoted only to making home telephone units will typically have lower costs per unit than a division that produces a diversity of communication equipment. (2) The structure will also affect the amount of concentrated attention given to *new* needs of the marketplace, such as computerized "dialing" in the example of home telephones; thus, a "new-product manager" would probably add to effectiveness.

Note, however, that company strategy determines where concentrated effort should be directed. In trying to secure a unique competitive edge, perhaps the company is more interested in mobile (automobile) communication than low-cost home units. If this is the objective, then a somewhat different organizational structure is likely to be more productive. The strategy and the structure must reinforce each other if high productivity is to be achieved.

FOR FURTHER DISCUSSION

1. Sears would like to use its many retail stores to help sell (a) its automobile insurance (Allstate), (b) stocks and bonds (Dean Witter), and (c) real estate (Coldwell Banker). How do you recommend that these additional activities be fitted into the organization of a Sears store? For example, should every salesperson in the merchandise departments also push insurance, stocks, and real estate?

2. Why do four-star restaurants usually have a separate wine steward, instead of the regular waiter, to take orders and serve the wine? Would a separate dessert steward also be desirable?

3. In designing an organizational structure, is it better to start at the bottom and organize around the work done there and then build up to higher-level departmentation, or vice versa? Discuss.

4. "We used to have a great safety record in this plant," said a first-line supervisor. "That is," he went on, "until we set up a separate safety department in the plant's human resources office. In the year and a half since this group was set up, accidents have gone up almost 20 percent." How would you explain this phenomenon?

5. Would you expect the number of standing plans written for compound groups to be more or less numerous than those for functional groups?

6. Describe the departmentation of the major activities of your university, including at least all the activities with which you have contact. Which of the key factors listed at the end of this chapter probably explain the organization that you just described? Would you prefer a different organization?

7. Arrangements have just been completed to transfer the franchise of a minor-league baseball team to your hometown. A ball park is being built to seat 18,000, and the owners of the team have offered you the job of organizing and managing the refreshment concessions. They will provide any capital and facilities you require. (a) Describe the operating work that would have to be carried out in running the concessions. (b) What alternative means of organizing this work are plausible? (c) In dividing the operating work, did you use the "top-down" approach, or the "bottom-up" approach, or did you trace the steps of the operation? What are the arguments for each of these approaches?

8. "Whatever the organizational structure, it should be changed significantly every five to ten years just to shake up things." Comment on this statement by the president of a large bank.

9. Professor Leonard Sayles proposes in *The Complete Book of Practical Productivity** that growing *specialization in management* is perhaps the most important source of productivity problems. "Each new unit creates the need for many coordination activities, which drain managerial time of existing departments and can create needs for more staff, more managers, and then still more coordination problems." Do you agree?

*New York: Boardroom Books, 1983.

FOR FURTHER READING

Gulick, L. "Notes on the Theory of Organization," in *Papers on the Science of Administration*, L. Gulick and L. Urwick, eds. New York: Institute of Public Administration, Columbia University, 1937, pp. 3–45. A classic study that is still fully applicable today.

Lorange, P., *Implementation of Strategic Planning*. Englewood Cliffs, N.J. : Prentice-Hall, 1982. An excellent guide to help managers implement a strategic plan.

Miles, R. H. *Macro Organizational Behavior*. Santa Monica, Calif.: Goodyear, 1980, Ch. 2–4. Good summary of the major studies exploring the relationship between technology and structure.

Mintzberg, H., *The Structuring of Organizations*. Englewood Cliffs, N. J. : Prentice-Hall, 1982. An excellent explanation of how to structure an organization in order to have the greatest strategic success.

Petro, F. A., "A Way Out of the Productivity and Innovation Morass?," *Journal of Business Strategy*, Fall 1983. This author says that to tackle the productivity challenge, companies will have to adapt their organizational reporting and compensation systems to the postindustrial era.

Randolph, W. A., "Matching Technology and the Design of Organization Units," *California Management Review*, Summer 1981. On the basis of behavioral studies, the author argues that the technology of an organizational unit should be chosen first, and then its structure, human resources, and interaction patterns should be fitted to that technology.

The 1983 consolidation of Apple Computer under Chief Executive John Sculley set the stage for a boardroom power play that triggered the traumatic departure of Apple Chairman and Cofounder Steven P. Jobs, which in turn spurred a follow-up reorganization that observers thought would help the troubled company in the long run.

Sculley was hired in May 1983 to teach Apple marketing and better the company's response to dealers and customers. He merged Apple's nine decentralized divisions into an organization structured on business functions such as engineering and marketing.

By 1984, Apple counted just three divisions: one for sales of all products, one for Apple II products, and one for the forthcoming Macintosh family of products.

Friction soon developed between the Apple II and Macintosh groups as the former turned in a record 1984 performance while the latter fell short of performance expectations.

While Macintosh bosses were glamorized as superstars, the less-publicized Apple II managers were producing more of the company's sales and much of the profit. Too, the Macintosh division—led by Jobs, who openly derided Apple II's "old" technology against Macintosh's newer designs—seemed to get more of the perks, including fruit juice and a masseur on call. This was in keeping with the creative structure Jobs used to build Apple, but as the company got bigger, Sculley moved to tighten that looseness with more structure.

Complicating the Apple II–Macintosh rivalry were increasing business problems. Mac sales fell short of projections, and executives blamed marketing and developmental flaws. Bickering between Jobs and Sculley intensified as Sculley, the corporate pro, urged Jobs, the headstrong entrepreneur, to be a more conscientious businessman and deliver new products on time. Jobs responded by questioning Sculley's competence in front of Apple friends.

At Apple's April 1985 board meeting, Chairman Jobs was relieved of his position as operational head of the Mac division. In late May, he plotted to convince directors to oust Sculley in favor of him. But Sculley had his ear to the ground and moved quickly to scuttle the scheme, revealing it at a meeting of Apple's executive committee. In the tense, three-hour meeting, executives could find no future role for Jobs—ironically Apple's largest stockholder.

Further attempts to find a place for Jobs failed. The man who had revolutionized the computer industry finally left the company he had helped build.

Sculley reorganized again in two marathon sessions in May. The new Apple was an almost entirely functional organization, with Apple II boss

Delbert Yocam heading engineering, manufacturing, and distribution, and William V. Campbell overseeing U.S. marketing and sales. Two weeks later, the company also announced it would close three of its six factories and lay off 1,200 workers.

But observers praised the new structure, saying it would allow Apple to present one face to dealers and customers. Observers predicted that it would help in particular with new business prospects, who had been put off by the turmoil between the rival product divisions.

Question

What advantages do you believe that John Sculley hoped to achieve from each of his reorganizations, one in 1983 and another in 1985?

For more information, see *Fortune,* 5 August 1985.

APPLICATION CASES

For practice in applying concepts covered in this chapter to managerial situations, see the following managerial decision cases. The case questions particularly relevant to this chapter are listed by number after each case name.

Grant Chemical Corporation (p. 59) 6, 10
Dayton Metal Works (p. 198) 8
GAIN Software (p. 303) 12
Clifford Nelson (p. 308) 9
Graham, Smith, & Bendel, Inc. (p. 442) 8

10

Designing the Hierarchy: Delegating and Decentralizing

LEARNING OBJECTIVES

After completing this chapter, you should be able to

1. Understand the difference between operating work and managerial work.

2. Discuss the three implied actions—duties, authority, and obligation—that stem from delegating.

3. Explain what happens to executives' obligations when they delegate a task.

4. Know the seven guides to how much decentralization is optimum.

5. Explain how decentralization can be useful in structuring business units responsible for their own profits or losses.

The growth of an organization inevitably leads to the formation of a managerial hierarchy. This is precisely the cause of the adjustment that occurred in the microcomputer industry in the mid-1980s, as it moved from an innovative *entrepreneurial* phase, in which inventions developed in garages became Apple Computers, for instance, to a *managerial* phase, in which free-flowing creativity and independence were supplanted by managerial basics and organization.

As a firm becomes larger, more levels of managers are needed to ensure coordinated planning, direction, and control. Centralization versus decentralization—the focus of this chapter—concerns the vertical allocation of *management action* across this hierarchy. In contrast, the discussion of departmentalization in the previous chapter focused on the horizontal allocation of *operating work*. Since these terms are critical, a brief review is in order:

- Operating Work: This embraces the basic activities necessary to create goods and services—the selling, machine-running, bookkeeping, and engineering in a manufacturing plant; the copywriting, art producing, media selecting, and campaign scheduling in an advertising agency; or the arranging of temporary care for children, locating foster homes, making placements, raising funds, and keeping records in a child-placement agency.
- Managerial Work: This refers to the guidance of other people. It includes the activities of all levels of supervisors, from first-line supervisor to president.

Persistence of the Problem

The question of how much work chief executives should do themselves and how much should be assigned to subordinates has concerned students of organization and administration for centuries.

The burden on executives is especially acute in enterprises that are changing and growing. As product lines are diversified and new employees added, executives find that they can no longer give proper attention to all the management problems that cross their desks. Unless they decentralize, they find that they are unable to cope with the job by themselves.

The allocation of managerial work is one of the most subtle aspects of the organizing process. The degree of decentralization may vary from department to department within a single company. The sales department, for example, may be highly decentralized. But the controller may retain direction over a great deal of planning, organizing, and motivating of the operations under his direction.

For insight into this web of relationships, this chapter first examines the delegation process and then considers factors determining the degree of decentralization that is desirable in a specific situation. The chapter closes with a penetrating look at profit decentralization—an organizational arrangement well suited to a dynamic society.

THREE INEVITABLE FEATURES OF DELEGATING

Delegation is familiar to anyone in a supervisory position; it simply means entrusting part of the work of operations or management to others. A filling station owner delegates car greasing to Bill and pump tending to Charlie. The president of Republic Aircraft Corporation entrusts financial matters to Ms. MacGregor, the treasurer. Or, as Figure 10.1 suggests, McDonalds headquarters delegates responsibility and authority for a single restaurant to its manager. Such delegations give rise to what we commonly call a *boss-subordinate relationship.*

Every time a manager delegates work to a subordinate—say, a president to a marketing manager, or a first-line supervisor to an operator—three actions are either expressed or implied, as Figure 10.1 suggests.

1. The manager assigns *duties.* The person who is delegating indicates what work the subordinate is to do.
2. He grants *authority.* Along with permission to proceed with the assigned work, the manager will probably transfer to the subordinate certain rights, such as the right to spend money, to direct the work of others, to use raw materials, to represent the company to outsiders, or to take other steps necessary to fulfill the new duties.
3. The manager creates an *obligation.* In accepting an assignment, a subordinate takes on an obligation to his boss to complete the job.

These attributes of delegation are like a three-legged stool; each depends on the others for support, and no two can stand alone.

Duties. Duties can be described in two ways. First, we can think of them in terms of an activity. For instance, we may say that Turner's duties are either to run a turret lathe, or to sell in Oshkosh, or to direct an employment office, or to discover and analyze facts about the money market and trends in interest rates, or to measure distribution costs. According to this view, delegating is the process by which we assign activities to individuals.

Second, duties can be described in terms of the results we want to achieve. Following this approach, we would say that in the first two examples, Turner's duties are to turn on his lathe a certain number of pieces per day according to engineering specifications, or to build customer goodwill and secure a prescribed number of orders in the Oshkosh territory. Here we are talking about objectives. We define the duties in terms of the goals we want to accomplish.

Because of differences in jobs, such goals may be stated as either

Courtesy McDonald's Corporation

Courtesy McDonald's Corporation

Figure 10.1 In a fast-food chain, carefully defined duties and limited authority are delegated from headquarters to the manager of each outlet. The manager, in turn, has an obligation to the executive who assigned the duties and authority.

long-run or short-run results. They may represent overoptimism or realistic expectation. Nevertheless, if the delegation of duties is phrased in terms of goals, a subordinate is likely to get psychological satisfaction from her work, and she will have advance notice of the criteria on which her performance will be judged. An employee's duties will be clear to her only if she knows what activities she must undertake *and* what missions she must fulfill.

Authority.   If a person is assigned duties to perform, is it not obvious that he must be given all necessary authority to carry them out? An advertising manager needs authority to buy space, hire a copywriter, and take other necessary steps if he is to gain his assigned objective of building customer demand for company products.

Unfortunately, assigning authority is not simple. It is important to understand exactly what kind of authority is within the power of a manager to grant; typically, several restrictions fence in the authority a manager has at her disposal.

Administrative authority consists of certain permissions or rights: the right to act for the company in specified areas (to buy raw material, accept orders from customers, issue press releases, admit people into a plant); the right as spokesperson for the company to request other employees to perform activities of various kinds; and the right to impose sanctions and discipline if a subordinate disregards his instructions. These rights are vested in the head of an enterprise by law and custom, and they are supported by the moral approval of society. They stem partly from concepts of private-property rights, partly from acknowledged authority of the political state, and particularly from the long-established human habit of looking to hierarchical leadership in cooperative undertakings. Because of this background, employees, and in fact our whole society, accept the idea that the head of an enterprise has certain rights of authority and that he may reassign these rights. This fundamental point finds its roots in the early management literature.[1]

When an employee takes a job, he also (1) expects to take orders from someone designated by the company; (2) looks to management for permission to use company property or to act as an official representative of the enterprise; and (3) expects a superior to review his work and bring pressure on him to improve if it is unsatisfactory.[2] Such socially accepted rights constitute formal authority, and management can assign these rights when it erects a formal organization.

Authority is an essential element of any modern enterprise, but it must not be confused with unlimited power. Not even a company president or section manager has the power to force customers to sign orders or suppliers to sell raw materials, or the power to compel the *enthusiastic* cooperation of associates and subordinates. The rights that an administrator may transfer are more akin to authorization than they are to power.

In addition to inherent limitations on the authority that an executive can delegate, virtually every company imposes limitations of its own. An executive is usually permitted to act strictly "within company policy" and "in accordance with established procedures." A manager may, in theory, have formal authority to hire and fire people in her division, but in fact

[1]C.I. Barnard, *The Functions of the Executive* (Cambridge: Harvard University Press, 1968) pp. 165-66.

[2]H.A. Simon, *Administrative Behavior,* 3d ed. (New York: Free Press, 1976).

she must adhere to myriad restrictive procedures that require her, for example, to refer job descriptions to the planning department before she can fill a new position, to satisfy the human resources department that no capable person is available within the company before she can hire an outsider, to set salaries within an established range for each job classification, and to refrain from discharging anyone without two prior warnings at least a month apart as well as other legal requirements. Another department head may have to endure comparable restrictions surrounding purchases of raw materials and, especially, of new equipment.

Because of these limitations on authority, when a task is delegated, the rights associated with it must be specified.

Obligation.   Obligation—the third inevitable feature of delegation—is the moral compulsion felt by a subordinate to accomplish his assigned duties.[3] When duties are delegated to him, a subordinate is not free either to do the work or leave it, as suits his convenience. A price checker is derelict in his duty if, on Friday afternoon, he mails out a batch of unaudited bids to customers merely because his work had piled up and salespeople were anxious to get the bids to their customers. Similarly, a clerk assigned to unlock the office in the morning fails in her obligation when she shows up two hours late with the excuse that her brother had unexpectedly stayed overnight for a visit.

Although agreement is usually implied rather than expressed, when a subordinate accepts an assignment, he in effect gives his promise to do his best in carrying out his duties. Having taken a job, he is morally bound to try to complete it and can be held accountable for results. A sense of obligation, then, is primarily an attitude of the person to whom duties are delegated. Dependability rests on the sense of obligation, and without it, cooperative business enterprises would collapse.

APPLYING CONCEPTS OF DELEGATION

Should Duties and Obligations Extend Beyond Authority?

A common saying in popular management literature declares that "authority and accountability should always be equal." Behind this statement lies the conviction that if a person is assigned duties, he ought to be furnished with enough authority—no more and no less—to carry them out; and if given authority, he has a corresponding obligation to use it wisely. Although there is an element of truth here, the statement is, unfortunately, an oversimplification.

The first difficulty is the word *equal*. Duties are concerned with objec-

---

[3]N.R.F. Maier, "The Subordinate's Role in the Delegation Process," *Personnel Psychology*, 21, 1968, pp. 179–91.

tives and activities, authority with rights, and obligations with attitudes. Although these three concepts are indeed related, it is hard to find a common denominator for measuring equality among them. Also, as was shown in the discussion of formal authority, there are only certain kinds of rights that an enterprise can pass along to its managers, and there are usually very substantial restrictions on how even these rights may be used. To permit anyone to charge into action without constraints would lead to chaos. An employee often must try to achieve objectives with authority far short of what he feels he needs.

It is more nearly accurate, though not so pat, to say to the boss—the person doing the delegating—"Duties, authority, and obligation depend on each other, and you should therefore correlate them thoughtfully"; and to the subordinate—the person receiving the delegation—"You are obligated to fulfill your duties to the maximum extent that is feasible in light of your authority and the conditions under which you have to work."

An Obligation Cannot Be Delegated

What happens when duties and authority are redelegated? Does this redelegation relieve the middle manager of *his* obligation? Suppose the treasurer of the Omaha Chemical Company delegates to the chief accountant the task of maintaining an accounts-payable ledger. The chief accountant, being too busy to maintain the records herself, assigns the job to a clerk.

The redelegation of the job by the chief accountant to the clerk does not at all change the initial relationship between the treasurer and the chief accountant. The chief accountant still has the same duties and as much authority, and even though she has turned over the major parts of these to the clerk, she can reclaim them if she wishes. More important, the chief accountant still has the same obligations to the treasurer. The additional obligation between the clerk and the chief accountant in no way relieves the chief accountant of her obligation. It is as though the treasurer lent ten dollars to the chief accountant, and the chief accountant in turn lent the money to the clerk; the chief accountant cannot satisfy her obligation to the controller by giving him the clerk's IOU.

If we were to abandon the principle that one cannot delegate obligation, there would be no way of knowing who was accountable for what.[4]

Dual Subordination

An issue faced over and over in delegating is whether each person should have only one boss. On this point, formal organization theory is clear. Workers—operators or managers—may have relationships with many people, but they need one supervisor whose guidance can be regarded as final. What are the reasons supporting this concept of a single chain of command?

[4]T. Heller, "Changing Authority Patterns: A Cultural Perspective, *Academy of Management Review,* July 1985.

All executives and all subordinate employees respond to a variety of influences, not just to those emanating from their line bosses. Nevertheless, the evidence indicates that as important as other people may be in influencing the behavior of an employee, the line boss is usually far more significant. Reasons for the overriding influence of the line boss are not hard to find. The boss usually trains and directs employees and explains what they should do; the boss authorizes what subordinates may do; he assists in getting necessary materials and tools and often represents "his" people throughout the organization; he checks results and initiates corrective action when necessary; he praises, blames, disciplines, promotes, recommends changes in pay, and otherwise motivates his subordinates. These activities are closely interrelated, and if they are to have their greatest impact, they should spring, integrated, from one source.

When two bosses try to share the fundamental role of immediate supervisor, their actions are likely to be inconsistent. One may praise, whereas the other may suggest improvements; the first may urge speed and initiative, whereas the second may withhold authority; they may make assignments that conflict. People can and do get along with two bosses, just as a child accepts guidance from two teachers or parents; but unless the two bosses have a very close working relationship, they may find many opportunities for maneuvering for advantage have been lost and may tend to be unjust to subordinates. When there is one boss, the likelihood of a consistent pattern of supervision is greatly increased. The experience of managers over the years indicates that it is wise to have one supervisor who resolves conflicting demands and has final say on priorities.

Duties Include Interactions

Clear-cut duties and authorities do not imply that everyone should work in his own isolated corner. Instead, in most delegation situations, managers make it very clear that subordinates should consult with others and keep them informed as they proceed with their own duties.

Furthermore, a few assignments are specifically joint undertakings. Some companies emphasize their concern with cooperation by saying that employees are accountable for both work and teamwork, and companies are dissatisfied with employees' performance unless they measure up on both counts. Cooperation is definitely part of the job and should be as clear as other duties.

Relations between supervisors and subordinates are subject to continual readjustment. Delegations should be modified as the work to be done and the people who do it change. Nevertheless, the vast number of relationships are stable—at least for some period of time. This stability is important. A worker learns what to expect of her boss; the boss learns how much he can depend on each of his subordinates; people doing related work learn how to deal with an established hierarchy. Such patterns of expectation are essential if we are to get day-to-day work done smoothly and quickly. If the delegating has not been done well, and if boss-subordinate relationships are unclear and become sources of friction, the company unity will be lacking.

HOW MUCH DECENTRALIZATION?

Focus on Planning

Experience has shown that *planning*—that is, identifying problems and deciding what action to take—is usually the most crucial element in thinking about decentralization. Organizing, leading, and controlling are also important, but assigning those activities to various executives typically depends on how planning duties have been allocated. In a later examination of leadership and control, we shall trace the interplay of these phases of management with decisions concerning decentralization.

There are several ways to divide the work of planning among executives, and these are important for describing varying degrees of decentralization.[5]

By subject. This is the simplest way to divide planning. An executive normally makes decisions only for the operations that she directs. However, when an operation affects several related departments, as does pricing or inventory control, she may stipulate that certain other persons are to be consulted before binding decisions are made.

Dividing planning by subject is especially useful in situations in which there is a senior executive and a lower executive who reports to him. A chief accountant, for example, might say to his office manager: "I'll decide what accounts to keep and where different types of items should be charged—that is, I'll set up the accounting system. But I want you to schedule the flow of work through the office, determine the number and types of people we need, and figure out whether it would pay us to get more automatic equipment." Or the vice-president in charge of sales might select the markets to be cultivated and then assign her sales manager the detailed planning of direct-mail publicity, personal contacts, and other activities designed to secure orders from the customers within these markets. Note that in each of these examples, certain subjects are decided by the senior person and other subjects by the subordinate.

By type of plan. A sharp division of administrative work by subject often is not feasible. A senior executive may want some say in the way a particular type of situation is handled, but may lack time to make daily decisions on individual problems. This partial involvement can be accomplished by relying on the various parameters of a planning system, described earlier, and shown schematically in Figure 10.2. For example, an

[5]A. Jay, *Management and Machiavelli* (New York: Bantam, 1974).

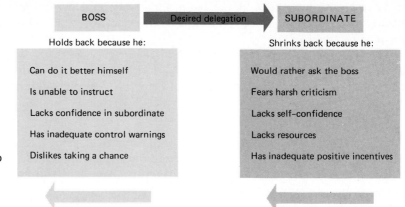

Figure 10.2 Personal obstacles to effective delegation. Even when organizational design calls for delegation, personal factors may obstruct the transfer.

executive can establish *objectives* and *policies* to set the direction and limits of action. Subordinates can then make decisions on specific cases within this guiding framework. For instance, the president of a telephone company can say, "No employee with more than two years of service is to be discharged as a result of installation of automatic-dialing equipment." The managers of local branches must act within this limit and plan for the transfer or retraining of any displaced workers with a two-year service record.

A senior executive may wish to be more specific. If so, he can lay out a step-by-step *procedure* (Chapter 6) to be followed, or a *schedule* (Chapter 7) of dates by which specific action is to be completed. Thus, advertising managers often set deadlines for drawings, magazine copy, radio scripts, and other parts of their promotion campaigns. Subordinates are free to make detailed schedules for their own work provided the master schedule is met.

In still other situations, an executive may announce that certain *premises* are to be adopted when plans are made for the future. For example, he tells the production manager to prepare his budget on the assumption that there will be a 20 percent increase in sales volume for the following year.

From the point of view of decentralization, the questions are *to what extent* these different types of plans should be used and *who* should set them up. Clearly, the more management circumscribes or regiments work by means of objectives, policies, and so forth, the more highly centralized the organization will be.

By phase of planning. Planning is not typically an isolated activity performed by a single person insulated from her associates. In fact, the more important the plan, the more likely that several people will participate in formulating it. As we noted earlier, planning consists of several identifiable phases: diagnosing and identifying a problem, finding possible solutions to the problem, gathering facts, projecting the results of each alternative, and, finally, choosing one alternative as the course of action to be followed. In practice, the work of each of these phases may be performed by different persons.

Except for final decision making, none of these phases need be regarded as the exclusive domain of a particular person. Anyone who spots a trouble area that needs to be cleaned up or has evidence that will contribute to the sound analysis of a problem should be encouraged to volunteer ideas. Eliciting such voluntary assistance, however, is not enough in itself. Someone must still be responsible for ensuring that each phase of the planning process is properly performed.

Just how these phases are actually handled depends a great deal on the atmosphere that prevails within each company. In one company, it might be presumptuous for a first-line supervisor to suggest a change in human resources policies, whereas in another company, the supervisor might get fired if he failed to spot potential trouble and recommend a plan for avoiding it. When a possible change is being studied, some companies expect lower-level supervisors to provide only the information requested, whereas others expect them to speak their minds on anything they believe pertinent, and perhaps, even to come up with counterproposals. These are all examples of how the burden of planning may be allocated in terms of phases or steps in the planning process.

Summary.   To decide who should do what in the planning process, the following questions must be asked:

1. What is the subject?
2. Is a *single* problem being solved, or is a *general* guide such as an objective, policy, procedure, schedule, or premise being established?
3. Do we want several executives to participate in the decision? If so, which phase of the decision-making process is each expected to take on?

Decentralization is concerned with how much of this complex planning activity should be assigned to each executive, from the president down to first-line supervisors.

Degrees of Decentralization

How are these concepts put into practice? The following two examples (illustrated in Figure 10.3) help answer this question. To make it easier to compare the degrees of decentralization, both examples concern sales activities.

Decentralized planning.   A company that manufactures materials-handling equipment has a field force of twenty-four representatives. Six are branch managers, and each has one to four sales representatives. The branch managers spend at least half of their time in actual selling. Be-

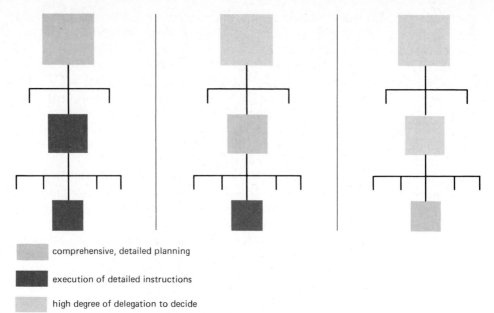

Figure 10.3
Centralized vs. decentralized planning. The degree of decentralization may differ for particular subjects, or for type or phase of planning.

comprehensive, detailed planning

execution of detailed instructions

high degree of delegation to decide

cause industrial equipment is purchased at irregular intervals, the salespeople have to follow new sales leads; they cannot depend on a regular flow of repeat business from established customers.

The management of this company thinks it has a highly decentralized sales operation. However, two important areas are definitely centralized: products and prices. Product planning is handled by the engineering department in the main office. A variety of standard equipment is described in a product book, and sales representatives sell this equipment whenever it is suited to the customer's needs. If special equipment is required, the sales representatives simply gather the operating data and submit these facts to the home office. The engineering department then decides what to recommend to the customer and prepares the necessary sketches. The setting of prices is also centralized. Prices of standard items and special orders are set by the sales manager. In making these decisions, the sales manager draws on field information on customers, cost figures from the estimating department, and his knowledge of the competitive situation.

Except for product planning and price setting, employees in the field have almost complete freedom. Which customers to call on, what selling methods to use, which conventions and trade association meetings to attend, when a long-distance phone call is worth its cost—all are determined locally. The branch manager is the key person in many of these decisions, but he may rely on an experienced sales representative to do her own planning.

The home office provides a variety of descriptive circulars, prospect lists, technical advice, and other services. Nevertheless, it is up to the branch manager and the sales representatives to decide what use, if any, they will make of these services.

Note that the planning of sales is rather sharply divided by subject. The chief engineer decides what products will be sold, the sales manager sets the prices, and the branch managers select the customers. Use of policies and standing procedures is limited. There is considerable cooperation in the planning process, particularly through the exchange of ideas and information. This exchange has not been formalized, however, to a point where the executive making the decision feels relieved of the preliminary phases of planning (except for the preparation of cost estimates used in pricing).

Not everyone in the company is convinced that the present method of dividing up the sales-planning work is the best. One manager advocates much more centralized planning and direction; he insists that sales quotas should be established, that sales representatives should be directed to specific prospects, and that direct-mail advertising should be tied in closely with sales calls. However, most executives believe that the local people can judge what will produce on-the-spot results better than anyone sitting in the home office.

Centralized planning. A quite different way of dividing sales planning work is followed by a successful Midwestern oil company. Each of the forty-two branch managers has a fuel-oil and industrial-sales manager, a gasoline sales manager who concentrates on sales through filling stations, and a branch engineer who leases, staffs, builds, and exercises financial control over company-owned filling stations.

Most sales planning is done in the main office. The marketing vice-president sets general prices and establishes policies covering any price reduction to meet local competition. Advertising is planned and executed at headquarters. Sales promotion, keyed in with the advertising program, is planned in detail at the home office and includes decisions on the color stations are to be painted and on the design of signs. A variety of training aids for station operators are also planned centrally, including instructions for waiting on customers, care of washrooms, methods of car greasing, and the like.

The branch managers, then, are primarily concerned with carrying out plans that have already been made. They hire, train, pay, direct, and motivate the key people in the branch office—all in accordance with company policy and other plans. If a price war breaks out, they adjust local prices in accordance with policy or, if necessary, request the home office to adjust them. They take care of the innumerable little problems that inevitably arise in the sale of a substantial dollar-volume of product. They often pass new ideas for sales promotion along to the main office. Their principal duty, however, is to carry out the sales program as effectively as possible, rather than to propose new ideas. The executives of this oil company would strongly resist any proposal to give branch managers the freedom in planning permitted by the manufacturer described earlier.

These two examples illustrate not only the general difference between a centralized and decentralized organization, but also the need to think specifically about each type of problem (for instance, pricing in the industrial-equipment company) even though a general pattern has been established. In practice, an endless variation in degrees of delegation exists, and properly so. Each company operates in its own unique circumstances of size, reputation, competitive strategy, existing equipment, abilities of key executives, and other factors. Each manager must figure out what allocation of executive duties best fits his needs. Nevertheless, certain factors can be identified that will help a manager make that allocation wisely.

Guides to "How Much Decentralization?"

The following seven factors should be carefully weighed when choosing the best place in the executive hierarchy for each category of decision making.[6]

1. *Who knows the facts?*
   Sometimes a single individual—salesperson, advertising manager, purchasing agent—is in constant command, through the normal course of her work, of all the facts needed to make a given type of decision. Such a person is naturally best equipped for decision making on the issue. Many decisions, however, require information from several different sources—a decision whether or not to buy a new machine, for example, requires data on production methods, plant layout, future volume, availability of capital, workers' attitudes, and so forth. Channels of communication must be established to funnel all this information to a single point; the question, then, is whether it will be easier to pass general information down the line or specific information up the line. This raises considerations of the accuracy, time, and cost of such communication.

2. *Who has the capacity to make sound decisions?*
   Clearly, if people at lower levels—engineers, office supervisors, branch managers—lack the ability and experience needed to make a wise decision, there is a compelling reason to withhold decision-making authority from them. Such capacity is usually a relative matter, however. Perhaps the president can make a very wise decision about granting credit, but the branch manager can make one that is almost as effective. Since the president's energies should be reserved for more important matters, and the branch manager's judgment on this subject is satisfactory, the planning for extending credit should be lodged with the branch manager.

3. *Must speedy, on-the-spot decisions meet local conditions?*
   The repair of airplanes or the purchase of fruit at wholesale auctions obviously requires that someone with authority be at the scene of action. A similar, though less dramatic, need for prompt action occurs in negotiating contracts, employing personnel to meet unexpected work loads, or adjusting the complaints of irate customers.

[6]V. H. Vroom and P. W. Yetton, *Leadership and Decision-Making* (Pittsburgh: University of Pittsburgh Press, 1973).

4. *Must the local activity be carefully coordinated?*

   Uniformity of action is sometimes so important that all decisions must be made centrally—for example, ensuring that all customers in a single area are charged the same prices, or determining the length of vacation for all employees in the same plant. Other decisions, such as determining a weekly production schedule or laying out a national sales-promotion program, require that activities in several areas be closely *synchronized*: here, at least some central planning is called for.

5. *How significant is the decision?*

   A relatively minor decision—one that will increase or decrease profits only by a dollar or two, for example—clearly should be left to a junior executive or beginning manager. The expense of communication up and down the chain of command, and of the time required for the senior executive to handle the problem, would be far greater than any savings that might result from his judgment. On the other hand, any decision that will have a major effect on the total operation—either a single transaction or a basic policy—should be approved at least by a senior executive.

6. *How busy are the executives who might have planning tasks?*

   In dividing up work among executives, overloads must be avoided. A top executive may already have so many duties that she will have to shirk additional responsibility for planning; or a plant superintendent may lack the time for careful analysis and thoughtful decision. If a busy executive has a distinctive contribution that only she can make, perhaps she can be brought in on one phase of the planning, while the rest of the chore is assigned to someone else.

7. *Will initiative and morale be significantly improved by decentralization?*

   Decentralization typically builds initiative and good morale in lower-level executives. Managers should be sure, however, that such feelings will be generated, and that they are desirable, in each specific situation. Companies that are faced with frequent shifts in consumer demand, in technology, or in the competitive situation must actively promote adaptability and initiative among their workers. In other enterprises, such as many public utilities, where the rate of change is much slower, too much originality and initiative among junior executives may actually create discontent and lower morale. Similar sharp differences in the need for initiative are also found in various departments of a single company.

In using these factors as guides to the degree of decentralization that is appropriate in a specific situation, a manager must determine how much weight to attach to each. Often the factors pull in opposite directions—the need for speed may suggest greater decentralization, while the desire for coordination may dictate greater centralization. Clearly, each factor must be carefully balanced against the others. Allowance must also be made both for traditional behavior and for growth in individuals' abilities. Again, the managerial task of organizing calls for a high degree of judgment.

PROFIT DECENTRALIZATION

One form of decentralization is highly important to larger companies: profit decentralization. Under this plan, a company is split into business units (discussed in Chapter 4), each of which is responsible for its own profit or loss.[7] Such an organizational design is shown in Figure 10.4.

Self-sufficient, Semiautonomous Units

Two characteristics lie at the heart of the plan. (1) All the major operations necessary to make a profit are grouped under the manager of a *self-sufficient* unit. This, of course, is a matter of departmentation (discussed in the previous chapter). Several such self-sufficient, self-contained units are usually established in a company. (2) The management of these units is so highly decentralized that each of them becomes *semiautonomous*. In effect, a series of little businesses operates within the parent corporation. The manager of each unit has virtually the same resources and freedom of action that he would enjoy if he were president of an independent company. He is expected to formulate his own strategy and to take whatever steps are necessary to ensure that his "little business" will make a profit.

Though profit decentralization is the key concept in organizing large concerns like General Motors, it is by no means confined to industrial giants. Smaller companies, such as Research-Cottrell and Dana Corporation, have found it admirably suited to their needs.

Ordinarily the business units are built around product lines, and the engineering, production, and sales of each line are placed within the decentralized division. However, the same idea has been applied to department-store chains, which place all their operations in each *region* on a profit-decentralization basis. In fact, this form of organization has become so successful and popular that most diversified companies use it in at least a modified form.

Benefits

A major advantage of profit decentralization is its stimulating effect on the *morale* of the key people in each of these self-sufficient, semiautonomous divisions. Executives are able to see the results of their own methods, to take the action they believe best, and to feel that they are playing an important role. The resulting enthusiasm and devotion to the success of their division tend to spread to employees at all levels.

[7]E. F. Finkin, "Developing and Managing New Products," *Journal of Business Strategy,* 41, Spring 1983.

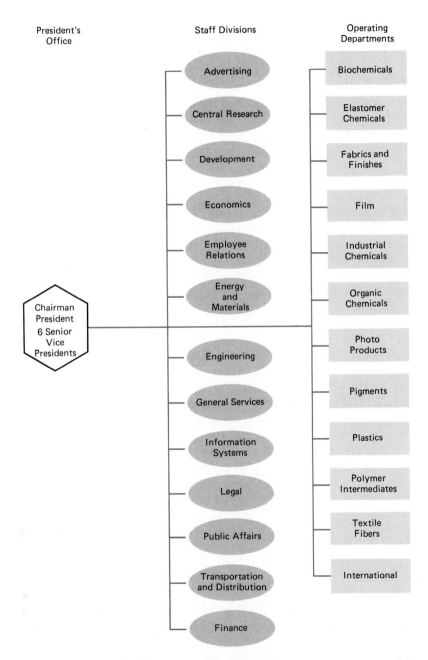

President's
Office

Staff Divisions

Operating
Departments

Chairman
President
6 Senior
Vice
Presidents

Advertising

Central Research

Development

Economics

Employee
Relations

Energy
and
Materials

Engineering

General Services

Information
Systems

Legal

Public Affairs

Transportation
and Distribution

Finance

Biochemicals

Elastomer
Chemicals

Fabrics and
Finishes

Film

Industrial
Chemicals

Organic
Chemicals

Photo
Products

Pigments

Plastics

Polymer
Intermediates

Textile
Fibers

International

Figure 10.4 Organization of a multibillion-dollar company. Each operating unit is a self-contained business with its own engineering, production, marketing, and finance activities. The staff divisions provide services to the departments and to the president's office.

Because business units established under profit decentralization are of a *manageable size,* fewer people have to exchange information, and they can communicate with one another swiftly and effectively. Thus, executives find it easier to comprehend the information that is funneled to them.

Situations requiring administrative action are more likely to receive *adequate attention* under profit decentralization. In a large-scale enterprise, it is all too easy to neglect a product or an operation that contributes only a minor part to the total sales volume. In a smaller business unit, however, such problems become relatively more important, and executives are much more likely to take the necessary corrective action.

The smaller size of the business units and the heightened ease of communication also lead to improved *coordination,* particularly in the critical areas of serving customers, matching production and sales, and keeping costs in line with income. Bureaucratic attitudes are less likely to interfere with voluntary cooperation.

By making both measurement and accountability more clear cut, profit decentralization promotes more effective *control.* The profit-and-loss statement of each business unit provides a significant measure of results, and there is less need to make arbitrary allocation of costs. Moreover, because a self-sufficient division is also semiautonomous, its manager can be held accountable for resulting profit or loss. If the results are poor, he can be required to take corrective action; if they are good, he can be, and often is, generously rewarded.

Limitations and Difficulties

If profit decentralization contributes all these impressive advantages, why are all large enterprises not organized in this fashion? Unfortunately, certain distinct limitations and problems are inherent in its use.

For one thing, not all companies can be *divided neatly* into self-contained business units. Technology may make it impossible for a large operation to be broken up into several smaller ones. A steel mill, for example, cannot be split down the middle. Or in operations such as wholesaling or retailing, which involve a large number of products, the sales volume of any one product may be insufficient to support the expense of a separate management and a staff of specialists. One of the limitations of profit decentralization, then, is that the operations of the company must lend themselves to being divided into self-sufficient units of manageable size.

A related problem springs from the auxiliary-service activities that the company must perform for the business units. Will a single, central *service unit,* such as purchasing or plant engineering, really be *responsive* to the needs of each of several business units? If so, what happens to their presumed autonomy and accountability for profits? These are not insurmountable problems, but they do emphasize that profit decentralization brings in its wake a series of potentially troublesome issues.

Although we have referred to this type of organization as profit decentralized, we must remember that profits, though important, may be an *inadequate measure* of the performance of a business unit, at least in the short run. A business unit may decide, with the full approval of top management, to spend money on advertising to improve its market position; for two or three years it may spend large sums developing a new product. In other words, the unit may be achieving its objectives even though it is showing a relatively small profit. Conversely, by keeping down expenses for nonrecurring or deferable items, a business-unit may make a good profit showing even though it is slipping in customer goodwill or development of potential executives. This means that the use of profits for purposes of control is valid only if it is interpreted with a full understanding of what is happening within the business.

Perhaps the greatest difficulty in the use of profit decentralization is to find executives with the *capacity and willingness* to work effectively within the system. The business-unit managers must be prepared to take the initiative on any matter that affects the long-run success of their units. They must be aware of the direct and indirect results of their own actions, instead of trying to rely on someone in the home office to keep them out of trouble. In other words, they must act as responsible stewards of the resources put under their direction.

Top administrative officials in the company, in turn, must accept their obligation to maintain a "hands-off" attitude toward the decentralized business. As the president of a successfully decentralized company put it, "This calls for confidence in the capabilities of other people, a belief in teaching rather than telling, patience while others are learning—perhaps through their own mistakes—and a willingness to let others stand out in the public eye."

And yet we must remember that many executives of business units have been trained to concentrate on a particular specialty rather than to take an overall view of an integrated business and that the top executives of many corporations have achieved their position through positive, aggressive action. This experience makes the behavior described in the two preceding paragraphs difficult to achieve in practice. The key managers in a company that adopts profit decentralization must have a realistic understanding of their new roles and must be flexible enough to adjust their behavior accordingly.

Restrictions on Autonomy

Clearly, there are many areas in which business units are *not* autonomous. Everyone agrees that corporate management should retain some influence over the separate businesses. In consultation with the business-unit managers, corporate management should (1) set business-unit strategy and annual goals, (2) establish the broad policies within which the units are to operate, (3) approve the selection of key executives within the unit, (4) approve major capital expenditures (which in effect means approving any major expansion), and (5) review any single transaction that might entail a major change in the profit or loss of the unit. In addition, the head-quarters office might want (6) to establish certain procedures for accounting, human resources, or purchasing to ensure consistent action throughout the corporation. Furthermore, corporate management can interpret all these limitations so broadly that it may retain the right to interfere with business-unit operations almost anywhere it wants to.

The manner in which these processes are performed can either support or vitiate the underlying concept of profit decentralization. Therefore, if a manager organizes along profit-decentralization lines, he must also plan, control, and lead in a manner compatible with profit decentralization.

CONCLUSION

In this chapter, we first discussed the process of delegating and then related this to the allocation of managerial work, especially its assignment to executives at various levels, from first-line supervisors to the president. Planning—that is, making decisions about actions to be taken—stands out as the crucial activity in managerial decentralization; once it has been decided who should do what planning, then other aspects of managerial work can be adjusted to fit into the pattern. Managers have to allocate planning work among their subordinates, and we have identified several factors that can help them design a pattern of decentralization suited to the particular conditions they face.

One special type of allocation, especially appealing to diversified companies, is profit decentralization. Analysis of profit decentralization highlights the intimate connection between the way a company is departmentalized and the forms of decentralization that are desirable. We need to consider, in the next chapter, how staff can be fitted into the total allocation of managerial work.

Impact on Productivity

There is a great deal of debate over how much decentralization will optimize productivity. One side stresses the potential efficiency of expert centralized planning and large-scale operations. The other side emphasizes local adaptability and high morale of self-directed workers.

In fact, the feasibility of decentralization depends substantially on (a) the technology being used for the activity, and (b) the type of employees at the various levels of the organization, and their desire to participate in decision making. As our discussion of degrees of decentralization indicated, some topics can be pushed down the hierarchy more readily than others. Productivity is strongly affected by the wisdom of the choice of what to centralize and what to decentralize in a specific setting.

1. What would be the advantages and disadvantages of making the business school (or department) of your university a semiautonomous division as described in the last section of this chapter?

2. According to centuries of tradition, the captain of an ocean ship has full authority to run his vessel as he sees fit while away from harbor. To a degree, similar authority is delegated to the captain of an airplane. Use the concepts of this chapter to recommend the degree of decentralization that you believe to be appropriate for the captain of a commercial passenger plane.

3. "We do a great deal of delegating in order to increase accountability for results, but we reserve the right to overrule lower levels of management on decisions in certain areas." Should these areas referred to by the senior vice-president of a small plumbing-supply company be spelled out in detail or just described in broad terms?

4. In delegating work, is it important to differentiate clearly between accountability for strategic versus tactical decisions? Can such distinctions be made? Should they be made?

5. In what ways will decisions on departmentation—particularly the choice between functional and com-pound groupings—affect decisions on how much and what kinds of duties to delegate?

6. The warehouse manager of a plumbing-supply company receives a phone call from a company salesperson requesting him to get a rush order out to an important customer. At 1 P.M., the warehouse manager assigns the job of preparing the shipment to three warehouse workers and stresses that they have to get the job done by 4 P.M. so that the shipment can get to the customer's plant an hour later. Although three hours is ample time to get the shipment ready, at 4 P.M. the three workers are not finished with their task. (a) Who is accountable if the order does not get to the customer by 5 P.M.? (b) Who had the obligation for getting the shipment loaded? (c) Discuss these forms of obligation in light of the authority that was granted. (d) How might better delegation have been achieved in this situation? (e) If three hours had not been ample time, how would this affect your answers to (a) through (d)?

7. "Phyllis Mason isn't my boss, but she is clearly the brightest, most experienced person in our laboratory. My boss is a great scientist, but a poor manager. Therefore, most of the people in the group look to Phyllis for direction." Comment on the benefits and drawbacks implied by this statement.

Chandler, A. D., *Strategy and Structure.* Cambridge: The M.I.T. Press, 1962. Traces the development of the decentralized, multidivision structure in American industry.

Drucker, P. F., *Management: Tasks, Responsibilities, Practice.* New York: Harper & Row, 1972, Chs. 41–48. Insightful discussion of the relationship between decentralization and organizational effectiveness.

Levinson, R. E., "Why Decentralize," *Management Review,* Oct. 1985. A business executive urges profit decentralization to rekindle innovative spirit.

Pascale, R. T. and A. G. Athos, *The Art of Japanese Management.* New York: Simon & Schuster, 1981. Contrasts the centralized direction of ITT by Harold Geneen with the much looser guidance of Matsushita Electric Co. by its founder.

Porter, M. E., *Competitive Strategy.* New York: The Free Press, 1980. An excellent guide to strategy development and implementation, with strong sections on issues of centralization and decentralization.

Ohmae, K., *The Mind of the Strategist.* New York: McGraw-Hill, 1982. Excellent insight into the strategic methods used by Japanese organizations and their leaders.

Vancil, R. F., *Decentralization: Managerial Ambiguity by Design.* New York: Financial Executives Research Foundation, 1979. Contemporary treatment of the managerial tradeoffs associated with decentralized organizations.

MANAGEMENT IN-ACTION CASE 10
The General Motors Reorganization

When Roger B. Smith took over as chairman of General Motors in 1981, he faced the unenviable task of pulling GM out of the worst doldrums in its oft-illustrious history. Ambushed by soaring oil prices, the invasion of fuel-efficient Japanese compacts, and costly engineering changes forced by a federal crackdown on safety and automotive emissions, GM in 1980 had suffered a $760 million loss, its first loss in sixty years.

Insiders put much of the blame on the company's management system. The decentralized management model created by the late Chairman Alfred P. Sloan Jr. in the 1920s had been bastardized to the point where GM's five operating divisions had become "mere instruments of corporate headquarters," according to author Cary Reich in his April 1985 profile of Smith in *The New York Times Magazine*.

Smith, an impatient man who had risen through GM's financial ranks in a 30-year career, moved quickly to rectify the situation. A task force was assembled and a consulting firm hired for a two-year examination of the corporation and the way it was run. Feedback from more than 500 executives indicated that GM had become a risk-averse company in which decision making was a cumbersome, time-consuming process.

GM adopted a radical solution in January 1984. The company's five car divisions and its Canadian car operations were reorganized into two groups: the Buick-Oldsmobile-Cadillac division, given responsibility for GM's higher-priced cars; and the Chevrolet-Pontiac-GM of Canada group, which oversaw GM's lower-priced cars and its Canadian operations.

The intent was to decentralize to the group level, but unite similar divisions there, and to increase decision-making power at every level of management and encourage risk-taking. The reorganization also enabled top management to more easily assess credit or blame for particular decisions, and it moved decision making into lower ranks that previously had not enjoyed such leeway.

Such "participative management," as the program was dubbed, allowed workers a greater role in making important decisions. Lloyd E. Reuss, first head of the Chevrolet-Pontiac-GM Canada group, called it "an important motivator in bringing out new ideas in people."

Question

In light of the discussion in this chapter, what benefits do you think will accrue to General Motors as a result of its 1984 reorganization?

For more information, see *The New York Times Magazine*, April 1985.

For practice in applying concepts covered in this chapter to managerial situations, see the following managerial decision cases. The case questions particularly relevant to this chapter are listed by number after each case name.

Fyler International (p. 68) 11
Dayton Metal Works (p. 198) 1, 9
Clifford Nelson (p. 308) 8,10
Peter Jeffries (p. 428) 8, 9
Unisa Sound (p. 530) 7
Norman Manufacturing Company (p. 538) 8

11

Staff-Line Roles: Matrix Management

LEARNING OBJECTIVES

After completing this chapter, you should be able to

1. Explain the difference between staff and line or operating jobs.
2. Discuss some of the potential difficulties and conflicts that can arise between staff and operating people.
3. Understand the rationale for having staff positions in a large organization.
4. Be able to discuss the four major problem areas in using staff members.
5. Explain the benefits of a matrix organizational structure and how such a structure works.

Once a manager decides how major departments are to be structured and what degree of centralization-decentralization will exist within them, it is time to consider staff units. The key questions are

1. What functions are highly specialized or take on organization-wide implications and need to be controlled across departments as a result?
2. Where should these functional experts be placed within an organizational structure?

Staff as Critical Elements

Especially in an increasingly complex society, in which change comes rapidly and fields become progressively more specialized, an executive's key staff members are critical elements in helping managers cope with their external environment. As such, staff members become people with whom the total management load can be shared—a device that supplements decentralization.

The key element within organizations that have people working in both staff and line, or operating, functions is how those two sometimes conflicting roles are connected within the organizational structure. One alternative that has been successfully used by a number of corporations—Corning Glass, General Motors Corporation, and Exxon, to name a few—is *matrix management,* a complex system under which managers report to both line officers, who oversee their specialized business, and staff executives, who oversee specific functions such as finance, human resources, and legal affairs.

Before we discuss the structural link between line and staff, it is important to get a clear picture of staff jobs and how they operate.

Definition of staff.   Staff work is managerial work that an executive assigns to someone outside the executive chain of command. If an executive wants to relieve himself of an administrative burden, it is sometimes preferable to assign the work to a staff assistant instead of delegating it to subordinates who also would be accountable for operations.

A president or head of a large department might use several staff people for different phases of a total management task. Some staff assistants might even have several subordinates of their own who form a staff department. But whatever the number and size of staff sections, their aim remains the same: to help an executive manage.

Because good staff assistants increase the workload that an executive can handle, the use of staff is one factor influencing the number of direct line subordinates that the executive can supervise effectively. This question is impossible to answer accurately. As Figure 11-1 suggests, availability of staff help is only one of four critical elements that roughly determine what an optimum span of supervision should be. The other key

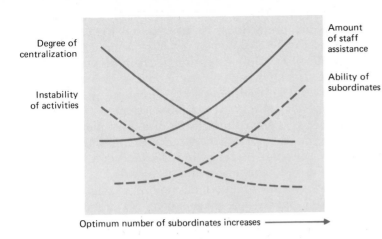

Degree of
centralization

Instability
of activities

Amount
of staff
assistance

Ability of
subordinates

Optimum number of subordinates increases ⟶

Figure 11.1 The optimum span of
supervision is not fixed. Rather, it
depends on several variables that
should be weighed in each situation.

elements are degree of centralization, instability of business activities, and
the abilities of the individuals being supervised. Clearly, then, using staff
in a management structure is closely entwined with the other features of
organization design. It is like increasing the horsepower of an automobile
engine: Some added horsepower will help, whereas too much will throw
the whole machine out of balance.

Examples of staff.   The concept of staff comes from the military, which
is the birthplace of many organizational models. But the business world
uses the term *staff* more loosely than does the military.[1] Practices
vary widely from company to company and from job to job, with the result
that there often is widespread confusion about what a staff person is supposed to do. Because there is no single pattern, managers must design each
staff position individually, as they do other jobs, deciding which activities
they can advantageously assign to each position.

    At the worst, General Archer H. Lerch contended, studies and other
projects undertaken by staff people accomplish two things:

1. They protect the chief from half-baked ideas, voluminous memoranda, and immature oral presentations.
2. Staff officers with real ideas to sell can more easily find a market for
   their ideas.

Assigning Staff Duties

In deciding which activities to assign to staff members, three examples
will indicate the range of possibilities:

Specialized staff.   Market research illustrates *specialized* staff work.
A typical market-research unit gathers a wide variety of information

[1]J.D. Hittle, *The Military Staff: Its History and Development* (Harrisburg: Stackpole Books,
1961).

ating executives advice on marketing problems. For example, market researchers can suggest sales projections to use in setting quotas for individual salespeople, and can test customer response to product change. Operating executives do not have time to gather such information themselves, and they hesitate to ask their sales force to do the work for several reasons: specialized skills are required, objectivity is essential, and salespeople should spend their time getting orders from customers.

An industrial engineer is a good illustration of a staff person in the production area. Typically he not only gathers information but also goes further than the market researcher in preparing specific plans. Layout of plant equipment, production methods, operating standards based on time studies, incentive plans, systems for production scheduling, quality-control techniques, preventive maintenance—these are among the problems an industrial engineer often tackles. Solution of such problems requires concentrated attention and may involve more technical knowledge than a production manager has.

General staff.   Not all staff people concentrate on a specific type of work. Managers sometimes want assistants to whom they can turn over a wide variety of problems. The assistant's duties can vary from functioning as a first-class secretary to serving as an alter ego to the boss in delicate negotiations. The staff person with such unspecified duties is often called "assistant to the _____."

On various days, an assistant to the president might gather information on the national economic outlook, edit a statement for the president to make before a Congressional committee, investigate a complaint about company service, or meet with a group of long-service employees who urge the company to advance the optional retirement age to seventy-five.

Corporate services.   Very large companies sometimes attach to the central headquarters staff units that work primarily as consultants to operating divisions.[2] In the General Electric company, for instance, one corporate "service" unit focuses on community relations, another on operations research, and so on. Each "service" is charged with anticipating external developments, advancing the state of the art in its particular field, organizing training courses to pass these advanced techniques on to executives and staff people in the business units, and being available as consultants on the invitation of the business units. Service is stressed. And to encourage operating people to use this service, senior executives at General Electric do *not* use these units for evaluation and control.

Some corporations have a few staff people who concentrate on strategic planning. Typically, this staff makes studies in areas outside the domains of existing business units for the purpose of locating areas or even

[2]B. Yavitz and W. H. Newman, "Corporate Input Strategy," in *Strategy in Action* (New York: Free Press, 1982), Ch. 4.

companies that are attractive expansion possibilities. A more controversial and less common assignment is independent evaluation of strategies recommended by existing business units. A third potential duty of a strategic-planning staff is to devise planning procedures to be used throughout the corporation, and to expedite the flow of paperwork and information that aids strategic decisions. However, the main responsibility for strategic planning remains with line executives; staff merely helps.

In these examples of staff and in the many others that will appear in this book, we find a delegation of managerial work to people who do not supervise operations. These delegations, like all delegations, carry with them duties, authority, and obligation. But the duties do not entail direct supervision over executives or operators.

When to Use Staff

Since staff complicates an organization, we should examine carefully the need for staff assistants. Generally speaking, managers can justify assigning duties to staff when they are overburdened or lack a necessary technical skill. Managers may hesitate to delegate more work to operating subordinates for any of the following reasons:

1. *Attention: Operating subordinates would not give an activity adequate attention.* For instance, a vice-president of human resources may be appointed if department managers are skeptical of modern techniques and central management fears they will slight this activity.
2. *Expertness: The work requires an expert.* Most managers lack knowledge of real estate, taxation, and the law, for instance, so staff assistants may be provided in these areas.
3. *Coordination: The company needs coordinated and consistent action among several operating units.* The need for consistency in fair-employment practices or in pricing may prompt a staff appointment. Or, coordination of a national advertising campaign with local sales promotions may need concentrated attention.
4. *Control: The manager wants help in controlling the operating departments.* Keeping track of local operations is especially difficult when activities are dispersed in many geographical locations.
5. *Analysis: The manager seeks aid in analyzing problems.* Managers may become so busy with pressing short-run problems that they need assistants who can help them think through basic questions.

Scope of Staff Work

The work of staff people can be defined in terms of both the subjects or problems they cover and what they do about them. Unless a staff person, his boss, and everyone he works with understands the scope of his work, his efforts may cause more trouble than help. It is not enough, for example, to say that a human resources director should handle staff services in the field of personnel relations. Rather it is more constructive to list the types of problems in the field and then decide how far we expect a staff person to go in dealing with them. Figure 11.2 indicates this general approach.

This chart reveals that the role of a human resources director may differ in various areas. In dealing with unions, for example, they are likely to serve principally as advisers. On the other hand, no appointment to

Figure 11.2   Chart for analyzing the duties of a human resources director.

Activities	Subjects							
	Recruiting	Selecting Employees	Training	Com-pensation	Benefit Plans	Health and Recreation	Union Relations	Employee Records
1. OPERATING WORK								
Supervises service operations	■				■	■		■
2. STAFF WORK								
Influences actions outside own department; to do so, he:								
A. Advises boss								
1. Identifies areas that need improvement				■			■	
2. Finds likely solutions				■			■	
3. Gathers and analyzes data bearing on choice of solution				■				
4. Gets concurrence or objections of people affected				■			■	
5. Recommends tentative solution			■	■			■	
B. Advises associates (mostly operating executives under his boss)								
1. Identifies areas that need improvement			■				■	
2. Finds likely solutions		■	■				■	
3. Gathers and analyzes data bearing on choice of solution		■	■				■	
4. Gets concurrence or objections of people affected			■				■	
5. Recommends tentative solution		■	■				■	
C. Prepares documents putting plans into effect		■		■			■	
D. Interprets and sells established plans								
E. Reports compliance to associates			■	■				
F. Reports on compliance to boss			■					
G. Concurs on specific acts		■		■				
H. Sets policies and systems			■					

vacancies can be made without the concurrence of the human resources director.

The chart also suggests that for some activities, such as recruiting employees, handling pension plans, or sponsoring company athletic teams, a firm may grant its human resources director operating authority; in these areas he ceases to be staff and becomes a supervisor of auxiliary services.

Each check mark on a chart such as Figure 11.2 represents careful thought about the functions of a particular staff person in a specific company. The chart is, of course, only a summary. For many duties under the heading of "Subjects," we must think through several subtopics. "Training," for instance, includes, by implication, considerations of what should be done for executive personnel, orientation of new employees, training on the job, personal-development plans, and so forth. All this detail cannot be shown on a single chart, but the same kind of analysis applies to each subdivision.

The same approach should be followed in determining the duties of each staff position. The principal task of market researchers is to gather and analyze data for their bosses and other operating executives—A.3 and B.3 on the chart. The industrial engineer, on the other hand, is likely to undertake all duties listed under A to F on the chart. Internal auditors are predominantly concerned simply with reporting compliance to their associates and their bosses—items E and F on the chart. Analyzing duties in this manner, goes a long way toward eliminating misunderstandings about the use of staff.

Although there is room for argument about some details of this proposal, such as the heavy use of written documents and the infrequency of personal discussions between a staff person and the boss, the central theme has much to recommend it. All too often, a staff person is willing to toss in ideas or information without thinking a matter through to a practical conclusion.

As useful as completed staff work may be, it is not ideal for all situations. It is expensive in terms of both the quality and the number of staff people needed. An additional expense is the interference with busy supervisors and operators involved in preparing a completed recommendation. Not many management posts warrant such extensive assistance.

Still another drawback in some companies is the tendency for a strong staff to undermine decentralization.[3] Staff people may initially emphasize help to managers in lower echelons, but if cooperation is not immediately forthcoming, they then turn to completed staff work and urge the big boss to issue an order. If the boss does so, of course, the center of decision making moves higher in the chain of command.

---

[3]V. Sathe, *Controller Involvement in Management* (Englewood Cliffs, N.J.: Prentice-Hall, 1982).

RELATIONSHIPS BETWEEN STAFF AND MANAGERS

Normal Staff Relationships

The relationship between a staff member and the operating executive with whom he works depends in part on the staff duties, as discussed on the preceding pages. A person who only gathers facts or only checks on performance, for instance, will have relations with his superior that differ from those of an assistant who has concurring authority. Nevertheless, there are several features that characterize almost all successful staff relationships.

1. A staff person is primarily a representative of her boss. She does things that the boss would do if he had the necessary time and ability. She is an extension of the boss's personality—advising, investigating, imagining, encouraging, following up on matters in his particular sphere. A staff person's position gives her stature and imposes an obligation *not to misrepresent* the boss. If occasionally she declares her own views, which may be at variance with those of her boss, she should be careful to make the distinction clear, for it is normally presumed that a staff representative is sufficiently close to her boss to be able to reflect accurately the thinking of the superior. Let us note in passing that bosses have an obligation to spend enough time with each of their staff assistants so that they can, in fact, establish a consistent point of view.

2. A staff person must *rely largely on persuasion* to get ideas put into effect. Lacking the power of command, she must build confidence in her opinions and must be sufficiently sensitive to the problems of those she would influence to win their acceptance of proposals. The staff person who cannot accomplish all, or at least most of, the things she wants done by winning voluntary cooperation had better look for another job.

3. A staff person must be prepared to *submerge her own personality* and her own desire for glory. She must be an ardent teamworker, recognizing that her boss or some other operating executive will get credit for carrying the ball. To achieve improved results, she must be prepared to see others receive recognition for ideas that she may have subtly planted several months earlier.

These three characteristics of staff work, when consistently maintained, go far in overcoming the inevitable friction that arises when a third party is interposed in what is otherwise a close relationship between a line supervisor and subordinate.

We usually speak as though staff people performed their jobs by themselves. In larger companies, though, they may in fact have several assistants. Multiplication of people does not, however, change the relationship between staff and operating executives. *Within* a staff unit, there are

the usual subordinate-boss, or "line," relationships. Just as any boss delegates—setting up duties, authority, and obligation—so the head of a staff
unit builds a series of line relationships between himself and others within
his group. We call these people "staff" because of their work, not because
they are in any way absolved from the customary subordinate-boss relationship.

Staff Influence Within the Chain of Command

A staff person charged with bringing about improvements in a particular
area has two courses of action open to him: He may make a recommendation to an operating executive who is directly or indirectly his boss and
then rely on the executive to issue the necessary orders to put the plan
into effect, *or* he may try to secure voluntary acceptance of his ideas without the support of formal orders transmitted down the chain of command.
The second, or voluntary approach is common, because a top operating executive is either too busy to bother with an issue, or he does not want to
impose his will on trusted associates unless absolutely necessary, because
he runs the risk of upsetting a pattern of decentralization.

In such circumstances, how does a staff person accomplish a mission?
Let us say a senior operating executive has delegated a task to his West
Coast superintendent; he has assigned duties and granted authority, and
the superintendent has a sense of obligation to him. Because of the direct
relationship with the senior executive, the superintendent is free (except
as noted below) to accept or reject the counsel of a staff person. Why, then,
can a staff person expect to exert any significant influence?

For one reason, people are inclined to accept the advice of a staff person because they regard him as a *technical expert*. Engineer, statistician,
repair mechanic, or lawyer—each has a specialized field in which his word
is likely to be taken as authoritative. Such expertise can lead to relationships such as the one shown in Figure 11.3.

For a second reason, when a staff person has an impressive title, reports high up in the organization hierarchy, and has an office that exhibits
the symbols of importance, he enjoys exalted *status*. His views will be
taken seriously by reason of his status alone.

Skill in presenting ideas, as we mentioned earlier, is still another reason why staff people are likely to be influential.

A perhaps more subtle source of influence is *potential backing* by a
senior operating executive. If people down the line believe that advice they
have rejected is bound to return as a command, they often conclude that it
is wiser to take the advice in the first place. Conversely, a staff person
soon learns when and how far he can push a particular point.

Finally, if a staff person's views may significantly *influence* an employee's salary increases or promotions, that employee will probably accord
the staff person's recommendations more than just polite acknowledgment.
This inclination is especially strong for employees away from the seat of a
company—for example, a branch human resources officer or a branch ac-

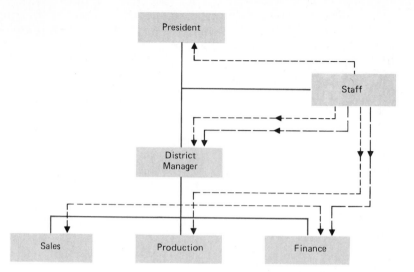

Figure 11.3 Typical relationships of central finance staff with managers in the regular line of command. The smaller dotted line indicates advice and assistance. The larger dashed line indicates functional authority.

countant who aspires to transfer within her functional field, perhaps to the home office.

In summary, then, even though staff people may have no command authority whatsoever, they may still get their recommendations accepted if they are intelligent, persuasive, impressive, and influential. Obviously, the potency of influence depends on each individual and each situation.

Compulsory Staff Consultation

Despite all the influence they can muster, staff people may find themselves on the sidelines watching the real action taking place without their participation. In a healthy organization, operating executives are strongminded, vigorous individuals. Not infrequently, such executives welcome staff assistance only on highly technical matters or when it suits their convenience. To counteract this tendency, some companies follow a practice of compulsory staff consultation. Under this arrangement, a staff person *must* be consulted before action is taken. For example, department heads cannot confront human resources managers with salary increases already promised or promotions already made; they must instead consult with them before they act. In other cases, a lawyer must have a chance to read a contract before a vice-president signs it. Under this plan, an operating executive is not blocked from proceeding as he thinks best, but he is required to stop and listen to advice from another point of view.

Compulsory consultation supplements a more general requirement for successful staff work—the requirement that a staff should have access to any information that relates to its field of interest. No mere directive, of course, can ensure that staff people will gain access to underlying motives that are often important for complete understanding of a problem; they can obtain such information only when they share with others mutual respect and confidence. Nevertheless, it is helpful for management to make clear to employees that they are to keep the staff fully informed.

A related practice that some firms follow is to require each staff unit to make a semiannual or annual report on any weak spots it has uncovered in its field. This requirement may put a staff person in the delicate position of revealing a weakness that an operating executive at a low level wants to conceal from senior administrators. The staff person finds himself playing detective and risks not being welcomed back later. On the other hand, the inevitability of the report may prod the operating executive into taking corrective measures, presumably with the help of staff, so that the latter can mention constructive steps along with unfavorable conditions. Fundamentally, what each company needs is a climate that nourishes bold statements of fact to anyone concerned, coupled with sympathetic and constructive efforts to help improve deteriorated conditions. Covering up facts because of fear of criticism is not healthy. Managers and staff people can count on a free flow of pertinent information on troublesome situations only if operating personnel are confident that they will receive constructive help in return.

Concurring Authority

Under some circumstances, a manager may desire to further strengthen the hand of his staff. If control over certain operations is very important, staff may be granted concurring authority so that no action can be taken until a designated staff person agrees to it.[4] Such concurring authority is probably most familiar in quality control, where an inspector usually must pass on raw materials or semifinished parts before they move to the next stage of production. Other examples include required legal approval before signing a contract, or the human resources manager's approval before making a promotion.

Whenever concurring authority is granted to staff, it is clear that a senior administrator wants to ensure that the staff viewpoint is incorporated into operating decisions. It is a "safe" arrangement, because operating executives cannot take heedless action. On the other hand, it slows down action, for if the staff and operating people do not agree, someone must appeal up the administrative line, perhaps even to a senior executive who is boss of all operations and staff. In addition, although management can hold both a staff and an operating person accountable for any actions they *do* take, both have plenty of opportunity for passing the buck when they do *not* take action.

These considerations suggest concurring authority should be granted only when the point of view represented by a staff person is particularly important, and when possible delay in action, while agreement is being ironed out, will not be serious.

Even when these conditions are met, it is important that we carefully define the grounds on which a staff may withhold its approval of a pro-

---

[4]For an innovative use of concurrent authority in long-range planning, see E. K. Warren, *Long Range Planning: The Executive Viewpoint* (Englewood Cliffs, N.J.: Prentice-Hall, 1966).

posal. For instance, it is one thing for a controller to block a capital expenditure because of lack of funds, and quite another if she blocks it because of her personal disapproval of a plan. An inspector may delay a shipment of goods because they do not come up to standard, but his company should not permit him to take over the engineer's function of deciding how a product should be redesigned. Dynamic action would be difficult under such a system.

Functional Authority

The most extreme formal technique for extending staff influence is the granting of functional authority. This means that a staff person can give direct orders to operating personnel in his own name instead of making recommendations to his boss or to other operating executives. His instructions then have the same force as those that come down the chain of command. As in direct-line relationships, a staff person probably consults with whomever he instructs, and the person receiving the instructions may point out difficulties in execution to the staff and to the line boss. But until orders are rescinded or revised, the company expects the worker to carry them out.

Naturally, a staff is given functional authority only over those areas in which its technical competence is recognized and its opinion would probably be accepted anyway. Thus, a chief accountant may have functional authority over accounting forms and systems, a medical officer over physical examinations, and a legal counsel over responses to any legal suits against the company. On such matters, the word of staff officers will be followed in at least 99 percent of the cases; it is simpler to have it clearly understood that their word is final.

The trouble with functional authority is that it is tempting in its apparent simplicity. For example, it is too easy merely to say that a human resources director will have functional authority over all personnel matters, a sales promotion director over sales promotion activities, and a controller over all expenses. Such sweeping assignments can wreak havoc in an organization. For if the human resources director can issue instructions that cover the selection, training, and motivation of all employees, he is virtually in a position to dominate all operations. And since expenses are fundamental to nearly every company decision, the controller with functional authority over such matters becomes tantamount to a general manager. In addition, wide use of functional authority may burden operating managers with conflicting orders; it tends to undermine the status of supervisors, and it complicates accountability. These difficulties arise from the indiscriminate use of a delicate arrangement.

What, then, are the circumstances in which a staff person may use functional authority? The following three conditions are desirable, and at least two should always be present before granting a staff person such authority:

1. *Minor Coverage: Only a minor aspect of the total operating job is covered.* Accounting forms and Blue Cross contracts, for instance, are only incidental to most operating jobs. Although these matters should receive the thoughtful attention of somebody, the plans adopted do not substantially affect the bulk of operations.

2. *Specialization: Technical or specialized knowledge of a type not possessed by operating executives is needed.* If a sales manager or a production superintendent is going to accept the advice of, say, a tax expert or a medical director anyway, decision making can be simplified by granting functional authority to such specialists.

3. *Uniformity: Uniformity, or at least consistency, of action in several operating units is essential.* For instance, pension rights of employees who are transferred among several divisions of a company should be treated consistently, as should credit terms extended to customers. A staff unit with functional authority is more likely to deal consistently with such matters than would divisions acting separately.

A Composite Pattern

Of the various means for strengthening the influence of staff, functional authority moves farthest from the purely assisting and counseling relationship first described. Compulsory consultation and concurring authority are intermediate positions. For reasons already noted, we should move cautiously from establishing an easy, simply helpful relationship toward insisting that a staff person must be heeded. Briefly stated, as staff is made more powerful, its scope should be confined.

In practice, a different kind of relationship is often provided for different duties of a single position. Company attorneys, for instance, might cover the whole range. On most matters they just *give advice,* but in one or two areas, *consultation* is compulsory; for a limited group of decisions, their *concurrence* is required; and possibly over a few technical matters they have *functional authority.* But such a composite set of relationships is apt to be confusing. The least trouble results when staff people are kept in *advisory roles.*[5]

PROBLEMS IN USING STAFF

Throughout this discussion, many difficulties that can arise in connection with staff have been suggested. Four common areas of trouble should be pointed out to those who will either use staff or serve in staff positions.

[5]A. C. Hax and N. S. Majluf, "Organization Design: A Case Study on Matching Strategy and Structure," *Journal of Business Strategy,* Fall 1983.

Vague Definition of Duties and Authority

Friction is common between operating executives and staff people, simply because the role of staff is misunderstood.[6] The word *staff* provides no formula for resolving questions of what the duties should be. Some people within an enterprise may assume that a staff person is merely a fact-gatherer or, at most, an adviser to the boss. A boss may want a staff assistant to make suggestions to people throughout the organization; and the staff person himself may be so zealous about his areas that he believes he should control as well as plan. With three such disparate views in competition, sooner or later a clash and perhaps hard feelings can be expected.

A common source of confusion is strengthening the influence of staff to meet a specific problem—through either required consultation, concurring authority, or functional authority—but failure to delineate the scope of this additional authority.[7] For instance, during an energy shortage, the chief engineer may be given "concurring authority over new uses of power." Trouble will arise unless everyone concerned recognizes that the new authority extends only to adding power-consuming equipment.

What is needed to overcome these problems is mutual understanding by all principal parties of the duties and authority of each staff person and, even more importantly, a working relationship built out of experience that translates the general understanding into smooth work habits and attitudes.

Scarcity of Good Staff

All too often, a staff failure can be traced back to a selection of the wrong people for staff positions. Staff people need both competence in their specialties and skill in staff work. Without technical competence, of course, they are hardly worth the nuisance they are to other executives. But technical competence alone is not enough. They must be affable, sensitive, discreet, and honest so that they may earn the confidence of other people; they must be articulate and persuasive so that they may win genuine acceptance of their proposals; they must be patient but persistent (rather than resort to commands) in their efforts to get results; they must find satisfaction in good team results rather than in personal glory; they must have a high sense of loyalty to the boss and of obligation to duty, even in the face of the frustration of highly circumscribed authority. Unfortunately, people with this combination of abilities and attitudes coupled with technical competence are sometimes hard to find.

Staff jobs are sometimes used as training posts for future operating executives, but also occasionally as dumping grounds or pastures for unwanted operating executives. If such executives are misfits in staff posi-

[6]P. Browne and R.T. Golembieski, "The Line-Staff Concepts Revisited: An Empirical Study of Organizational Images," *Academy of Management Journal*, Sept. 1974.

[7]B. Yavitz and W.H. Newman, "Resource Allocation: Power of the Purse Strings," in *Strategy in Action* (New York: Free Press,1982).

tions, the company creates a new problem in trying to solve an old one. Staff work, by its very nature, creates delicate relationships, and if a company has only unqualified people available, it had better sharply curtail staff jobs in scope or eliminate them entirely.

Mixing Staff and Operating Duties

It is not always practical to completely separate staff duties and operating duties into different jobs. For example, a controller usually directly supervises corporate accounting and also has staff duties in connection with budgets and analysis of expenses of other departments.

Small companies that can afford only a limited number of executives may ask a single individual to fill two positions. For instance, a sales promotion manager may also supervise selling in one district. Or a company with one large plant and two or three small assembly plants may have its production superintendent run the main plant and also maintain an undefined staff relationship with the assembly plants.

Still a third type of mixture of staff and operating duties—one found in both large and small companies—is to have senior operating executives serve as staff to the president on companywide problems. A large operating department may follow a comparable arrangement by having key executives wear two hats: one when they run their own divisions and another when they act as advisers on whatever problems face the whole department.

Theoretically, such a combination of duties should cause no difficulty as long as the executive and the people with whom she works understand which role she is playing at any one time. The practical difficulty is that this distinction is hard to maintain. The executive herself may be unable to shift gears from being a hard-driving operating executive to being a reflective staff counselor. Even when it is clear in her own mind, she may fail to tell others which role she is playing. When this difficulty is compounded by failure to clearly define duties and authority in each kind of work, the result is a "staff" that has a vague assignment to dabble in other people's problems.

The remedy lies in real understanding of what staff work is, agreement of what each person should do, and care in assigning individuals who are both technically and temperamentally qualified.

Disregard of Staff by the Boss

A fourth source of staff difficulties may be the very manager who has created staff positions in the first place. He undoubtedly finds his total administrative burdens more than he himself can carry and sets up one or more staff positions to relieve him of part of the load. But if he falsely assumes that he has solved his difficulties and can forget about them, he is certainly sowing seeds of future woe.

A boss must maintain close enough and frequent enough contact with a staff person to enable the latter to serve effectively as an extension of the eyes, ears, and mind of the superior. It is by no means necessary for a specialized staff person to see the boss daily. What is essential is that the two maintain sufficient contact to ensure their general accord on approaches and values.

Even more devastating to confidence than lack of contact is the willingness of some executives to make decisions in an area assigned to a staff person without ever consulting him. Suppose a senior executive specifically charges his budget director with preparing capital-expenditure budgets. But later, when an operating subordinate presses him, the senior executive approves a large expenditure without first talking to the budget director. The next time the operating executive needs capital, he will probably again bypass the budget director and go directly to the senior executive. The budget director will soon be a useless adjunct.

In contrast, the budget director will have greater status if the senior executive insists that his operating executives talk through all matters of capital expenditure with the budget director before bringing any request to him. The operating people will soon learn that to get approval for capital expenditures, they must work with the budget director. In short, when an executive creates a staff position, he must be prepared to discipline *himself* to use the staff if he expects others to do so.

MATRIX ORGANIZATIONAL STRUCTURE

One way an executive can create linkages between line managers and staff experts is through a design known as *matrix organizational structure*. While the matrix concept caught popular attention as an aid to landing a man on the moon, it has many other applications, including the dovetailing of staff expertise with delivery of complex products or services.[8]

Matrix organization basically gives an operating manager two bosses. One boss deals with mobilizing resources, techniques of production, and other aspects of creating the product (or service). The other boss is concerned with producing an output that pleases the customer—the right performance characteristics, quality, delivery time, and so on. To avoid too much or too little attention to either the input side or the output side, the two bosses negotiate do-able instructions for the operating managers (Figure 11.4). Whether the task is building a space shuttle or delivering an advertising program for a new soft drink, such integration of inputs and outputs is a complex task.

In most matrix organizations the inputs come from (1) functional operating departments, such as engineering, production, and purchasing, and (2) staff services, such as human resources, research, contract administration, and specialized technical experts. Thus, staff people get drawn into the field of action because they have vital contributions to make to the

[8]A.R. Janger, *Matrix Organization of Complex Business* (New York: Elsevier North-Holland, 1983).

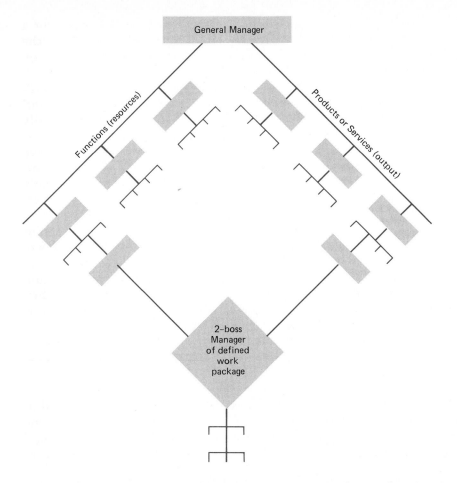

Figure 11.4 Example
of a matrix design.
From S. Davis &
P. Lawrence, *Matrix*, p. 22,
Fig. 2-1. © 1977 Addison-
Wesley Publishing Co., Inc.,
Reading, MA. Reprinted with
permission.

integrated program. The matrix structure can facilitate this integration much more effectively than more traditional organizational structures.

Need for Coordinated, Focused Action

A drawback of the typical organization with its functional departments is that unusual, complex projects often get shunted about, progress slowly, and are the cause of endless meetings of key departmental executives. The more innovative and complicated the project, the more likely is fumbling to occur.

Matrix organization strives to (1) ensure the coordinated, focused attention that such projects require and (2) retain the benefits of specialized expertise and capabilities that only functional departments and staff units can provide. For example, the production of reactors for nuclear power plants calls for unusual engineering, materials and parts with heat-resistance far beyond any previously fabricated, scientific knowledge concerning reactor design, a special and very large assembly operation, and a whole array of new inspection techniques. Production is complicated by high uncertainty about how to achieve required quality and safety margins, by a desire to keep costs low enough to allow nuclear power to compete with coal- and oil-generating stations, and by the pressure to complete such units in time to overcome national electric-power shortages.

Companies making nuclear reactors do have staff units that are expert in science, engineering, purchasing, fabrication, and inspection, but each of these departments has twenty to a hundred different orders to work on at one time. Also, they do not have standard answers for dealing with nuclear reactors, and do not know what related decisions other departments may make for a specific order. Many conferences within and between departments become necessary. Disagreement on design or manufacture is likely to arise. Production falls behind schedule, and costs rise. To overcome these typical difficulties on an important piece of business, some mechanism is needed to channel part of the company's store of talent into the specific project and to ensure open communications on interrelated issues and prompt agreement on action to be taken.

This kind of situation is not peculiar to heavy-equipment manufacturers. An advertising agency, to pick an example far removed from physical hardware, is in the same predicament. It has departments staffed with experts in market research, copywriting, art work, television production, media selection, and other functions—all useful to various clients, whose accounts are managed by line salespeople known as account executives. Client A wants a specific advertising mission accomplished, one suited to its particular situation. The organization problem is how to draw on the outstanding capabilities of the expert departments and staff units and at the same time get an imaginative, tailored program for Client A when they need it. Comparable situations in management-consulting firms and in large building-construction firms are easy to visualize as well.

Matrix as problem-solver.   The matrix-organization answer to the problems just posed is to appoint a project manager for each clear-cut mission and then to assign talent from the functional departments and staff units as needed.[9] The project managers operate like line managers who are running a business, line account executives in an advertising agency, or building specialists overseeing a nuclear reactor construction project. They bring in staff or functional specialists as they are needed. And the specialists are linked to both line project managers and their expert departments, as shown in Figure 11.5, which indicates the working arrangement for a nuclear-reactor builder.

A matrix relationship can last a few weeks or several years, depending on the duration of the specific project for which an expert's special skill may be needed. Such relationships can even be relatively permanent, as in the case of a General Motors public-relations staff member who is functionally linked to the corporate public-relations staff, but simultaneously

---

[9]I.C. MacMillan and P.E. Jones, "Designing Organizations to Compete," *Journal of Business Strategy,* Spring 1984.

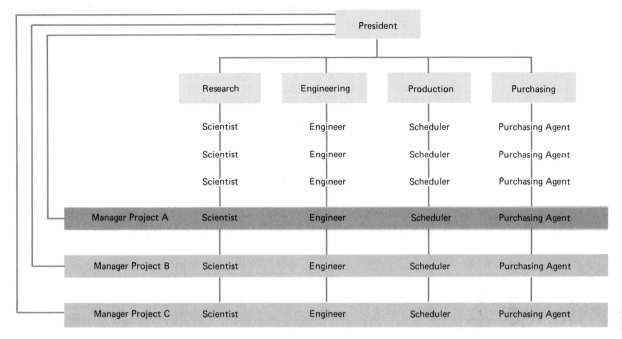

Figure 11.5 Matrix organization. The project managers are bosses for their projects borrowing the talent they need temporarily from the functional departments. The heads of functional departments develop capable people—and perhaps other services—but do not supervise them while they are assigned to the project team.

serves as the public-relations adviser to the general manager of a GM division, such as Cadillac. This functional expert maintains an operating responsibility to the Cadillac general manager, but also retains a functional linkage to the corporate vice-president in charge of overall public-relations activities.

During the time a functional or staff specialist is working on a job, he looks to the project manager for direction; he is "out on loan." When the project is finished, or when he is no longer needed, each specialist returns to his functional department for assignment to other duties. The project manager must rely heavily on these assigned people for counsel and decisions in their respective areas. If the team is small, its members will have frequent contact with one another and will be fully informed of the current status of the project. In these circumstances, most of the coordination will be voluntary. From time to time, tough, trade-off decisions (sacrificing in one place to gain in another) may be necessary, and these will be made by the project manager.

The personal relations within a project team are delicate. [10] Although the project manager is the nominal boss, each member of her team is on

[10]P.R. Lawrence, H. Kolodny, and S.M. Davis, "The Human Side of the Matrix," *Organizational Dynamics,* Summer 1977.

temporary assignment and will return to his functional department, where his long-run career is primarily determined. To draw the best from her group, the project manager must therefore rely both on the challenge of the job and on her personal leadership. Because of this heavy reliance on voluntary cooperation, project teams work best on projects for which the quality of the finished product or service, its deadline, and its costs are clearly specified.

While such formalized situations are the exception rather than the rule when it comes to linking line and staff functions, they show the extent to which formal relationships can be established to bring operating and functional people together. Their working together can be encouraged through joint performance review sessions and through agreement by line and staff bosses on the size of a raise or on a person's promotability.

While it is usually not necessary to go the extent of forming a matrix organizational structure to bring line and staff people together in the workplace, it has become an increasingly popular model by which many organizations achieve that outcome.

CONCLUSION

The concept of staff is appealing, for it permits executives to extend their capacity. Staff assistants perform managerial work that executives are too busy to do or for which they may lack technical competence. However, the arrangement is easily abused. Unless mutual understanding exists regarding the subjects covered and the action expected of the staff, relations between supervisors and subordinates may become confused.

Moreover, anything as delicate as staff relationships rarely continues on an even keel. Somebody will undoubtedly become too aggressive, one person will step on another's toes, people will observe consultations in the letter rather than in the spirit, jealousies will creep in. To keep emotional flare-ups at a minimum and to maintain relationships between staff and operators, managers must take time to provide continuing coordination and guidance. They must know whether the staff has become autocratic or lazy, whether their assistance is constructive, whether they are persuasive of their viewpoint, and whether operating people are too submissive or too independent.

In other words, by creating a staff, executives may facilitate their total jobs, but they also impose upon themselves new burdens: contact with staff, supervision of relations between staff and operating executives, and self-restraint so that they use the staff according to their own prescriptions. In some cases, such line-staff relationships can be enhanced by a matrix organizational structure.

Impact on Productivity

Staff, when properly used, is very effective for expanding the capabilities of key managers. It can help managers to deal with an ever-increasing array of external and internal pressures, and it can provide more thorough and expert counsel on how to respond constructively to such pressures. In these ways, staff has in the past increased the productivity of companies, and should continue to do so in the future, especially in changing situations.

Staff is no panacea, however. Once established, often for a good reason, a staff unit tends to continue to expand and to elaborate its mission. There are no simple measurements for when to check this self-induced growth, a problem that can be especially troublesome when the staff unit is physically and organizationally distant from the scenes of action.

A further drawback is continuing focus on yesterday's problems. Critical issues on which managers need help change over time, whereas experts tend to stick with their specialty. Companies in U.S. "smokestack" industries, for example, typically have large, technically advanced staff units, but they often focus on questions that are obsolete.

As a result, companies may become overloaded with staff that reduces, rather than enhances, productivity. To benefit from staff, central managers must keep the size lean, locate staff people close to actual operations, and redirect attention from old to new problems.

FOR FURTHER DISCUSSION

1. "Staff-line distinctions are obsolete in today's complex organizations," a management professor said recently. What might have prompted him to say that? To what degree is he right? Wrong?

2. A regional manager with line authority to change prices in his region consults with the corporate director of market research (a staff position) and is given several "pieces of data" that the market research manager feels would dictate a price reduction. If the regional manager accepts this advice and later finds that his revenue was adversely affected, who should accept the obligation for this loss?

3. "Our company plans to hire more female MBAs and engineers and place them in staff positions. These women are bright, articulate, self-effacing, and able to compromise. If we could just hire some that are independently wealthy, we would have perfect staff candidates." Discuss.

4. If you had a full-time job as an attorney ("company counsel") in a company making pesticides,

what sort of authority over operating managers would you seek?

5. Chapter 2 predicts an increase of uncertainty and volatility in the business environment. What effect will this have on companies' need for staff? Give specific examples of (a) subjects, (b) scope of work, and (c) relationships of staff to operating managers.

6. In U.S. firms, industrial engineers are typically located in a separate organization unit reporting to the plant manager or to the manufacturing vice-president. In Japanese firms, industrial engineers are dispersed throughout the plants and report to local superintendents. What are the pros and cons of each arrangement?

7. Citibank has made such wide use of matrix organization (for example, customer account officers in a matrix with managers of regional offices) that bank employees use the word *matrix* as a verb, as in "I matrix with J.P. Jones of the Singapore office." What does *matrix* mean to you in this usage?

FOR FURTHER READING

Davis, S.M. and P.R. Lawrence, *Matrix*. Reading, Mass.: Addison-Wesley, 1979. Concise review of matrix organization and its diffusion among companies in the United States and abroad.

Dubin, R., *Human Relations in Administration*, 4th ed. Englewood Cliffs, N.J.: Prentice-Hall, 1974, Ch. 10. Summarizes behavioral views on the role of the staff specialist.

Hax, A.C. and N.S. Majluf, "Organization Design: A Case Study on Matching Strategy and Structure," *Journal of Business Strategy,* Fall 1983. Alternative organization designs for a computer-systems company are presented, and a method for making the final choice is discussed.

Janger, A.R., *Matrix Organization of Complex Business.* New York: Elsevier North-Holland, 1983. Explores use of matrix organization in sixty European and U.S. companies, and the internal relationships involved.

MacMillan, I.C. and P.E. Jones, "Designing Organizations to Compete," *Journal of Business Strategy,* Spring 1984. Recommends combining activities into focused departments that can respond more quickly than competitors to market opportunities.

Sathe, V., *Controller Involvement in Management.* Englewood Cliffs, N.J.: Prentice-Hall, 1982. Good exposition of a company controller's dual staff role as an outside evaluator and an inside service provider.

MANAGEMENT IN ACTION CASE 11
The TRW Matrix

Early in the 1960s, the TRW Systems Group was experiencing a major organizational transition. In a short three-year period, the company moved from being a "sheltered captive" supplier to the U.S. Air Force to a fully independent, competitive aerospace company. Along the way, the number of employees increased from fewer than 4,000 to more than 6,000.

After that strategic business decision was made by TRW, the face of its business changed dramatically. From only 8 customers and 16 contracts in 1960, by 1963 TRW had 42 different customers and 108 contracts. And TRW needed a major change in its organizational structure to match the change in its business and strategy.

Things were complicated because TRW needed to sustain the high-skilled specialization that allowed it to develop technological and research firsts in such areas as rocket propulsion systems, guidance and control systems, electric power systems, telecommunications, digital systems, mechanical design, metals technology, and a host of other areas. At the same time, TRW recognized that its new customers—primarily nongovernmental businesses—were not interested in buying functional competence. They were buying specific outputs from project and program offices. The office worked closely with their customers—interpreting their needs, modifying them when necessary, and converting them into specifications that would relate to the functional resource groups.

To provide an organizational form that matched the needs of its changing constituencies, TRW—like numerous other aerospace companies before and after it—moved to a matrix organizational structure.

Under that system, the functional specialists were assigned to specific project teams—say, the Saturn rocket team. In their early planning and shakeout stages, such teams would be relatively small. But as they came closer to producing viable products, the teams grew exponentially.

Through it all, in the matrix structure, the specialists—engineers, metallurgists, physicists, and the like—reported to their project manager as well as to the chief executive of their particular functional areas. True, they were violating a long-held management principle that a worker could serve only one master, but in so doing the organization's designers decided it was preferable to have decentralized communications on a project-by-project basis rather than a functional structure that might have been inappropriate to serving TRW's new-found niche of customers.

The strategy apparently worked—and TRW became one of the country's most successful high-technology companies, today doing relatively little of its overall business with the federal government.

Question

One of TRW's most successful civilian divisions operates the largest nationwide network supplying credit information on millions of individuals to retail stores, auto dealers, local credit bureaus, and the like. The heart of the operation is a large computer storage of people's repayment behavior, and high-speed communication links to TRW's customers. How do you think this division fits into TRW's matrix organization?

For more information, see S.M. Davis and P.R. Lawrence, "The TRW Systems Group Case," in *Matrix* (Reading, Mass.: Addison-Wesley, 1977).

APPLICATION CASES

For practice in applying concepts covered in this chapter to managerial situations, see the following managerial decision cases. The case questions particularly relevant to this chapter are listed by number after each case name.

Grant Chemical Corporation (p. 59) 4, 6, 11, 12
Fyler International (p. 68) 12
Clifford Nelson (p. 308) 11, 13, 14, 21
Graham, Smith, & Bendel, Inc. (p. 442) 9
Scandico (Singapore) (p. 546) 6, 7, 8

12

Human Resources Management: Matching People and Jobs

LEARNING OBJECTIVES

After completing this chapter, you should be able to

1. Discuss how personal differences can influence how well people and jobs fit together.

2. Understand the major personality characteristics of managers and explain why they are so important.

3. Explain four techniques for gathering data for personnel selection.

4. Know which criteria should be considered most important in choosing between potential methods of matching people and jobs.

5. Cite some reasons that short-term planning and long-term planning of human resources might not always be consistent with each other.

ADJUSTING FOR PERSONAL DIFFERENCES

An organization can have a wise strategy and an appropriately designed structure and still not succeed. The reason is simple: No matter how sophisticated management techniques become, they still rest on how well an organization matches individuals with specific skills to jobs with specific needs.

This matching process was less difficult a hundred years ago, because most skills relevant to the workplace tended to evolve from brawn and muscle. Today, with "knowledge" work becoming more common all the time, skills, especially the skills of a manager, are difficult to identify. In the old days, one needed only to spy a man's muscle to know he could shovel coal. In contrast, the skills that make a manager unique today are increasingly the less obvious ones dealing with mental ability, values, and emotions.

Whole new fields have developed to study these modern issues, including human resources management, human factors analysis, applied areas of cognitive psychology. In just one area—commercial aviation—researchers from those three fields have joined to learn how individual differences and interrelationships might contribute to plane crashes. Different, but strongly related, findings have resulted:

1. Human resources experts found that cockpit crews are more effective when pilots and copilots are trained together as teams, learning each other's strengths and weaknesses, and developing confidence and a working relationship over time, rather than individually bidding for particular flight schedules with the right days off and best layover stops.

2. Human factors specialists, who study the linkage between people and technology,[1] found that some cockpit technical equipment was so ill-suited to human performance that crew members routinely turned off or ignored devices designed to warn them of danger, or did not adequately communicate the information to each other.

3. Cognitive psychologists found that the key may well lie in how readily individuals search for and assimilate new information in situations that may seem familiar, but are in fact unique.[2] An important factor seems to be whether an individual operates with relatively few mental models of how the world works and forces information into those visions, or whether a person is open to new ideas and willing to adapt his thinking accordingly.

---

[1]C. Perrow, *Normal Accidents: Living With High-Risk Technologies* (New York: Basic Books, 1984).

[2]M.J. Driver, and A.J. Rowe, "Decision-Making Styles: A New Approach to Management Decision-Making," in C.L. Cooper, ed., *Behavioral Problems in Organizations* (Englewood Cliffs, N.J.: Prentice-Hall, 1979), p. 143.

These considerations take on even more importance as organizations that for decades have operated in stable, noncompetitive environments—such as consumer banks—now face competition from a variety of sources. One researcher has found that in such changing external environments, those who are most open to new ideas and those who seek out the most information perform best.[3] In fact, those managers who conform to the way things have traditionally been done around the bank, rather than maintaining a degree of independence, tend to be the poorer performers as times change.

These issues are important because each specific job within an organization must be filled by a specific person with specific skills. Some fill a job well and some badly, because individuals differ in ability, learning, attitudes, and behavior. Moreover, the same person changes over time as he gains experience and his interests shift. As these changes occur, it may be a case of trying to fit square pegs into round holes—which requires an adjustment of the peg, the hole, or both.

Such staffing problems can be aggravated by basic changes in an organization's strategy. A manager who is well suited to rapid expansion, for instance, may lack the caution and concern needed when a strategy shifts from emphasizing growth to generating cash. One airline company had to "kick upstairs" its outstanding promoter and then try two other presidents before getting a good match with its new earnings-focused strategy. Similarly, labor unions often find that an aggressive union president who is suited to a period of organizing is too restless and unbending after union recognition is well established.

PREPARING INDIVIDUAL SPECIFICATIONS

The overall process of matching jobs and individuals resolves itself into the following subproblems: What kind of person is needed for each job? What are the abilities of the people now in the organization? How can individuals and jobs be best matched in the short run? Should the individual be trained or replaced, or should the job be adjusted? How can people be obtained to match long-run needs?

Clarifying Job Specifications

The first step in matching jobs and individuals takes up where organizational analysis left off. If an organization is designed properly, a series of *job descriptions* is available. A job description sets forth the objectives, duties, relationships, and results expected of a person in the job. A controller's job description, for instance, might include this duty: "Prepare

[3]A.R. McGill, Unpublished doctoral dissertation, The University of Michigan, 1987.

monthly profit-and-loss statement." A hospital administrator's description might include statements such as, "Coordinate all community relations" and "Promote outpatient services so as to relieve pressure on bed facilities."

In order to match jobs and individuals, job descriptions must be more explicit and concrete. The declaration that a controller should prepare a monthly profit-and-loss statement, for example, does not say whether she personally must compute the state, local, and national taxes, or whether she can delegate this task to an expert. The hospital administrator may be in charge of all community relations, but does this duty involve delivering speeches, appearing before medical boards, or conducting health programs for school children?

The *relationships required* by a position must also be made explicit. Does the job require a lot of talking with many different people, or is it independent, calling for only short, terse communication? With what kinds of people must an incumbent deal? Are they sharp traders or indifferent, uneducated operators? Will they interpret "democratic" advice-seeking as a weakness, or have they learned to be independent and to resent orders? Do they want friendship mixed up with their work relationships, or would they prefer to keep their contacts at work matter-of-fact and impersonal?

A job description may have to be amplified in other ways, so that it spells out, for instance, how much decentralization is intended, what frequency of innovation is expected, or what managerial techniques are to be used. In clarifying job descriptions, thoughts need not necessarily be put in writing, but they should be clear in the minds of everyone involved in the delicate task of matching specific individuals with specific jobs. The central point is to think through the nature of a job completely and carefully, as Figure 12.1 suggests.

Translation to Individual Specifications

The second major step in matching jobs and individuals is translating the duties in the amplified job description into "individual specifications." A statement of duties often does not specifically tell what to look for in appraising an incumbent or a candidate for a position. Suppose a controller is being sought for a large company, and one of his duties is to "report any critical developments, as shown by accounting records, to the board of directors." How is it possible to tell whether a candidate is skilled at this work? If a plant manager must "coordinate sixteen foremen," how can a person who can do so be recognized?

Of course, in appraising an individual already in a position, past performance, compared with the behavior and results desired, will be the main evidence used. But when a new candidate is being considered or a position changed, a list of the crucial characteristics of a person in that job is needed.

Specifications should not be so closely tied to those exhibited by previous successful executives that people with different experience and personality are automatically excluded. In particular, highly qualified women

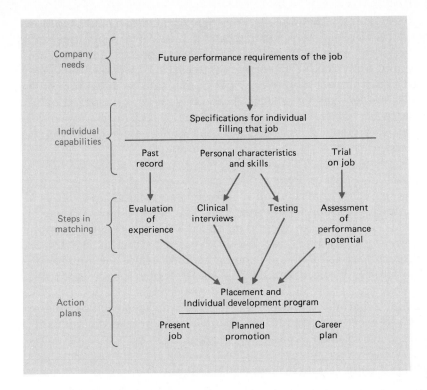

Figure 12.1 Matching individuals and jobs.

and members of minority groups must be kept in the talent pool used to fill vacancies.

Actually, three quite different ways of stating individual specifications are in common use.

1. Certain standardized tasks can be *tested directly*. Candidates for a lifeguard job can be run through a series of tests in a pool; prospective typists can be asked to type a sample passage; often an aspirant can be observed on an actual job for a brief period. Unfortunately, such standards cannot be applied to complicated and unusual tasks (which are typical of many executive jobs), and they tell little about how a person will fit into a working group. So additional specifications, especially for executive positions, are needed.

2. Past *work experience and accomplishment* may be useful as an indication of ability to do similar work in the future. For example, a large chemical company specified that its vice-president of finance "should have served as chief financial officer for a medium or large chemical-processing company for a period of eight years; should have been responsible for tax accounting in a medium-sized company for at least two years; should have had at least fifty people reporting to him." A water company specified that its plant manager should have demonstrated ability to "reduce costs, develop subordinate personnel, and avoid stoppages and breakdowns."

3. Specifications may include a list of *personality characteristics* that are stated either in the technical jargon of behavioral scientists or in more general terms, such as "friendly temperament" and "apparent energy and ambition." The reason for resorting to personality characteristics is that experience may be an inadequate indication of the qualities needed for a position. A job may be so unusual that few candidates have pertinent experience, and experience may fail to demonstrate clearly all the qualities that might be needed for success in a new situation.

In practice, most statements of individual specifications for executive and staff jobs include a combination of desirable experience and personality characteristics phrased in lay terms,[4] as Figure 12.2 shows. Preparing the "experience" section of an individual specification is relatively simple and grows directly from analyzing the duties of a particular job. Experience specifications are valuable and should be used whenever appropriate. The fact that much of the discussion on the following pages deals with personality characteristics means not that such characteristics are more important than experience, but merely that personality specifications are more difficult to prepare and that the opportunity is greater for managers to improve this aspect of individual specifications.

Important Personality Characteristics of Managers

Psychologists, psychiatrists, sociologists, and cultural anthropologists have identified and classified hundreds of human characteristics. None of the classifications is "right" or "wrong." Some are useful in studying individuals in the family, others in dealing with the mentally ill, still others in analyzing small work groups. This discussion includes suggestions from both science and business practice of certain characteristics that are most *useful to managers* in writing individual specifications, in appraising people, and in planning personnel development.[5] For convenience, these will

[4]J. P. Kotter, *The General Manager* (New York: Free Press, 1982).
[5]L. R. Flanders, and D. Utterback, "The Management Excellence Inventory: A Tool for Management Development," *Public Administration Review,* May 1985.

Figure 12.2 Selection of a television news interviewer can be based on past record, interviews and auditions, and trial-on-job. Each of these evaluation steps is complex, making evaluation especially difficult for young or relatively inexperienced managers.

be discussed under five headings: knowledge, decision-making talent, self-reliance and self-assertion, social sensitivity, and emotional stability.

Knowledge

In matching an individual with a job, an inevitable question is, "What does the candidate need to know?" The knowledge an aspirant to an executive position should have can often be specified in terms of specialty, depth, coordination, and management. Managerial positions call for specialized knowledge of, say, selling methods, water pollution, petroleum economics, or bond discounts. Some jobs require in-depth knowledge, whereas others demand only general acquaintance with a field. The president of a company, for instance, may need some general knowledge of public relations, but the public-relations manager should have thorough knowledge of sociology, politics, communications media, and kindred subjects.

It must be considered, then, what coordinating knowledge a manager will need to tie in his activities with related jobs; such knowledge includes an understanding of operations—facts, technology, and problems—and of the people whose work is related to their area of the company. Managerial knowledge is a grasp of management principles and techniques applicable to a variety of situations. Of course, other kinds of knowledge may be necessary for specific decisions, but consideration of specialty, depth, coordination, and management provide a good start in identifying knowledge requirements for a particular job.

Decision-making Talent

Jobs differ in the complexity and novelty of problems that must be solved. The president of a large aerospace firm needs a different type of decision-making ability from that needed by the head of a motel chain. These are several of the personality factors that contribute to decision-making talent:

▫ *Analytical ability* This ability enables a person to break a problem into parts, identify relevant facts, interpret the meaning of facts, and project the consequences of a decision. Because so many facts bear on a typical management problem, an executive needs what might be called an *intuitive analytical sense* in order to select key facts and eliminate the rest.

▫ *Conceptual-logical ability* To get meaning from a vast array of facts, they must be assembled under large concepts. For instance, an executive may take a chart that shows declining sales, information from competing companies, and reports on the activities of the company's own sales representatives, and pull them all together into one concept—"poor customer service." Synthesizing facts involves both inventing concepts and using logic to connect concepts in causal relationships.

▫ *Creativity* Tough problems usually cannot be resolved by known methods. A fresh approach, a new twist, a novel arrangement of recognized parts, or the addition of a different material or system is often necessary to find an acceptable solution.[6] Preferably, an executive can create original ideas herself; at a minimum, she needs acumen in spotting the good ideas of others.

▫ *Intuitive judgment* This resembles the "hunch." Up to a point, a decision maker looks at a problem analytically and logically and then suddenly seems to "know what to do." Even though the process is only partially systematic and conscious, a decision does emerge. Intuitive judgment is particularly important when all facts cannot be gathered, when conceptual and logical arguments are fuzzy, or when immediate action is required without waiting for long, rational analysis.

▫ *Judgmental courage* Unlike a scientist, an executive must often act without careful research and foolproof logic to back up his decision. Psychologists associate ability to do so with a person's *tolerance of ambiguity* (capacity to deal with uncertainties without breaking down) and with *frustration tolerance* (ability to deal continually with difficulties without becoming discouraged). Courage is needed to make decisions when confronted by uncertainties and frustrations.

▫ *Open-mindedness* The sixth component of decision-making talent, particularly important in individual specifications, is receptivity to new ideas. Does a person conscientiously listen to others and try to determine the relevance of their ideas in solving current problems?

▫ *Risk-taking desire* Finally, some managers, because of the way they were raised as children or socialized into organizations as adults, are averse to taking risks; others thrive on the challenge and uncertainty of operating in a risky environment. An individual's desire to take or avoid risks clearly affects where that person should fit in an organization. Jobs requiring new ideas and innovation cry out for the risk taker, but those resting more on stability and maintaining the status quo not only would fail to fulfill the risk taker, but in all likelihood they would be more effectively filled by the person who is averse to risk.

In summary, although decision-making talent is difficult to pin down, some of its elements can be identified. An executive who is analytical, logical, creative, open-minded, intuitive, courageous, and a seeker of reasonable risk is more likely to make useful decisions than a person who is weak in these qualities.

Self-reliance and Self-assertion

In satisfying needs and solving problems, people differ in how much they rely on themselves and how much on others. Jobs, too, differ in what they require of a person in the way of taking initiative, asserting ideas with

[6]R. G. Shaeffer, *Staffing Systems: Managerial and Professional Jobs* (New York: Elsevier North-Holland, 1983).

persistence over those of others, and presenting ideas forcefully and ener-getically.

Psychologists have studied this trait and describe degrees of self-reliance—or lack of it—in terms of a range between extremes. Some talk of dominant↔submissive characteristics; others speak of independent↔dependent or of active↔passive behavior. Practical business executives of-ten use the expressions "initiative," "drive," or "self-starting ability" to identify the same qualities, at least for the end of the continuum they are most interested in.

This trait is one that is revealed in everyday activities. To check yourself on this quality, observe what you do when you wake up in the small hours of the night because you are cold. Do you try pulling the cov-ers closer around your neck hoping the chilly air will go away? Or do you face the problem, climb out of bed, and get another blanket? Many execu-tive jobs need the type of person who gets another blanket.

Closely allied with self-reliance is ambition, or "achievement moti-vation." Having mastered one problem, most persons set higher goals for themselves and start working toward them. Individuals differ, however, in how much they advance their aspirations. Some aspire to make "big jumps," whereas others are content with modest progress, and still others may actually level off and rest for a while.

Social Sensitivity

Some people react to a problem largely in terms of the feelings of those involved. They have a high capacity for *empathy*—the ability to project imaginatively into the thoughts, feelings, and probable reactions of an-other. A socially sensitive manager might empathize with an auditor or a salesperson in Alaska without necessarily approving of his feelings and behavior; but because the manager really senses his reactions, the man-ager is likely to be sympathetic to, or at least understanding of, the Alas-kan's point of view.

Social sensitivity may be helpful, of course, in almost any job, but it is of critical importance for most selling, staff, and executive positions.[7]

Emotional Stability

Emotional stability indicates a good adjustment to life. People who are emotionally stable tend to act in the following ways: (1) they accept differ-ent people, including those they do not like, calmly and objectively; (2) they react to obstacles by steadily increasing their efforts or finding new ways to achieve their desires, rather than by denying that the obstacles exist, becoming overly depressed, lashing out aggressively, or rationalizing their inabilities; (3) they know when they cannot achieve a given goal, and shrug their shoulders and turn their attention to other matters that inter-

[7]J. L. Kerr, "Diversification Strategies and Managerial Rewards," *Academy of Management Journal,* March 1985.

est them; (4) they react happily to moments of success but remain objective, without experiencing childlike exhilaration and becoming overly optimistic; (5) they behave simply and naturally without artificiality or straining for effect.

The test of emotional stability comes, of course, when people are subjected to conflict and tension; and some jobs test people more than others. For instance, the tension experienced by the sales manager of a newly formed pharmaceutical company is likely to be greater than that felt by the chief accountant of a savings bank. So a higher degree of emotional stability would be needed in the sales job than in the accounting job.

Perceptive Use of Personality Factors

The personality factors we have been talking about will be of greatest usefulness if a list of specifications is prepared for each job. The following examples suggest how a manager should tailor specifications to a job.

It is a good idea to provide complementary abilities in executives and their key subordinates. Thus an executive who has intuition, courage, and a penchant for fast action might want an assistant who has analytical skill and a predisposition for research and fact-finding. If a new supervisor is to be appointed over a group of subordinates who are highly dependent, he will need considerable self-reliance and self-assertion.

The position of production scheduler presents a different problem. His work must interlock frequently and closely with that of a wide variety of people—perhaps a dozen shop supervisors, inventory clerks, purchasing agents, maintenance people, sales representatives, and others. Anyone appointed to such a job should have considerable emotional stability if he is to remain problem-centered and get along with everyone.

In contrast, the jobs of researcher and development engineer typically require persons with specialized knowledge and keen decision-making talent. Social sensitivity and emotional stability, although desirable, would not be so essential for such jobs as they would be for a production scheduler. The position of sales representative calls for still different abilities, social sensitivity and self-reliance ranking at the top of the list.

Executives need considerable courage and self-assertiveness when a company is making frequent changes to adapt to new competition or rapid changes in technology. A high degree of emotional stability is also desirable, as major changes mean stress for everyone whose job is affected by new practices.

A final remark about individual specifications. The preceding discussion has been couched in terms of fixed and set working environments, including a stable array of subordinates, associates, and social structure. This approach implies that an individual must adjust to fit a position. But sometimes adjustment may run in the other direction. A job may be shaped, at least to some extent, to fit the person. A manager must always think closely about both the job—however it may be revised—and the characteristics of a person who could fill such a job well. Also, jobs change over time. If a new strategy is likely to be adopted, then the qualities needed in the people who are to meet the revised priorities should be specified.

Job analysis and individual specifications are not ends in themselves; they are vital preparations for a third step—assessing specific individuals to see how well they match the jobs created by an organization design. Specifications provide standards, and the manager must now evaluate people in terms of those standards.

Appraising Experience

Measuring what a person has done is relatively simple and direct. For example, if the specifications for a vice-president in charge of production state, "Should have ten years experience as head of manufacturing in a medium-sized company," then matching work record to the specifications is all that is necessary. The same is true if experience specifications are stated in terms of *results* rather than years—for instance, "Should have increased the sales in assigned territory significantly during tenure as branch manager." But when the specified results are intangible—such as having developed good subordinates or maintained goodwill with suppliers—there are measurement problems. In a complex situation, it is often difficult to know how much the person being appraised influenced the outcome, and how much of the outcome was caused by other forces. In such cases, it may be desirable to pool the subjective judgments of several people.

Appraisal of experience is somewhat analogous to what a statistician does when he predicts the gross national product by fitting a trend line to the experience of the past ten or twenty years. He is not sure of the precise values and weights of all underlying forces; hence, without knowing the forces, he simply projects a line that is the result of all of them. Similarly, it is often possible to use past achievement to predict a person's likely future success, without being sure which personal abilities determined success. Although such prediction is admittedly risky, it is often the best way to size up an individual. The method does have two attractive advantages—it is inexpensive, and it can be used by executives who lack technical training in psychology.

The reliability of an appraisal based on experience depends partly on the *relevance* of past experience to the new job. If a person is being evaluated in her present position, naturally the pertinent issue is whether current results are satisfactory. But when a person is being considered for transfer or promotion, her past experience must be related to a job with different specifications. And if the candidate's background does not quite fit the new specifications, is the fit close enough? In this event, past experience is probably used as evidence about personality factors, and judgment may be improved if it is recognized that a shift has been made from one kind of criterion to another.

A common safeguard in making promotions in many companies is a policy of testing a person in several different jobs. These assignments are useful *both* for training and for appraisal. If there is any doubt about Claire's or Pete's ability to get work out on schedule, they can be assigned a task in which they can gain experience and their development can be watched closely.

Personality Appraisal by Executives

A job may be unique or so new that no previous work closely resembles it; it is useless to insist on full experience in this case, and the appraisal must be made on the basis of a person's ability and personality. For years, managers have depended on their intuitive judgment in selecting personnel. Because such selection is so crucial, measures that can improve the quality of judgment should be adopted. Here are three practical rules that are applicable to large and small companies.

1. Make individual judgments on sophisticated grounds. Instead of resorting to vague terms like "personality" or "a good worker," define specifically the qualities needed in a job. By doing so, an appraiser can detect his own biases and cultivate objectivity, which will enable him to judge people realistically.

2. Use group judgment. In order to prevent mistakes in perception and judgment, many companies insist that three or four executives appraise a person on each specification.

3. Maintain a file of key incidents in each person's performance. Recent events tend to be remembered and overemphasized. A more balanced appraisal can be made with the help of a systematic record that includes revealing incidents about the person over a period of years. Such a record should denote both strengths and weaknesses, and it may indicate the directions in which an individual is developing (perhaps he has overcome earlier knowledge deficiencies, and he may be showing more—or less—self-reliance).

Tests and Clinical Interviews

Personality and aptitude tests provide useful information for certain types of well-defined positions, such as salesperson, computer programmer, and routine production worker. Clinical interviews by skilled psychologists are also useful when simpler methods do not clearly indicate certain characteristics, like emotional stability. As our knowledge about human behavior in work situations increases, the value of such tests should also improve.

Unfortunately, psychological tests have only limited value as predictors of success in specific jobs.[8] The diversity of job specifications, along with the complexity of individual motivation and behavior, makes the design of a reliable test extremely difficult. Tests may be invalid for minority candidates. Furthermore, only the largest companies can afford the great expense of designing and giving tests that are adapted to specific jobs. Except for preliminary screening of a large number of raw recruits, psychological tests and clinical interviews will probably continue to be used largely as supplements to managerial judgment. For executive posts especially, the chief value of tests lies in corroborating or questioning personal estimates. Assessing people on the basis of experience and observable personality characteristics are sure to endure as an important management duty for a long, long time.

Assessment Centers

The assessment center is a relatively new concept for identifying managerial potential.[9] In an assessment center, candidates participate in several performance simulations while trained observers evaluate their behavior.

One widely used assessment device is the "in-basket exercise," in which participants are asked to deal with a realistic set of messages, telephone calls, letters, and reports. Assessors evaluate the candidate's decisions with respect to such abilities as willingness to take action, organizing ability, memory and ability to interrelate events, and ability to delegate. Similarly, leaderless group discussions are employed to assess a candidate's persuasiveness, flexibility, self-confidence, and aggressiveness. As more and more firms have introduced assessment centers, simulation exercises have been customized to fit the firms' particular situations. Thus, in the assessment center operated by a large department store chain, an assessor places an "irate customer phone call" in order to rate the candidate's ability to control emotions, demonstrate tact, and satisfy the complainer.

Some assessment centers have achieved impressive accuracy in predicting which candidates will advance to higher managerial ranks. Some disadvantages offset this predictive capability, however. Since an assessment typically involves a number of assessors working with a small group of candidates over a number of days, assessment centers are very costly. Care and sensitivity are required to manage the stress situations created by the competitive aspects of assessment center simulations. In addition, low assessment center ratings may demotivate people who are competent in their present positions.

[8]J. P. Campbell et al., *Managerial Behavior, Performance, and Effectiveness* (New York: McGraw-Hill, 1970).

[9]A. Howard, "An Assessment of Assessment Centers," *Academy of Management Journal,* vol. 17, 1 Mar. 1978, pp. 115–34.

Present job occupants will seldom match completely the specifications prepared for existing positions, as Figure 12.3 indicates. An appraisal of personnel typically reveals that some people have less ability than desired, whereas others have unused talents. What can a manager do to improve this match of human resources and organization needs? Both short-run and long-run adjustments are necessary. In the short run, concentration on present employees and present jobs is necessary. The long run allows much more flexibility, as will be discussed later.

The Weak Incumbent

Probably the most difficult and unpleasant short-run problem arises when an individual already in a job fails to measure up. In such cases, there are three alternatives for improving the congruence of person and job.

1. Change the job. This procedure is a matter of "tinkering" with the organizational structure. Three examples of such tinkering are withdrawing a duty from one position and assigning it to another, adjusting the degree of decentralization, and providing additional assistance in the area of weakness.[10]
2. Change the incumbent. Perhaps through counseling and training, the employee may overcome the gap between his present performance and what the company desires.
3. Remove the incumbent. If a person cannot be expected to become competent in a reasonable time or if the job cannot be changed to fit him, it may be necessary to transfer or dismiss him and fill the position with someone who more nearly fits the individual specifications.

Action in such situations is often painful because it upsets both expectations and established behavior. But procrastination may undercut the effectiveness of a whole department or company.

Deciding on a Matching Method

In deciding on which of the three methods to follow in matching person and job, several questions should be answered carefully.

How closely does the job interlock with other positions? The degree of interdependence between a given job and other jobs directly affects the ease or difficulty of changing the organization to fit a person. For example, if the Montana sales representative of a Midwestern paint company is ineffective, the company can accept a somewhat reduced volume of busi-

---

[10]E. H. Schein, *Career Dynamics: Matching Individual and Organization Needs* (Reading, Mass.: Addison-Wesley, 1978).

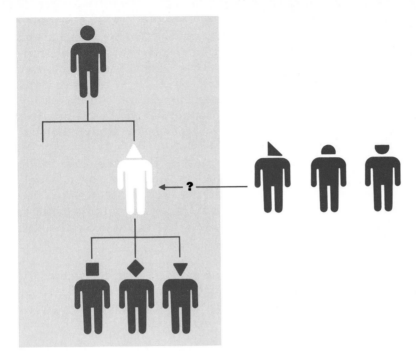

Figure 12.3 Short-run personnel
planning. Neither subordinates nor
available candidates outside the
company are able to fill effectively a
gap that has occurred in the company
organization. There is a mismatch
between the jobs as now conceived
and the qualifications of candidates who
are available to fill them.

ness, cut the representative's territory, or have him concentrate on a limited number of customers, so that his duties match his abilities. But poor
performance by a billing clerk may have far-reaching repercussions. Customers may get too many items of one color and not enough of another;
the accounts-receivable clerk may spend extra time trying to straighten
out invoice difficulties; salespeople may have trouble with customers; inventory records may be snarled up; and so on. To adjust the billing job to
fit the capacities of the present clerk is not practical because it would set
off a chain reaction that would alter several other positions.

Will training make the person acceptable?   Some personal deficiencies can be corrected fairly promptly, whereas others can be altered little—
if at all. For instance, product knowledge or specific company knowledge
can often be quickly acquired, but conceptual-logical abilities require na-
tive capacity plus many years to develop. This distinction is important,
because it is tempting to keep people in positions because they are familiar
with current facts and routines, even though they lack the imagination
and drive to perform satisfactorily over a period of time.

Is a good replacement available?   One small firm had a chief engineer who was cantankerous, uncompromising, and slow. But the company
retained him because his technical knowledge of the product line was far
superior to that of any subordinate or of engineers in other firms who
might be attracted by the salary the company could afford to pay. Even-

tually, it was hoped, one of the younger engineers could take on responsibility for contacts with the sales department, production department, and customers, thereby permitting the current chief to concentrate on developing new products. Pending the event, however, the president took over some of the duties that ideally should have been the chief engineer's; the assistant production superintendent was assigned the task of expediting plans for new products; and a coordinating committee that met weekly was formed. In this instance, the organization was changed to fit an individual because a good replacement was unavailable.

In thinking about promotions and transfers, the manager must be wary of chain reactions. Perhaps the Canadian branch manager is well qualified to replace an ailing vice-president, but how will the work of the Canadian branch be carried on? Although analysis starts with matching a particular candidate to a specific job, it can lead to thought about the best arrangement of the whole structure of jobs and people.

How long will the person remain on the job?   If an unsatisfactory employee is within a few years of retirement, or can be transferred soon, then temporary and expedient adjustments in work assignments may be warranted.

Is superior performance urgent?   The president of a large soap company, which was heavily dependent on advertising to compete with such companies as Lever Brothers and Procter & Gamble, was saddled with "a grand old man" as advertising manager. He was not up-to-date on advertising research, use of cable television, and other new developments in sales promotion. The pressure of competition forced the company to bring in a competent advertising manager in short order, despite the consequences for the senior man. Urgency, in terms of time and importance, required such a course.

Most cases are not so clear-cut. Just how important is it to have a job filled exactly according to specifications in the organization plan? What obligations does a company owe a person who has given long and perhaps distinguished service? Should any weight be given to long personal friendships? Must the need for change be clearly evident, or can changes be made on the basis of uncertain estimates of the future? Because answers to such questions of value tend to be personal and subjective, executives should check their judgments with two or three associates.

How will removal affect morale?   Removing a widely known, well-liked individual may cause other employees to say, "Don't go to work for this company—they fire people at the drop of a hat." Even if everyone else remains in his job, a pervasive feeling of insecurity may be created in a department by removal of one popular individual. Negative effects on morale can be lessened by letting it be generally known that the person dismissed was given a fair chance to demonstrate his ability, that he was offered a transfer with dignity to another position, and that he was given a dismissal benefit for early retirement.

Sometimes, on the other hand, morale is improved by the removal of a person from a position for which he is not qualified. If employees see that someone is kept on a job even though his performance is mediocre, they may develop the general attitude expressed by the question, "Why push yourself?" And many a competent young person has been discouraged to find his advancement blocked by a series of inadequate people in key posts. In such situations, removal of a weak incumbent will be a signal that management is prepared to distinguish between good and poor performance, and this will boost morale among the more able employees.

The foregoing list of questions certainly indicates that no universal answer can tell managers whether they should fit their organizations to people or find people to fit the organizations. Because managers have an obligation to carry out company strategy, it is important that they give independent and detailed study to the design of an organization that is well suited to that strategy. But in the short run, managers must clearly meld this ideal design—as reflected in person specifications—with the abilities of available personnel.

An Unexpected Vacancy

Resignation, death, or unanticipated transfer may create a vacancy with little warning, and the empty position must be filled as soon as possible. In such cases, there is usually a choice of replacements, but rarely will any of the candidates completely match the specifications for the vacant position. Again the question must be addressed of how much a job should be modified to fit an individual.

Consider the sudden death of your professor or the manager of a local supermarket. The issues to be faced in seeking a successor are similar to those already discussed. Must the job be structured so that it readily interlocks with other positions? What requirements for the job can be learned after the person is appointed, and what qualities must she already possess? How will the position vacated by the new appointee be filled? Is top performance immediately important, or is gradual learning and adjustment feasible? If duties are to be reassigned, what will be the impact on morale? Does this unanticipated event present an opportunity to correct previous faults in the organization, or to move toward a long-range organization plan?

Expedient, compromise steps—such as having one executive cover two jobs—may be unavoidable when an unanticipated vacancy first occurs. But these moves should be clearly announced as temporary. Then prompt action should be taken to work out a more satisfactory arrangement. The danger, of course, is that the expedient action may be allowed to continue for so long that later adjustments will not be made; or if they are, people will be upset by what they regard as another reorganization.

The Strong Incumbent

Some people in every organization will have greater ability than their jobs call for. A familiar question arises: Should the job be adjusted to fit the person? In fact, such adjustment tends to happen. There are four common situations that call for it. (1) If the work that interlocks with a person's regular duties is poorly performed, a capable individual often gives advice and checks on performance that lies beyond his assigned sphere; by doing so, he sets the stage for having duties transferred to him. (2) When a special problem arises, a capable person is often asked to help with its solution. Repeated assignments to such special projects may lead to his having additional duties as a regular part of his job. (3) Further, to paraphrase an old rule of science, "Organization abhors a vacuum"; if important activities are not being taken care of at all, the most capable person around often steps into the breach. (4) Finally, quite aside from assigned duties, the influence of a strong individual is apt to extend beyond his prescribed area.

Such natural, if unplanned, expansion of a job creates no difficulties until the person becomes so involved in unofficial activities that he neglects his regular duties, or until he gets promoted. The first danger can be avoided if the supervisor insists that the individual keep his main assignments in clear perspective. Promotion is likely to cause a more severe jolt, however. The shock is like that on a football team built around a backfield star who leaves the game with an injury. Weaknesses formerly covered up suddenly become serious. A wise manager, therefore, should keep abreast of how work is actually getting done and should use his outstanding subordinates for special assignments or in other ways that do not make his organization vulnerable to serious upsets when the exceptional performer moves on to another job.

A final observation applies to all shifts of personnel, whether initiated by a manager or by a worker leaving her job. No two persons are identical; each has her own strengths and limitations. Consequently, when a person takes a new position, she will—and should—perform the work in ways that are somewhat different from those of her predecessor. At first, she may not be prepared to carry the full load, but later she will probably take on some duties that were not assigned to her predecessor; on the other hand, other duties may be more fully delegated, or initiative for them transferred to staff advisers. Inevitably, then, at least minor adjustments will occur in the assignments of duties and in social structure. During this transition, while people are learning new relationships, a manager has an opportunity to make alterations in organization without treating them as special problems. Such a period is also a natural occasion in which to introduce features of a long-range organization plan. For all these reasons, *placement of an individual should be considered in terms of organization* as well as from a strictly personnel viewpoint.

LONG-RUN HUMAN RESOURCES PLANNING

Human resources planning for the long run differs in several particulars from the short-run problems just discussed. It is concerned with all jobs and all employees at once, with matching a complete roster of people to total job requirements; it is concerned with filling future vacancies rather than existing jobs; and it allows time for long-term learning, especially through rotation of personnel.[11] Three major steps are involved in the process of long-run human resources planning: (1) projecting the organization structure and the personnel who are required to operate that structure, (2) matching the projected personnel requirements with present employees, and (3) planning for individual development so that people will be qualified when job openings occur.

Projecting Personnel Requirements

The first essential step in long-run human resources planning is to forecast the organizational structure that will best meet the future needs of the company. The environment of any company is constantly changing—new products are introduced, existing products are modified, production processes altered, automation is introduced, advertising policies shift, competition changes, and so on. Public-service enterprises are changing even more rapidly. The whole job structure should keep pace with such changes. Adding positions because of growth and new activities may be necessary, and existing positions may be assigned quite different duties ten years hence.

With this future organizational structure as a basis, specifications for each position can be prepared. Naturally, some aspects, such as personality characteristics to complement people in related jobs, cannot be included in these early individual specifications. Nevertheless, the main elements of each job should be thought through. The aim is to develop a clear understanding of what future human resources requirements will be.

Matching People with Requirements

The second step in long-range human resources planning starts with appraising all key people and cataloging their characteristics without reference to specifications for a particular position. This *inventory of talent* should include, in addition to present executives, younger men and women, and members of minority groups. Even if these younger members are not yet in key spots, a good deal of positional shifting will undoubtedly occur during the subsequent three to ten years.

With a list of individual specifications for jobs and an inventory of talent, jobs can be matched to individuals. First consideration for any position similar to a present job goes, of course, to the incumbent. Does she have the abilities that will be needed in the future? She may be highly qualified; perhaps she needs further development; possibly she should be replaced. Her age must also be considered. If she will retire within the period covered by the long-range plan, obviously a replacement should be

---

[11]G. F. Brady, R. M. Fulmer, and D. L. Melnich, "Planning Executive Succession: The Effect of Recruitment Source and Organizational Problems on Anticipated Tenure," *Strategic Management Journal,* July 1982.

found. As an analytical device, some companies draw up an organizational chart with colored bands around the boxes; red, say, to denote a vacancy within three years, amber for five years, and purple for ten.

From the preceding steps, the initial set of vacancies have been spotted—new jobs in which the incumbent should be replaced, and jobs that will be vacated by retirement. The individual specifications for each of these vacancies, plus the inventory of talent, will identify the *most probable* candidates to fill the vacancies. Some companies pick a single candidate for each post; others pick two or even three (at least for major positions) because they are not certain which candidate will be best qualified by the time the vacancy opens up.

A second set of probable vacancies is created as soon as people have been identified as candidates for promotion. Are there employees qualified to move into the present positions held by these candidates? Again, a list of most-probable candidates can be prepared by comparing individual specifications with the inventory of talent. Theoretically, a third set of vacancies could be studied to find replacements for the replacements, and so on. In practice, complete plans for replacements are rarely carried beyond the second set; because so many uncertainties exist, such a projection is unwarranted. Instead, division managers simply recognize that some turnover will undoubtedly occur; consequently, they develop—often with the help of the central staff—junior people for promotion, without knowing just who will move where.

The important result of this analysis is that management foresees, several years in advance, both its need for people to fill certain key vacancies and the most promising individuals for those jobs. Management can then develop those individuals accordingly, as Figure 12.4 shows.

Planning Individual Development

Few if any candidates will have all the essential characteristics for the positions to which they might move. To overcome these deficiencies, man-

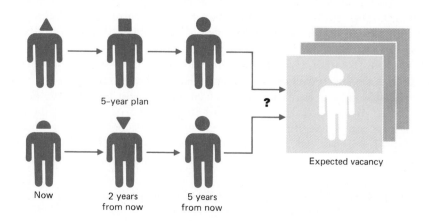

Figure 12.4 Long-run human resources planning. To prepare for an anticipated future need, the organization guides the development of candidates, so that when the vacancy occurs, one or more individuals will have qualifications that match the requirements of the vacated position.

5-year plan

?

Expected vacancy

Now

2 years
from now

5 years
from now

agement must determine what experience is needed and what capabilities should be developed. Some companies call the forms on which this information is listed "gap sheets."[12]

At this stage of planning, any major difficulties in staffing the projected organization will become apparent. It may turn out to be so hard to find satisfactory executives to fill certain positions that a firm will have to reconsider its organization design, at least at those points. In small firms whose owners will undoubtedly continue to occupy key posts, adjustments may be necessary because of the owners' strengths and limitations. A three-year program, of course, is more likely to require adjustment of organization to personnel than a ten-year program, for there is obviously more opportunity to acquire and develop suitable personnel during the longer period.

Once a decision has been made on the gaps—the improvement and abilities a person needs to qualify for promotion—development of the individual can begin. Management can help in individual development, especially in providing needed experience. For example, a sales representative who is a candidate for branch manager might first be placed in a home-office staff position for two years. This service would broaden her perspective and thoroughly acquaint her with home-office activities and people. Executives who need broader perspective can be offered an opportunity to take part in a university's executive-development program.[13]

Most of the individual development, however, will depend on the person himself. He will have to choose, at several points in his development, a career path—looking toward more intensive specialization, overseas assignments, managerial tasks, or other alternatives. He will probably not be told exactly what management plans for him, but an ambitious person will guess and will act on any suggestions about where he should try to improve.

Long-run human resources plans, like any other long-range plans, should be revised periodically. With the passage of time, forecasts of operating conditions and concepts of an ideal organization for the company will change. Assessments of people will change, too, because some will develop faster and others more slowly than anticipated. In addition, resignations may require a revision of proposals for replacements. Nevertheless, if the whole process of long-range human resources planning successfully serves its purpose, qualified people will be available to fill vacancies as they arise, and short-run organization adjustments made necessary by inadequate personnel will occur less often.

---

[12]M. London, *Developing Managers: A Guide to Motivating and Preparing People for Successful Managerial Careers* (San Francisco: Jossey-Bass, 1985).

[13]R. J. House, *Management Development: Design Evaluation and Implementation* (Ann Arbor: University of Michigan Press, 1967).

RESTRUCTURING FOR PRODUCTIVITY

One of the most startling changes in human resources management during the past several years has been a strong and pervasive push to reduce the number of managers and specialists needed to carry out a given quantity of work. In most instances this calls for a reduction in the number of professional personnel, at least in the short run; in other cases it means adding new people more slowly.

The pressure for increases in productivity of managerial and professional people appears to be more than a short-term cost-reduction effort. Instead, the driving force is greater global competition, which is expected to continue for a long time. To meet this competition, reductions may be as high as 25 percent in organizations not facing significant loss in sales volume. In companies that are losing sales, such as several steel and electronics firms, the reductions have exceeded 50 percent.

A recent conference sponsored by Columbia University's Center for Career Research and Human Resource Management explored the implications of such reductions in higher-level personnel. Representatives from fifteen major corporations, all of which were in good health, reported on their experiences with "downsizing," as such reductions are often called. The following are among the major implications:

1. Human resources planning becomes much more sensitive and vital. Nevertheless, the basic approach is the one already outlined in this chapter: (a) Redesigning the organization and restructuring jobs to produce higher output per person; (b) matching existing personnel with the new jobs; (c) fairly treating those whose talents no longer fit new job descriptions; (d) selecting and developing newly hired people for positions left vacant in step (b).

2. Personnel who no longer fit into the redesigned organization must be terminated very carefully—in order to preserve long-run morale and to conform with equal opportunity laws. Among the measures used are (a) offers of early retirement with no cut in the level of retirement benefits; (b) assistance in finding a new employer—that is, "out-placing"; (c) termination pay for several months during the search for a new job. Note that such measures have large short-run costs, so the company may actually experience no cut in expenses during the first year.

3. The remaining people must promptly adapt to a major reorganization. Job content is likely to be expanded; decentralization and other relationships will be changed; many information flows will be new; and so on. Even more important is a recommitment to the revised set-up; disheartened yearning for the "good old days" cannot be tolerated. A sharp shift in company culture is called for, as will be explained in Chapter 17.

4. In the future, managers will need more versatility. Most of the new jobs comprise a wider range of duties. And, as individuals are transferred or promoted, they will face a wider scope of problems. In addition, the expected rate of change in company activities, discussed in Chapter 1, will call for versatile managers.

Each of these implications of downsizing points to increasing changes in the work that managers will be expected to do. Personal development to prepare for these specific assignments, as recommended earlier in this chapter, will be important. Because job requirements will change often, however, such personal development will be an ongoing task.

CONCLUSION

Matching individuals and jobs, as set forth in this chapter, consists of rather sharply defined steps: clarifying jobs, preparing individual specifications, appraising personnel, making short-run adjustments, and planning long-run development of people to fit predicted organization needs. This step-by-step presentation is a useful approach to a dynamic problem. But the approach is not intended to provide a fixed blueprint.

Organizations are never completely established. Even the best plan soon becomes outdated by changes in work and personnel. The need for adjustment—often minor, occasionally major—is continual. Instead of being a static machine, an organization is an evolving social system.

We have been principally concerned with designing a system for getting work done. Clearly, such a plan is essential in order to achieve the mission of an enterprise. But emphasizing work alone tends to be too mechanistic. The wise manager conceives of an organization as a social system, not simply as a machine. Consequently, we devote our full attention in the next Part to the stuff of which an organization is made—people and their leadership.

Impact on Productivity

A good fit between job assignments and key individuals is essential for high productivity. Both effective use of a major resource (people) and getting necessary work done well are at stake.

Where people are concerned, good fits are vital if the organization is to be staffed with persons who are competent and committed. With respect to the work, high quality performance depends on having individuals suited to their respective assignments.

In practice, such neat fits are not always possible. Jobs may therefore have to be modified to match the capabilities of the available people. The danger, of course, is that such adjustments extend to a degree where productivity suffers. A related issue is merging all the diverse people into a harmonious social system. *Productive* performance includes a requirement that each specialized job activity be performed in a manner that dovetails with related work. While each individual contributes, productivity shows up as a group output.

FOR FURTHER DISCUSSION

1. "Human resources management is a glorified name for the personnel department. They don't do anything different. It's just a highfalutin name for the same old thing." Comment on this statement by a long-time professor of management.

2. Joe Wells, a twenty-five-year veteran of your company, has been assistant controller for the last ten years. With the death of the controller, Joe is promoted to the job. After several months, however, it appears that although he was a good assistant, Joe's boss never really developed his initiative. As a result, Joe is barely adequate in the top controller position. You are his supervisor. What action might you take? What factors would influence your action?

3. Give an example from your own experience (concealing the real names of the people involved) of a good and bad fit between a person and a job. The goal is to recognize the unique and specific requirements of certain jobs.

4. If, as a senior manager, you had to deal with a weak executive, which of the following alternatives would you be most inclined to choose, given your present preferences: (a) change the job, (b) change the executive, or (c) remove the executive? Why?

5. The chapter suggests three potential methods of matching people and jobs. Which would you tend to favor and why?

6. What role—if any—should a candidate's sex have in key staffing decisions?

7. Since jobs will certainly change over time, how much obligation has an organization for helping its employees change, and how much of the obligation should lie with the employees?

8. "This corporation has a human resources planning system that lists—for every one of its top 5,000 employees—three jobs, one of which will be the person's next job. We also have at least three candidates for every job that could open up at the management level." Comment on this statement by the chief executive of one of the country's largest corporations.

FOR FURTHER READING

Kotter, J. P., *The General Managers*. New York: Free Press, 1982. An in-depth look at fifteen general managers—what they actually do and how they do it.

Schein, E. H., *Career Dynamics: Matching Individual and Organization Needs*. Readng, Mass.: Addison-Wesley, 1978. Part 3 argues for an integrated human resources planning and development system based on an analysis of individual careers and key job dimensions.

Shaeffer, R. G., *Staffing Systems: Managerial and Professional Jobs*. New York: Elsevier North-Hol-land, 1983. Includes case studies of staffing systems in four different kinds of organizations.

Sonnenfeld, J., *Career Management: An Introduction to Self-Assessment, Career Development, and Career Systems*. Chicago: Science Research Associates, 1984. A nontechnical but sophisticated guide to personal career planning and the design of company career systems.

Yavitz, B. and W. H. Newman, *Strategy in Action*. New York: Free Press, 1982. Includes discussions of executive compensation and of bringing managers in from outside the organization.

Only a very special individual can withstand the psychological pressures of living in Antarctica.

The U.S. military personnel stationed in that barren iceland are literally cut off from the rest of civilization for months at a time. Unlike at the Arctic stations, nothing moves into or out of Antarctica during the winter, a season of 100-below-zero temperatures and days of hurricane-force winds.

Such horrid conditions, coupled with the six-month-long days and six-month-long nights, give rise to rampant alcoholism, drug abuse, depression, insomnia, claustrophobia, and paranoia. Indeed, the psychological burdens of living in Antarctica may be greater than the physical.

That's why the U.S. Navy conducts extensive psychological testing of winter personnel in an attempt to screen out those likely to take too much of a mental beating. More specifically, the testing is aimed at weeding out potential alcoholics, a breed that thrives on the white continent.

In fact, though, many Navy people scorn the testing. "It's a joke," said Henry Koch, a South Pole communications technician. Koch took a 536-question test that queried him about everything from harassing animals to the supernatural.

Moreover, despite the testing, alcoholism and drug abuse abound in Antarctica. A University of Oklahoma study in 1970 estimated that the average man at the Antarctic outpost outdrinks his U.S. counterpart by nine to one. "We work ourselves to death," said Barton Prentiss, a Navy steelworker who underwent an alcohol rehabilitation program only to return to drinking. "Then we drink ourselves to death."

Some denizens of Antarctica find ways to cope other than drinking, though. One peculiar group spliced together bits from westerns, Disney features, and pornographic films into their own production, and adopted a vocabulary based on the creation strange enough to unnerve relief crews that arrived the next spring.

Others pursue hobbies, teach themselves foreign languages, or just take time to reevaluate their lives. On these people, perhaps, the Navy testing has worked well.

Question

Besides testing, what methods of selection of personnel for the Antarctic assignment do you recommend?

For more information, see *The Wall Street Journal*, 10 December 1985.

APPLICATION CASES

For practice in applying concepts covered in this chapter to managerial situations, see the following managerial decision cases. The case questions particularly relevant to this chapter are listed by number after each case name.

Fyler International (p. 68) 10
Consolidated Instruments-B (p. 189) 12, 21
Delphi Insurance (p. 316) 12, 13, 22
Peter Jeffries (p. 428) 7, 11, 22
Petersen Electronics (p. 435) 6, 12, 13
Scandico (Singapore) (p. 546) 14

GAIN Software was founded three years ago by Gerald Mandel, Alice Barber, Ignacio de Santos, and Norma Zimmer. During their senior year in college, the four worked on the idea of forming a business based on developing and selling computer software specifically oriented to the needs of small retail businesses. These establishments typically deal with service bureaus or companies that handle their payroll, billings, accounts payable, and other standard services. Few grow large enough to afford to do their own computer or data processing work internally.

"We felt," said Gerry [Gerald Mandel], "that with the development of the PC [personal computer] and breakthroughs in telecommunications, we could offer something to even small retailers that they couldn't buy anywhere else. We developed software to help them with their purchasing, inventory control, pricing, and promotions. Our software isn't designed to handle big, basic operations like payroll, billing, etc. It is supposed to give small-to-medium-sized retail stores a means of making better decisions on what to buy in what quantity, where, and for what terms. Then it helps them with inventory control, pricing, and special promotions."

"Using basic hardware, owners or managers of such businesses can have daily—in some cases, hourly—access to information they need to make key decisions," said Norma Zimmer. "At reasonable prices, we can hook them up to regional data sources and through low-cost telecommunications give them access to information and sources that only large stores or chains could tap into before."

"We tested our ideas," Ignacio de Santos said, "as a project in a new ventures course and created a business plan. We wrote some of our own software—Alice is a real genius in that area—and then designed systems using readily available equipment for several small stores. We offered to *give* them the software and our services in selecting equipment and show them how to use it if they paid for the equipment and paid telephone access charges and so on. We did three stores for under $8,000 each and all three are convinced they got their money back in months."

After graduation, Gerald, Ignacio, and Norma created a partnership and launched their venture. Alice Barber decided to accept an attractive offer from a large company, but agreed to let them use software she had written and to develop new software for the company.

"We agreed to pay her a relatively small sum for each package she puts together," said Gerry, "and to pay her a royalty for every system we sell that incorporates it. Alice is still our biggest software developer, but we have three or four others we can contract with if she is too busy."

The three partners have done extremely well since graduation. While the first year was difficult, they believe they now have a winning formula and team.

"For the last two years," Norma said, "We have each earned six-figure salaries and bonuses. While we have been putting in incredible hours, we are making more money than we ever dreamed of at this stage. In addition, we have paid off our original loans and have money in the bank. We have access to a sizable line of credit if we choose to expand; I know we could attract equity money."

Expansion—how, and how fast—has created the first serious disagreement among the three partners. Each has a quite different view on how to capitalize further on their current success. The plans are outlined as follows.

Gerry's Plan

"I want us to keep doing what we are doing now. We have thousands of good-sized communities and cities to target. What we have been doing is picking one and spending a few days to a week researching it. We get data on retail establishments, analyze it, and select a small target group of three to six businesses. Then we really study these businesses and design, in rough form, systems for them. We all work on these systems jointly. When we are ready, we each take one or two stores and go in for the sale. We often haven't even been in the store before and the owners are amazed at what we know about their businesses.

"We can usually tell them not only the key characteristics of their business and their key numbers, but the names of their grandchildren and pets as well. We show them brochures and testimonials and then demonstrate what we can offer them. Sometimes we cart in our own hardware and rent a hotel suite for a week or two. Sometimes we rent space and equipment from a local service bureau, and in large cities sometimes we set up our own office when we plan to stay a month or more. Norma says we are like a traveling vaudeville team. We do our magic and move on.

"Every time, if we have done our homework, we sell 75 to 100 percent of our initial target group. We 'low ball' the cost and really custom-tailor the product for them. With them as our base, we then blitz the rest of the town. The companies we sell initially become our strongest support team, as long as we stay away from their major competitors.

"We do much more standard packages and charge full price as we move through town. When we have covered the biggest and best stores, we head for home, pick our next target, and start our research and plans again.

"Except for demonstration equipment, we have no real investment. We sell our software, we design the systems, and we order equipment if asked to do so. When it arrives, we move back into the community and set it up and either teach them to use it or hire local people—believe it or not, often high school or college kids—to teach them to use it.

"We have an answering service and a twelve-hour-a-day hot line to handle any questions or problems that crop up. Finally, we *charge* them a small fee to receive our 'newsletter' and our special reports on new equipment and software. We now have a big enough customer base to use the newsletter and reports to set up a good mail-order operation, if we could find someone to run it for us.

"My plan is to keep right on doing what we are doing. We travel to some neat places, work real hard for a while, make lots of money, and then pull back. We could work six cities or sixty in a year. We could take a couple of weeks off for each month of high-pressure work and still make big money, or we could pile through six months and then spend a month visiting Katmandu. Later, if we want, we could add one, two, or three new partners, teach them a piece at a time until we know we can trust them, and grow slowly without risk.

"What I love about what we do now is that *we* are in charge. No big capital tie-up, no bureaucracy. We decide where we work, how hard we work, and how much we make. We get along fine, so why spoil a good thing?"

Norma's Plan

"I find a lot of what Gerry says appealing," said Norma, "but his approach has a number of flaws. While I'm not nuts about trying to keep up this pace, I can handle it. What I can't handle is the realization that we may be giving up millions. We have a winning formula but we must leverage our time and capitalize on it. Second, if we don't build a bigger, stronger organization *fast,* we may lose not only opportunities but the whole program. A few 'copycats' have already tried to imitate our approach and are using it with some success. They haven't hit us head-on in the same town, and probably won't for a while, but this thing may pyramid and we may have fifty carbon copies to deal with in the near future.

"One of our imitators will do what I want to do and will become a large, well-organized regional or national organization. Maybe even worse is if one of them decides to take their version of our formula to an existing large company and sells them the idea. That's what Ignacio wants us to do before someone else has the same idea.

"My plan is to get big as fast as possible. We must set up an organization—not a big one, but one that can do what we do now on a regional or even national basis. We can hire specialists in software, hardware, and telecommunication to design systems. Then, through either our own sales group or by franchising, we can sell, install, and maintain the systems.

"With a larger organization, we can look for better prices and/or commissions from the equipment companies and we can really organize and exploit our potential mail-order system as well. *What* we do isn't that complex. Unless we get bigger and stronger so that we can offer better service at lower prices, we will lose what we now have.

"I want us to borrow what we can, incorporate, and sell up to 40 percent of our stock to either a venture capitalist or to the public. I am sure we can raise enough money to operate not only on a larger scale, but a lot more professionally and not have to kill ourselves in the process.

"Unfortunately, I am having trouble convincing either Gerry or Ignacio that this is not just the best approach, but the only way to *survive*. At least I have Gerry convinced that we need to change our name. GAIN was corny enough when we were in college, but now with Alice no longer active, we should drop the *A*, and I can't see us as GIN Software. Right now we aren't so well known that a name change would hurt us, but if we grow we need to have a name that fits.

"I like 'Strategic Information Systems' or 'SIS.' We have to make sure it isn't taken, but Gerry is willing to check it out. Ignacio feels it doesn't matter, so why waste the money on name research. He wants to 'cash in his chips' and look for another game.

"Frankly, I think he is just worn out. We have been working hard for the last couple of years. I want us all to just take a month off, rest up, and then spend the next several months getting the money, designing our structure, building systems, and hiring people."

Ignacio's Plan

"Norma may be right," mused Ignacio. "Maybe I will feel differently after a month off, but I doubt it. While we are all exhausted, I don't think I will feel any different after a vacation. Even if I do, I don't think Gerry will go along. I don't mind working for a big company, but I don't want to be a manager! I don't mind working very hard, but I don't want responsibility for other people's lives. I manage myself quite well but not others. I am impatient with people who aren't as quick or as willing to sacrifice as I am. I hate having to criticize them or even depend on them.

"If we followed Norma's plan, I would want no part of management. Just give me a territory, some support people supervised by others, and turn me loose—not in this 'gypsy' approach we now take but in a given geographic area. Then let me work it in a steady way. With salary, commissions, and equity, I can make enough money not to need even a big title.

"Gerry isn't like that; he doesn't want any part of a big organization even if it was his own. He hates bureaucracy. He loves to freewheel and work on his own, but I don't think he would be happy doing what I described for myself. I don't want to manage, but I can be managed. Gerry would have to be the top manager to rise above the bureaucracy, and I don't think he would be a good executive.

"My recommendation is that we sell out and sell out fast while we have something to sell. Sooner than later, a big computer or telecommunications company is going to either buy out one of our imitators or set up their own operation. Once they realize just how much there is to make, they will go for it.

"I believe we should spend our month off studying possible buyers.

Then we should show them our books—not our 'tricks,' but our books. If we get a good lawyer or 'finder' to help us, I'll bet we could get a big chunk of money up front and either royalties or stock.

"I would be willing to work for the big company to help them get started and Norma might, if she had no choice, do the same. In fact, she might parlay this into a big executive job with the acquiring company running this operation for them.

"Gerry might help during the transition but if he wants out, that's okay. There should be enough money for him to start up something new on his own. Who knows—maybe I'll join him.

"Out of respect for Norma, both Gerry and I have agreed to take a month away from the business and relax. Then we will get together and try to resolve this."

QUESTIONS

Part I

1. In what ways may the introduction of new information technology impact the role of managers? Explain.

2. Which external environment factors will have the greatest impact on what GAIN should do next?

Part II

3. Evaluate the viability of the current strategy against what is implied by Norma's plan.

4. What is GAIN's best strategy for dealing with "copycat" competitors?

5. How would adoption of Norma's plan affect the number and type of standing plans needed to manage GAIN effectively?

6. In what ways will "higher-level" ends have more to do with selecting the best strategy than detailed means of implementing each?

Part III

7. What will be key organizational considerations if Gerry's approach prevails? How could he increase the likelihood of selling his approach through organizational suggestions?

8. What will be the major delegation problems associated with Norma's preferred strategy?

9. Do you feel Ignacio would be effective in the role he describes for himself in his plan? What would determine whether he succeeded in helping a large company succeed with GAIN after acquisition?

10. How may increased use of personal computers and good software affect the organization of small stores (delegation and degrees of centralization)?

11. What key staff groups will be needed under Gerry's plan? Norma's plan?

12. *Summary Report Question for Part III.* How will the different strategies employed in each partner's plan affect selection of a proper structure? Please be specific with respect to basic departmentation, degrees of decentralization, and delegation. What will be the most significant staffing decisions (matching people and jobs) under *each* strategy?

Part IV

13. How may changing needs affect these three partners' motivation?

14. How should they motivate others if they gradually added partners and followed Gerry's plans for growth? Consider more than monetary motivation.

15. What kind of leadership style would be needed if Norma's strategy were to succeed? Do you believe she can supply this leadership, or would it be better to bring in professional managers?

Part V

16. What control mechanisms do the partners have at their disposal under their current strategies? How effective do you feel their current control systems probably are?

17. How would control systems have to change under Norma's proposal? Consider the mix between steering and budgetary controls.

18. Would the controls used by a large company if it acquired GAIN be similar to what is needed under Norma's plan? How would they differ?

Summary Report Question for Solution of Case as a Whole

19. Develop a report supporting your choice of the best approach for GAIN to take. Do not limit your alternatives to the three given. Seek a creative approach that might best satisfy all three partners.

Decision Case III–2
CLIFFORD NELSON

The Simmons Simulator Corporation is the largest producer of process analysis equipment in the world.* Since 1940, Simmons has been a leader in applying advances in data processing technology directly to the monitoring and active control of operating systems.

The company designs and manufactures three main product lines. Of these, the simulator line has been the most profitable for the company. Simmons simulators differ from computer-based simulators in that a Simmons simulator is a small-scale mock-up that physically reproduces the actual operating process, rather than mathematically modelling the process. However, simulator systems do utilize analytical computational capabilities as part of the total simulation process.

Simmons designs and manufactures control devices, instruments, and simulator components, but also purchases these and computer components from other companies. While Simmons holds some key patents, particularly in the simulator-component and control-device areas, the major strength of the company, in attaining its position of market leadership, has been its capacity for developing total systems. Simmons' continued dominance of its industry has been based on a combination of technological innovation and a reputation for reliability and quality service. This combination of product leadership and client service has enabled Simmons to grow rapidly in size, market penetration, and profitability; in the last fiscal year, Simmons realized profits of $600 million on total sales of approximately $3 billion.

H. J. Simmons and the Simmons Philosophy

The company was founded in the late 1930s by H. J. Simmons. At the beginning of World War II, Mr. Simmons turned his attention to the development of effective means of controlling total production processes. He recognized the potential of electronic computers as high-speed analytical processors and began developing computer-assisted simulators. By coupling the computer technology with the simulator concept in his emphasis on total process control, Mr. Simmons was able to move his company to a dominant position in the total process control market in the early 1950s.

Simmons employees throughout the organization spoke warmly of Mr. Simmons and pridefully of their contribution to the organization. The "Simmons philosophy"—technical excellence, product innovation, customer service, and employee satisfaction and security—was a real factor in forming decisions and attitudes throughout the company. As Mr. Simmons stated at a recent annual meeting:

"As you know, the success that we have been fortunate enough to enjoy at Simmons has been based on our continued adherence to two basic tenets of good management.

"One, the highest purpose of business is to produce quality products to serve today's needs and to be prepared with quality products for tomorrow's needs when they emerge.

"Two, a Simmons product is a Simmons product while it is being

---

*Other Simmons Simulator cases are the following: "Simmons Simulator Corporation," in W. H. Newman and E. K. Warren, *The Process of Management,* 4th ed.(Englewood Cliffs N.J.: Prentice-Hall, 1977), Chap. 28; and a longer version by T. P. Ference, I. C. MacMillan, and W. A. Benson, prepared for use in executive programs, 1978.

manufactured, when it is sold, and for as long as it is in use by the customer.

"Thus, we will continue to forego short-run profits in the interests of continued investment in product development and product excellence, we will continue to rest our name and reputation on the provision of quality service for all Simmons products at all customer installations, and we will continue to attempt to insulate our employees from fluctuations in the economy or in the levels of business activity through the practice of steady employment. We will also continue to honor our obligation to stockholders and to consolidate it through continued improvements in return on investments and realized profits achieved through diligent and demanding management."

The Structure of Simmons Simulator Corporation

Although he is approaching seventy H. J. Simmons remains as chairman and president. Two executive vice-presidents and the corporate treasurer report directly to Mr. Simmons. One executive vice-president has all staff groups reporting to him. The other has the five operating divisions under him. The operating company is divided into five major divisions, each headed by a division president. The corporate staff is composed of five major groups, each headed by a vice-president. Mr. Simmons, the two executive vice-presidents, the treasurer, and the chief counsel serve as the Management Committee. As will be described next, the Management Committee is the primary mechanism for integrating corporate policy with divisional operations and for reviewing and approving divisional operating plans. The organizational structure reflects two major concerns:

1. The operating divisions have been established to reflect basic product/customer markets. Organizational policies and structure have been developed in an effort to allow divisional presidents maximum flexibility and freedom in day-to-day operations.
2. The corporate staff groups are small, and are intended to reflect technical expertise available to the executive group in determining policy directions and in monitoring the implementation of policy.

The corporate staff groups are located at corporate headquarters in Southern Connecticut. Divisional headquarters are scattered throughout the Northeast.

The Simmons Planning System

Corporate planning at Simmons is a combination of a two-year operating plan and a five-year strategic plan, each reviewed and updated annually at both the corporate and division levels.

The corporate-planning process at Simmons is a year-long effort, repeated annually, and therefore goes on continuously. At the beginning of each planning cycle, each division president receives a detailed statement of the overall strategic plan and the objectives and needs established at the corporate level. This strategic plan includes an updating of performance against strategic objectives established in previous planning cycles, an identification of specific planning questions that each division is to consider in the present planning cycle, a description of the business environment for the coming year as estimated by the corporate staff, and an identification of special problem areas. The planning document also includes a review of established corporate policies and, typically, a detailed set of specific questions and objectives aimed specifically at each of the operating divisions.

With the strategic planning mandate in hand, division management is required to produce an operating plan with three main components:

1. A two-year operating plan to be initiated at the end of the present operating year. This plan should contain, by the end of the planning cycle, projections of sales, costs, resource needs, and staffing plans for all programs, ongoing and new, for the two-year planning period. This two-year operating plan should contain detailed responses to all strategic objectives and needs raised by the corporate planning guidelines, should be consistent with corporate resource constraints, and should incorporate all information available from corporate and divisional staff on economic conditions, competitor behavior, and technological developments. The planning process is intended to be an interactive one, reflecting continuous contact between division level planners and corporate staff experts; division management is expected to notify relevant corporate staff groups of its plans as they develop in order to elicit useful information, as well as possible instances of corporate nonconcurrence with the divisional plans. Division management is required to make a formal, preliminary submission of its plan to the corporate staff groups at least two months before final review of the plan. Finally, all divisional plans are presented for review and approval to the Management Committee in the fourth quarter of the planning cycle.

2. In addition to the two-year operating plan, each division is required to produce in each year's planning cycle a detailed, qualitative discussion in its program planning proposals of the opportunities and challenges it faces over the longer period of the five-year strategic plan.

3. Finally, division management is required to present in each planning cycle a detailed response to specific questions raised by the corporate-planning guidelines.

Clifford Nelson is in charge of "Product Test: Measurement Methods," a section of the engineering department of SSD, the largest of Simmons' divisions. Cliff has been with Simmons for three years, having joined them after completing an engineering degree. His job is to review all testing procedures used to determine whether products and components produced by SSD meet standards set for them.

"I don't determine the standards, nor do I conduct the actual tests. My job is to direct and coordinate a group of engineers," explained Nelson, "who develop and evaluate testing procedures. Standards are set elsewhere for everything that has Simmons' name on it. My job is to see to it that we have tests that will assure the division president that those standards are met. It is a very challenging job and I have spent many nights burning the midnight oil working on a technical problem, but up until now I have always had my boss's support."

SSD recorded sales of $1.2 billion last year but saw profits challenged by numerous smaller competitors. None could offer the full range of systems and service offered by SSD, but several made component elements that matched Simmons' in quality and performance. Recently, SSD learned that several smaller companies had begun announcing components that were compatible with both Simmons and competitive systems, and that could substantially increase the productivity and flexibility of the total system. These components would be available in about six months.

SSD has been working for almost eight years to develop a fully integrated system of its own to offer these features.

Nels Ohlberg, division marketing director, stated, "We have the system almost ready to go. It will not only replace much of our existing Series G stuff but will knock out many competitors' ability to sell systems wired together with a hodgepodge of peripherals. Within a year or so, we can offer, for less money, something better than anything now available." Still, Ohlberg had reason to be concerned. He learned that the new components being announced by competitors were gaining wide praise in the industry. He approached the division president, Lou Mertz, and told him that unless SSD announced its new system within thirty to sixty days, a substantial segment of the market would purchase the peripheral units of competitors and tie them into existing systems.

At roughly $100,000 to $150,000 each, these peripherals represent a sizable investment to the purchasers. Ohlberg fears that once they have bought them and tied them in, they will not be able to justify the immediate purchase of Simmons' new system.

"We have waited years to knock out those ragtag systems made up of some of our equipment and lots of odds and ends," Ohlberg said. "At last, we are almost there. We can offer the market a fully integrated system with Simmons' name on it for only a bit more than the Rube Goldberg stuff they have now. If we don't announce, however, before they commit to these latest add-ons, we will face a market in which companies will have to wait at least three or four years to write off their new investment. Our only other option would be to price our new system at levels that would not be profitable and even risk the Justice Department coming in and claiming unfair pricing. We stand to lose millions unless we announce what we have coming in the next two months."

Mertz, the division president, asked for a special report on the matter.

All department heads except engineering agree that an earlier announce-ment is needed. The head of manufacturing is certain, based on prototypes, that he can produce what would be promised at currently estimated costs. The division human resources director fears that failure to announce could lead to major sales losses and threaten layoffs. The division controller con-firms that not announcing in the next sixty days would cost the division millions in lost profits.

Engineering executives have indicated that they are confident that the new system they have designed will pass all tests and can be produced in volume at cost and quality levels currently forecasted.

"The only reservation I have," said John Weir, director of engineer-ing, "is that several key components have not met final test standards, and thus the whole system cannot be said to have passed final tests. Corporate has made it very clear in the past that they will not even look at a new product announcement until all final tests have been passed. Since this is a very important new system, standards have been set very high and tests not only have been designed to meet high confidence levels but are layered in a manner that offers even higher degrees of certainty. If we use the tests as currently set up, it could be a year before standards are met. I have asked Cliff Nelson's boss, Gene Gulden (director of product test), to have him find a way around our dilemma."

Gulden made it clear to Nelson that everyone was counting on him. "Cliff is the best we have," Gulden said. "No one knows more about this area than he. At first he told me the problem could not be solved by chang-ing the tests, but when I relayed this up the line, I got blasted. Ohlberg was almost apoplectic.

" 'No third-level technician is going to hold us up,' he bellowed. 'You tell that narrow-minded, provincial jerk that if he can't see the big picture, you'll find someone who will!' Of course, I had to tell Ohlberg not to give me orders—that I would handle my own people. But basically I agree with him. Cliff just wants to play it extra safe. If there are problems later, he is afraid he will be blamed. I have told him not to worry."

Cliff is worried nonetheless. He feels that he could alter certain tests and, by shifting their sequence, probably squeak through final tests in the time requested.

"But," he says, "we would be cutting all kinds of corners. Anyone looking at these changes compared to normal division practices would know we really twisted this one. My boss, Gene Gulden, has told me not to worry—that, while the division president said he wants to hear all sides of this issue, he knows he can't afford to be late. Therefore, they say no one will question our changes. I'm not sure. Normally, when all depart-ments agree and the division plan meets corporate guidelines, it sails through corporate review. But what happens if corporate engineering staff or even legal gets wind of this? They might not concur, and if they force debate, I could be in trouble. I hate to seem like a narrow technician who can't see what is best for the division but, damn it, the tests they want would be shoddy and could easily be misleading, even if applied rigor-ously."

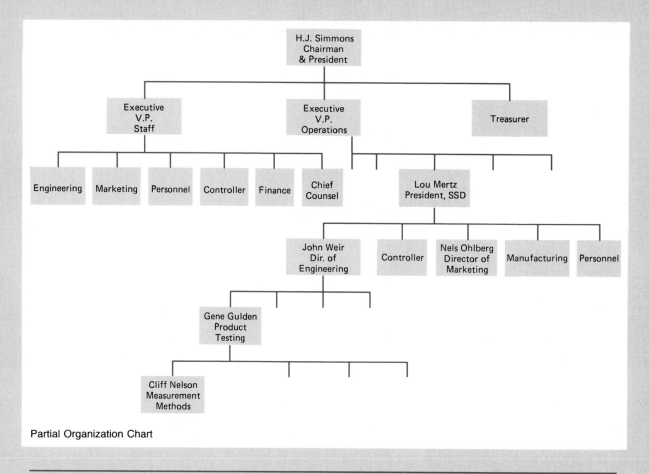

Partial Organization Chart

QUESTIONS

Part I

1. How might better monitoring of the environment have avoided the dilemma now facing Lou Mertz?

2. Is a giant company, an industry leader, more or less free to do what is needed when faced with the problem facing Mertz?

Part II

3. What elements of Simmons' master strategy might help provide important criteria to guide Mertz in his choice of actions?

4. In what ways may standing plans prove to be important in dealing with this situation? What are their limitations or drawbacks?

5. Why might the announcement "problem" be stated differently by Nelson, Ohlberg, Mertz, and Simmons? How would each state it?

6. Develop a means-end diagram that shows how one might *link up* the several problems as defined by Nelson, Ohlberg, Mertz, and Simmons.

7. From Nelson's perspective, is it more important for him to push toward root causes of his gap or move toward higher-level goals by asking "Why?" Explain.

Part III

8. Should this decision be elevated to the president or be resolved at the division level? Why?

9. In what ways does Simmons' organizational structure contribute toward making a decision that is consistent with overall corporate strategy? In what ways might the structure detract from the decision being made in a corporate, strategic context?

10. Who should have what kinds of authority in making a decision on when to announce?

11. Discuss the role that (a) division and (b) corporate staff should play in decisions such as this. What authority should each level have?

12. How might the talent and temperament of Cliff Nelson influence his ability to play the role most helpful to Lou Mertz, or even H. J. Simmons, in arriving at a sound decision?

13. What role, if any, should corporate staff play in influencing Mertz's decision?

14. How much weight should H. J. Simmons give to corporate staff if it argued against announcing early and Mertz argued for it? Why?

15. *Summary Report Question for Part III.* Assume you are H. J. Simmons. Using this case to illustrate your answer, indicate (a) the key steps that should be taken, (b) the people (management levels or positions) who should make the decision, and (c) the checks built into the system to ensure that this kind of decision is made well.

Part IV

16. When or how would conflict be desirable (healthy) in this situation? When and how would it be destructive?

17. What should H. J. Simmons do to increase the chances of desirable conflict emerging and being resolved satisfactorily?

18. How may H. J. Simmons' personal leadership style affect the quality of the decision on this announcement?

Part V

19. What should be included in corporate level controls to ensure that divisional decisions on matters like this are made in the context of corporate strategy?

20. Would broad corporate controls suffice to ensure a good decision at the division level in this case, or are detailed corporate controls needed? Explain.

21. How should corporate staff be used in "controlling" divisions in situations such as this?

22. The two-year operating plans at the Simmons Simulator Corporation replaced annual financial budgets. How do these two-year plans differ from the typical budgets used by most companies? What advantages do you see in the Simmons Simulator planning process?

Summary Report Question for Solution of Case as a Whole

23. What action would you take if you were Cliff Nelson? Be specific as to *how* you would carry it out. If you were the division head (Mertz), what action would you take once you learned of Nelson's decision?

Decision Case III-3
DELPHI INSURANCE

"During the next ten years, we will find out who the best managers are," said George Hankinson, chairman of Delphi Insurance. "There just aren't that many 'tricks' in this business. Most of the industry leaders, by now, have evolved a strategy and determined which niches to go after. The companies that come out on top are going to be the ones who implement well . . . who can make it happen, and that means management."

Hankinson was addressing the top twenty-four executives at Delphi. As the first speaker, he set the theme for a three-day meeting held at the Spring Vale Country Club. He had called this meeting to consider how to (1) identify, (2) develop, and (3) utilize more fully middle-management talent.

"This company, despite the fact that we have already moved into the top five in our industry, will be number one in profits, if not in volume, in the next ten years, and we are going to do it through better management and more highly motivated personnel. While I hope for new services, new markets, new wrinkles, we are not going to count on them as the key to our continued growth. We are going to get there primarily by doing the same basic things our competition does but doing them better and doing them for less. Through motivation and management, we will get there. We must get more from *fewer* people, not so much to reduce payroll costs, but to improve effectiveness by challenging people with more demanding jobs.

"Ladies and gentlemen, I am proud of you! I believe that the group in this room includes the finest top executives in this industry. I also believe that we have at the bottom of this organization thousands of outstanding hourly people. Our agents, actuaries, underwriters, analysts, etc. are, in my judgment, the best as a group in the world.

"But—ladies and gentlemen, our *middle* is flabby and very, very mediocre! We are a company whose success stems from two dozen geniuses at the top and thousands of highly competent, well-motivated workers at the bottom, but our middle-management ranks are overstaffed in terms of numbers and layers and understaffed in terms of ability. We have too many mediocre people shuffling papers and keeping each other busy. We undoubtedly also have in these layers too many good, once-good, could-be-good managers being suffocated by the absence of challenge and our continued acceptance of mediocre performance on their part and that of their peers.

"This will change! I want us to develop plans to reduce the number of layers, combine jobs, and do whatever is necessary to develop *fewer, more challenging* positions. Then, through attrition and dismissal, we will thin the ranks and shift to the new structure. Simultaneously, we must develop systems to find those who want to grow, help them grow, and give them *bigger* jobs, not necessarily *high-level* jobs. The purpose of this meeting is to work through what has to be done, *this year,* to move quickly in these directions."

Leroy Carthage, a senior vice-president and a man of considerable independent income, was the first to respond to Hankinson's statements.

"George," he said, "I have been part of Delphi for almost forty years now. In four or five more, I'll collect my clock and retire, so I don't care too much if we try out your notion but, frankly, I think you're making a big mistake.

"You are dead right in your description of what *is* right now. I don't know about that genius stuff, but you have twenty-four of the best senior vice-presidents in this industry. You are also right when you describe our lower-level people as outstanding individual contributors. Finally, you are dead right in describing our middle-management ranks as 'havens for hacks.' But George, I truly believe you are wrong to try to change it. Most of those middle-management jobs require detail-oriented bureaucrats to somehow get all the papers shuffled properly. They are dull, routine, uninspiring, non-growth supervisory and middle-management positions, but they are *necessary*.

"If you put really good high-potential people in those jobs, they will go nuts in a year. Face it George, there are lots of dull, boring jobs that have to be done. I don't think you can change these jobs. Let's just be grateful that there are enough dull, boring people to do them."

"You were born two hundred years too late, Leroy," Hankinson quipped. "You could have been a great Louis XIV, or at least Marie Antoinette's baker. If we don't try to strengthen the quality of people by creating more demanding jobs, where will we find replacements for those in this room when the time comes?"

"This group can be replaced," said Leroy, "the same way it was built. There will always be a few people with talent who want *so badly* to escape the mediocrity of middle management they will somehow rise above it. If we don't find someone at the right time, we will do just what we did with Jeb and Franklyn [pointing to the corporate counsel and executive vice-president of finance]; we'll go hunting at IBM or Exxon or General Electric. George, all you are going to do is raise a lot of people's expectations and ultimately disappoint them when we can't keep delivering new challenges. It's better that you just let them write notes to each other and snooze a bit. Finally, George, if you do try to change things, you are going to have one hell of a transition. What do we do with several thousand long-service, middle managers who are very well suited to their current jobs but can't handle a bigger one and won't accept a smaller one?"

The other senior officers remained silent throughout this exchange. Some looked uncomfortable, several smiled and exchanged winks.

"I hear you, Leroy," said Hankinson, "loud and clear, but we *will* change things. Do you realize that with 'assistant to's' and deputy 'this and thats', there are seven levels of management between you and the hourly people in your division? I'm not singling you out as the worst offender, either, This is, to me, totally unacceptable. I want fewer layers, better people, and probably fewer people. We have sound strategies for our several businesses. In fact, they were sound five years ago, but by the time things creak up and down this pyramid, we waste millions of dollars and many opportunities. We must get fewer, better, more self-motivated managers *throughout* this organization.

"I've heard Leroy's views. What do the rest of you think? We *will* get started; the question is how."

QUESTIONS

Part I

1. What environmental forces in the period from 1946 to 1983 contributed to recent trends toward flatter organizations and the need for increased productivity through people?

2. What do you think of Hankinson's "strategy" to concentrate on implementation of existing strategies rather than seek to modify or add to them in any significant manner?

3. Hankinson seems to place a great deal of emphasis on the role of managers in bringing about improved results. How appropriate do you feel his optimism is for a company such as this in the insurance industry?

Part II

4. If Hankinson succeeds in reducing the number of layers of management and increasing the quality of middle-management personnel, how *should* that affect the need for, and types of, standing plans?

5. Hankinson and Carthage apparently disagree on *means* of improving productivity, not *ends*. How might a good diagnosis of the whole situation help them reconcile their differences?

6. How should Hankinson test his choice of the best way to improve company results before making major changes in the organization? Might the current task forces help? What are their other roles?

7. How appropriate, in your opinion, is Hankinson's participative approach to implementing his decisions? In what ways might it be better or worse to have involved only a few key people and developed more detailed plans before informing or involving others?

Part III

8. Can Delphi do a sound job of restructuring without first reassessing its master strategy?

9. How should the strategy influence the resizing effort Hankinson has proposed?

10. Estimate the likely impact of Hankinson's plans, if they are successfully implemented, on each of the six key factors in departmentation.

11. How might an educated outside analyst determine whether Hines has decentralized too much to his "can do" section?

12. How might Hankinson test the validity of Carthage's statement, "If you put really good . . . people in those jobs, they will go nuts in a year"?

13. What will be needed in Delphi to meet short-run and long-run personnel planning needs if Hankinson's decisions are to be implemented effectively?

14. *Summary Report Question for Part III*. Can Delphi accomplish Hankinson's objectives without carefully reviewing the top twenty-four jobs as well? Who should consider reorganizing the senior-level jobs?

Part IV

15. Comment on Carthage's statement that "there are lots of dull, boring jobs that have to be done. I don't think you can change these jobs. Let's just be grateful that there are enough dull, boring people to do them."

16. Hankinson's plans will have a major impact on informal groups, customs, and roles in middle-management levels. What steps should be taken to deal with this impact?

17. How would you characterize Hankinson's leadership style based on his approach to senior management at the Spring Vale meeting?

18. How important a role will internal politics play in affecting the implementation of Hankinson's decision? What might he do to channel political behavior in a constructive direction?

Part V

19. What effects would a significant movement toward Hankinson's goals have on control systems used by and for middle management?

20. Will strategic control be made more difficult or easier if Hankinson's plan succeeds? Explain.

21. How should Hankinson measure progress toward his resizing goals?

Summary Report Question for Solution of Case as a Whole

22. Develop your recommendations for the eight to ten key steps in developing a flatter, leaner Delphi organization. BE specific as to *what* should be done, by *whom,* and in what *time frame*.

13

Motivation: Adjusting Jobs to New Values

LEARNING OBJECTIVES

After completing this chapter, you should be able to

1. Identify common changes in personal values that affect the kinds of jobs people want.
2. Explain how managers' understanding of the potency of their workers' needs can aid in leadership.
3. Discuss the strengths and weaknesses of trying to satisfy workers' needs on the job.
4. List ways organizations can be redesigned to improve motivation.
5. Describe the role of financial compensation in satisfying human needs.

PART IV: LEADING

Making all the strategic and structural changes that have been suggested in preceding Parts of this book still does not insure an organization's success. Critical though these planning and organizing elements are, they do not actually get work done. Success requires that individuals throughout the organization not only do the tasks assigned to them, but that these individual employees—to a large degree—internalize these expectations and come to own them as if they were their own values.

One of the trickiest and most critical aspects of managing is to secure the actual execution of plans by people in their jobs. This requires leadership, the subject of Part IV.

Leading is the process by which a manager directly and personally influences the behavior of subordinates. It is a two-way relationship—with feedback running the gamut from highly subjective, personal responses from subordinates to dry, raw data. In Part IV we will explore individual motivation, leadership styles, interpersonal communication, managing conflict, and managing change. The more systematic arrangements for controlling will be examined in Part V.

CHANGING VALUES

Since people are a manager's chief resource, and since organizational success is so dependent on such individuals' actions to achieve results, it is vital for a manager to understand why people behave as they do. Formal organization is but one part of what guides the behavior of people at work. In addition, managers must understand the full range of influences, formal and otherwise, on the behavior of organization members. Personal drives as well as the results of social interactions heavily influence such outcomes.[1]

The experience or reward that "turns you on" probably differs from the things your grandparents valued. Your grandmother did not even dream of being an executive vice-president of a Wall Street bank. As pointed out in Chapter 3, several major influences are altering our hopes and attitudes. Here are a few of the social forces that are reshaping people's values:

- Higher educational attainment
- Changing life-styles, including the influence of television watching, weekend travel, sex, and child care

[1]T. Mitchell, *Motivation and Performance* (Chicago: Science Research Associates, 1984).

322

Increasingly splintered loyalties

New (unlimited) roles for women

Increased sense of entitlement, and legal means to pursue them

Shift in job opportunities to the service sector

Because of such changes, and the foregoing list is by no means complete, we must be careful in making assumptions about what motivates workers. Note, however, that individuals continue to have strong desires; the specifics may have changed, but the opportunity to motivate people by fulfilling their needs remains.

The fact that values are changing underscores two facets of a manager's task of motivating subordinates. (1) Values differ from person to person. To be effective, the manager should try to identify and understand what is currently important to each subordinate. (2) The challenge then is to structure the total work situation such that each person gets substantial fulfillment of personal values. Of course, there will be sharp limitations on what can be provided; nevertheless, a reasonable fit must be achieved if motivated behavior is to result. The focus in this chapter will be on ways to fit the employee's values (needs) with the work situation. The following chapters then turn to a manager's own behavior in leading and communicating.

WHY PEOPLE WORK

The leadership phase of managing involves both creating a challenging work situation and building favorable one-to-one personal relationships. Both dimensions can be improved by thoughtful attention to the ideas and feelings of the individuals involved.

Motivation as a Process

One might be tempted to try to oversimplify a manager's task of motivating employees. The easy assumption is that providing selected benefits or working conditions will almost automatically result in motivated workers. For instance, a manager might assume that paying double the minimum wage and using consultative supervision will ensure that subordinates will work hard. Indeed, early behavioral science research took this view.

Recently, much more recognition has been given to the linkage, or process, that connects benefits or working conditions with specific behavior desired by the manager. Unless workers see a linkage, they will not be motivated. According to the *expectancy theory*, motivation occurs when a worker expects—anticipates—that a particular behavior will help him to satisfy his needs.[2]

The theory doesn't presume that workers make a mathematical calculation for each of their actions—"If I finish this report on time, the payoff will be $73.45." Rather, the linkage is often less clearly defined. It may be just a *belief* that a particular sort of behavior will increase (or decrease) one's chances of obtaining certain satisfactions. Nevertheless, that expectation is essential if managers are to motivate workers.

For managers to use the expectancy theory, of course, they must have a sound sense of what workers want to obtain by working. And because managers are concerned about specific individuals performing specific tasks, they should be sensitive to differences among subordinates "want" lists. As just noted, people's wants are changing and becoming less uniform; this complicates the task of motivating.[3]

Fortunately, we do have several analytical frameworks that suggest a variety of satisfactions that people are likely to seek. We also know of an array of things managers might do to create such satisfactions. These valuable aids are discussed in this and the following chapters. From these frameworks a manager can construct at least a preliminary picture of (1) what will motivate T. V. Smith, (2) what the company can do to make these rewards potentially available to Smith, and (3) what behavior will be required of Smith in order to convert the potential rewards to reality, as suggested in Figure 13.1.

Nature of Needs

The term *needs* is sometimes used to refer only to essential requirements for survival. Here, however, it is helpful to follow the practice of psychologists and adopt a much broader meaning. Needs include both what people *must* have and what they merely want. Psychologists say that as long as a person wants something, he has psychological need for it, regardless of what someone else may think of the justification for this desire. This concept of need leads us to avoid making subjective judgments. We would not

---

[2]E. E. Lawler, *Motivation in Work Organizations* (Belmont, Calif.: Brooks/Cole, 1973); and E. E. Lawler, *Pay and Organization Development* (Reading, Mass.: Addison-Wesley, 1981).

[3]L. Roth, *Managing the Technical Professional Workforce* (New York: Career Center Publications, Columbia University, 1984); and C. J. Fombrun, N. M. Tichy, and M. A. Devanna, *Strategic Human Resource Management* (New York: John Wiley & Sons, 1984).

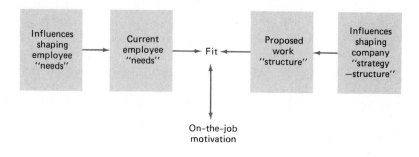

Figure 13.1 Analysis for building on-the-job motivation for each employee

judge, for example, whether it is a matter of necessity or desire for a college student to have a car on campus.

Needs vary widely among individuals, and as we just noted, such variation appears to be widening. Nevertheless, the underlying types of needs are quite stable, and such a classification helps a manager to understand the individuals in his work group.

Needs have been classified in various ways. Our attention will be limited to those needs that can be satisfied to a significant degree by working in a business enterprise, for these are the needs a manager may be able to do something about. Drawing on A. H. Maslow's classic hierarchy of needs, we can classify these job-related needs as physical needs, security needs, social needs, and self-expression needs.[4]

Physical needs.   All human beings need to survive and to physiologically maintain their bodies. Thus, they require food, drink, shelter, rest, and exercise. Until such needs are reasonably well satisfied, they remain strong, driving forces. Our society is prosperous enough, however, to enable the minimum physiological requirements to be met for most people most of the time. Management has devoted a good deal of attention to providing adequate ventilation, heat, and light to ensure working conditions that make a workplace physically satisfactory, if not attractive. If computerized communication enables more people to work at home, a new set of physical needs may arise.

Security needs.   This is an age in which entire Western society seems to have an obsession with security. We all want the satisfactions we now enjoy to continue and hope that no misfortune will cross our path. Guarantees are impossible, particularly in a dynamic society, and we must couch our hopes for security in realistic terms. Both economic and psychological security are involved.

With respect to work, most of the attention of social reformers has been focused on *economic security*. People worry about steady employment, provisions for old age, and insurance against catastrophes that might call for large financial outlays. Both private enterprise and government have sought ways of providing at least minimum financial protection against these risks. Discussions of pensions, unemployment insurance, health insurance, and similar plans have made all of us sensitive to economic security.

A more subtle matter is the need for *psychological security*. This need relates to people's confidence in dealing with the problems that confront them. An ability to meet future job requirements, the fairness of present and future supervisors, the balance of benefits and losses that result from economic and technological changes—all conjure up hopes and fears. Everyone needs assurance that he will be able to adjust satisfactorily to such new conditions.

[4]A. H. Maslow, *Motivation and Personality* (New York: Harper & Brothers, 1954).

One source of psychological security is knowing the rules of the game. For example, the student who at the beginning of a course wants to know what the final grade will be based on or how long research papers should be is trying to remove an irritating uncertainty. Uneasiness about the effect of a rumored reorganization on one's job can lead to high anxiety because the rules of the game may change. Somehow people need to develop confidence that they will be able to cope with new situations successfully.

Social needs. Social needs are satisfied through relationships with other people, and in most of us, the desire for *sociability* is strong. We need contacts with informal groups as well as with close friends. Such contacts include friendly greetings, casual conversations, and amusing luncheons that a person—whether a mimeograph operator, foreman, or vice-president—engages in with associates at the office or plant. Companies have found that when employees have friendly relationships on the job, absenteeism tends to be low. In fact, people often go to their jobs or to a social function, despite a headache or a lack of interest in the activity itself, just to associate with other people.

Closely related to sociability is a sense of *belonging*. People want to feel that they are recognized members of a group; that they will be included in group plans and will share informal information, both gossip and fact; that others will help them in trouble and that they will be expected to help others as well.

A third social need is desire for *status*. In a business, status depends on the value of a position in the eyes of others. Status always implies a ranking along some kind of scale, and the hierarchy of a formal organization is one of the commonly accepted gauges. In addition, occupations differ in status value in various companies and communities. For example, being an actuary at the Metropolitan Life Insurance Company may command much more respect in "upscale" suburbs than being a pier boss at an ocean dock, even though the pier boss is paid more. Within companies, distinctions may be drawn between computer programmers and credit analysts, between locomotive engineers and firemen, or between sales clerks and cashiers. Status distinctions are drawn within classes of occupation. Everyone in a company usually knows who is the top person, the fastest typist, or the manager of the most profitable branch. Status inevitably implies competition, and competition is especially vigorous in the United States, where most people seek to improve their status. But perhaps even more pronounced than the desire to rise is the desire not to lose status. A lathe operator may refuse to sweep around his machine or an executive may refuse to answer her own telephone—even though to do so might be the simplest way to get work done—merely to maintain status in the eyes of coworkers.

Self-expression needs. Aside from what others may think each person is ultimately concerned with his private aspirations, and in this matter he measures himself. He asks, "Does this job permit me to do what *I* would like to do, to be what *I* want to be?" Everyone needs to express himself. At the nucleus of the cluster of needs for self-expression, we find self-asser-tion, power, personal accomplishment, and personal growth.

Mature adults want to assert themselves, to be independent at least to some extent. As we grow from childhood to adulthood, we rely less and less on other people to help us survive, to make decisions for us, and to show us how to behave and act. We want increasing control over our own destiny. In short, as we mature we progress from dependence toward in-dependence.

By the time a person reaches maturity, he attains a level of *self-as-sertion*—we might say independence or initiative—that he must maintain if he is to stay happy. Being independent makes life more pleasant for him than taking advice from others. Although this drive for self-assertion var-ies in intensity from person to person, nearly everyone has at least some need to be independent and to exercise initiative.

In some persons, desire for self-assertion slips over into a strong urge for *power*. Like the thrill a teenager gets from driving a car, the ability to make things or persons respond to one's own will can be a strong motive.

Most of us also desire a feeling of personal *accomplishment*. Crafts-people take pride in their work, whether it be a neatly typed letter, a dif-ficult surgical operation, or a welded joint that may never be seen by the public eye. Some people feel deeply about educating children, making highways safer, or otherwise contributing to the general welfare. For them, satisfaction comes from knowing that they have done a worthwhile job well; regardless of public acclaim or the size of tasks, they enjoy an inner sense of accomplishment. Few people, in fact, can do their best work unless they feel satisfaction of this sort.

In addition, people normally want an opportunity for *growth*. Satis-faction comes from the *process* of achieving as much as from the accom-plishment itself. A college graduate in accounting may be happy while she first learns a small part of a company's cost-accounting system, but after she has solved problems there, she wants to move on to something else. She at least wants variety, but she probably also wants a task calling for greater skill. Individuals vary greatly in the kind and amount of growth to which they aspire. Psychologist David McClelland gives us impressive evidence that even the growth of nations is closely tied to their peoples' need for achievement.[5] We can anticipate that with increasing education, travel, and technological change, the desire for growth opportunities will become even more pressing than it has been in the past.

Potency of Needs

The array of human needs seems overwhelming.[6] Even those needs related to work—physical, security (economic, psychological), social (sociability, belonging, status), and self-expression (self-assertion, accomplishment,

---

[5]D. C. McClelland, "Business Drive and National Achievement," *Harvard Business Review,* July 1962.

[6]D. A. Nadler, M. L. Tushman, and N. G. Hatvany, eds., *Managing Organizations: Readings and Cases* (Boston: Little, Brown, 1982), section II.

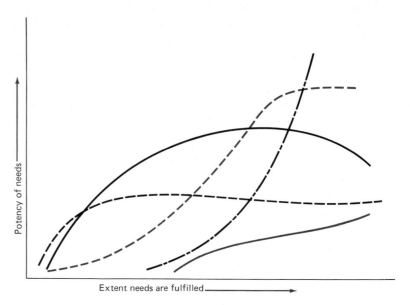

Figure 13.2 Marginal potency of
needs varies with fulfillment. Some
needs, such as physical protection from
weather, are fully satisfied and drop off;
others, like esteem of friends, keep
expanding. The shapes of these curves
differ among individuals, and even for
the same individual, over time.

growth)—make us ask, "Can human beings ever be satisfied?" Part of the
answer lies in the relative potency of these various desires. In this connection, it helps to consider marginal values, aspiration levels, and emotional
factors.

Marginal values.   How intensely individuals want more of a thing—
say, food, social recognition, or job security—depends partly on how much
they already have, as Figure 13.2 shows. What is an additional, or *marginal,* unit worth to them? One might sell one's birthright for air to
breathe if one were suffocating; when fresh air is in plentiful supply,
though, it loses its marginal value. In times of earthquake or war, starving
people have traded diamonds for food; once adequately fed, however, these
same people become more interested in security and self-expression.

At a given moment, each person has a hierarchy of needs, ranging
from those that seem urgent to those that are relatively unimportant. As
the most basic needs become satisfied—that is, when a person has sufficient water, shelter, and so on—the next most important needs, such as
job security and good supervision, become the real governors of behavior.
Some needs become dormant then, but others, such as a drive toward personal achievement or desire for social recognition, tend to keep expanding.
Those needs that keep growing are called the *motivating factors* by Herzberg.[7] Whether a need continues to be potent as a person derives increased
satisfaction depends largely on his levels of aspiration and on his ability
to draw qualitative distinctions about those needs.

[7]F. Herzberg, *Work and the Nature of Man* (New York: World Publishing, 1966).

Aspiration levels. The potency of a need depends on whether a person expects the need to be met. A desire to become company president, for instance, is not a strong motive for one who says to herself, "I know I'll never make it." On the other hand, a design engineer who expects ample opportunity for self-expression will be very dissatisfied if he is assigned routine drafting. To understand human needs, then, the analyst must identify each need and note how well it is already being met, but also consider how much more satisfaction of each type of need a person really aspires to attain.

Incidentally, many workers—especially those on routine jobs—do not expect great things from their work. A majority are satisfied with their present jobs, primarily because their aspirations are not very high. We are kidding ourselves if we assume most of these people want tough, varied, and ever-expanding jobs. Nevertheless, a large minority would welcome more meaningful work, and this number will probably rise as educational levels go up and as women and minorities shift their expectations after becoming comfortable in the workplace.[8]

A person's self-image strongly influences his aspiration levels—that is, what he believes his abilities are, and what he thinks his role should be. If he regards himself as the best salesperson in a company, he will work harder to achieve a top ranking than someone who considers himself a plodder, "about as good as the average." Similarly, the executive who views herself as a natural leader will be highly concerned about social approval of her ideas. Of course, self-images change over time. Repeated failures to achieve an expected satisfaction normally lead to a downward adjustment in aspiration, whereas successes encourage new dreams of glory, especially if one's friends or others close to one are experiencing similar failures or successes. These adjustments in self-image are made quite slowly, however.

Social scientists have observed three things about such aspiration levels that are especially pertinent for a business manager.

1. Change in the extent of need fulfillment—either up or down—is especially potent. For instance, a drop below a level that has become accepted is felt as a severe deprivation.

2. For many needs, people expect improvement from year to year. Indeed, the improvement is often more important than the absolute standard.

3. Operators and managers recognize that in every firm there is a certain amount of dirty, routine, and otherwise unattractive work to be done. Performing such tasks satisfies few human desires directly; it is simply necessary work. Nevertheless, most people realistically expect to do some unattractive but necessary work as part of their jobs. Even though it does not contribute directly to meeting needs, it may

---

[8]S. Peterfreund, "The Challenge of the 'New Breed,'" in M. D. Richards, ed., *Readings in Management,* 7th ed. (Cincinnati: South-Western Publishing Co., 1986) pp. 64–70.

be consistent with levels of expectation. Throughout life, everyone learns to mix the bitter with the sweet; the effort is simply to devise a more pleasant mixture.

Rational vs. emotional factors. Rarely do people calculate marginal values and aspiration levels systematically and logically; the potency of a need is more often based on feelings. Even the person who wants to act logically is confronted with a formidable task. The list of work-related needs is already complex, but there are still others, connected with family, religion, and other aspects of life, that also demand satisfaction. There are many ways to satisfy each of these needs, especially when we recognize *degrees* of satisfaction. For instance, we may use numerous foods of varying quality to satisfy the hunger need; we may satisfy social needs by a wide range of activities, from going to parties to working in an office together. For any given need, we may select from numerous alternative goals to fulfill it. Furthermore, we may adopt any of several alternative actions to attain each goal. We are therefore confronted with almost unbelievably complex decisions about what to do at any one time—or *would be* if we logically determined each action. We cannot carefully calculate all the pros and cons, so we rely chiefly on habits, attitudes, and emotional response.

No one can prove that as much as 95 percent of people's actions are uncalculated, but this is a useful approximation for a manager. It is a warning that attempts to change people's behavior by logical argument will meet with limited success. Instead, managers must try to learn which needs have high potency for their subordinates and then try to create a work situation in which each subordinate finds satisfaction while helping to achieve company goals.

SATISFYING NEEDS ON THE JOB

On-the-job vs. Off-the-job Satisfactions

This discussion of human needs has concentrated on those desires that can be met, at least to some degree, by working at a job. Such satisfactions, however, may arise either directly or indirectly from work; this distinction has an important bearing on how a manager seeks to motivate subordinates.

Work itself can be satisfying. A sense of achievement, for instance, arises from doing a job well. When a person performs an assigned task and at the same time satisfies his basic needs, he enjoys "direct," or "on-the-job," satisfactions. In such a case, it is the work itself and the relationships with coworkers that provide satisfying experiences.

In contrast, there may be rewards for work that are not generated as an aspect of work activity. Familiar forms of this kind of reward are pay, vacations, and pensions. The satisfactions that arise from such rewards take place *outside* the management system or work situation, and mostly outside the company. Work is simply a means of obtaining satisfaction at

Table 13.1 HUMAN NEEDS RELATED TO WORK

Needs	Direct, On-the-Job Satisfactions	Indirect, Off-the-Job Satisfactions
Physical needs	"Working conditions"	Money to buy necessities of life
Security needs	Psychological security	Economic security
Social needs	Sociability, belonging	Money to attain social status
	Status within company	Recognized title in reputable company
Self-expression needs	Self-assertion, power, sense of accomplishment, growth possibilities	Improved ability to engage in hobbies
		Money to seek power

a later time and place. These are referred to as "indirect," or "off-the-job," satisfactions.

When these distinctions are applied to the human needs discussed in this chapter, it may be surprising to note how important on-the-job satisfactions are in the total picture (see Table 13.1). Most of the literature in economics and scientific management stresses financial, or off-the-job, compensation. But behavioral scientists have insisted—and this is one of their major contributions—that on-the-job satisfactions are also highly important.

Limitations on Off-the-Job Satisfactions

In our society, off-the-job satisfactions from work depend largely on money. We use money to buy things that satisfy physical needs and contribute to social status. Economic security during old age or in time of catastrophe is also ensured by money. But the lack of direct association between work and such satisfactions has a serious drawback—it too often leads to this familiar attitude; "I don't care about the job as long as the pay keeps rolling in."

Not all off-the-job satisfactions come through money, however. Employment with a well-known company and a good title contribute to social status away from work. Some people would rather be vice-president of a local bank than sales representative for Chilean Nitrates at a higher salary, simply because the bank job carries more prestige among their friends.

Companies may provide housing, recreation, and other off-the-job benefits. During recent years, however, most companies have withdrawn such forms of compensation because of changes in income tax laws and because of worker resistance to such "paternalism." Due to a desire for independence, which has been discussed in connection with self-assertion, most employees prefer that their employer keep out of their private affairs.

They are likely to resent even a generous program if management clearly expects them to be appreciative of the good things bestowed on them. A company can and should help build a wholesome community, provided it maintains the independence and self-respect of the citizens.

On-the-Job Satisfaction: A Challenge to Management

Many social, self-expression, and security needs must be fulfilled on the job if they are to be satisfied through work. But providing on-the-job satisfactions is not a simple matter for two reasons. First, the principal difficulty lies in meeting needs for social contact, self-expression, and psychological security. Fulfilling each of these needs calls for the active participation and often the initiative of a worker himself. A manager cannot *force* a worker to enjoy his associates, be independent, take pride in his work and be confident of the future; a manager can only create an environment in which such feelings can flourish. For a manager who is accustomed to moving equipment, shaping raw materials, and otherwise achieving goals by positive action, an approach limited to facilitating action by others may seem slow. Yet all he can do is encourage growth and foster independence.

Second, on-the-job satisfactions should arise only while *people are doing the work that is necessary to meet company goals*. The sequence of events is not that a manager first ensures worker satisfaction and then hopes that the happy workers will decide to do the tasks assigned to them; as emphasized in our discussion of potency, a satisfied need does not motivate behavior. Nor does a benevolent boss parcel out satisfactions as rewards. Rather, actually doing a task that leads to company success must, at the same time, be what workers derive their satisfactions from. Both parties to the transaction benefit, just as a bee in the process of making honey from a blossom fertilizes the potential fruit.

Because work must be done if an enterprise is to remain in existence, a manager may prefer to organize work purely on the basis of technology, and then, as a separate issue, use "indirect" incentives to stimulate good worker performance. However, if he expects his subordinates to be self-reliant, eager, and dependable instead of apathetic, indifferent, and lazy, he must try to set up the work in ways that offer people substantial, direct, on-the-job satisfactions—all the while remembering that the people are unique individuals and are likely to differ in their wants as well as in what it takes to satisfy them.

MEETING HUMAN NEEDS THROUGH ORGANIZATION

The structure of a company defines an environment of formal rules, job descriptions, and communication networks in which people live during working hours. This environment can satisfy needs or block them; it can develop good attitudes or bad; and it can determine, in part, what people think and learn. Therefore, structure—as well as planning, face-to-face leadership, and control—is highly important in getting results.

The following paragraphs present a variety of ways in which organizational structure may contribute to, or detract from, the satisfaction of human needs. There may be other more compelling considerations in making the final choice of an organization pattern, but the purpose here is merely to point out some ways that an organization itself can affect the satisfactions of the people in it.

As already noted, people's needs are changing, and this means that adjustments may be necessary in the on-the-job work structure. A simple example is the need to modify working hours to accommodate workers (usually women) who also care for school-age children. One scheme is to create "permanent" part-time jobs—say, 9 AM to 3 PM five days a week. Or, "flextime"—starting and stopping work at the worker's option—may be feasible in some circumstance. Such an arrangement may convert a strained relationship with high absenteeism into a welcome opportunity to pursue two careers.

Creating Small Units

When many workers are required for an operation, the social satisfactions will be greater if we can assign the workers to small groups of, say, three to ten. For instance, an insurance-company typing pool of perhaps sixty typists is too large to serve as a social group. The typists would form small, informal friendship groups, of course, but their socializing would probably be a thing apart from their work. On the other hand, if their work could be organized into small units, the typists could, to some extent, serve their sociability needs *while doing assigned work*. Moreover, a sense of *belonging* would probably be stronger in the smaller unit, and if we could measure the group output, we might find that the small groups engendered a sense of personal achievement.[9]

The use of project teams for usual planning needs, or for customized output in a matrix organization, typically creates small work groups. While these teams are temporary structures, they do provide for intense and unstructured social interaction. Social satisfactions are a byproduct of their use. In this connection, the much-praised "quality circles" of Japanese firms are a special form of problem-solving teams.[10]

Avoiding Organizational Isolation

Taking social needs into account in organizing should make us wary of carrying to the extreme the process of cutting down the size of work groups. We should not isolate an individual.[11]

[9]R. J. Boyle, "Designing an Energetic Organization: How a Honeywell Unit Stimulated Change and Innovation," *Management Review,* Aug. 1983.

[10]E. E. Lawler and S. A. Morhman, "Quality Circles: After the Fad," *Harvard Business Review,* Jan. 1985.

[11]J. R. Hackman and G. R. Oldman, *Work Redesign* (Reading, Mass.: Addison-Wesley, 1980).

The personal secretary to the president of one of the country's largest corporations once remarked that in many ways she was not as happy as she had been when her boss was a lower-level executive. "This office is beautifully furnished and has the latest equipment, and I do have prestige as the president's secretary. But it is quiet in here, and the door is always closed. We're so busy that I never have a minute to get out and talk with Jean and Betty and Ken like I used to." This woman was isolated by space and walls, but the same result can be produced by breaking down work into such *extremely specialized and independent parts* that a person lacks opportunity to interact with fellow workers while working. This amounts to *organizational isolation*.

Consider a roomful of design engineers. One engineer might be assigned to a small, specialized project with which no other engineers are concerned. Day in and day out, she designs perhaps only pipelines, whereas all other engineers collaborate in designing chemical-processing units. Because she has little reason to discuss her work with others, she must either sacrifice social satisfaction during working hours or steal time from the company to have conversations on other matters that are either partly or wholly irrelevant to the job of designing pipelines.

As an alternative, this person could be included in a unit of engineers who design processing units and pipelines at the same time. Both her enjoyment of work and the amount she does might increase. She would derive social satisfaction from discussing problems with colleagues and from talking to construction supervisors who come into the drafting room to seek advice on construction operations. Such "socializing" is inherent in the position and does not involve serious interruption of assigned work.

Job Enrichment

In addition to inhibiting social interaction, narrow specialization takes a toll on worker satisfaction. The assembly-line worker who spends day after day tightening a single bolt has become a classic example of a person who has a routine, monotonous job. Although many workers do not object to such work because of off-the-job satisfactions, they enjoy little pride of accomplishment from the work itself.

Dividing work into highly specialized jobs may also affect a person's opportunity for growth. To take a simple example from office work, a large oil company meticulously divided up work in its billing department among four employees: one typist listed in separate columns on an invoice all types and quantities of products from customer orders; a second clerk entered prices next to the products typed in the list; a calculator operator multiplied quantity by price and entered the total for each product; finally, a fourth clerk added up product totals, adjusted for special transportation charges, and entered the total amounts customers owed. With each person doing such small tasks, these workers found little room for growth on the job; only through promotion was there hope for growth. The company, however, changed the organization of this operation. Instead of restricting each person to a specialized task, management divided up the work so that each operator completed a whole invoice, from typing to totaling. Output went up and the number of errors down.

Other companies have found that similar job redesign has improved results.[12] Part of the benefit comes from technical improvements. Coordination is simplified, less time is wasted in moving work from one worker to another, and only one person has to give attention to each piece of work. Another benefit is increased worker satisfaction. A job becomes more challenging than under the former setup; a worker becomes aware of a natural completeness, or wholeness, to his task, and this affords him a greater sense of accomplishment. A worker on an enriched job also becomes better prepared for other assignments.

Rearranging Work Flows

In order for people to satisfy their social needs, their relationships with others must be *reciprocal*. We do not enjoy always giving and never receiving, any more than we enjoy a one-way conversation. For a high degree of satisfaction, the initiation of contacts and the exchange of information should be roughly equal and reciprocal.

An easy give-and-take is hard to establish when a staff expert with functional authority simply tells other people what to do. Relationships in such a case tend to run in one direction. Similarly, companies often set up controls so that information flows only upward from the operating level to a staff person who measures and analyzes results. Either arrangement may accomplish its primary purpose, but it would not provide for satisfying social relationships.

The General Hardware Manufacturing Company had an organization that illustrates this point, as shown in Figure 13.3. A staff engineer who reported to the president was assigned the duty of operating a research

---

[12]Goodmeasure, Inc., *The Changing American Workplace: Work Alternatives in the '80s* (New York: American Management Association, 1985).

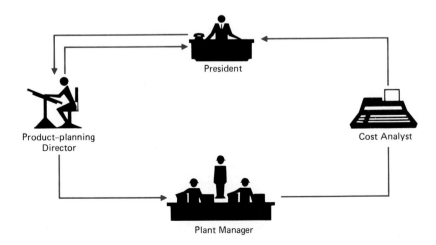

President

Product-planning
Director

Cost Analyst

Plant Manager

Figure 13.3
Relationships in the General Hardware Manufacturing Company. Arrows indicate the main flow of information and the initiation of contacts among selected executives.

department to plan new products and new uses for existing products. After top management approved product innovations, this product-planning director was expected to help the president convey and clarify instructions to the plant and sales managers. This one-way flow of decisions did not provide opportunity, especially for the plant manager, to enter into give-and-take discussion with the product-planning director about the work itself. Physical separation and the status of "an expert from the head office" contributed to the difficulty of establishing reciprocal relationships. The same company also located in the home office a cost expert who watched over all expenditures—labor, overhead, and manufacture of specific products. His principal duty was to request data and explanations from plant managers and pass an analysis of this information on to the president. Again, the flow was one-way, as indicated in Figure 13.3. As might be expected, the plant managers did not look forward to their meetings with either the product-planning director or the cost analyst; similarly, dealing with plant managers was just one of the crosses the central staff had to bear.

If the company would modify the work structure so that the people concerned with product development, plant operation, and cost analysis could come together in frequent discussions of how to operate each plant in order to contribute most to company profits, the feelings and social satisfactions would be different. One organizational change that might bring this about would be to combine all three functions under a single executive—a plant manager with expanded duties. Another possibility would be to locate cost analysts physically in each plant, where they could serve the plant manager as well as prepare reports for the president. Even shifting greater responsibility for product development to the plant managers, with the result that they would make suggestions and ask for help from the central research group, would encourage reciprocal relations. The company would have to make any such modification with its total situation in view, but the alternatives mentioned indicate how the organization could be restructured to meet social needs more effectively.

Splitting Up Established Roles

Some jobs become firmly structured and embrace a fixed range of duties, particularly when a long period of formal training is required and when professional associations are active in the field. In hospitals, for instance, the roles of staff physician, graduate nurse, and dietitian are sharply defined by tradition. Similarly, in a manufacturing company, a first-class machinist or mechanical engineer may have a clear self-image of what he should and should not do. He has a professional pride in his job and the way he performs it.

Efficiency occasionally suggests reshaping such a role. Perhaps a draftsperson can take over some duties that for years have been done only by engineers; or perhaps—this would be even more devastating to the engineers' pride—some aspects of design work might be shifted to salespeople. Part of the price of any such change will be a loss of self-esteem by the people who see their professional job being split up. The probable resistance may be strong enough to cause management to doubt whether a new organization is worth the rumpus. One large electronics firm, for instance, delayed a major reorganization because it would hurt the status and pride of its electrical engineers; at the time, good engineers were hard to recruit and hold, and the firm felt it had to provide a full range of satisfactions to retain key people.

Organizational Status

Most people take pride in reporting to a high-level executive. It enhances their status, even though the executive may be too busy to see them frequently. Indirectly, it may also impart independence—if the executive has many people who report to her, she *must* grant considerable freedom of action. Perhaps pride of place in an organization's hierarchy explains why over one hundred important officials report directly the President of the United States.

Adding a supervisory level in an organization structure cuts into satisfactions from status, especially of those who report to the newly established supervisor. In one advertising agency, for instance, two department managers resigned when they discovered that they would no longer report directly to a vice-president. The people in their departments felt demoted, even though no one would have suffered a reduction in pay or a change in duties.

Related to the matter of place in the hierarchy is the question of titles. Titles provide significant status satisfactions both within and outside a company. Theoretically, titles (or rank in military establishments) could be assigned on individual merit, irrespective of job duties or position in an organizational hierarchy. But because titles are important in helping people understand a formal organization, they should describe where a job fits into a total organization structure. Even within this limitation, however, managerial ingenuity in devising attractive titles can make substantial differences in employee satisfaction. "Let's give the guy a title instead of a raise" is not just a wisecrack; the right title may increase a person's satisfaction with his job more than a small, routine salary increase. Participation in decision-making also can help, as Figure 13.4 shows.

Decentralization

By its very definition, decentralization means increasing a subordinate's freedom of action. This freedom naturally affects the fulfillment of self-expression needs. At one extreme, a job description for a sales representative might simply specify, "Call on all customers in the Norfolk territory at least once a month and present company products that appear to offer most appeal at that time." At the other extreme, the guides and rules defining the same job might spell out exactly how the representative should approach customers—for instance, by presenting samples first and mentioning price only incidentally, or even by spouting a canned sales talk that has been memorized from the company manual. In the first case, the

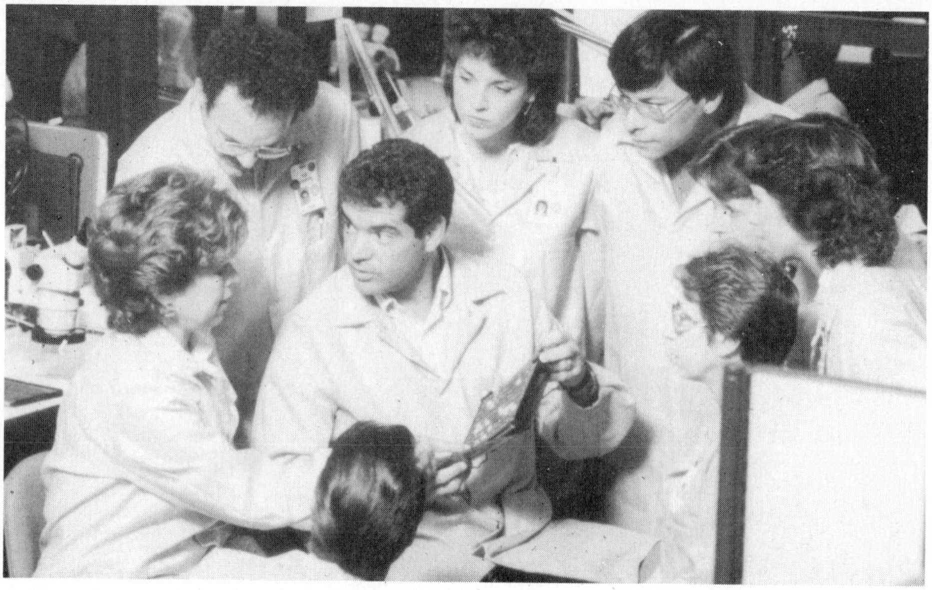

Figure 13.4

Workers share their opinions in reaching a decision, which makes everyone feel better in terms of participation and motivation.

Danford Connolly Picture Group

representative could give his initiative free rein, but in the latter circumstance, he would have much less opportunity for independent self-assertion.

The issue of opportunity for independence is also of concern to managers throughout a company. The supervisor of a cost-accounting department in a factory, for example, may have either a high or low degree of delegation from the plant controller. She may or may not be free to work out her own methods for gathering data from heads of operating units; she may or may not be allowed to plan the vacation schedule for employees in her department; she may or may not be permitted to determine the schedule for sending summary reports to the controller.

The higher the degree of decentralization—that is, the greater freedom allowed—the more satisfaction a subordinate can expect from asserting his own ideas. Moreover, the more a person feels he is "running his own show," the more he will enjoy satisfactions of achievement. With greater decentralization, there is more opportunity to grow and, in so doing, to prepare for more complex assignments. Clearly, decentralization ministers to self-expression needs by providing opportunities to satisfy them.[13]

Freedom Versus Order

A recurring issue in matching personal needs with an organization's is how to balance individual freedom against established order. Today non-

[13]M. Green and J. F. Berry, "Trimming Corporate Waste Lines: The Participation Solution," *Management Review,* Nov. 1985.

conformity is common and many young people regard fitting into any regulated system as a sacrifice. The issue calls for sensitive balance.

One cluster of basic human needs hinges on security. A known, orderly way of working together is an important source of such security. Established roles, normal procedures, and planned change all help members of an organization to feel psychologically secure. They know what to expect, and they have a recognized place in the total activities. People also want opportunities for self-expression, but a completely unstructured, unpredictable environment goes too far. As we have already noted, however, after the need for security is fairly well satisfied, it drops in importance. The practical questions, then, deal with *marginal increments* of security and self-expression.

Our reaction to orderliness depends substantially on our feeling about the necessity for it. Musicians, artists, and researchers voluntarily submit to all kinds of disciplined behavior—with no sense of lost freedom—if they regard the drill as necessary to their personal expression. Similarly, when committed to an objective, people often accept all sorts of necessary guidance in reaching their end.

For centuries most people have satisfied their self-expression needs off the job, and now the dramatic reduction in the work week provides increasing freedom for the pursuit of independent personal interests. People neither want nor expect to depend solely on their jobs for opportunities for self-expression.

So we don't face a simple trade-off between the orderliness required by technology or economics on the one hand and individual freedom on the other. Nevertheless, rising living standards, increased mass education, and higher aspirations raise the marginal value attached to individual self-expression. Perhaps as a general guide, we should start with the assumption that organization designers tend to overdo systems and formal assignments. This means that we should look for opportunities to leave discretion with individual operators and managers and should be ready to modify existing organization to keep it relevant to current social moods.

INTEGRATING PAY, NEEDS, AND ORGANIZATION

Although to say that "people work for a paycheck" is a gross over-simplification, financial compensation is a vital source of satisfaction. The size of a paycheck *does* matter to virtually every worker, from president to office boy.

The real question is how pay fits into the relationship between jobs and need satisfaction.[14] To be sure, pay enables workers to meet their physical needs and those of their families. If a paycheck is large enough,

[14]E. E. Lawler, "Reward Systems," in J. R. Hackman and J. L. Suttle, *Improving Life at Work: Behavioral Science Approaches to Organization Change* (Santa Monica, Calif.: Goodyear, 1977).

they may have steak instead of hamburgers, two cars instead of one, or a color television set with a videocassette recorder in the bedroom. But a paycheck means more than just what it buys. It is a symbol of status, a source of self-respect, an avenue to security. These primarily noneconomic aspects of the paycheck often have more impact on how people behave in their jobs than does the check's mere purchasing power.

Several of these indirect influences of pay on behavior are closely related to organization design. They also intertwine with on-the-job satisfactions. Because an alert manager will want to give attention to such interrelations, we now turn to several key issues in this area: Can we substitute money for other kinds of satisfaction? How should a pay system be related to formal organization? Can we use pay to reinforce the influence of staff and of executives? How should individual raises be related to assigned duties and company objectives? What burdens does the use of incentive pay place on organization structure?

Pay Instead of Other Satisfactions

Can a company pay high salaries and wages and disregard security, social, and self-expression satisfactions? For instance, provided pay is high, will a capable individual work as a subordinate for a supervisor who is highly critical, insists on making even minor decisions, and gives no opportunity for growth in the job? Experience answers, "Money isn't everything." Competent people shift to other jobs where the work is more attractive even if the pay is lower. Those who do stay on an unpleasant job are likely to develop negative attitudes toward their work and the company, to show little initiative, and perhaps even to restrict their output. Even though high pay may attract a worker, it does not win his emotional support if his job is low in direct satisfactions.

However, a job so brimful of direct satisfactions that it is actually fun still requires reasonable pay. The pay cannot be much below the prevailing rate for comparable work because of the psychological aspect of pay. The amount of compensation reflects the importance a company attaches to the work; it is a symbol recognized by other people inside and outside the company. Even when workers like their jobs, they also want others to think well of them and of the job. We can conclude, then, that a wise manager must consider *both* direct and indirect satisfactions. Most people are willing to substitute one for the other only to a limited extent. We can apply the principle of marginal value to both situations: extra-high pay cannot compensate for the reduction of on-the-job satisfactions below a commonly accepted level, *and* a high degree of job satisfaction will not keep a person working if his pay significantly degrades his self-respect or social standing.

Exceptions to this general proposition can be found, of course. Some jobs, such as preaching or teaching, carry enough social prestige and ego satisfaction to attract people, even though business pays for comparable ability at a significantly higher rate. Employers can also fill dirty or risky jobs by paying premium rates. In general, however, both fair pay and satisfying work are necessary to attract and motivate good people.

This conclusion still leaves open the question of what compensation is reasonable for specific jobs in a specific company. One important guide for both a manager and those who receive the pay is this: A pay rate should reflect the difficulty of a job. Jobs that require more skill, longer training, or more obligation should command higher pay. This guide is based on formal organization, for job descriptions specify duties and, at least by implication, the abilities needed to fill each position. Any pay system that is inconsistent with formally assigned duties may lead to discontent.

Status is the chief issue. A difficult or important job should have a high status. Because pay level—along with title and place in the official hierarchy—is the most conspicuous evidence of status, great care should be taken in matching duties and pay. Employees at all levels are sensitive to this point. Strikes have been called over the amount of difference in wages between, say, electricians and machinists, not because of a few cents per hour, but because of what the difference meant in relative status. On the executive level, a vice-president of a certain department store was quite satisfied with an $85,000 salary until she learned that another vice-president, whose job she considered no more important than her own, was earning $100,000; immediately, she felt insulted, downgraded, and discriminated against.

Management usually dovetails salaries and duties by a procedure called "job evaluation."[15] Steps in an evaluation include: (1) comparing all jobs on many counts—such as scope of duties, skills and working conditions—and placing the jobs in a series of grades; (2) establishing a general salary level for each grade based on going rates for comparable work among other firms; and (3) creating a salary range for each grade that will permit increases from minimum to maximum as an individual progresses from beginner to expert in any one job. Such a system for a small bank is reflected in Figure 13.5.

No matter how elaborate the job-evaluation technique for a pay system, it will not be successful unless it is *accepted* by the employees to whom it applies. They must believe that it fairly reflects differences in jobs; the grades assigned must coincide with the relative standing of various roles as the workers conceive of them. Without such acceptance, the status and self-esteem of some workers will suffer, and the pay system will have a negative effect on their eagerness to do their work.

Reinforcing Staff and Executives

Management has a further reason to be concerned with the relative pay levels of people in supervisory and staff positions. The feeling is common in American society that we should respect the opinions of persons who earn more money than we do, whereas the opinions of persons earning less are open to challenge. The simple assumption is that earnings are a mea-

[15]E. B. Flippo, *Personnel Management,* 6th ed. (New York: McGraw-Hill, 1984).

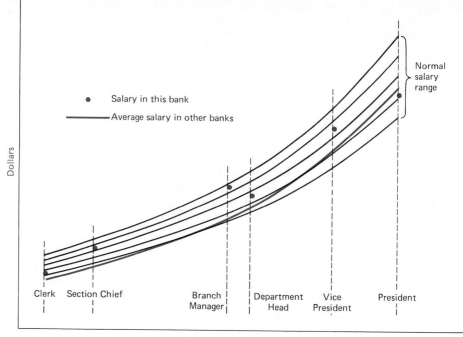

Figure 13.5 A possible salary structure for a small bank. The structure reflects the difficulties, duties, and status of jobs, the rates paid by other firms, and the possibilities for salary increases in any given position.

sure of the soundness of a person's views. Although this is an unwarranted assumption, it exists whether we like it or not.

Because of this feeling, a low-paid staff person will have more difficulty winning acceptance for his ideas. An operating executive may say to himself, "Why should I take that fellow's advice? He doesn't earn half as much as I do." Thus if management wants to increase the influence of a particular individual, one way to achieve its aim is to give him the prestige of a high salary. Similarly, a supervisor should get paid more than his highest-paid subordinate.

Raising a person's salary is not the only way to build his influence, but the impact of salary on an individual's ability to operate within an organization should not be overlooked.

Tying Raises to Company Objectives

How a company grants merit increases has a direct influence on behavior in the organization. To an individual himself, an increase is a sign of his personal progress; he will try to continue behaving in the way that he thinks led to his raise. His colleagues are likewise alert. They know who gets raises more often, and who gets none at all, and they take their cues accordingly. At the same time, workers typically have strong opinions of what they feel is "fair"—that is, who deserves a raise.

Consequently, management should be careful to grant increases to those who are, in fact, improving their effectiveness and should try to get everyone to agree that the policy on giving raises is reasonable and fair. In this matter, as with most others, management's actions speak far louder than its words. Playing favorites or being soft and giving everybody a small increase just to avoid arguments will undermine appeals to do a better job. On the other hand, if management consistently matches merit increases with known contributions toward company strategy, it reinforces the whole structure of formal plans and organization.

Incentive Pay and Organization

If merit increases should go to people who perform their assignments well, how about extending the idea to incentive pay, which varies directly and immediately with performance? Commissions for salespeople and piece rates for factory workers are common examples of incentive pay; at the managerial level, we find executive bonuses based on profits, on actual results compared with budgets, or on other quantified measures of results. Occasionally, when a whole group of people must cooperate to achieve results, a firm will offer a group bonus.

Desire for security has become so intense that today few employees on any level—president, sales supervisor, or machine operator—subsist entirely on incentive pay. Instead companies ensure a degree of security either by guaranteeing minimum earnings regardless of results or by paying a base salary and adding incentive pay as a bonus. Even though incentive pay may be a small percentage of total compensation, it focuses on the particular achievements that management uses in determining the amount of bonus.

Incentive pay introduces several requirements in organization design. The mission—the end result—of a job eligible for a bonus must be sharply defined, and the results must be measurable. Many jobs, such as that of chief accountant or human resources director, cannot be defined in this manner. Even the work of a sales representative is not simple to describe. The primary task may be to obtain orders, but in addition the representative is expected to cultivate new customers, obtain information on new products, deal with complaints, and keep expenses low. If the bonus is based solely on new orders, the representative is likely to slight other duties.

For an organization, this means one of two things. Either (1) authority should be highly decentralized—for instance, authorizing division managers to change prices, hire people, and take other action that is necessary to achieve profits, on which bonuses are based—or (2) management should standardize and control the work conditions that affect output—for a production worker who is paid a piece rate, this means that material should be readily available, machinery in good operating condition, helpers adequately trained, power and light dependable, and so forth. In both instances, the location and adequacy of staff and service work are important to the person who receives incentive pay. Again, we see that an organization design and a salary system are closely interrelated. If we use incentive pay, we get into questions of delegating authority, providing service and staff, and defining duties so that they conform to the bases of bonuses.

CONCLUSION

In this chapter, we have focused our attention on the personal needs of managers and their subordinates—especially on their physical, security, social, and self-expression needs, because these can be met to a significant extent through working. A manager should not only identify the specific needs of the people he directs, but also be sensitive to the relative potency of these various desires. Such an understanding provides a manager with a foundation for deciding how to motivate individual subordinates.

A manager should be alert to the connection between on-the-job satisfactions and organization. The organization can often be adjusted to increase the direct satisfactions of the people working in it. By tying the amount of pay to the importance and influence that managers wish to attach to various jobs, they increase the chances that the organization will actually work as they want it to. The objective should be to design a structure in which on-the-job satisfactions are enhanced at the same time company aims are furthered.

Impact on Productivity

Motivation of its employees to do the work needed by the company obviously has a direct tie to company productivity. For this reason, the subject of this chapter is critical. And as companies seek to improve quality and lower costs so as to meet foreign competition, the urgency increases.

The chief hurdles to future improvement in productivity from this source are identifying what the new generation of workers and managers really want, and then readjusting the work structure so that desired satisfaction is directly linked to high performance. Devices such as flextime and quality circles will help managers build these bridges. To a large extent, however, the adaptations that must be made are local, undramatic adjustments that will come from perceptive and imaginative effort in millions of specific work relationships. This is a task that no good manager of the future can sidestep.

FOR FURTHER DISCUSSION

1. The shorter work week and the increase in attention by employees to off-the-job activities has increased the relative importance they attach to the size of their paychecks. On-the-job satisfactions are, therefore, becoming less important. Do you agree? What can company management do about it?

2. How may the increasing number of dual-career families affect management's ability to motivate such employees? (Assume that both do not work for the same organization.)

3. What do you consider the most significant changes in America over the last two or three decades that are likely to influence the attitudes of people toward work as a means of satisfying their potent needs? Consider your answer to the first part of this question in terms of the age of the people you have in mind. Would the changes you consider significant have as much, more, or different kinds of influence on people under twenty-five than they would on those over thirty?

4. "Widespread use of computers tends to emphasize the quantitative aspects of business decisions and measurements of performance. This leads to poor performance because employees are no longer motivated to give attention to qualitative aspects of their work." Do you agree with this statement? What other effects do you think computers have on motivation?

5. "I have no use for all this job-enrichment stuff that is supposed to fulfill me. I get all the fulfillment I need by being a mother, wife, member of the school board, and Sunday School teacher. I work because I'm bored between 7:30 AM and 3:30 PM and we can use the extra money. I wish these unfulfilled psychologists who keep running around the office would leave me and my job alone." Consider this statement from a forty-year-old woman.

6. Job rotation is used by some companies to make work more appealing. How do you think employees in a restaurant would feel about job rotation? Where might job rotation be more popular?

7. (a) Does "equal opportunity for work" increase or decrease workers' motivation? (b) Laws in most states now prohibit discrimination (in the selection of individuals for jobs and in their compensation) on the basis of sex, race, religion, age, sexual behavior, political affiliation, and so forth. Threats of fines and damage suits are causing companies to be very cautious on such matters. How does this trend affect a company's ability to motivate its employees?

8. It is generally agreed that rewards are very strong motivators when they are closely linked to specific performance. How does this affect an organization's ability to motivate its people toward achieving strategic objectives?

FOR FURTHER READING

Goodmeasure, Inc., *The Changing American Workplace: Work Alternatives in the '80's.* New York: American Management Association, 1985. A report on how companies are redesigning work to improve personal motivation.

Hackman, J. R., "Work Design," in J. R. Hackman and J. L. Suttle, eds., *Improving Life at Work: Behavioral Science Approaches to Organizational Change.* Santa Monica, Calif.: Goodyear, 1977, pp. 92–162. Clear review of concepts and research findings on worker satisfaction, motivation, and the effect of job enrichment.

Mitchell, T. R., *Motivation and Performance.* Chicago: Science Research Associates, 1984. A short, insightful psychological analysis that stresses importance of arousal as an early element in motivation.

Rappaport, A., "How to Design Value-Contributing Executive Incentives," *Journal of Business Strategy,* Fall 1983. Ties compensation arrangements into company planning.

Staw, B., ed., *Psychological Foundations of Organizational Behavior,* parts I–IV. Santa Monica, Calif.: Goodyear, 1977. Excellent series of articles on motivation and individual behavior in organizations.

Steers, R. and L. W. Porter, *Motivation and Work Behavior,* 3d ed. Santa Monica, Calif.: Goodyear, 1983. Articles present a wide array of behavioral studies relating individual behavior to the characteristics of the work being done and especially to the job design.

MANAGEMENT IN ACTION CASE 13
The Human Touch at Herman Miller

One sunny fall morning, the shirt-sleeved chairman of Herman Miller Inc. strolled through his company's main office-furniture plant in tiny Zeeland, Michigan, greeting workers, asking questions, warmly clapping a shoulder here and there.

That wasn't unusual at all for Max De Pree, a man who once said that, "In addition to all of their ratios and goals and parameters and bot-

tom lines, it is fundamental that corporations have a concept of persons."
At Herman Miller, designer and maker of state-of-the-art office furniture,
De Pree practices what he preaches.

Herman Miller made participatory management a part of its business
long before the concept became a Fortune 500 fad in the 1980s. In 1950,
company founder D. J. De Pree, Max's father, adopted a plan developed by
labor leader Joseph Scanlon. The program has been revised several times
since, and today all Herman Miller employees meet monthly to disucss
ways to better their performance.

The company offers profit sharing bonuses, which have averaged 10
percent of salary over the past 30 years. Nearly all of the employees own
stock in Herman Miller through an employee stock-ownership plan instituted long before ESOPs became the vogue in corporate America.

De Pree is a man of strong moral conviction who stresses "roving
leadership" as opposed to hierarchical command. Instead of contractual
agreements with his employees, he favors "convenantal relationships" that
are "based on shared commitment to ideas, to issues, to values, to goals,
and to management processes," he said. "Words such as *love, warmth, personal chemistry* are certainly pertinent. They fill deep needs and they enable work to have meaning and to be fulfilling."

Workers like the Herman Miller atmosphere. Rusty Ridgely, production supervisor at the company's Roswell, Georgia, plant, said, "I was with
a very well-known firm before this, a national company, and it was very
cold and hard and businesslike and bottom-line oriented. When I came to
Herman Miller, it was just such a tremendous change."

Workers' appreciation is reflected in their work. The world's No. 2
office-furniture maker behind Steelcase Inc., Herman Miller saw its sales
soar from $30 million in 1973 to $512 million in 1985. The same year,
Herman Miller was chosen as one of the "100 Best Companies to Work for
in America" by the authors of the popular book.

Question

Do you see any dangers in Max De Pree's approach to motivating employees?

For more information, see R. Levering, M. Moskowitz, and M. Katz *The 100 Best Companies
to Work for in America*. (Reading, Mass.: Addison-Wesley, 1985).

APPLICATION CASES

For practice in applying concepts covered in this chapter to managerial
situations, see the following managerial decision cases. The case questions
particularly relevant to this chapter are listed by number after each case
name.

14

Achieving Personal Leadership

LEARNING OBJECTIVES

After completing this chapter, you should be able to

1. Understand the key elements of personal leadership.
2. Discuss the contingency approach to leadership, in which the manager adjusts to the situation.
3. Describe some of the key attitudes for effective leadership.
4. Better understand how leadership can be a key element in implementing an organization's strategy.

A number of popular books published in the mid-1980s distinguished between managers and leaders.[1] The fundamental difference most often mentioned was that *leaders* were the pivotal characters who, through charisma, determination, downright fear, or combinations of all three, changed people's fundamental views of themselves and their businesses.

This was true of Chrysler Corporation savior Lee A. Iacocca, ITT mastermind Harold Geneen, the banker who molded Citibank's vision of the future, Walter Wriston, and dozens of other heroes who led their organizations through major transitions—often from the brink of failure. In contrast to such dominant personalities, *managers* are viewed as those people who operate in more limited and less personally dramatic ways to run an organization using more normal methods under more normal circumstances.

Gap Between Decision and Action

In fact, both the dominating CEOs and all other managers have a leadership role to play. All are concerned, in part, with closing any gap between plans and likely results. If the gap between goals and current reality is canyon-like—as it was when Chrysler was fighting for survival or when Citibank needed a transformation to confront a difficult future—frame-breaking action may be necessary to reshape and revive a self-pitying organization.

In still other situations, something done in a routine managerial fashion, but not implemented as it should have been by an executive's subordinates, may require the most skillful of leadership to overcome a much more volatile result.

That was the case when President John F. Kennedy ordered the removal of U.S. missiles from their locations in Turkey. Kennedy's decision came after a careful review of alternatives submitted by the Joint Chiefs of Staff, the State and Defense Departments, and the National Security Council. Once the final decision was made, clear written directions began to make a spiral path from the White House to the silos in Turkey.

Months later, though, during the height of the Cuban Missile Crisis, Kennedy learned that his decision had not been carried out.[2] In his famous confrontations with Soviet Premier Nikita Khrushchev, Kennedy was told that the Russians would withdraw their missiles from Cuba if we would

---

[1] L. A. Iacocca, *Iacocca: An Autobiography* (New York: Bantam, 1984); H. Levinson and S. Rosenthal, *CEO: Corporate Leadership in America* (New York: Basic Books, 1984); H. Geneen, *Managing* (New York: Doubleday, 1984); W. Bennis and B. Nanus, *Leaders* (New York: Harper & Row, 1985); E. H. Schein, *Organizational Culture and Leadership* (San Francisco: Jossey-Bass, 1985).

[2] G. T. Allison, *Essence of Decision: Explaining the Cuban Missile Crisis* (Boston: Little, Brown, 1971).

remove ours from Turkey. Kennedy was shocked to discover that his earlier decision had not been followed—and that his control system had failed to keep him as well informed as was Khrushchev about the status of the U.S. missiles in Turkey. But more important from an organizational standpoint, it meant Kennedy needed to put forth a high level of leadership skills to remedy the situation and to ensure that his orders were followed to the letter the second time around.

What went wrong? Is it possible that those responsible for carrying out this decision did not understand what they were to do? Were they unwilling to comply with the decision? Or did they lack the commitment necessary to execute the decision when confronted by obstacles? If this could happen to one of the two or three most powerful executives in the world, imagine how much more likely it is to happen to the average manager.

Although many forms of human effort are required to build organizations, develop plans, and design control systems, they are all for naught unless their outcomes are put into action.[3] A construction superintendent has to convert blueprints into a power dam. A football coach has to transform plays that look foolproof on paper into touchdowns on the field. A director has to turn a Gilbert and Sullivan score and libretto into a lively stage production. Such a conversion of ideas into results is an essential element in every manager's job, and how skillfully he does it profoundly affects the return from all other phases of management.

The role of leadership in management.   Broadly speaking, leadership deals with the steps that a manager takes personally to get subordinates and others to carry out plans. It bridges the gap between managerial decisions and actual execution by other people. Here the focus is on *personal* leadership; that is, on human relationships between the leader and the led, in which the distinct personalities build mutual understanding and trust.

Effective leadership generates close person-to-person relationships. It is rooted in the feelings and attitudes that have grown up between people over the entire time they have worked together. It is a never-ending process, with actions and reactions flowing both ways.

Such personal, active leadership serves two broad purposes. One stems from the impact of the leader on others—he cultivates cooperation and commitment.[4] The second results from the impact of the others on the leader—they give him information and responses that modify his behavior and future plans.[5] This is a two-way interchange.

[3]K. Davis, ed., *Organizational Behavior: Readings and Exercises,* 6th ed. (New York: McGraw-Hill, 1981).

[4]J. J. Cribbin, *Leadership Strategies for Organizational Effectiveness* (New York: AMACOM, 1982).

[5]H. Mintzberg, "The Manager's Job: Folklore and Fact," *Harvard Business Review,* July–August 1975, 49–61.

ELEMENTS OF PERSONAL LEADERSHIP

Behavioral science studies have confirmed a variety of managerial actions that help a leader develop cooperative attitudes, as Figure 14.1 shows.

Structural Prerequisites to Voluntary Cooperation

The total process of managing must be reasonably well performed for voluntary cooperation to flourish. We cannot do a poor job of organizing, planning, and controlling, and then expect a kindly leader to miraculously pull us out of our troubles.

Managerial leadership operates within a structure—a structure of plans, organization, and controls. On the basis of this formally designed structure, a social structure develops. Many of the habits and persistent feelings of workers (both managers and their employees) arise from the formal and social structures that are created as a part of managing, and these feelings affect workers' responses to a leader's request. Major points at which structural design may have a significant bearing on the responses of workers follow:

Clear role to play.   When a person has known duties—and corresponding authority—he can develop a pride in his work, a recognized status, and a sense of inner security. By making clear the role of staff, a source of confusion and perhaps conflicting obligations can be avoided.

Individuals well matched with jobs.   A person's feeling about his work also depends on whether his job is suited to his abilities. Through human resources planning and development, organizations try to make full use of an individual's abilities, but at the same time try not to put him

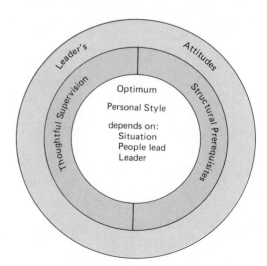

Figure 14.1   Elements in personal leadership.

in a spot where he becomes discouraged and defensive because he cannot meet his obligations. Minor modifications in organizational structure are often made, either enlarging or contracting an assignment, so that the person and his job are well matched. Such matching fosters a cooperative feeling.

Effective communication networks.   With each person necessarily doing only a piece of the total work in an organization, systems must be designed to provide the worker with the information he needs, promptly and accurately. If well informed, his work can proceed smoothly and he can take pride in his accomplishment; poor communication, on the other hand, leads to confusion, frustration, and negative attitudes toward meeting company goals.

Sound objectives.   To create personal satisfactions, broad goals should be translated into specific aims that are meaningful to each employee, and then reasonable levels of achievement should be agreed on. Such specific goals can become the basis for a great deal of voluntary cooperation, and achieving them can give a worker a significant sense of accomplishment.

Workable policies, methods, and procedures.   A structure of plans for handling repetitive problems creates a necessary stability and a pattern of behavior that make work more satisfying to most employees, for aside from an occasional rebel, most people derive a sense of security from an established, known set of norms. A good body of standing plans also eases work tasks. In addition, if some flexibility can be introduced by using many of the plans as guides rather than as fixed rules, employees are likely to be even more cooperative.

Balanced control systems.   Control systems, too, can be designed in a way that minimizes the usual negative reaction to controls and provides constructive help to people in meeting their accepted goals. To achieve this, it is necessary to select the right criteria of performance, set reasonable standards, measure output reliably, and provide prompt and direct feedback. A poorly designed control system, in contrast, can give rise to a good deal of discontent and make a manager's job of developing voluntary cooperation difficult.

Progressive off-the-job benefits.   The most conspicuous way to cultivate cooperation is to be progressive (generous) with off-the-job benefits. In addition to paying relatively high salaries, a company may be a leader in cutting hours of work or making them more flexible, granting holidays, providing paid vacations, giving liberal pensions, guaranteeing employment, arranging for health and other insurance, sponsoring recreational activities, and providing still other fringe benefits.

Such added compensation obviously increases the attractiveness of employment by a progressive company. Here again, the way employees feel about what they are receiving is crucial. To create positive sentiments, a benefit must (a) be generous relative to historical patterns and (b) be at least as good as benefits provided by other well-known employers. Thus there is a built-in escalation in the costs of such provisions and a risk that even slowing down on increases will lead to disappointment because worker expectations have not been fulfilled. In addition, such programs must be consistent, despite the fortunes of an organization. Providing generous compensation packages in good corporate financial times, only to extract concessions when business isn't as good, sends mixed signals to employees and can serve to drive them from the company at the time when you need them most.[6]

All the preceding ideas are examined more thoroughly in other parts of the book. The purpose of this quick review is merely to refresh our memories on how often the feelings of employees and the design of plans, organization, and controls are intertwined.

In the following discussion of personal actions by a manager that help develop voluntary cooperation, we are assuming that the total management structure is conducive to effective person-to-person leadership. The entire structure may not be completely to everyone's liking, of course, but on balance it must be favorably regarded by subordinates if through personal behavior a leader is to generate enthusiasm in them for carrying out company plans.

Thoughtful Supervision

What can supervisors do in person-to-person relations with subordinates to build a sustained feeling of cooperativeness? The following pages examine a series of managerial actions that nourish a cooperative work climate.

Friendliness and approval. The kind of friendliness referred to here runs deeper than mere cordiality and politeness. Subordinates are dependent on their supervisor for a variety of things—job assignments, information, help in overcoming problems, and the like—and they want assurance of *approval* from this strategic person. Being friendly is one way a supervisor can convey approval.

Consistency and fairness. Inconsistent treatment by a manager in a few key areas of a job can anger people to a point where they become disgusted with their entire job, as the differences in Figure 14.2 suggest. The president of a medium-sized import-export company, for instance, was so unpredictable in his demands that his chief accountant resigned. The accountant explained: "I can't live with a guy like that. One day he's

[6]A. R. McGill, "Reward Systems: Practical Considerations: A Case Study of General Motors Corporation," in C. J. Fombrun, N. M. Tichy, and M. A. Devanna, *Strategic Human Resource Management* (New York: John Wiley, 1984).

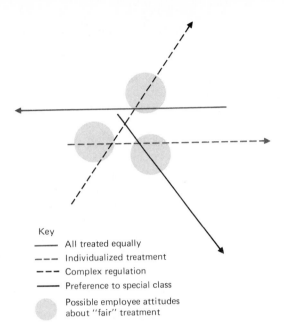

Key
———— All treated equally
– – – Individualized treatment
‐ ‐ ‐ Complex regulation
———— Preference to special class
● Possible employee attitudes
about "fair" treatment

Figure 14.2 Attitudes differ about how managers should treat subordinates. Four possible patterns of treatment are shown. Circles indicate which methods three separate groups of subordinates consider "fair."

hounding you for figures—'guesstimates' if necessary. The next day accuracy is all important, right down to the last penny. The Dr. Jekyll–Mr. Hyde act was driving me nuts." Consistent supervision enables subordinates to develop normal patterns of behavior. Knowing what to expect and how to respond, they feel more secure and self-confident.

Even more important to a spirit of cooperation than consistency over time is consistency—or fairness—of treatment among subordinates. A feeling among people that management plays favorites ("Joan gets all the soft assignments; she can take a day off and nobody kicks.") can quickly reduce voluntary cooperation to zero.

Here it can be difficult to determine just what is fair. The principle of equal treatment clashes with another strong belief. Every person should be treated as an individual. If Joe has thirty years of service with the company, or his leg is in a cast because of an automobile accident, or he is going to be sent abroad in six months, should he be given special consideration?

To build a spirit of cooperation, rewards and punishments must be given fairly and managers must perform other supervisory acts in a manner that *subordinates feel* is consistent, or at least reasonable. Equal treatment is only a starting point. Many exceptions to strict equality are regarded as fair. Joe can be given special treatment—because of his long service, or accident, or future job—if the reason is known and accepted as legitimate and if subordinates believe that future exceptions will be made consistently for others in a similar situation. Among many employees, in fact, fairness actually requires that those with long service or in poor health be given special treatment.

Support for subordinates.   Managers can provide a wide range of support for their subordinates. One is simply to help in getting a job done. For example, machines may need repairing, tough customers may need to be impressed by an executive from the home office, letters should be answered while a subordinate is in bed with the flu, and so on. Subordinates will feel more secure and confident if they know they can get help from their boss *if and when* they ask for it.

Managers may also support their people outside the department. They may vigorously seek every salary increase their people deserve; they may try to keep work flowing to their people at a steady pace—that is, avoid critical demands one week and layoffs the next; they may negotiate frictions with related departments—perhaps getting engineers to modify unworkable specifications or answering complaints from customer-service people; they may push for better offices or equipment; and they may keep their people informed about changes that affect them. When subordinates know their boss is representing their needs with a fair measure of success, they are inclined to follow his lead.

Law of the situation.   Whenever possible, supervisors should let the facts of a situation tell their subordinates what should be done—rather than saying, in effect, "Do this because *I* tell you to." An American manufacturer of electrical equipment lost a big order to a foreign competitor who quoted an appreciably lower price, and the domestic firm faced the prospect of losing substantially more business for the same reason. The general manager might well have issued a lot of edicts about cutting costs. Instead, he laid the full facts before his engineers and production people, announcing, "We have a problem." The situation, rather than the general manager, issued the order to cut costs.

Reliance on the law of the situation can be used for small problems as well as large ones. For instance, a customer's complaint about an error in billing or the illness of a key person in a department obviously requires some kind of action. A manager may in the end decide precisely what is to be done, but the *need* for action is accepted by subordinates not because the manager says so, but because they recognize an objective to be met. When people respond to a situation rather than to an order, they have a sense of self-expression and self-importance. Their identification with the desired result fosters a willingness to cooperate with a program of action.

Prompt settlement of grievances.   Over time a manager can expect subordinates to have occasional work-related grievances. Most of these will be *minor:* discrepancies of a dollar or two in the computation of overtime on a paycheck, a chair that snags stockings, lost telephone messages, failure to announce a new title, and the like. Any minor grievance by itself is not particularly important, but until it is settled, it is a continuing source of annoyance. By giving prompt attention to such matters, a manager not only removes the irritation but also shows concern for the feelings of subordinates. Even if a grievance cannot be resolved in just the way the subordinate wishes, the manager clearly demonstrates that even minor needs are worthy of respect.

The leadership concepts just listed fit so many situations that they can be regarded as constants. With rare exceptions, *any* manager will be a more effective leader if he utilizes the precepts of friendliness and approval, consistency and fairness, support for subordinates, law of the situation, and prompt settlement of grievances. In contrast, the next two concepts—participation and permissive supervision—should be treated as variables. The *degree* to which each can be wisely employed varies with the situation.

Use of Participation

Participation in decision making should be regarded primarily as a means of arriving at better decisions.[7] But if participation is justified as a method for improving decisions, we can also anticipate a strengthening of the motivation of those who participate. A simple case will suggest the difference in the way subordinates feel when participation is and is not used.

Pat Harrison, a young woman recently graduated from business school, has a job as a trainee in a medium-sized factory that makes dungarees for sale to large companies. After a year with this company, she has now been in the production control department for six months, where she reports to Ms. Baker, the department supervisor. At this point, Baker could treat her in two ways.

High Participation	Low Participation
Almost every day, Baker comes over to Pat's desk and asks her for some kind of advice. One day it may be whether a large order can be run in between the two small ones on Pat's list; the next it may be what Pat thinks ought to be done about a bottleneck in the cutting department. Over the six months, Pat has seen Baker's real interest in Pat's ideas, and about 30 percent of them have been put into effect.	Pat thinks that Baker likes her as a person. Baker is always courteous, she shares jokes with Pat and even invited her to dinner a couple of times. When it comes to actual work in the department, Baker is tough but fair. She tells Pat what to do, lets Pat do her job, but expects her to keep her mind off departmental problems. She does not believe that anyone in the department should take care of problems that are rightly assigned to her as supervisor.

If we compare these two ways of treating Pat, we see that the high-participation approach (left column) gives Pat more opportunity for self-

[7] A. G. Jago, *"Leadership: Perspectives in Theory and Research," Management Science* (Boston: The Institute of Management Sciences, 1982).

expression; she probably enjoys her work more and feels surer of Baker's approval. With such treatment, Pat undoubtedly feels more closely identified with results in the entire plant, and will spontaneously cooperate in overcoming plantwide problems.

As a general proposition, the higher the degree of participation (that is, the more the initiative, the wider the scope, and the greater the influence of a subordinate) the stronger will be the resulting inclination to cooperate with company plans.

However, the participation must be genuine. Managers must really want contributions of knowledge, diverse viewpoints, or decision-making skill from their subordinates and must be prepared to devote the time required to obtain their counsel. If they are merely putting on an act, their subordinates will soon detect their insincerity. Then, asking for participation is likely to do more harm than good. As one realistic, autocratic manager put it, "My people already know I am an SOB, and I don't want them to think I'm a hypocrite too."

Closeness of Supervision

An operation is closely supervised when a manager frequently observes it and makes suggestions to the employee. The boss in such situations acts much like a backseat driver, who calls attention to things the driver has already observed, is free with suggestions about just how the car should be driven, and plays "Monday-morning quarterback" for every minor mistake. We often hear people say of this sort of person, "He's a good boss in a way, but he's always needling those who work for him." The most disconcerting action of such a boss is to transfer an assignment before a subordinate has an opportunity to finish it or to give the assignment to two different workers, forcing them to compete with each other.

Such interruptions of a previously assigned task tend to have adverse effects on a subordinate's cooperative attitude. The boss may well be trying to be helpful, but the subordinate is likely to interpret the boss's actions as a lack of confidence or as a negative reflection on his ability. Even if the subordinate overcomes his discomfort and impatience with the interruptions, he is apt to feel like an automaton and to become quite indifferent about his work.

In contrast, when assignments are made in terms of results to be achieved and a supervisor becomes involved in the actual performance of the work only on the request of a worker, a feeling of self-reliance is encouraged. Subordinates can rightfully take more pride in their work, and they have clear evidence of their boss' confidence in them.

During a training period, close supervision is normally expected, but an experienced worker—from vice-president to janitor—finds close supervision somewhat insulting. If close supervision is continued after reasonable training, a worker develops neither the inclination nor the work habits to take the initiative voluntarily in meeting new problems.

Throughout this book, managers are urged to select the type of planning, the particular form of organization, and the system of control that best suits the specific problems confronted. There is no universal solution to different types of problems; instead, wise managers look at their needs and available resources, then chart their course to fit that contingency. The specific issues, options, and factors affecting final design provide guidelines for adjusting the way of managing to a particular set of circumstances.

Leading should also be shaped by a contingency approach.[8] The measures adopted should be suited to the situation. This concept is not always accepted. Instead, we find advocates for Theory Y, management by objectives, self-actualization, and a variety of other motivational techniques.[9] The originators, or more likely some of their disciples, have missionary zeal for what they believe to be the "one best way." Such single-mindedness can perhaps be explained because (1) advocating a single technique is simpler, or (2) the technique fosters some human values that appeal to the advocate. Such techniques usually have considerable merit when used in the proper setting, but they may waste time and actually be harmful when the necessary support for them is lacking.

Adjusting to the Situation

A key to finding the right combination of leadership actions—often called "leadership style"—is to consider carefully (1) the situation in which the leading takes place, (2) the people being led, and (3) the personal characteristics of the leader himself.[10] Because differences occur in all three of these factors, there can be significant variation in leadership styles, all of which are effective, as Figure 14.3 indicates.

The situation in which managers are striving to get action often constrains or encourages the leadership style they use—that is, the extent to which they use participation, share information, are permissive, and supervise only in general terms.

Two factors that affect the choice of a leadership style are the amount of discretion permitted by the technology and the practicality of close supervision. In any organization, there are numerous tasks where technology provides workers with limited discretion. Because an assembly line is designed to control as much of the environment as possible, the opportunities for participation in decision making and permissive supervision are re-

[8]B. Kellerman, *Leadership: Multidisciplinary Perspectives* (Englewood Cliffs, N.J.: Prentice Hall, 1984).

[9]R. Likert, *The Human Organization* (New York: McGraw-Hill; 1967); D. McGregor, *The Human Side of Enterprise* (New York: McGraw-Hill, 1960); R. R. Blake and J. S. Mouton, *The Managerial Grid* (Houston: Gulf, 1964).

[10]B. M. Bass, *Leadership and Performance Beyond Expectations* (New York: Free Press, 1985).

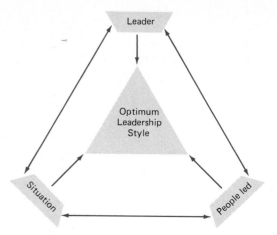

Figure 14.3 In order to determine the best leadership style, three factors must be considered: (1) the leader; (2) the people who are led; and (3) the situation in which leadership is necessary.

duced. One might argue that such mechanistic tasks that require minimal flexibility and creativity should be eliminated. Clearly, much of the job-enrichment literature strives to make that point. In fact, the auto industry—birthplace of the manufacturing assembly line early in this century—has in the 1980s even moved toward greater teamwork and pooled decision making. If such a careful analysis of an individual's or group's total tasks leads to the decision to reorganize the job, then indeed a new leadership style may be practical. Until such a change in duties takes place, however, close supervision is an acceptable means of achieving these tasks.

The practicality of close supervision and strong control must be considered when selecting a leadership style. The service people who maintain complex computers are subject to close supervision and control when they are being trained. As they learn their trade in the classroom, or under the eye of an experienced person, they can be closely supervised. But when that service engineer goes out in the field, close supervision and control become too costly. How well he performs now is much more a function of his skills and his motivation. An assembly-line operator, on the other hand, is traditionally almost continuously subjected to close supervision and tight controls. Because of technological constraints, close supervision and control were seen as necessary.

In the examples shown in Figure 14.4, we see the desirability of matching a leader's permissiveness to the degree of discretion permitted by technology and the practicality of close supervision, as well as other situational factors such as the need for fast action, risks involved, and creativity desired. Theoretically, congruence between leadership style and a situation can be achieved either by leaders adjusting their style to suit the situation or by changing the situation to fit the leader (or by a little of both). In the examples given in the first column, changing the situation would be difficult, so, at least in these instances, most of the adaptation should come in the behavior of the leader.

Low Degree of Permissiveness	Determining Factor in Situation	High Degree of Permissiveness
Running a subway train	Degree of discretion technology permits	Running a sightseeing bus
Overcoming a blackout due to power failure	Need for speed	Locating a new power plant
Operating sanitation equipment (garbage truck)	Satisfactions built into job	Finding ways to reduce water pollution
Flying a passenger airplane	Risks involved	Teaching history in college
Operating TV broadcasting equipment	Creativity desired	Producing a TV show

Figure 14.4 The impact of the situation on leadership style. Activities that are similar may dictate a high or low degree of permissiveness and participation. Although the activities in the box at left are similar to those at right, permissiveness and participation vary.

Adjusting to the People Led

Participative, permissive leadership affects the behavior of some subordinates more than others. One simple distinction is the rate of turnover. On some jobs employees are not around long enough to grasp, and have an interest in, the ramifications of their job. Similarly, routine work often attracts workers who do not expect or want their jobs to be too demanding; they get their kicks elsewhere, such as from hobbies, sports, or their families. Such employees may not be looking to their jobs for fulfillment of self-expression needs. We are not suggesting that these employees will have a negative response to, say, minor participation. Rather, the point is that it would be a mistake to assume that such people welcome deep involvement, nor do they relish the self-discipline that is entailed under a permissive leader who expects subordinates to set their own high goals and regulate their behavior to achieve the goals. On the other hand, if the group to be led comprises energetic, ambitious people who regard themselves as professionals, expect to be with the company a long time, and hope to find personal challenge and self-expression in their work, then participative, permissive leadership is called for.

Different types of work naturally attract different types of people. College professors differ from maintenance people, computer repairers differ from security analysts, and so forth. The differences in values and orientation of production, research, and marketing people are a potential source of conflict.[11] This suggests a different leadership style for various departments, partly because the work situation calls for different kinds of behavior and partly because the people to be led differ. In other words, from the viewpoint of leadership, the situation and the type of people to be led may be mutually reinforcing factors.

[11]A. J. DuBrin, *Foundations of Organizational Behavior: An Applied Perspective* (Englewood Cliffs, N.J.: Prentice-Hall, 1984).

Adjusting to the Leader

A third factor to be considered in picking an effective leadership style is the leaders themselves. From experience, and under many other influences, each of us develops a set of attitudes, values, beliefs, and habitual ways of coping with our environment. This set of personal characteristics may make it easy for some managers to be highly permissive and participative. Such managers have a strong respect for other people, believe that virtually everyone has high potential, take a keen interest in helping people reach their potential, and are willing to take personal risks on the success of other people. They are said to be *people-oriented*.

Other managers are less sure of the capacity of their fellows. They prefer to put their trust in system, law and order, and checks and balances. These managers are not antisocial, but when they have heavy obligations and want to be sure to accomplish a mission, they tend to rely on facts and figures, regulations, cross-checks, and their own direct involvement. We can say that they are *systems-oriented*. These managers have difficulty when there is a high degree of permissiveness, participation, and sharing; they tend to supervise closely.

In the hurly-burly of running an enterprise, mismatches occur. A situation and the people to be led may call for a people-oriented leader, but the actual manager may be systems-oriented—or vice versa. Behavioral scientists have given much attention to this predicament. They are especially concerned about a shortage of people-oriented managers. This preoccupation reflects (1) higher expectations of workers regarding job satisfactions, (2) a high degree of voluntary cooperation required by more jobs, and (3) the personal values of many behavioral scientists. The emphasis is in tune with the times, but leaders should not overlook the possibility that some managers need conversion in the other direction—toward a systems orientation.

When confronted by a mismatch, we can (1) try to adjust the situation and subordinates to fit the leadership style suited to the present manager, (2) replace the manager, or (3) convert the manager. This first alternative may be unattractive because the adjustment of subordinates, either through a job transfer or through training efforts, can be very disruptive. Similarly, the adjustment of the situation may result in a less-than-optimum organizational design.[12] Actually, Sears did just this, because good overall store managers were scarce, and the loss due to a less-than-optimum organizational structure was smaller than the cost of trying to force the managers to use a style unsuited to them.

The alternative of replacing managers is rarely used because in all managerial functions, an equally effective replacement (never mind a better one) is hard to find. Therefore, most effort goes to converting systems-oriented managers to people-oriented managers.

Conversion of mature managers is tricky. Intellectual reasoning is not enough; a person's beliefs and attitudes have a deep emotional basis.

[12]Kellerman, *Leadership*.

Only when we can achieve a propitious match of the situation, the led, and the leader will the fullest degree of participation and permissiveness be feasible. Many managers may conclude that some lesser degree of participation and/or permissiveness is more suitable in the particular circumstance they face. Such a choice does not, of course, preclude the substantial amount of cooperation attainable through the other leadership concepts outlined earlier in this chapter.

Compatibility Among Leadership Styles

Up to this point the clear message has been that leadership style should be adapted to individual situations. A manager's desire for varying permissiveness and participation in dealing with the same individual is, in fact, quite common. Both parties expect different leadership styles to be employed. This mutual expectation that some aspects of work will be treated differently from others has a parallel in planning and in decentralizing, which vary from subject to subject. Leadership styles are normally adjusted to these variations in planning and decentralizing.

A final aspect of using different leadership styles is the need for consistency in the eyes of subordinates. As noted, varying leadership styles are normal and expected. But unpredictable shifting from one to another can be disturbing. If a manager utilizes high participation one month, then next month permits only limited participation, subordinates will not only be confused, they will also question their boss's integrity. The key here is communication. If managers choose to modify their previous leadership style, subordinates should be told about the change and given the reasons for it.[13]

Leadership in Frame-Breaking Changes

An especially difficult leadership task arises when companies must make a frame-breaking change. Such a need occurs when external pressures or rapid growth forces a fundamental shift in strategy. With the strategy shift comes a revised organizational structure, new planning and control procedures, and a lot of reshuffling of key people into new positions. It is a new ball game, often with new players.

If frame breaking is necessary, the leadership task involves (1) convincing members of the organization that a fundamental shift is necessary, (2) creating a motivating vision of the new future, (3) winning enthusiasm—or at least acceptance—of key people for their new roles, and (4) making the new policies and relationships a normal, customary pattern of behavior.[14] As Chapter 17 will point out, a revised culture must be developed.

[13]P. Selznik, *Leadership in Administration: A Sociological Interpretation* (Berkeley: University of California Press, 1983).

[14]N. Tichy and M. A. Devanna, *Transformational Leaders* (New York: John Wiley, 1986); H. Hornstein, *Courageous Leadership* (New York: John Wiley, 1986).

Because resistance to this sort of change is to be expected, the managers promoting the change must draw on all their leadership knowledge and skills. Experience indicates that many executives who are very competent managers of relatively stable situations cannot pilot a frame-breaking change. New persons, unencumbered by past commitments and loyalties, may be required in several jobs. Nevertheless, either a new person or a converted manager must make a fresh appraisal of subordinates' needs, work requirements, communication channels, and all the other factors discussed in the last two chapters. The leadership attitudes identified in the next section are especially valuable in rebuilding the social structure to fit the new strategy.

LEADERSHIP ATTITUDES

Developing an understanding of leadership attitudes emphasizes the key role that personal relations play in the management process. Managers are dealing with the reactions of individual personalities to one another. To improve their ability to lead, then, they have to be perceptive about people. Most managers will never become trained psychologists, but they can develop an awareness of the more obvious factors that might confront them in a given situation. Even such an awareness, however, requires a set of attitudes that often need cultivating: *empathy, self-awareness,* and *objectivity.*

Knowing about the importance of these attitudes will not ensure their development, of course—just as knowing we should not get mad and actually controlling our anger are quite different matters. Still, by understanding which attitudes contribute to good leadership, problems can be better diagnosed and managers may discover where they personally should try to improve.

Empathy

Empathy is the ability to look at things from another person's point of view. If a leader is to guide, motivate, and get information from another, he needs the capacity to project himself into that person's position. How does that person feel about the company and about her job? What values does she attach to friendships, security, titles, and the many other things affected by her work? How will she interpret the words and actions of her boss, her associates, and her subordinates? What are her hopes and aspirations? What difficulties are bothering her at the moment? Whom does she trust, and whom does she fear? Note that empathy is not a case of asking, "What would *I* do if I were in your position?" because any one of us might bring to the position quite different knowledge and feelings. We are empathetic only when we can sense and feel, almost intuitively, *how another person reacts* to a given situation.

An executive may set up a new vacation policy or make some other change he intends as an aid to his subordinates, but if he thinks of the change in terms of how *he* would like it rather than how the people affected will like it, the move is likely to misfire. To be empathetic we need *respect* for the other person as an individual. We may disagree sharply with his values and consider his reasoning false, but we should still recognize that his feelings and beliefs seem just as valid to him as ours do to us. A salesperson, for instance, often finds he needs such attitudes; if he is a good salesperson he has a lot of empathy for his customer, but he does not necessarily endorse the customer's behavior or beliefs.

Self-awareness

Knowing oneself ranks with empathy as a requisite for leadership. An executive needs to be *aware* of the particular impact she makes. She should know her own predilections for, say, taking action hastily, being brusque with people who don't understand instructions the first time, getting so involved in specific problems that she bypasses supervisors in resolving them, and so forth.

Moreover, a leader should know how she appears to other people. Many of us have an image of ourselves that differs from the way others see us. A manager may think of herself as fair and objective, for example, but some of her subordinates may consider her to be biased in favor of young women with college degrees. Regardless of which view is correct, the manager may have difficulty in motivating and communicating with a subordinate who is convinced she is biased unless she knows that the subordinate thinks so.

Finally, with an awareness of his own preferences, weaknesses, and habits, and of what others think of him, a manager should learn what impression his actions make on other people. One high-ranking executive, for instance, growled over the telephone at the secretaries and assistants of his immediate subordinates when the latter were "not in." In so doing, he unwittingly created morale problems for his subordinates and virtually cut himself off from any voluntary help from lower-level personnel. But this executive, whose manner with his immediate subordinates was much less gruff, was unaware that by expressing his displeasure to secretaries he was creating difficulties.

Objectivity

A third quality that is crucial to good leadership is objectivity in person-to-person relations. People have reasons for behaving as they do. To identify the influences on Joe Jones' actions is to take an important step toward guiding his behavior. Instead of getting angry with Joe for resisting a new method, for instance, his response should be recognized and an attempt made to find out what caused it. Or if a salesperson is unusually energetic, understanding what motivates her suggests a way to induce similar behavior in other salespersons.

Such detachment may not be easy to maintain. People commonly react to the behavior of others emotionally instead of analytically. Besides, managers are often deeply concerned with the outcome of their subordinates' activities and therefore let their intense feelings cloud their objectivity.

In addition, empathy fosters sympathy and personal identification with other people; yet a good leader should be both objective and empathetic. The viewpoint of a physician is similar to what a leader needs to reconcile these two attitudes. A good physician understands her patients' feelings—she is highly empathetic; but her *own emotional involvement* with her patients must be limited if she is to make an objective diagnosis and perhaps take action that she knows involves substantial risk. She is well aware of the problems of her patients as individual personalities, and at the same time she deals with such problems in a detached, scientific manner. A good manager, likewise, understands the feelings and problems of her subordinates; yet she keeps enough psychological distance to be fair, just, and constructively concerned with performance.

Many qualities contribute to a manager's ability to lead. It is impossible to make a complete and unassailable list of such qualities, partly because they vary with the people being led and with the circumstances in which the leading takes place. Nevertheless, these three qualities—empathy, self-awareness, and objectivity—are needed in the vast majority of cases.

CONCLUSION

Managerial leadership is primarily concerned with converting plans into action, and in an enterprise this involves highly personal, one-to-one interaction between managers and subordinates. In their roles as leaders, managers are in a particularly tight spot. They must act within the constraints imposed by technology and their environment, must fulfill company objectives, and at the same time must be responsive to the individual needs of their subordinates.

To be effective leaders, managers must understand the feelings and problems of their individual subordinates. Such feelings change, partly as a result of the behavior of managers themselves, and problems change with the ebb and flow of events. To keep in tune with these personal "facts," the manager needs empathy, self-awareness, and an objectivity about behavior.

Managers are concerned with both productivity and the personal satisfaction of their associates. Such a merger is not easily accomplished. We have noted that it is built upon a wisely designed managerial structure, a prerequisite for effective leadership. Then, objective, empathetic managers can work with their subordinates in a manner that gives all individuals the continuing support and encouragement they need. The various guides suggested here give no formula, but they do point to the quality of relationships that build sustained cooperative attitudes.

Leading is an endless process for a manager. Not only do the problems and plans of an enterprise keep changing, thereby creating new issues calling for leadership, but individuals also change. This makes the continuous adaptation to change one of the greatest challenges facing future managers.

Impact on Productivity

Opportunities for improvements in personal leadership are widespread. Although significant and desirable, most of these improvements will probably add small increments to the effectiveness of company operations. Over a period of time, these changes could lead to a marked lowering of costs and smaller deviations from quality and delivery targets.

In a few situations, however, such as those noted in the opening of the chapter, personal leadership by senior executives can make dramatic contributions. Such major shifts usually occur in turnaround settings where a forceful personality leads the organization to unexpected success. Here, the leader often changes the nature of the company's services as well as inspiring exceptional efforts by the employees. Productivity leaps ahead.

These dramatic transformations are so rare that it is a mistake to think of leadership only in such terms. Like so many other facets of managing, the larger contribution to productivity will come from an accumulation of smaller refinements in personal leadership by thousands of managers in diverse positions. The responsibility rests on all of us.

FOR FURTHER DISCUSSION

1. Describe the supervision practices and the leadership style of the best boss you ever worked for. Why was this person effective as your leader? Was that person similarly effective with other subordinates?

2. "I'm continually amazed," said a national sales manager of a company selling office equipment, "at the failure of many outstanding salespeople to become effective leaders when appointed to branch management posts. A good salesperson has very little power over customers. Sales are made with good products and the attributes of a leader. Why can't those same attributes be used to lead the branch when the salesperson is put in charge?" What do you think of this observation?

3. "A labor union organizer does not make a good president of the union after it is recognized as the bargaining agent because the situation has changed from a fight to maintaining a negotiated agreement. Similarly, the manager of a start-up airline such as People Express is unlikely to have a leadership style suitable for the CEO of one of the top half-dozen national airlines." Do you agree?

4. Identify the key factors that will determine the leadership effectiveness of women moving into senior management positions.

5. What is the distinction between *paternalism* (which is strongly criticized by both unions and human resources experts) and the measures for securing voluntary cooperation discussed in this chapter? Is paternalism wise in other countries such as Japan or India, but not in the United States? Why?

6. List all the reasons you can think of why you might elect *not* to use high participation with a subordinate of yours. Are there any ways to adjust your behavior so as to obtain the benefits of participation and still recognize the obstacles or reservations on your list?

7. Assume a division of a large company shifts from a strategy of aggressive pursuit of market share to one of seeking less growth but more stable profits. How would such a shift in strategy affect the leadership style needed by the division's general manager?

8. Individuals vary in the kind of leadership behavior to which they respond. Does this suggest that a manager with a diverse set of subordinates (different ages, experience, personalities, and so on) should adjust his leadership style to fit each subordinate? How much variation can most managers muster? What happens to equity (equal treatment) among the group?

FOR FURTHER READING

Bass, B. M., *Stogdill's Handbook of Leadership.* New York: Free Press, 1981. Encyclopedic revision of the classic handbook on leadership. Twenty-five references for each page!

Burns, J. M., *Leadership.* New York: Harper & Row, 1978. A distinguished political scientist looks at leadership in social and political settings. An insight into charismatic leaders.

Hersey, P. and K. H. Blanchard, *Management of Organizational Behavior: Utilizing Human Resources,* 4th ed. Englewood Cliffs, N.J.: Prentice-Hall, 1982. Concise summary of major theories of leadership.

Hunt, J. G., *Leadership and Managerial Behavior.* Chicago: Science Research Associates, 1984. Concise view of a progression of contingency models of leadership. Includes exercises and other self-help aids.

Hunt, J. G. and J. D. Blair, eds., *Leadership on the Future Battlefield.* Elmsford, N.Y.: Pergamon Press, 1984. Military and civilian scholars address future leadership in the high-tech arena.

Kantor, R. M., *The Change Masters: Innovation for Productivity in the American Corporation.* New York: Simon & Schuster, 1983. Describes use of participation management by large companies to foster innovation.

Yukl, G. A., *Leadership in Organizations.* Englewood Cliffs, N.J.: Prentice-Hall, 1981. Useful condensed survey of leadership literature.

MANAGEMENT IN ACTION CASE 14
Al Davis and His Football Misfits

Few owners of professional sports teams identify with their players—and their players with them—as intensely as Al Davis of the Los Angeles (nee Oakland) Raiders.

While other owners distance themselves from the rank and file in corporate offices and luxury box suites high above the playing field, the man whom *Time* magazine called "a middle-age rock n' roller in a '50s hairdo and a black leather jacket" roams among his black-and-silver-clad Raiders like a member of one of the special teams, instilling fear and a chilling contempt for the opponent.

Among his National Football League peers, Davis is regarded as a renegade. As commissioner of the American Football League in the 1960s, he prompted the NFL to consider a merger with the upstart AFL by trying to lure away the NFL's top quarterbacks. As owner of the Raiders in 1982, he infuriated fellow owners and NFL Commissioner Pete Rozelle by unilaterally relocating his team from Oakland to Los Angeles, where crowds of 90,000 were bigger than even the sell-out audiences up north. In a bitter court fight that followed, Davis prevailed over the NFL and was awarded $35 million in damages.

In similar style, Davis' players revel in their image as league villains. "The three *P*'s of Raider football," linebacker Matt Millen once said, "are pointing, pushing, and penalties." The great Raider teams of the 1980s have been ragtag bands of malcontents and castoffs, players who speak with affection of Davis, the mentor who has the audacity to renegotiate contracts on the practice field. Yet they fear him too, as anyone might fear a man who once boasted, "If I have a guy with a (drug) problem, I put a guy on him twenty-four hours a day. I'm not sensitive to his rights. I don't let up on him."

With Davis as their inspiration, the Raiders are consistently one of the NFL's winningest and most intimidating teams. In 1984 they became the biggest winner of all by whipping the Washington Redskins, 38–9, in Super Bowl XVIII. The lopsided score was emblematic of Davis' ruthless ambition. "We can dominate anybody," he said. "We don't sit around hoping for turnovers or time of possession or those other clichés. We beat you up, knock you out early. We dominate."

Question

What are the advantages and the disadvantages of Al Davis' style of personal leadership? Do you recommend that other managers—say, the dean of a business school—try to use the same style?

For more information, see *Newsweek*, 6 February 1984; *Time*, 23 January 1984.

APPLICATION CASES

For practice in applying concepts covered in this chapter to managerial situations, see the following managerial decision cases. The case questions particularly relevant to this chapter are listed by number after each case name.

Grant Chemical Corporation (p. 59) 13
Fyler International (p. 68) 13
Heartland Union Bank (HUB) (p. 183) 15,16
Consolidated Instruments (p. 189) 17
Norman Manufacturing Company (p. 538) 11
Scandico (Singapore) (p. 546) 13

15

Informal Groups and Communicating Within Organizations

LEARNING OBJECTIVES

After completing this chapter, you should be able to

1. Understand the power of informal groups that form within organizations.

2. See how three potential managerial responses to group activities can be effective in an organization.

3. Identify the major obstacles to effective personal communication within organizations.

4. Summarize the major guides for empathetic listening, and know when to use this technique.

5. Describe ways that you can improve your two-way communication in an organizational setting.

THE INFORMAL ORGANIZATION

This chapter explores two kinds of interpersonal relations in organizations—informal groups and person-to-person communications. Managers must understand and deal skillfully with both if they are to provide effective leadership.

The organization chart of a business reflects the formal aspects of the organization—who is responsible for what, who reports to whom, and the formal chain of command. Such plans are often even more elaborate and describe duties and official intentions.

But there is another side to organization—an informal side—that many researchers contend may be every bit as important as the formal structure. Whenever people work together, they quite naturally drift into informal groups—groups that soon influence behavior and beliefs. Understanding how these informal groups function, how they support or detract from the formal organization, and how communications flow to and from them is critical for the manager who expects to oversee the total, living organization.[1]

Social Groups Within Organizations

Small social groups significantly affect the way a formal organization actually works. Informal groups of from three to perhaps a dozen members spring up in response to social needs. They rally wherever people work, and are common among college students and in large government offices as well as in business firms. Members of such groups see each other frequently on the job, at lunch, or riding home from work. They discover common interests and exchange ideas. A group thus forms spontaneously. If one or two members tend to be leaders, their position arises naturally out of the situation rather than from formal selection.

Most people get many of their day-to-day satisfactions from such groups. Among the "rewards" for belonging to such a group are sociability, a sense of belonging (which contributes to feelings of inner security and personal worth), a sympathetic ear for troubles, aid on the job (both information and occasional direct assistance), and some protection through a united stand against pressure from a boss or outside force.

Small-group rewards are especially prized by people who work in large organizations, where, too often, the work itself provides few satisfactions. If the work is fragmented and remote objectives are not felt to be significant, then the social satisfactions derived from subgroups become a major force in behavior on the job.[2]

A small informal group—whether composed of computer operators, members of a vice-president's staff, or senior executives in an electrical-engineering department—falls into routines for its activities. Members sit

[1]A. Zander, *The Purpose of Groups and Organization* (San Francisco: Jossey-Bass, 1985).
[2]P. Gyllenhammer, *People at Work* (Reading, Mass.: Addison-Wesley, 1977).

together in the lunchroom; Mary stops to chat with Steve before going home in the evening. When the members work near one another, interchange may take place from time to time throughout the day. Sometimes a pattern of contact is extended to include off-the-job activities, such as bowling, golf, bridge, or union meetings. In addition, a group tends to evolve a pattern of attitudes, at least toward subjects of common interest. Members frequently discuss their feelings toward their boss, company, rates of output, young MBAs from college, or the accounting office; often, they all hold similar views on such subjects.

Most people belong to several small informal groups. One may be founded on physical proximity at work, another on a common interest in baseball, and a third on an interest in a professional society—for example, the Society for Advancement of Management. A political protest group draws together quite a diverse collection of people. Some of these groups may be fairly inactive, and people may drift in and out of them. But those based on daily work relationships are likely to be the strongest and most enduring.

Effect of Social Groups on Worker Behavior

It is typical of social groups to put pressure on members *to conform to group norms,* which are standards and expectations governing behavior. This push to conformity is, of course, common throughout life. A school child gets teased by his classmates if his clothing is too fancy. Young couples who move to suburbia match their neighbors by selling the compact and buying a sports car. Even nonconformists in college express their defiance in ways endorsed by fellow nonconformists—for instance, new polished shoes must *not* be worn even if the owner has to go to a lot of trouble to get them dirty and scuffed up. Of course, the particular matters on which to conform vary from group to group and from time to time.

In addition to such standards of conduct, groups also *provide many beliefs and values* to the individual. Joe or Kathy may believe that the personnel director is a "good guy" and that the advertising director is a "screwball"—not from any personal observation or conviction, but merely because these are the sentiments passed on to them by their group. They may believe that all senior executives draw fabulous salaries, that only a Stanford graduate can get ahead in the firm, that their company has the best engineering department in the industry, and many other articles of faith, because they are strongly held by their social group. A group can also influence feelings about such matters as pilfering, accuracy in keeping reports, importance of efficient quality control, service to customers, or even how to treat the boss.

The potential influence of beliefs fostered by informal groups is illustrated in the odd case of one chief executive who moved into government. His new "advance man" (a person who arranges travel, sets up appointments, and so forth) was told that the executive had back trouble and required a board under his mattress to make the bed harder when traveling.

The government advance man went to great extremes to be sure his new boss always got a bed board, only to hear him complain about not sleeping well on the road. It wasn't until the advance man announced one day, "I even have them put a board under your mattress," and noticed the shocked look on his boss' face that both realized that a hoax had been played on both by a small group back at the executive's former corporation.

Employee groups may strongly support the company strategy, as has been the tradition at IBM, or they may be indifferent or even opposed to it.

Even when an individual has direct evidence contrary to group sentiment, he may accept group judgment. For example, in a classic series of experiments with groups of college students, all persons except one in each group were instructed to give incorrect answers to a simple question about which of several lines was longest. As different sets of lines were flashed on a screen, the exception in each group found his judgment consistently at odds with that of a half-dozen other people in the same room; eventually he began to distrust his own perception and started giving the group answer.[3] At work, when facts are less clear-cut, and group pressure is even greater, the temptation to accept group opinion is strong. Fortunately there continues to be a good sprinkling of rugged individualists who maintain their independence of judgment. Even these people, however, are likely simply to remain silent rather than challenge some cherished bit of lore.

[3]S. E. Asch, "Effects of Group Pressure Upon the Modification and Distortion of Judgments," in H. Guetzkow, ed., *Groups, Leadership and Men* (Pittsburgh: Carnegie Press, 1951).

Figure 15.1 As group members work together over time, group cohesiveness develops. A cohesive group is likely to exert pressure on a member who disagrees with the majority.

Irene Springer

The pressure of a group on its members is substantial, for an individual gets many of his satisfactions in his job through group responses. If he deviates too far from group standards, other members may no longer want to associate with him and may treat him as though he were a deviant, if not a traitor. Group influence is particularly strong in *cohesive* groups. The members of a cohesive group strongly identify with group norms; the close attachment to common beliefs and to other group members produces high group solidarity.

The member of a cohesive group who deviates from an accepted norm will be subjected to severe social censure. For this reason, cohesive groups exert considerable control over the output of individual members. If a group of production operators agrees to restrict daily output to an accepted group standard, low productivity will result. On the other hand, if group norms favor high output, a highly cohesive group can be very productive. Low performers are likely to be considered outcasts in such high-producing groups.

Behavioral research has found one further characteristic of group behavior that is of direct interest to management. A group will probably *resist any change* that upsets its normal activities, especially if the change is initiated by an outsider. A new method, a change in office layout, or a reassignment of duties modifies established patterns of social relationships. Social groups may be broken up, and this disruption means loss of known satisfactions in exchange for an unknown future. Consciously or unconsciously, people resist such changes, even when offsetting advantages may benefit individual members of a group, and new groups may replace old ones. Managers should thus anticipate resistance when they upset social patterns.

Managerial Response

Since informal organization is a prevalent and influential aspect of business life, wise managers try to understand and use it. Here are three possibilities.

Gain better understanding of motivations. Informal organizations are voluntary and rather private relationships, but they are not secret societies. A perceptive manager can learn much about these informal associations, and one major advantage of doing so is the light such understanding sheds on the behavior and motivations of members of the organization. As already noted, beliefs and values—and their impact on behavior—are often tied to informal groups. Thus, managers can predict and interpret actions of subordinates better if they are well informed about the informal social structure.

Armed with this kind of insight, managers may elect to adjust their personal leadership actions or even modify explicit plans and controls. Or, if employee behavior is being influenced by mistaken assumptions, the manager can pump accurate data into the communications network. For the latter purpose, actions speak louder than words. Attitudes and beliefs are more emotional than rational, and verbal explanations need to be buttressed by direct experience. But note that any of these managerial responses rely on a good understanding of the informal ties among social groups.

Foster informal groups related to meaningful work.   A second sort of managerial response is to encourage informal groups where they can also serve company purposes. An example of this, already noted in previous chapters, is a *task team*.

To form an integrated task team, we should identify blocks of work that have a natural unity, whose end result we can clearly visualize. An example of such a block may be all activities that pertain to securing a customer's order, or to making a particular product or part. Then, we should place authority for doing such a specific, complete block of work squarely on a small group of people. These people will constitute a team, and it is up to them to complete the effort. One person may be captain, but the assignment belongs to the entire task team, as Figure 15.2 shows.[4]

By assigning meaningful jobs to a task team, we hope that a social group will form that is interested in achieving results.[5] In fact, there is considerable research evidence to indicate that there will be less indifference to company goals and fewer restrictions on output under the task-team organizational structure than in a highly functionalized organization. Although such research deals mostly with operating tasks, task teams at the management level have a similar result.

This suggestion about managers creating situations that foster informal groups does not presume that managers can prescribe informal orga-

[4]E. J. Poza and M. L. Markus, "Success Story: The Team Approach to Work Restructuring," *Organizational Dynamics,* Winter 1980.

[5]F. M. Gryna, *Quality Circles: A Team Approach to Problem Solving* (New York: AMACOM, 1981).

Figure 15.2   In an integrated task team, each member has an assigned role, but it is the immediate task itself that calls for action and voluntary coordination of effort.

nization. The most they can do is design the formal organization in a way that is conducive to informal groups at locations where a merging of informal and formal grouping would be beneficial. The hope is that the influence of the informal group will reinforce the formal structure.

Seek political support through informal groups.   Since informal groups often have a strong influence on values and behavior, they obviously have political clout. Company politics will be discussed in the next chapter, so here we merely observe that political support in a company for a particular cause or change is likely to be sought through informal channels. (The formal organization is presumed to act objectively and rationally in pursuing *company* objectives.) Thus, we see another reason why a manager needs to understand the informal grouping.

Informal groups by their very nature are intangible, shifting, and lacking in explicit doctrine. A manager learns about them almost entirely by talking with individuals. Also, a manager deals with subordinates in an official capacity predominantly through face-to-face contact. Consequently, personal communication—the subject of the next section—is a crucial element in the broad process of leading.

PERSONAL COMMUNICATION: FOUNDATION FOR LEADING

One way to make change more palatable is through fair, open, and honest communication. The mutual understanding that can result is essential to lasting leadership. Throughout this discussion of leadership, it has been assumed that the manager understands his subordinates and associates, and that they understand him. In practice, deficiencies in such understanding are a major stumbling block.

The critical element here is an ability to communicate person-to-person. A manager must learn from his associates the latter's thoughts, feelings, and motivations. He must also clearly convey his explicit and implicit instructions, along with their significance and the feeling that lies behind them.

To improve one's ability to communicate person-to-person, one should: (1) be aware of common obstacles to gaining understanding, (2) understand the process of empathetic listening, (3) convey meaning to others, and (4) get feedback confirmation by testing the signals. Throughout discussion of these topics, however, the reader should think of their relevance and suitability to each of the leadership styles explored earlier. In person-to-person communication, as in virtually all other areas of managing, the value of a concept or technique depends upon the situation to which it is being applied. To simplify the following discussion, we will use the supervisor-subordinate relationship as the setting.

Obstacles to Understanding

Differences in viewpoints.   One reason that communication is often difficult lies in the different points of view of receiver and sender. Take this example: Joan Brown is sales manager for one of the leading American manufacturers of men's and women's apparel; her salesman in the Atlanta territory is Al Williams. Brown has always gotten along with Williams, enjoys talking with him, and likes to help Williams when she can. Brown has recently been looking at figures on population and buying power; these indicate that the Atlanta district has greatly increased in both categories. So on a visit to the Atlanta office, Brown said to Williams, "I've been wondering if the Atlanta territory is the right size for one person to cover."

In making this apparently simple observation, Brown meant to imply that the work load in Atlanta has apparently increased, and that some arrangement must be made to keep the company growing and profitable in relation to its competitors. She is also trying to convey to Williams the feeling that she likes him and is concerned about his satisfaction with his job.

Al Williams, however, has just returned from 300 miles of travel on a July day with temperatures over ninety degrees, a trip that included sixty miles of dusty, unpaved road. Before his boss came in, he read his mail and found a routine communication from New York asking him to fill out a complete set of forms on forecasting purchases by each customer and to "get these back to us next week if possible." Williams knows that he will have to work a couple of nights to finish the forms in time. In addition, Brown is the first woman Williams has ever worked for. So when Brown says "I've been wondering if the Atlanta territory is the right size for one person to cover," this series of thoughts runs through Williams' mind: Brown has never been over the back part of the territory; she doesn't know what the territory is really like; she thinks of it as a big smooth map; now she thinks I'm not working hard enough so she's asking why I'm not producing more sales.

Situations like this occur in industry every day. An executive makes a seemingly simple statement, and a responsible subordinate who gets along well with his boss receives quite a different communication. Why was Brown's communication ineffective?

First, we should note that to Brown and Williams, the word *territory* means different things on the factual level. Williams has seen thirty towns in the back part of the territory, known forty-five customers in those towns, traversed thirty roads connecting them, and experienced how much time it took to talk to Al Jackson in Marietta compared with the time it took to talk to Jack Freeman in Valdosta. These 107 facts, along with hundreds of others, he has lumped together in his head, into a construct called the "territory." From literally thousands of things he has heard and seen, Williams has abstracted a "territory." It has *meaning* to him. Brown, on the other hand, has looked at many maps, reviewed statistics on the number and names of customers, measured distances, looked at population and buying-power statistics, and has lumped all these facts together into something *she* calls a "territory"; the word clearly has another meaning for her.

In addition to such differences in factual content, the feelings a person intends to transmit may not correspond to those that are received. Joan Brown, when she spoke, actually felt friendly toward Al Williams; but Al did not receive that impression. He may generally feel that Brown likes him, but this statement did not reinforce that feeling. At this point, then, just as each person is thinking of different intellectual abstractions, so each one is feeling different emotions.

If Al Williams is to understand Joan Brown, then Brown must find some way to overcome this semantic barrier, a barrier created by both the difference between her own factual experience and that of Williams and the differences in her feelings and his.

Incidentally, Brown will gain very little by asking Williams, "You know what I mean by the Atlanta territory, don't you?" Williams can really only answer yes. If he says anything else, his boss is likely to think that he is not too bright. Furthermore, if by saying yes Williams really believes that he does understand, he can only mean, "I understand what I heard," not "I understand what you heard yourself say."

Organizational distance.   Subordinates naturally want to look good in their bosses' eyes. Consequently, they select the information they pass up the line so as to create a good impression, and they hold back information that makes them look bad. In organization jargon, they protectively screen the information that they transmit. Likewise, bosses may feel that, because of their position, they should not be completely candid with their subordinates. Individuals differ, of course, in the extent to which they permit a status discrepancy to interfere with a free exchange of ideas and feelings: in extreme instances, organizational distance blocks all except formal communication.[6]

Perfunctory attention.   In our conversations with others, we often only half-listen to what they say. We are so busy with our own thoughts that we tend to give attention only to those ideas we expect to hear. When an accountant talks to the controller, the controller may pay attention only to how work is progressing and may disregard clues on morale or friction with staff. In fact, psychological studies show that many of us ignore information that conflicts with our established patterns of thought; we simply do not believe that Steve is serious about quitting or that a key customer would buy foreign-made equipment, because such thoughts do not conform with the ideas we already hold. Especially if we are deeply committed to,

[6]K. Davis, ed., *Organizational Behavior: Readings and Exercises,* 6th ed. (New York: Mc-Graw-Hill, 1981), Chap. 12.

or emotionally involved in, some matter, we prefer to pay no more attention to bad news than Hitler did to reports of inadequate supplies during the latter part of his regime. We tend to retain our private concept of the world by saying to ourselves, "I just don't believe it."

A manager is especially likely to give perfunctory attention to incoming communications when he is very busy with other matters. He simply has so many other distractions that he selects those parts of a total communication that can be readily used. Novel and irreconcilable bits of information or unexpected feelings get brushed aside. Under some circumstances, an executive may be justified in such cursory treatment of messages, but he pays a price for being superficially informed.

Repressed feelings. Western culture stresses objective evidence, full knowledge of the facts, and exchange of information. At the same time, however, we are taught to hide our emotions. Unlike small children whose feelings are openly expressed, mature adults are expected to moderate their emotions, or at least *appear* to moderate them. Likewise, our culture encourages us not to publicly recognize emotions in others. Except with one's closest friends, it isn't polite to discuss strong feelings.

As a result of this repression of feelings, we are inept in communicating them. Of course, there are such cues as body language.[7] But particularly in a business or other organizational setting, special effort is required to detect how people feel, and we rarely find an opportunity to verify our guesses directly.

Inferred meanings. Still another difficulty faced in developing a clear, mutual understanding with a boss or a subordinate is the meaning— or interpretation—given a message. We do—and should—consider the source of a message: The sender may be biased, she may draw her ideas from an unrepresentative sample, or she may deliberately twist the evidence. But trouble is caused by lumping everyone into broad classes—for example, assuming all salespeople exaggerate. True, the typical salesperson tends to be too optimistic, but that doesn't mean that everything he says is unreliable. Moreover, hopes may lead us to infer a meaning that was never intended; for example, a friendly talk with the boss does not necessarily mean we are in line for a promotion.

Then, too, the particular situation at the time a message is received may *accidentally* affect the meaning attached to it. If Al Williams had been working over his prospect list instead of just returning from a hot, dusty trip, the meaning he drew from Joan Brown's comment about the size of the Atlanta territory might have been quite different. To take a similar example from another company, a plant superintendent was talking with one of his foremen about the high cost of certain products on the same day that the company controller distributed a bulletin on keeping time cards posted accurately. The foreman inferred that the superintendent thought

[7]K. H. Roberts, *Communicating in Organizations* (Chicago: Science Research Associates, 1984), Chap. 3.

he was faking his time reports. Actually, the superintendent had no such idea in mind; the arrival of the two messages on the same day was pure coincidence.

Sensitivity to these common difficulties with person-to-person communication within organizations helps managers to spot misunderstandings. They may not be able to correct the difficulties—most are imbedded in social customs—but they can sharpen their communication skills so as to work around them.

Empathetic Listening

The kind of communication being explored requires the mutual exchange of ideas and feelings between managers and subordinates. Managers must *listen* and must also *impart* facts and feelings. But for the interchange to be most effective, they should emphasize listening. If they start by giving their views to subordinates, as many managers are inclined to do, they are likely to stifle upward communication because of their status and latent power. Of course, managers do give directions, as we shall soon note; but the form of communication being examined here builds understandings and relationships that underlie and greatly simplify the task of directing.

What empathetic listening involves. When listening empathetically, a person opens the way for another to talk freely about his ideas and feelings without having to justify each statement he makes. The listener reserves his own views and preconceived ideas, while giving close attention to what the other person is trying to express. The listener is simply trying to gain insight into what is "on the other fellow's mind." This is a valuable skill at all levels, but it is probably most valuable to the high-level manager who, because of his status, has difficulty getting subordinates to give him their "whole message."

Empathetic listening makes use of certain psychotherapeutic techniques whereby a patient first expresses his feelings, then recognizes the facts of his problem, and finally develops a workable adjustment of these facts. Most managers, of course, are not about to undertake psychotherapy, but they can use some of its concepts to nurture a mutual understanding of day-to-day problems at work. The manager can listen sympathetically, without injecting his own views, to a subordinate's attitudes and emotions about his job; in so doing, the manager may help the subordinate to gain a more objective appreciation of the total situation.

For managers, this kind of nondirected interview may be the only way they can learn the full feelings and operating problems of subordinates. Without such an understanding, managers are in a poor position to predict responses to requests or to energize forces to shift those responses.

Example of empathetic listening. An illustration of empathetic listening will give concreteness to the technique in general terms. Let us compare the way two different executives approach the same situation. The following facts were presented to executives at a management-development program; then members of the group interviewed a person who knew the full story and who responded as Tony Flynn probably would have.[8]

Tony Flynn works in the assembly department of a company that manufactures television-broadcasting equipment. The operation requires that people work in teams. Tony has been employed by the company for six years. During the first two years he showed aptitude for the job, but his attendance record was so irregular that he was warned twice that he would be dismissed unless he got to work steadily. For the past four years he has had a good attendance record and is a competent, experienced worker. Although Tony gets along with his fellow workers, he has always been very quiet and reserved, and company records do not contain any explanation of his early absences. Three days ago (Monday) Tony did not show up for work, nor did he phone that he was sick—which company rules require employees to do in cases of illness. Tuesday the same thing happened, and the employment manager got no answer when he tried to call Tony's home. Again, on Wednesday, no Tony. This morning Tony appeared on time, but looking a bit disheveled and glum. The superintendent of the assembly department asked the supervisor under whom Tony works to send him to his office.

One interview with Tony developed as follows:

SUPT.: Hello, Tony, it's good to see you. Sit down a minute.
TONY: (*Taking chair beside desk*) Thanks.
SUPT.: Tony, we've missed you the last few days.
TONY: (*Half to himself*) Yeah, been out all week, until this morning.
SUPT.: That's right, I'm sorry to say, and you know how one man out upsets your crew. We didn't have a substitute most of the time.
TONY: (*Pause*) Yeah, afraid I caused some trouble.
SUPT.: And not calling in, Tony, that made matters worse because we didn't know what to plan on. You've been here long enough to know how important it is to keep full crews in assembly.
TONY: (*Again, half to himself*) Should have called in, that's right.
SUPT.: Tell me, when you realize how important it is, how could you just disappear for three days? We couldn't even get an answer at your home.
TONY: I just couldn't make it, and been too messed up to call in. Sorry I caused so much trouble.
SUPT.: Tony, I've looked over your record. The last four years have been fine. We need good men like you. A few years back the absences were pretty seri-

[8]Professor Alex Bavelas assumed the role of Tony in both of the "role-playing" views digested here. The persons who took the position of superintendent were given only the facts known to management before the interview; they were free to conduct the interview as they chose and did not listen to anyone else before their turn. The two interviews selected represent contrasting approaches. The conversations have been condensed to conserve space.

ous, and I sure hope we're not going to slide back to that trouble again. Yet, the recent record looks real good. *(Pause)* What do you think, Tony, can you keep that record as clean as it has been the last couple of years?

TONY: I'd sure like to. I've been trying. *(Pause)*

SUPT.: We need good men like you. You know the work, and you pitch in when we have to get work out in a rush. But we have to be able to depend on the men we keep in your spot. If you think this won't happen again, we're mighty glad to have you back.

TONY: Well, I need my job, and I'll do the best I can.

Another executive took a different tack with Tony.

SUPT.: Hello, Tony, we've been missing you. Sit down and let's talk about it.

TONY: *(Taking chair beside desk)* Thanks.

SUPT.: You been under the weather, Tony?

TONY: I'm all right, I guess.

SUPT.: Gee, Tony, the way you say that, you don't sound very sure.

TONY: *(Half to himself)* Well, I've got to feel all right.

SUPT.: Hmm?

TONY: *(Pause)* I just gotta keep going somehow.

SUPT.: It takes some real push, sometimes.

TONY: Lost three days' pay already. Not sure I can stay awake today.

SUPT.: Been losing sleep?

TONY: Can't sleep even when I get to bed. *(Pause)* Took Mary to the hospital Sunday—no, that would be Monday—about 2 AM. She darned near died that morning. Went home to see about Patsy that evening. She was bawling to see her mother, but I left her with the neighbors anyway. Spent most of the night at the hospital. Tuesday, Mary at least knew who I was. Tuesday night I took Patsy home—the neighbors got kids of their own—and she cried and fussed most of the night. Last night I tried to give her supper. I was awful. Mary's getting better, they say, but she still looks like a ghost. Well, I figured I had to get back to work this morning.

SUPT.: No wonder you look bushed. Think you can keep going?

TONY: Guess I can get through to the weekend. The neighbors will keep Patsy in the day and a high school girl is coming to sit with her in the evenings so I can go see Mary. But we can't keep this up forever, and I don't know how to pay the doctor's bills and blood transfusions and all that. (Pause) Guess I'd better take Patsy down to Mary's sister's. Could do that Sunday without losing any more pay.

SUPT.: Tony, you don't have to settle everything right away. You say your wife is getting better, and that's most important. If you can get Patsy taken care of for a couple of weeks, maybe the public nursing service can help your wife get back on her feet. The personnel department could tell you about that.

TONY: Sure, we might make out that way for a while.

SUPT.: I'll phone Joe [Tony's supervisor] to find a few minutes you can talk with the personnel people today. And if you do have to take time off, be sure to phone us, Tony. You know how important it is to make up a full crew.

TONY: *(Leaving)* Yeah, thanks. I'll call in if I have to be out any more, but I don't think it will be necessary.

In the first conversation the superintendent was not unfriendly, but he was so preoccupied with the problems of staffing his department that he failed to get information from Tony that was needed in order to deal with the situation constructively. In the second interview, the superintendent said very little until Tony had talked about *his* problems. Then the superintendent was in a much better position to take action that would avoid future absences.

Guides for listening.   From studies in clinical psychology and psychiatry and from experience with nondirected interviewing in industry have come a series of guides for empathetic listening.[9] The most useful of these guides for the manager are the following:

1. Listen patiently to what the other person has to say, even though you may believe it is wrong or irrelevant. Indicate simple acceptance (not necessarily agreement) by nodding or by interjecting an occasional "Um-hm," or "I see."

2. Try to understand the feeling the person is expressing, as well as the factual content. Most of us have difficulty talking clearly about our feelings, so careful attention is required.

3. Restate the person's feelings, briefly but accurately. At this stage, you simply serve as a mirror and encourage the other person to continue talking. Occasionally, make summary responses such as, "You think you're in a dead-end job," or, "You feel the manager is playing favorites"; but in doing so, keep your tone neutral and try not to lead the person to your pet conclusions.

4. Allow time for the discussion to continue without interruption, and try to separate the conversation from more official communication of company plans. That is, do not make the conversation any more "authoritative" than it already is by virtue of your position in the organization.

5. Avoid direct questions and arguments about facts; refrain from saying, "That just is not so," "Hold on a minute; let's look at the facts," or "Prove it." You may want to review evidence later, but a review is irrelevant to how the person feels now.

6. When the other person touches on a point you want to know more about, simply repeat his statement as a question. For instance, if he remarks, "Nobody can break even on his expense account," you can probe by replying, "You say no one breaks even on expenses?" With this encouragement he will probably develop his previous statement.

7. Listen for what is *not* said—evasions of pertinent points or perhaps too-ready agreement with clichés. Such an omission may be a clue to a bothersome fact the person wishes were not true.

[9]R. Hopper, *Human Message Systems* (New York: Harper & Row, 1976).

8. If the other person appears genuinely to want your viewpoint, be honest in your reply. But in the listening stage, try to limit the expression of your views, for these may condition or repress what he says.

9. Do not get emotionally involved yourself. Try simply to understand first, and defer evaluation until later.

A great deal of practice and self-awareness are needed before most managers can follow these guides for listening. Much of the time, a manager must assume a positive, self-confident role, making decisions and giving orders. Clearly, empathetic listening calls for a sharp change in pace. But unless they can develop the self-discipline and humility to listen respectfully, managers are likely to lose touch with the reality of the people who work for them.

When to use empathetic listening.   The process of listening just described will be effective only under several necessary conditions. One requirement is *time*. That kind of conversation takes more than a minute or two. An executive must be willing and able to give her subordinate uninterrupted, private attention for fifteen minutes, half an hour, or perhaps longer—just for listening. With other demands on her time, an executive must value highly the benefits of listening before she will take such a block of time out of her busy day. Moreover, she must be willing to listen when a subordinate wants to talk.

Another requirement is recognizing the unique qualities of each subordinate. A person cannot understand the feelings and problems of another person unless he respects *his individuality*. R. L. Katz has pointed out that each person has his own values, which

> stem from his previous experiences (his expectations of how other people behave), his sentiments (the loyalties, prejudices, likes and dislikes which he has built up over a long period of time), his attitudes about himself (what kind of a person he is—or would like to be), the obligations he feels towards others (what he thinks others expect of him), his ideals (the ways he thinks people should behave and how things ought to be done), his objectives and goals (what he is trying to achieve in a given situation), and perhaps many other things.[10]

For empathetic listening to be successful, we do not have to know everything about an individual, but we must be prepared to respect individual differences in personalities.

The *personal discipline* of the executive is a third requirement. Most people are inclined to respond emotionally to what others say. We normally approve, challenge, get angry, or react in other ways. Yet for em-

[10]R. L. Katz, "Skills of an Effective Administrator," in M. D. Richards, *Readings in Management,* 6th ed. (Cincinnati: South-Western Publishing, 1983).

pathetic listening, a person must remain objective, and objectivity calls for practiced self-discipline.

Finally, a passive, nondirected approach by a manager presumes that his *subordinate has feelings or problems he wants to talk about.* Perhaps the subordinate is disturbed by something that has happened, or he may have a strong response to a proposal his boss or some other executive has made. But when a person is content with—or indifferent to—his work, then "Um-hm" tactics by his boss will result in a fruitless conversation indeed.

Empathetic listening is a valuable process, but it should be used only when a manager can devote the necessary time, remain objective, and respect the individuality of the person he is talking to, and when that person apparently has repressed feelings that the manager wants to understand.

Conveying Meaning to Others

Listening deals with one direction in two-way communication. But a manager also has to *transmit* his ideas. Here again, the aim is to develop a mutual understanding of ideas, problems, and feelings; and again, the difficulty is that each party—the manager and the subordinate—may assume the other assigns the same meaning to a message that he does.

Technical communication model.   A simple model, used in analyzing electronic communications such as television or bouncing messages off satellites, may help identify the reasons why B does not always understand just what A meant to say. Figure 15.3 shows the basic elements.[11]

In electronic communication, the message usually consists of words or physical forms. Encoding and decoding involve converting the message to and from electric impulses, and major difficulties of distortion and noise may arise in the channel. In face-to-face communication, there are fewer channel difficulties, but in encoding and decoding we run into many subtle psychological problems.

Many of the concepts used to analyze listening apply equally well to the job of imparting ideas. The meaning of words, for instance, enters directly into encoding and decoding, and the effect of emotions on what we

[11]K. H. Roberts, *Communicating in Organizations* (Chicago: Science Research Associates, 1984), Chaps. 4 and 5.

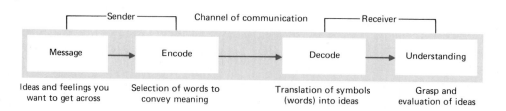

Figure 15.3 A
simple technical
communication model.

attend to can garble the meaning of a message as it flows in either direction. The following suggestions for improving the transmission of ideas from supervisor to subordinate review insights about the kind of behavior that should permeate a leadership relationship.

The world of the receiver.   When an executive has a message he wants to get across to a subordinate, he should take time to reflect on the attitudes and interests of that person. The subordinate will probably be preoccupied with other matters that seem important to him, and he will be inclined to pay attention primarily to those ideas that are related to his personal needs. Moreover, his emotional state will affect his receptiveness to new messages.

Consequently, if a manager wants to get across an important idea, a new meaning—not just routine information—he must be sensitive to the world of the person who will receive the message. How that person perceives it will depend as much on what is already in him as on the content of the message. If the manager has a close relationship with him, based on previous empathetic listening, he will know something of his world and how he is likely to interpret the new message. Of one point the manager can be sure: "Logical" arguments will not go far if the message requires the subordinate to alter his values. Therefore, as a sound starting point, the manager should consider the personality of the person to whom he wishes to convey a meaningful message. In addition, he should ask himself: How will the idea look to him? Can anything be done to prepare him for the point to be transmitted?

Meaningful language.   As we have seen, words—even ordinary terms like "territory"—may mean different things to the sender and the receiver of a message. To get meaning across, a communicator must try to use words in the sense that the receiver will take them. Long and technical words, although perhaps more precise, often have to be discarded in favor of short terms that are easily grasped. Maybe the other person *should* be smart enough to understand our language, but our aim is to reach a mutual understanding—not to test his literacy.

Some repetition helps in most learning—assuming that the learner is trying to understand. So a message may be repeated, preferably in different words or with new examples. It is even more effective to draw attention to an idea by relating it to a current experience of the subordinate; he then sees the meaning of the words in terms of his personal behavior.

Free, face-to-face interchange.   It takes a while for a person to assimilate an important idea, to get used to it. One has to roll it around in one's mind and savor its implications. When trying to communicate a significant message to subordinates, managers should provide them the time for such assimilation. One way to do so is simply to exchange thoughts with them about the message, to talk it over. The subordinate may think out loud, "'Wow, that new product would louse up our production schedule

. . . . We could promote a couple of those young engineers who are getting restive . . . . How would the shipping department handle it? . . .," and so forth. Executives may also express their thoughts—both pro and con—about the proposition. This interchange is highly informal, and neither person states firm conclusions.

During such a give-and-take discussion, many doubts and misunderstandings come into the open. If the executive is skillful at listening, she can probe long enough to uncover misunderstandings and then restate her meaning or intention. Frequently the executive herself has not thought through all aspects of an idea, and a discussion of this sort may result in clarification—and perhaps modification—in her own mind.

Note that during this assimilation stage, authority is set aside while both people seek a mutual understanding. Mutual respect and trust are necessary, because each person is exposing tentative, speculative, unconsidered reactions. If the conversation has rambled, the executive may well summarize the message as it has been redefined at the end, but the free, face-to-face interchange should have clarified the meaning substantially.

Communicating through behavior.   One of the best ways executives can give meaning to a message is to behave as they ask others to.[12] The new president of a sugar refinery wanted to break a tradition that pay increases and promotions for executives depended primarily on long, loyal service. He stated on several occasions that raises would be awarded only on the basis of demonstrated improvement in performance. Most executives let the statement slip by as just another part of a pep talk. But at the end of the year, a good many executives (including the president's son) did not get raises even though they had worked hard; a few people who could show significant improvement in results received good bonuses. The grapevine spread the word, and at this point the president's message took on meaning.

In contrast, the vice-president in charge of sales of another company became worried about low gross-profit volumes and told each of her district managers not to grant special discounts to large—or tough—customers. Within a few weeks, however, the vice-president herself made several concessions to two customers she handled personally. This action changed the meaning of her "no special discount" statement to "no special discounts except by the vice-president." It created resentment on the part of the district managers because they felt the vice-president was inconsistent in what she said and did.

Subordinates sense quickly the presence, or lack, of consistency in their boss's words, spirit, and action. In fact, subtle feelings and values may be conveyed better by example than by words, although there is no reason for not using both. The poet Emerson put it this way: "What you are [do] thunders so loud I cannot hear what you say."

---

[12]O. W. Baskin and C. E. Aronoff, *Interpersonal Communications in Organizations* (Santa Monica, Calif.: Goodyear, 1980).

These general guides—recognizing the interests and attitudes of the person receiving a message, expressing the message in terms that are meaningful to him, have a face-to-face discussion of the idea, and accompanying the words with consistent action—aid the manager in conveying meaning to subordinates. But how can he be sure they actually receive a message as he intends it? It has already been noted that merely asking listeners whether they understand provides scant assurance.

To confirm that a communication has resulted in mutual understanding, a manager needs to keep alert to any feedback that is available. The simplest check is to observe whether the subordinate behaves in accordance with the message. When direct observation is not practical, as is often true for executives, they can watch various reports and results for cues. And for more intangible or subtle messages, the listening process described earlier may be the most reliable feedback. If a manager has developed a close leadership relationship with a subordinate, he should have enough frank interchanges of ideas and feelings to provide indications of how well he has communicated.

CONCLUSION

The complexities of human relationships within organizations require that the successful manager understand the informal side of the organization as well as the formal structure. This focus allows a manager to understand how informal traditions and interactions influence organizational performance. A key to dealing with gaps between formal desires and informal realities is better communication, which can allow a manager to steer through difficult obstacles. This is a subtle process, however, and empathy—the ability to see things from another's point of view—is critical. The effective manager must understand potential barriers to effective communication and must learn how to overcome them through better listening and feedback.

Impact on Productivity

Full understanding of subordinates and informal organization places a manager in a better position to build enthusiastic cooperation. Such cooperation, in turn, is a prime factor in internal efficiency and effectiveness. Productivity improves.

This source of productivity illustrates again that most improvement will come, not from some grand invention, but from persistent effort. Such an accumulation of numerous small gains arises from an attitude about workers and work and from a habit of considering the psychological and social setting. However, most managers can upgrade those attitudes and habits by at least occasionally assessing their customary behavior. Maintaining a flow of incremental gains warrants systematic attention.

FOR FURTHER DISCUSSION

1. Cheaters on examinations are often protected by fellow students even though the students who do not report the violators may suffer in their comparative rankings. How do you explain this sort of behavior? In what respects is informal group behavior in business organizations similar? In what ways is it dissimilar?

2. Do you think that cultural differences between Japan and the United States may explain why quality circles are more common in Japan and contribute more to their company (and national) productivity than is typical in the United States? Does this suggest that informal organization is not very strong in the United States?

3. In what ways is the significant increase in the number of women moving into managerial ranks likely to affect the informal organization?

4. In what ways should decisions on delegation (discussed in Chapter 9) be based on knowledge of the existing informal organization?

5. Try the following as an experiment in empathetic listening. Have one participant play the role of a top-notch young executive who has just informed his (or her) boss about plans to take another position. Have a second participant play the role of the boss. The young executive, while being honest with the boss, should be somewhat reticent about revealing the real reasons for quitting. With the person who is to take the role of the boss out of the room, agree on the real reasons that the young executive is quitting; for example, you might select any of the following: fear that nepotism will block advancement; a feeling that the company president is stubborn and not too bright; desire to move away from the mother-in-law, who is a close friend of the boss' wife; or belief, based on grapevine information from a source that cannot be revealed, that the company will be sold to a much larger firm. Then, role-play a talk between the boss and the subordinate. See if the boss can uncover the subordinate's reasons for leaving by using the guides for empathetic listening. Following the role-play, write down illustrations of (a) where the superior succeeded in employing these guides, (b) where he failed, and (c) how a different approach might have been more successful.

6. "I have just one question for those who advocate empathy and understanding of subordinates' problems. To whom do I go for treatment when I get through? Am I supposed to sit and listen to a lot of silly mistakes, alibis, and complaints, and just say, 'Uh-huh—you're late because you resent your mother's domination'? It seems a lot better for their performance and my psychological well-being that, when there is something wrong and I know what to do about it, I come right out and speak my piece." Comment on this statement.

7. What is meant by the term *body language*? Give examples of, or demonstrate, how it may be a part of interpersonal communication in an organization.

8. Use a common slang expression in a sentence. Then show how the communication model in Figure 15.3 can be applied to analyze what meaning you probably sent to a specific listener.

9. What factors should a manager consider in deciding when to follow up an oral communication with a written summary?

FOR FURTHER READING

Baskin, O. and C. Aronoff, *Interpersonal Communication in Organizations*. Santa Monica, Calif.: Goodyear, 1980. Explores basic communication relationships in organizations and their impact on organizational efficiency.

Davis, K., ed., *Organizational Behavior: Readings and Exercises*, 6th ed. New York: McGraw-Hill, 1981. Reviews studies of communications barriers, especially at the first level of supervision.

Gryna, F. M., *Quality Circles: A Team Approach to Problem Solving*. New York: AMACOM, 1981. A thorough introduction to the process of controlling quality through teamwork in the workplace.

Gyllenhammer, P., *People at Work*. Reading, Mass.: Addison-Wesley, 1977. A detailed look at Volvo's innovations in work redesign and the resulting changes in the social system of a plant.

Johnson, B. M., *Communication: The Process of Organizing*. Boston: American Press, 1981. Distinctive treatment of communication from organizational perspective.

Roberts, K. H., *Communicating in Organizations*. Chicago: Science Research Associates, 1984. Clear, short discussion of psychological aspects of interpersonal communication and of communication networks in organizations.

Zander, A., *The Purpose of Groups and Organizations*. San Francisco: Jossey-Bass, 1985, Chap. 9. Insightful discussion of activities that make groups more or less effective in attaining their objectives.

MANAGEMENT IN ACTION CASE 15
A High-Tech Communicator

Lots of high-tech companies are fond of offering unusual perquisites believed to nurture creativity, loyalty, and teamwork among employees. Few firms treat the task so seriously—or lightly, depending on your point of view—as Odetics Inc., an Anaheim, California-based maker of robots and digital, audio, and video recorders.

The small company, appropriately headquartered across the street from Disneyland, has three official committees—two for management and one for fun. A book called "The 100 Best Companies to Work for in America" called Odetics one of seven firms that throw the best employee parties. Odetics' 13-point philosophical manifesto says, "At Odetics, we work hard but we also play hard."

They sure do. In November 1984, the company held a morning sock hop followed by a cheeseburger-and-milk-shake lunch and contests in bubble-gum blowing and hula-hoop dancing. A belly dancer gave an impromptu performance one Good Friday, prompting a religious controversy. One Halloween, when all Odetics workers were encouraged to work in costume, Chairman and Chief Executive Joe Slutsky showed up as a fly. Employees also kept a six-foot alligator named Gordo, which escaped one evening and was found under a secretary's desk.

The architect of this madness is Slutsky, a white-haired, white-bearded man who, if you haven't guessed already, disdains conventional management methods. When the company pool opened, Slutsky arrived in a nightshirt, fins, goggles, snorkel, and mask, and was tossed in the drink by a subordinate. "If you don't have fun," he said, "then I think it's going to detract from the business."

But is having fun always good business? Slutsky said it encourages development of innovative, profitable products. "More than anything, we want a creative, innovative atmosphere in which people like to come to work."

Odetics had some trouble in 1985, reporting a loss of $510,000 in the quarter ended June 30. However, officials said the friendly ambience helped employees weather an uncharacteristically serious period during which Slutsky discontinued some bonuses, delayed pay raises, and required some workers to put in extra hours. The company made a small profit the next quarter.

The bottom line aside, Odetics workers enjoy their jobs. "I have never seen a place like this in my life, and I've had eighteen jobs," manufacturing engineer Paul Chvostal said. He should talk. He once put on a bunny suit and hopped around the company handing out eggs. And it wasn't even Easter.

Question

Would you expect the communication between managers and their subordinates at Odetics to be completely frank and open? Would you like to work at Odetics?

For more information, see *The Wall Street Journal,* 4 December 1985.

APPLICATION CASES

For practice in applying concepts covered in this chapter to managerial situations, see the following managerial decision cases. The case questions particularly relevant to this chapter are listed by number after each case name.

Grant Chemical Corporation (p. 59) 16
Heartland Union Bank (HUB) (p. 183) 14
Consolidated Instruments (p. 189) 16
Delphi Insurance (p. 316) 16
Peter Jeffries (p. 428) 12, 13

16

Managing Conflict and Politics Within Organizations

LEARNING OBJECTIVES

After completing this chapter, you should be able to

1. Identify the major sources of intraorganizational conflict.
2. Describe ways of organizing to deal with conflict.
3. Understand why organizations create desired conflict.
4. Explain how individuals obtain power within organizations.
5. Describe the relationship of power to internal politics.
6. Explain the benefits and drawbacks of political behavior within organizations.
7. Understand how a manager can effectively channel political behavior.

MANAGERS AND CONFLICT

Conflict is an inevitable part of organizational life. As people assume managerial roles within organizations, especially at the executive level, they must be willing to risk being unloved to operate with some level of success.

Take the contrast cited by presidential historian James MacGregor Burns between former presidents Lyndon Baines Johnson and Harry S Truman.[1] Johnson wanted every American to love him; but Truman opined, "If you can't stand the heat, get out of the kitchen." Truman understood that national leaders—like organizational leaders—must settle for less than universal affection and must deal with conflict to succeed.

Conflict surrounds managers every day—in disagreements with colleagues, superiors, and subordinates over how to approach a problem, how to forecast the pros and cons of a prospective business venture, whom to place in charge of a project, where to make a large capital investment. The outcome in such relationships often leads to one person "winning" at the expense of another's loss—or so it seems—thereby creating substantial conflict within an organization.

Sources of Conflict in Organizations

Since conflict and its resolution have a sharp impact on the effectiveness of any organization, managers should be skilled at analyzing its sources. Research data indicate at least four major sources of intraorganization conflict.

Competing for scarce resources. Organizations offer their members the opportunity to accomplish the most they can with a limited bundle of resources.[2] Hence, committed members want the resources necessary to achieve their goals. The marketing department wants promotional, adver-

[1] J. M. Burns, *The Power to Lead* (New York: Simon & Schuster, 1984), and *Leadership* (New York: Harper & Row, 1970).

[2] J. Galbraith, *Designing Complex Organizations* (Reading, Mass.: Addison-Wesley, 1973).

Figure 16.1 Historical conflict over scarce resources has sometimes been redirected toward constructive ends. Although the weapons differ, similar conflict in organizations may likewise be destructive or constructive.

tising, and entertainment funds; the production executives want the latest version of a particular piece of equipment; the systems department wants better computers; and the treasurer's office would rather save as much money as possible to enhance the look of earnings and the funds available for dividends. Since the total of all those requests for money inevitably exceeds the amount available, a scramble for that money results.

Capital is not the only scarce resource. Increasingly, in fact, competition for highly skilled people has surpassed the battle over money in many industries.[3] The problem has become especially acute in businesses experiencing rapid change; these companies find only a limited number of managers inside the organization able to adapt to those conditions quickly. One executive tells the story of a manager whose name showed up on lists of top candidates for vacated jobs no less than 115 times in less than six months, all of which underscores the competition for good people during critical times.

Built-in conflicts.   Another form of organizational conflict is quite deliberately anticipated. This results from the way that jobs are linked together. Many staff jobs have this characteristic, as do positions in the research and new-product engineering areas from time to time. An industrial engineer, for example, may be assigned to find more economical methods of making tape cassettes. But if he is successful, the new approach will complicate life for the manager supervising cassette production; quality will be hard to maintain, and schedules—even delivery schedules—may have to be revised as a result. While such conflict is bad enough, it can be aggravated when a staff person is cocky or young and the line manager is experienced, older, and has less formal education. This opens the door to another potential source of conflict.

Divergent personal values and aims.   The personal values of people attracted to various kinds of jobs can also influence how their departments interact and can create job conflict.[4]

Research people, for instance, usually identify more closely with scientific-researcher types throughout their area of expertise rather than with many other members of the organization. Researchers are usually intrigued with the unknown, place a high value on scientific "truth," are prepared to wait months or years for the right answer, and expect others to be as patient as they are. In contrast, most production workers prefer to deal with what's in front of them, have a practical and intuitive sense of what is right, want prompt and positive action, and are more comfortable with authoritarian relationships. And values will be different again for accountants, marketing managers, and chief executives.

[3]C. Fombrun, N. M. Tichy, and M. A. Devanna, *Strategic Human Resource Management* (New York: John Wiley, 1984).

[4]P. R. Lawrence and J. W. Lorsch, *Organization and Environment: Managing Differentiation and Integration* (Boston: Harvard Business School, 1967).

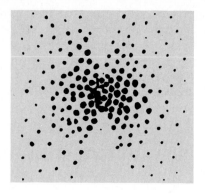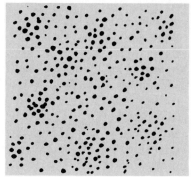

Figure 16.2 Polarization and depolarization of conflict. At left, lines of conflict are clearly defined, the clash is sharp, and all elements rally on either side of the issue. At right, vague clusters hint at potential issues, but there is some mingling of feelings; and the cluster that is forming in the center at the bottom suggests a genuine coalition.

A critical issue for managers is how much to encourage people with similar values to form close-knit groups that are distinct from other close-knit groups. The danger, as suggested in Figure 16.2, is that such groups will fight rather than cooperate with each other.

Ambiguous organization. Still another source of conflict can come from hazy organizational design, which makes it unclear who will do what and under what circumstances. In one company, for instance, the president thought the accountant's job was to establish accurate accounting records, to compare actual expenses with the budget, and to point out deviations. The controller himself thought he should press executives to avoid budget overruns and report only unresolved deviations to the president. And still a third person—a newly appointed computer-systems executive—believed that the controller's job was only to count, maintain records, and make information available to him and fellow executives on request. The ill will that resulted from such role ambiguity lasted much longer than the few months it would have taken to reach an agreement on who would do what.

Jurisdictional squabbles can arise anywhere, from the senior level down to the operating level. Job scope is not a trifling manner, as nationwide strikes over jurisdictional issues demonstrate. Many firms prepare written job descriptions only every few years, and even then such descriptions can never be complete and are soon outdated. And the more dynamic the company, the more likely it is that conflicts will result from ambiguous organization.

Organizing to Harness Conflict

Students of management have long assumed that conflict within organizations should be avoided and have concentrated on how it could be minimized. More recently, though, the focus has shifted to the channeling and harnessing of constructive conflict.[5] There are several ways that a manager can deal positively with such conflicts.

[5]K. Thomas, "Conflict and Conflict Management," in M. D. Dunnette, ed., *Handbook of Industrial and Organizational Psychology,* rev. ed. (New York: John Wiley, 1984).

Create—but separate—competitors.   To get adequate, expert, independent attention to a special aspect of an organization, it may be necessary to establish a separate staff unit. In the 1970s and 1980s, for example, many corporations established special units to counsel, train, and promote minority workers. Separate control units are common, especially when independent action is required for such tasks as auditing, cost control, and quality control. Such independence and divergence of objectives may promote conflict, but the net result is worth it.

In more routine work situations, competition can be introduced by setting up a series of similar operations and making regular comparisons of their results. Retail sales, banks, television, computer maintenance, and insurance sales are only a few of the areas where this concept can be applied. And when such units operate at separate locations, conflict between them largely centers on status and allocation of resources—and tends to be minimized. Hence, conflict can be useful and nondivisive when properly directed.

Establish an umpiring system.   Whenever conflict units are deliberately set up, a mechanism for guiding the conflict becomes necessary, as Figure 16.3 shows.[6]

An organization's formal strategy and other plans set the framework within which such guidance can take place. To prevent such conflicts from escalating, someone is needed to act as an umpire so that decisions can be made promptly and the game can go on. Not everyone may like the decision, but everyone usually knows that there will be another day and will return to work once a decision has been made. And because the criteria for judging are known, parties in conflict can often anticipate the result without even going to the so-called umpire for a decision.

Design integrated units.   When conflict resolution calls for frequent or varied adjustments in the activities of several people or units, an umpiring system is too slow and unwieldy. Under those conditions, it is usually better to group interrelated activities. Examples include jet crews and microsurgery teams, both of which contain varieties of specialists working together toward a common goal. Conflicting pressures are still present, to be sure, because specialists, with their idiosyncrasies and different values, are still specialists. But the compound groups are small enough that the need for coordination is evident and pressure mounts for self-management through personal, face-to-face communication.

Such integrated units can be quite helpful in avoiding destructive conflict. The arrangement is not always practical, however; the cost of pulling a functional unit away from its major department may be high, and intense disturbance may result. Technology may be another thing that prevents the separation, or the departments may lack employees with the competence to exercise the decentralized authority needed in an integrated team. Hence, integrated units can be helpful, but they are not a panacea.

[6]B. M. Bass, *Stodgill's Handbook of Leadership,* rev. ed. (New York: Free Press, 1981).

UPI

Figure 16.3   When conflict is deliberately built into an organization, safeguards are needed to prevent the escalation of conflict. One useful device is an "umpire" to "call the plays" promptly.

Separate the contestants.   In those circumstances in which the integrated unit seems inappropriate, the opposite design may be in order—separating the people involved. If conflicting parties cannot work together in harmony, then organizational separation plus a liaison can be a useful alternative.

A classic example involves cooks—the skilled elite in a restaurant.[7] They strongly dislike pressure from waitresses or runners, who have less status. Yet waitresses, under pressure from customers, are persistent in their requests. All too often, conflict over priorities and quality escalates into personal feuds, with disastrous results for customers. A mechanical system—a computer into which orders are punched—can remove the cooks from personal interactions with the waitresses. And the cooks feel their status is not jeopardized by receiving a series of written requests. The waitresses wait outside the kitchen until their numbers are called or flashed on a screen. The opportunity for conflict is thus reduced. This kind of procedure can be used in many types of work, from plastics, to international trade, to the news media.

These organizational arrangements for lowering the disruptive effects of conflict—creating conflict where it can be beneficial, establishing umpires, designing integrated units, and separating the contestants—can harness conflict. The conflict is not eliminated; rather, it is constrained and

[7]W. F. Whyte, *Men at Work* (Homewood, Ill.: Richard D. Irwin, 1961), Chap. 8.

channeled so that the natural desire to do one's job well contributes to the company goals.

While such arrangements are indeed helpful, opportunities for conflict persist in many areas within an organization. Differences in personal goals and competition for scarce resources inevitably create tension.

The way any organization responds to such tensions depends upon *who* has effective power, and upon informal company politics.

POWER AND POLITICS

Power is intertwined with conflict. Sometimes a powerful person steps in and settles the dispute by decree. Few people possess enough power to really settle all conflict, however, and almost no one likes to be overruled by another person with a big club.

A second way, then, that power enters into a conflict situation is through company politics, as indicated by Figure 16.4. People with power exchange favors and, in the process, develop "friends." Then when a conflict arises, or just threatens, they call on their friends to support their cause. In this cheery view of life, organizations make choices by continuously exchanging favors and by friends helping friends!

Here again, able managers need to analyze what is taking place in their particular organization. They need to understand (1) how people become powerful, and (2) how such power can be used in the game of company politics.

Roots of Power

Research on the subject of power has been actively pursued for the last half-century,[8] but some of the most revealing information about how organization members come to receive power is found in a classic three-decade-old study[9] which lists five bases of power:

[8] J. P. Kotter, *Power and Influence: Beyond Formal Authority* (New York: The Free Press, 1985).

[9] J. R. P. French and B. Raven, "The Bases of Social Power," in D. Cartwright, ed., *Studies in Social Power* (Ann Arbor: Institute for Social Research, University of Michigan, 1959).

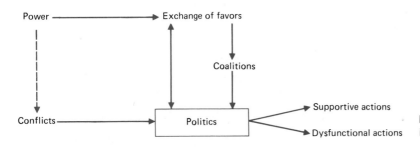

Figure 16.4 Elements in intraorganizational political behavior.

□ REWARD POWER—The ability to have power over others because you can control the rewards they receive.

□ COERCIVE POWER—The ability to manipulate the behavior of others who fear they will be punished if they do not conform to attempts to influence.

□ LEGITIMATE POWER—The ability to control others' behavior because they perceive you to have the legitimate or positional standing to tell them what to do.

□ REFERENT POWER—The potential to have power over others because they identify with or admire you, and strive to emulate you; they thus tend to do what you suggest because of that strong internalization.

□ EXPERT POWER—Because of specialized knowledge—perceived or actual—you can exert power over others because they regard you as specially skilled in a critical subject area.

Establishing Power Cautiously

The foregoing list deals with the roots of power—why one person is inclined to follow the wishes of another person. Note that the powerful person is not necessarily a direct line supervisor. In addition, some of these roots, such as expert knowledge and referent power, are attached to specific individuals;[10] senior managers cannot move power of this sort around the organization as they wish.

Nevertheless, senior managers can influence who does, or does not, have power through the following five sorts of assignments:

1. Formal appointment to a line position that by tradition and by control of human and financial resources gives the incumbent authority to make key decisions.
2. The opportunity to review and veto plans.
3. Direct supervision of the resources necessary to carry out essential steps in the plan.
4. Access to and control over the flow of information—especially computer data—that is needed to identify or monitor key issues.
5. Quick, direct access to people with even more power, plus the ability to influence them.

Power of Coalitions

An individual often lacks sufficient power to achieve a goal by acting alone. A common alternative is to form a *coalition*—a temporary partnership with other people to support a particular action. Members of a coalition do not give up their independence, and they may continue to differ

---

[10]Bennis, Warren and Nanus, Burt, *Leaders* (New York: Harper & Row, 1985).

sharply on some issues, but they do agree on joint action to promote a common cause.

For several years the marketing manager of a furniture company had recommended adding upholstered chairs and sofas, but other executives had a coalition that was preoccupied with dining and bedroom furniture. When sales dropped, however, and upholstered products offered a chance to keep the plant busy, a new and more powerful coalition pushed through a decision to add the new line.

Coalitions are easier to form in opposition to a proposed change, as was true for a long time in the furniture company just cited. Agreeing on a positive action is more difficult. Among people with diverse goals, we are more likely to agree on what we don't like.

Coalitions in most companies are quite informal and spontaneous, although on major issues the coalition leaders may systematically seek support and may modify the proposed plan to obtain crucial backing. It is the combination of power that wins the day. Company politics strongly influences the way power may be combined.

POLITICAL BEHAVIOR IN ORGANIZATIONS

For some, *politics* is a dirty word. E. E. Jennings, for instance, implies that company politics are "devious, indirect, and under-handed."[11] In contrast, for a political scientist, political behavior is a normal, essential element in "winning the consent of the governed."

We regard politics as necessary and unavoidable, and consequently we must deal with it. From the viewpoint of effective management, political action can have both good and bad effects, so this behavior should be guided into those areas where it is a constructive influence.

The Nature of Company Politics

Politics begins with the exchange of favors. You might car pool with a colleague, share work when he's busy and you aren't, or even suggest how he could dress to conform to what is expected of people at your level within the corporation. In turn, your colleague does things for you, too, because an implied obligation arises, as Figure 16.5 suggests. So, for instance, if the accounting supervisor has bent the rules a little so that you could buy some small items without going through the purchase-order procedure, he may ask you to submit next year's budget proposal a week early as a personal favor to him, so that he can begin evaluating it without waiting until the last minute.

Such relationships are especially important in large, bureaucratic or-

---

[11]Jennings, E.E., *The Mobile Manager* (Ann Arbor: University of Michigan Press, 1967).

Figure 16.5 The exchange of favors in business is usually unspecified. Here, setting budgets and handling rush orders are presumably handled in a purely objective fashion. But if a production manager receives kindly treatment in his budget request, he is likely to ensure that the rush order of interest to the budget officer gets prompt attention; or perhaps the sequence is reversed. The favors may consist of prompt attention and sympathetic attitudes.

ganizations where excessive policies and procedures can hamstring anyone trying to accomplish something quickly. If the sales representative can call on the service manager, for whom she has done favors in the past, she may be able to get a same-day service call made that would otherwise take three or four days—which makes her customer that much more satisfied. Clearly, in such cases, things can get done faster and better with friends at key points at which help is needed. There is nothing inherently sinister about such behavior, contrary to what some critics of politics imply. Much voluntary coordination and efficiency improvement result from these relationships, and it is only when they are taken to excess—so that you can't get a service call at all without knowing somebody, for example—that such relationships can lead to complications.

Risks Arising from Internal Politics

Obviously, people within organizations can extend their scope and influence through political behavior. But unless such efforts are carefully channeled, intraorganizational politics can undermine the effectiveness of an enterprise.

Four influences are worthy of specific attention.

1. Pursuit of the personal goals of politicians (either self-selected causes or personal drives for power or promotion) usually detracts from the central strategy of the organization. And if political action causes a diversion of resources or blocks efforts toward target results, effectiveness suffers.

2. If internal politics escalates into major struggles for control, a substantial amount of attention and energy can become misdirected.

3. The organization's incentive mechanisms aimed at implementing the strategy may be undermined by the rewards and punishments or personnel moves made by those with political power. The more imprecise the measurement-and-reward system, the more vulnerable it will be to counterproductive internal political pressure.

4. Politics often focus on short-run trade-offs, which means important long-term issues can be sacrificed because the measurements and payoffs from them will not occur until well into the future.

To increase congruence of political action
and enterprise goals:

Sharpen enterprise objectives

Tie resource allocation and rewards to objectives

Punish deviant power seekers

Isolate resource acquisition from internal operations

Figure 16.6 Ways to harmonize political and company goals.

Channeling Political Behavior

The preceding analysis indicates that, although some features of political behavior can be beneficial, there is serious danger that it will dissipate the concerted effort that the organization is intended to deliver. Needed, then, are ways that managers can harness and direct the energies of people who have a bent for politics, as Figure 16.6 indicates. The following measures will move managers a long way toward this end.

Sharpen the strategy.   When political pressures pull away from the central strategy of an organization, trouble is the result. To help avoid such negative outcomes, the organization should sharpen its strategy, clarifying and agreeing upon desired results. Once that is done, numerous activities—including the political maneuvering—can be evaluated in terms of their contribution toward achieving strategic goals.[12]

While sharpening strategy is easier said than done—because of multiple and sometimes competing desires, shifts with the times, and conflicting subobjectives—mechanisms do exist for identifying what strategy is most important at a given time. This must be articulated if undesirable political activity is to be flagged and checked. And with such thrusts and targets known, political efforts may work more in the direction of strategic achievement.

Tie resources and rewards to strategy.   Since the capacity to give or withhold resources and rewards is a foundation of political power, management must structure the allocation of resources and rewards so that the best payoffs clearly go to people who are actively contributing to the achievement of official goals—not to mere political allies.

In accomplishing this, these procedures and criteria must be carefully followed:

1. For standard, repetitive situations, the steps to be taken to obtain resources and rewards, and the criteria used in allocating them, should be known in advance. Individual discretion—save for assess-

---

[12]Kotter, J.P., *Power and Influence: Beyond Formal Authority* (New York: Free Press, 1985).

ing the facts in each case—is reduced to a minimum. And there is relatively little occasion for intramural politics.

2. While such approaches are inappropriate for promotions, research, assignment to high-potential project teams, and the like, decisions on such matters can be made jointly and openly among executives, their staffs, and the affected staffs. Such open consultation provides opportunities to check political maneuvering and to test the compatibility of a proposed action and a strategic goal.

3. Because the power to influence rewards is so strong, procedures and jobs that give people power to interrupt communications and work flows should be avoided whenever possible, even at some extra expense, thereby reducing a potential political base. If such positions are unavoidable, however, such jobs should be filled by individuals loyal to the overall company strategy.

The underlying goal of such an approach is to create a situation in which virtue is rewarded and crime does not pay.

Punish deviant power seekers.   When that isn't enough, another way to avoid undesirable political activity is to create a setting in which the desired results are known, and if people still prefer to promote their own private goals, then they should be punished. Such negative behavior should be promptly and openly reprimanded and, if continued, dealt with even more severely.

Every organization develops a set of traditions, values, and standards that subtly shape behavior. Tolerance or intolerance of independent power bases is part of those customs. If an organization wants to avoid becoming infested with petty power players, the practice must be explicitly frowned upon. If the right message is given, most managers will usually get it. And if one doesn't, his dismissal is certain to reinforce the message in the minds of all those who remain.

Isolate resource acquisition from internal operations.   Every company must attract a variety of resource suppliers—people with various skills, capital, material, government support, customers, and the like. Some bargaining over the terms of cooperation will inevitably take place.

If this external bargaining with resource suppliers gets mixed up with internal decision making, the likelihood of deviant internal politics jumps sharply. For instance, if a banker is given a veto on expenditures or a union leader controls work assignments, they may become members of internal coalitions. The outsider has a narrow, parochial interest—not the company interest. To allow such a person to mix into internal politics adds a bias to an already delicate situation.

These four proposals for channeling company politics deal with actions that management can take. They neither eliminate nor deny the existence of political maneuvering. Rather, they help to tie such give and take to the company mission.

Every vigorous organization has its unique mixture of conflicts, power, and politics. Wise managers should seek to understand how these forces interact in their own companies. Clear perception is a necessary first step in dealing with these facts of life.

If given a loose rein, conflicts-power politics can be disruptive. It can absorb human energy that is badly needed for the pursuit of the company mission, and can block innovative steps.

Fortunately, managers can, to a large extent, lower the disruption and harness the emotional forces stirred by conflict or politics. Suggestions for confining conflict, creating power cautiously, and channeling company politics have been made throughout this chapter. The effective use of these suggestions calls for leadership skill rather than mathematical calculations.

Impact on Productivity

Conflicts and company politics occasionally become so rampant that the internal feuding has a devastating effect on productivity. Attention is diverted from providing superior service and seizing new opportunities to merely protecting one's turf. In contrast, when mutual help is focused on common objectives, the give-and-take can be an additional source of enthusiasm.

For most companies most of the time, company politics has a mixed impact, diverting some effort while also generating some emotional drive. However, a balance on the constructive side may give particular companies a clear advantage over their competitors. Consequently, managers dare not disregard political currents within their organizations.

Power, coalitions, and politics are normal, unavoidable aspects of organized human activities. Natural divergence of personal values always generates some tugs and pulls, and these conflicts can become emotional when people are pursuing a cherished "cause." Often the resulting behavior is not fully rational. In such circumstances, the leader must somehow harness the social forces if full productivity is to be achieved.

FOR FURTHER DISCUSSION

1. In government political parties, the various local "leaders" (precinct captains, for example) build strength for their party by "taking care of"—doing favors for—their constituents. On election day, these constituents are then expected to vote the party ticket. (a) Compare this process with the description of internal company politics presented in this chapter. (b) How do company strategy and policy fit into this picture? (c) How does an individual with "personal principles" fit into this scheme?

2. If you wish to build some political power in a company for which you work, what kind of positions would you seek and what else would you do to develop political clout?

3. How does a coalition differ from a close-knit group that contributes greatly to an organization's objectives? Are coalitions usually good or bad in terms of their impact on an organization's effectiveness?

4. "I not only believe conflict, when it arises, to be potentially valuable, but in many situations I will seek to create conflict between evenly matched individuals or departments. There's nothing like a little competition to help find the fittest." What is your opinion of this statement by an advocate of "managerial Darwinism"?

5. "The way to avoid politics is to confine behavior to only those individuals who are committed to company objectives." Do you agree?

6. Do you think that the new generation of smart, sophisticated, educated employees (like yourself) will act more rationally and less politically in their job assignments than the older generation? Why?

7. "Since managers don't have to get elected, they don't have to keep trying to please everybody. They should be more concerned with what is *best*. I don't want politics in my bank." Comment on this statement from the president of a large bank.

8. In general, do you feel that effective use of organization politics is more important at high management levels or among first-line supervisors?

FOR FURTHER READING

Bacharach, S. B. and E. J. Lawler, *Power and Politics in Organizations: The Social Psychology of Conflict, Coalitions, and Bargaining*. San Francisco: Jossey-Bass, 1980. Thorough analysis of conflict and politics from a psychosociological viewpoint.

Bennis, W. and B. Nanus, *Leaders*. New York: Harper & Row, 1985. Profiles and descriptions of leadership as shown by dozens of the most important leaders in the world, from both public and private sectors.

Culbert, S. A. and J. J. McDonough, *Radical Management: Power Politics and the Pursuit of Trust*. New York: Free Press, 1985. Urges that managers take a positive approach to organizational politics and adapt the underlying forces to create a feeling of trust.

Hayes, J., "The Politically Competent Manager," *Journal of General Management,* Autumn 1984. Describes how effective managers use power constructively to achieve company goals.

Kotter, J. P., *Power and Influence: Beyond Formal Authority*. New York: Free Press, 1985. An analysis of how people jockey for power in the informal systems within organizations.

MacMillan, I. C. and W. D. Guth, "Strategy Implementation and Middle Management Coalitions," in *Advances in Strategic Management,* Vol. 3. Greenwich, Conn: JAI Press, 1985. First-rate discussion of internal politics.

Miles, R. H. *Macro Organizational Behavior*. Santa Monica, Calif.: Goodyear, 1980, Chap. 5. Good summary of sources of conflict and ways of managing conflict.

Mintzberg, H., *Power In and Around Organizations*. Englewood Cliffs, N.J.: Prentice-Hall, 1983. Explores a broad spectrum of power related to organizations, including internal and external coalitions.

Yates, D., *The Politics of Management*. San Francisco: Jossey-Bass, 1985. Stimulating analysis of the sources of political conflict and what managers can do to avoid and correct problems.

MANAGEMENT IN ACTION CASE 16
Internal Politics at ABC

While executives may share a mission or an idea, maybe even agree on the strategies of how to accomplish it, from time to time other dynamics come into play. Namely, the rivalry that exists among individuals competing for the same resources, attention, time—or even competing for the same job.

Such was the case in 1980 at the ABC television network. On Thursday, 21 August 1980, ABC's "World News Tonight" ran an over-four-minute segment detailing alleged criminal fraud, conspiracy, and conflict of interest by a number of ABC executives.

The so-called "Charlie's Angels" scandal, involving one of the most popular television shows of the time, was uncovered by *The New York Times*. But ABC News subsequently investigated it in more depth and turned up even more damaging information.

The allegations were that ABC executives were involved in a scheme to defraud "profit participants" in "Charlie's Angels" of close to $1 million, diverting a large part of those funds to a production company by way of "creative accounting," and that an ABC lawyer in California was fired when she tried to bring the scandal to the attention of ABC executives, and—most political—that a very close friend of the owners of the production company was ABC President Elton Rule.

The question becomes: What are the internal political ramifications of such a situation?

The answer came a few months later, in December 1980, when *Fortune* added a political dimension to the earlier ABC report. It seems that the 74-year-old chairman of ABC was about to retire—and Elton Rule was his heir-apparent. A dark horse for the job was aggressive and ambitious Roone Arledge, the head of ABC News.

Some suggested that Arledge used his news organization's investigations and news program to blemish Rule and maybe cloud the likelihood of his becoming chairman because, as one ABC employee said, Arledge and Rule were "about as friendly as Iran and Iraq."

While pejorative, such examples evidence the importance internal political situations can take on in modern organizations.

Question

Assume that you were in Mr. Rule's position in 1980 at the time the "Charlie's Angels" news report was broadcast. What would you do?

For more information, see "ABC Covers Itself," *Fortune*, 17 November 1980.

APPLICATION CASES

For practice in applying concepts covered in this chapter to managerial situations, see the following managerial decision cases. The case questions particularly relevant to this chapter are listed by number after each case name.

17

Organizational Culture and Managing Change

LEARNING OBJECTIVES

After completing this chapter, you should be able to

1. Understand the critical importance of a company's internal culture to managers who wish to bring about change.

2. Know how organizational cultures develop.

3. Identify dimensions of internal culture that strongly affect managing.

4. Discuss how you would go about changing an organization's culture.

5. Develop a set of tactics that you would use to implement change within a company.

ORGANIZATIONS AND CULTURES

Companies that are consistently regarded as the most successful share one common characteristic: They never get so big and so accomplished that they can rest on their laurels for long; they realize it takes a relentless, dynamic quality for an organization to adjust to new challenges in a rapidly changing world.

So it is that a company's strategy and the resulting policies cannot remain fixed and rigid in a changing technical, political, and cultural climate. Just as the environments within which companies must operate are constantly changing, so too must the internal organization itself continuously seek to adapt to that changing world. As such adaptation takes place, the values of key managers change, as do attitudes about certain aspects of business, such as government regulation, risk taking, entering new markets, or creating new products. These on-going changes affect company decisions, politics, and the capability of individuals to fill important jobs.

When an internal organization must change, it requires people within the organization to alter both their social structure and their personal values. Managers who understand the development and evolution of so-called corporate cultures operate with a distinct advantage in such circumstances, because they at least have the tools to understand the magnitude of a desired organizational change and can develop a program of changing their organization against that backdrop.

THE DEVELOPMENT OF CULTURE WITHIN ORGANIZATIONS

When analyzing the internal culture of their internal organizations, managers should distinguish between (1) how they want people to behave and what company objectives, policies, and procedures prescribe, and (2) the actual values and behavioral patterns that workers follow, including the informal (unprescribed) relationships discussed in the last few chapters. Of course, there is a lot of overlap between these two factors, but to bring about real change, managers must focus on the second.

Customs and Roles

A good way to start to understand a culture is to objectively observe its customs and roles. This approach is just as appropriate for the culture within a company as it is for pygmies in the Kalahari Desert.

How customs develop. Only a small fraction of human behavior is consciously chosen. It would be practically impossible to analyze every movement or remark before acting. In those cases in which the pros and cons of every step are not weighed, people rely heavily on customs and habits in tailoring their behavior. Such reliance takes place in both personal and business parts of our lives. Most companies, for instance, have fairly standard customs for greeting new employees: They get them to sign income tax withholding forms, explain and sign them up for insurance and other benefit programs, issue an identification card, and explain policies and expectations.

Once established, a customary way of doing business becomes natural—and often far too intractable. As members of the organization learn these customs through personal experience, they become comfortable with them. Hence, once the new employee has mastered the forms and bureaucracy involved in getting a new journal subscription, she will likely follow that same procedure whenever she needs a new subscription. Efforts to change such a system will be met with resistance, because people who have learned the old system can merely follow those norms on a mental "automatic pilot" and get what they want—a far more desirable situation for them than another new system that requires rethinking of each step.

Expected roles. Work customs are especially important when several people work together. Each person learns to rely on the others to perform certain roles in routine, customary ways. Thus, the hospital emergency room physician assumes high levels of exact behavior on the part of x-ray technicians, laboratory analysts, diagnostic specialists, on-call surgeons, nurses, paramedics, security officers, administrators, and support staff members. All these workers must act in unison and in a well-synchronized fashion in order for the emergency room to function successfully. When each person learns what to expect from the others with whom they work, coordinated behavior is greatly simplified. This is especially true in professional work, where there are preconceived ideas beyond the workplace as to the skills of a certified public accountant, or a commercial jet pilot, or an architect, or an insurance underwriter.

Established roles strongly influence the behavior that is expected of anyone filling those roles. Established roles are common throughout society. CPAs should be able to file tax returns, jet pilots to fly airplanes, and so on. This is true even in less glamorous or professional jobs. One applicant for a waiter's job in a fashionable new upscale restaurant was asked if she owned a tuxedo and could do "French service." She answered yes to both questions—untruthfully—fearing that she would not get the job otherwise. But she neither owned a tux nor even knew what the spoon-service French style was all about. Her interview was short indeed because the expected norms for the role she was hoping to fill were clearly beyond her knowledge and experience.

In business—and especially within a single enterprise—the role for any position may be firmly established (Figure 17.1). For instance, what an insurance adjuster should and should not undertake and what his attitude toward traditional adjusting should be may be clearly defined in the minds of all who will come in contact with him. The existence of such definite roles gives a stability to work relationships, allowing people to predict behavior.

It is more difficult, however, when complete agreement is lacking on

Figure 17.1 When persons assume a given role, their duties and authority, and sometimes even their gestures and clothing, are well defined.
Courtesy Bill Mark

all features of a role. Top executives may be inclined to think of a job in terms of a formal organizational plan that is embellished with details contributing to company objectives. An incumbent may have a somewhat different point of view based on her own preferences and experiences. Her subordinates may attach importance to still other features of the job, and her associates may be most concerned with how her position interrelates with their work.[1] Such divergence can be minimized, however, if the norms and customs of the organization clarify these issues, making them part of the overall understanding of how things operate within the organization.

Organizational Culture

The full body of such understandings and traditions about work form a large part of an organization's *culture*. The whole subject of culture became the focus of major study in the 1980s, as scholars and popular authors alike addressed the subject across a broad dimension from religious fervor to relatively objective inquiry.[2]

What is culture?   Because of such roots, the word *culture* has many meanings and connotations. People within organizations generally find it

[1]D. R. Hampton, C. E. Summer, and R. A. Webber, *Organizational Behavior and the Practice of Management*, 4th ed. (Glenview, Ill.: Scott, Foresman, 1982).

[2]T. E. Deal and A. A. Kennedy, *Corporate Cultures* (Reading, Mass.: Addison-Wesley, 1982); and T. J. Peters and R. H. Waterman, Jr., *In Search of Excellence* (New York: Harper & Row, 1982).

easy to agree that culture exists and is very important, but they have difficulty defining it.[3] Schein provides the following definition of culture:

1. Observed behavioral regularities when people interact, such as the language used and the rituals around deference and demeanor.
2. The norms that evolve within working groups.
3. The dominant values espoused by the organization, such as product quality or price leadership.
4. The philosophy that guides an organization's policy toward employees or customers.
5. The rules of the game for getting along within the organization.
6. The feeling or climate that is conveyed in the organization by the physical layout and the way in which members of the organization interact with customers or outsiders.

These cultural norms are learned and taught through a variety of formal and informal activities within the organization. They do not start from scratch, but rather are the product of organizational founders or group members with the power to change things. Cultural norms change as an organization evolves from its birth and early growth stages through stability, maturity, and, finally, organizational death.[4] As an organization evolves, culture often becomes less the philosophical glue that holds things together and more a political tool used to divide competing factions jockeying for the success of themselves or their ideas at the expense of others in the competition pool.

Cultural messages are embedded and reinforced primarily by:

1. What leaders pay attention to, measure, and control.
2. How leaders react to critical incidents and organizational crises.
3. The degree to which leaders encourage deliberate role modeling through teaching and coaching.
4. The criteria used by leaders for allocating rewards and status.
5. The criteria used by leaders for recruitment, selection, promotion, retirement, and dismissal from the organization core group.

IMPACT OF CULTURE ON A COMPANY

Managers are not much concerned about hair styles or fertility rites—aspects of culture observed by anthropologists studying primitive tribes. In-

[3]E. H. Schein, *Organizational Culture and Leadership* (San Francisco: Jossey-Bass, 1985).

[4]E. H. Schein, "The Role of the Founder in Creating Organizational Culture," *Organizational Dynamics*, Summer 1983, 13–28.

stead, managers should pay close attention to the following elements within their organizations.

Cultural Dimensions that Affect Managing

As leaders signal organization members about what they like and dislike, sanction and frown upon, a cultural model of the organization develops. It can serve as a road map for members of the organization in dealing with critical issues. The following are among the elements of such a culture:

Personal values.   What is desirable and important to people? In a company, these values often relate to concern for customer service, equity among workers, regular dividends, good citizenship in the community, promotion of minorities, and so forth. Widely held values are typically endorsed, and even promoted, by senior executives, although this is not always the case. One executive, for instance, refused to permit operating officers in a bank to promote anyone who the chief executive thought was overweight. Another executive, a staunch neoconservative, insisted that senior managers share his political philosophy in order to get promoted in his company, although government politics were irrelevant to the work.

Attitudes and beliefs.   The culture also embodies attitudes and beliefs about how or why things occur. Things like, "We didn't get the order because their purchasing manager golfs with one of the competitor's vice-presidents," or "You can't rely on members of a labor union to take responsibility or pride in their work because the union doesn't let them." Such beliefs tend to reflect deeply held biases—filters through which organization members evaluate what goes on around them. These can be the most inaccurate, destructive, and difficult-to-change aspect of culture.

Rewards and punishment.   What pays off in this company? Bosses may verbally encourage risk taking, for example, but if the behavior they actually reward over time tends to be more akin to not making mistakes, then that is probably a more appropriate behavior—and risk aversion is certainly the behavior desired by most corporate executives.

Informal information flows.   Mary has noticed that other managers always seem to hear about what's going on in her department before she does. She is certain that Pete, a member of her department, is informally passing along that information to the other managers—either to seek advice, or to encourage them to confide in him, or to cause Mary political trouble or embarrassment. Other sorts of information travel quickly along the "grapevine." For example, salespeople usually learn that shipments will be delayed long before they are formally notified; the arrival of internal auditors is often anticipated even though the visit is supposed to be a surprise. Indeed, smooth functioning of the culture depends on these informal communication links.

How decisions are made.　　What gets attention? Who controls the agenda? Generally the person within the organizational structure who gets to keep the records on performance—like the official scorer in a baseball game—tends to have a very powerful position. Answers to the questions of who has such powers and over what provide a reliable indication of the cultural directions of an organization.

Every Organization Has a Culture

Customary methods for dealing with issues such as those just outlined form the basis of a corporate culture. Much of such culture is formally recognized in manuals and policy statements, but another large part is informal, often unwritten, but nonetheless important because it suggests "the way we do things around here." This real signal of how things are done is critical for members of an organization to understand. In a conservative company, for instance, the culture is rigidly enforced by social pressure, whereas a more liberal organization may permit—even encourage—small deviations in some areas. Such flexibility adds to the subtlety of culture, because organization members have to sense how much variation is acceptable. A new employee needs to know, for example, whether whistleblowing is ever acceptable.

　　Culture does change—usually slowly and in one area at a time. Because of external pressures, for instance, it is becoming commonplace to find women in managerial roles. But such changes must be managed so that the appropriate changes take place when and where they are needed. Too often in the past, unsuccessful managers ordered changes and then just waited in vain for the changes to come. They never did, because the managers were not actively addressing the cultural issues that required change as readily as they focused on strategic issues of change.

CHANGING AN ORGANIZATION AND ITS CULTURE

Broadly speaking, managers can change the way an organization operates by (1) altering the prescribed management processes or (2) altering the behavior of people within the organizational system—changing the organizational culture.[5] But the most effective changes come from changing *both* the managerial process and the organizational culture, as Figure 17.2 indicates.

Changing Strategy and Culture

When American Motors merged into Renault, the giant French auto firm, a change was required in the prescribed way of doing things at American Motors as well as in the company's culture.

---

[5]L. Porter, E. E. Lawler, and J. R. Hackman, *Behavior in Organizations* (New York: McGraw-Hill, 1982).

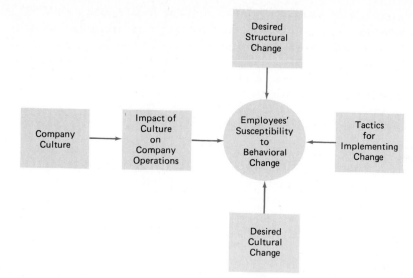

Figure 17.2   Considerations in
modifying unstructured behavior in a
company.

New processes.   From a formal operating standpoint, American Motors needed to alter its domestic engineering department because after the merger, AMC would rely heavily on Renault for engineering improvements—lighter engines, reliable front-wheel-drive capabilities, and the like. AMC also needed to alter its dealer network, which would be used to sell French-built cars as well as improved American products.[6]

Cultural change.   The American Motors culture also underwent substantial change. After decades of being the number four domestic auto maker in the United States and developing a corporate culture that accepted that state, AMC found its corporate headquarters outside Detroit filled with French executives sent over by Renault to change things. Risk taking was encouraged again—more than it had been in years. Labor negotiations were met with renewed vigor and aggressiveness. French executives actually took over the top management positions, placing their deputies, with whom they had worked in the heavily competitive European market, in other key jobs throughout AMC. This brought about such a dramatic positive cultural change that AMC line-worker attitudes were actually more positive than those of workers at a much-heralded Toyota plant south of Tokyo.[7]

Why Structural Changes Alone Are Inadequate

Designing a well-integrated management structure, carefully fitted to some new objective, does not guarantee that a desired change will take place. Even a neat system—ordered into place and making sense to orga-

[6]For an overview of structural approaches to change, see M. Beer, *Organization Change and Development: A Systems View* (Santa Monica, Calif.: Goodyear, 1980), Chap. 10.

[7]A. R. McGill, "Personal Communications from then–American Motors Chairman Paul Tippett," Detroit, March 1981.

nization members—will not necessarily work. Such a design takes no account of an organization's social structure, and it may not meet the needs of organization members.

Social fiber.   Any new design lacks social support because the plans have yet to take on full meaning from varied experience. The organizational relationships have to be worked out among people. The use of power has to be tested. Controls have to be felt before they become effective. Numerous other gaps in formal prescriptions have to be filled by the doers themselves. And while all these things are going on, slippage occurs. Uncertainty saps energy. Politics alter the designed structure. The interpretation of words twists their meanings.

Human needs.   Such a new structure also may not meet the needs of the people and groups that make up the organization. Managers typically design new structures to achieve new goals. But members of the organization may have personal goals that do not precisely match those of the organization. In fact, organization and worker goals may be very much in conflict. If a manager expects commitment—or even compliance—from employees in a new structure, the organization must meet their personal needs reasonably well. Some adjustment in the initial design may be necessary to make this happen. More likely, concessions will be made to win better motivation.

Such problems can be overcome if efforts are made to alter the behavior of people by affecting their culture as well as ordering change. The key reasoning here is that people—not goals or procedures—take center stage.

People Approaches to Change

Modifying individual behavior.   The simplest way to redirect the actions of an individual is to use some variation of the management-by-objectives technique discussed earlier. This helps the individual to understand new organizational goals and to develop personal goals that work toward that end. Such altered behavior must be strongly tied to rewards, in order to reinforce in the employee's mind the idea that this is what the company wants. To verbally support such changes but not redesign the reward system suggests to the employee that changing isn't really important, but that continuing the old behaviors that led to rewards in the past is still most important.

Organizational development.   As an organization moves to improve effectiveness by enhancing the degree to which individuals identify with the organization and its goals, the techniques of *organizational development* (OD) can be helpful.[8] OD seeks to treat all group members as self-

[8]N. Margulies and A. P. Raia, *Conceptual Foundations of Organizational Development* (New York: McGraw-Hill, 1978); also D. D. Warrick, *Managing Organization Change and Development* (Chicago: Science Research Associates, 1984).

fulfilling individuals; it encourages open and candid communication, and awareness of group norms and processes and their impact on group members. From this base, group members can mutually seek new attitudes, values, and ways of relating to each other. One drawback is that these discussions sometimes become far too focused on individuals—what's wrong with Joe, why no one can work with Alice—rather than on the overall group issue. Social pressures can be used to push aside such individually focused considerations for the greater organizational good. Group discussions can facilitate this process by (1) unfreezing individuals' beliefs, (2) objectively exploring new approaches, and (3) when consensus is reached, refreezing beliefs in a new way that can alter organizational culture and enlist group commitment.[9] Most important is the underlying identification with accomplishing a shared mission.

Personnel shifts.   Since any change affects an organization's employees, one alternative is to replace a few key people with some "new blood"—just as was done at American Motors. The issue of retraining versus replacing affects everyone whose work is significantly altered by the organization's new direction. Retraining has some advantages in that it allows an organization to retain people who already know each other and the environment. But arguments for bringing in at least a few new people are strong: Such people will be less culturally wedded to older norms, they are less likely to be defensive about past decisions, and they are unencumbered by social obligations of the past. Hence, such newcomers bring with them a clean slate, free of bias and fresh with energy.

Every change situation is different and must be honestly evaluated on its own merits; the magnitude of the change, the adaptability and values of current employees, the availability of new key people, and the urgency of the situation must be considered.[10]

TACTICS FOR IMPLEMENTING CHANGE

There are many alternatives for bringing about change within an organization. Change can be implemented quickly or slowly, or at a pace in between. Rapid action is sometimes required, as in the case of a crisis precipitated by an unanticipated hostile takeover attempt, or in the case of a massive external threat such as that faced by Lockheed when the Air Force banned further contracts because of quality control problems. Some changes can be implemented at a more moderate pace, and these situations provide the best opportunity for the time-consuming efforts needed to modify a culture while simultaneously changing strategic direction.

---

[9]I. Adizes, *How to Solve the Mismanagement Crisis* (Homewood, Ill.: Dow Jones-Irwin, 1979).

[10]M. A. Devanna, C. Fombrun, and N. M. Tichy, "Human Resources Management: A Strategic Perspective," *Organizational Dynamics,* Winter 1981, pp. 51–67.

In general, the decision of whether to pursue organizational change slowly or rapidly depends on the following circumstances:

The Nature of Objectives

Urgency.   The need for prompt results suggests a mass concentration from within the organization toward a unified goal, regardless of conflicting attitudes or disagreements. The person with final authority must determine what should happen and deserves complete support—although he will be subject to much second-guessing afterwards.

Agreement on objectives.   The extent to which employees agree with the organization's objectives must be assessed. When everyone is seeking a different result, it may be difficult to move quickly. A slower approach that offers hope of eventually unifying beliefs may be more appropriate.

Desire for continuing cooperation.   In most business relationships, we expect to deal with the same people over and over. Consequently, today's actions become tomorrow's experience. It may make sense to move slowly and think a great deal about the long-term impact before risking unpopularity by moving too quickly.

The Present Situation

Resources available.   A firm with relatively strong reserves of workers and capital may be able to move quickly in several different directions, whereas one with limited resources may have to move more gradually and choose which directions to invest in more carefully.

Managerial temperament.   Some managers are psychologically inclined to move quickly and decisively. Others like to operate at slower and more reasonable paces. The chances of success are improved if strategic directions match the managerial temperaments of the people asked to implement the changes.

Cultural norms.   Some organizations have rigid cultural norms that limit flexibility in the rate at which change can occur. While consumer-product firms often have lean structures and traditions that allow for rapid adaptation to change, other institutions, such as banks or insurance companies, are structurally and culturally designed to change much more slowly. These factors affect the speed with which an organization should be programmed to change.

The Chances of Success

Future environment.   What does a manager expect of the future external environment? Will there be barriers to entry in a few months or years that are not present now? Will there be more or less competition? How will costs change? If a manager feels that the conditions within an environment warrant moving rapidly, then that is what should be done. But if the risks involved in waiting are minimal, then taking a more deliberate approach is a viable alternative.

The Costs Involved

Disruption.   How disruptive would moving rapidly be, as opposed to taking a slower approach? This cost is concerned with the socio-cultural costs of moving too quickly when it may not be warranted. Some disruption is inevitable, but it is beneficial to keep it to a minimum.

Side effects.   If change occurs too quickly, will there be undesirable side effects—such as succeeding in a business, but alienating organization members? Are negative consequences associated with moving too slowly— such as loss of top personnel because of the organization's hesitancy? These considerations are critical and go far beyond the initial focus of a single strategic alternative; they emphasize the secondary and tertiary effects of a managerial act.

TIMING OF A CHANGE

Once these considerations have been weighed, managers must decide when and how fast, to seek a change. Among the alternatives are the following:

1. Pushing through a plan despite active opposition and obstacles.
2. Seeking gradual changes rather than revolutionary ones.
3. Making a quick showing. This may be a viable option when there is skepticism about an idea, but not necessarily active opposition to it. This alternative is a prompt and favorable way to erase skepticism and create a unified effort toward a desired goal.
4. Initiating change by boring from within. People within the organization come up with the necessary changes themselves and then implement them; managers do not get actively involved.
5. Letting things get worse before they get better.
6. Striking when the iron is hot. This option is best in a propitious situation that offers an opportunity of limited duration.

BUILDING A NEW STABILITY

Conversion to a new management system and a new culture takes time. Business strategies, social structures, and personal beliefs cannot be altered over night. But managers can assist in the transition by dealing with the psychological factors of learning, anxiety, and confidence.

Learning new relationships and attitudes—like any other learning—is aided by clear explanations, opportunities to try new alternatives, further questions and explanations, more trials and adjustments, and still more practice. If a manager helps everyone involved in the change recognize this process, then an otherwise tedious period can ultimately reduce confusion and expedite a total transformation.

Any change that alters a person's primary source of satisfaction for security, social, and self-expression needs is sure to create anxiety (Figure 17.3). Uncertainty about how a new system will affect each individual is unsettling. Such anxiety often causes odd behavior, including irritability, resistance, and lack of enthusiasm. Managers should do all they can to relieve such anxiety during a transition. Stating facts, explaining future plans, stressing future benefits, having people meet new associates, scotching rumors, showing awareness of political problems—all help allay anxiety. With rare exceptions, bad news faced promptly is better than extended worry. If answers to specific questions cannot be given, assurances about when and how the information will be available can be helpful.

Both learning and relief of anxiety help to rebuild confidence. In addition, a manager can bolster confidence by reinforcing desired behavior. Public recognition and reward of employees who successfully use the new design will discourage reversion to old ways and encourage acceptance of new patterns, thereby helping to change the organizational culture. Continuing acknowledgement of success will restore a sense of competence that has been threatened by the need to alter familiar behavior.

These personal and social adjustments take time. Experience indicates that major reorganizations require at least a year to digest, even with strenuous efforts to speed the conversion. Because of the necessary investment of time and energy, such changes should not be undertaken lightly or without a thorough understanding of the time factors at work.

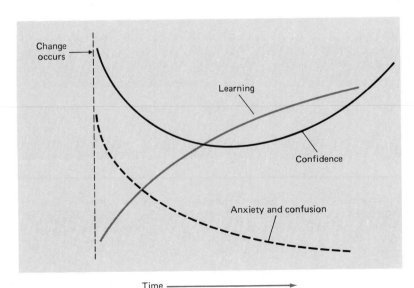

Figure 17.3 Psychological factors involved in a change of systems. Diagram indicates how response to change shifts over time.

CONCLUSION

All organizations evolve cultures that pass along information on norms and values—"the way we do things around here." Such cultural traditions form the underpinnings of any organization, and thus must be considered a major contributor to organizational change. Managers can use several alternative methods for implementing change. The overriding theme of this chapter is that along with structural or strategic changes, there must also be cultural-change efforts to bring about new directions in that strong, informal part of the organization.

If change is to be internalized by employees, it must be accepted by them—not merely ordered from above. The magnitude of the change desired, the urgency, the resources available and their fit into a new thrust, tolerance for risk and for frequent change—all affect the blend of elements that suit a specific change process. Because so many diverse considerations are involved, some overriding objective or mission is needed to clarify priorities and values, and the organizational culture must be altered to be consistent with those priorities and values. The situation determines which programs are strategically feasible. But at least equally important—and maybe more important—is the cultural condition of an organization and the degree of change required to make it consistent with an organization's new strategy.

Impact on Productivity

Like individualized motivation, personal leadership, clear communication, and harnessed politics—all subjects examined in the preceding chapters—cultural change is vital to productivity. It is a dimension that no leader can bypass. A young company just doesn't change very much until its internal culture has been modified.

To alter the culture, a leader must exert consistent and persistent pressure. Time is required because many individuals have to develop new habits and revised attitudes. These new habits and attitudes must be intertwined into a lively social fabric. The leader secures a lasting change in productivity by developing such revised patterns of teamwork—patterns that are then internalized by the numerous players.

FOR FURTHER DISCUSSION

1. Give an example of a custom that has evolved within an organization with which you are familiar. How deeply embedded in the culture is that custom? What would it take to change it?

2. What implications do the cultural issues described in this chapter have for the manager who wants to bring about change in an organization by altering the structure? Is that manager likely to im-

plement a successful change if he only alters the structure without also trying to change the culture? Why?

3. Given what you now know about implementing change, take an organization with which you are familiar and develop a list of tactics you will use to bring about change. Which of these changes are likely to face the most resistance within the organization?

4. Two management scholars were debating the cultural issue within organizations. One said: "With what we've learned in the last ten years, it's quite clear that cultural issues are *the* single most important ingredient in bringing about organizational change. If you can modify the culture, you can change the organization for the better." The second person responded, "I'm skeptical about that. It sounds like an interesting enough theory, but no one has really proven it yet to my satisfaction. Basically, I think, most people in most organizations will change when you tell them to because you're their boss." Which of these two sides comes closest to your beliefs and why?

5. Which of the three "people approaches" to change described in this chapter do you personally find most appealing? Why?

6. Give an example of a situation best served by gradual change and an example of a situation requiring revolutionary change. What are the key differences between these two types of situations?

7. Three major factors in the early success of People Express (airline) were: (a) low fares and low service on all flights, (b) flexible work assignments to make full use of employees while they were at work, and (c) stock ownership by all regular employees. It was a stripped-down, cooperative venture. Then, the management decided that the airline had to fly over most of the country to succeed. Coast-to-coast flights were started, but to attract business passengers at higher fares, more services were added. Also, Frontier Airlines, with a network of routes in the Rocky Mountain region, was purchased, but Frontier did not follow the three policies listed in the first sentence of this question. Explain the cultural problems People Express faced in its expansion program. Assuming that the expansion was economically sound, what would you have done to develop a consistent culture for the enlarged operations?

FOR FURTHER READING

Beer, M., *Organization Change and Development; A Systems View.* Santa Monica, Calif.: Goodyear, 1980. Comprehensive treatment of major approaches to organizational change, with particular emphasis on conceptual foundations and empirical research.

French, W. L. and C. H. Bell, *Organization Development: Behavioral Science Interventions for Organization Improvement.* Englewood Cliffs, N.J.: Prentice-Hall, 1984. Good overview of the techniques and approaches used by organization development practitioners.

Goodman, P. S. et al., *Change in Organizations: New Perspectives on Theory, Research and Practice.* San Francisco: Jossey-Bass, 1982. Ten articles written by leading academics in the field.

Kantor, R. M., *The Change Masters: Innovations for Productivity in the American Corporation.* New York: Simon & Schuster, 1983. Intensive look at how innovative changes are brought about in leading U.S. companies.

Kimberly, J. R. and R. E. Queen, eds., *Managing Organizational Transitions.* Homewood, Ill.: Richard D. Irwin, 1984. Good collection of articles dealing primarily with behavioral aspects of major changes in organizations.

Schein, E. H., *Organization, Culture and Leadership.* San Francisco: Jossey-Bass, 1985. An excellent assessment of the cultural influences within organizations and their implications for politics and leadership.

Tichy, N. M., *Managing Strategic Change: Technical, Political and Cultural Dynamics.* New York: John Wiley, 1983. Develops an integrated framework, based on extensive fieldwork, for dealing with technical, political, and cultural aspects of strategic change.

It was 1979, and stodgy, bloated Chrysler Corporation was teetering on the brink of financial collapse. The invasion of imported cars made by Chrysler's Japanese rivals had devastated America's no. 3 auto maker, which faced heavy losses and enormous cash-flow problems.

Enter Lee A. Iacocca, a straight-talking salesman and ex–Ford Motor Company star, whose job it was to rescue Chrysler from bankruptcy and rebuild it into a feisty, flexible competitor.

It wasn't a pleasant job, but Iacocca took to it with characteristic aggressiveness and gusto. He closed plants, sending hundreds of hourly workers to the unemployment lines. He gutted Chrysler's overcrowded management ranks. To get contract concessions from the United Auto Workers (UAW), he took the bold step of putting UAW chief Douglas Fraser on the Chrysler board of directors.

Iacocca miraculously talked the U.S. government into guaranteeing $1.5 billion in loans to Chrysler. He refocused the company's marketing strategy on small cars and encouraged development of risky new products, such as the highly successful minivan. He pushed for investment in high-tech automation to improve Chrysler productivity. And he even joined with a Japanese rival, striking a deal for a joint venture with Mitsubishi.

He also became the company's most visible spokesman, appearing in television commercials to tout "the New Chrysler Corporation." The jowly chairman arrogantly challenged consumers with a line that became famous: "If you can find a better car, buy it."

By 1984, Chrysler was solidly back in black ink. Although the jury on its small-car strategy was still out, the company was leaner and more aggressive than ever. Chrysler workers rallied to the radical shift in company direction and tenor that Iacocca had orchestrated. "I owe it all to Iacocca," said Sarah Haynes, a Chrysler assembly-line worker who returned to work after five years on layoff. "If the workers are saying he's great, it ain't no jive."

In a cover story on Iacocca in 1985, *Time* magazine said, "By 1983, everyone could see that Iacocca had, in fact, carried out his immense logistical mission. He had managed to whip a sprawling company into shape, and saved American autoworkers' jobs by the tens of thousands."

Indeed, Iacocca's changing of the mood at Chrysler rubbed off on the nation. Political pundits talked seriously of a Lee Iacocca bid for the presidency of the United States in 1988. Iacocca's autobiography stayed atop best-seller lists for almost a year.

Said *Time*, "After a long period of feeling cranky and skeptical, the country seems in the mood to have a hero or two. Moreover, (Iacocca's) life embodies just the kind of happy ending that Americans like to celebrate: He had reverses, he fought back, he came out on top."

Question

Was Iacocca's reputation for personal leadership during his first five years at Chrysler due primarily to (a) his personal charismatic qualitites, (b) bold and determined action with a company that stakeholders did not want to see die, or (c) a basic change in Chrysler's internal culture?

For more information, see *Time* 1 April 1985.

APPLICATION CASES

For practice in applying concepts covered in this chapter to managerial situations, see the following managerial decision cases. The case questions particularly relevant to this chapter are listed by number after each case name.

PART IV MANAGERIAL DECISION CASE STUDIES

Decision Case IV-1
PETER JEFFRIES

Occasionally after a long day's work, Pete Jeffries and his wife wonder whether he has made the right career choices. As an undergraduate at a small, prestigious college, Pete majored in economics and marketing. "I wasn't a 'Phi Beta,'" he said, "but I held a solid *B* average and did a number of other things as well."

Among the "other things," Pete had won varsity letters in football and track, and played intramural rugby and basketball. Between seasons, he averaged twenty hours a week working as a bouncer and later as a bartender at a campus oasis. During athletic seasons, he worked as a tutor. An officer of his fraternity, he also averaged enough hours of "housework" and maintenance to cover his meal charges.

"In some ways," he commented, "I probably got more out of college than a lot of people who didn't have as much to do. When you don't have much free time, you have to use what you have carefully. I was lucky to get to college and I wanted to make the most of it."

Pete is the youngest of eleven children. His mother died when he was two and Pete's father placed the eight youngest brothers and sisters with relatives and friends in the Boston area and worked for the next three years at two full-time jobs. He sold their house and lived in a small apartment in order to pay for the children's support. He brought them together for holidays and birthdays whenever possible, and saved until he was able to purchase a large old house in Charlestown, Massachusetts, bring the remaining children back together, and afford part-time help.

"None of my brothers and sisters had a chance to go to college," Pete related. "Even when we were together again, money was tight and the older kids had to take care of the younger ones. By the time I got to high school there was a little money and lots of encouragement. I did well academically and, as a big kid, attracted attention as an athlete. Everybody helped to make sure I got to college."

At 6 feet 4 inches and 235 pounds, Pete was a fine linebacker on weak football teams and a good, but not outstanding, shot-putter.

"We played tough competitive football, but we were the smallest school in our league. With no athletic scholarships and high academic standards, we had a rough time, but we generally held our own. Many a Saturday I wished we had 'built less character' and scored more points, but it was worth it."

After graduation four years ago, Pete accepted a job as a sales management trainee with a highly regarded consumer goods company and was quite successful during his first year, ranking in the top ten percent of his peer group.

"I was pleased to be one of two out of thirty-seven applicants to get an offer," Pete said. "They were so professional in their recruiting and so choosy, I took the job just because I 'won' it. Their training programs were extremely valuable and I liked the challenge, but frankly, I just couldn't see myself making a career with them. It was just too structured, too pat. My supervisor was encouraging, but I felt I was just going through the motions.

"I competed with the others they hired only because I wanted to be the best in the group. I competed to be the top sales rep, and I was for seven out of ten months, but I felt I was trying to prove I *could* do it rather than that I *wanted* to do it."

Pete's supervisor, Susan Waters, was disappointed when he indicated that he was leaving after fourteen months on the job. "I tried to get him to give it more time," she said. "He was doing so well and I felt he was being hasty. Few trainees enjoy setting up displays and doing the things they have to do at the start, but he had so much going for him; I know he would have moved up rapidly into sales management. Unfortunately, he had made up his mind, and Peter is a strong-minded person."

"Susan just couldn't understand," Pete said. "I really tried to anticipate what was ahead. I talked to people two, three levels up in the hierarchy and tried to get a feel for what they did. Maybe I would have changed my mind in five years, but at the time I felt that it wasn't impatience, but a bad fit. I couldn't see myself just fine-tuning well-tested programs as they did. Further, there was no real sense of a group or group support. I felt like my 'team' was the company, and that's too big a team for me.

"My friends thought I was nuts to quit. 'Why leave such a great company where you have so much to learn and such strong professional support?' they asked. That was just it; it was *too* well organized, *too* supportive, and I simply couldn't identify with soap and toothpaste."

To the dismay of many of his friends as well as his supervisor, Pete then accepted a job as a management trainee with the Greatway Trucking Company. "It was a real tough decision," he said, "because I had gotten married only six months before and Marie was expecting."

Greatway Trucking

Greatway Trucking is one of the largest and most profitable national firms in the trucking industry. With over 550 terminals, Greatway handles both long- and short-distance shipping throughout the continental United States, offering a full line of freight-forwarding and transit services.

In recent years there has been a considerable shake-out in the trucking industry, with almost one-third of the larger nationwide firms either merging with others or failing. Overinvestment in rolling stock and fierce discounting have made for tough times in the industry. A few firms, like Greatway, have survived and grown in volume, but all have experienced some erosion in profits.

"The survivors are the ones who work harder and smarter," said Luke Spagnola, president of Greatway. "While we continue to invest heavily in the latest information technology, there are no real secrets to this business. You need smart people who work hard and have the guts to make tough judgment calls on rates, service, and investment. This starts with picking the right people, starting them near the bottom, and teaching them not only our methods but our culture."

The company's approach to hiring, training, and developing candidates for sales and operations management is a rather unorthodox one. Spagnola recognizes that his approach carries risks.

"We look for special young men," he said, "and a few women. We pick the best, then break most of the rules in terms of leadership, communication, motivation, and compensation. We look for college grads, mostly after they've worked for one or two years for some big company with fancy formal programs and too little challenge. While our turnover is high during the first two years, I doubt it's much higher than that of our competitors or even companies in other industries. We feel, however, that the ones who stay with us are really our kind of people and are committed to carrying on our way of doing things."

Spagnola went on to outline a profile of the kind of people they recruited as trainees for management positions in sales and operations. "Ten years ago," he said, "we started to look exclusively for young men who were fair-to-good students and who played football for Ivy League or Ivy League-type colleges. We wanted kids smart enough to get into a tough, smaller school and tough enough to maintain good—not great—grades and play football in an environment where 'jocks' not only weren't heroes but were often sneered at by the majority of grade grubbers who go to these kinds of schools.

"Usually we let the big, better-known companies screen and hire them and teach them some real-life basics. Then we would go after the ones our grapevine said were doing well but who were tired of big-company ways. Sometimes we hire right out of college, but we do better after they have already quit one job and are hesitant to quit again. If it weren't for that, our turnover would be even higher, given how hard we work them.

"We tried a few former college wrestlers recently, but they didn't work out as well. I think it's the team thing with football players plus the physical demands we want. While wrestlers may be team-oriented to some extent, on the mat it's one-on-one. My personnel director wants me to try crew members—you know, the rowers—but I figure, why experiment when we have a good formula now?

"When I first told my personnel director what I wanted and how I wanted them handled once hired, I know he figured I'd gone bonkers, but my inspirational leadership and his mortgage payments led him to make my plan a success.

"In recent years we have tried to get some women in. I'm not against women in management, but our formula is a bit hard to follow with women."

Vincent O'Connor, personnel director, agreed that his first reaction to Spagnola's ideas was skepticism. "Luke is a persuasive guy, though, and smart. He hasn't much formal education, but he reads a lot and is a good thinker. You don't succeed in this industry just by being tough; you have to be smart, too, and he is. He's also a good leader. He's always kidding about how he will fire people, but everyone knows that's just talk. We just don't fire people who have been with us for a few years unless we catch them breaking the law."

"The law," subsequent discussions revealed, did not mean just local, state, and federal law, but Greatway "laws," as well. While these laws were never written down, Greatway employees—hourly, union, nonunion, and managerial—somehow knew not only what was allowed and what wasn't but also how much "punishment" was associated with violations. Many employees indicated that seldom did management have to enforce the law. "We just play by the rules," said one loading-dock supervisor. "They are fair, clear, and you give up too much if caught to take a risk."

"Management is very tough," said an hourly worker, "but they are fair. We don't have to worry about a lot of 'chicken stuff,' but they won't put up with us breaking the rules. We've got a strong union here [Teamsters], but they don't fight management on most discipline calls because they know they will lose one way or another. What I like best is that the same rules apply to the big shots [management] as to us, and they are just as tough when they screw up."

"Like I said," O'Connor added, "Luke's bark is worse than his bite, but when he bites he takes big pieces. On his hiring plan, I admit, ten years ago I didn't think it would work, but when he outlined how he wanted us to handle our recruits, I was really worried. God bless him, though—as usual, the old man knew what he was up to."

O'Connor then outlined the system that has been in operation for the past ten years and its results as he sees them.

Starting salaries are roughly 20 percent higher than those offered by national, well-known companies for comparable positions as management trainees. But the average work week is often 40 percent longer.

"We don't try to compete with the real high bidders," O'Connor said, "but we match or top most insurance companies, banks, and industrial and consumer goods companies."

In addition to salaries and comparable benefit packages, Greatway offers year-end bonuses, based on "team performance," which can run from 10 percent to 40 percent of base pay. "Teams" vary depending on the size and location of the facility, as well as on the nature of the work. Hourly workers and managers know what their teams are and roughly how bonuses will be distributed.

A team typically includes drivers (Teamsters), maintenance people, freight handlers, schedulers, and sales personnel.

"Most of the hourly personnel belong to several teams," Pete said. "They are also members of functional departments. I think the fancy term for what we do in the terminals is 'matrix management.' I have a team reporting to me, but each of my team members also reports to a department head. Each team leader has a full complement of skills necessary to do his job. As a supervisor, I often have to compete to get more effort from individuals who are members of my team and others'. Occasionally we have to go to a shift supervisor for arbitration, but most of us try to settle things among ourselves.

"I know my success depends on my team. They range from high-school dropouts to some computer types with master's degrees; from a fork-lift driver in his early twenties to a maintenance chief pushing seventy. They know they can make or break a young supervisor like me, so it is a real challenge to win them over and get that extra something when I need it. This is particularly true of the union members of the team, who don't participate in the bonus pool."

"The higher up you get, the more you get, percentage-wise," one supervisor said. "There isn't any published rule and no one knows exactly what anyone else gets," he added, "but we know enough to feel it's fair."

The most unusual part of the program is that all college hires, whether aiming for sales management or operations management (facilities and headquarters) begin by working at a terminal. For roughly three years they work 50 to 60 hours a week, typically five 10-to-12-hour days or, more accurately, nights.

One year they work from 7 PM to 6 AM or 7 AM, the second year from 9 PM to 8 AM or 9 AM. They work at scheduling and supervising inbound and outbound freight. Not only are the hours long, but the work is demanding, requiring a great deal of flexibility and team involvement to meet many and varied problems; one of the laws is that shipments don't sit around on the loading docks.

"In ten years, despite high turnover in the first two or three years," O'Connor said, "we have built a strong team of bright, young, 'can-do' managers and have grown in sales and profits while many of our competitors merged or went broke."

Pete Jeffries' Current Situation

Two and one-half years after joining Greatway, Pete Jeffries is now working the "day shift," from 9 AM to 8 PM or 9 PM, five days a week. He and his wife are now proud parents of an almost-two-year-old daughter.

"The first two years were rough," he said. "My wife and I would pass like ships in the night. When the baby arrived, things got even more hectic, but after a while we got things organized and my being home and awake in the afternoon and early evening let me relieve my wife. Since we rotate our five days around all seven, I'd often have to give up all or part of weekends and holidays, too. That can pose problems, but the worst is behind us now.

"By my fourth year, if I stay with it, I'll have enough seniority to avoid the worst shifts and probably be on my way to a new location. I'm not sure where they will send me or even what I'll be doing. They make no promises and give fewer hints.

"I'm sure that if I keep performing, I will have some choice, although usually you move when offered a promotion or wait a long time for another good offer. Hell, if they don't come up with something good, I can always leave. I'd hate to give up the bonus because no one else offers as much as I would get after four years. I'd also hate to leave my team; they are a great bunch, but I'd have to start again in a new location anyway.

"Lots of other trucking firms, as well as industrial and consumer goods companies with large fleet operations, would probably offer me a good deal after my training at Greatway. While our competitors make fun of our conditions, they know the result is a well-trained person who has shown enough intelligence and discipline to have succeeded in a rough environment. While Greatway doesn't fire people who have proved their worth, almost 40 percent of their annual new hires for my job category are gone for one reason or another in two to three years.

"I figure I'm over the hump now and can start looking forward to more challenging work, better money, and more civilized hours within a year, whether it's with Greatway or someplace else."

QUESTIONS

Part I

1. Which would have better prepared Pete for a position in general management with a firm other than the two he has worked for—the training at his first job, or the training at his second job?
2. Could a large bank or service industry company follow Greatway's recruiting and development strategy?
3. How are changing family values, the increase in the number of dual-career families, and other environmental factors likely to affect Greatway's current personnel approaches?
4. How has the evolution of managerial roles affected the success of Greatway's approach? Do you feel it would have worked as well before a decade ago? Do you think it will work as well, better, or worse ten years from now?

Part II

5. Which of Pete's two jobs require better planning by his supervisors to ensure that Pete learns but also performs well? What kind of planning (standing versus adaptive) would be more valuable to Pete's supervisor?
6. In what ways will a firm's master strategy determine the nature of its approach to recruiting management trainees? Illustrate your answer using this case.

Part III

7. How good a job do you feel Greatway has done in matching people and jobs, given the high turnover among its trainees?

8. Which company would be more likely to delegate work to trainees after six months—Pete's first company or Greatway? Explain.

9. In what ways will the degrees of delegation and decentralization affect the composition of bonus teams and the effectiveness of group bonuses?

10. Do you feel that Pete's training at Greatway will be equally beneficial in preparing him for higher-level staff jobs or line jobs?

Part IV

11. Can Greatway's approach succeed in attracting and motivating a large number of capable women? How would it have to be modified, if at all, to do so?

12. What might Susan Waters (his first supervisor) have done to better understand Pete's needs and values?

13. Had she better understood what motivated Pete, could his first supervisor have persuaded him to stay?

14. In what ways will shifts in Pete's needs and priorities influence his effectiveness at Greatway?

15. What do you think of Spagnola's leadership style? What seem to be its key elements if it has been successful?

16. What techniques account for the apparent effectiveness of the "grapevine" at Greatway?

17. Identify several areas that should be watched carefully at Greatway to avoid undesirable conflict and politics affecting the work of employees like Pete.

18. *Summary Report Question for Part IV.* What should Greatway do to increase the likelihood of Pete's staying with the company in the future? Consider the broader implications of your answer.

Part V

19. How would performance measurement of trainees probably differ between Pete's first company and Greatway?

20. What are the key considerations when building control systems in a setting that offers sizable group bonuses?

21. To what degree should attitudes toward Greatway's "laws," and discipline for violation of these laws, influence the formal controls within the company?

Summary Report Question for Solution of Case as a Whole

22. What general lessons may be learned from this case about the recruiting, training and development, and compensation of young professionals such as Pete?

Petersen Electronics was founded by its current president, Benjamin Petersen, in 1954. The company grew rapidly during the 1960s and 1970s, reaching sales of $200 million in 1978. Growth since then, however, has been uneven and at an average of less than 5 percent per year. However, 1984 was a good year, with sales and profits leaping 12 percent and 18 percent, respectively.

Despite the good year, Benjamin Petersen is concerned about the company as he nears retirement. One of the problems on which he would like advice involves George Briggs, vice-president of marketing, and Thomas Evans, national sales manager, who is one of Briggs' four subordinates.

Each of the key characters is described below and his comments on the problem are presented for your consideration.

Benjamin Petersen, 61, president and board chairman. Petersen's views on the dilemma he faces are as follows: "When we started, a handful of people worked very hard and very closely to build something bigger than any of us. One of these people was George Briggs. George has been with me from the start, as have almost all of my vice-presidents and many of my key department heads. For the first five years, I did almost all of the inventing and engineering work. Tom Carroll ran the plant, and George Briggs knocked on doors and sold dreams as well as products. As the company grew, we added people and Briggs slowly worked his way up the sales organization. Eight years ago, when our vice-president of marketing retired, I put George in the job. He has market research, product management, sales service, and the field sales force (reporting through a national sales manager) under him, and he has really done a first-rate job.

"One of the problems of having built this business with so many people who started with me at the beginning is that we are all approaching retirement at about the same time. We realized this about ten years ago and began bringing in more bright young engineers and MBAs. We have moved them along as fast as we can. Turnover has been high, and we have had some friction between our 'Young Turks' and the 'Old Guard.' When business slowed in the '70s, we also had a lot of competition among the newcomers. Those who stayed have continued to move up and a few are now in, or ready for, top jobs. One of the best of this group is Tom Evans. He started with us nine years ago in the sales service area. Later, he spent three years in product management. George Briggs got him to move from being head of the sales service department to being an assistant product manager. After one year, George Briggs named him manager of the product management group, and two years later, when the national sales manager retired, George named Evans to this post.

"That move both surprised and pleased me. I felt that Evans would make a good sales manager despite the fact that he has little or no direct sales experience. I was afraid, however, that George Briggs would not want someone in that job who hadn't had years of field experience. I was even more surprised, though, when six months later (a month ago), George told me he was afraid Evans wasn't working out and asked if I might be able to find a spot for him in the corporate personnel department. While I'm sure our recent upturn in sales is not solely Evans' doing, he certainly seems to be one of the keys. Despite his inexperience, he seems to have the field sales organization behind him. He spends much of his time traveling with them and from what I hear has built a great team spirit.

"Despite this, George Briggs claims, he is in 'over his head' and that it is just a matter of time before his inexperience gets him in trouble. I can't understand why George is so adamant. It's clearly not a personality clash since they have always gotten along well in the past. In many ways, George Briggs has been Evans' greatest booster, until recently.

"Since George is going to need a replacement someday, I was hoping it would be Evans. If George Briggs doesn't retire before we have to give Evans another move or lose him, I'd consider moving Evans to another area. When we were growing faster, I didn't worry about a new challenge opening up for an aggressive young manager—there was always a new division or a new line or something to keep him stimulated and satisfied with his progress. Now I have less flexibility; my top men are several years from retirement, and yet I have some people, like Evans, whom I would hate to lose, always pushing and expecting promotion. Evans is a good example of this; I could move him but there are not that many *real* opportunities. He could go to personnel or engineering or even finance. Evans has the makings of a real fine general manager. I'd hate to move him now, however. He really isn't ready for another shift—although he will be in a few years—and despite what George Briggs claims, I think he is building team work and commitment in the sales organization as a result of his style. Finally, while I don't want to appear unduly critical of Briggs, I'm not sure he could get the job done in these competitive times without a bright young person like Evans to help him."

George Briggs, 53, vice-president of marketing.   The following is George Briggs' account of the situation: "Before I say anything else, let me assure you there is nothing personal in my criticism of Evans. I like him. I have always liked him. I've done more for him than anyone else in the company. I've tried to coach him and bring him along like a son. The simple truth is that he is in way over his head and showing a side of his personality I've never seen before. I brought him along through sales service and product management, and he was always eager to learn. While I couldn't give him a lot of help in those areas (frankly, there are aspects of them I don't yet fully understand), I still tried, and he paid attention and learned from others, as well. The job of national sales manager, however, is a different story. In the other jobs Evans had—staff jobs—there was always time to consult, to consider, to get more data. In sales, however, all this participative stuff he uses takes too long. The national sales manager has to be able to make quick, intuitive decisions. What's more, like the captain of a ship, he has to inspire confidence in those below him. If the going gets rough, the only thing that keeps the sailors and junior officers from panicking is confidence in the skipper. I've been there and I know. Right now, with orders coming in strong, he can get away with all of his meetings and indecisiveness. The people in the field really like him and are trying to keep him out of trouble. In addition, I have been putting in sixty to seventy hours a week trying to do my job and also make sure he doesn't make any serious mistakes.

"I know he is feeling the pressure, too. Despite the fact that he has been his usual cheery self with others, when I call him in to question a decision he has made or is about to make, he gets defensive. He never was that way with me before. Now, whatever I suggest he disagrees with me. I may have lost a little feel for what's going on in the field over the years, but I suspect I still know more about the customers and our sales people than Tom Evans will ever know. I've tried for the past seven months to get him to relax and let the 'old man' help him, but it's no use. I'm convinced he just is not cut out for the job, and before we ruin him I want to transfer him somewhere else. He would probably make a fine personnel director some day. He's a very popular guy who seems genuinely interested in people and in helping them.

"I have talked with Ben Petersen about the move and he has been stalling me. I understand his position. We have a lot of young comers like Tom Evans in the company and Ben has to worry about all of them. He told me that if anyone can bring Evans along, I can and asked me to give it another try. I have, and things are getting worse. I hate to admit I made a mistake with Tom Evans, but I plan on seeing Ben about this again tomorrow. We just can't keep putting this off. I'm sure he'll see it my way, and as soon as he approves, I'll have a heart-to-heart talk with Tom Evans."

Thomas Evans, 34, national sales manager. The following is Thomas Evans' account of the situation: "This has been a very hectic but rewarding period for me. I've never worked as hard in my life as during the last six months, but it's paying off. I'm learning more about sales each day and more importantly, I'm building a first-rate sales team. My people are really enjoying the chance to share ideas and support each other. At first, particularly with our markets improving, it was hard to convince them to take time to meet with me and their subordinates. Gradually they have come to accept these sessions as an investment in team-building. We come up with more good new ideas and figure out ways to help each other to a greater degree than ever before according to them.

"Fortunately, I also have experience in product management and sales service. Someday, I hope to bring representatives from this department and market research into the meetings with regional and branch people but that will take time. This kind of direct coordination and interaction doesn't fit with the thinking of some of the old-timers. I ran into objections when I tried this while I was working in the other departments. I'm certain, however, that in a year or so I'll be able to show, by results, that we should have more direct contact across department levels.

"My boss, George Briggs, will be one of the ones I will have to convince. He comes from the old school and is slow to give up what he knows used to work well. George likes me, though, and has given me a tremendous amount of help in the past. I almost fainted when he told me he was giving me this job. Frankly, I didn't think I was ready yet, but he assured me I could handle it. I've gotten a big promotion every few years and I really like that—being challenged to learn new skills and getting more responsibility. I guess I have a real future here, although George won't be retiring for a good many years and I've gone as high as I can go until then.

"George is a demanding person, but he is extremely fair and is always trying to help. I only hope I can justify the confidence he has shown in me. He stuck his neck out by giving me this chance, and I'm going to do all I can to succeed.

"Recently we have had a few run-ins. George Briggs works harder than anyone around here, and perhaps the pressure of the last few years is getting to him. I wish he'd take a vacation this year and get away for a month or more and just relax. He hasn't taken more than a week off in the nine years I've been here, and for the last two years he hasn't taken any vacation. I can see the strain is taking its toll. Recently he has been on my back for all kinds of little things. He always was a worrier but lately he has been testing me on numerous small issues. He keeps throwing out suggestions or second-guessing me on things I've spent weeks working on with the field people.

"I try to assure him I'll be all right and ask him to please help me where I need it with the finance and production people, who have had a tough time keeping up with our sales organization. It has been rough lately, but I'm sure it will work out. Sooner or later George will accept the fact that while I will never be able to run things the way he did, I can still get the job done for him."

Victor Perkins, 39, vice-president, personnel.   The following is Victor Perkins' opinion on the cause of the present conflict and his thoughts on how to deal with it: "I feel that George Briggs is threatened by Evans' seeming success with the field sales people. I don't think he realizes it, but he is probably jealous of the speed with which Tom has taken charge. In all likelihood, he didn't expect Tom to be able to handle the field people as well as he has, as fast as he has. When George put Tom in the job, I have a feeling that he was looking forward to having him need much more help and advice from 'the old skipper.' Tom does need help and advice, but he is getting most of what George could offer from his own subordinates and his peers. As a result, he has created a real team spirit below and around him, but he has upset George in the process.

"George not only has trouble seeing Tom depend so much on his subordinates, but I feel that he resents Tom's unwillingness to let him show him how he used to run the sales force.

"I may be wrong about this, of course. I am sure that George honestly believes that Tom's style will get him in trouble sooner or later. George is no doddering old fool who has to relive his past success in lower-level jobs. In the past, I'm told he has shown real insight and interest in the big-picture aspects of the company. The trouble is he knows he was an outstanding sales manager, but I am not sure he has the same confidence in his ability as vice-president. I have seen this time and again, particularly in recent years. When a person begins to doubt his future, he sometimes drops back and begins to protect his past. With more competition from younger subordinates and the new methods that they often bring in, many of our experienced people find that doing their job the way they used to just isn't good enough any more. Some reach out and seek new responsibilities to prove their worth. Others, however, return to the things they used to excel in and try to show that theirs is still the best way to do things. They don't even seem to realize that this puts them in direct competition with their subordinates.

"What do we do about this? I wish I knew! At lower levels, where you have more room to shift people around, you have more options. When the company is growing rapidly, the problem often takes care of itself. In this case, I am not sure what I would recommend if Ben Petersen asks my advice. Moving Tom to Personnel at this time not only won't help me (I

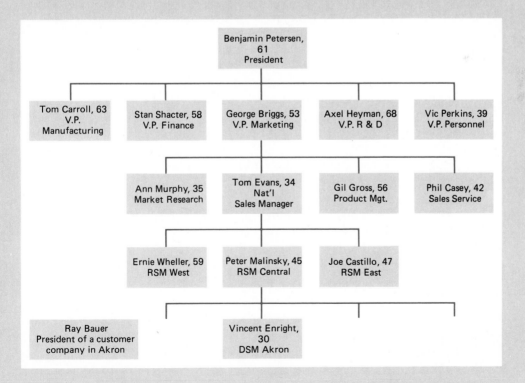

really don't have a spot for him), but it won't help Briggs or Evans either. Moving Evans now would be wasteful of the time and effort we've put into his development. It may also reverse some important trends Tom has begun in team-building within the sales force.

"If Briggs were seven or eight years older, we could wait it out. If the company were growing faster we might be able to shift people. As things stand, however, I see only one approach as a possibility and I'm not sure it will work. I would recommend that we get busy reinforcing Briggs' attention on the vice-president's job and get him to see that that is where he has to put his time and effort. Perhaps the best thing would be to send him to one of the longer senior-executive programs. Don't forget he is a very bright and experienced person who still has a great deal to offer the company if we can figure out how to help him."

Benjamin Petersen has agreed to talk with George Briggs about Tom Evans tomorrow afternoon. What would you advise him to do?

QUESTIONS

Part I

1. To what degree may the Briggs/Evans problem stem from changes in the role of a manager? Relate your answer to the fact that until recently Briggs has been a stronger supporter to Evans and has furthered his career.

2. How may have environmental pressures contributed to the Briggs/Evans conflict?

Part II

3. How might standing plans relieve Briggs of some of his concerns about Evans? How might such standing plans affect Evans' ability to manage the field-sales organization?

4. In what aspects of planning does Evans most need help from Briggs? How should he go about getting this help?

5. In what ways does Evans' lack of field-sales experience affect the chances of his contributing to creative solutions to field-sales problems? Consider both pluses and minuses in your answer.

Part III

6. How might the Briggs/Evans conflict be dealt with by making structural changes in the organization? What would be the effect of any changes in organization on (a) Briggs, (b) Evans, (c) Evans' peers, and (d) Evans' subordinates?

7. Why didn't Briggs' concerns about Evans surface when Evans occupied either of his two previous staff positions?

8. If Evans continues to "succeed" in developing more participative, team-building techniques with his peers and subordinates, how will Briggs' duties, authority, and accountability be affected?

Part IV

9. How does Evans' style of management affect the potential for his subordinates and peers to satisfy a fuller range of needs through work?

10. How does Evans' style of management affect Briggs' capacity to satisfy his higher-order needs through work?

11. How will the power and influence of the vice-president of marketing change if Evans is permitted to continue doing things his own way and sales continue to improve?

12. What would be the advantages and disadvantages to (a) Evans and (b) the company of shifting Evans to a job in personnel at this time?

13. If Evans is shifted to another division or leaves the company, what characteristics should Petersen press for in his replacement?

14. How do you explain Evans' success in changing the attitudes of his field subordinates to acceptance of his more participative style? Why has he not been as successful with Briggs?

15. *Summary Report Question for Part IV*. Assume that the president refuses to move Evans at this time and decides to shift Briggs' focus to the broader, longer-range, strategic aspects of his job as vice-president of marketing. Develop a detailed action plan for implementing this solution. Specify what steps Petersen should take and in what sequence, and give a rough timetable indicating when each step should be taken.

Part V

16. In what ways might Briggs measure and evaluate Evans so as to reduce his concern that Evans may get into serious difficulties?

17. Using your answer to question 16, what effect might this control system have on Evans (a) personally and (b) in terms of his effectiveness?

Summary Report Questions for Solution of Case as a Whole

18. Assume that Petersen has decided not to approve Briggs' request to transfer or remove Evans at this time (see question 15). Prepare to play the role of Petersen and illustrate, in a role-play, how this decision should be communicated to Briggs. Should Petersen seek compliance or commitment from Briggs on this decision?

19. If you were Petersen, what action would you take in the Briggs/Evans situation? Consider answers to questions 15 and 18 in particular, but do not feel constrained to follow these approaches. Be specific about what steps you would take and how you would evaluate the success of your plan. If your primary plan appeared unsuccessful, what would be your contingency plan?

Introduction

The Graham, Smith & Bendel organization is a highly respected management-consulting firm. Though not among the industry leaders in gross billings, GSB has a highly impressive list of past and present clients. For more than 30 years, under the direction of William Graham, GSB had been a profitable but conservative consulting firm.

> Our fees are a bit higher than our competitors' [Graham said], but our clients know we will not take on an assignment unless we have the expertise to do it right. We have been very cautious when adding staff, and we bring them along slowly until we and our clients are confident that they have proved themselves ready.

While their competitors were expanding rapidly during the 1960s, GSB refused to recruit inexperienced staff. They frequently turned down assignments rather than add "unproven" staff to do the work. As a result, the 1970s found GSB with a solid profit picture but with slow growth and a declining market share.

At the time of his retirement two years ago, eleven functions reported directly to Graham. Basic consulting services were grouped in five departments. Each was headed by a senior consultant, who reported to Graham. In addition, six service departments also reported to the president.

Before his retirement, Graham named Aaron Nettles as his replacement. Nettles, 59, has been with the firm for 27 years and was director of consulting projects, which deals with marketing issues.

Aaron Nettles, President

> Mr. Graham was a consultant's consultant [said Nettles]. He headed up a number of our key account projects even while running the business. His secret was his ability to find good people, groom them slowly, and then give them almost complete freedom to do their job. Once he felt you were ready, he told you explicitly what objectives he wanted met, listened, altered them if you made a good case, and then gave you autonomy. If you did well, you heard from him only once a year to congratulate you and update your goals. If you did poorly, he would call you in and ask how he could help. If you could tell him, he would provide what you asked for and possibly adjust your objectives. Normally, if you did not show marked improvement within a year, he let you go. He followed this practice with all of his subordinates and expected them to do the same with theirs. He was extremely tough but very fair. Although some very senior people were fired in this way, I never heard anyone blame Graham.
>
> With this highly decentralized style and his many talents, he probably could have had 50 people reporting to him.

Nettles went on to explain that, though he respected Graham, he was neither comfortable with Graham's style nor content with slow growth. Within six months, he acquired two smaller consulting firms. One, Executive Recruiting and Placement, was regarded as an ethical and effective management-search firm, which operated on a regional basis from Los Angeles. The second, Arista, Inc., was also a highly regarded firm that specialized in sophisticated research and engineering studies. With its headquarters in Cambridge, Massachusetts, and offices in Houston, Texas and San José, California, Arista had a growing reputation in high-technology industries. About three months ago, Nettles acquired Filer Associates, a New York-based market-research firm. Filer, highly regarded for the quality and integrity of its work, had become overextended and resisted laying off personnel during recent slow periods. As a result, it was close to bankruptcy when agreeing to join GSB.

Although all three acquisitions were made by exchange of stock, Nettles felt that the firm would have to accelerate its growth and generate more volume and profits. As he stated,

> We have an excellent reputation and great opportunities to grow. Mr. Graham built an outstanding group of people but never really tried to capitalize on what he built; his view was that our sales promotion should be as "professional" as that of a physician. I believe we must seek to make fuller use of the talents of our three new divisions, and we have to get more synergy out of our existing groups.

Reorganization

After the Filer acquisition three months ago, Nettles announced a major reorganization. Three long-service GSB consultants, Shamtun, Reldan, and Leon, were named vice-presidents and put in charge of groups that had hitherto reported directly to the president (see Exhibit I). In addition, several service activities were divided into smaller departments.

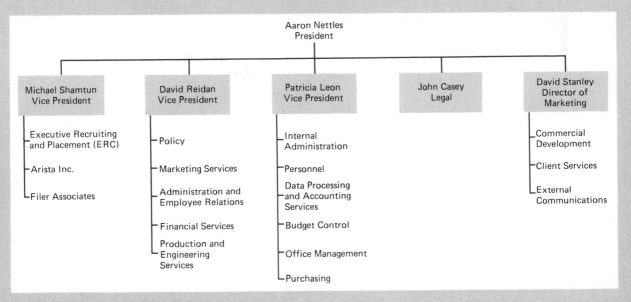

Exhibit I Partial organization chart.

I want to maintain our decentralized structure, but I also want more coordination among key departments and more time to devote personally to key accounts [Nettles explained]. When we get a project, it usually falls within the scope of one of our five consulting departments (policy, marketing, administration, finance, or production and engineering). It is assigned to a senior consultant from that area and he builds a project team. He may draw on people from other areas by checking with their department heads. This works pretty well, but with Reldan heading up all five groups, he can save me a lot of time overseeing the makeup of key project teams and balancing workloads.

I also expect Reldan to get more business from our current customers. Frequently, for example, while working on a financial project with a client, the potential for a marketing or personnel project will emerge. In the past, our people were virtually conditioned not to seek such a project for another group within our firm. Mr. Graham felt this was "solicitation" and not ethical. "If the client needs more work and feels we can handle it," he used to say, "then he will invite us to make a proposal." We have missed too many opportunities this way.

David Stanley, Director of Marketing

To assist Reldan and Shamtun in marketing GSB services, Nettles named David Stanley to the new position of director of marketing. Stanley is a relative newcomer at GSB, having been brought in less than two years ago by Nettles. Stanley, at 37, had been a professor of marketing at several leading business schools before accepting Nettles' offer to join GSB.

I had hoped Stanley would become head of our client-marketing group [Nettles said], but he had problems with some of our older consultants. They are slow to accept a newcomer and a few regarded him as too much of an academic. It was really unfair stereotyping on their part. I have watched Stanley and he will make a first-rate consultant. Dave Reldan didn't want him to head up his marketing group, though; so I put Stanley in charge of our firm's personal-marketing efforts. This is a new job and it will be up to Stanley to make it work.

Stanley has one man and one woman working for him who carry out commercial-development activities.

They do some missionary selling with prospective clients [Stanley said], but their main function is to work with our consultants and our acquisitions and to help them develop and sell proposals to existing clients.

Stanley also has a small client service and an external-communications department under him. But he considers his most important responsibility to be his post as chairman of the New Business Committee, which was created by Nettles at the time of the reorganization.

New-Business Committee

To foster greater exchange of ideas within the firm and to promote new business, Nettles has asked David Stanley to chair this committee. The head of each of the five consulting groups under David Reldan also serves on this committee. In addition, one representative from each of Shamtun's three divisions was designated by Shamtun. Since GSB's headquarters are in New York, of Shamtun's people only the representative from Filer attends the committee's fortnightly meetings. The representatives of Executive Recruiting and Arista are kept informed of committee work and are expected to attend three major meetings held in March, September, and December.

In addition to these, Patricia Leon, vice-president of internal administration, is also a member of this ten-person committee.

I wrote a memo to each member as soon as the committee was announced three months ago [Stanley explained]. In it I laid out two basic objectives and suggested some procedural guides. But I left things open until we met and sorted things out face to face.

The two basic objectives stated in the memo were:

1. To facilitate communication among organizational units with an eye to sharing successful techniques and helpful data.
2. To develop an integrated mission for business that will foster growth greater than the sum of what is possible in individual segments.

So far [Stanley observed], I am getting nowhere. Over the last three months, eleven meetings have been scheduled, but three were cancelled because key people were out of town on client business. Of the eight we held, only our last one included all ten members, and that was the biggest fiasco of all. I prepared a detailed agenda and asked each representative to be prepared to make a one-hour report on his department's plans and opportunities for synergy. They had all agreed to do their homework, and I blocked out two days to give us ample time to hear and criticize each unit's inputs.

I was optimistic that we would really develop the basis for a more integrated marketing approach because our earlier two meetings generated a lot of good discussion. These previous two meetings dealt strictly with exchange of techniques, and everyone there said they got a lot out of them. As soon as we shift from information to planning, however, they clam up.

I'll bet that half of the people from Reldan's group hadn't spent more than ten minutes preparing their presentations. It was particularly embarrassing because it was the first meeting the Arista and Executive Recruiting representatives attended; and they had both put a lot of time into their presentations, even if they were more descriptive than prescriptive.

I specifically asked Reldan to assign the heads of each of his five groups to this committee to get their commitment, and he went along. Perhaps they are just too busy and I ought to get them either to name an alternate or send their junior people to the fortnightly meetings. Then the top people would need come only to the three meetings attended by Arista and Executive Recruiting. Perhaps I could get more debate and honest exchange of ideas from their subordinates. Reldan's department heads virtually refuse to dig in and criticize one another's operations. Nettles is looking to me to generate a lot of new business from existing clients, and I know I can do it if these people would take off their department hats and try to think in terms of the whole organization. He promised to help when he gave me this job and I certainly need it. It's just that I'm not sure what to ask for. He is very busy and has a lot of confidence in me. I would hate to let him down.

Following the most recent committee meeting, Stanley asked his two subordinates (who constitute the commercial-development department) to develop a list of planning possibilities which, if approved by Nettles, would improve GSB's marketing efforts.

They each developed a number of ideas [Stanley said], and then we discussed them and added some more. It was a real brainstorming session. Though we eliminated the wildest ones, the following list of ideas still needs further pruning before going to Nettles for approval. (See Exhibit II.)

Exhibit II Market-Planning Possibilities

1. *Codification of Marketing Techniques* A manual listing the marketing techniques that had been presented and discussed at previous committee meetings. Make this a looseleaf manual to encourage additions.

2. *New-Business-Opportunity Reports* Require each project manager, before completing a major consulting project, to fill out a form (prepared by commercial development) listing and describing opportunities for additional consulting work. (No decision on whether Stanley or Nettles should determine who receives copies of this report and on who pursues each lead.)

3. *Client-Review Meetings* Require each project manager to meet monthly with Stanley, Reldan, and Shamtun to discuss potential for additional business.

4. *Market-Analysis Reports* Seek funds to develop a detailed market analysis for each of eight major industry categories.

5. *Assessment of Internal Capabilities* Develop a detailed report on GSB strengths and weaknesses relative to the five areas under Reldan's direction and the three subsidiaries under Shamtun's direction.

6. *Strategy Formulation Workshops* Get Nettles to hold several strategy-formulation workshops. Here, the top twelve to fifteen people in the firm would use the results of items 4 and 5 (above) to recommend overall GSB strategy and specific planning programs.

7. *Research and Publications Policy* Develop a policy that directs GSB consultants to seek opportunities, wherever possible, to contribute to business research and writing. These activities would be coordinated and evaluated by Stanley, though client clearance would remain with the project managers.

8. *International-Expansion Policy* Seek funds to have market analysis carried out with regard to expanding GSB activities overseas. (At present all GSB work overseas is based on U.S. contracts and coordinated in the U.S.) Stanley would be authorized to study and recommend programs for greater involvement in markets outside the U.S.

9. *Assessment Standards* Develop standards to use for evaluating how well each segment of the firm is meeting its market potential. These standards would be developed jointly by Reldan, Shamtun, and Stan-

ley, and would then be reviewed, modified (if necessary), and approved by Nettles and administered by Leon.

10. *Policy Clarification of Marketing Responsibilities* Request that Nettles carefully review the authority and accountability needed by Stanley to play a more active role in shaping policies and carrying out programs designed to generate new business.

> As I reread this list [Stanley said], it seems clear that we can't push for all of these. I don't want people thinking I am trying to build an empire. On the contrary, I would rather that most (if not all) of the things contained in these ten proposals were carried out by Reldan's and Shamtun's people. I just don't think they will do it, however. Too many of the things we should be doing are foreign to the firm's history. The only written policies we have were last reviewed twenty years ago and deal with ethics of client-firm relationship and expense-account procedures.

> Next week I will meet with my people again and try to trim this list of ten and assign priorities to the ones that remain. Then I will meet with Nettles and see just how far and how fast he is willing to move.

QUESTIONS

Part I

1. In what ways may changing environmental factors help Nettles reshape the strategy of the firm?

2. If the old strategy were not to be changed, how might sufficient growth be accomplished to ensure challenge?

Part II

3. Should Nettles attempt to develop a written master strategy for GSB at this time? If not, indicate your reasons and note when, if ever, he should do so. If you feel he should, indicate how he would go about developing and writing it.

4. If Nettles were to seek explicit profit goals from Reldan and Shamtun for each of their departments, how should he go about getting these goals set? Should he follow the same approach with each? If yes, why should they be the same? If no, how and why would they differ?

5. Consider your answer to question 4. If Nettles took your advice, how might his action help or hinder Stanley's tasks as director of marketing?

6. Which of Stanley's ten market-planning possibilities would result in standing plans? Indicate for each whether they are most nearly policies, standard methods, or standard operating procedures?

Part III

7. What are the pluses and minuses of the GSB departmental structure in terms of "harnessing" specialized efforts?

8. Assume that GSB decided to seek further growth by establishing small offices and offering the five major services now under Reldan's direction.

These offices would be located in Washington, Chicago, Los Angeles, Brussels, and Tokyo. (a) What changes in overall organization would you recommend? (b) Might the larger New York office be organized differently from the "branch" offices? Discuss.

9. How might a more complex structure, such as a matrix organization, fit GSB's current needs? How might it contribute to Nettles' growth objectives?

10. Based on Nettles' objectives, does Stanley seem to fit the specifications of the person who should occupy the director of marketing position?

Part IV

11. How might differences in customs and roles between the subsidiary divisions and Reldan's group be dealt with? Should differences be (a) maintained, (b) encouraged to increase, or (c) encouraged to decrease?

12. What forms of conflict may arise from each of the ten market-planning possibilities being considered by Stanley? In *each* case indicate whether such conflict is likely to be constructive or destructive.

13. Was the idea of a New-Business Committee a good one?

14. How, politically, might Stanley have acted to increase the success of his New-Business Committee?

15. For each of the ten market-planning possibilities, if approved by Nettles, forecast Reldan's likely response.

16. Based on your answers to question 15, for which of the ten would you seek compliance and for which commitment? Where the forecast response differs from the desired response, what energizing force should be applied, how, and by whom?

17. *Summary Report Question for Part IV.* Develop a list of means that might be most helpful to Stanley in motivating key personnel to assist in making necessary changes.

Part V

18. For each of the ten market-planning possibilities, indicate (a) which you consider standing plans and (b) how controls could be developed to ensure compliance. What standards would be set, and by whom? What measures would be taken, and by whom? How frequently would they be measured? How would the results be analyzed, and who would recommend corrective action?

19. Which of the controls discussed in answer to question 18 would be most likely to evoke negative response from Reldan?

Summary Report Question for Solution of Case as a Whole

20. Based on your analysis of this situation, what action would you take if you were in Stanley's position?

Basic Elements of Control

LEARNING OBJECTIVES

After completing this chapter, you should be able to

1. Understand why control is necessary in an organization.
2. Describe the three main types of controls and know when each is appropriate.
3. Identify the major stages in the control process.
4. Understand how symptoms, predictions, and sampling are used for purposes of management.
5. Identify who in an organization should receive control reports.
6. Describe how corrective action is carried out.

Controlling is the follow-through of managing. Planning, organizing, and leading—discussed in previous Parts of this book—set the stage and start the action. However, it is control that focuses on achievement of target results. Without control, productivity sags and targets are missed. In fact, the skillful use of control processes—discussed here in Part V—is essential for sustained success in today's competitive environment.

Controlling is the task of every manager—from the chief executive officer to the most humble supervisor. Since its elements are the same at all levels, we will first examine simple control problems and then, in later chapters, consider controlling more elusive outcomes such as progress toward strategic targets.

Managerial Control

The primary aim of controlling is to ensure that results of operations conform as closely as possible to established goals. A secondary aim is to provide timely information that may prompt the revision of goals. These aims are achieved by setting standards, comparing predicted and actual results against these standards, and taking corrective action.[1]

In practice, controlling is often poorly done; conflict arises about when to control and who should do it. One way to avoid part of this difficulty is to distinguish three different types of controls (Figure 18.1).

1. *Steering controls*. Results are predicted and corrective action taken before the total operation is completed. For example, flight control of the spacecraft aimed for the moon began with trajectory measurements immediately after take-off, and corrections were made days before the actual arrival.

2. *Yes/no controls*. Here, work may not proceed to the next step until it passes a screening test. Approval to continue is required. Examples are legal approval of contracts, quality checks on food, and test flights of aircraft.

3. *Postaction controls*. In this type of control, action is completed; then results are measured and compared with a standard. The typical budgetary control and school report card illustrate this approach.

All three types may be needed to control a department or major activity. But it is steering controls that offer the greatest opportunity for constructive effect. They provide a mechanism for remedial action while the actual results are still being shaped.

Yes/no controls are essentially safety devices. The consequences of a faulty parachute or spoiled food are so serious that we take extra precau-

---

[1]W. G. Ouchi and M. A. Maguire, "Organizational Control: Two Functions," *Administrative Science Quarterly*, 20, 1975, pp. 559–69.

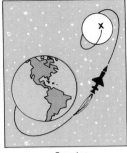

Postaction   Yes-No   Steering

Figure 18.1 Three basic types of control.

tions to make sure that the quality is up to specifications. Avoidable expense or poor allocation of resources can also be checked by yes/no controls. If we could be confident that our steering controls were effective, the yes/no controls would be unnecessary; unfortunately, steering controls may not be fully reliable, or may be too expensive, so yes/no controls are applied.

Postaction controls, by definition, seem to be applied too late to be very effective. The work is already completed before it is measured. Actually, such controls do serve two purposes. (1) If rewards (a medal, a bonus, discharge, self-esteem) based on actual results have been promised, these results must be measured and the appropriate rewards granted. The aim is psychological reinforcement of the incentive scheme. The payoff in this reinforcement lies in future behavior. (2) Postaction controls also provide planning data if similar work is undertaken in the future.

Phases in Controlling

Even though controls are placed at different stages of operations, as the preceding classification suggests, three phases are always present in each control cycle.

1. *Control standards that represent desired performance.* These standards may be tangible or intangible, vague or specific, but until everyone concerned understands what results are desired, control will create confusion.
2. *Measurement of predicted or actual results against the standards.* This evaluation must be reported to the people who can do something about it.
3. *Corrective action.* Control measurements and reports serve little purpose unless corrective action is taken.

Regardless of what is being controlled, these elements are always involved.

Expense control, from the use of electric lights to the total cost of goods; quality control, from the appearance of a typed letter to the dependability of an airplane engine; investment control, from the number of spare parts in a repairman's kit to the capital investment in a fleet of tankers—all involve standards, evaluation, and corrective action. A closer look at each of these phases will help us design controls for specific purposes.

The first step in setting control standards is to be clear about the results desired. What will be accepted as satisfactory performance? This question must be answered in terms of (1) the outcome characteristics that are important in a particular situation and (2) the level of achievement, or "par," for each characteristic.[2]

Characteristics that Determine Good Performance

Operating objectives, already discussed in Chapter 5, serve as starting points in setting control standards. Usually, however, these must be amplified. For instance, we noted in Chapter 5 that companies with separate business units have found that profits are an inadequate measure of success. In addition to profits, such companies often consider market position, productivity, leadership, personnel development, employee attitudes, and public responsibility. It is possible to focus on only one aspect, such as profits or market position. But to do so without first thinking through *all* characteristics that contribute to good performance is to court trouble.

A furniture store, to cite another example, found that it had to think about the following factors in appraising its credit department: the attitude of customers who had dealings with the department; the total credit extended; the operating profit earned on goods sold on credit; credit losses; department operating expenses; gross income from credit charges; net expense of running the department; and departmental cooperation with the treasurer, sales manager, and other company executives. It was decided that the credit manager had to perform well on all these counts if her work was to be rated as satisfactory.

Each time managers design a new control, they face this question of what characteristics to consider, as Figure 18.2 suggests. An approach that could benefit some jobs would be to give thought to these three matters.

1. *Output.* What services or functions must be performed? Perhaps each of these services can be defined in terms of quantity, quality, and time.
2. *Expense.* What direct dollar expenses are reasonable to secure such an output? What should be normal indirect expenses in terms of supervision, staff assistance, interference with the work of other people, and opportunities foregone to perform other kinds of work?
3. *Resources.* Does the operation require capital investment in inventories, equipment, or other assets?[3] Are scarce human resources or company reputation being committed? If so, effective use of resources should also be considered.

[2]K. A. Marchant, "The Control Function of Management," *Sloan Management Review,* Summer 1982.

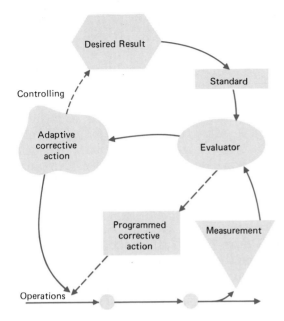

Figure 18.2 Control Cycle for Repetitive or Continuous Operations.

Par for Each Characteristic

Having identified the characteristics of good performance, we must then determine how high a level of achievement is desired for each characteristic. More precisely, what is a reasonable expectation, or par, for good performance? For example, pars for the credit department in the furniture store mentioned earlier might be as shown in Table 18.1.

Table 18.1 **PARS FOR A FURNITURE STORE CREDIT DEPARTMENT**

Characteristic	*Standard*
Attitude of customers	90 percent of furniture purchased on time, financed by the store
Total credit extended	Outstanding loans approximately equal to last 90 days' sales
Operating profit earned on goods sold on credit	$500,000
Credit losses	0.5 percent of credit extended ($7,000 in normal year)
Department operating expenses	$24,000 per year
Gross income from credit charges (above interest paid to bank)	$28,000 per year

[3]Although the cost of developing a well-trained corps of workers, a smooth-running organization, or a good reputation with outside groups does not appear on a company balance sheet, such assets do require investment in the same way that machinery does. Such investment is essential if future "output" is to be achieved within desired future "expenses."

For most performance characteristics, par is simply an ordinarily feasible achievement level. Variations beyond this level are usually desirable—such as output above par or expenses below par. But in special circumstances, such as the rate of production on an assembly line, there may be only narrow tolerance limits for deviation above or below the established par.

On highways, the speed limit is a single standard that is applicable to all drivers. Similarly, in business, a single standard may be applicable to such things as quality of delivery service. But for many other situations we may adjust the standard for a particular individual or local circumstance. A branch manager of a national sales organization who tried this individualized approach reports as follows:

> Don't compare an individual to the group average, but rather to a standard set for that person. I have tried this on quotas for growth and for new customers and during the current canvass the results are good. The salespeople are more quota-conscious than I have ever before known them to be. I find they will work much harder to make their own standards than they will to "beat the high person" or surpass crew average. Also, each one is much more aware of his own quota (through interest) and the total book standing than previously.

Securing flexibility through adjustment of par.   In control, as in other phases of management, we have a legitimate need for flexibility. A firm may increase inventories if there is reason to anticipate a shortage of raw materials; it may cut its price to meet competition, knowing that dollar sales figures will be thrown out of line; during a depression it may decide not to cut employment in proportion to the drop in production; and so forth.

Unfortunately, "flexibility" is sometimes used as an excuse to disregard control entirely. Because the standards are no longer reasonable, there is a temptation to say that control is not feasible. A more sensible way of dealing with unforeseen conditions is to adjust par. The performance characteristics being watched, the measurements, and the reports continue to be useful; we need to change only the levels of expectation. As we shall note in Chapter 19, this is precisely the result of "flexible" budgets, and this concept may be adapted to many other control standards.

Both automatic and semiautomatic adjustments of par are usually based on a variation of a key external variable (that is, external to the domain of the person being controlled), such as volume, price, or wage rates. The original pars are based on a set of *planning premises;* and when these premises shift through no fault of the controllee, some offsetting revision of pars is called for. In a broader scope, this kind of adjustment suggests that when control is used for personal evaluation, the key planning premises should be identified and then *their accuracy,* as well as the results of a person's efforts, observed.

Relating results to individual accountability. Control standards are most effective when they are related to the performance of a specific individual.[4] Thus both the person himself and his supervisors can know whether he should be praised or blamed. In addition, fixing accountability for a deviation helps focus the search for causes and thereby sharpens corrective action.

But accountability for a desired result is not always simply assigned. A company's investment in inventory, for example, is affected by purchases, rate of production, and sales. Each employee to whom one of these three activities is assigned looks on inventory from his own point of view, as does the treasurer, who is concerned with the financial strength of the company. In some companies, only one person, who has the task of coordinating these different viewpoints, is accountable for the level of inventories. In other companies, the task is divided. For instance, the sales manager estimates sales, the plant manager schedules production and indicates the quantities of raw materials she will need each month, and the purchasing agent decides when it will be advantageous to buy the materials specified by the plant manager. In such a situation, in which no one person is accountable for the level of inventories, standards may be set for each step. Then if there is trouble with inventories, the point at which the system broke down can be determined.

An alternative to dividing complex tasks into separate steps that can be assigned to single individuals is dual accountability. When cooperative effort is crucial and contributions of each person are hard to distinguish (as in a surveying crew and in many methods-improvement studies involving both line and staff personnel), we may say that each member is accountable for the team result. The control then keeps the focus on results, with strong emphasis on cooperation.

Clearly, the establishment of standards for control purposes is heavily dependent on the previous management decisions on plans and organization. Specifically, objectives (discussed in Chapter 5) are the direct counterpart of "desired results"—the starting point in a control cycle. Similarly, the assignment of duties (discussed in Chapters 9 and 10) is the key to the assignment of accountability for achieving control standards. Theoretically, setting objectives and defining job duties need not be reconsidered when control standards are set. But in practice this is rarely so. Workable control almost always calls for refining and clarifying objectives and duties. Without fail, though, we should start with the plans that have already been developed. Then the process of developing standards for purposes of control is really a matter of refinement.

Checking at pivotal points. "Desired results" have been urged as a good starting point for designing managerial controls.[5] We now turn to several refinements of this principle.

---

[4]G. P. Latham, L. L. Cummings, and T. R. Mitchell, "Behavioral Strategies to Improve Productivity," *Organizational Dynamics,* Winter 1981.

[5]E. C. Schleh, *How to Boost Your Return on Management* (New York: McGraw-Hill, 1984).

1. To attempt to evaluate all the results of everyone's work would be very burdensome. Instead, results are usually measured only at various intervals. For instance, a dairy farmer may measure his output only in terms of pounds of butterfat produced per week. Moreover, as we shall discuss in the section on evaluation, sometimes only samples of the output are measured. The aim is to watch enough to keep track of what is happening, without going to the expense of watching everything. That is, the aim is to pick *pivotal points* that will, at least indirectly, reflect the total operation. If results at these points are off standard, a more detailed check can be made of intermediate stages to find the reasons for the deviation.

   The president of an automobile-parts manufacturing company keeps his eye on four key items that reflect operations in the plant: total output, efficiency, back orders, and inventory. By watching the ratio of standard worker-hours to actual worker-hours every month, the president believes he can detect any major difficulties with equipment or with operating personnel, and so keep track of overall efficiency. The back orders indicate whether the plant is meeting sales requirements. The inventory figures show whether good deliveries and plant efficiency are being achieved by large accumulation. There are, of course, many other local controls, but the four points are what the president watches closely.

2. Steering control is used so that a move can be made before the final results have occurred. For this purpose, points which will serve as warning posts are sought. Here the aim is to *direct attention* rather than to evaluate. The Hilton Hotels, to cite an example, keep close tabs on advance bookings of conventions—one, two, or even three years ahead. With this warning of the ups and downs of business volume, they can undertake special promotions to fill in valleys. On a month-to-month basis, when it is too late to change booking volume, knowledge of advance bookings is used to expand or contract staff to fit the expected level of operations.

   In safety work, control is achieved largely through training in safety methods and through maintaining safe operating conditions. In other words, management locates pivotal control points in the formative stages, and inspections are made to try to prevent trouble from ever arising.

3. Yes/no controls allow screening devices to catch serious errors. Actual results to date are measured, and work is permitted to proceed only if the results are satisfactory. Such controls may be placed anywhere in the flow of work at which safety can be checked—the earlier the better.

In many companies, requests for capital expenditures for such things as new buildings, equipment, and sources of raw materials have to be presented in writing with an explanation of why each investment will be advantageous to the company. The request then passes a yes/no hurdle. By controlling approval of the projects at this formative stage, the president or financial officer can exercise an influence that would be futile after orders are placed and contracts let.

Checking on methods of work.   In the preceding discussion of control standards, we have emphasized the results of work rather than the method for accomplishing it. Even strategic control points at early stages are basically devices for anticipating results. This emphasis is consistent with our stress on objectives, in the earlier discussions of planning and decentralizing. Nevertheless, there are times when control over method is more expeditious than control over results.

Sometimes controls are set on work methods simply because it is more economical to watch the methods than the results. Diamond-cutting and quality control in the manufacture of spacecraft or parachutes are undertakings in which control will probably be exercised over methods as well as results.

Then there are baffling situations for which it is extremely difficult to know just how good results should be. Cancer research, or negotiating with a group that is protesting ecological abuses, are examples. In these situations the manager may resort to evaluating the method by which work was done.

Whenever control is undertaken, then—from the entire company down to the work of a single employee—the manager needs to consider what kinds of results and what level of par to incorporate into company standards. And since busy executives cannot give regular attention to a complete array of standards, they must identify pivotal points to watch: summaries of overall results, results of key activities, warnings of impending trouble, and—for some jobs—*methods* of work. One of the arts of good management is setting the right standards at the right control points.

THE TASK OF MEASURING

Once standards are set, the second basic step in control is the evaluation of performance. This step involves (1) measuring the work that is done, or predicting what will be done, in terms of the control standards, and (2) communicating the appraisal to persons who search for reasons for deviations and take corrective action. Broadly speaking, control measurements seek to answer the question, "How are we doing?"

Auditing is concerned with control, but not the type of managerial control we are discussing in this chapter. A manager focuses on achieving certain results. Financial auditing, on the other hand, is designed chiefly to ensure that no skullduggery has taken place. An auditor deals with the accuracy of financial reports—be they bearers of good tidings or bad—and especially with making sure that there has been no pilfering of cash or valuable inventory and no fraud or embezzlement.

The specific methods of measuring results are almost as diverse as the activities of business. Because at best we could give only a few suggestive examples here, it will be more useful to examine some of the common difficulties in measuring for control and to note several promising ways of dealing with these difficulties.

Need for Ingenuity

Engineers are far ahead of managers in their ability to measure what is going on. For one thing, managers have tended to rely on accounting far beyond its intended purpose and inherent capacity. To be sure, surveys of employee attitudes and morale, and Nielsen reports (which provide current data on the sale of goods in the grocery and drug fields by brand, region, and type of outlet) are steps in overcoming this deficiency. But great opportunity remains for improvement.

Actually, many companies have information they do not fully utilize.[6] An employment office may be able to provide a lead on labor costs long before these figures show up in accounting reports. A market-research department may be able to provide both control data and planning data. The information necessary for production scheduling can be used to measure productivity. Facts for use in control may be found in a variety of places.

Leadership in product design was set as a major control point for the engineering department of one electrical equipment company. Because product leadership is very difficult to measure, the company decided to try to summarize personal opinion systematically. Each year, a committee composed of the general manager, sales manager, chief engineer, and two outside experts try to agree on the following points:

1. The number of the company's significant "firsts" introduced each year versus competitors' "firsts."
2. A comparison of company products with competitors' products in terms of market requirements for performance, special features, attractiveness, and price.
3. The percentages of sales of products appraised to be superior to competition, equal to competition, or inferior to competition, together with corresponding market position and gross margin ratios of each category.
4. The percentage of company products in the total electrical equipment used in the plants of the twenty most efficient customers in the country.

In spite of the high degree of personal judgment involved in some of these criteria, this company has substantially better control over its prod-

---

[6]J. O'Shaughnessy, *Competitive Marketing* (Boston: George Allen & Unwin, 1984), Part III.

uct development than before it undertook such measurement; the design of managerial controls can benefit greatly from ingenuity.

Balancing Qualitative Versus Quantitative Results

Because measurement is often difficult, it is only natural to use any available figures. This is to be commended. There is the danger, however, that those characteristics of an operation that can be easily measured will receive far greater attention than their importance warrants.

An office-equipment manufacturer relied heavily on dollar-sales figures to control its ten regional sales representatives. As the sales manager was fond of saying, "The signed order tells who's on the ball." The representative in the Southern territory was an older man, and for two years before his retirement, he and the company had a clear understanding that he planned to settle down in Florida when he reached sixty-five. His sales held up reasonably well. But when he was replaced, it was discovered that he had neglected to cultivate new customers. He had called only on his old accounts, and even with them he had glossed over troublesome service problems and had failed to cultivate the younger people in the customers' organizations. Several years of hard work were required before the territory again produced the volume it should. This unsatisfactory condition developed because the firm relied only on the easy measurement of results. If other, more intangible factors had been watched, the deficiency in the representative's performance would have been noted before too much damage was done.

The danger that ease of measurement will dictate what gets attention is even more serious in operations in which quantitative results are hard to pin down. The public-relations department of a pharmaceutical company kept close track of the number of letters received as a result of the news releases it issued. "Letters received" became one of the department's few quantitative measures of performance, and public relations was soon issuing news releases written expressly for the purpose of creating a flow of mail. Unfortunately, although controversial subjects and hints that a remedy was being developed for a wide-spread malady did produce a lot of letters, publicity on these topics distorted the public image of reliability that the company wished to establish.

Expense control is often characterized by an imbalance between quantitative and qualitative considerations. Zealousness in controlling, say, travel or telephone expenses occasionally causes people to pay as much attention to these minor aspects as to the results of the work.

Using Symptoms for Control

Just as the smell of smoke is an indication of fire, or bloodshot eyes and a haggard look at examination time are an indication of cramming, so in business we may use symptoms as indications of what is going on.

Employee attitudes, for example, are hard to measure directly and economically. Consequently, several companies have used such criteria as turnover, the number of absences and tardinesses, the number and content of grievances, and the number of suggestions submitted in a formal suggestion system. Under normal conditions, such factors probably do reflect employee attitudes. But we must exercise care in using symptoms as measuring devices, because (1) outside factors may cause a symptom to vary, and (2) when it becomes known that a symptom is being used as a measure, it may be possible to manipulate the measuring stick—for instance, tardiness in one office may be low because the office manager is a tyrant and not because employee attitudes are good.

Using Predictions in Control

In steering controls, predictions are often used as a basis for corrective action, as Figure 18.3 shows. As with the use of symptoms, actual results are not measured. But here the reason for using less-reliable criteria is a desire for prompt action. Customer inquiries may be used to predict a rise or fall in sales; a machine's vibration may be used to predict a breakdown; or grievances may be used to predict a strike. The prediction in such a case initiates corrective action; the manager doesn't wait for the predicted event to occur.

One of the large can companies has a control procedure that encourages corrective action based on predictions. A monthly profit-and-loss budget is prepared for each operating division and plant. Then, ten days before the start of the month, the various managers are asked to estimate how close they will come to the budget. Each prepares a revised estimate

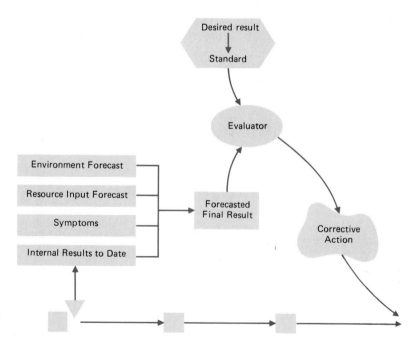

Figure 18.3 Steering control is based on predicted results.

about ten days after the beginning of the month. A major advantage of preparing these two estimates lies in forcing the manager to predict what is likely to happen and to adjust operations to current conditions. Because local demand for vegetable cans varies with the weather, short-run expansion or contraction of operations—and of expenses—is important. Top executives compare the performance of each division and branch against the original budget, but they give more emphasis to their managers' ability to predict results accurately and take prompt corrective action.

Sampling

A familiar way of simplifying the measurement task is to consider only a sample, which is presumably typical of the whole. For example, the quality of most food products, from kippered herring to corn meal, is tested by sampling. And students are well aware that an examination is only a sample of what they know, just as office workers realize that in his periodic visits, their supervisor samples their behavior.

Sampling is better suited to some activities than others. If a machine set to perform a particular operation turns out good-quality products both when the run is started and at the end, we can usually assume that the intervening production has also been satisfactory in quality. In a check of routine sales correspondence, if a random sample indicates that letter-writers are using good judgment and diplomacy, a supervisor will probably assume that all the work is satisfactory. On the other hand, a 100-percent check is desirable for some operations. A manufacturer of hearing aids, for instance, may sample at the early stages of production, but will undoubtedly insist on a careful inspection of every finished product for performance before it is shipped.

Broadly speaking, to determine what portion of an operation should be measured, we try to balance the cost of incremental measurements against the increased value that might accrue from catching more errors. "Statistical quality control" is a special application of this general idea. When products are produced in large quantities, statistical probabilities can be used to determine when the number of errors is large enough to warrant stopping production and finding the cause. Substantial economies in inspection costs may result in situations in which this technique applies. However, the vast majority of managerial control situations do not involve the large number of similar actions that are needed for this refined statistical technique.

Personal Observations and Conferences

Even with all the measurements that have been suggested in the preceding paragraphs, a supervising executive still needs to hold informal discussions with the persons whose work is being controlled; and, at least occasionally, she should visit the actual operations. Anyone who has corresponded over a period of time with another person whom he knows only by letter, and then has an opportunity to meet and talk with him, knows that there are certain impressions that can be conveyed only in face-to-face contact, personal observation, and conversation.

More importantly, personal observation has a flexibility that permits an executive to keep his eye on what is "hot" at the moment. Ability to make prompt delivery to customers may be crucial at one moment and the number of executives worthy of promotion at another. When a person is new in a job, a supervising executive will want to watch her work more closely than he would that of an experienced operator. Even if these factors could be incorporated into a formalized, continuing flow of information, to do so would probably be undesirable because of the cost and the added burden.

Discussions in other parts of this book dealing with organization, planning, and leading present compelling reasons for close personal contact between executives and those who work with them. To those reasons we should now add this: effective measurement of results.

CONTROL REPORTS

Measurement of performance is of little value until the resulting appraisals are communicated to executives who can take corrective action.

The smaller the operating unit, the simpler the control reports need to be. In fact, in a small company or within a small unit, a supervising executive often evaluates results herself, and the only report is an oral discussion with the person doing the work that is being evaluated. A great many controls, perhaps the most effective ones, have this informal character. The basic steps of control are present—setting standards, evaluating results, taking corrective action—but the formal recording of results and of comparisons with standards is simple and rudimentary. Few people are involved and the facts are known to everyone, so the control deals primarily with initiating corrective action.

As more people are involved, the task of reporting and evaluation becomes more important. People work in different places, they are concerned with different parts of a total task, and there are more detailed facts than any one person can keep in mind. A need arises, therefore, for control reports that summarize and communicate the conclusions of the measurements that have been undertaken.[7]

Who Should Receive Control Reports?

Control information should be sent immediately to the person whose work is being controlled. He is the one most likely to be able to do something about it. Of course, the information should not go to a machine operator or a clerk who is merely carrying out specific instructions. Rather, it should

---

[7]A. L. Patz and A. J. Rowe, *Management Control and Decision Systems* (New York: John Wiley, 1977).

go to the purchasing agent who decides how much to buy, to the supervisor who decides when overtime work is necessary, to the sales representative who may be able to secure additional orders for slow-moving products, or to the foreign manager who might decide to withdraw from a market. In other words, information should reach the person who, by his own actions, can have a strong influence on final results.

Prompt feedback to the point of action encourages use of the "law of the situation," one of the means for obtaining voluntary cooperation discussed in Chapter 13. In most instances, the person on the firing line will start corrective action as soon as she knows that results are falling short of the established norm, as Figure 18.4 suggests.

In addition, control information should flow, perhaps as a summary at a later date, to the controllee's boss. The person on the firing line may need help or she may need prodding; it is the duty of the supervisor to see that she gets either or both, as the situation warrants.

These elementary observations about the flow of control reports are meant to emphasize that action resulting from control measurements should be taken by the people who have primary responsibility for an activity being measured. Only in rare circumstances is it desirable to separate the action, or dynamic, phase of control from the duties of the one who initiates and supervises performance of the activity. But other people are often interested in these reports, to be sure: (1) executives who will use the control information to help formulate new plans, and (2) staff personnel who are expected to be familiar with, and give advice about, the particular activity under control. These people should be provided with such reports if they find them helpful. But their claim is secondary to those of operators and immediate supervisors.

Figure 18.4 Alternative flows of control reports.

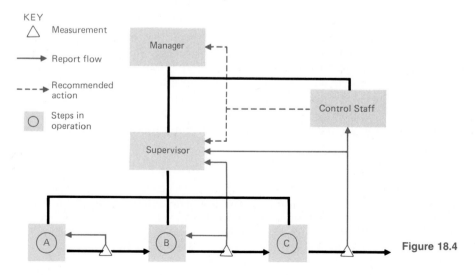

Figure 18.4

Timeliness Versus Accuracy

Promptness is a great virtue in control reports. If some job is being mishandled, the sooner it is reported and corrected, the less damage will be done. Moreover, if the cause of a difficulty is not obvious, a prompt investigation is more likely to turn up true causes.

The distinction between postaction controls for overall evaluation and steering or yes/no controls affects the importance of promptness. Timeliness is especially urgent with the latter group, because they lose most of their potency if they are tardy.

Unfortunately, it is often difficult to be both prompt and accurate. An accurate evaluation may require a certain amount of investigation and double-checking. The person making an evaluation naturally wants to be sure he can justify his conclusions, especially if they draw attention to inadequacies in someone's work. In addition, delay is likely to be compounded if a report is prepared by someone who is trained to balance accounts to the last penny. A hospital administrator, for example, was having great difficulty keeping down expenses, partly because expense reports—laboriously compiled at the end of each month—did not become available until six to eight weeks following the events presumably being controlled.

Executives who use control reports should be fully aware of the kind of information they are getting. If they insist on prompt reports, they must learn to disregard insignificant variations and to expect some false alarms. On the other hand, if they are interested in having the full facts and being deliberate in taking action, then they need a different kind of report.

Form and Content of Reports

Most control reports can be kept simple and present only key comparisons.[8] They are not intended to present a full analysis; furthermore, the people using them are intimately familiar with the operations they reflect. These reports are not designed to impress the public; they are valuable if they give the operating people the facts they need quickly and understandably.

In addition to showing a comparison of performance against standard, control reports often reveal whether a situation is getting better or worse. They do so by comparing present performance with that in the recent past and with that during the same period a year ago. Such "trend" information is a helpful guide to a manager in deciding what kind of corrective action is appropriate.

---

[8]Computerization of management information systems does not alter this guideline. Detailed control information need not accompany the summary report. Instead, the detail will be stored in the memory bank and retrieved on request. For a comprehensive discussion of such systems, see D. R. Moscato, *Building Financial Decision-Making Models* (New York: AMACOM, 1980).

Control reports call attention to deviations of performance from plans, but they only signal trouble. The pay-off comes when corrective action is taken. The control information should lead to investigating difficulties, promptly deciding how to overcome them, and then adjusting operations.

Sometimes a control report will start a new management cycle: new planning and organizing, more active leadership, and another set of measurements and reports. But often, the original objectives and program are retained, and managers simply make minor adjustments at one point and push a little harder at another. These adjustments may be necessary anywhere along the line—needling a supplier; pinch-hitting for Joe Jones, who is ill; running Department A overtime; and so on. In such situations, a manager is like a captain who gets information on the location and bearing of his ship, and then adjusts his course in order to arrive at his planned destination.

The distinction between replanning and corrective adjustments is not sharp. For convenience, we speak of "corrective action" if plans and the final result remain the same. If an appraisal indicates that major changes in plans or goals are in order, then the manager should replan. In both kinds of action, data from measuring is fed back to executives, who modify their operation.

Finding Reasons for Deviation

That actual operations do not always turn out just as planned is not surprising when we think back over the planning process described in Part II. To proceed with planning, the manager must often adopt predictions as premises—predictions of sales, competitive prices, availability of capital, research results, productivity of new machines, and a host of other things. Such premises are the best estimate at the time, although it is recognized they may not be accurate. Also, many plans involve a calculated risk; there may be, say, about one chance in five that an assumed event will not occur.

So, when control measurements indicate that all is not well, it is necessary to investigate many possible causes to discover the one that is creating the difficulty. Perhaps some person is at fault, but it is likelier that one of the manager's premises is wrong or that he has unluckily run into the one chance that he hoped could be avoided. At this stage, he is more interested in identifying the cause than the culprit, so that necessary adjustments in operations can be made promptly.

Moreover, the control measurements themselves may lead him astray. He may deliberately watch symptoms or estimates for early warnings of trouble—sales inquiries or employee absences, for instance. But symptoms can be misleading. A similar situation is possible if the "exception principle" is used—that is, if watch is kept only for exceptionally high or low performance. An exception may flag serious trouble, or it may be a unique instance that probably will not recur.

In some highly routinized operations, a manager can act like a servomechanism on a machine, automatically making a given adjustment when certain conditions are detected. Automatic pilots on airplanes and thermostats on furnaces work this way. But most managerial situations are not so simple; it is necessary to identify which of many possible causes is creating difficulty and then devise appropriate corrective action.

Corrective Adjustments

Once a difficulty is spotted, as a result of an investigation prompted by an unfavorable control report, the manager must move quickly to corrective adjustments. If the operating situation has shifted from what was planned—perhaps raw materials are delayed by a dock strike or the computer breaks down—he will take steps to get the working conditions back to normal. If subordinates are ineffective, he will clarify directions to them, provide additional training where necessary, consider motivational lacks, and perhaps reassign work. Or, if it is not within his power to overcome the difficulties—say, customers simply will not buy the company's product—he must then recast goals and programs. From a managerial point of view, a control is not effective until such corrective action as may be necessary has been undertaken. Figure 18.5 shows key elements of such a system.

Figure 18.5 DIFFERENCES IN DESIGN OF THREE BASIC TYPES OF CONTROL

	Elements in the Design of Three Basic Types of Control		
Design Elements	*Steering Controls*	*Yes/No Controls*	*Postaction Controls*
Define desired results	√	√	√
Look for predictors of results	√	–	–
Select composite feedbacks	√	–	–
Set par for each predictor and desired result	√	√	√
Specify information flow	√	√	√
Evaluate	√	sometimes	√
Take corrective action	√	sometimes	–

Controlling, like many other aspects of management, is simple in its basic elements but calls for ingenuity and deftness in its application. Setting control standards at pivotal points, sampling and measuring qualitative results, balancing timeliness and accuracy in reports, translating reports into corrective action—all are examples of the many issues that must be skillfully resolved for a control system to be potent.

Distinguishing between steering, yes/no, and postaction controls assists greatly in control design. The selection of pivotal control points, the use of predictions before work is completed, the balance of promptness versus accuracy in reporting, and the nature of corrective action are all affected by a choice among these control types.

Although this chapter has explored a range of issues that managers should consider in the controlling phase of their work, other vital factors remain to be considered. Financial control techniques will be illustrated in the following chapter. Next, we will review the responses of people to controls, and finally, the integration of controls to other areas of management. These further considerations are important in making control an integral and consistent part of the total management structure and behavior.

Impact on Productivity

Control should be the watchdog on productivity. It tells us whether we are reaching our productivity targets and, more useful in week-to-week operations, it helps guide our current activities in ways that make those targets attainable.

As already stressed, productivity is achieved by supplying desired goods or services efficiently. And every business firm, large or small, develops plans about the particular goods or services it will supply and plans for producing that output efficiently. The role of control is to ensure that all these noble productivity intentions are carried out.

Because many distractions and obstacles are likely in our troubled world, and because one may be tempted to do merely what is convenient at the moment, a persistent reminder of productivity goals is needed. A vigilant monitoring system keeps us on track and up to speed. Without an array of supportive controls, such as those sketched in this chapter, productivity will decline instead of rise.

FOR FURTHER DISCUSSION

1. In what ways do you think high-speed computers will affect the elements of control? Where are they likely to be most helpful? Where least? Are computers affecting controls to which you are subject?

2. How are detailed objectives and standing plans likely to affect the type and effectiveness of controls?

3. In a college course, is postaction control, such as

a final grade, an adequate control? What else, if anything, do you recommend? Should yes/no controls be used?

4. How would you apply a complete control cycle to an intangible objective such as customer goodwill or employee morale?

5. In most foreign countries, the Pepsi-Cola Company grants a franchise to a local bottling and distributing firm. The franchised firm must use Pepsi's secret extract shipped from the United States. All other activities are performed by local nationals. The American company provides advice on production and distribution and permits use of the well-known Pepsi-Cola trademark. The company in the United States is naturally concerned about both short- and long-run profits in the foreign countries and about the worldwide reputation of Pepsi-Cola. What controls should the company establish over the activities of a franchise dealer in a foreign country?

6. A major shift is occurring in the United States from blue-collar jobs to white-collar jobs. This reflects both the automation of heavy physical work and the increasing relative importance of service industries. How, if at all, is this shift likely to affect human problems in managerial control?

7. Are detailed controls likely to be more important (1) when an organization is following a strategy to obtain growth and profit in a new market for a new product or (2) when following a strategy of maintaining profits and market share for an established product in mature markets?

8. Especially since the tragic leak of toxic fumes in Bhopal, India, Union Carbide Company has been concerned about environmental safety around its chemical plants. What type of control—steering, yes/no, postaction—should Union Carbide focus on to reduce the danger of injuring people living close to its plants?

FOR FURTHER READING

Anthony, R. N., et al., *Management Control Systems,* 5th ed. Homewood, Ill.: Richard D. Irwin, 1984. Text and cases examining quantitative and management aspects of the control process.

Flamholtz, E., "Organizational Control Systems as a Managerial Tool," *California Management Review,* XXII, No. 2 (Winter 1979), pp. 50–59. Discusses criteria for judging the effectiveness of a control system.

Marchant, K. A., "The Control Function of Management," *Sloan Management Review,* Summer 1982. Good approach to deciding what controls a company needs.

Newman, W. H., *Constructive Control: Design and Use of Control Systems.* Englewood Cliffs, N.J.: Prentice-Hall, 1975. Comprehensive analysis of managerial control, including—in addition to topics in this Part—chapters on control of repetitive operations, projects and programs, resources, creative activities, and strategy; and a chapter on balancing the total control structure.

Newman, W.H., *Managerial Control.* Chicago: Science Research Associates, 1984. Condensed version of preceding book, with short cases and other aids for self-study.

Richards, M. D., *Readings in Management,* 7th ed. Cincinnati: South-Western Publishing Co., 1986, Section C. Convenient source of a selection of pioneering articles on control.

Yavitz, B. and W. H. Newman, *Strategy in Action.* New York: The Free Press, 1982, Ch. 12. Suggests ways to control the dynamic aspects of strategic management, such as external monitoring and milestone reviews.

MANAGEMENT IN ACTION CASE 18
"Racy" Jones

For "Racy" Jones, attendance at State University will be possible only with financial help. The University is 160 miles from Racy's home, so there will be living expenses as well as other costs. Racy's father died one year ago, and two younger brothers eat up most of the meager income their mother can provide. Fortunately, Uncle Kirby offers to help—if Racy is really serious about professional education.

Racy's Scholastic Aptitude Test scores are quite good—much more impressive, in fact, than his high school grades. Racy's attention has vacillated between track (the source of his nickname), music, love, and parental reform—with book learning coming in big gulps just before tests. The overall record, however, is good enough to secure admission to State University next fall.

"My father's death made me take another look at what I want to do," says Racy. "Running around the track is fun for me, but it's no way to earn a living. So, at State University I guess I'll have to major in Business Administration, with only a minor in Physical Education. Besides, that fits in with Uncle Kirby's talk of 'facing life's responsibilities,' and he's going to pay most of the bills the first year."

Uncle Kirby, a minister of the Gospel, has a church 200 miles from State University. He has young children of his own, and helping Racy will put an unexpected strain on his family finances. Consequently, Uncle Kirby is loath to see his money "wasted."

What little Uncle Kirby knows about Racy's behavior to date does not inspire complete confidence. Instead, he wants assurance that his money is being well spent.

Question

Assume that Uncle Kirby has asked you for advice on the kinds of controls he should establish on Racy's activities at State University. What do you recommend to Uncle Kirby?

APPLICATION CASES

For practice in applying concepts covered in this chapter to managerial situations, see the following managerial decision cases. The case questions particularly relevant to this chapter are listed by number after each case name.

19

Budgetary Control Techniques

LEARNING OBJECTIVES

After completing this chapter, you should be able to

1. Express in dollars the anticipated results of future plans.
2. Understand the link between strategy and budgetary support to achieve that strategy.
3. Realize that there are both benefits and potentially limiting dangers in budgetary control.
4. See the link between budgetary control and the improvement of organizational efficiency and productivity.

ELEMENTS OF BUDGETARY CONTROL

Financial budgeting is a widely used control technique that aids in planning and in coordination as well. By discussing budgetary control techniques here in Part V, we underscore the interdependence between planning and control.[1]

Basically, financial budgeting involves these three steps.

1. *Expressing in dollars the results of plans anticipated in a future period.* These dollar figures are typically set up in the same way as the accounts in a company's accounting system. The budget shows how the accounts should look if present plans are carried out.

2. *Coordinating these estimates into a well-balanced program.* The figures for sales, production, advertising, and other divisions must be matched to be sure that they are mutually consistent; the financial feasibility of all plans added together must be ensured; and the combined results must be examined in terms of overall objectives. Some adjustments will probably be necessary to obtain such a balanced program.

3. *Comparing actual results with the program estimates that emerge from step 2.* Any significant differences point to the need for corrective action. In short, the budget becomes a standard for appraising operating results.

These steps will be illustrated first in an extended example of a small company. Then we shall discuss the implications of the budgeting concept for larger firms and for special situations. Finally, we shall look into ways of securing flexibility and also into some of the dangers and limitations of budgetary control. Our aim is to see how financial budgeting fits into the management processes; we are not concerned here with the details of budgetary procedure.

BUDGETING IN A NEW ENTERPRISE

Examining budgets for a new, small company enables us to see readily how operating plans can be translated into financial figures and how budgets provide an opportunity for overall coordination. For this purpose, we shall use Belafonte Fashions as an illustration.

General Plans of Belafonte Fashions, Inc.

After working as a stock boy, presser, and, more recently, foreman in several apparel plants, Paul Bailey went into business for himself. He had an

---

[1]Other management techniques also serve a dual planning/controlling function. For instance, PERT, which was discussed as a planning tool in Chapter 7, is also a control device.

opportunity to buy all the equipment of a defunct ski-suit plant and to take over a lease on the space it occupied. The $90,000 price was attractive, especially since the equipment was already installed and experienced labor was available in the area. Bailey, a black himself, had a strong desire to establish an all-black enterprise in a depressed area on the Near-West side of Chicago. His new venture was made possible by an investment by High Horizons, a private urban-renewal corporation. High Horizons matched Bailey's capital contribution of $67,500, arranged for an equipment mortgage with a bank, and made a temporary working-capital loan of $50,000. Because Bailey had little background in finance and accounting, High Horizons stipulated that he use the "MBA Consultants" from Midwestern University for help in this area; Morris Barkin is the student assigned to this client.

Bailey's strategy was to concentrate on a limited line of women's pants, which are relatively simple to manufacture and use the existing skills of the work force. Purchased fabric of polyester and cotton or wool is cut, sewn, and pressed; permanent-press finishing is subcontracted to a nearby company. Bailey started in business in the autumn, a season when the demand for pants is brisk, and by the end of the year he had a going concern. The balance sheet at that time is shown in Table 19.1.

Morris Barkin, after a careful industry survey, urged Bailey to prepare a profit-and-loss budget for his new company. At the beginning of the new year, Bailey had the following plans in mind:

1. The company would first establish itself by making four fairly standard pants at low cost. With this operation as a base, more highly styled and novelty items could be added later to provide wider profit margins. But to attempt to operate a business on novelty items alone was too risky.

Table 19.1 BELAFONTE FASHIONS, INC. BALANCE SHEET—JANUARY 1

Assets			Liabilities		
Cash		$ 18,700	Accounts payable	$ 48,000	
Accounts receivable		75,200	Accrued taxes, etc.	1,300	
			Current liabilities		49,300
Raw material	$45,900				
Finished goods	37,600		Mortgage on equipment		35,600
Inventories		83,500			
Total current assets		177,400	Loan from High Horizons		50,000
			Total liabilities		134,900
Equipment	90,000				
Less depreciation	3,300	86,700	Equity Common stock	$135,000	
			Loss for first 3 months	−5,800	129,200
Total assets		$264,100	Total liabilities & equity		$264,100

2. The four types of pants Bailey had in mind usually sold to retailers at an average price of $102 per dozen. Even with allowances and markdowns, Bailey hoped his average selling price would be at least $94 per dozen.

3. Selling would be done through manufacturers' agents, one in New York, covering the territory east of the Mississippi, except for Illinois and Wisconsin, and one in Chicago, covering the remainder of the United States. In the plant, Bailey figured, he needed an experienced cutter and a sewing foreman, each of whom would be paid $500 a week. He expected to take care of designing, buying, marketing, and general administrative work himself. However, he had hired someone to act as bookkeeper and general office assistant at $22,000 per year. All other employees were to be paid on an hourly or piece-rate basis. While the business was getting on its feet, Bailey planned to pay himself only $1,600 per month.

4. Experience during the fall had indicated that fabric, zippers, and other materials would cost about $48 per dozen finished pants. Provided the work was well planned, direct labor amounted to $22.50 per dozen.

5. Every apparel company is torn between being able to make prompt deliveries and avoiding a large obsolete inventory. Bailey sought to meet this problem (1) by keeping well stocked with fabric (each month he would purchase the fabric needed for producing the pants he expected to sell during the next 30 to 60 days) and (2) by restricting his stock of finished goods to expected shipments during the following two weeks. This plan was intended to permit him to adapt the sizes and styles of pants being produced to the orders being received (assuming the right kinds of fabric were on hand).

Profit-and-Loss Budget for the Year

After talking with his sales agents, Bailey estimated he could sell 10,000 dozen pants during his first full year of operations. In fact, the New York agent talked of large sales to chain-store buyers, but this would have involved making price concessions and maintaining a large inventory that Bailey wanted to avoid at this time.

By translating his plans and estimates into dollar values, Bailey and Barkin came up with an estimated profit-and-loss statement, which is shown in Table 19.2. The young proprietor was pleased about two features of this budget: it indicated that he should be able to earn a modest profit, and it showed that a large part of total expenses could be adjusted downward if sales volume did not develop. Thus, through close control of "variable expenses" he should be able to avoid large losses, even if sales were smaller than anticipated. He now saw more clearly the financial results he might expect, and he had a standard to guide him while attempting to achieve these results.

Table 19.2 BELAFONTE FASHIONS, INC. PROFIT-AND-LOSS BUDGET FOR THE YEAR

Net Sales (10,000 dozen @ $94)	$940,000
Expenses:	
Materials ($48 per dozen)	480,000
Labor ($22.50 per dozen)	225,000
Plant supervisors' salaries	58,000
Repairs	16,000
Heat, light, janitor	16,000
Rent	18,000
Depreciation	13,200
Office salaries	41,160
Travel expenses	4,500
Office miscellaneous	2.700
Sales commissions (2.5%)	23,500
Shipping (1.0%)	9,400
Interest and financing charges	14,452
Total expenses	921,912
Operating profit	18,088
Income tax	2,038
Net profit	$ 16,050

Monthly Cash Budget

Morris Barkin was dubious. He did not challenge the annual-profit budget, but he was worried that the company might go bankrupt before the end of the year. He pointed out (1) that wide seasonal fluctuations in sales would cause temporary demands for larger inventory and accounts receivable; (2) that High Horizons hoped to get back $22,500 of its loan by the middle of the year; and (3) that the company might have to make additional investments in equipment. An examination of this last point revealed that Bailey was using his personal car for company business and that a company car ($9,000) would be needed before the end of the year. Additionally, a different kind of fabric was needed for the autumn lines, and this would require the purchase of second-hand sewing machines for a total of $10,750.

Faced with these facts, Bailey and Barkin undertook to prepare a monthly budget of cash receipts and disbursements. For this purpose Bailey assumed that customers would pay for merchandise within thirty days after shipment and that he would pay for his purchases within a similar period. But it was more difficult to estimate how his annual sales volume would be distributed by months throughout the year. Industry figures supplied by the local sales agent indicated that the distribution would probably be as shown in Table 19.3.

With the data he already had and with his inventory policy, Bailey was now able to budget his monthly flow of cash. This analysis indicated that he might just squeeze by the March sales peak and that cash would accumulate rapidly in April and May, as he collected from customers and

Table 19.3 **BELAFONTE FASHIONS, INC.: ESTIMATED MONTHLY SALES**

Month	Sales (dozens)	Month	Sales (dozens)
January	800	July	400
February	800	August	500
March	1,100	September	1,200
April	900	October	1,300
May	600	November	1,200
June	400	December	800

reduced his inventories. May and June, then, appeared to be the best time to buy the new equipment and reduce the loan to High Horizons.

Serious trouble would arise in August and September, however, as inventories and accounts receivable would rise to an autumn peak. Without financial aid, Belafonte Fashions could not possibly meet its budgeted annual sales.

The crucial assistance was found in a finance company. An agreement was made for Belafonte Fashions to borrow whatever it needed up to 80 percent of its accounts receivable. The accounts were pledged as collateral, and special records and collection procedures were established. For its services, the finance company would be paid both a flat annual fee of $1,600 to set up the arrangement and also interest on any money borrowed, at the rate of 16 percent per annum. With this assistance, the estimates indicated, Paul Bailey would be able to weather the financial crisis forecast for the autumn.

The budget that reflects all these plans is shown in Table 19.4. Note that the preparation of this budget required some adjustment in financial plans in order to arrive at a feasible balanced program.

Comparison of Actual Results with the Budget

During the first six months of the year, the operating results of Belafonte Fashions were surprisingly close to the budget. Sales during March, April, and May were 400 dozen below the budget, but the comfortable accumulation of cash tended to obscure the influence of this drop. More serious trouble arose in November and December when business failed to meet expectations. Mild weather in the fall left retailers well stocked with the type of pants Belafonte made, so reorders did not come in as anticipated. This in turn left Bailey with a high inventory of raw materials; also, Bailey could not pay off the finance company in December because of inadequate receipts. Price-cutting was necessary in order to move the finished stock, and even with this action sales were 800 dozen below the budget forecast for the last two months. The final profit-and-loss figures for the year compared with the budget are shown in Table 19.5.

A first glance at actual results compared with the budget indicates that virtually all the unsatisfactory showing can be ascribed to the drop in

Table 19.4 BELAFONTE FASHIONS, INC: BUDGET OF MONTHLY RECEIPTS AND DISBURSEMENTS

	Jan.	Feb.	Mar.	Apr.	May	June	July	Aug.	Sept.	Oct.	Nov.	Dec.
Sales (dollars)	75,200	75,200	103,400	84,600	56,400	37,600	37,600	47,000	112,800	122,200	112,800	75,200
Sales (dozens)	800	800	1,100	900	600	400	400	500	1,200	1,300	1,200	800
Goods produced (dozens)	800	950	1,000	750	500	400	450	850	1,250	1,250	1,000	800
Cash received from sales	75,200	75,200	75,200	103,400	84,600	56,400	37,600	37,600	47,000	112,800	122,200	112,800
Disbursements:												
Materials	38,400	38,400	45,600	48,000	36,000	24,000	19,200	21,600	40,800	60,000	60,000	48,000
Direct labor	18,000	21,375	22,500	16,875	11,250	9,000	10,125	19,125	28,125	28,125	22,500	18,000
Plant supervision / Repairs / Heat, light, janitor / Rent	9,000	9,000	9,000	9,000	9,000	9,000	9,000	9,000	9,000	9,000	9,000	9,000
Depreciation	0	0	0	0	0	0	0	0	0	0	0	0
Office salaries / Travel expenses / Office miscellaneous	4,030	4,030	4,030	4,030	4,030	4,030	4,030	4,030	4,030	4,030	4,030	4,030
Sales commissions / Shipping	2,632	2,632	3,619	2,961	1,974	1,316	1,316	1,645	3,948	4,277	3,948	2,632
Interest & finance charges	0	0	3063	0	0	3063	0	1,600	2,163	0	800	3,763
Disbursements for operations	72,062	75,437	87,812	80,866	62,254	50,409	43,671	57,000	88,066	105,432	100,278	85,425
Cash gain or loss from operations	3,138	–237	–12,612	22,534	22,346	5,991	–6,071	–19,400	–41,066	7,368	21,922	27,375
Loans received or paid						–22,500		20,000	40,000		–20,000	–40,000
Investment in equipment				–9,000	–9,000	–10,750						
Cash balance at end of month	21,848	21,611	8,999	31,533	44,879	17,620	11,549	12,149	11,083	18,451	20,373	7,748

Table 19.5 **BELAFONTE FASHIONS, INC. COMPARISON OF ACTUAL PROFIT-AND-LOSS WITH BUDGET FOR YEAR**

	Budget	Actual	Difference
Net Sales	$940,000	$817,520	$ − 122,480
Expenses:			
Materials	480,000	418,400	− 61,600
Labor	225,000	206,800	− 18,200
Plant supervisors' salaries	58,000	58,000	0
Repairs	16,000	13,320	− 2,680
Heat, light, janitor	16,000	16,930	930
Rent	18,000	18,000	0
Depreciation	13,200	13,720	520
Office salaries	41,160	41,160	0
Travel expenses	4,500	5,700	1,200
Office miscellaneous	2,700	3,110	410
Sales commissions	23,500	20,438	− 3,062
Shipping	9,400	8,260	− 1,140
Interest and financing charges	14,452	14,452	0
Total expenses	921,912	838,290	− 83,622
Operating profit or loss	18,088	− 20,770	− 38,858
Income tax	2,038	0	− 2,038
Net profit or loss	$ 16,050	$ − 20,770	$ − 36,820

sales. This is somewhat misleading. Price-cutting to an average of $92.90 explains almost $10,000 lost in revenue even on the 8,800-dozen volume. In addition, direct-labor cost was $1 per dozen higher than the budget, which points to an inefficiency here; the total labor cost went down, but not as much as it should have. Fortunately, material costs dropped even more than might be expected from the shrinkage in volume. Variations in other expenses were minor: sales commissions and shipping naturally went down, and tighter control of other expenses would have made only a minor difference in the final outcome. In short, this comparison points directly to sales volume, price, and direct labor costs as the areas where improvement must be made if the company is to become profitable.

The revised budgets that proved suitable for the first year of operation of Belafonte Fashions provide a simple example of the three basic steps in budgeting. Plans were translated into accounting results, plans were adjusted where the combined picture proved to be unworkable, and the resulting budgets served as a useful standard in highlighting places that need corrective action. For Paul Bailey, planning became more comprehensive and rigorous, and postaction control became a reality. Clearly, budgets need not be elaborate to be a useful management tool.[2]

[2]R. M. Powell, *Budgeting Control Procedures for Institutions* (Notre Dame, Ind.: University of Notre Dame Press, 1980).

Company size does not affect the essentials of budgeting, but it does influence the complexity of the budgetary system. As a company grows, several things are likely to happen to the budgeting process.

1. Separate budgets are prepared for each department or division of the company. Because each operating unit is somewhat independent, standards to measure its particular performance are needed. Moreover, detailed budget information is often helpful for control within the division. In a large company there may be literally hundreds of subsidiary budgets dealing with the sales, expenses, or other appropriate items of many different operating centers.

2. Communication of "planning premises" is important if these numerous subsidiary budgets are to be prepared consistently. Each person who prepares or interprets a budget needs to know what assumptions to make about, for instance, wage increases during the budgeting period. The plant manager is dependent on the sales department for information on volume of activity. Are prices and the availability of raw materials going to change? How soon will a new product be ready for the market? Such matters will affect the budgets of several departments. Therefore, someone must provide a forecast that can be used consistently in all subsidiary budgets.

3. Coordinating the many subsidiary budgets into a balanced program becomes complicated. A big company tends to have a large number of specialized units, and a good deal of effort is needed to synchronize their activities. Even in highly decentralized companies, the total activities of the business units, as reflected in their budgets, must not exceed the company's resources. Moreover, all business-unit and service division budgets should be reconciled with their respective strategies and with corporate strategy. Only a balanced program that supports strategy will be in the best interest of the corporation as a whole.

4. A special unit that concentrates only on budgeting may be desirable. Such a unit can help design the budgetary emphases and procedures that are best adapted to the particular needs of its company. A budgeting unit may provide routine clerical services in processing figures and in compiling and circulating reports; perhaps it will also make substantive analyses of both proposed budgets and actual experience, with recommendations for action. This staff unit, however, should neither prepare the budgets nor try to enforce them; budgeting is a tool for operating executives to use and not a device for usurping their duties.[3]

---

[3]J. Bacon, *Managing the Budget Function* (New York: National Industrial Conference Board, 1970).

Securing Flexibility

A budget is a prediction. Using the language of accounting, it tells how the financial accounts should look at some future date. Like any prediction, it is subject to error because of unanticipated events. Strikes may occur, competitors may introduce a new product, prices may skyrocket, or some other *unmanageable* influence may prevent the prediction from coming true.

A budget is also used as a standard in the control process. Insofar as the budget is in error, because of these unmanageable influences, it loses its validity as a standard. A district sales manager, for example, cannot be held accountable for a drop in sales if a truckers' strike prevents delivery of merchandise to his customers. Obviously, there must be some means of adjusting budgets if they are to be used as standards of performance.[4]

Variable Budgets

One way of introducing flexibility into budget standards is to compute in advance any adjustments for shifts in volume of work. If a plant superintendent is asked to step up output above the budgeted figure, her material and labor costs will also probably be over the budget. The question is, how much increase in expenses is justified? We need a revised par to serve as a control standard.

Variable budgets are a device for computing such expense standards for any volume of work within a broad range. The underlying approach is simple. A budgeted expense is set for both a high volume and a low volume, and a plan is prepared for interpolating between these figures. Then, at the end of the budget period, when the actual volume is known, it is possible to compute the appropriate expense for this particular volume. The variable budget approach is illustrated in Table 19.6 and Figure 19.1. The figures developed either in the table or the chart may be used to set a standard for labor costs in the housekeeping department of the hotel at occupancy rates varying from 200 to 500 guest-days. A similar analysis could be made for all the expenses of the hotel, and by adding these elements the manager could obtain a budget standard for the entire operation or any of its subdivisions for the actual level of occupancy for any day or week.

This brief explanation of variable budgets suggests their limitations as well as their benefits. They deal only with changes in volume; no adjustment is made for other unmanageable variables. Adjusting costs at a steady rate, as the straight line on the graph implies, may be unrealistic; hotel maids, for example, may have to be hired by the week rather than by the fraction of an hour. And costs may not vary in a straight line outside of the initial volume range. Of course, more elaborate cost curves can be used, but they would complicate the calculations. Finally, the flexibility

---

[4]A more comprehensive discussion of these techniques for securing flexibility is contained in G. Shillinglaw, *Managerial Cost Accounting,* 5th ed. (Homewood, Ill., Richard D. Irwin, 1982).

Table 19.6 THE VARIABLE BUDGET APPROACH

	Low Volume		High Volume
Guest-days	200		500
Labor costs	$620		$980
Increase in labor costs		$360	
Average increase per guest-day			
($360 ÷ 300)		$1.20	
Variable portion of total:			
($1.20 × 200)	$240		
($1.20 × 500)			$600
Fixed portion of total:			
($620 − $240)	$380		
($980 − $600)			$380
Budgeted cost if volume is 275 guest-days:			
$380 + ($1.20 × 275) = $710			
Budgeted cost if volume is 437 guest-days:			
$380 + ($1.20 × 437) = $904.40			

achieved to improve control makes the budget less useful as a planning and coordinating device. The purchasing agent, for example, cannot wait until the end of the period to find out how much raw material will be needed. This means that variable budgets will probably be an addition to, not a replacement for, the traditional single-volume budget.

Standard Costs

Variable budgets are hard to apply when *different* products are handled. Making three television transmitters, for instance, costs General Electric a lot more than making a dozen radar receiving sets. For such situations, there is no simple measure of volume. Standard costs are one way to deal with this difficulty.

   In a standard cost system, budgeted costs—for materials, labor, and so on—are computed per unit for *each* different product. Then, at the end

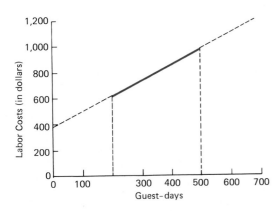

Figure 19.1 Variable budget for labor costs in housekeeping department of a hotel

of a given period, the number of units of products A, B, C, and so forth, that were processed are multiplied by their respective costs. By adding these figures, the manager can get a total for materials, a total for labor, and a total for overhead that all together reflect the specific product mix for this period. Such totals become control standards that can be used to evaluate performance for that period.

Unfortunately, this flexibility for a product mix carries with it some weaknesses. Most seriously, the cost per unit is assumed to be the same no matter what volume of work is processed. This assumption is not valid, especially for overhead costs. Consequently, when using control standards based on standard costs, we must still make some allowance for the level of activity. And standards lose their potency when we have to make a variety of subjective allowances about their reasonableness.

But standard costs do have additional accounting conveniences, quite aside from control, that contribute to their continuing popularity.

Periodic Budget Revisions

Although variable budgets and standard costs do provide flexibility in some situations, by far the most common type of adjustment is periodic revision of the normal budget. A common practice is to prepare a budget for twelve months in advance, but to revise it for a particular month just before the beginning of that month. In this revision, we can adjust for volume, price, wage rates, or *any* other factor. Presumably, this modified budget is a realistic statement of results that can and should be achieved.

One large container company distinguishes between its "budget," which gives monthly figures for a year ahead, and "revised estimates." The budget, once adopted, is not changed, but an estimate for month X is made up ten days before the beginning of the month, and a revised estimate is made ten days after the beginning of the month. The manager of each operating division plays a leading part in preparing these estimates. Obviously, the performance of any good executive should come close to the revised estimate. The principal advantage the company finds in this system is that it puts incentive with the executives to adjust their plans to fit current conditions (for example, the effect of weather on demand for vegetable cans) and to cut expenses when volume drops. The pressure develops when there is still time to make adjustments in actual operations. The effectiveness of this system, then, depends fully as much on the way standards are set and on an executive's anticipation of being measured as it does on the evaluation after a period closes.

Budget revisions must be held within bounds, of course. Confusion arises if changes are made too often. (Just recall how college students react if course schedules are modified even twice during a year.) One of the chief advantages of a regular, specified time for budget revisions is that people learn to expect modifications then. Desirable adjustments are "saved up" for the relatively few revision sessions, and changes do get made, yet people are not unduly upset by these changes in plans and control standards.

The budgets we have discussed thus far are concerned mainly with managerial actions that produce observable results within a given accounting period—a month, a quarter, or at most a year. Other managerial actions are taken that are not expected to yield results for two years, five years, and often longer. Such actions pose special control problems; appropriation budgets help meet this need. These budgets cover expenditures for items such as

1. land, building, and equipment;
2. research for new products and new processes;
3. institutional advertising;
4. human resources development;
5. new-market development.

Expenditures of the type just listed deserve management attention for several reasons. When wisely made, they are often crucial to the long-run success of the company. But on these items management has a wider latitude of discretion—it can expand, contract, or even discontinue them—than it has for most current expenses, which must be met in order for the company to continue operations.[5]

Typically, all large requests for new buildings and equipment are submitted once a year to top management, which examines the justifications for each project, compares prospective yields, considers the relation of each to company strategy, matches the total requests against available financial resources, and finally makes an overall appropriation. This appropriation, which usually includes an allowance for small and emergency requests, becomes the approved budget for the year. A similar procedure is often followed for research and advertising appropriations. Budgets for development expenses, however, are apt to be less formally established.[6]

A great deal of work is devoted to preparing these appropriation budgets, and in large companies we find elaborate procedures for review and approval—especially for new equipment and buildings. In essence, these procedures provide yes/no control to proceed with—or hold back on—proposed expenditures *before* any money is spent or contracts signed.

Usually, purchasing or hiring commitments are not permitted unless they are covered by an appropriation. But note that this provides a one-

[5]For a classic case study of how capital allocation in large corporations takes place, see J. L. Bower, *Managing the Resource Allocation Process* (Boston: Harvard Graduate School of Business Administration, 1970).

[6]M. F. Van Breda, "Integrating Capital and Operating Budgets," *Sloan Management Review,* Winter 1984; N. Piercy, and M. Thomas, "Corporate Planning: Budgeting and Integration," *Journal of General Management,* Winter 1984.

sided check. It does not even attempt to measure the results—which is the original purpose of making the investment.

Unfortunately, a useful check on the results of long-term investment is extremely difficult to devise. The period from initial decision to fruition is long—extending far beyond the time when corrective action during the formative stages would be possible. During this long interval, many other events occur, making a clear chain of cause and effect difficult to establish. Such efforts as we can make to match an appropriation with specific results are more for "learning-from-experience" than for control. (One company does check results of capital expenditures two years after installation, however, "just so operating executives won't forecast all sorts of benefits they can't deliver.")

Nevertheless, appropriation budgets have some clear benefits. (1) They keep disbursements for the purposes they cover within known limits. (2) They provide an opportunity for key executives to review and compare alternative uses of limited funds. (3) They enable executives to tie major investments to strategy. (4) They provide important information for cash budgets and permit coordination of investment and financing plans.

BENEFITS AND DANGERS OF BUDGETARY CONTROL

Budgeting is no panacea. We need to understand its strengths and weaknesses so that we may fit it into the total control structure of a company or subdivision.

Unique Advantages

First, the greatest strength of budgeting is probably its use of a single common denominator—dollars—for many diverse actions and things. Television advertising, tons of coal, and liability insurance can all be reflected in a budget of dollar cost and dollar result. Dollar language has its limitations, as we shall see, but it does lend itself to summaries and comparisons. The dollar, more than any other measuring device in business, government, or even military and church administration, can be applied to a wide range of work; and financial budgets capitalize on this unique feature of a monetary unit.

Second, budgeting uses records and systems already in existence. We must keep elaborate accounting records for tax returns, financial reporting, and internal management. In budgeting we utilize this system, rather than a new set of records. Figures on past experience are likely to be already prepared. Some new accounts or reports may have to be added, but the basic information system is available and easy to use.

Finally, budgeting deals *directly* with one of the central objectives of a business enterprise—making a profit. What shows up in budgets is what affects recorded profit or loss. Thus the relevance of items being controlled by a budget can be easily traced to the profit objective.

Stimulus to Good Management Practices

Budgeting often makes its greatest contribution as a stimulus to other good management practices. These are practices an executive might wisely use without budgets, but the adoption of budgetary control may bring them to life. For instance, here are several critical management requirements, with suggestions of how budgeting can help vitalize them.

1. Formal organization should be clear. An understanding of who is assigned to make each type of plan should be a prerequisite to the translation of such plans into budget form. Similarly, accountability for execution has to be clear if comparisons of actual performance with a budget are to have their full impact.
2. Financial accounts must be set up for each department or other unit of administration. When expenses, investments, and income are readily traceable to specific managers, they are more easily controlled. Such correspondence between accounts and departments is especially important in both the preparation and the evaluation phases of budgeting.
3. Planning must be done well in advance and should be highly specific. Without such plans, a budget for the year ahead would be little more than a guess. Precision in planning, in turn, calls for clarifying objectives and for coordinating the plans of interrelated departments.
4. Once annual budgets are well established, tentative budgets for three to five years become feasible. Experience with budgeting is also very useful in what some companies call "profit planning"—setting targets for profits and related matters and then working back through financial accounts to determine the actions that will be necessary to achieve these targets.[7]
5. When line managers use budgets as a key management tool, they provide at least an opportunity for clear directing and constructive counseling. Because budget figures are objective and tangible, everyone can avoid misunderstandings and all parties can focus on improving results.

When we dream about a "turkey dinner with all the fixins," it is hard to tell whether the turkey itself or what goes with it is the more attractive. And so with budgeting. Budgets are useful as a financial control, but when they are accompanied by other elements of good management, they can be an even more cogent force.

---

[7]G. A. Welsch, *Budgeting: Profit Planning and Control*, 4th ed. (Englewood Cliffs, N.J.: Prentice-Hall, 1976).

The most serious risk in using budgets is an *unbalanced emphasis* on factors that happen to be the easiest to observe.[8] For example, the operating expenses of the engineering or human resources department stand out clearly in budget reports, and the supervising executives are under pressure to keep expenses within prescribed limits. But the services such departments perform are of even greater importance. Inadequate service, unfortunately, is reflected only indirectly in the profit-and-loss figures—perhaps in costs or in low sales—and is difficult to trace back to the service division. In terms of budget controls, a service department can look good by keeping expenses in line even though it performs its major mission poorly.

At the same time, a budget emphasizes the orders received by the sales department and low cost in the production department. Executives of these departments make a good budget showing by demanding more, rather than less, help from related operating and service divisions. Consequently, a budget tends to create *internal conflict* and pressures. Intangible results may not be measured at all, or they may not be properly associated with the units that produce them.

A related danger of budgetary control is that a manager may *treat symptoms* as though they were basic problems. He may become involved in a numbers game rather than probe the reality that lies behind the numbers. If total office salaries look high, for example, a manager may withhold merit increases and fill vacancies with low-salaried, inexperienced help. This remedy may make a bad situation worse. Perhaps the salary figure is a symptom of poor office organization, and a realignment of jobs is what is really needed.

To cite another example, high material costs do not necessarily mean that the supervisor in the processing department is ineffective. Such costs may be a symptom of any of the following weaknesses: unnecessarily rigid specifications, competition for limited supply of raw stock, inept purchasing, inadequate inspection of materials put into the production process, poor process engineering, or old or poorly maintained equipment. A financial budget cannot and should not be expected to reveal the real cause of difficulty. A related danger is that three-year or five-year budgeting will be *substituted for strategic planning*. Budgets and strategy differ. Strategy is more selective, probing, and innovative. Budgets should buttress strategy, but they are too detailed and finance-focused to serve the leading role of strategy.

A budget system opens the way for *dictatorial* action. The terse, objective figures of a budget make it easy for an executive to say, "Cut that expense by 30 percent." If the executive is pressed for time or does not

[8]B. Yavitz and W. H. Newman, *Strategy in Action,* Chapter 11, "Resource Allocation: Power of the Purse Strings" (New York: The Free Press, 1982).

know what else to do, he may order a change in the budget without thinking through its ramifications.[9]

Finally, there is the danger that a company will go through the *form* of budgetary control *without the substance*. All too often some staff person in the controller's office merely predicts what the accounts will look like several months in the future, with little or no actual planning by operating managers. In other instances, budgets are prepared routinely and mechanically, with no thought given to how operations might be improved. Later the managers simply make excuses if performance compares unfavorably with the budget. In such circumstances, budgeting is a nuisance rather than an aid to management; it simply adds paper work and red tape to an already complex task. Budgetary control can be helpful only if key executives incorporate it as a dynamic part of their way of managing.

CONCLUSION

One striking aspect of budgetary control is the need for careful planning before the control feature can be effective. In fact, the pressure to refine and clarify plans when setting up budgetary controls may be a major contribution in itself. Also, although budgetary controls do not ensure corrective action at early stages, they do permit prompt identification of trouble. Both aspects provide us with a framework for making adjustments that recognize the ramifications of the actions taken.

In this review of budgeting, we have made only passing reference to the way people respond to controls. Actually, the effects of budgetary controls depend heavily on getting executives and operators to accept and use the data provided, as the next chapter will show in detail.

Impact on Productivity

Budgets are widely used to help managers control the *efficiency* aspects of productivity. They provide the standards, the financial pars, for expense control at many levels, from company-wide accounts to single-office outlays for labor or specific materials. Budgets are also a convenient device for allocating capital among departments, and for monitoring the use of funds in inventories, accounts receivable, and the like. Moreover, financial ratios such as return-on-investment and inventory turnover tersely summarize several elements of productivity.

Budgetary control is less powerful in guiding company effort into *new forms of service*. Although budgets may include allocations for expansion of some activities and set targets for quantitative results in new markets, budgets are permissive rather than leading for the dynamic aspects of productivity. At best, budgetary control reflects a new strategy; the initiative of new thrusts normally precedes the preparation of budgets.

[9]V. Madsen and T. Polesie, *Human Factors in Budgeting* (London: Pitman, 1981).

Indeed, the serious danger is that tight budgetary control will obstruct managerial efforts to move a company or department in creative directions. The outputs of product development, market research, and personnel upgrading, for instance, are too intangible to appear in financial results; the costs show up much sooner in budget accounts. Consequently, from a budgetary control viewpoint, productivity appears to be dropping. Then, the pressure to make the clear, short-run efficiency numbers look better squeezes out the necessary preparation for adapting to new consumer desires.

The crucial skill in using budgetary control to gain productivity is to retain attention on efficiency, but at the same time provide the resources necessary to tool up to serve the changing needs of society.

FOR FURTHER DISCUSSION

1. Budgets are commonly used as postaction controls. What are the advantages and disadvantages of using them for yes/no controls? Can they be used as steering controls?

2. (a) Many items of income and expense are affected by inflation—which managers cannot control. How can budgets and comparisons of actual results versus budgets appropriately recognize inflation? (b) Foreign exchange rates are also volatile. What provision, if any, should companies with foreign operations make in their budgets and reports for changes in exchange rates?

3. Many companies prepare a twelve-month budget in December for the following year, and then the budget for the next month is revised each month on the basis of more up-to-date estimates. At the end of the year, for comparing actual expenses and income to the budget, which set of budget figures for any one month should be used—the figures prepared the previous December for the entire year or the revised monthly budgets? Support your answer.

4. Management by Objectives (MBO) is a planning device that tailors short-run objectives to specific individuals and provides for frequent readjustment of these objectives. How can MBO be reconciled with annual budgets?

5. "The key to measuring progress toward accomplishing long-range strategies is the use of short-term budgets." Comment on this statement by the controller of a steel company.

6. If a company has a formal five-year plan, would it be wise to have detailed budgetary controls developed for all five years? Consider pros and cons in your answer.

7. "The greater the decentralization in a company, the greater the need for detailed budgetary controls at the corporate level." Discuss.

8. (a) Do you recommend that annual bonuses paid to managers be based primarily on how the actual performance of their respective departments compares with their budgets? (b) What are the implications of granting bonuses based on such budgetary control; for instance, will budgeted amounts be higher or lower? Will managers be more or less committed to achieving their budgets? Will managers cooperate with each other more actively in achieving overall company objectives?

FOR FURTHER READING

Camillus, J. C. and J. H. Grant, "Operational Planning: The Integration of Programming and Budgeting," *Academy of Management Review,* July 1980. The usual three-phase cycle of strategic planning, long-range programming, and budgeting often creates problems. Merging programming and budgeting into one integrated activity should increase both flexibility and control.

Jones, R. L. and H. G. Trentin, *Budgeting: Key to Planning and Control,* revised ed. New York: AMACOM, 1980. Describes the budgeting process from a managerial viewpoint.

Madsen, V. and T. Polesie, *Human Factors in*

Budgeting. Marshfield, Mass.: Pitman Publishing Co., 1981. Explores behavioral responses to budgeting.

Shillinglaw, G., *Managerial Cost Accounting,* 5th ed. Homewood, Ill.: Richard D. Irwin, 1982. Thorough explanation of budgeting, standard costs, responsibility accounting, and reporting systems; emphasis is on managerial use of data.

Sweeny, H. W. and R. Rachlin, eds., *Handbook of*

Budgeting: Systems and Controls for Financial Management. New York: Ronald Press/John Wiley, 1981. Chapters on everything a financial manager needs to know about budgeting.

Yavitz, B. and W. H. Newman, *Strategy in Action.* New York: The Free Press, 1982, Chapter 11. Explores difficulties of getting strategic goals incorporated into budgetary decisions regarding both capital outlays and operating expenses.

MANAGEMENT IN ACTION CASE 19
Matching Money and Strategy

Organizations are constantly adapting to changes in their external environment, but sometimes their budgeting procedures don't keep pace. Take the case of the Metropolis Bank.*

The bank could see the major opportunities in the era of high technology, which afforded opportunities to serve customers across the country, and even in many places overseas, through electronics. Consequently, the bank made it a strategic priority to penetrate much deeper into the consumer area through the use of computers and electronic telecommunications.

While this deliberate commitment was made explicit in policy statements, strategic plans, business plans, and all sorts of conversations all over the bank, it faced a wall of tradition when it came time to commit the financial resources to pay for the multimillion-dollar system.

At Metropolis Bank, budgeting was done on a business-group-by-business-group basis. And because this new electronic system would be used mostly by individual consumers, it fell to the bank's Consumer Division to make the financial commitment—even though the strategic decision had been made by the higher-level Executive Committee and approved by the bank's board of directors.

In that budget-making session, senior consumer bankers argued that they couldn't cut back operating costs in their various businesses. They couldn't cut enough, they said, even to dedicate a relatively small $30 million to the project from a $500 million overall group budget.

The result was that a final budget was proposed allocating only $10 million for the new electronic project, which meant that the strategic decision made by the bank's top executives was not being given the budgetary support necessary to make the program succeed.

The message is simple: If you want a strategic program to work, you'd

*Disguised name.

better be willing to pay for it. And when that strategic program involves something new and controversial—as it did at the bank—it pays for senior executives to follow up to make sure the appropriate funds have been set aside.

That's exactly what happened at Metropolis Bank. When the Executive Committee saw the proposed Consumer Division budget agreed upon by senior executives of that department, they sent back the budget for revisions, ordering that the full $30 million be allocated for the computer-electronics banking system.

Question

Why do you think that the managers of the bank's Consumer Division allocated only $10 million of their capital budget to the new computer-electronics project? What impact is the Executive Committee's allocation of $30 million likely to have on the computer-electronics project, and on other activities of the division?

APPLICATION CASES

For practice in applying concepts covered in this chapter to managerial situations, see the following managerial decision cases. The case questions particularly relevant to this chapter are listed by number after each case name.

Heartland Union Bank (HUB) (p. 183) 17
Dayton Metal Works (p. 198) 15
Clifford Nelson (p. 308) 22
Unisa Sound (p. 530) 12

20

Behavioral Responses to Controls

LEARNING OBJECTIVES

After completing this chapter, you should be able to

1. Understand the importance of employees' acceptance of controls.
2. Realize the importance of setting tough but attainable standards, or pars.
3. Recognize the importance of feedback within the behavioral control system.
4. Contrast the likely responses to steering, yes/no, and postaction controls.

A fire siren never put out a fire. Nor has an on-line computer printout secured a new customer. Only when some person responds to the signal or takes action in anticipation of it does a managerial control become effective. An adjustment in behavior is crucial.

In the two preceding chapters, we have considered controls primarily from an engineering, or mechanistic, point of view. Control standards derived from company strategy and operating objectives, control points selected in light of technology and administrative organization, financial budgeting made attractive by the existence of an accounting system—these are valid considerations, but they are not enough. The payoff comes only when somebody—manager or operator—does his work better because the controls are in operation.

In fact, responses to controls may ill serve the purpose for which they were designed. The controls may be mistrusted and disregarded, with significant negative side effects. This chapter explores ways to create positive responses to controls—and ways to minimize the negative reactions. Although people's feelings about controls vary widely, we do have some data on typical responses; behavioral scientists have described controlled behavior, and executives have reported on an even wider range of experience.[1] Our aim here is to translate these findings into guides that can be used in designing and operating a control system.

Each element in a control cycle can provoke either constructive or negative responses. The standards set, the reliability of measurements and reports, and the manner of corrective action all affect the eagerness or resistance of the people affected by the controls. So in addition to the rational, mission-focused aspects of control design discussed in the preceding chapters, we must incorporate behavioral dimensions, as Figure 20.1 suggests.

MEANINGFUL AND ACCEPTED CONTROLS

Meaningful Controls

A desirable end result from the viewpoint of a central manager may be regarded as vague and inapplicable by an operating supervisor. The operating vice-president of a large textile firm, for example, is deeply concerned that each company mill keeps its production costs in line with the quarterly budget; for her the financial budget provides the natural criterion for cost control. However, the mill supervisors, who are in the best position to change costs, regard budgets as a nuisance. Most of them realize the competitive necessity of keeping costs down, but in their eyes budgets merely absorb time that they could better devote to actually doing something about costs. The supervisors think—and act—in terms of machine loading, output per worker-hour, spoilage or material usage, ma-

[1]G. P. Latham, L. L. Cummings, and T. R. Mitchell, "Behavioral Strategies to Improve Productivity," *Organizational Dynamics*, Winter 1981, pp. 4–23.

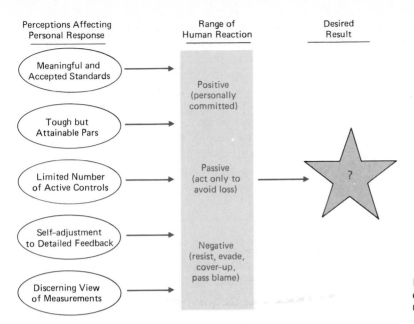

Perceptions Affecting Personal Response

Range of Human Reaction

Desired Result

- Meaningful and Accepted Standards
- Tough but Attainable Pars
- Limited Number of Active Controls
- Self-adjustment to Detailed Feedback
- Discerning View of Measurements

Positive (personally committed)

Passive (act only to avoid loss)

Negative (resist, evade, cover-up, pass blame)

Figure 20.1 Critical aspects of controls that affect employee responses.

chine maintenance to avoid stoppages, and indirect labor on the mill payroll. They know what happens to these factors long before budget reports are received, and explaining budget variances is merely a chore imposed upon them by "the pencil pushers in the office." Therefore, controls that have a constructive impact on the mill supervisors must provide prompt data on operating factors.

"Client satisfaction," to cite another example, is a poor control criterion for the printing shop superintendent of a public-relations firm. This person has unique talent for producing beautiful brochures, announcements, and reports, but takes no part in deciding what message is important or what media are most suitable. The finest creations may or may not satisfy clients. Instead of the broader goal of client satisfaction, relevant control criteria for the printing superintendent are unique and attractive publications, on-time production, and reasonable costs.

A control criterion is meaningful to a person (1) when it is expressed in operational terms—that is, in terms of actions and results within his sphere of activities; (2) when he can significantly affect the outcome being considered; and (3) especially when the outcome is clearly measurable.[2]

Accepted Controls

To spark a constructive response, a control criterion must also be *accepted* as reflecting a valuable part of the job. Psychologically, the person being influenced should feel that measuring his results in this respect is normal and legitimate.

[2]E. Flamholtz, "Organizational Control Systems as a Managerial Tool," *California Management Review*, XXII, No. 2 (Winter 1979), pp. 50–59.

Controls may be accepted for a variety of reasons. The person accepting them feels that they are relevant to his job, they are the way the game is scored, they are worthy, they represent "professional" conduct, they bring punishment or reward. Whatever its origin and reinforcement, psychological acceptance is a prerequisite for the success of any control. Without acceptance, the control is sure to be resented; evasion, manipulation of reports, and buck-passing then become normal responses.

Acceptance is often passive. The person being controlled recognizes the objective as part of his responsibility, but beyond that he is indifferent to the outcome. The typical taxi driver, for example, conscientiously takes her passenger to the stated destination without the slightest concern with why the trip is being made. Many of us, as was pointed out in Part IV, have wide "zones of acceptance" with respect to parts of our work.

Although passive acceptance permits the control to function adequately, active commitment is obviously superior. Psychologists speak of a goal being "internalized"—the individual includes the goal as one of his own. When an individual gains personal satisfaction from achieving a result that is also a company goal, his feeling about control shifts. Control now helps him to gain personal satisfaction. Steering controls, especially, become aids rather than irritants.

Active acceptance is common. Typically, carpenters do take pride in the quality of their work; teachers do want their students to learn; gardeners do like to see flourishing flower beds. Although questions arise about levels of achievement and competing goals, a completely indifferent person is very rare.

Control, then, is much easier and more effective when it is based on goals that are meaningful and actively accepted by the people who really shape the result.[3] When designing a control system, then, it pays to seek out ways to match company objectives and personal values.

Participation to Secure Understanding and Acceptance

Participation in setting standards is widely advocated as a way of gaining positive commitment to control. Sales representatives in a large frozen-food company were asked to develop a picture of a first-class representative in terms of duties and performance. Following a thorough and frank discussion of this ideal person, everyone was asked to prepare, for his use the following year, a statement of what he thought he would accomplish. The representatives were expected to cover all the functions that had been listed, but they were free to set whatever outputs they believed were reasonable. Management then used these statements as standards of performance for the following year. The only adjustments—and these were made with the concurrence of the people involved—were to scale down some of

[3]L. D. Parker, "Control in Organizational Life: The Contribution of Mary Parker Follett," *Academy of Management Review,* Oct. 1984.

the outputs if the representatives had set too high a standard for themselves.

Participation has been successful in a wide variety of instances. But the way participation is employed is critical. Hypocrisy is an ever-present danger. The end result sought by a control is usually fixed by plans that are already settled. To pretend that these goals can be changed in participative discussions is misleading, and the participants will soon recognize this. Such discussions lead to a cynical mistrust of the whole system.[4]

Participation does help, however, (1) to develop a mutual understanding of the aims and mechanisms used, (2) to translate broad goals into criteria that are meaningful and operational for the people whose work is being controlled, and (3) to set stimulating pars, as indicated in the following pages. These are the subjects on which the controllee can make definite contributions; having done so, he is more likely to psychologically accept—and possibly feel a commitment to—the control endeavor.

SET TOUGH BUT ATTAINABLE PARS

Meaningful and acceptable control targets create a situation in which various control mechanisms can function. There is agreement about the aims of cooperative effort. However, further refinement of goals is necessary. The specific level of quality, amount of output, and expected degree of perfection must also be agreed upon. So we turn now to the psychological aspects of establishing pars.

Much criticism is aroused by attempts to enforce unreasonable levels of achievement. Some kind of speed limit, sales quota, or deadline, for instance, may be quite acceptable, but tempers rise if the standard is felt to be impossible or unnecessary. Unacceptable pars turn positive effort into all sorts of scheming to evade the pressure.

Dual Purpose of Pars

Pars serve two distinct purposes: (1) a motivational target we hope to achieve, and (2) an expected result used in planning and coordination. Although actual practice varies, most evidence indicates that people generally respond to a challenging target.[5] We get more personal satisfaction and pride out of meeting a tough assignment than from exceeding an easy standard. Not everyone will meet the tough standard every time, but some will, and the overall result will be higher. Note, however, that with such high pars, some deficiencies will occur. For planning and coordination, these shortcomings must be anticipated; thus, the estimated sales volume

[4]M. Beer, "Performance Appraisal: Dilemmas and Possibilities," *Organizational Dynamics,* Winter 1981, pp. 24–36.

[5]G. P. Latham and E. A. Locke, "Goal Setting—A Motivational Technique That Works," *Organizational Dynamics,* 8, No. 2 (Autumn 1979), pp. 68–80.

used for coordination purposes will be lower than the total sales quotas for individual sales representatives or separate product groups.

Pars That Motivate

Tough pars will motivate people only if several conditions are met. The individuals responding must feel that the target is attainable with reasonable effort and luck. Perhaps, as with a handicap in golf, the person will privately set her aspirations a bit lower than the stated standard. But to stimulate determination and willingness to be inconvenienced, she needs a personal belief that she has a reasonable chance of success in achieving the adjusted target.

A supportive atmosphere is necessary. Supervisors and staff can provide help; they *join in the game* of meeting a challenge—like climbing a mountain or swimming the English Channel. Success is emphasized and rewarded; failure is a disappointment but is not treated as a catastrophe. If the par can be adapted to unpredictable, external variables—as with quotas tied to industry activity or cost tied to orders processed—the feeling of being supported in the venture is increased.

Motivating pars cannot flaunt social norms. Peer groups have their own ideas about acceptable behavior—output ceilings in a factory being the classic example. If a control pushes a person to take actions that are not approved by his friends, he is likely to abide by their social standards. Of course, there are plenty of instances—especially in the executive ranks—in which social pressures support controls. The attitudes that really count are those of associates whose friendship and respect the individual wants to keep. If these persons feel that a control standard and its measurement are fair and that cooperating with management is the right thing to do, they will constitute a social force supporting that standard.

Between the two extremes of direct opposition and strong support are many shades of group attitudes. Perhaps a group is indifferent to what management wants to accomplish, but it may have certain norms of its own, such as keeping the gang together or deciding who may legitimately set a standard. So exactly how peer groups affect responses to controls should be examined for each case.

Pars That Breed Dissension

If a par is so difficult that controllees consider it "impossible" to achieve, a strong negative emotional response is likely. In fact, the behavioral-science literature is so full of gruesome cases of unattainable pars that naive readers assume that control always produces bad results. Sending incomplete or shoddy work to the next department, falsifying records, and transferring blame are common devices used by workers under the pressure of appearing to meet a standard.[6] If such defenses are inadequate, people

---

[6]V. Madsen and T. Polesie, *Human Factors in Budgeting* (London: Pitman, 1981).

may become indifferent about their jobs, irritable to work with, and hostile to their bosses. To relieve his frustration, an employee may join in horseplay, slip a dead mouse into a can of soup, and take an active part in any available protest movement.

Confronted with such behavior, a supervisor who wants to meet her commitments often increases pressure on the alienated operator. She is then faced with a vicious circle—more pressure, more resistance, the adverse response undermining the social system of which the operator is a part.

One way to avoid such a collapse is to lower performance standards to a level that the performer regards as realistic, as the pole vaulter adjusts the height of his bar (Figure 20.2). Even if this lower par is insufficient to attain some broader output or quality objective, it is better than a standard that precipitates negative behavior of the kind just described. Fortunately, there are a variety of other steps that can be taken to reconcile gaps between what is needed and what the person responsible for the

Chris Sheridan

Figure 20.2 People usually obtain much satisfaction and pride from carrying out a tough assignment. In pole-vaulting, the "par" is adjusted so that the jumper considers the height of the bar "tough, but attainable."

work regards as realistic; redesigning the job, training, demonstrating, and transferring employees are examples.

Participation in Setting Pars

Since feelings about what is reasonable and unreasonable so sharply affect the response to a control, extra effort should be made to uncover those feelings. Participation in setting the pars provides this communication. Each supervisor—from the president to the foreman—can frankly discuss with subordinates the levels of expected results that will be used in each major control.[7]

Such participation includes fact-finding, communication, prediction, negotiation, and mutual agreement. Although the supervisor has the stronger bargaining position, sincere agreement by the subordinate is essential if the control is to induce a positive response. And this feeling cannot be ordered by the boss. The process of participation itself has beneficial side effects, but these depend on consenting to standards that the subordinate really feels are attainable.

Technical pars, such as worker-hours per telephone installed or credit losses per dollar of sales, tend to be stable and must be renegotiated only when significant changes occur in the environment or technology. On the other hand, broader-output pars, such as sales quotas or budgeted profits, are reset for each period of time. Participation in setting the broader-output pars is akin to bidding in contract bridge. A player first negotiates a tough but realistic standard based on his new situation and then strives to achieve the contract.

Thus, if controls are to induce positive responses, the establishment of pars must be approached not just in terms of company needs. These standards also connote fairness, challenge, self-respect, social norms, winning, and other positive attributes for people. Consequently, the manager must perceive the attitudes and values of the people whose behavior he hopes to influence—a process explored in Part IV.

LIMITING CONTROLS

A third cluster of behavioral considerations relates to the total load. "The straw that breaks the camel's back" must be avoided. We are all subject to an array of controls, a situation which can cause psychological problems. We may feel the controls to be so oppressive that we rebel or our responses become irrational.

Consider the controls on a purchasing agent. Quality of materials and supplies obtained must meet exacting production standards. Delivery dates must anticipate actual use. Inventory levels will be checked against capital allocations. Prices paid will be measured in terms of cost estimates.

[7]S. R. Hinckley, "A Closer Look at Participation," *Organizational Dynamics*, Winter 1985.

Departmental operating expenses must stay within budgets, and a wide variety of personnel and accounting procedures should be followed. No personal gifts can be accepted. In addition, there are informal controls on intangible factors, such as obtaining data on new materials, responding to normal pressures for reciprocity, and minimizing risk arising from strikes and other shutdowns of suppliers. Tight controls over all these facets add up to a great deal of pressure; the purchasing agent can justifiably feel that he is buffeted from all sides.

Psychological Tolerance for Controls

People differ in their desire for freedom, and in the areas in which they feel that controls are repressive. One person may feel that regular working hours and scheduled tasks infringe on her rhythm of work, whereas another welcomes specific work assignments and checks on her progress, but is irritated by controls designed to monitor how she gets the work done. To some extent, by carefully selecting people for specific jobs, we can match these individual differences in security and freedom needs with the number of controls inherent in the work assigned. However, the number of controls necessary for management can seem excessive to many people.

An emphasis on steering controls, rather than yes/no controls, will reduce feelings of constraint. Although steering controls signal a need for action, they do not restrict the action. Also, participation in selecting criteria and in setting pars—already recommended—helps to incorporate the resulting controls into the normal activities associated with the job.

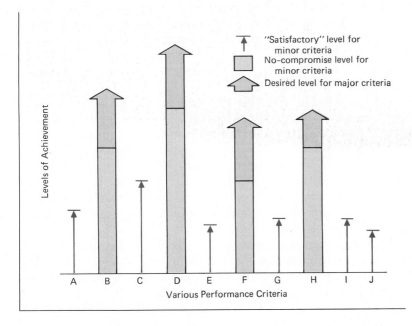

Figure 20.3 Pars for multiple goals.

"Satisfactory" Targets for Minor Criteria

The main way to make a variety of controls tolerable is to associate "satisfactory" levels of achievement with most of them (Figure 20.3). As long as a satisfactory level for personnel turnover or equipment maintenance is achieved, no one gives it much attention; there is little or no pressure to improve performance beyond a satisfactory level. In any going concern, experienced personnel carry on many activities in this fashion. Controls exist, but most of them are rarely brought into play, for people have learned to do satisfactory work; and these satisfied controls do not seem oppressive.

Obviously, if satisfactory achievement is accepted for a particular criterion, additional improvement in that area is being sacrificed. In effect, the manager is saying that the potential benefit of a tighter control here is not worth the psychological cost and the reduced effort in other areas. So he must select carefully areas in which the effects of not pushing hard are relatively minor. Experience indicates that most people can give serious attention to only four to six different objectives. This rule of thumb suggests that controls above this number should require merely an adequate level of performance. Even four prime controls may be too many if they deal with complex and urgent matters. A simple arrangement for dealing with targets that merely need to be "satisfied" is *management by exception*—a signal is raised only on the exceptional occasions when the satisfactory level of attainment is not being met.

Reducing Competition for Attention

Even a limited number of controls, each with a tough par, can place an operator in a psychological vise. For instance, the purchasing agent just mentioned may find pressures for ready availability of materials, high quality, low cost, and low inventories competing for his attention. He may be forced to trade off low cost for higher inventory, low cost for less quality, and so on. He feels frustrated because he recognizes that meeting one goal will hurt him on some other front.

Such compound pressures can be relieved in several ways. Simple priorities may be established—in the preceding example, instructions might be given to meet targets in the following sequence: quality, availability, cost, inventory level. A more sophisticated guide would set "no-compromise" levels below the desired pars, and then set a priority to fill the gaps between the "no-compromise" levels and pars. In financial budgeting, three levels are sometimes specified for various accounts—optimistic, expected, and minimum. More often, an implicit tolerance range is understood by people using the controls.

The key in all these arrangements is to relieve the pressure, at least to the extent of providing guidance for allocating effort along competing controls. Each control by itself may be desirable and acceptable, but we must also consider how that control fits into the whole.

Interference with employees' work can be very annoying to them. A branch manager may be fully committed to training new sales representatives and have in operation her steps to meet an agreed-upon training target. But if she is then subjected to detailed control over the selection of trainees, their job assignments, and how they are supervised, she is likely to resent the control. Most experienced workers—from bus drivers to atomic scientists—have a set of activities that they feel they know how to do well; they regard interference by outsiders as lack of confidence and respect for this skill.

Expense budgets are another case in point. Such budgets frequently include great detail. (The amount of detail often arises mainly from the availability of expense records.) Once specific items for telephone or overtime are in the budget, a supervisor or staff controller is tempted to watch these items closely and to insist on an explanation each time actual expense exceeds the budget. The typical manager will resent such "needling," especially if his *total* expense is in line.[8]

Feedback and Self-control

In behavioral terms, the person who feels that his domain is being invaded by a control is likely to be the one who can best initiate corrective action. He knows the local facts and is aware of the effect of manipulating one part of a total operation. Consequently, the control on overtime, for instance, will probably be most effective if the standard and the feedback on overtime become an integral part of *local* management.

In controlling detail, then, a desirable arrangement is to (1) design control mechanisms for elements worthy of systematic attention, but (2) route the feedback to the lowest level of decision making for that element. The aim is to encourage self-control and to avoid interference by an outsider. Obviously, such a scheme will work best when some evaluation of the overall results can be made, and when the local decision maker recognizes that the detailed feedback will help him to achieve that desired overall result. In other words, for important details, quick, operational feedbacks must be designed—and then the person who wants to run his own show must be encouraged to use them.

Conrad Hilton applied a variation of this arrangement in the management of his hotel chain. Each hotel, from the Waldorf-Astoria to the Shamrock, regularly computed and reported many ratios (for example, number of meals per guest-day and coffee shop sales per guest-day). Occasionally, at an unpredictable time (one manager claimed 1 AM to 3AM was most likely), Mr. Hilton phoned a hotel manager to ask what was being done to correct an off-target situation. If corrective action was underway, Mr. Hilton was satisfied; he relied on the hotel manager to decide what

[8]K. E. Said, "The Human Side of the Budgeting Process," *Managerial Planning,* Jan. 1978.

action fit the local situation. The effect of the system was that local managers retained a feeling of autonomy in operating their hotels, but they were alert to the control mechanism that central management had designed for local use.

This situation of considerable freedom in selecting local means to achieve an overall result is also well suited to participation in setting pars for local performance. Theoretically, the supervisor could withdraw entirely. In many cases, however, the supervisor wishes to strongly encourage the local operator to use particular controls, and periodic participation in setting pars is one way to indicate continuing respect for a control mechanism.

Control System Integrity

The human problems discussed thus far relate to the design of a control system—what criteria are acceptable, how tough standards should be, how many controls a person can tolerate, how to build on desires for self-control. We now turn to a different kind of issue—the *integrity* of the system, as Figure 20.4 shows. Can we believe what the control reports say?

Your response to the gasoline gauge on your auto or to the scale in your bathroom depends heavily on your belief in the accuracy and significance of the message the device is sending to you. Neither device is fully reliable, so you allow for a margin of error. But if the error is unexpectedly large, you become annoyed about the false alarm (or lack of alarm). Here, as with all controls, one's feeling about the measurement can significantly affect the response.

Promptness versus Accuracy

A prompt but vague warning is often more useful than a tardy precise one, as we pointed out in Chapter 18. For instance, we heed flood warnings by the weather bureau even if they are "wrong" (a flood does not occur) 50 percent or more of the time. It's preferable to respond to an imprecise warning than to wait until the water is at our doorstep before starting suitable action.

Psychologically, early but unreliable measurements are a potential source of tension. The person making the measurement (or prediction) may be criticized because of his "mistakes," and the person receiving the report may become resentful if he is pushed to act on "wrong" information. Only when all persons concerned recognize the inherent limitations of such measurements (or predictions) can such friction be avoided. Some individuals are so reluctant to take risks that they are incapable of dealing with unreliable data. These people either cry "wolf" for every distant shadow they see or do nothing until they are sure the wolf is at the door. They are misfits in a dynamic-control job.

Preliminary estimates and probabilities can be used for control in a variety of ways. Perhaps they merely alert the operator, or they may set in motion a series of more elaborate measurements. If a large number of

Tom McHugh/Photo Researchers

Figure 20.4 The
complex facility
monitoring a power
plant system.

similar events are involved—as in quality control of long runs of machine-made parts or in extending credit to customers of mail-order retailers—statistical ranges of normal variability help distinguish between random and significant deviations. In all such uses, a clear awareness that the measurement itself may be misleading is coupled with precautionary action. Everyone knows that uncertainty exists. They are prepared to shrug off the false alarms.

Credibility Attached to Control Data

Uncertainty arising from a small, early sample (as just discussed) is fairly easy to understand and to accept psychologically. A different sort of problem arises from the use of symptoms and subjective measurements. Here the significance of the measurement is open to question. For instance, how valid a control instrument is the number of laughs at a Broadway play or the number of lunch dates scheduled by an aspiring young management consultant?

Such information is often helpful; it provides some additional "feel" about what is happening. But both the measuring and the evaluating can be challenged. And this doubt about its meaning makes such data poor input for strict controls.

Such "soft" data can be used for *self*-control, and for supplementing more objective measurements. But until such a measurement has gained credibility in the minds of both the controller and the controllee, its use for yes/no controls or for postaction evaluation is likely to evoke a negative response.

RESPONSES TO THREE TYPES OF CONTROLS

Behavioral reactions to each control element (goals, pars, measurements, feedback, and the like) are vital parts of every control design. To ensure that these human dimensions are recognized, we can also relate normal rsponses to each of the three basic types of control singled out in Chapter 18. The underlying response patterns are those already described, but regrouping them by types of control shows their significance in a new light.

Positive Response to Steering Controls

The great virtue of steering controls is that most people regard them as helpful rather than as pressure devices. If the goal is accepted, then the various feedbacks are treated as aids in achieving the desired result. Even though a control report sometimes conveys unwelcome news and prods a person to extra effort, the warning is constructive. Coming before work is completed, the signal is seen in terms of action needed rather than personal evaluation.

Since steering controls provide inputs early enough for the principals concerned to use the data in their own decisions, their personal involvement in the control cycle is high. And this close involvement adds to the positive response.[9]

Goal acceptance is crucial. Unless the sales representative wants to increase her sales, reports of deviation from course and of potential obstacles are merely so much static. And an unreasonable par can sour the reaction of the latest word about competitors or planned shipping dates. Steering controls stimulate a positive response only when the people on the giving and receiving ends of the control effort are steering in the same direction.

Who steers is also an issue. As already mentioned, outside regulation of detailed operations annoys those who see themselves as experts in that area; consequently, self-regulation is more welcome. This suggests that steering controls should be translated into action as close to the actual operation as possible. The positive response to the control activity then spreads among operating personnel.

Too many reports can swamp the system. Unimportant information diverts attention from the main goals; frequent needling is irritating. So for many dimensions, "satisfactory" conditions should not be reported. Feedback should center on key variables and on major shifts in the work

---

[9]D. A. Nadler, P. Mirvis, and C. Cammann, "The Ongoing Feedback System: Experimenting with a New Management Tool," *Organizational Dynamics,* Spring 1976.

environment. Steering can then focus on goals we wish to maximize and on serious obstacles.

Behavioral Impact of Yes/No Controls

Yes/no controls set hurdles to be crossed. They ensure that quality standards are met, that a proposed action is within budgetary restraints, and the like. For the "professional" who takes pride in his work, being able to clear such hurdles easily may provide reassurance. But the check is only whether work is good enough to pass. If it is better than standard, little or no praise is given; if it is below standard, the work is rejected. And rejection of work often creates delays and resentment. On the whole, when yes/no controls demand attention, they proclaim bad news.

Negative feelings about yes/no controls are often increased (1) when a person is unable to achieve other goals because his work is blocked by this hurdle; (2) when the par is felt to be unreasonable (for example, the budget is too tight or the requirement for a salary increase is too strict); or (3) when the standard is vague and unpredictable. The legality of a contract, the impact of a public-relations release, or the qualifications required for promotion are typical examples in which standards are likely to be vague and unpredictable. Unpredictable standards are particularly troublesome, for people lack guides on how to prepare for the control. Then if the standards applied to separate cases appear to be inconsistent, charges of favoritism and politics will follow.

Such reactions to yes/no controls can be reduced. First, it must be made clear that the control is necessary for attainment of company or department objectives. Both the aspect being measured and the par should be directly traceable to a basic objective. Second, the measurements must be kept as objective as possible, and they must be applied consistently. (Occasional exceptions will, of course, be necessary. In fact, people working under the system may strongly advocate exceptions, to achieve justice or meet an emergency, for example. But exceptions have little meaning until we have established a stable, predictable social system as a base.) These steps will rarely make the control popular, but they will cut down frustration and foster a feeling of fair play.

Postaction Controls as Scorecards

In a strict sense, measurement and evaluation after work is completed cannot alter what is already done. Like Monday-morning quarterbacking, talking about what might have been won't change matters. Nevertheless, as previously indicated, postaction controls do serve two general purposes. (1) If we are going to play another game next week, the Monday-morning review of successes and failures help us *plan* the *next* engagement. (2) If some kind of reward is tied to how well actual results match selected goals, then the *anticipation* of that comparison and payoff may be a strong incentive.

The influence of anticipated rewards depends upon the strength of the rewards (or punishments) and upon the perceived basis on which the rewards will be allocated. We are not here exploring the nature of rewards—they vary from bonuses and promotions to commendations and scoring well in the game. But we are directly concerned with the scorecards that determine, in fact, when a person receives a reward. Postaction control reports are such scorecards.

Control design affects what is put down on that scorecard—the factors that are watched, how they are measured, and the expected levels of performance.[10] Their impact on behavior has several dimensions.

1. People in the system will be sensitive to factors measured and reported; if valued rewards are closely allied to control reports, the participants will watch the scoring like bettors at a racetrack watch the horses. Consequently, tying controls to the desired emphasis among objectives is important.

2. A lack of confidence in the reliability of measuring and reporting mechanisms will create a feeling that granting of rewards is probably inequitable.

3. In a rapidly changing environment, people may discover that their final score is affected more by their skill in renegotiating pars after the fact than by efforts to improve actual results.

When the purpose of a control is to produce a scorecard, several ways of automatically adjusting par after the fact are available. A flexible budget that is adjusted on the basis of actual volume—sales quotas adjusted for actual disposable income in each territory—illustrates an attempt to make the final standard reflect changes in the environment. Such devices usually increase the chances that the participants believe the par is fair, even though they recognize that the par may move up as well as down.

CONCLUSION

Managerial controls are concerned with achieving results—with a balance between inputs and outputs that pushes toward the company mission. These controls, however, take effect only when they influence the behavior of people. It is behavioral response, not the mechanics of a control, that really matters. So when designing a specific control or a control system, we must consider how executives and other people involved will react. This chapter highlights conclusions drawn from behavioral-science studies that relate to the process of controlling.

Controls typically have a poor reputation, at least in terms of their popularity with persons being controlled. Fortunately, such negative feel-

[10]E. E. Lawler, A. M. Mohrman, and S. M. Resnick, "Performance Appraisal Revisited," *Organizational Dynamics,* Summer 1984.

ing need not prevail. By including behavioral aspects in the design and execution of controls, these devices can become normal aids in cooperative effort. Important in this respect are meaningful and accepted goals, challenging but attainable pars, restraint on the number of controls, means for resolving conflicting pressures, encouragement of self-adjustments, and acknowledged uncertainty in some of the measurements. Participation in designing and setting standards also helps.

All these ways to secure positive responses to controls are only parts of a total management design. Remember that the need for controls arises from managerial planning and that controls function in an organization structure. So as the manager shapes the control process, he must also be sensitive to harmony with planning and organizing.

Impact on Productivity

The way employees respond to controls affects company productivity in two ways. First, the specific controls are important. Control on quality, prompt delivery, costs, use of assets, and waste disposal—to cite only a few examples—all bear on some aspect of efficiency or effectiveness. If you and I react favorably to a control, we are probably adding a bit to our company's productivity. If we drag our feet, productivity drifts downward. Of course, the importance of our action depends on what is being controlled and how much clout we have in that operation.

Second, response to controls is contagious. What you and I do affects our fellow workers, and vice versa. And a disregard, or enthusiasm, for one control tends to color the attitude toward other controls. Such feelings about controls in general are a significant aspect of company morale. And the pervasive attitude can profoundly influence productivity. Disrespect for controls drags down current output and makes managers timid about seeking improvements. In contrast, support of controls leads to dependable—even aggressive—pursuit of company goals and creates a climate in which modifications of activities can be tried with confidence.

Because a positive, constructive response to controls is a necessary ingredient for major productivity improvement, the "people approach" to controls outlined in this chapter has a double benefit.

FOR FURTHER DISCUSSION

1. List two controls that influence your actions in some significant ways. Make one of these a control that you accept as *necessary* and regard as a useful instrument to guiding your behavior. Make the other a control that you feel to be *unnecessary* and that you would circumvent if you could. (a) What accounts for the differences in your feelings about the two? (b) What, if anything, would you substitute for the second control?

2. "As people become better educated and have the capability to understand their jobs, the number of controls—especially yes/no controls—should be reduced. Educated people can manage themselves." Do you agree? Explain.

3. What is the distinction between a satisfactory level and a maximum level of achievement? Why in managerial control do we often use the satisfactory level?

4. "Detailed control systems let people know where they stand and make reward and punishment fairer. Thus they are a key to positive motivation." "No matter how you develop them, controls show lack of trust and must be considered as obstacles to positive motivation and thus a necessary evil."
With which statement do you more nearly agree? Why?

5. How far should participation be used in setting control standards for students at a university? Consider standards for (a) social behavior on the campus, (b) behavior in class and when taking examinations, and (c) academic achievement.

6. "One of the major advantages of using Management by Objectives (MBO) in our planning is that now my subordinates have no basis for objecting to controls. Since the controls are based on jointly set standards, they must regard them as fair." Discuss this assertion.

7. Can steering controls also be used as the basis for determining appropriate rewards and punishments?

8. (a) Assume that you are employed by an automobile dealer as a salesperson. Would you prefer to work under no controls? Many controls? Selective controls? If so, which ones? Why? (b) Now assume that you are the manager of the dealership. Would you adopt the control pattern you described in response to (a)? Why or why not? (c) Would your answers be the same for the repair shop of the dealership? Why or why not?

FOR FURTHER READING

Ewing, D. W., *Do It My Way or You're Fired*. New York: Wiley, 1983. Interesting examination of how control and motivational aspects of work have changed over the years.

Latham, G. P. and K. N. Wexley, *Increasing Productivity Through Performance Appraisal*. Reading, Mass.: Addison-Wesley, 1981. Good overview of techniques for obtaining more positive response to measurement and evaluation systems.

Lawler, E. E. and J. G. Rhode, *Information and Control in Organizations*. Santa Monica, Calif.: Goodyear, 1976. Uses behavioral-science research findings to explain responses to control mechanisms in organizations.

Lorange, P. and D. Murphy, "Considerations in Implementing Strategic Control," *Journal of Business Strategy,* Spring 1984. Experience of twenty-five companies reveals systemic, behavioral, and political difficulties in controlling the execution of strategic plans.

Rosenbaum, B. L., *How to Motivate Today's Workers*. New York: McGraw-Hill, 1982. Several methods of motivation and control are described.

MANAGEMENT IN ACTION CASE 20
Zephyr Hi-Fi, Inc.

Mona Sharp, a recently promoted district manager of Zephyr Hi-Fi, was meeting with her replacement as sales representative, Toni Barr. While waiting for Mona to get off the phone, Toni leafed through *Guide to Better Selling—The Zephyr Way*. The headings included the following:

Dealer Sales Organization—check:
▫ Inventory of Zephyr equipment
▫ Display of Zephyr equipment
▫ Number and quality of sales personnel
▫ Loyalty to Zephyr vs. competing brands

□ Other product lines carried

□ Advertising—amount, media, producer tie-ins

Dealer Service Organization—check:

□ Skill of service personnel

□ Knowledge about Zephyr equipment

□ Use of Zephyr-supplied parts

□ Promptness of service

□ Prices charged

□ Credit Arrangements

This was only a fraction of the *Guide,* but Mona was now ready to talk.

"Did you get a copy of this memo on 'work down dealer inventory—new models coming soon'? That's just one more thing to think about."

"I guess it's here someplace," replied Toni, "but I thought we tried to keep the dealers well stocked."

"Of course, most of the time, except you'll have a lot of returned goods if you load up the dealers just ahead of a new model. That's not what concerns me. Only two months ago we got that packet about building up *new* dealers. Remember, we have to file a report on our coverage versus competitors', relative strength of present dealers, new prospects, and plans for building your territory. What happens to that?"

"You told me to think in terms of 100 percent. More attention on one place means less on another. What do you want me to do?" asked Toni.

"Look, I think the most important thing for this territory is more dealers—good ones if we can get them. We agreed on 50 percent there. Let's stick to that. Now this new inventory memo—put it on the back burner; nobody's going to check up unless there is a whole truckload going back to the warehouse. You do need to call on the present dealers regularly, but if no problems have surfaced, you can move on. Of course, you'll have to fill out call reports with their 1001 questions. But I'm sure that if we can show an expansion in dealerships, no one will make too much noise about all the rest of those good things. I'll cover you if somebody is upset. Meanwhile, we'll do what's really important—build the territory."

"That's okay with me," said Toni, "at least until I get called on the carpet."

Questions

1. Is Mona acting as a good supervisor should?
2. What is happening to Zephyr's control system?

APPLICATION CASES

For practice in applying concepts covered in this chapter to managerial situations, see the following managerial decision cases. The case questions particularly relevant to this chapter are listed by number after each case name.

21

Integrating Controls with Other Management Processes

LEARNING OBJECTIVES

After completing this chapter you should be able to

1. Understand the need to link control to the total planning system.
2. Know how to modify control—without losing it—when decentralizing.
3. See the important role people with staff-level positions can play in an overall control process.
4. Discuss how to harmonize departmentation and controls.
5. Explain how to make leadership styles compatible with the control system.
6. Explain how management information systems and control systems should reinforce each other.

MANAGEMENT SYNTHESIS

The intimate relationship of controls to other management processes has been indicated throughout the last three chapters. Strategy and operating objectives, for instance, underlie the selection of control standards; programs find their financial expression in budgets; decentralization and participation have a marked influence on the acceptance of controls; and so on. Many control designs can be made more effective by modifying the company's organizing, planning, or leading. Conversely, sometimes the control design should be adjusted to aid the planning, organizing, or leading. Obviously, such tradeoffs should be considered, especially if synergistic effects in the total management design are possible.

In this chapter, we shall single out several ways controls can be fitted together with other management processes. These opportunities do not begin to cover all the interrelationships. Rather, they are issues that arise time and again in actual practice, and resolving them wisely can be a great aid to effective management. These issues include the following: linking control to planning systems, decentralizing without loss of control, using staff in control, harmonizing departmentation with controls, and enhancing controls by leadership action.

LINKING CONTROL TO THE TOTAL PLANNING SYSTEM

Since control becomes effective only through modifying people's behavior, the broad objectives of an enterprise need to be translated into the *specific* results required from individuals. The elaboration of strategy into single-use plans and standing plans (Chapters 6 and 7) requires continuing managerial attention. Similarly, we need to be sensitive to the influence of control information on *new* planning.

Elaborating Plans and Specifying Results

The basic concept that planned results become the goals of control is simple enough. However, deciding to increase the ratio of women executives or to obtain more stainless steel from European sources merely states an end result. Planning must be pushed from broad objectives to successively narrower and more specific tasks, until each necessary move or component is assigned to a particular person. Then controls at the subsidiary level will contribute to the final result.[1] If the completed plans for the construction of a building are properly integrated—and then controls set up over the work of the foundation subcontractor, the structural-steel subcontractor, the electrical subcontractor, and everyone else who makes a contribu-

---

[1]P. Lorange, *Corporate Planning: An Executive Viewpoint* (Englewood Cliffs, N.J.: Prentice-Hall, 1980), Chap. 5.

tion to the total structure—the final result should be a building as conceived by the architect.

Unfortunately, this sort of matching of the control structure with company objectives is hard to achieve. Often the planning is not extended to the point where we can safely rely on individual discretion to complete the task. And if a new objective is unusual, normal measuring devices may not reflect its distinctive features. So two questions should be asked (1) Who must achieve what results if the new objective is to be obtained? (2) How will we know that the necessary contributions to the final result are being made? *Planning is incomplete until concrete steps have been identified and provision made to control this implementation.*

The elaboration of a plan down to results required from the many individual operators or units need not be prepared by a single central-planning body. A large block of the total work may be delegated to one division, and the elaboration of plans for that block developed within the division. Such decentralization does not reduce the need for full planning and subsequent control, however; only the location of who does the planning and controlling is changed by the decentralization (Figure 21.1).

Control and New Planning

When steering controls and yes/no controls are used to adjust activities so that a predetermined objective will be achieved, corrective action may prompt action in any of the other managerial processes. Nevertheless, objectives usually remain the same, and the adjustments are like those of a ship's pilot who modifies his course with the winds and tide to reach home port. Only if there is a terrible storm or breakdown is the pilot likely to change (replan) his destination.

In contrast, postaction controls almost always lead to planning. For example, if a sales campaign is only partially successful, both the objec-

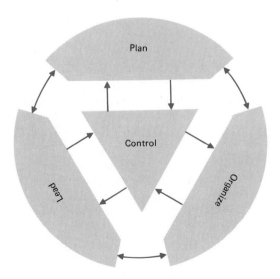

Figure 21.1 Interaction of Different Phases of Managing. By integrating the subsystems, the effectiveness of the combined effort is greatly increased.

From *Constructive Control: Design and Use of Control Systems* by W. H. Newman (Englewood Cliffs, N.J.: Prentice-Hall, Inc., 1975), p. 145. Used by permission of Prentice-Hall, Inc.

tives and methods of the next campaign are likely to be modified; similarly, executive-development activities planned for next year will be strongly influenced by an appraisal of results achieved this year. In situations such as these, control reports serve as a basis for an entirely new cycle of managerial activity—planning, perhaps organizing, leading, and controlling the new activities.

But the concept that postaction controls rather than steering controls are of principal use in planning needs two important qualifications. First, we must often lay plans for new activities before a present cycle is completed. University budgets, for example, are often prepared in preliminary form in December and January for the following school year. This means that the results of the fall semester activities are not yet known, and the spring semester has not even begun, when the first steps of planning for new courses and size of classes have to be taken. Automobile companies have an even greater lead time in planning for their new models; commitments on design and engineering are often made with little or no measure of the popularity of the current year's model.

When new plans must be made before the results of the old ones are known, the results must be predicted. Control information of the steering type is naturally used in making these predictions. In some situations, then, we use information on how we are doing both as a guide to current operations and as part of the data on which the outcome of present and new plans are predicted. The benefits of control to planning, however, should not be exaggerated. If we want planning to be dynamic, we must consider new ways of performing work. Operating conditions change, and future opportunities may improve or diminish; consequently more complete, or different information is often needed for planning than control activities provide.

Second, as objectives are changed, established controls tend not to be readjusted. Take even the simple matter of a cutback in the sales of a product line because of a change in competition or technology. It is entirely possible that although the overall income and expense objectives will be adjusted to the new conditions, the control standards for engineering and other service departments will remain unchanged. Or suppose the company president decides to increase the number of broadly trained young men and women in the organization as a reservoir for filling top management positions. If the job specifications that control the representatives who actually hire college students are not adjusted, the specific actions at the various recruiting centers will not be attuned to the new objective.

The several steps involved in translating the new company objective into new patterns of individual behavior all take time and effort.[2] In extreme cases, inertia is so great that inconsistency between company objectives and ineffective controls continues indefinitely. So the need to link

[2]N. W. Dirsmith, S. F. Jablonsky, and A. D. Luzi, "Planning and Control in the U.S. Federal Government: A Critical Analysis of PPB, MBO and ZBO," *Strategic Management Journal*, Oct. 1980.

planned results to control standards arises over and over. Whenever new plans are laid, the question "What corresponding adjustments in controls must be made?" should be asked.

Tie to Management Information Systems

The flows of information needed for both planning and controlling are, of course, large parts of the overall management information system of any company. For instance, a whole array of measurements are made as one step in the control process, and these data can be sent to anyone concerned with the progress of the measured activity. Similarly, postaction control reports are regularly used in planning next year's actions.

For normal, repetitive activities, these flows of information fall into a pattern. Sales data, production rates, regular expenses—often expressed as ratios—are circulated to many managers. They learn to rely on these reports as a source of data for making new plans. The management information system, especially since the introduction of computers, can be designed to ensure a regular and prompt flow from and to key decision or control centers. Of course, as just noted, someone must keep such data flows up to date; for instance, when an organization change increases the authority of a branch manager to cut prices, additional information should probably be sent to that person on a regular schedule.

Nonroutine data are more difficult to circulate. For example, a control report may indicate that Congress will soon restrict the imports of Italian shoes; as a result, our sales manager plans to sell more high-priced U.S.-made shoes. How does the management information system process this sort of data? Up to now, nothing has actually happened. Clearly, the system should provide for irregular flows in addition to the customary reports. Face-to-face contacts will probably have to supplement the computer printouts.

DECENTRALIZING WITHOUT LOSS OF CONTROL

Each time a manager delegates work (operating or managing) to a subordinate, he creates the problem of knowing whether the work is performed satisfactorily; hence, delegating inevitably raises the question of control. The degree of decentralization a manager will adopt often depends on how far he can decentralize without feeling that he is losing control.

Modifying Control

A manager need not lose control when he delegates a large measure of planning, but he should be prepared to change his controls.[3] This alteration is illustrated in Table 21.1. First, the appropriate control standard

[3]N. Piercy and M. Thomas, "Corporate Planning: Budgeting and Integration," *Journal of General Management*, Winter 1984.

Table 21.1 **EFFECT OF DECENTRALIZATION ON CONTROL**

| Degree of Decentralization | Nature of Control | |
	Type of Standard	Frequency of Measurement
Centralization of all but routine decisions.	Detailed specifications on how work is to be done, and on output of each worker.	Daily for output; hourly to continuous for methods and for quality.
Action within policies, programs, standard methods; use of "exception principle."	Output at each stage of operations, expense ratios, efficiency rates, turnover, and the like.	Weekly to daily for output; monthly for ratios and for other operating data.
Profit decentralization.	Overall results, and a few key danger signals.	Monthly for main results and for signals; quarterly or annually for other results.

changes. When decisions are centralized, the manager himself will establish rather detailed standards for the method and output of each phase of the work. But as he delegates increasing amounts of authority to plan and decide, the manager should shift his attention away from operating details to the results that are achieved.

The frequency of appraisals also changes. Because the manager is no longer trying to keep an eye on detailed activities, most, if not all, daily reports can be dropped. As his attention shifts more and more toward overall results, the span of time covered by reports can typically be lengthened. For a business unit that operates on a profit-decentralization basis, monthly profit-and-loss statements and balance sheets come as frequently as most top managers want reports. Other factors, such as market position or product development, may be reported only quarterly.

Retaining Safeguards

The shift from frequent, detailed control reports to periodic, general-appraisal reports does not preclude the use of a few danger-signal controls, as Figure 21.2 shows. A common practice is to expect a subordinate to *keep his manager informed* of impending difficulties rather than bother him with control data when conditions are satisfactory. A manager may ask to be notified when deviations from standard exceed a certain norm, thus applying the "exception principle" to control. Moreover, yes/no controls can be used for certain major moves, such as large capital expenditures or the appointment of key executives. Here again, the number of proposed actions that *require confirmation* will decrease as the degree of decentralization increases.

Still another kind of safeguard is to *insist that lower levels of man-*

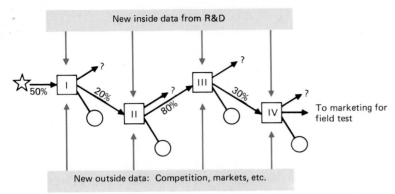

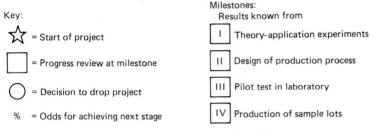

Key:

☆ = Start of project

☐ = Progress review at milestone

◯ = Decision to drop project

% = Odds for achieving next stage

Milestones:
Results known from

| I | Theory-application experiments |

| II | Design of production process |

| III | Pilot test in laboratory |

| IV | Production of sample lots |

Figure 21.2 Progress review of R & D Project at Critical Milestones. Major projects, such as the development of a new product, can be controlled by full-scale reviews at "milestones" in the process. Such reviews often prompt replanning.

From *Constructive Control: Design and Use of Control Systems* by W. H. Newman (Englewood Cliffs, N.J.: Prentice-Hall, Inc., 1975), p. 103. Used by permission of Prentice-Hall, Inc.

agement use specific control devices even though an upper executive himself neither sets the standards nor receives reports on performance. A vice-president in charge of production may be vitally concerned that a reliable quality-inspection plan is in use, but he may take no personal part in its operation. He expects sufficient control data to be handy if the need for determining the cause of any problem arises.

As more authority is delegated, *self-control* by the subordinate becomes crucial. Such self-control is partly a matter of attitude and habit. In a situation in which centralized control has been the traditional practice, operating personnel naturally rely on senior executives or their staff to catch errors and initiate corrective action. If authority is then passed down to them, they need to develop a new attitude. It may also be necessary to redirect the flow of information so that these people down the line have what they need to do their own controlling.

With heavier reliance on self-control by subordinates, the manager should act more as a *coach* than as the one who decides on corrective action. Ideally, the initiative for corrective action comes from the subordinate. This degree of decentralization clearly requires the right people. Subordinates able to perform the delegated duties must be selected, trained, and properly motivated. An executive himself must be able and willing to adjust his behavior, and the two people involved in each delegation must trust each other. Remove or significantly diminish any one of these aspects of an operating situation, and there will be a corresponding reduction in the degree of decentralization possible without loss of control.

Staff assists in performing managerial work, as Figure 21.3 shows. As we explained in Chapter 11, most staff assistance is concerned with planning, but it is not necessarily limited to this one process of management. To what extent, then, should staff also be used in control?

We have noted that people naturally dislike controls, and they are especially sensitive about who may legitimately exercise control. Consequently, as we think about assigning control duties to staff, we must be sure (1) that the tasks are well suited to a person in an auxiliary position, and (2) that the control duties will not make the performance of other staff work more difficult.

Setting Standards

Staff is often used in setting control standards. Since the early days of Scientific Management, industrial engineers—by employing time-and-motion study—have set output standards; product engineers have set quality standards; and cost accountants have set detailed standards for product and process costs. A market researcher often takes part in establishing sales quotas for individual sales representatives.

The reasons for using staff to help set standards are clear. Special skills in engineering or research methodology may be required. Besides, setting standards is often very time-consuming, and an operating manager

Figure 21.3 Staff may take various roles in the control process. In these three examples, staff assumes the roles indicated in color.

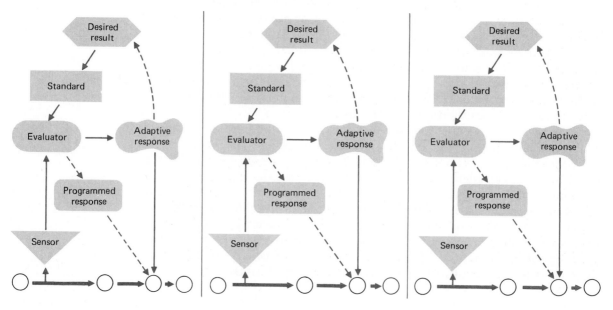

cannot give attention to all the necessary details. Of course, when we think of the whole range of control standards a company uses, it becomes evident that many standards are established without the aid of staff. However, when controls are formalized and detailed, staff help may lead to better standards.

The active participation of staff is also a major source of human problems with control. All too often the people being controlled feel that standards are unreasonable and that control pressure comes from illegitimate sources. The technical jargon of a staff person, his preoccupation with certain aspects of a problem, his values, and his desire to make a good showing all contribute to a lack of confidence by workers and lower-level supervisors in the standards he sets. If, in addition, the staff person applies pressure to meet the standards and suggests corrective action, fuel is added to the flames. "Who does that graphite engineer think he is?" is likely to be the response.

The remedy appears to lie in two directions. (1) Operating managers should be instructed to give more attention to the review of standards before they are put into effect and to discuss these standards with people who will be expected to live up to them. (2) Staff people should be made to realize that their most constructive contribution lies in providing sound advice up and down the organizational hierarchy without usurping the functions that legitimately belong to the line managers.

Objective Appraisal

When control standards are expressed in terms of inches or dollars, the comparison of actual performance—as in auditing—is relatively simple. But measurements are often vague, and the allowances we must make—for illness, competition, and numerous other influences—are a matter of subjective judgment. There is widespread debate about the value of staff participation in this kind of appraisal.

Operating managers, it is pointed out, often lack objectivity in making appraisals. They are committed to a program, and the drive they need to make the program succeed calls for optimism and a determination to "do the impossible." Besides, a manager must appraise the work of his friends, and he is sensitive to the effect of appraisal on their morale. On the other hand, it is argued that although a staff person has greater objectivity, he also has a less intimate knowledge of the facts. He, too, may have a bias, especially if he is looking at a situation only from the point of view of, say, human resources, engineering, or public relations.

Management needs both kinds of appraisals. The objective views of staff can be extremely valuable. But such appraisal finds its greatest use when we are formulating *new* plans rather than attempting to control activities so that they conform to *existing* plans. Corrective action is predominantly a line activity; so inevitably, an operating manager will rely primarily on his own judgment. When formulating new plans, however, an operating manager normally has more time for contemplation; and in this activity both the appraisals and proposals of staff can make their greatest contribution.[4]

Yes/No Control

In special circumstances, a staff unit, like an operating manager, may exercise yes/no control. The human resources department, for example, may have to give its approval before the sales manager can make a final commitment to hire a new representative. Similarly, capital expenditures may require the approval of the controller; changes in organization, the approval of the management-planning section; or property leases, the approval of the legal staff. When yes/no control is exercised by a staff person, he is said to have *concurring authority*.

Concurring authority works best when the criteria on which a staff person can either approve or reject a particular proposal are specified. And, for those transactions in which a mistake would be very serious and in which time is not critical, concurring authority may be desirable as a safety measure. Serious difficulties with yes/no staff control arise when a decision to turn down a proposal is based principally on subjective judgment. It is one thing for a controller to say that an advertising appropriation has been used up, and another for her to turn down a proposal because she believes that advertising is unwise during a recession. An alternative arrangement is simply to have the staff person give advice; we may insist that a consultation take place, but specify that the operating manager's judgment prevails.

A final reason for carefully defining and restricting staff participation in control is that it undermines the constructive role staff usually plays in other areas. An unpopular assignment makes a staff person unwelcome, so his ability to be a friendly adviser is lessened if he goes too far into control.

HARMONIZING DEPARTMENTATION WITH CONTROLS

The ease of control is significantly affected by the way the company is grouped into departments and divisions.[5] Important here are the concepts of clean breaks, deadly parallel, and direct interaction.

The simplest way departmentation can aid control is by separating departments or sections where a *clean break* in work occurs. Thus, a farmers' buying co-op will separate bulk fertilizer, seeds, fuel oil and gasoline, and garden supplies; each requires distinct storage and delivery equipment. Likewise, a well-run ski resort will have separate divisions for its ski run, its ski shop, and its housing and food; to separate control of its

---

[4]E. K. Warren, *Long-Range Planning: The Executive Viewpoint* (Englewood Cliffs, N.J.: Prentice-Hall, 1966), Chaps. 5 & 6.

[5]W. G. Ouchi, "The Relationship Between Organizational Structure and Organizational Control," *Administrative Science Quarterly,* 22 (March 1977), pp. 95–113; H. Mintzberg, *Structure in Fives: Designing Effective Organizations* (Englewood Cliffs, N.J.: Prentice-Hall, 1983).

restaurant from its bar, however, becomes more difficult because the service is so interrelated. Control is easier when either the physical separation of operations or distinct stages of work make it simple for everyone to understand the organizational structure.

A second suggestion is to set up two or more operating units in *deadly parallel.* A telephone company may create a series of nearly identical divisions; or finance companies may organize each of many offices on the same general pattern. Control is enhanced because the results from any one office may be compared with performance in the others. This deadly-parallel arrangement removes a great deal of personal opinion in setting standards. As we noted in the last chapter, it is important that employees accept standards as reasonable; if one branch meets a given standard, an aura of reasonableness is created for that standard, and a wholesome attitude toward it tends to develop throughout all branches.

A proper grouping of activities can aid control in still another way. By placing together activities that are closely interdependent, so that workers are in *direct interaction,* we can reduce the amount of "overhead" control. When interrelated work is done in several different departments, we have to control with precision the quality and flow of work as it moves from one department to another. Even with the best of controls a mistake is likely to result in arguments and buck-passing. Thus, a more satisfactory arrangement is to assign the interrelated work to a single department or "project team," or to an individual. Two of the best examples of this basic idea are *profit centers* and *project teams* in a matrix organization, as shown in Figure 21.4.

Figure 21.4   Matching controls with alternative approaches to product management and organization. Product divisions, shown on the far right, serve as clear-cut "profit centers."

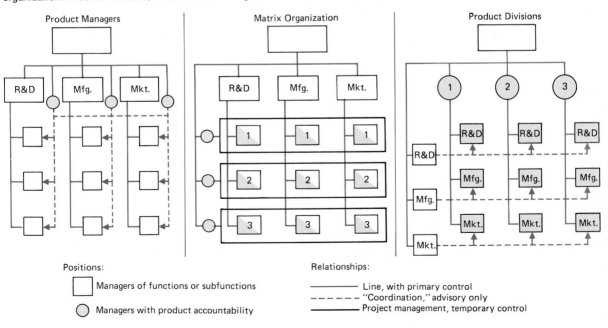

Creating Profit Centers

Profit centers are a valuable control device if organization and controls are well matched. A business unit with its own engineering, production, and marketing can be judged in terms of the profit it earns. Since the profit figure shows the *net* result of all unit activities, its use as a control standard encourages coordinated and balanced effort. Also, executives within the unit must keep their activities in tune with the external environment in order to sustain profits. Although insensitive and slow to reflect intangibles, the profit standard is the best comprehensive measurement available.

The temptation is to overuse the idea of the profit center. Some companies try to make each plant, each branch office, each warehouse, and even service units (such as purchasing) a so-called profit center. A profit is calculated for each unit. In effect, each unit buys its materials (often from other units), hires its own labor, and sells its products or services (perhaps to other units). Then, after charges for overhead, a profit for the unit is computed. But how suitable is this resulting profit figure as a control standard?

Many profit-center managers devote more energy to negotiating the artificial prices used to transfer goods in and out of their units and the amount of overhead charged to them than they give to improving the activities they can actually improve. Because of the profit control, they spend a lot of unproductive time playing games with transfer prices. The trouble arises because the control measurement—profit—is much more comprehensive than the activities assigned to the unit they measure. Most plant managers, for instance, do not decide the specifications of what they make, how much to produce, or whom to sell it to at selected prices. Consequently, control standards focusing on cost, quality, and delivery are more appropriate for such a plant manager than total profit.

Profit-center control makes sense when (1) semiautonomous, self-contained business units are part of the organization structure, and (2) the primary objective of such a unit is profit. Managers of the semiautonomous unit are free to adjust to new opportunities, and their initiative must be encouraged but controls must direct that initiative to the desired result. If the main purpose of a district office is to build sales volume, it would confuse matters to call it a profit center. The control selected should reinforce the intent of the organization.[6]

Adjusting Controls to Matrix Organization

Distinct control issues arise when a matrix form of organization is used.[7] As noted in Chapter 11, a matrix organization has two types of units—

[6]P.Lorange, "Strategic Controls: Some Issues in Making It Operationally More Useful," in R. Lamb, ed., *Competitive Strategic Management* (Englewood Cliffs, N.J.: Prentice-Hall, 1984).

[7]A. R. Janger, *Matrix Organization of Complex Business* (New York: Elsevier North-Holland, 1983).

resource departments that develop pools of specialized talent, and project teams to which talent is assigned to work on specific projects.

In a matrix organization, scheduling and control is carried out primarily within each project team. The program scheduling and control tools normally will be those described in our discussion of adaptive programming in Chapter 7. And the director of each project team—the interim line boss—will be the person to balance the impact of the diverse controls so that the major mission of the team can be achieved. Selected reports on progress will be made to senior executives in charge of the respective teams. In all these respects the control design represents the straightforward application of the guidelines examined in Chapters 18 through 20.

The troublesome issue is what role the resource departments should play in controlling. For instance, in a ship-building company, should an engineering department (or marketing, legal, purchasing, finance, or the appropriate resource department) actively participate in controlling the quality and amount of engineering work done on a new container cargo vessel? Or in a large legal firm, should the criminal-law department control the briefs prepared by a young criminal lawyer assigned to a major antitrust case? Having provided the needed personnel and perhaps other services, the resource departments take on the role of staff. The question then arises of what control, if any, the resource departments should exercise while in this staff posture.

Three control designs indicate the array of possible relationships.

1. Full delegation to project teams. In a decentralized matrix design, each project team has virtually full independence in the action it takes. The presumption is that the uniqueness of the project, the need for prompt and coordinated action, and/or the high competence of the various specialists assigned to the team make localized control preferable. The team is on the field and it is up to the players to win the game.

Such independence relates to the running of specific projects. Postaction review by the resource department will, indeed, be carried out so that improvements in training for future projects can be made. These postaction reviews also seek to evaluate the effectiveness of persons assigned to the teams (insofar as this can be unscrambled from the group effort). Future assignments as well as advice on bonuses or other rewards will be influenced by this evaluation. Obviously, this postaction review is of personal concern to team members, so they are unlikely to disregard the training, suggestions, and values of their resource "home" department.

2. Periodic concurrence. A second arrangement is for the resource department to participate in milestone reviews. These milestone reviews are typically yes/no control points when the progress to date is used as a basis for authorizing continuation of the project as planned. Resource departments may join in such assessments and their concurrence may be necessary for the work to proceed.

All yes/no controls are introduced to improve safety, and adding an evaluation by resource departments increases the chances of catching serious errors. The chances for delay are also increased, however, so the desirability of requiring concurrence of resource departments at milestones depends on the relative weight attached to safety versus speed and some expense. Much depends upon how provincial the resource department is in its standards; it is possible, though by no means common, for the resource department to be as customer-oriented and results-oriented as the project managers themselves.

Naturally, the people on the operating teams will try to anticipate possible objections by the resource departments (and those whose views will be sustained if a difference of opinion is appealed to higher authority). This anticipation of control at the review points will temper actions in advance because prompt clearance simplifies the operating task. So even though reviews are occasional, any resource department whose consensus is required exercises substantial influence.

3. Continuous monitoring. A highly centralized control by resource departments is possible, usually by making the departmental representative on the project team merely a communicator of reactions and decisions made by the control staff group. This arrangement will undermine the project team concept. It can be tolerated only for those functions that make minor and intermittent inputs to the team's action, as may be true of, for example, a legal or real estate department. In effect, these fringe functions are withheld from the matrix. The staff groups perform an occasional service and exercise yes/no control at a few points when their specialty is involved.

Control in a matrix organization, then, does involve more or less double-checking by the project teams and their line supervisors, and by the resource groups. The scope and frequency of the double-checking calls for a careful balancing of greater freedom for the project team and closer scrutiny by the control staff group.

MATCHING LEADERSHIP STYLES AND REWARDS WITH CONTROLS

Since leadership style is intertwined with the application of control standards, leadership style and control design should be compatible.[8] For instance, to couple a control system predicated on close observance of standards with a permissive leadership style invites trouble.

Our previous analysis of control design clearly indicates that some situations call for tight control whereas loose control is preferable in others. The same situational factors bear upon the choice of leadership style.

[8]C. Cammann and D. A. Nadler, "Fit Control Systems to Your Managerial Style," *Harvard Business Review,* Jan. 1976.

Some trade-offs of benefits may be involved in the final selection of controls and leadership style, but it is vital that the controls support the leadership style, and vice versa.

Leadership style is not established by public announcement; it is based on executive behavior. Regardless of what a boss or a manual may say, those controls that are enforced are to the persons being controlled an unembellished guide to what they must do well and what they can do indifferently. They soon learn, for example, whether a "no smoking" rule means what it says or is merely a suggestion of desirable behavior. It is the action of the supervisor in disregarding or insisting that that standard be maintained that gives meaning to the control. Enforced standards communicate.

The permissive leader obviously faces a tough decision on which control standards he will seek to enforce. If he does not follow up on, say, established quotas, antipollution standards, or routine matters of attendance, his subordinates will infer that he is indifferent to their actions in such areas. This kind of permissiveness results in no control. On the other hand, if he consistently checks up on deviations of actual performance from standard but then confines his response to mild suggestions for improvement, the amount of control will be a function of the motivation of the subordinate. Of course, even a permissive leader may single out a few subjects on which no permissiveness is tolerated; the key here is to pick these subjects carefully.

Consistent rewards and controls. The company reward system, like leadership style, should reinforce the controls. Every production worker knows that a bonus based on volume alone leads to neglect of quality. Similarly, if professors get promoted on the basis of publications, their teaching suffers. Perhaps the most common error in management practice is to reward people for short-run results while urging them to take a long-run viewpoint; such short-run payoff is particularly insidious because long-run results are hard to measure and control. With a recognized reward (or penalty) associated with one kind of result, even the best designed controls on other results will receive secondary attention.

Individuals respond to many kinds of rewards, tangible and intangible, on the job and off the job. Tying these rewards to controls is not simple. Only part of the rewards can be granted or withheld by management. Persons who take actions that lead to rewards—for instance, making promotions or providing challenging assignments—are often not the same as the persons who exercise control. The timing and occasion for rewarding action is often separated from evaluation of results, sometimes by several years. Actions viewed partly as a reward may be subject to other considerations—promotions, for example.

Consequently, a careful review of the reward system should be made along with any major redesign of the control system. Insofar as flexibility permits, the granting of rewards should be clearly and explicitly related to desired performance as reflected by the controls. The line supervisor will usually carry the primary part in this mating of rewards and controls. The interconnection is so important, however, that an occasional independent check by someone with an objective viewpoint is desirable.

CONCLUSION

Like the nervous system in the human body, control is only one of the vital subsystems in effective management. Planning, organizing, and leading are also essential; and all these subsystems interact. If one is changed, the others may need to be redesigned also.

This interaction is a potential source of strength. By designing an organization suited to company plans, and by reinforcing both with compatible leadership styles and controls, we can create a highly synergistic force.

Several ways to obtain such an integrated management design have been flagged in this chapter: linking controls to the total planning system, decentralizing without loss of control, creating departments and profit centers that aid control, using staff properly, and enhancing control with consistent leadership styles and rewards.

The design of good controls is an intriguing task. Fitting them neatly into a balanced management structure is even more challenging—and rewarding.

Impact on Productivity

Even a quick review of the productivity sections at the close of each chapter in this book will underscore three aspects of improving the productivity of a company.

(1) Many factors are involved. There is no single quick fix. Rather, a lot of grass-roots activities have to be carefully designed and then done right. For example, if a radio program is to go on the air at 7 AM to catch the commuter audience, or if Barcelona engineers are to be thoroughly trained in the use of CAD-CAM computer programs by the end of the year, both goals require persistent effort, and they must pervade their organizations to achieve the desired levels of productivity.

(2) Moreover, these numerous refinements must fit together synergistically. As we stressed in this chapter, a move in one department or function must be compatible with work elsewhere. We don't focus just on our own convenience; side effects are identified and the trade-off of benefits and costs weighed. Japanese engineering has demonstrated that production simplification and customer repair service can be reconciled with selling appeal. One of the benefits of clear-cut strategy is the consistency of targets that it introduces. Strategy provides a unifying direction around which the many adjustments can be coordinated and integrated.

(3) Such a finely tuned, productive social structure takes effort and time to build. But while we are in the process of building the structure, we also know that the productivity achieved today may be obsolete tomorrow. Customers' needs change, technology changes, supply and competition change. Preeminence in making automobiles or consumer loans is an unstable achievement. Thus, a third vital aspect of productivity is a capacity to keep adapting to new conditions. Managers have to understand the process of managing—the subject of this entire book—well enough to be tooling up for future requirements at the same time as they are stressing effectiveness and efficiency in today's operations.

Fortunately, the three aspects of achieving high productivity just listed are do-able—at least for company managers as a group. We have a set of management concepts that, although far from perfect, help us to improve the many pieces, to knit these together, and to adapt to shifting requirements. The know-how is available. Everything does not have to be changed at once, however. Custom and learned behavior provide continuity for the vast majority of everyday activities. Changes are built on this established base. With proper leadership, organizations will put forth joint effort toward identified and unified goals. The productivity challenge is to get this total act together.

FOR FURTHER DISCUSSION

1. In many companies, managers' bonuses are based on profits. However, controls may direct managers to take actions that reduce current profits—spending money on research, for example, or on public goodwill. How do you suggest that controls and incentives be reconciled?

2. "The results of staff work essentially overlap the results of line executives' work. Therefore, you must define the results you expect of staff people so that they will be harmonious with the results of line people. Both the line and staff should get full credit for whatever is accomplished, just as though either had done it themselves." Do you agree? What difficulties might arise in applying this concept?

3. "A plan is no more than a rough roadmap until it is translated into a control system. Only then does an organization have a useful plan!" Do you agree with this comment by the president of a small paper company?

4. Senior officers of a large brokerage firm, E. F. Hutton, were penalized by the Securities and Exchange Commission (SEC) because several Hutton branch managers made a practice of illegally overdrawing various bank accounts. The officers ob-

jected; they claimed that because of a high degree of decentralization, they did not know of the practice. However, the SEC said that even if the officers did not know of the practice, they were still responsible because of "poor controls." Do you agree with the officers or with the SEC?

5. "The most critical controls for strategic plans are steering controls." "Strategic plans require the most detailed controls so that people can be encouraged to carry them out by knowing they will be monitored closely." With which statement do you more fully agree? Discuss.

6. Profit centers can be very valuable as control devices in businesses. Can centers of a similar character be created in not-for-profit organizations with corresponding benefits? Explain why or why not. As illustrations, consider schools, hospitals, fire departments, cemeteries, national parks, and so on. How do planning processes and rewards affect your response?

7. How does one develop good control systems for a matrix management structure?

8. What steps do you recommend to increase the "productivity" at your campus bookstore?

FOR FURTHER READING

Anthony, R. N. and D. Young, *Management Control in Nonprofit Organizations,* 3rd ed. Homewood, Ill.: Richard D. Irwin, 1983. Text and case studies explaining how the control process is applied in nonprofit organizations.

Cammann, C. and D. A. Nadler, "Fit Control Systems to Your Managerial Style," *Harvard Business Review,* Jan. 1976. Relates selection and design of controls to leadership style and internal motivation of subordinates.

Horovitz, J. H. and R. A. Thietart, "Strategy, Management Design and Firm Performance," *Strategic Management Journal,* Jan. 1982. One of few studies that looks at many elements in management design—including planning, organizing, and controlling—and matches these with growth and profit of a sample of comparable companies.

Hurst, E. G., "Controlling Strategic Plans," in P.

Lorange, *Implementation of Strategic Planning.* Englewood Cliffs, N.J.: Prentice-Hall, 1982, Ch. 7. Perceptive analysis of issues in designing controls for strategic management.

Newman, W. H., J. P. Logan, and W. H. Hegarty, *Strategy, Policy, and Central Management,* 9th ed. Cincinnati: South-Western Publishing Co., 1985, Chs. 22 and 23. Discussion of central managers' use of controls to secure united action, and the role of control in managing multinational enterprises.

Yavitz, B. and W. H. Newman, *Strategy in Action.* New York: Free Press, 1982. Part II focuses on the use of planning, organizing, leading, and controlling concepts to effectively execute company strategy. Part III deals with the integration of these activities into a moving game plan.

MANAGEMENT IN ACTION CASE 21
The Bhopal Disaster and International Management

On 3 December 1984, a Union Carbide pesticide plant in Bhopal, India, sprang a leak and spewed a lethal, poisonous gas that killed more than 2,000 people and blinded or otherwise harmed thousands more.

The catastrophe—easily the worst industrial accident in history—and its aftermath of accusations and lawsuits raised serious questions about how a U.S. corporation should conduct business in a foreign land.

India, like most developing countries, wants to manufacture within its boundaries products that are used locally. Moreover, India is a strong advocate of technology transfer and the employment of its own nationals to build and run local plants. Such "indigenization" is one of the pillars of economic and social development of the Third World.

Union Carbide's rather extensive operations in India, including the Bhopal plant, had been regarded as excellent examples of application of these principles. Union Carbide's technical staff in the U.S. provided specifications for the plant (a close copy of a similar U.S. plant) and other know-how for the production of insecticides—products that are used to increase the food production of the country. The plant was built and operated by a subsidiary located in India and staffed almost entirely by Indians. The entire subsidiary was run on a highly decentralized basis. The parent company did continue to make technical advice available; it supplied a few managers to help get the company running; and as part of its usual oversight of foreign operations it sent, about two years ago, an engineering team to review quality and safety practices.

Questions

1. What are the advantages of decentralizing an operation such as this?

2. What controls should the parent company retain? (Do *not* confine your answers to safety.)

3. Will the exercise of such controls undercut the advantages that you listed in answer to question 1?

4. Would your answers to questions 1 and 2 be the same for a subsidiary based in Europe? In Texas?

APPLICATION CASES

For practice in applying concepts in this chapter to managerial situations, see the following managerial decision cases. The case questions particularly relevant to this chapter are listed by number after each case name.

Fyler International (p. 68) 18
Consolidated Instruments (p. 189) 20
GAIN Software (p. 303) 17, 18
Unisa Sound (p. 530) 15
Norman Manufacturing Company (p. 538) 18

MANAGERIAL DECISION CASE STUDIES FOR PART V

Decision Case V-1
UNISA SOUND, INC.

Three months ago, Unisa Sound reached the $1 billion level in sales again and showed profits before taxes of over $120 million. Return on investment was higher than it had ever been, and yet the price of Unisa stock remained far below its previous high. This was the strongest showing in several years, during which losses in two divisions and divestiture of a large portion of a third division brought the company record losses.

An analyst who had followed Unisa stock for some time explained the lack of market excitement over Unisa's fine year as follows:

> They are like the little girl with the little curl. When they are good they are very, very good but when they are bad . . . For almost twenty years this company has gone through boom and bust cycles. They launch a new product or catch a piece of a growing market and they exploit it well and make lots of money. But then, almost as regularly, they hit a down market or make a mistake about a product and they suffer more than their competitors. I'm not sure whether they simply get sloppy in their management thinking after a success or what. It's clear, however, that they have experienced too many big ups and downs during the past twenty years for their stock to sell as it might with somewhat more stable performance.

Management's Response

The top four executives of Unisa have received clear signals from the board that, while pleased with last year's profit showing, they were not pleased with the stock market's low interest in the company because of its reputation for unstable earnings.

Samuel Parker, chairman, met with George Hayes, president, and Henry Cunningham, vice-president of corporate affairs, and Jervis Reiling, vice-president of finance, to discuss the company's future.

"Here we have one of the best years in our history," said Parker, "and our stock price barely moves. Two years ago when we lost $11 million as a result of divestitures and a bad market, we promised to turn things around and sure enough, we have, but the market doesn't nearly reflect that."

"The problem," said Hayes, "is that they are waiting for the next drop. The 'street' sees us as a company that can't sustain our profits for more than a year or two without at least one segment of our business taking a deeper nose dive than our competition."

Reiling nodded and said, "Well, George, it is hard to blame them. A look at our record over the last few decades tends to support that attitude.

We simply have to try to stabilize our growth and profit through more conservative investment and tighter budgeting. In the past, whenever a division has had a good year or two, they got everything they asked for and frequently spent far too much, too fast. Then, if they got in trouble, we tended to chop off a few heads, tighten down too far on expenditures and new capital, and unduly punish them."

"Well, that may be a bit of an overstatement, Jervis," said the chairman, "but what you describe is substantially true. When we were smaller, we tried to create a real sense of entrepreneurial drive in our divisions by giving the division presidents a great deal of freedom. If they delivered, they were rewarded, both personally and in terms of capital for expansion and greater freedom to call their own signals. When they failed, we tended to change personnel and tighten up control of funds. Perhaps we have gotten too large to continue this style of management. I want each of you to give real thought to what we must do. Don't be bound by the past or by personalities. I want to do what is necessary to change our image by changing our performance. I want growth in sales and profits, but I want more of it to come from greater *productivity* than from rolling dice on exotic new products or markets. Growth achieved through productivity is more stable growth. I don't rule out new ventures, but I want a more solid, stable business as a base. We will meet again in three weeks and I want your thoughts on how we make this happen."

Henry Cunningham, vice-president of corporate affairs, nodded in agreement and said, "I'm sure we can come up with a great deal in three weeks, Sam, but to get the most in terms of ideas and commitment to carrying out those ideas we have to develop programs that have every manager in this company working with his people to get them involved. This will take time, but it is essential if we are to avoid further labor problems. You know that our hourly and managerial work force may be even more upset than our stock holders with our recent peaks and troughs. The key to holding their confidence and commitment is to get them more fully involved in the solution."

"I quite agree, Hank," said Parker, "but before we start hanging suggestion boxes in every toilet, let's be sure we have a good idea of at least the major things that need to be changed. Let's plan on meeting here in three weeks."

Following this meeting, Hayes met with Cunningham and Reiling. "There are any number of ways we can move on this," he said. "I don't see us making dramatic changes in our product lines or markets, however, or spending more on R&D. Basically, our business is sound. My concern, and I'm sure it is Sam's concern as well, is whether our current structure and management processes really fit the business that has evolved in recent years. While we may want to make some changes in personnel, I don't see any major purges. We have good people, but have we organized them properly and designed the kinds of management systems to get the most out of all of us? "Jervis [Reiling, vice-president of finance], I want you to look at our present planning and control systems and think through how they might be altered to meet Sam's objective of stable growth through more productive use of our internal resources and existing market potential. Henry [Cunningham, vice-president of corporate affairs], I'd like you to consider our current organizational structure and our personnel systems. Have we got the right basic design? Are we too decentralized? Do we hire, develop, identify, and utilize our human resources as well as we should? We don't have a great deal of time before we meet with Sam again, so let's not try to come up with final answers; instead, we need a better set of criteria and guides for testing what we have and, if necessary, knowing what we are looking for."

Over the next two weeks, Cunningham and Reiling moved towards carrying out their assignments. Prior to developing recommendations on "criteria and guides" for Hayes to consider, they sought to describe the company's current organization, planning, control, and people systems.

Company Background

Unisa Sound came into being in the early 1950s as a result of a merger of two firms. One, United States Acoustics, was a $200 million firm, which produced acoustical equipment. They sold certain products directly to the federal government for military use and others to large electronics firms that produced radar and sonar equipment for both military and private use. The second firm, Phoenix Sound Equipment, was a smaller company, which produced extremely high-quality, high-fidelity components for the consumer phonograph market and the recording industry. Phoenix had a number of valuable patents, and excellent research and engineering personnel but lacked the capital and marketing know-how to exploit its products fully. Over the next five or six years, Unisa developed, under its chairman, Sam Parker (former president of U.S. Acoustics), into a major factor in four areas, or "businesses." Each "business" was headed by a division president and reported to George Hayes, the corporate president. Hayes was brought in after the merger by Parker. He had been a successful marketing and then group executive with one of the giant electrical-product firms. Also reporting to Hayes were two senior vice-presidents, Cunningham and Reiling. (See Exhibit 1.)

Government Systems Division (GSD)

Approximately one-third of the company's volume and an average of 20 percent of its profit comes from the sale of electronic components and sound systems to various governmental bodies and agencies. Unisa has a solid reputation in these markets and is respected by its competitors. Though sales to government sometimes tend to fluctuate more dramatically than Unisa's sales to other markets, Unisa's market share of government sales is more stable than its share in other markets. Julius Katz, president of this division, explains:

> We are so highly regarded in the markets we sell that when there is a cutback, we usually feel it less than our competitors. Except for a few areas where we have exclusive products or know-how, government buyers hedge by

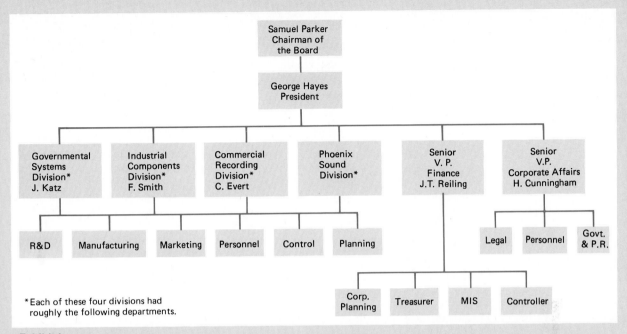

Exhibit I

*Each of these four divisions had roughly the following departments.

dealing with several suppliers. We not only get the lion's share of most of the government markets we go after, but we usually are the last to be cut back when government spending declines. Thus, while we are vulnerable to changes in governmental spending, these changes are relatively predictable at least a year or two in advance, and we can prepare for them.

Industrial Components Divisions (ICD)

Industrial Components' sales in recent years have accounted for almost 40% of the company's sales, but profits have fluctuated greatly. Within the past fifteen years, this division was the largest profit maker in the company for eight years, had record losses for five years, and realized modest profits for two years.

An executive with another Unisa division described ICD as follows:

They are in the most exciting and most dangerous part of the business, selling the most sophisticated acoustical components. They must stay on top of component technology, but they must also be constantly on the lookout for cost-reduction programs that don't hurt quality. When they were making money, their division head, Tom Ashe, was king. He got everything he wanted from corporate and ran that division like a separate, but not equal, kingdom. His people looked down on the rest of the divisions, and for a while they were coining money. They slipped one year but came right back, stronger than ever. Then, five years ago, they lost us a bundle of money. It's funny, but they seemed to do worse than the competition once they started. In the good years they always seemed to do better. After three straight years of record losses, Ashe resigned, and his replacement, Fran Smith, managed to break even last year and make good money this year. The trouble is, thanks to Ashe, I still don't think anyone at corporate understands the various parts of that division, its specialized markets, nor how it is set up.

Commercial Recording Division (CRD)

Smaller than GSD and ICD, CRD accounts for approximately 20 percent of Unisa's average sales. Its profits, like ICD's, have fluctuated widely. With lower peaks and valleys, CRD's profit-and-loss cycles have been shorter, but more numerous. The current president, Charles Evert, explained,

> We are in a very tough business. There is a great deal of competition, and we have to work hard to get the right balance of quality and cost. We periodically have to sell for less than full cost to hold key customers.
>
> In the past we used to sell audio equipment and components to a dozen or so large recording and film companies. Now there are literally hundreds of companies, most smaller than in the past, doing commercial recording work. This makes the market more difficult and more subject to fluctuation, as well.
>
> The basic business is sound and we can make good money if we get enough to invest in new-product development and marketing when we need it, which is often when we have to catch up on the competition. In fact, it's great to have the freedom we get when the going is good, but frustrating to have everything freeze up on you when you take a dip.

Phoenix Sound Division (PSD)

The PSD division now accounts for only 6 to 8 percent of Unisa's total sales. Its product line consists of extremely high-quality home sound systems. The division manufactures amplifiers and speakers and purchases turntables and other components and sells one of the most expensive high-fidelity stereo systems on the market.

In past years, PSD had also assembled and sold a line of less expensive hi-fi systems, tape decks, and other audio equipment, but foreign competition virtually drove the division out of this business. Four years ago, it sold to a Japanese firm the trade name and product designs that once accounted for 80 percent of its volume in less expensive systems. Though much smaller now, the division has cut its losses greatly but remains marginal in terms of its profit contributions.

Previous Management Philosophy

After a short period of readjustment following the merger, Unisa was organized along much the same lines as it is today. Parker, an engineer by training, and Hayes, whose early background had been in marketing, worked well together. They, along with J. T. Reiling and, later, Henry Cunningham, serve as an executive committee and make most major financial decisions by consensus. Hayes commented, "Sam is a Quaker and knows how to manage by consensus. Make no mistake, though, if he really has his mind set, he gets his way, but he likes to have the four of us agree."

Except for financial controls, the four operating divisions typically enjoy great freedom. In Parker's words, "As long as they set tough goals and meet them and maintain the overall company image for high-quality and ethical standards, the divisions pretty much call their own shots."

When a division fails to live up to these standards, the executive committee has tended to move in quickly. Tom Ashe, former president of ICD, said,

> I still respect Parker and Hayes as people, but I am terribly disappointed in their lack of patience. I gave them eight outstanding years of performance and, due to a tough market, lost money for two years. I know I could have turned it around, but they insisted on trying to run my division for me with a lot of ratios and budget cuts. None of them really knows the business, so either they should have *fired* me and brought in someone like me who *understands* the situation, or they should have left me alone. When they tried to "help," all they did was turn a depressed situation into a disaster.

Planning and Control Systems

While Parker has stated that the company as a whole does not develop a formal strategy plan, each division is asked to generate its own strategic plan.

"We set broad growth and profit goals," said Hayes, "and approve their five- and one-year financial plans, and occasionally step in when there is a major decision to be made, like when the divestiture of most of our consumer products took place. We don't have central staff or a big planning group. Reiling runs our financial and information services; Cunningham, our legal, personnel, and public relations services. They don't second-guess the divisions or do their work for them; they provide them with service, and Sam and me with information and advice."

Reiling agreed with that description: "We discuss with each division president his last year's performance and his next year's plan in February. This is done in light of a five-year plan, which he presents or updates at the same time. We try to understand the major directions, opportunities, and problems reflected in the plant, but we really dig in only on major new capital requests or when a division has been in trouble several years in a row."

Cunningham feels these systems worked well when the business was smaller but believes they now are deficient. "Our problems with ICD and Phoenix are perfect examples of our weaknesses. With better planning and control systems, we should have spotted the difficulties in these divisions much sooner. We don't get enough detail from the divisions with regard to the qualitative assumptions or premises on which they base their plans. We have only a general idea of how the plans are put together within each division and of what lies behind the single set of numbers we receive.

"Thus, we have little basis to either challenge their plans or, after the fact, evaluate their results. This makes it very difficult to learn the business or evaluate what is needed when they get in trouble.

"Of course, if we were to get the data I want, I wouldn't know what to do with it. I have neither the numbers nor quality of top staff people I would need to really assess the division plans or evaluate their results the way we should.

"Jervis Reiling had a director of corporate planning reporting to him, and he set up our current planning and budgeting procedures several years ago. He rubbed a few of the division people the wrong way, however, and left the company as a result of the personality clashes. Jervis has never really replaced him. Although we still use the same systems, the chap who now has this job is really not a planner. He heads up a budget consolidation process, which includes some review. I have suggested to Jervis that he look for a stronger person or that I take over the planning area to try to get away from what I believe to be the undue emphasis on numbers.

"I am trying to figure out how we might reorganize or shift job descriptions enough to allow central management to play a more active role in directing, or at least better evaluating, the divisions. We must do this if we are to meet Sam Parker's goal of more stable growth through productivity."

Reiling and Hayes seem to share Cunningham's objective but are less than certain about how to carry it out without a major change in management philosophy.

Human Resources

Unisa is regarded by most of its employees and managers as a fair, ethical organization. Most of its operations are nonunion, and it has gained a reputation for being a bit paternalistic. As one union organizer put it, "They want so badly to keep us out that they pay more to keep us out than we could get if we got in." Cunningham feels that the recent problems have created grave potential problems for personnel.

"We had our ups and downs in the past and, despite some short layoffs or cutbacks, we have generally kept most of our good people employed. Because much of our manufacturing and engineering work has a lot in common, we have been able to transfer workers and managers across division lines when one or the other was having a slow time. Recently, however, our ups have been higher, our downs lower, and several divisions were affected at the same time. This has led to build-ups in employees and then the need for larger reductions than we could handle by transfers. When we unloaded most of Phoenix at about the same time as ICD was falling from its prior heights, we had to effect major layoffs for the first time.

"We have never really involved lower-level managers, professionals, or hourly workers in decisions affecting their work, so they find it difficult to understand why they must pay for our mistakes."

Hayes is concerned about personnel, but for slightly different reasons. "In the past, we were very generous during good years with all our people," he explained. "We paid higher wages, big bonuses, and had a great incentive compensation system. Each time things went well, the base got bigger. Each time we had a downturn, we would cut back, but not as much as we should have, thus increasing our difficulty in the next cycle.

"To maintain a more stable growth picture through productivity increases, we are going to have to be less generous across the board and at the same time reward those who can save or generate big dollars for us. For this reason, I share Hank's desire to get more participative planning, but we must first get a clearer picture of where we want to take this company and whether we have the proper organization, procedures, and people to get us there."

QUESTIONS

Part I

1. How should an analyst attempt to determine the extent to which Unisa's widely fluctuating results stem from uncontrollable environmental changes and to what extent from a poor or incomplete master strategy?

2. What do you think of Parker's comments on achieving growth and profits through strategies that focus on productivity rather than "rolling dice on exotic new products"?

Part II

3. How might Unisa's different divisions contribute to strategic growth by playing rather different strategic roles? Illustrate your answer by sketching out strategic roles for any two divisions.

4. Review your answer to question 3. How would operating objectives vary in the divisions you describe as playing different strategic roles?

5. Will developing more standing plans at the corporate level contribute to more stable divisional results? What kinds of standing plans would be most helpful?

Part III

6. Would greater centralization be likely to reduce fluctuations in Unisa's performance? Explain.

7. Might one or more of Unisa's divisions be highly centralized and others very decentralized? What factors would you consider in permitting such disparities?

8. How might strengthening corporate staff affect the emphasis on longer-term stability and productivity at the group level? Would staff groups that seek to help the divisions be more or less desirable than staff groups that evaluate division efforts and seek to pressure them in various directions?

Part IV

9. How should leadership styles in the Governmental Systems division differ from those most needed at the top of Phoenix sound system?

10. In what ways may Parker's efforts to deemphasize "rolling dice" positively and negatively affect motivation throughout the divisions?

11. What will be key parts of the change process needed to move toward more formal integrated planning?

Part V

12. Will more detailed budgetary controls be necessary if more detailed plans are required of each division?

13. During a transition period, what will be most important in creating controls that help both division *and* corporate managers to learn what works and what doesn't work under more formal plans?

14. How would you monitor the reaction of key creative people at the division level to more stringent corporate controls? Should corporate or division personnel do the monitoring.

15. How should control systems be altered to make sure compensation and bonuses are tied to objectives that now are to be given greater emphasis?

16. How should Unisa ensure that movement toward greater participation in planning will not reduce accountability for results?

17. *Summary Report Question for Part V.* Based on your answer to question 18, develop a detailed control system indicating what to measure, when, how, how often, by whom, and so forth to determine the degree to which *any one* of the four divisions was moving toward playing the strategic role most needed of it to increase stable growth for Unisa as a company.

Summary Report Question for Solution of Case as a Whole

18. Develop (a) strategies, (b) key action plans, (c) staffing changes, and (d) motivational and leadership techniques needed to bring each of Unisa's four divisions to play different roles in producing more stable growth for the total company.

Decision Case V-2
NORMAN MANUFACTURING COMPANY

The Norman Manufacturing Company produces a variety of industrial machinery and equipment, including electrical switches and relay boxes; the smaller items of coal-mining equipment; and chains, hoists, conveyors, and other materials-handling products. In addition to these lines, the company has expanded, through acquisition in the past ten years, into two lines less closely connected with its original product line: the manufacture of sporting goods and of furnishings (hardware, plumbing, furniture) for pleasure yachts. Its annual sales last year approached $70 million.

Norman Manufacturing Company originated thirty years ago as a family-owned company that specialized in manufacturing and selling chains and hoists, with a plant located in Bridgeport, Connecticut. The company has experienced rapid growth through the years. Products allied to heavy industry have been added during the past fifteen years. Company headquarters were moved from Bridgeport to New York City seven years ago.

Regarding the objectives of the company, L. D. Norman, Jr., the president, states:

"Since my father's death thirteen years ago, we have endeavored to stress even more strongly the objective of growth over the years. The public now owns 63 percent of our stock, but they, as well as our family and our management, have certain principal accomplishments in mind: to have this company grow in assets, market coverage, profitability, and prestige over the years; and to have it gain a national reputation for quality and service to our customers. This is why we have taken on two new divisions that are not connected with our past experience. We feel that the company has a future in many product lines. Technology and consumer tastes mean you can't stand still with your traditional products and ways of doing things."

The Lange Division

Seven years ago, the Norman Company purchased the Lange Sporting Goods Company and established it as the Lange Division of NMC. The research bulletin of a New York investment firm at that time carried the following statement:

> The Lange Company, with a good, stable line of products, has suffered in recent years from a lack of vitality in keeping its products, production methods, and advertising up to the "zip" displayed by its competitors. We believe that Norman's record of capable and aggressive management should enable this company to show good growth over the intermediate-term future.

The management of Lange had been in the hands of four members of the Lange family, all of whom retired at the time of the merger. L. D. Norman, Jr., immediately replaced them with Fred K. Gibbs as general manager of the Lange Division, and with two Norman middle-management executives as controller and production superintendent.

Fred Gibbs, 42, had been executive vice-president of a competing sporting-goods manufacturing company. After graduating from the University of Washington, he held positions as production-scheduling trainee, salesman, sales manager, and marketing vice-president for that company. Reference checks at the time of his employment by Norman Manufacturing Company indicated that he was well liked by his fellow executives, possessed an unusual degree of energy and drive, and had initiated many of the ideas that later, in the form of company policies, led to sales increases and the growth of his company.

Management of the Norman Company

L. Donald Norman, Jr., has been president of the Norman Manufacturing Company for thirteen years. At age fifty, he has worked for the company twenty-six years, first in the plants, then as a salesman, and for ten years as an assistant to his father, designing and supervising procedures to co-ordinate production, sales, shipping, and inventories. As president, he has spent most of his time planning new customer strategy and sales incentive programs, and projecting financial statements to plan increases in plant investment. Together with T. M. Farish, executive vice-president, and C. A. Langford, treasurer, he sits on the executive committee. This committee meets three times a week to discuss all important matters in sales, production, and finance.

At the time the Lange Division was established, the executive committee minutes show, Farish and Langford were somewhat apprehensive about the ability of Norman Company management "to take hold of this new venture and manage it successfully, since we do not have experience in consumer products."

Mr. Norman, the minutes also show, gave the committee a summary of the study he had been making of decentralization. He pointed out that such companies as General Motors and Du Pont were able to grow by creating independent divisions, selecting capable people to run them, and retaining only broad measures of performance. In this way, he said, the Norman Company could delegate virtually the entire management task "to Fred Gibbs and his team. We do not have to know much about the details of the division, as long as we establish broad controls."

In the five months after the acquisition, the three top Norman officials drew up the following control points. They were careful to make clear, Norman says, that Gibbs' own performance would be measured only in terms of these controls. "Everything else—all of the details of running the division—would be left to Fred."

▫ *Rate of return on investment:* Lange was earning an average of 14 percent (before taxes) on book value, and it was agreed to raise the target to 19 percent within five years. *Sales as a percentage of industry sales:* Norman judged that the Lange Company had been performing as indicated below, and new targets were set for Lange's three principal products:

Product	Present	Five-Year Target
Tennis equipment	11%	15%
Golf bags	8%	12%
Gym clothing	10%	25%

In setting these figures, all three executives agreed that there was no accurate way to be "scientific" about what percentages could be reached.

All recognized that the Lange Company had been, in the words of Norman, "conservative, lacking in morale, and complacent." It therefore seemed reasonable that "with a hard-hitting management and some new ideas, the targets are neither over nor understated—they are realistic."

Gibbs at first expressed the idea that the gym-clothing sales target was too high. But Langford and Norman showed him the results of their study of profits in this line compared to others. The profitability of selling gym clothing, particularly to institutions, was much higher than that of the other items. Gibbs, too, agreed that his target was a wise one.

Operating Results: First Six Years of Operation

Lange Division has been in operation for six fiscal years. Rate of return on investment and percentages of industry sales appear in Exhibits I and II, respectively.

During the first four years, the executive committee of the Norman Company had a verbal agreement, of which they frequently reminded themselves, that none of Norman's management should initiate inquiries about *specific* operations in Lange. Langford reports, for instance, that when he noticed, on the expense statements furnished for the first year,

Exhibit I RATIO OF PROFIT (BEFORE TAX) TO INVESTMENT IN THE LANGE DIVISION

Year	Method 1*	Method 2**
First	14%	12%
Second	14%	11%
Third	15%	13%
Fourth	15%	13%
Fifth	17%	16%
Sixth	17%	16%
Present***	17%	16%

 *Used by Lange Division controller, charging advertising and research to capital investment, the lower half of the ratio.

 **Used by Norman Company management, charging advertising and research to current expense, thus decreasing the top of the ratio.

***First quarter adjusted.

Exhibit II SALES AS A PERCENTAGE OF TOTAL INDUSTRY SALES

Year	Tennis Equipment	Golf Bags	Gym Clothing
First	11%	9%	10%
Second	12%	10%	15%
Third	12%	9%	21%
Fourth	13%	11%	22%
Fifth	12%	10%	23%
Sixth	12%	10%	22%
Present (lst quarter)	12%	10%	21%

that telephone and telegraph expenses of Lange were, in his opinion, far out of line with those of the rest of the company, he felt that he should not use these statements as detailed controls.

The committee also agreed that Norman should make fairly frequent (perhaps bimonthly) visits to Lange headquarters in Providence for the purpose of inquiring about overall sales improvement. He should also encourage Gibbs to come to New York whenever "*he* feels the need to discuss any matter—broad, detailed, or otherwise."

As a matter of practice, Norman, Gibbs, and Langford did meet about three times a month, at which time they discussed overall sales results for ten to twenty minutes, and they discussed and approved lump-sum amounts of money requested by Gibbs to be budgeted for both capital expenditures and current expenses.

At the end of the fourth year, Langford, who had been raising questions with Norman all along about the wisdom of Gibbs' expenditures, suggested that investment return and sales targets were "far less than satisfactory. We have been holding off telling him how to manage various phases of his budget for too long. There is little doubt but that he has gone too fast and too far in increasing expenditures for advertising, salespeople's bonuses, and salespeople's expense accounts. Furthermore, his expenditures for employee-recreation facilities and increases in factory salaries have been unwise when we are trying to increase return on investment. The former increased the investment side of the ratio, and the latter decreased the income side."

Langford, incidentally, received expense summaries regularly—as he says, "not as control reports, but for the purpose of consolidating the figures with the rest of the company divisions for the profit-and-loss statement." These summaries contained thirty-five account captions (for excerpts of five of the captions, see Exhibit III).

After reviewing Langford's cost statements, the executive committee agreed that "Gibbs needs some helpful guidance." Since Langford knew more about the details of expense and capital budgets, they also agreed that he should visit Gibbs once a month to go over the thirty-five expense accounts, and see how each progressed during the year.

Exhibit III **SELECTED EXPENSE CAPTIONS AND AMOUNTS FROM LANGE DIVISION EXPENSE TABULATION**

Expense Caption	Fourth Year	Year Prior to Merger
Advertising	$1,200,000	$ 280,000
Salespeople bonuses	1,010,000	223,000
Salespeople expense	245,000	168,000
Factory salaries	1,265,000	1,050,000
Employee service	180,000	22,010

Gibbs recalls that early in his fifth year at Lange, when Langford first came to Providence and told him what the executive committee had decided, "I was surprised. I guess it scared me a little right off the bat, since I had no idea they were thinking like that. The targets weren't being met, but I thought that surely they must know that things were going quite well, considering all of the things that must be done to put this division on a solid footing for the future. After my initial anxiety and surprise, I got downright mad for a few days."

Gibbs also states that, "Early in the fifth year, I began to cut back on some of the spending inaugurated in the beginning. I got the salespeople together on four occasions and gave them a talk about the necessity of cutting their expense-account expenditures, and the fact that we would have to stop making some of the purely promotional calls, and concentrate on those customers that looked more like immediate prospects. I also cut the number of direct-mail promotional brochures from twelve mailings a year to six, and decided to let one person go who had been hired as a merchandising person. He had helped, in the four years he had been with us, in designing the products for eye-appeal, in creating point-of-sale displays, and in improving the eye-appeal of our packages. I did not cut down on the number of salespeople employed, however."

The Question of Advertising and Research Costs

As early as February of the second year, Gibbs objected—in his words, "mildly"—to Norman "because of the way Langford entered on certain financial statements the money spent for advertising, the market-research department, and the product-research department." When the first-year statement of return was prepared by Lange's own controller, Gibbs and he felt that these outlays represented an investment, rather than a current operating expense. They reasoned that the increase in new products, and the increase in goodwill or consumer acceptance, would not begin to pay off for two or three years. Since return on investment is the ratio of income to investment, charging these three items to investment showed a higher performance (14 percent in the first year) than the same statement prepared by Langford (12 percent in the same year). It seemed to Gibbs that subtracting the outlay from one year's profits "was a real injustice. Tom Farish and Norman family stockholders have pretty much stayed out of my end of the business, but I don't want them to get the wrong impression. They will, from that kind of misleading figure."

Gibbs and Langford both feel that, in spite of this disagreement, the relationship of the Norman management group to Gibbs is "a pretty good one." Gibbs says, "I pretty much go along with their guidance, though at one time it looked like interference. The only thing I'm still darn mad about is this way of figuring return. Norman overruled me when Langford and I had it out in front of him one time, but it's still such a hot subject that Langford and I won't bring it up anymore. Why, just look at the figures for the whole period that the division has been in existence!" (See Exhibit I.)

QUESTIONS

Part I

1. How successful do you feel Norman will be in attempting to manage his traditional industrial-product line, sporting-goods division, and yacht-supply division? What factors will determine whether he can play the several roles needed?

2. What do you think of Norman's strategy for diversification? What are its strong and weak points?

Part II

3. From the facts in the case, draw conclusions about the broad objectives of the Norman Manufacturing Company.

4. From a study of the case, make a list of policies and procedures that might help to solve the conflicts between top management and division management.

5. Describe in some detail how participation might work in this case to improve the quality of decisions in Norman Manufacturing Company. Specify who would do what. Then discuss the advantages that might accrue to various people in the case and to the company.

Part III

6. Should the Lange division have its own controller's (accounting) department? Why? What disadvantages does the company incur by having a separate accounting department in this division? What advantages?

7. What effect is the economic function of the company having on its internal organizational structure? What effects are the people (executives) having on the structure?

8. At the end of the case, how did the "real" organizational structure differ from that visualized as the "formal" structure at the beginning of the case? Describe the process that brought about this change.

Part IV

9. How should Norman go about getting Gibbs to accept the directions of the headquarters management? What means does Gibbs have for resisting these directions?

10. What can be done in the way of building communication networks that might help to solve the problem of the Norman Manufacturing Company?

11. After studying the case carefully, do you think the leadership function is being performed effectively in this company? State the underlying causes that support your answer. What changes are necessary to improve Norman's leadership? Gibbs' leadership?

12. What factors in this case seem to be causing a lack of understanding between Langford and Gibbs? How might personal communication improve the operation of the company?

Part V

13. What are the key objectives of the Lange Division? Has management adopted strategic measures for their attainment? List other key measures they might have instituted.

14. List the objectives Gibbs was trying to reach by the expenditures listed in Exhibit III. Then state the objectives Langford was trying to reach when he opposed the increase in expenditures. Why do these conflict? How do they relate to the broad objectives of the company? In light of this conflict, what strategic control points should Norman establish?

15. After careful study of the case, diagnose the underlying reasons why Gibbs objected to the controls proposed by Norman headquarters. Then outline what actions Norman top management might take to eliminate these reasons.

16. Given the type of organizational structure (division of work and delegation of authority) Norman envisioned, what is indicated for designing control points? (Illustrate with facts from the case.)

17. Will Norman have an easier or more difficult time measuring results now than they did before permitting Langford to suggest changes to Gibbs?

18. *Summary Report Question for Part V.* After thorough study of the case, write a report that (a) states the central problems of measuring and controlling results faced by the Norman Company top management; (b) traces the basic causes of these problems, in terms both of standards and measurements themselves and of the reaction of people to controls; (c) recommends what actions management should take to remove these causes and prevent the recurrence of the problems in the future.

Summary Report Question for Solution of Case as a Whole

19. Answer the following questions, considering not only the control system employed in Norman Manufacturing Company, but also the organizational structure, decision-making methods used by executives, and their leadership patterns: (a) What are the goals to be attained, and the problems faced, by management? (b) What are the basic causes of the problems that have arisen in the company in seeking to reach its goals? (c) What actions should be taken by various executives in the company to achieve goals and remove the causes of the problems?

Nels Engberg is managing director of Scandico (Singapore), a wholly owned subsidiary of Scandico, Ltd., a large Swedish shipping company. He has had this position for almost four years, having been hired away from a competing shipping company. Scandico, Ltd., with headquarters in Stockholm, owns and operates a large fleet of commercial vessels (freighters, tankers) that produce over 70 percent of the company's revenues and profits. Most of the remaining revenue comes from its freight forwarding division, which handles a variety of transportation services for large industrial customers. Wherever possible, the freight forwarding division seeks to use Scandico vessels, but they are not limited to them as means of transport.

Scandico has offices in more than a hundred locations. The large offices are headed by a managing director who typically will have two general managers reporting to him. One integrates all shipping activities, while the other looks after freight forwarding. While there is a great deal of direct contact between these two general managers, it is the reponsibility of the managing director to coordinate these two groups to ensure the greatest benefit not just to his office but also to Scandico's international operations.

Scandico (Singapore) is a large operation with almost 85 percent of its volume managed by Axel Lindt, general manager of shipping. Profits have recently been very good, and headquarters management feels this is due to Engberg's knowledge of the market and skills as a negotiator. While Lindt is regarded as an excellent administrator, Engberg is seen as the key to the office's successful maintenance of high margins.

Michael Day, who is forty, came to Singapore about two years ago as general manager of freight forwarding, after serving for several years as shipping manager in Sao Paulo, Brazil. Prior to that he had worked in various positions for another shipping company. His performance in Brazil was regarded by corporate management as acceptable, but not outstanding.

"His biggest problem as head of a shipping operation was his lack of skill in negotiating with large customers," said Peter Alstrop, Scandico's president. "He just didn't seem capable of driving a tough bargain. He generated a good bit of business and maintained the clients he took over, but our margins were almost always lower than we felt they should be. When we called him on the margins negotiated, he always had a good reason for getting less than we thought he should get. We had real trouble pinpointing where he was 'wrong' because of the distance, but his overall results, though acceptable, just weren't up to what we thought they should be. Day is a charming, bright man and knows shipping well. He just doesn't seem to have the skills to negotiate the few extra points that spell the difference between acceptable margins and good margins. In other respects, he appears to be an excellent manager and developer of people. We transferred him to Singapore with high hopes. He is a manager we feel has the potential to head up one of our large operations, and we have told him so. By having him work for Engberg, we hoped he would develop the skills and toughness he needs. Engberg was not anxious to have him. He has produced good results recently and did not feel he needed Day.

"We couldn't convince him to take Day on as general manager of shipping, but he did agree to name him as general manager of freight forwarding if we promoted his current general manager of freight forwarding to a key job in Australia. Engberg drives a hard bargain even with us, but we went along with him with the understanding that while Day would manage freight forwarding, Engberg would include him in negotiations with large Chinese customers of the shipping division. The Chinese are among the best and toughest bargainers in the world. We felt Day would learn a lot by watching and gradually helping Engberg negotiate with them. We felt he could do this and still manage our service operation there since it is small and runs very smoothly."

After Day's first year, he was evaluated by Engberg, and the appraisal, along with Day's responses, were forwarded to the company's personnel office in Stockholm. Walter Nielsen, corporate director of personnel, indicated he was "a bit unhappy" with what he deduced from the forms.

"Overall," Nielsen said, "Engberg has given him a satisfactory rating, but has criticized him for not paying enough attention to details in his freight forwarding group. Engberg feels that Day wants to avoid the nitty-gritty and let his subordinates handle details that he himself should get into."

Day, in his comments on his appraisal (in diplomatic terms according to Nielsen) says that "he isn't getting what he came to Singapore for—namely, experience in negotiating." Day feels that he can give his subordinates the freedom he does, that it is good for their development, and that he doesn't let them make any serious mistakes. He has asked Engberg to include him in more big projects in the shipping division and to let him take on a few small negotiations on his own.

Since we sent Day over to learn," Nielsen said, "and Engberg knows this, Day's requests seem reasonable. Besides, we hoped Day could show Engberg how to delegate and develop his subordinates. Engberg needs to develop this talent if he is to manage a larger operation."

Nielsen communicated these views in a long letter to Engberg and indicated that he had discussed the situation with Peter Alstrop, the company's president, and Mark Hammersmith, vice-president, Far East, Engberg's direct superior. Both, according to Nielsen, agreed with Nielsen's views.

Reluctantly, Engberg began to bring Day into several large shipping projects and over the next year gave him three small shipping projects involving negotiations to manage himself. When Day received his second appraisal from Engberg, he again was given an acceptable overall rating but was strongly criticized on two counts.

"Day is a smart man," says Engberg, "but he can't or won't face up to conflict. He doesn't want to hear about problems unless they are purely technical problems. These he dives into and solves them well. People problems, particularly conflicts among people, seem beyond him. He will either walk away from them or give in and compromise *his* goals to try to get others to come to agreement.

"This means he often neglects important details in running his freight forwarding division. He will give good technical advice, but if two or more of his subordinates can't agree on something, they have learned not to come to Day, but to solve it themselves. This would be all right except they often lack the perspective to come to good decisions.

"My second concern is more serious. With his desire to avoid conflict, he just cannot handle tough negotiations. He gives away too much. This not only costs us in the specific deal he is working on but also has ramifications on many other current or future deals.

"In short, I do not believe he will ever make a good negotiator or a good manager. He is a walking encyclopedia, though, and could make a fine staff resource, and I have tried to encourage him to take this route, but he won't listen. For some reason, he thinks I don't like him and that I am undercutting him with the people here and in headquarters. As a result of this, despite my efforts to correct this impression, he has started politicking and trying to line up allies here and at headquarters. While I was away for two weeks of meetings in Stockholm, he wheedled his way into several negotiations and we ended up with deals I do not like. I have reprimanded Lindt, the general manager of shipping, for not keeping Day out of these deals. Lindt said he was under the impression that Day had important friends at headquarters who wanted him to get as much exposure as possible to negotiations involving the shipping division. I asked Lindt where he got this idea and he said it came from comments Day had made and from a Telex he had received from Nielsen [corporate director of personnel], requesting that he, Lindt, give personal attention to Day's development in shipping.

"When I heard this, " said Engberg, "I hit the ceiling. I had never seen this cable. I regard Nielsen's actions as most inappropriate and I fired off a Telex to him telling him how I felt and demanding that Day be transferred as soon as possible to another location. We do not need what he has to offer in Singapore, and his presence here is becoming increasingly disruptive to my operations.

"Nielsen's response completely ignored my protest of his high-handed behavior and invited me to come to Stockholm to discuss this matter. I'll be damned if I see the value of traveling so far to discuss this matter and I Telexed Nielsen to this effect, repeating my request that Day be transferred.

"I sent copies of all correspondence on this matter to my boss, Hammersmith. In the past he has always been very supportive, but in this case, he seems to be passing the buck. A week passed and I received an invitation from Peter Alstrop [president] to come to Stockholm and discuss the Day case and 'other related issues.' I really don't understand this and I am tempted to ask Alstrop for clarification, but this may not be wise. I called Hammersmith and he suggested that perhaps I should go and find out what Nielsen's been up to. The rumor mill has been very active here lately, and for the first time since I've been here, I see signs of polarization.

"If Day isn't moved, he may well build a following among my weaker people who like his "laissez faire, don't-make-waves" approach to things. Day has been telling them, I'm sure, that I am too tough, and that by always trying for the extra points, he says I am creating good short-term results but not developing an organization or customer relationships that can stand up over time. Rubbish! I have produced good results here for three straight years. Hammersmith says I'm his best producer, but he has an enormous geographic area to oversee and I don't see him more than two or three times a year. Frankly, I don't expect much help from him. I'll probably have to straighten this out myself."

QUESTIONS

Part I

1. To what degree may the *role* of a manager differ in countries such as Singapore? How may the role be the same regardless of culture, economic development, and so forth?

2. Is the role of a general manager who attempts to manage over vast geographic distances significantly different from the role of one who manages a large but local company? Explain and illustrate using Alstrop and Hammersmith as examples.

Part II

3. To what degree might Engberg's differences with Day have been caused by failure to set proper operating objectives?

4. Should an operation like Scandico (Singapore) operate within a large or small number of standing plans developed in headquarters? What kind of standing plans would be most helpful? Least helpful?

5. List what you feel are four or five different problems (gaps) presented in this case. Develop a means–end network that shows the relationships among these problems. Which should Engberg tackle first? Which should the president, Alstrop, tackle first?

Part III

6. What do you think of Nielsen's statement, "Since we sent Day over to learn . . . Day's requests seem reasonable. Besides, we hoped Day could show Engberg how to delegate and develop his subordinates"? To what degree might these dual objectives be complementary? Contradictory?

7. Assess Nielsen's action against the concepts of corporate staff presented in Chapter 10. Consider both good and bad aspects of his behavior.

8. To what degree might a matrix organization be appropriate to Scandico? If it were in place, how would it affect Day's situation in Singapore?

9. How good a match of structure and people appears to exist with respect to Engberg and his position in the company? With respect to Day?

Part IV

10. Assuming that Day remains in Singapore, what steps should Engberg take to deal with his concerns about polarizing the group?

11. Does the conflict that appears to be building in Singapore have any potential benefits to the organization, or is it likely to be only destructive?

12. How should Nielsen and/or Alstrop have sought to motivate Engberg to train and develop Day? Is it still possible for them to motivate him to carry out his task? How?

13. Do you think it possible for two such apparently different leadership styles as Engberg's and Day's to function in the Singapore division?

Part V

14. How should Engberg's performance be appraised and his career planned?

15. What controls might contribute to Day's improvement as a negotiator?

16. How might controls be developed that will help headquarters assess the degree to which Engberg may be building or detracting from longer-term results?

17. To what degree may the large number of offices make control of individual offices (a) easier and (b) more difficult than if there were ten offices?

18. What role(s) should headquarters staff play in control of the hundred offices?

19. *Summary Report Question for Part V.* What steps do you recommend Alstrop and Hammersmith take to prevent, or deal more effectively with, problems such as those surrounding Nielsen and Day? How would you measure and control the effective implementation of these steps?

Summary Report Question for Solution of Case as a Whole

20. Assuming Alstrop wanted Day in Singapore for his career development only, what action should he take now?

22

Managing Multinational Organizations

LEARNING OBJECTIVES

After completing this chapter, you should be able to

1. Recognize that multinational corporations face added complexities because of cultural and geographic differences.

2. Discuss some of the pressures that host governments can bring to bear on multinational corporations.

3. Understand the complexities of leading and planning in multinational organizations.

4. Develop ideas for better control in multinational organizations.

5. Apply the framework and most of the management concepts developed in this book to a company operating in several different countries.

Manufacturing companies were the birthplace of most of the management concepts discussed in the first five parts of this book. But the concepts are contagious, and we have frequently used examples showing how such ideas arising in manufacturing also apply to other kinds of business. Even so, the original arena for "how to manage" typically has been a U.S. company that makes *things*.

In the next three chapters we want to reemphasize that (a) basic management issues arise in all sorts of enterprises—manufacturing is just one setting, and (b) the specific management design that you select should be tailored to the needs of your particular setting. Thus, in the following chapters we will take a closer look at three different types of business: multinational corporations, small firms and new ventures, and service companies.

For each type, the main distinctive characteristics will be identified. The way these distinctive characteristics affect appropriate management practice will then be illustrated.

Chapter 22—Managing Multinational Organizations. The impact of four distinctive characteristics of international management are discussed in this chapter. At the same time, the applicability of the framework of this book to complex situations is illustrated.

Chapter 23—Small Business Management and Entrepreneurship. Here the managing of small firms that are dominated by entrepreneurs is considered, primarily through a series of short case examples.

Chapter 24—Managing Service Businesses. Because service enterprises take so many shapes and forms, this chapter provides an impressive example of the "contingency theory" of management.

Each of these business types has a critical role to play in future society, and it is important to understand how to manage them effectively. A more immediate benefit for readers of this book, however, is a further drill in applying our management-process model to diverse situations.

DISTINCTIVE CHARACTERISTICS OF MULTINATIONAL CORPORATIONS

Multinational corporations (MNCs) perform dynamic, and often upsetting, functions in business affairs. Because they both produce and sell products in several countries, they are agents of change. They speed up the transfer of production to countries that offer low cost or other supply advantages, and they invade markets with modernized products and services. No longer does the United States dominate this sort of activity. MNCs with home bases in foreign countries are now active within our boundaries (with watches, cameras, computer chips, shoes, banking services, automobiles, machine tools, and many other products); they also compete with U.S. firms in foreign locations.

Of course, this greatly enlarged range of operations complicates the task of managing such a corporation. Our concern in this chapter is to flag several of the distinctive characteristics of MNCs that make managing much more complex, and to indicate the impact of these features on planning, organizing, leading, and controlling.

Four aspects of multinational operations, among others, add to management's burdens.

1. Pressure of Host Governments

When an MNC sets up a plant or a distribution organization in country X—whether it be a developed country like France or a developing one like Peru—the local government has a set of objectives that differ from those of the MNC. The growth and stability of local employment, conservation of cherished resources, tax revenues, military vulnerability, foreign balance of payments, interference in local politics (the situation in South Africa is an example)—any or all can be vital issues to the host government.[1]

The political party in power has a normal desire to survive, yet bungling on any one of the issues just noted might lead to turmoil. Past history, local pride, competing leaders, and other pressures all help shape what the host government can do and must do. And these forces shift over time.

No MNC can disregard these concerns of the host government. Locally, the economic interests of the MNC are *not* paramount. Somehow, a plan must be devised that helps the host government while also contributing to the MNC's objectives. Note that localized pressure is repeated for each country in which the MNC operates, and the demands of the several host governments may be conflicting.

2. Cultural Differences Affecting Management Practice

The way a business firm is run varies from country to country; a practice that works well in one country may flop in another. These differences are often linked to religion and other deeply rooted cultural beliefs. The feeling in Sweden about employee participation in decision making, for example, differs from that in Saudi Arabia.

Americans typically assume that our democratic, individualistic beliefs are desired in all cultures, and we are not very perceptive of divergent viewpoints. For example, a high degree of decentralization would be puzzling in an autocratic society. Or, consider "bribery." Payoffs that are normal in some countries could send a manager to jail in the United States. More subtle are the rights, or authority, of a manager. How much consistency from day to day is expected? Must all employees in comparable situations be treated equally, or is favorable treatment of relatives acceptable?

[1]See T. N. Gladwin and I. Walter, *Multinationals Under Fire: Lessons in the Management of Conflict* (New York: John Wiley, 1980); A. Desta, "Assessing Political Risk in Less Developed Countries," *Journal of Business Strategy,* Spring 1985; and I. Frank, *Foreign Enterprise in Developing Countries* (Baltimore: Johns Hopkins University Press, 1980).

3. Diverse Competitive Structures

When an MNC deals in several countries, even in the same product line, it will face quite different competitive conditions. The number, size, and competence of competitors will vary. The MNC will, of course, have to adjust its efforts accordingly.

Moreover, demand patterns will differ. Income per capita will shift some products from necessities to luxuries; automobile ownership will help shape the effectiveness of supermarkets. On the supply side, countries vary in availability of resources such as oil and gas, steel, good telephones, and, of course, capital. The resulting divergence among countries in opportunities and in requirements for success adds complexity to the management task.[2]

Local laws, financial structure, government agencies, trade associations, and other institutions will also have a marked effect on the way competition is carried out. Here again, the more countries in which an MNC operates, the greater will be the burden of reconciling local patterns.

4. Communication: Distance, Language, Loyalties

By no means the least of an MNC's distinctive characteristics is its task of communicating across national borders. Sheer distance makes face-to-face meetings difficult. Language is an even higher hurdle, especially in conveying subtleties of meaning and feeling. Although these difficulties can be overcome, managers' valuable time and energy will be consumed.[3]

Individual loyalties and values are less yielding. Perhaps unconsciously, we all screen a problem and proposed solutions through our own view of what is important. Such views are likely to reflect national origin. For instance, you and your Nigerian friends may inevitably perceive South African problems differently; and even though you try, you probably have difficulty communicating about that situation.

The four MNC characteristics just noted are far from a complete list of features that give a special flavor to multinational management. Nonetheless, they do provide a useful backdrop to a discussion of managerial issues that must be confronted by MNC managers.

STRATEGY ISSUES FACING MULTINATIONALS

An MNC faces all of the strategy issues encountered by a domestic company—product/market domain to be served, differential advantage in serving that domain, strategic thrusts as steps toward the desired position, and

---

[2]S. H. Robock, K. Simmonds, and J. Zwick, *International Business and Multinational Enterprises,* 3d ed. (Homewood, Ill.: Richard D. Irwin, 1983).

[3]H. W. Wallender III, *Technological Transfer and Management in Developing Countries* (Cambridge, Mass.: Ballinger, 1979).

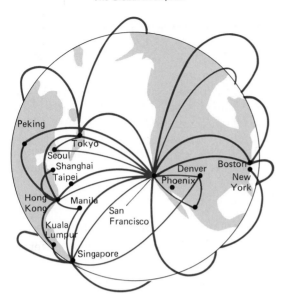

Figure 22.1 Complex Product Flow of
an MNC Pursuing a Global Strategy

Copyright © by Arthur D. Little, Inc., 1984.

target results expected from these activities. However, operating in several
countries adds a complicating dimension as Figure 22.1 suggests. Here are
three examples.

Global Strategy versus Portfolio of Outposts

Worldwide competition is becoming more intense. In several industries—
including automobiles, agricultural chemicals, computer chips, corporate
finance, aluminum, even Cabbage Patch dolls—the path to competitive
survival appears to require an *integrated global strategy*.[4]

Global strategy views the entire world (or much of it) as a market,
and designs products or services that can be sold in worldwide segments of
that market. Similarly, supply of these products or services is to be obtained from the most advantageous sources anywhere in the world; if this
means producing some parts in one place and assembling them in another,
that will be done. When conditions change, as they surely will, the MNC
with a global strategy will revise its pattern of markets and of supply.[5]

---

[4]See W. H. Davidson, *Global Strategic Management* (New York: John Wiley, 1982); C. Lorenz,
The Design Dimension: Product Strategy and the Challenge of Global Marketing (New York:
Basil Blackwell,1986); and G. Hamel and C. K. Prahalad, "Do You Really Have a Global
Strategy?" *Harvard Business Review,* July 1985.

[5]See J. A. Young, "Global Competition: The New Reality," *California Management Review,*
Spring 1985; Y. L. Doz, "Strategic Management in Multinational Companies," *Sloan Management Review,* Winter 1980; and D. C. Shanks, "Strategic Planning for Global Competition," *Journal of Business Strategy,* Winter 1985. See also A. M. Pettigrew, *The Awakening
Giant: Continuity and Change in ICI* (London: Basil Blackwell, 1985).

Note the contrast of a global strategy, which treats each country as only one piece in its total system, with an "outpost strategy," in which each country—or outpost—designs a strategy that fits its local opportunities and needs. This outpost strategy may include some importing or exporting, but those trade relations are features of a country-oriented plan that centers around local country considerations.

Because a global strategy requires coordinated action between several countries, it is more complex. Communication between local operations and the central planning unit must be extensive and accurate. The competitive structure shifts dramatically. The players are larger and more powerful, and face much bigger risks. Not all MNC managers welcome such a global approach.

Clash with Host Government Interests

Host governments are wary of the global-strategy approach. They object to being mere pawns in a global game, being treasured or abandoned because of developments in other parts of the world over which they have little influence. As just noted, host governments want the actions of any outpost in their territory to be compatible with the total array of local problems confronting them—employment, defense, tax income, and so on.

Consequently, a global strategy must be constrained so that continuing cooperation of host governments is obtained. The MNC must provide at least some local benefits. The presumption that MNCs can disregard social costs is a drawback in the global-strategy concept.

Partners in Promoting Outpost Activities

The traditional alternative to a global strategy is the establishment of a series of outposts in different countries. Each outpost, often a partnership with local managers, has its own strategy based on (1) local opportunities and resources, and (2) distinctive inputs from the MNC. These inputs may be technological know-how, machinery or other forms of capital, marketing assistance, or the like. With this help, the outpost follows a course that makes the most sense locally.

Lever Brothers, the large U.S. soap company, is such an outpost of Unilever, Ltd., and grew quite independently of its parent. The accounting firm of Price Waterhouse is likewise a spin-off of British expansion. Occidental Petroleum (a U.S. corporation) has a large joint venture in the People's Republic of China. Each of these examples reflects an outpost strategy rather than a global strategy. In the circumstances under which each outpost was established, a global strategy would have been unworkable; communication difficulties, host-country institutions, and the absence of centralized power all favored an outpost approach.

An MNC's choice between a global strategy and an outpost strategy is an issue that has no close counterpart for a domestic company. In resolving that issue, we must weigh the four distinctive characteristics of MNCs noted earlier—pressure of host governments, cultural differences, diverse competitive structures, and barriers to communication. Despite these differences from strategy design for domestic companies, however, the underlying need for and role of "company strategy" is a powerful concept in multinational and domestic companies alike.

PLANNING MULTINATIONAL OPERATIONS

As with strategy, the planning concepts discussed earlier in this book have direct application to MNCs, although the specific subjects relate to particular issues faced by MNCs. The following examples illustrate how managers in MNCs can and do put the basic planning concepts into practice.

Use of Standing Plans

A recurring problem in MNCs is how closely *products* should be *standardized*. In IBM—which pursues a global strategy—the computers made and sold worldwide are almost identical. In contrast, the cooking oil sold by Unilever varies from country to country. IBM wants known, dependable performance and interchangeable repair parts. Consequently, its product policies are strict and detailed. In cooking oil, Unilever wants to cater to local tastes and ways of preparing food, so its centralized policy is limited to ensuring purity and freshness.[6]

Transfer pricing of products within an MNC is another perpetual issue. A high transfer price increases the profits earned in the exporting country and decreases the profits of the importer; this affects who pays more income tax and which local managements "look good." The transfer price is also likely to affect long-term investments, selling prices, and local allocation of effort among products. Consequently, an MNC like Mobil Oil Corporation—which ships crude oil from the Middle East to its refinery in the Netherlands, and then ships refined products from the Netherlands to Germany for sale to consumers—needs a policy regarding transfer pricing.

Possible influences on transfer prices include currency exchange rates, market price (if a market for the product exists), direct cost plus a markup percentage set by headquarters, total actual cost including a normal profit on local investment, and selling price less distribution costs. The internal wrangling about any one of these options is hard to believe. One useful guide in setting the policy is to put the variability—the residual profits—in those operating divisions having the greatest maneuverability to make or lose money. That places an incentive where the most can be done about the final outcome. But whatever the choice, some well-defined standing plan is essential.

Because the issue arises less often, many MNCs have no predeter-

[6]See R. L. Tung, "Selection and Training Procedures of U.S., European, and Japanese Multinationals," *California Management Review,* Fall 1980; R. L. Tung, "A Framework for the Selection and Training of Personnel for Overseas Assignments," *Columbia Journal of World Business,* Spring 1981.

mined policy regarding the *proportion of local ownership* they will seek in each foreign subsidiary. In any subsidiary, domestic or foreign, sharing ownership with the local managers provides a strong long-run incentive to those managers. However, 100 percent ownership gives the parent company much greater flexibility in assigning duties, setting transfer prices, and shifting business to another division. The choice becomes even more complicated and emotional in multinational settings because of national pride and all the host government interests noted earlier in this chapter. If (1) a natural resource is involved and (2) a major sector of the economy is affected—as is true of oil in Nigeria and coal in Australia—then governments can rise or fall on the ownership issue. With so many pros and cons involved, the MNC managers may decide *not* to have a policy but to work out the ownership arrangement case by case. Only a few MNCs that want flexibility to follow a global strategy, such as IBM, will consistently insist on 100 percent ownership even though doing so may prevent them from operating in significant markets, like India.

Application of Single-use Plans

MNCs commonly utilize single-use plans just as they do standing plans. Here, again there are questions of what topics should be covered in how much detail, and how the decisions will be made.

Annual financial plans are very common, typically prepared first by the local companies and then approved at headquarters. Vertically integrated MNCs will also prepare quarterly and annual plans for commodity flows, as is implied by Figure 22.2, which shows world movements of crude oil. Expansion programs are still another typical kind of single-use plans; these will probably be initiated at headquarters for MNCs having a global strategy and locally for MNCs with an outpost strategy.

While both single-use and standing plans have vital roles in managing an MNC, as the previously cited examples show, they deal with fewer

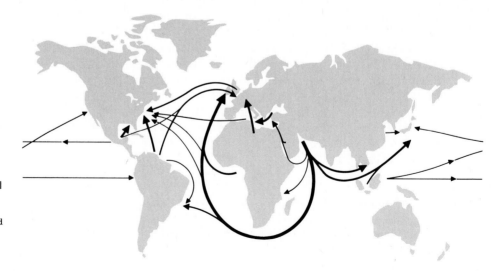

Figure 22.2 Principal Oil Movements by Sea—1983

Source: "Middle East Oil and Gas," Exxon Corporation, Dec. 1984, p. 12. © 1984 Exxon Corporation.

subjects than is common domestically. Communication hurdles and cultural differences among countries make the formulation of such plans a slow and costly process. Thus, managers are selective in the number of subjects covered by plans that are international in scope.

557

Chapter 22 Managing
Multinational
Organizations

ORGANIZING INTERNATIONAL ACTIVITIES

Worldwide locations of MNCs' activities make their organizational problems more complicated than similar issues faced by domestic firms. The pressures of host governments, cultural differences, diverse competitive structures, and communication barriers are additional considerations. We can see the impact of these on three organizational issues: Where should foreign operations be placed in the basic structure? What degree of decentralization is desirable? How can corporate expertise be made available to local managers?

Place of Foreign Activities in Structure

The basic structure of any company should fit its strategy. This is especially important in MNCs because geographical dispersion makes informal cross-boundary communication difficult.[7] Figure 22.3 shows, in abbreviated form, three structures that suit three quite different strategies.

Structure A, which matches an outpost strategy, is widely used by companies just entering the international arena. Because major departments of the company are preoccupied with domestic problems, each foreign division is allowed to fend for itself in its "strange" environment. If there are such outpost operations in several countries, an "international vice-president" may be appointed as an overseer and a bridge into the domestic production, domestic marketing, and other functional departments.

An alternative structure, B, may be used by a company that has a narrow line of products and seeks additional revenue by extending its domestic production and marketing know-how to ever-wider territories. To get closer attention of its functional specialists, the corresponding foreign activities are placed within the separate functional departments. Such a structure enabled Singer sewing machine, during its heyday, to sell its products in remote hamlets throughout the world. Digital Equipment Company's foreign expansion was substantially of this sort.

Structure B works well when (1) the company is a leader in marketing and production technology and (2) modifications for local needs are minor. Because coordination of production and marketing is centered at the top of the pyramid, however, changes to meet local needs are slow. Also, when competitors catch up with the technology, or perhaps leapfrog ahead, a new industry's competitive structure may force more adaptability than the staid home office can manage.

---

[7]W. G. Egelhoff, "Strategy and Structure in Multinational Corporations: An Information Processing Approach," *Administrative Science Quarterly*, Sept. 1982.

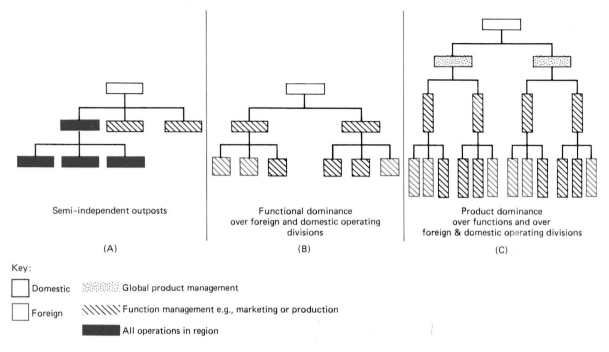

Key:

▢ Domestic   ▦ Global product management

▢ Foreign   ▨ Function management e.g., marketing or production

■ All operations in region

Figure 22.3 Structural Alternatives for Multinational Operation

If an MNC moves on to a global strategy, the third structure, C, is desirable. The global competition will often focus on a rather narrow group of high-volume products, each of which calls for its own fast-acting organization. Consequently, an MNC may need two or more separate product sectors, as indicated in Figure 22.3.

The three structures just identified focus on the major design features. In practice, an organization is never that simple. First, other necessary functions have to be fitted in with the major design. Second, some arrangement is needed in structures B and C to enable an MNC to develop a unified posture in each country that hosts two or more operating units. The general manager of the largest unit often takes on this coordinating and spokesperson role. Third, confusion will be invited if design A is used in some countries, design B followed in other countries, and design C superimposed on both.

Design of Decentralization

Sharp differences in decentralization will be linked with the three organizational structures identified in the preceding section. In the semindependent outpost design, A, most of the decision making will be delegated to the operating divisions in each country. Here, local adaptability is stressed, and coordination between countries is given minimal attention.

In contrast, major decision making is highly centralized in the functional dominance design depicted in B. The presumption here is that managers at headquarters possess expertise and wisdom, and that local divi-

558

sions are predominantly executors of centrally made decisions. In the global design C many decisions, especially competitive tactics, are centralized in the top product-management group just below the president. These people not only have the technological wisdom presumed for senior managers in design B, they also keep well informed on competitors' moves and can orchestrate appropriate responses.

These patterns of decentralization and centralization apply to major decisions. In each case, the location of decisions on some other topics will run counter to the primary design. For instance, an MNC following the outpost strategy in a type-A organization will probably elect to have at least some corporation-wide "policies," as illustrated in our earlier discussion of standing plans. Likewise, central managers in both B- and C-type organizations will undoubtedly delegate to operating divisions the choice of plans for customer credit, warehousing, labor relations, and the like; these activities depend largely on local conditions.

Decentralization, then, is not a simple issue. The managers in each organization will have to sort out the kinds of decisions that, in their setting, should be centralized, and also those decisions that can be made most advantageously in local units. And, having defined the dimensions of freedom at various levels, the multinational manager must try to ensure that the structure is widely understood—a substantial task because of the communication barriers described early in this chapter.[8]

Providing Expert Counsel

A perpetual problem in MNCs is how to obtain full benefit from the expertise that exists in various parts of the corporation. How can this accumulated wisdom be conveyed to the decision points established by the departmentation and decentralization discussed in the last few pages?

Of course, the managers on the spot will have part of this knowledge in their heads as a result of their experience and training. But technical know-how and data about competition in other parts of the world may be known best by people thousands of miles and several national boundaries away from the decision makers.

A common solution is to establish "staff" positions at corporate headquarters (or product-line headquarters in a type-C structure). These liaison people ferret out the latest techniques—or problems—in domestic operations or in other foreign divisions, and then use this knowledge to advise managers in other distant locations. Sometimes a decision maker may ask for advice; at other times the staff travel and inspect local practice, giving advice when warranted.

This expert counsel does not flow easily. In addition to the normal transnational communication hurdles, local pride may interfere with acceptance. Union Carbide's disaster in Bhopal, India, is an example. Staff engineers from Union Carbide's U.S. headquarters "advised" the India division regarding design of the Bhopal insecticide plant and periodically

[8]C. A. Bartlett, "How Multinational Organizations Evolve," *Journal of Business Strategy,* Summer 1982.

inspected local operating practice. However, because of the Indian government's legal insistence that such a plant be run by Indians, the advice was not thoughtfully and carefully followed. As a result, thousands of people were killed, and Union Carbide's long-run future was placed in jeopardy. This experience indicates that the policy of having headquarters staff travel to foreign outposts sharply limits headquarters' influence over local decisions.

An alternative to advisory staff is a matrix form of organization. The most common matrix in MNCs is to overlay product divisions on geographical (or country) divisions.[9] At Corning Glass Company, for instance, a product division for television tubes may plan all activities from engineering and production to marketing of its products. At the same time, the geographical divisions that have plants making such products or marketing organizations selling them also plan for television tubes along with other products. By having *both* the product division and the geographical divisions responsible for television tubes, the expertise of each is brought to bear on the television-tube business. The divisions are expected to negotiate an agreement on the plans for action insofar as overlap exists.

In practice, the matrix concept is much more difficult to use than the advisory staff concept.[10] Sooner or later one division dominates the decisions, and the other division takes on an advisory or service role. In the interim, decision making is slow and accountability is blurred.

Few MNCs are satisfied with the spotty success they have achieved in getting good advice focused on local problems. Opportunities for improvement abound in this facet of organization.

More broadly, economic forces are pushing many MNCs toward a global strategy as Figure 22.4 suggests; this, in turn, calls for a global type-C organization, with its corresponding realignment of centralization/decentralization and counseling networks. But such globalization often conflicts sharply with the nationalistic aspirations of host governments. Reconciliation of these opposite trends is a major challenge to MNC managers. In the background is concern with "national sovereignty" and the dawn of a superstate that might set ground rules for MNCs playing off one nation against another.

DISTINCTIVE LEADERSHIP PROBLEMS OF MULTINATIONALS

Leadership, at home or abroad, involves person-to-person interaction. Inevitably these relationships are strongly influenced by the values and beliefs that each of us treasure. Motives, aspirations, attitudes toward work, per-

---

[9]The matrix described in the latter part of Chapter 11 overlaid project managers on functional divisions, but the underlying matrix concept is similar.

[10]S. M. Davis, *Managing and Organizing Multinational Corporations* (New York: Pergamon Press, 1979).

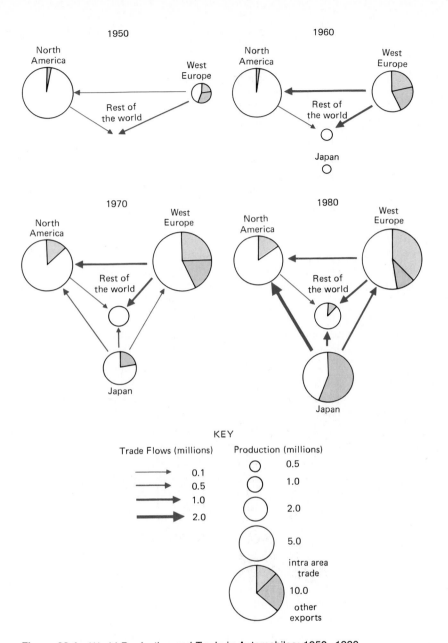

Figure 22.4 World Production and Trade in Automobiles: 1950–1980

Source: D. T. Jones, "The Internationalization of the Automobile Industry," in *Journal of General Management,* vol. 10, no. 3, Spring 1985, p. 26. Used by permission.

sonal obligations are all shaped by the culture in which we were reared. As a result, one of the most subtle and stubborn problems MNCs face is leadership of their polyglot personnel.

We can illustrate this problem by a brief look at a few of our own cultural assumptions that are not shared by many people in other parts of the world.[11]

Assumptions That Underlie our Leadership Concepts

Confident belief in self-determination.   Most Americans believe that they exercise considerable choice in what they do and, through this, in what happens to them. To be sure, we may run into "bad luck," but even here we are inclined to place at least part of the blame on ourselves.

This belief in self-determination is in sharp contrast to a fatalistic viewpoint found in some Moslem countries. It also differs from a mystical view that holds that events are determined by perhaps the capricious influence of spirits that must be appeased. Whatever the explanation, the critical issue is whether people believe that events will occur regardless of what they do, or whether they share with Americans and most Westerners the belief that they can help shape future events.

Results come from persistent hard work.   Both our lore and our experience underscore the necessity for hard work if objectives are to be achieved. Even if one does not accept the Puritan ethic that hard work is a virtue in itself, there is a strong belief that persistent, purposeful effort is necessary to achieve high goals. Hard work is not considered to be the only requisite for success; wisdom and luck also play their part. Nevertheless, the feeling is that without hard work a person is not only unlikely to achieve desired objectives, but also that any expectation of achieving them under these circumstances is unjustified.

This belief in the efficacy of hard work is by no means worldwide. Sometimes a fatalistic viewpoint makes hard work seem futile. In other instances, one needs merely to curry the favor of the right person, and in still other situations hard work is "unmanly."

Time is a crucial aspect of performance.   To an American, *timing* is an important factor. Effective use of one's own time and effective scheduling of independent activities requires precise timing. This concern with precise timing is reflected in our daily lives; for a television program to start three minutes later than announced is a national disgrace.

Virtually all studies of comparative management have noted the wide variation in attitude towards time in various cultures. Part of the charm of some Latin American cultures is their relaxed view of the clock and the calendar. People in many other parts of the world fail to understand why the normal rhythms of life should be twisted to fit a schedule.

---

[11]The following list is selected from a more comprehensive treatment by W. H. Newman, "Cultural Assumptions Underlying U.S. Management Concepts," in J. L. Massie and J. B. Luytjes, *Management in an International Context* (New York: Harper & Row, 1972); see also S. Ronen and O. Shenker, "Clustering Countries on Attitudinal Dimensions: A Review and Synthesis." *Academy of Management Review*, July 1985.

Appoint the best person available for the specific job.   The pre-sumption is that we start with the needs of the enterprise. The mission, policies, and other plans call for a particular array of activities; these activities are then organized into jobs. Specifications based on the duties of each job are then prepared, and these specifications would then be used in selecting a person to fill each post. Furthermore, executives who fill positions are expected to make a diligent search of all likely sources of candidates. If well-qualified persons are not readily available, this search should extend to all divisions of the enterprise, as well as to outside sources.

In societies in which each person has a moral responsibility for the immediate family (and perhaps for the extended family), or in other societies in which the exchange of personal favors is an integral part of the social structure, such Western beliefs about how appointments should be made generate serious difficulties.

Remove "second-raters."   The belief just described extends beyond the initial appointment. The underlying assumption is that if a person is not continuing to perform well, he should be replaced with someone who will. The cost to the enterprise of poor performance, especially the poor performance of an executive, is far greater than the person's salary; this poor performance complicates the task of people whose work interrelates, and may undermine the effectiveness of the entire operation.

In a number of countries, the removal of a person from a recognized position involves so much loss of prestige that the action is rarely taken. This is particularly true when the appointment was initially made on the basis of family or friendship. Poor performance is an inadequate excuse for disgracing a relative or friend.

Although far from complete, this partial list of our cultural assumptions suggests that we must be cautious in using U.S. leadership styles abroad. Many aspects of U.S. management concepts may seem odd to a foreigner. Long-range planning, for instance, will appear futile to someone who normally submits to Allah's will. Unless managers believe in hard work, decentralizing is dangerous. Consultative supervision with an incompetent relative is probably a waste of time. Motivation based on expected promotion lacks vigor when attractive appointments are, in fact, based on friendship.

Empathetic Leading

Any MNC manager who has to "lead" foreigners is well advised to first learn how their attitudes toward work, rewards, and the like match—or depart from—his own. The leader and the followers may have much in common. However, a few points of mismatch may undercut an approach that may have worked well in another country.

Where a mismatch of cultural assumptions exists, some managers will be able to adjust their style accordingly. They will have a good "feel" for what will be effective in a strange setting. Most of us, however, are not so flexible. We may have to devote special effort to find subordinates who are more like us and to invent a hybrid leadership style that bridges the two cultures.

The role of leadership—the tying together of managerial plans and their actual execution—is the same in multinational and domestic organizations. It is the manner of leading—the way that leadership is achieved—that requires distinctive skills in MNCs.

CONTROLLING MULTINATIONAL OPERATIONS[12]

Distance and diversity of operating conditions also create problems of control within a multinational enterprise. The three dimensions of these control problems, discussed next, illustrate the special burden MNCs undertake in addition to the normal control tasks in each of the operating units.

Understanding the Concept of Constructive Control

For cultural reasons, the control process is poorly understood in many countries. The significance of completing work on time and of maintaining quality often is not accepted. Local life proceeds more casually, so when Western control standards are imposed, the action appears to local workers as unwarranted and capricious.

Similarly, accounting records in many countries are scanty, inaccurate, and often manipulated to reduce taxes. Naturally, managers do not look to such records as aids to prompt coordination of activities.

In some cultures, business relationships are closely entwined with personal friendship, kinship, reciprocal favors, and simpatico feelings. In such situations, objective appraisal and tough corrective action are too irritating to be tolerated.

A first step, then, for the MNC manager in securing control is to win acceptance of the concept. Executives in operating units must understand that survival in world business requires realistic objectives, performance standards based on these objectives, regular measurement of performance, prompt feedback of control data to people who can undertake corrective action, overall evaluation, updating of targets, and correlation of incentives with results. Without acceptance of this process, the best-designed control systems will achieve only moderate effects.

Operating Controls that Encourage Optimum Performance

Every MNC must have dependable, understandable accounting reports from each country. Due to local variations in bookkeeping practice, the

---

[12]This section is adapted from W.H. Newman, J.P. Logan, and W.H. Hegarty, *Strategy, Policy, and Central Management,* 9th ed. (Cincinnati: South-Western Publishing Company, 1985), pp. 613–15. Reprinted with permission.

establishment of a worldwide accounting system is no small task. But once in place, it does permit the introduction of annual and five-year budgets, measurement of growth in sales and profits, and other usual financial control devices.

Essential as such financial controls are, reliance on financial reports alone is especially dangerous in a multinational business. The opportunities and the difficulties in each country make necessary more complete and sensitive yardsticks.[13] In addition to financial reports, criteria such as market share, government relations, quality maintenance, customer service, cultivation of new customers, physical productivity, employee training and turnover, plant maintenance, innovation and modernization, protection of assets from inflation, cooperation with other units of the company are all control measures that the MNC headquarters should watch in each country.

Frequent evaluation is inappropriate. A thorough semiannual review plus prompt evaluation of major changes or deviations from plans serve most MNC's better than monthly reporting, which is likely to become routine.

Periodic Product Stream Evaluation

The controls just described help keep each operating unit "on course," but they do not check the continuing desirability of the course itself. This broader evaluation is difficult because most multinational firms sell the same product in different countries, ship materials or parts from one country to another, and in other ways seek synergistic benefits from joint activities. Separate controls in each country do not tell whether the desired overall benefits are being obtained.

Consequently, special studies that consolidate the incomes, costs, and investment from all countries dealing with a *product line* are needed. Since several lines are typically handled, at least when all countries are considered, a lot of unscrambling of assets and joint costs may be necessary. The analysis thus becomes too involved for routine periodic reports. Fortunately, a special appraisal, say every two years, is adequate because changes in product line or production strategy can only be made in relatively long time cycles.

With an analysis of how product lines are measuring up to original plans, a reappraisal of markets, competition, technology, and other external factors is also in order. This may lead to significant shifts in company strategy. We thus find ourselves completing the full management cycle of strategizing, implementing plans, organizing, leading, and controlling, which provide the basis for a revised strategy and a new cycle.

---

[13]See J.H. Horovitz, "Strategic Control in Three European Countries," in *Top Management Control in Europe* (London: Macmillan Press, 1981); and C.K. Prahalad and Y.L. Doz, "An Approach to Strategic Control in MNCs," *Sloan Management Review,* Summer–Fall, 1981.

CONCLUSION

Two conclusions emerge from this chapter:

1. The management process model, the framework of this book, fits a multinational corporation. It puts the array of MNC management issues into an orderly pattern that managers and others dealing with the enterprise can readily grasp. The interplay between strategy, planning, organizing, leading, and controlling can be anticipated and built into an integrated, reinforcing system.

2. At the same time, the multinational dimension does add very significant issues. Aside from substantive matters, which are outside the scope of a *management process* book, MNC managers face several distinctive problems.

    a. Host governments demand attention to their parochial interests. Not only do these pressures restrain what MNCs can do locally, but the variation among demands from several countries make unified action difficult, and global competition may be especially hampered.

    b. The culture of each country in which an MNC operates affects the workability of American management techniques. Likewise, the competitive and institutional structures within each country affect how local activities must be conducted. These environmental factors again create a dual task of adapting to the characteristics of each country and meshing these diverse practices into some kind of an overall system.

    c. Communication hurdles are present in all the relationships between countries. They impede resolution of the two issues just noted and matters that are even more routine may become the source of misunderstandings. Inferences and the significance of what is not said may also convey meaning that a foreigner fails to grasp.

In spite of the added complexities of conducting business in several countries, MNCs are becoming increasingly important both economically and socially. It is imperative that a leading country such as the United States be adroit at MNC management. Consequently, adapting our domestic concepts to multinational needs is a vital task.

Impact on Productivity

MNCs bear on productivity both directly and indirectly. Their very survival in international trade depends on their being more productive than domestic firms in serving market needs and in finding low-cost sources of supply. Which countries benefit from the productivity that MNCs uncover or develop is a controversial question. But there can be no doubt that productivity is increased someplace.

Indirectly, MNCs spur their competitors, including domestic companies in the United States, to improve their practices. Our automobile companies, to mention a conspicuous example, are in the midst of a major overhaul of their design and production practices because of the pressure of foreign-based MNCs. Indeed, our whole foreign trade balance is under attack. Fortunately, recent evidence from many of our industries indicates that U.S. productivity is improving enough to meet this challenge. We no longer have a comfortable lead, however.

FOR FURTHER DISCUSSION

1. Compare the desirability of a global strategy for a well-financed MNC dealing in (a) civilian aircraft, (b) shoes, and (c) cookies.

2. "Business managers are facing so much more uncertainty and risk, I think that long-range programming only rarely pays off. And the uncertainty is even greater in the international arena. My recommendation is that we restrict our foreign programs to two years or less." Do you agree with this view? If not, how do you propose dealing with uncertainty abroad?

3. (a) What type of organizational structure best fits the Coca-Cola Company's worldwide operations? Justify your answer. (b) Where should the company focus its control efforts, assuming the organization that you propose is in place?

4. The customs and attitudes toward giving and accepting side-payments for business favors differ from country to country. What we consider bribery is, within limits, acceptable in some foreign countries. Assume that you are employed by a U.S. company and assigned to work in a country where side-payments of about 15 percent are expected, in much the same way that tipping in a U.S. restaurant is expected; however, the sums involved are much larger. Would you make such payments? Accept such payments?

5. A U.S. manufacturer of girls' dresses makes most of its dresses in its Georgia plant, but it contracts with a Taiwan firm for additional supply to fill increasing demand. Past policy has been to keep the U.S. plant running at near capacity, and to use the Taiwan suppliers for fluctuating peaks. Because the annual Taiwan volume is growing, the local owners are proposing that the U.S. manufacturer buy 60 percent of the stock in the Taiwan firm. (Most of this new capital would be used for expansion in Taiwan.) (a) Assuming that the investment is made, a possible revision of the policy regarding allocation of production must be considered. What are the main factors that U.S. management should consider? What do you recommend? (b) Should the Taiwan government establish any requirements or restraints on the way the new controlling owners run the Taiwan plant?

6. What controls should Union Carbide Company exercise over its foreign activities like those at Bhopal, India? (See page 561 for a brief description of the Bhopal set-up.)

7. Several Japan-based MNCs are opening their own manufacturing plants in the United States to help supply their already-established national marketing operations. What leadership style do you recommend that the Japanese managers who are assigned to head these new plants utilize? Should they rely on practices that have been highly successful in Japan, or should they use good U.S. practice?

8. Which group of MNCs do you predict will be managed most effectively over the next ten to twenty years—those with a home base in England, in Japan, in Switzerland, in the United States, or in some other country? Why?

FOR FURTHER READING

Bartlett, C. A., "How Multinational Organizations Evolve," *Journal of Business Strategy,* Summer 1982. Thoughtful, well-documented report with focus on organizational issues.

Davidson, W. H., *Global Strategic Management.* New York: John Wiley, 1982. Comprehensive text based on Harvard's Multinational Enterprises Project.

Farmer, R. N., *Advances in International Comparative Management,* Volume 1. Greenwich, Conn.: JAI Press, 1984. An entry into recent scholarly literature on comparative management; takes a research viewpoint.

Gladwin, T. N. and I. Walter, *Multinationals Under Fire: Lessons in the Management of Conflict.* New York: John Wiley, 1980. Rigorous analysis of MNCs behavior on critical issues.

Pascale, R. T. and A. G. Anthos, *The Art of Japanese Management.* New York: Simon & Schuster,

1981. Thoughtful comparison of U.S. and Japanese management styles, using contrasts of IT&T and Matsushita as illustrations.

Prahalad, C. K. and Y. L. Doz, "An Approach to Strategic Control in MNCs," *Sloan Management Review,* Summer–Fall 1981. A way of analyzing head office–subsidiary control relationships.

Shanks, D. C., "Strategic Planning for Global Competition," *Journal of Business Strategy,* Winter 1985. Practical requirements for success with a global strategy.

MANAGEMENT IN ACTION CASE 22
The Wall Street Journal

One of the great management dilemmas when it comes to international organizations is whether they should be controlled locally or by distant executives.

Increasingly, strategy in successful organizations is determined at the home office, but local officials are given wide latitude—virtual autonomy—in determining how that strategy should be implemented.

Such was the case at *The Wall Street Journal,* which decided in the early 1980s to establish daily editions in Asia and Europe, but had several options as to how those editions would come together.

In the end, the *Journal* exported its national-regional concept from the United States and appointed editors and publishers in each of the key world regions. They would determine the content of the locally distributed newspapers. They would determine the editorial policy. They would not be bound by the daily *Wall Street Journal* policies set in New York, but rather could edit their products locally for the needs of their local audiences.

But there was one key caveat: All must be done within the "corporate conscience" as established in New York. The *Journal* couldn't be conservative in the United States and liberal in Asia. Save for that exception, the Asian and European editions would have local autonomy.

As things turned out, it was the right blend. Not only were both the Asian and European editions of *The Wall Street Journal* financially successful, but they spawned a publisher, Peter T. Kahn, who was called the heir-apparent to the entire Dow-Jones corporation.

What made both the Asian and European editions successful was that they appealed to local interests from a local perspective while reflecting the overall worldwide appearance, journalistic credibility, editorial philosophy, and news quality that the *Journal* had become famous for in the United States.

Hence, the *Journal* successfully diversified geographically, while maintaining its quality and image.

Question

Do you think *The Wall Street Journal's* approach to multinational expansion should be followed by Kentucky Fried Chicken? By Avis car rental?

APPLICATION CASES

For practice in applying concepts covered in this chapter to managerial situations, see the following managerial decision cases. The case questions particularly relevant to this chapter are listed by number after each case name.

Fyler International (p. 68) 3, 4, 18, 19
Scandico (Singapore) (p. 546) 1, 2, 17, 19

23

Small Business Management and Entrepreneurship*

LEARNING OBJECTIVES

After completing this chapter, you should be able to

1. Describe distinctive characteristics of small businesses, especially those marked by a strong innovative spirit.

2. Explain the economic significance of small businesses, especially their impact on productivity.

3. Discuss the benefits and drawbacks of having a vigorous entrepreneur be the senior manager of a small company.

4. Understand the distinctive aspects of managing (planning, organizing, leading, and controlling) a small business.

5. Describe typical characteristics and problems related to the functional aspects (finance, production, and marketing) of a small entrepreneurial business.

*This chapter has been contributed by Narendra C. Bhandari, Professor of Management at Pace University in New York, and founding editor of the *American Journal of Small Business*. The author wishes to thank Professor William Newman for his help in finalizing this chapter. Thanks are also due to Pace University and Vidur Bhalla, this contributor's graduate assistant, for their research support; and to Chitra Bhandari, for her untiring assistance with typing this chapter.

SMALL BUSINESS ENTREPRENEURS

A small partnership was formed in 1837 between William Procter, a British candlemaker, and James Gamble, an Irish soapmaker. Today it is a multimillion-dollar conglomerate. Many of Procter & Gamble's brands are used all over the world.

Similarly, in the mid-1950s, Dr. An Wang, an immigrant from China, decided to put together a typewriter, a display screen, and an elementary computer. The word processor, so invented, has revolutionized office work. Wang Laboratories, founded by Dr. Wang, is one of the leading firms in the computer industry today.

Small business and entrepreneurship play crucial roles in the well-being of society. They not only often lay the foundation for a large company, as in the examples just cited, but they also provide the bulk of retailing and service activities for the public. Small business firms are also responsible for providing an increasing number of jobs, especially to women and minorities.

Focus on Small Business Entrepreneurs

Although many large corporations are now seeking ways to encourage intrapreneurship, economic vitality in the western world is being spurred by entrepreneurs who establish their own small businesses. The management of these firms poses special problems. The founders of such businesses tend to be zealous in promoting ideas but often lack broad managerial experience. Yet if the firm is successful, a full array of managerial problems is sure to arise.

The critical need is to provide freedom of action and expert support to the entrepreneur while also keeping the managerial structure soundly coordinated. In exploring this dilemma, we shall (a) briefly note several features of small businesses in general, then (b) observe how the managerial processes of planning, organizing, leading, and controlling are applicable to a small business. With this background, a series of examples will then be presented to demonstrate the difficulties of applying good management practice to highly dynamic, individualistic new ventures.

FEATURES OF SMALL BUSINESS FIRMS

Before turning to our primary concern with managing small entrepreneurial businesses, we need a brief look at what such firms are like.

Definitions

Small business. The terms *small business* and *entrepreneurship* have been variously defined. Generally speaking, a small business is independently owned and operated and is not dominant in its field of operation.

Table 23.1 SMALL BUSINESS SIZE STANDARDS (MAXIMUMS)

A. *For Loans*	*Annual Receipts Maximum*
Services	*$2,000,000
Retail	*$2,000,000–$7,500,000
Wholesale	*$9,500,00–$22,000,000
General construction	*$9,500,000
Farming and related activities	*$1,000,000
	Average Employment Maximum
Manufacturing	*250 to 1,500
B. *For Procurement*	*Annual Receipts Maximum*
Services	*$2,000,000–$9,000,000
General construction	*$12,000,000
	Average Employment Maximum
Manufacturing	*500 to 1,500

*Varies by industry

Source: Adapted from Public Communications Division of the U.S. Small Business Administration, *Facts about Small Business and the U.S. Small Business Administration,* U.S. Government Printing Office, Feb. 1981, p. 8.

Table 23.1 presents a set of business size standards that generally apply to firms seeking assistance from the Small Business Administration (SBA).

Clearly, these standards are quite vague and broad. In 1961, using a similar guideline established by the SBA, American Motors, then the fourth largest automaker in the United States, was classified as a small business and thus enjoyed special privileges in bidding for government contracts.

Entrepreneurship.   Joseph A. Schumpeter, a noted scholar in the field of entrepreneurship, defined entrepreneurs as individuals whose function is to carry out new combinations of means of production. He emphasized the innovative nature of the entrepreneur in doing new things or in doing in a new way things that are already being done. Risk taking is also widely regarded as an entrepreneurial attribute. Further, some scholars regard ownership of a business as a prerequisite to entrepreneurship.

Intrapreneurship.   The conspicuous success of entrepreneurs like Steven P. Jobs (cofounder of Apple Computers) and William Gates (Chairman of the Microsoft Corporation), has aroused big companies' interest in the field of entrepreneurship.

"Intrapreneurship"—innovating and risk taking by employees within their firm—is increasingly welcome by firms that are tired of losing their highly talented employees to more free-wheeling start-ups. Employees, in turn, see intrapreneurship as a way to inject excitement and urgency into otherwise dull jobs. It was this intrapreneurial environment that enabled Arthur Fry, an employee at 3M, to develop Post-It notes, the highly successful yellow pads with the gentle adhesive. Similarly, Texas Instruments' successful Speak-n-Spell electronic learning aid was developed by engineers who received financing outside the company's normal funding channels.

The Lure of Starting a Small Business

People start their own businesses for many reasons. Some of these are personal, such as a desire for independence, a wish to eliminate the frustration of working for someone else, a need for self-achievement, and the potential for flexible work hours. Economic reasons include lack of alternative employment opportunities and the potential for profits and personal wealth. Social reasons include the potential for gaining visibility and the respect of friends and relatives.

In a survey conducted by Control Data Business Centers and *Venture* magazine, the majority of entrepreneurs reported that the impetus for running their own show was emotional, and it was usually expressed in a negative way. They felt victimized by their former employers.[1]

Variables of success. There is a sharp difference between wanting to start one's own business and being successful with that undertaking. Entrepreneurial or small business success depends upon a number of variables. Most important are the abilities to find a viable business opportunity, to innovate and take risks, to obtain financial support, to work with people, and to maintain technical competence.

Causes of failure. In fact, most new business ventures fail. Most experts agree that there is a 25 percent chance that a new firm will fail in its first year, a 50 percent chance that a business will not survive through two years, an 80 percent chance that a new product won't make it.

Reasons behind small business failure include neglect, fraud, lack of field experience, lack of managerial experience, incompetence, and natural disaster. But Dun and Bradstreet conclude that incompetence is the most important cause of business failure.

Legal Forms of Small Business

One issue faced by small business managers but rarely by managers of large enterprises is the choice of an appropriate legal form. Most of the small business firms that have received significant visibility are incorporated. In terms of sheer numbers, however, sole proprietorship remains the most popular form of organization.

Sole proprietorship. The owner of a sole proprietorship owns all of its assets and is solely responsible for all its debts, operations, and management. The owner takes all of the firm's profits and bears all its losses. The sole proprietorship is the easiest form under which to start a business.

The "unlimited liability" aspect of sole proprietorship should be em-

---

[1]A. Feinberg, "Inside the Entrepreneur," *Venture,* May 1984, p. 80.

phasized. Under the law, the firm's creditors have the right to sue not only the firm but also its owner to recover the debt. The owner's personal assets (house, jewelry, furniture, and so on) may have to be sold to pay the firm's creditors. This aspect of sole proprietorship could be disastrous to owners and their families.

Partnership.   According to the Uniform Partnership Act, a partnership is a voluntary association of two or more persons to carry on as co-owners of a business for profit.

A partnership form of organization, as compared with sole proprietorship, allows a firm to pool the talents of several people (partners) and generate larger amounts of capital. It also allows for diversified viewpoints and skills, greater visibility, and larger credit-worthiness. However, similar to a sole proprietorship, each partner is personally liable for the firm's debts.

For a partnership to work effectively, it is desirable to have a partnership agreement prepared by an attorney. The agreement should contain information, guidelines, and rules on matters such as the rights, obligations, and duties of each partner in terms of participation in equity, assets, liabilities, profits, losses, management, operation, and dissolution of the partnership.

Corporation.   In 1819, Chief Justice John Marshall, in the Dartmouth College case, declared that a corporation is "an artificial being, invisible, intangible, and existing only in contemplation of the law." A corporation thus became a legal entity in its own right; thus, a corporation can buy, sell, and hold property, and sue and be sued in the same manner that a private individual can.

For a corporation to exist, it should be registered under the applicable laws of a state. A corporation is owned by its shareholders, who elect its board of directors. They, in turn, appoint officers to run it according to its charter.

Unlike a sole proprietorship and a partnership, a corporation's life is independent of its shareholders. It does not die with the death of its shareholders, nor do its shareholders have unlimited liability.

The corporation form of organization has enabled people to pool large amounts of capital (by selling shares to several investors) in order to finance projects requiring such large funds. Acquistion of such funding might not be possible through sole proprietorships and partnerships.

In practice, the legal form of a small business does not substantially change its managerial problems. Except for financing, the issues of planning, organizing, leading, and controlling are not significantly different in a corporation versus a proprietorship. As a company gets larger, however, the potential for raising capital—and the associated characteristics of limited liability and perpetual life—does become more attractive. So, sooner or later most successful ventures adopt the more formal structure of a corporation.

PROCESS OF MANAGEMENT IN A SMALL BUSINESS

Managers of small firms conduct their activities through the basic processes discussed in Parts II through V—planning, organizing, leading, and controlling. However, the extent and formality of several of these processes vary widely.

Planning

Although the act of planning can help managers identify and implement goals and objectives in small business firms, it is usually done informally, if at all. Robinson and Pearce found that lack of time, technical expertise, and openness are among the reasons for low emphasis on comprehensive planning in small businesses.[2]

To overcome these shortcomings, some experts recommend the use of outside consultants in initiating planning in a small business. Company directors, accountants, lawyers, bankers, or advertising agencies frequently prove helpful in this effort.

Similarly, in a comparison of small business firms that received assistance from outsiders (small business development centers, in this case) with those that did not receive such assistance, it was found that the firms receiving such help were significantly more profitable than were those that did not receive such help.

Organizing

Staffing. Founders of small business firms are generally quite competent in one or two areas of business (they may have founded their firms to take full advantage of their skills). They might not be as skilled in other areas, however. Many firms cannot afford to hire full-time experts to fill the gaps. In addition, many young people may be reluctant to take jobs with small firms because the prospects for promotion are limited.

A possible solution to this kind of dilemma is the same as that proposed for planning. A small business firm should consider using part-time consultants to fill those "gaps in expertise."

In family-owned firms, the entrepreneur's children may be recruited—with results that can be positive or negative. An able offspring may provide the firm with talent that could not otherwise be attracted. Alternatively, an unsuited or poorly motivated child may block opportunities for nonfamily personnel.

When selection of key personnel is dictated by family connections, instead of by strategy, the causal direction is reversed. Strategy should be set according to the given staff member's abilities.

---

[2]R. B. Robinson and J. A. Pearce, Jr., "Research Thrusts in Small Firm Strategic Planning," *Academy of Management Review,* 1984, p. 129.

Division of labor. Dividing a firm into various departments, establishing communication channels, and determining the rights, duties, and responsibilities of staff members in each department are among the major tasks of organizing.

In a small firm, however, formal job descriptions are uncommon. The chief executive of a small firm—often its founder—observes much of what goes on and often makes all the important decisions. Consequently, there is little decentralization in most small firms. However, because of the informality of relationships between boss and subordinates and because there are fewer people involved, small firms can respond more quickly to changes in their environment. Bureaucracy doesn't get in the way. Although the range of available expertise may be limited, the small firm can often respond faster and more effectively than a large company. The small company's first-hand knowledge of local facts also contributes to this edge.

When a firm is small, this kind of organizational pattern and set of practices may be effective. As the firm grows, however, poorly established organizational structure and policies can be damaging.

Leading

Leading involves motivating people to do their jobs as planned. The ultimate success of a small business depends on how well its leaders can motivate employees. The Ztel company provides a classic example.

> Ztel, Inc.,[3] a high-tech start-up in sophisticated telephone switching equipment, experienced a very different leadership style.
>
> Its riches-to-rags saga began in 1981, when Henry A. Zannini, Richard A. Epstein, and Michael Lento left a Boston software company and set up shop in Burlington, Massachusetts. Along with William Y. Tao, a software expert from Eastman Kodak, they set out to make a better private-branch-exchange (PBX) telephone system than those offered by AT&T, Northern Telecom, and Rolm. The Ztel founders envisioned a PBX that would carry computer messages over telephone lines at very high speeds, doing away with the need for separate computer and telephone networks.
>
> To obtain more management know-how, Ztel hired Peter S. Anderson to be its president.
>
> Unlike most presidents of small companies, Anderson managed at arm's length. He set up a formal structure and separate operating plans for each division, with little interaction among the units. Kevin P. Moersch, vice-president for sales, says Anderson made decisions based only on information from key lieutenants. "I was never involved in any meeting [with Anderson], and I ran all the sales operations," says Moersch.

[3]L. Therrien and M. Maremont, "How Ztel Went from Riches to Rags," *Business Week,* 17 June 1985, p. 97.

Even cofounder Epstein found Anderson aloof: "I don't know how many times I asked Peter to come to the lab, but he stayed in his office. He wasn't that visible to the troops."

During its final two years, Ztel frittered away $52 million in start-up funds, making it one of the largest venture capital failures ever. Opinions vary about who made what mistakes. But Anderson's failure to build a close-knit team was clearly a major contributing factor. Leadership that promoted communication and voluntary cooperation was lacking.

Controlling

Controlling is a process by which performance is compared with preset goals by identifying major deviations and taking corrective action to prevent unfavorable deviations from recurring. Taking corrective action brings us back to the planning function. The process of managing is an ongoing, continuous cycle of activities.

As we have noted, small companies often have difficulty controlling their operations because their plans are vague and their organization is poorly defined. Fortunately, these prerequisites to good control are found in some new enterprises. The following description of Advanced Technology, a firm with 1,000 employees, indicates that big-company practices can be adapted to small-company settings.

> Much of Advanced Technology's success has come from providing plans and reports to assist the Navy in its acquisition programs. But market niche is only one factor in its growth. Others are the well-thought-out policies that its founders (Robert LaRose, Ronald Hobbs, and Girish Jindia) developed before launching the company. The discipline of management by objectives is the largest single reason for Advanced Technology's success. The company clearly stated its principles and goals in five crucial areas: staffing, management development, marketing, contracts to be sought and fulfilled, and finance.

> Advanced Technology gives every employee a chance to be an entrepreneur and rewards top performers before they request salary reviews. The growing company would create new positions and add layers to its organizational chart so that no executive would supervise more than six entrepreneur-managers.[4]

OVERALL MANAGEMENT OF SUCCESSFUL SMALL BUSINESSES

Small companies, just like large ones, must achieve a reasonable balance and integration of total operations. Not all busy entrepreneurs do this well.

[4]R. C. Wood, "Every Employee an Entrepreneur," *Inc.,* 4 March 1983, p. 107.

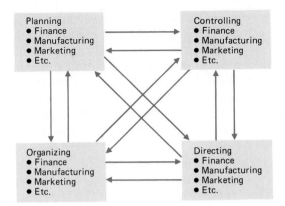

Figure 23.1 Relationship Between Management Processes and Functional Areas

The overall integration task comprises several elements, as is indicated in Figure 23.1.

1. Attention must be given to each of the key functions within the business—marketing, production, finance, and so on. In small companies, the dominant managers often concentrate on only one or two functions, neglecting the others.

2. Each key function has to be managed in a way that makes that function at least adequate and preferably strong. This calls for planning, organizing, leading, and controlling suited to the functions. Because small firms often lack managers who recognize the distinctive needs of various functions, some of these needs are likely to be overlooked.

3. Moreover, both the functions and the management techniques must be integrated. The functional activities must be compatible and balanced, and the management design (the planning, organizing, leading, and controlling) must promote adequate attention and good coordination. Few entrepreneurs think in such abstract terms; most simply deal with problems as they arise. Nevertheless, the informal procedures for conducting the business that do emerge should include these integrating features.

In Chapter 4 we emphasized the useful role of company strategy in securing integrated, overall management. Strategy provides guidance for balancing various functions, and the strategic thrusts set priorities for immediate action. Strategic aid of this sort is fully as important for small firms as it is for large ones.

The Need to Integrate Functional Viewpoints

Apex Equipment Company provides a real-life example of how differently managers from various functions approach the same problems.

The Apex Equipment Company is embarking on its first venture in foreign manufacturing. The company has a successful record in the automobile equipment replacement industry. Auto supply jobbers sell Apex products to the thousands of shops, garages, and filling stations that repair autos and trucks. Of course, the original equipment manufacturers (OEMs) also sell their products in the replacement market. However, Apex has designed its manufacturing activities to handle short production runs, and is thus able to compete with OEMs in the replacement end of the industry.

Apex sees an opportunity to be an OEM supplier in Brazil, and later in other such countries. They are not sure, however, how bold to be in this new thrust. One Brazilian company is already in the business, but its quality is considered inferior. A European producer may set up a Brazilian plant. So, if Apex opens a local plant, it can promptly become a leading supplier for local OEM and replacement parts, probably with tariff protection. Here is a summary of how Apex's functional managers view the Brazilian venture.

Joe Androtti, Apex Production Vice-President. "The fastest way to get started, and with the least risk now, is to rent a small plant in the Sao Paulo area. Then when we are successful and know our way around—say, in three years—we would have to move, presumably to our own larger plant in Belo Horizonte [Brazil's third-largest city, with a vigorous industrial development program].

"A second alternative is to build a somewhat larger—though still small—plant in Sao Paulo. We would just postpone deciding what to do when we outgrow such a plant."

Maude Weaver, Apex Treasurer. "If we located in Belo, we can, in effect, get our new building at half-cost, have no real estate taxes for five years, and also receive a subsidy for training new workers.

"My figures on our capital requirements boil down to this: Renting in Sao Paulo gives the lowest investment, but with rent expense figured in, the production costs per unit would be at least as high as those in our owned plant in Sao Paulo, and we would have to move in a couple of years.

"If we go to Belo immediately, we would hold back on some of the equipment until we needed it. Of course capital is (or should be) a function of actual volume rather than capacity. So our capital investment when sales are running $6 million would not be much higher at Belo than at Sao Paulo—about $3 million total. Production costs per unit should also be about the same. When volume moves above $6 million, the advantages of the larger plant at Belo would really show up."

Paul Nichols, Apex's President. "Key personnel will be our bottleneck in this Brazilian venture, in my opinion. We will need a Brazilian general manager and a Brazilian production manager. I wish we had a Portuguese-speaking financial person to send down, but we don't.

"From a personnel angle, a modest start where we can test and train executives would be preferable. It is particularly difficult to select executives in a foreign country where you don't know the subtleties. I'd feel better about going the Belo route if I had full confidence in the general manager.

"Another consideration is our organization here at headquarters. We have only an export manager who concentrates entirely on foreign sales. I'm not sure how involved our key department managers should or will get in far-off Brazil. Maybe we should be thinking in terms of an international division."

Howard Schaller, Apex Export Manager. "It is always difficult to know how hard to push in a foreign situation. There are at least two reasons for moving fast in Brazil. First, if we are going to stake out a major position, we should get there before others do. There is room for only a couple of manufacturers in Brazil. If we move aggressively, maybe we can discourage others from entering. Second, the government attitude about foreign investments might change quickly. I don't think it will in Brazil, but other countries have had sudden shifts in governments and in economic policy. If we are already set up inside the country, our position is much more secure.

"According to one estimate, we can develop a $12 million volume in our line of business within four or five years. It may be optimistic, but the potential is there. With profit margins there 50 percent higher than in the U.S., this should be a real money maker."[5]

Apex Company expansion is a clear example of interdependence of management processes and functions. In order for Apex to take up the Brazilian venture, they have to determine various functional moves, such as choosing location, selecting size of plant, raising funds, and recruiting personnel. Each functional area in turn has to be planned, staffed, organized, led, and controlled properly. For example, Apex must project its short-term and long-term sales before decisions about plant location and equipment purchase can be made. Qualified people have to be hired for each functional area, including finance, production, and marketing. An appropriate organizational structure must be established to allow the U.S. firm to stay in effective contact with its Brazilian unit. In a complex situation of this nature, a small firm like Apex probably should start by hiring management consultants who are familiar with Brazil to help it evaluate the local environment and make advantageous strategic and tactical decisions.

[5]W. H. Newman and J. P. Logan, *Strategy, Policy and Central Management,* 8th ed. (South-Western Publishing Company, 1981).

Financing Early Growth

Although the basic problems of acquiring capital and overseeing cash flow are similar in large and small companies, the managers in small firms are often so absorbed in other matters that they fail to plan for their future capital requirements. Others use too many controls over cash flow, which also may lead to crises. Many of the financial needs of a small business can be anticipated in a carefully prepared budget. For example, Belafonte Fashions, described in Chapter 19, came to grips with its seasonal cash flow problems when its first monthly cash budget was prepared.

Budgeting helps departments and people work with each other and understand their mutual interests, strengths, and weaknesses. Further, once a budget has been prepared, it acts as a standard of expected performance. Finally, a budget becomes a source of motivation to achieve the budgeted targets.

Figure 23.2 presents a conceptual model of a master budget. It may be noted here that depreciation, a noncash expenditure, is a source of cash inflow; dividends are a cash outflow.

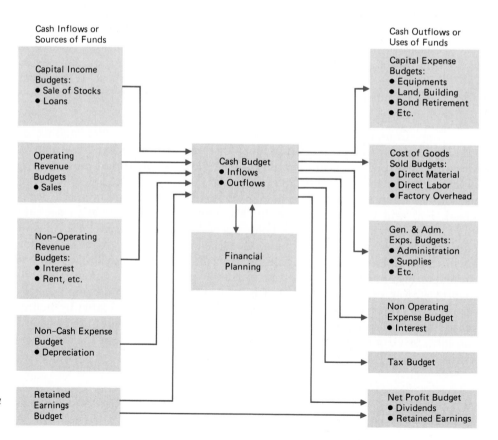

Figure 23.2 Cash Budget and Financial Planning

Source: Adapted from N. C. Bhandari, "Flexible Budgeting for a Small Business," *Journal of General Management,* vol. 7, no. 4, Summer 1982, p. 50.

Data needed to prepare a budget can generally be obtained with foresight and planning. It is not an exclusive domain of large firms.

Producing a Desired Product

Small firms need to find a niche in an attractive domain, just as large businesses do. The difference between small and large companies in this regard is the close tie in small firms between the personal skills of one or two key people and the niche selected. Because the principals of the firm will be directly involved in creating the product or service to be provided, their capabilities tend to dictate the niches that are chosen.

Finding a niche helps a small firm survive in a competitive world. Exploiting that niche requires sufficient financing, quality production, adequate facilities, and effective marketing strategies. From an economic viewpoint, a good idea can become worthless if it cannot be converted into a marketable product or service. We discussed certain financial aspects of small firms in the previous section. This part of the chapter is devoted to some of its production aspects, such as location, product innovation, design, quality, and inventory management.

The Kron's Chocolates case highlights the practical applications of these and other aspects of production management in the backdrop of small business firms.

Kron's Chocolates

Chocolates are made and consumed the world over. It's an age-old business, and competition is keen and widespread. But there is always a place for a high-quality product established in the right location. Kron insisted on locating in New York's fashionable Upper East Side, even though it meant setting up both manufacturing and retailing facilities in a tiny unfinished basement. He priced his chocolates at five times the cost of most American chocolates; his confections go for as much as $25 a pound. But Kron was convinced that his product was worth it. "I have always given my customers the best," he says. "No oils. No artificial anything. I use pure cocoa butter and world's finest cocoa beans." He makes imaginative specialty items, such as golf balls, tennis rackets, and telephones. His customers include celebrities like Barbara Walters and Elizabeth Taylor.

He sold $250,000 worth of chocolate in 1972, the first year of production. Last year, his fifteen-employee, semiautomated manufacturing operation generated an estimated $3 million in revenues. Kron has relied on franchising to build a nationwide chain of chic confectionary boutiques. In twelve major markets, these shops bear Kron's name and sell his products.[6]

Georgena Terry presents another illustration of a small business base

---

[6]A. Fooner, "The Thomas Kron Affair," *Inc.*, July 1982, p. 56.

established around distinctive product design and quality production. It is appropriate to note that both Kron and Terry produce products that they personally like. Like many small entrepreneurs, their early decisions reflect their own preferences rather than a national response to market research. For better or worse, planning is personalized.

Georgena Terry Precision Bicycles For Women

Georgena Terry is a New York frame builder who recently began offering a custom-quality line of production bicycles designed for women's body proportions. She's a painstaking and conscientious frame builder, and quite knowledgeable about frame design and workmanship. It's common knowledge that women and men are differently proportioned. For the same overall height, a women will have longer legs, a shorter torso, shorter arms, narrower shoulders, a wider pelvis, and smaller hands and feet. And, of course, the same overall height is rare: The median woman in the United States is about five feet, three inches tall; the median man, about five feet, eight inches. It's also common knowledge that the bike business has tended to neglect these facts, despite market statistics showing that women form a 55 percent majority of adult bike riders and account for 70 percent of all new participants.

Terry's bikes differ from traditional bikes in several important ways. They are available in sizes that run from 17 to 22 inches, not the customary 19 to 25 inches. Corresponding top tubes are also shorter. The smaller front wheel allows the designer to endow the bike with optimum steering geometry for good handling, the best possible top tube length and seat tube angle to fit the rider, a suitably low bottom bracket for good handling and low standover height, and no toe clip overlap with the front wheel.

Components are chosen to fit smaller people. The smaller frames have 165-millimeter crankarms; stock saddles are Avocet women's Touring I; the handlebars are 36 or 38 centimeters wide (4 centimeters narrower than you'll find on men's bikes), and the brakes use Weinmann levers designed for smaller hands.

Terry's frame building methods are completely conventional. All frames are lugged and brazed. The final hand-filing and sandblasting processes do indeed produce a frame worthy of the slogan "custom quality." The frames that enter the paint booth are smooth and satiny throughout, with nary a nick or rough edge anywhere. When they leave the paint booth with their DuPont Imron coats, they compare favorably with any frames in their price range. (Bare frames are $450.) Some dealers have said that these bikes are underpriced; they may be right.

None of these design attributes is exclusive to or original with Terry. But she is the first to package them all and shout, "Here, women. This is for you." She offers custom-quality $750 bikes, made well enough to be worth more than every penny.

Terry graduated from Pittsburgh's Chatham College in 1972 with a degree in drama. Realizing that there were no jobs in drama, she picked up an MBA from the University of Pennsylvania's Wharton School of Finance and Commerce and a BS in mechanical engineering from Carnegie-Mellon. Before starting her own firm, Georgena Terry Precision Bicycles for Women, in 1982, she worked as a product engineer with Xerox in Rochester, New York.

Her director of marketing, Chris Rugh, in his fifties, has decades of experience in advertising, corporate communications, and the like.

The reason, according to Rugh, the big bike companies aren't offering bikes more suitable for women is that some vice-presidents of the big companies aren't getting out and riding. "They're looking at their 'what-if' market research!"

The Rugh touch is immediately apparent. Terry's brochure is more informative and enticing than brochures from some companies that sell 100 times as many bikes as the 1,000 Terry plans to build and sell this year. A point-of-purchase display card is similarly impressive—and particularly unusual for a small bike company like Terry. And Rugh is rapidly building a first-rate dealer network. His correspondence file bulges with letterheads from the most prestigious shops in the nation. Rugh uses a clever trick to speed the penetration of Terry bikes into the shops. When he receives a sale directly from a consumer, he routes the bike through whatever bike shop that consumer regularly patronizes. The bike shop is called and told, "You just sold Terry." Without any cash commitment, the shop makes a good retail markup—and is told about the even better markup that awaits dealers who stock Terrys.

"There's no substitute for an order," Rugh said. "You can talk marketing all you want, but an order, and cash in the pocket, gets their attention."

And Terry's own charisma is a major factor. In her workshops for women cyclists at events such as the New England Area Rally and Bicycle USA's Great Eastern Rally, she charms the crowd like no man could.[7]

Building Market Recognition

Being newcomers, small entrepreneurial companies always need to build customer recognition. And because the entrepreneur often (though not always) thinks in terms of making a better product, the world of sales promotion is a strange environment. Successful small ventures find some way, within their limited resources, to become favorably known by an appropriate clientele.

[7]J. Schubert, "Georgena Terry," *Bicycle Guide,* April 1986, p.33.

Abington Shoe Company presents an excellent example of how an obscure outfit can transform itself into a successful manufacturer of fancy boots.

Abington Shoe Company[8]

Abington Shoe Company was bought by Nathan Swartz, a Russian immigrant, in 1951. His sons, Herman and Sidney, joined him in 1955. They made a glossy oxford, a moccasin-toe workboot, and a functional, if not handsome, workshoe.

The principal attraction of Abington's products was price; they sold for roughly $4.95 a pair, even in the middle 1960s, which made them very popular with discount stores. "We tried to make a nickel or dime on each pair," says Herman.

In 1968, they decided to buy equipment for injection molding. This process forms thick rubber soles onto any leather upper without stitching, thus eliminating needle holes that leak. The process also eliminated the costly, hard-to-find hand-stitchers themselves. "Injection molding," Herman says, "had the reputation of being used only on the cheapest shoes. But we decided that there was no reason we couldn't make a quality shoe by combining high-grade leather with injection molding. The labor savings were enormous."

Between 1969 and 1973, their sales almost doubled every year. Their leather construction boots, named Timberland, were selling very well. A lot of young people, college students, were buying them.

Herman and Sidney had spotted the first flickers of what was to become a fashion bonfire called the "outdoor" or "survival" look. The corduroy pants, the flannel shirts, down parkas, and rugged boots normally worn around backwoods campfires were soon to appear as any-day dress in the big city. And in a celebration of function, comfort, and durability, the survival look would even become fashion chic.

Most of the initial problems with Timberland stemmed from the Swartz brothers' unfamiliarity with marketing. They were trying to reach a totally new market with the same methods of distribution and advertising they had used in the high-volume business.

So Herman and Sidney were really shocked when Len Kanzer, President of Marwin and Leonard Advertising, recommended that the Timberland boot—heavy leather, mile of thong, thick rubber sole, and all—should be marketed as a fashion item. It had the outdoor look, he said, and the look was in. So take the boot to the "upscale" buyer, that growing crowd of well-heeled and well-educated urban backpackers that wanted the "look" and didn't care what it cost. Put it in Saks, he said, right up there with those sleek, imported slip-ons from England and Italy. Advertise it, of all places, in the *New Yorker*. And finally, he told them to increase their price by five dollars a pair so they could put the difference in advertising.

[8]L. Rhodes, "Sole Success," *Inc.*, February 1982, p. 44.

In effect, Kanzer had asked the brothers to abandon 20 years' worth of business practices. Says Sidney, "We agonized over it. Even raising the price was hard to accept. I mean, we were used to raising prices by nickels, not by five dollars."

Ads began appearing in the *New Yorker*. They were masterpieces of creative advertising and eventually won more than 50 industry awards. They featured a colorful cast of straight-talking backwoods characters who clearly knew a good boot when they saw one. There was a family of moonshiners that included a mother whose face, even in wire-rimmed granny glasses, looked like a pick-ax, and her three boys sporting shotguns, suspenders, and outrageous high-water pants. They all thought Timberland was just fine.

And there was an old man testifying for Timberland from the seat of a log hauler. Not only was he satisfied with his own boots, but he also said he asked the Timberland salesman for "a pair of 13-wides for cousin Luther, double-wide on the left foot where the tractor run it over." Every ad closed with the refrain "A whole line of fine leather boots that cost plenty, and should."

The ads had just the right touch of down-home sincerity to attract the "upscale" buyers—when they could find the boots. Unfortunately, the company hadn't yet signed up any of the big-name upscale stores where the upscale buyers are supposed to go. Most of the company's salesmen didn't know how to sell to upscale department stores. "They were used to the Army-Navy-stores relationship," Herman says. Things changed when they hired Stanley Kravetz, 48, as their executive vice-president.

Kravetz joined them in the summer of 1976. By July, he was tramping up and down Fifth Avenue in New York with a green plaid suitcase stuffed with samples. In the next two years, Kravetz and his remodeled sales team signed up 2,000 new accounts, including a crowd of fancy department stores and an assortment of smaller, upscale retailers.

Even the competition was properly amazed. Says Rick Sherwin, vice-president of Dunham's, "I was very impressed with their marketing approach. It's the kind of thing where you ask yourself, 'Now why didn't we think of something like that?' "

In 1979, the Abington Shoe Company changed its name to the Timberland Company.

The New-Venture Syndrome

Although small businesses face many of the same kinds of problems that confront large companies, and although they can adapt many large-company management practices to their simpler settings, the climate is different. Two common sources of this difference keep reappearing in examples such as those cited on the preceding pages.

1. The personal interests and capabilities of the founders of small companies exert a life or death influence on their ventures. The excitement and commitment that these entrepreneurs bring to the enterprise breathe life into the new undertaking. There is no "going concern" reputation and inertia to provide momentum. Instead, the start-up energy comes from the self-appointed leaders.

   There is a price to pay, however. The founding managers often have strong biases when it comes to priorities. They tend to stress what they personally can do well. There is a lack of breadth. Even when the founders recognize new managerial needs, they usually lack the time and the knowledge to deal with these problems. And they can't afford to hire full-time specialists. Consequently, achieving balanced overall management is very difficult.

2. Transitions in successful start-ups arise often and require rapid adjustment. Capacity expansion, new financing, reorganizations, more formal planning and control—these are the essentials of success. To grasp the growth opportunities that the founders have worked so hard to create, such readjustments frequently must be made within a few months. Strong-willed founding managers may resist these changes, preferring to "do their own thing" in their own way. Thus we see that managerial versatility and adaptability are added prerequisites for managing small businesses. It is often necessary to recruit new executives to manage these transitions.

   Even in the face of these hurdles, small businesses continue to spark much of our economic growth.

CONCLUSION

According to the Small Business Administration's Office of Advocacy, 97 percent of the nation's business firms are small. In addition, 43 percent of the U.S. gross national product is generated by small business. Table 23.2 shows that 39.7 percent of employees are working for small firms with fewer than 100 employees. Small business has also been a leader in offering women and minorities the opportunity for economic advancement through employment and entrepreneurship. Minorities own 5.7 percent of all U.S. businesses, account for 3.5 percent of gross receipts, and tend to be concentrated in the areas of retail trade, services, and construction.

According to a Dun & Bradstreet survey, small business firms planned to create nearly 3 million new jobs in 1986, a decided increase over the 2 million added in the previous year.

Impact on Productivity

A research project conducted for the National Science Foundation concluded that small firms created four times more innovations per research-

Industry	Percentage
All industries	39.7
Wholesale trade	73.0
Contract construction	71.8
Retail trade	54.4
Services	50.3
Finance, insurance, and real estate	36.2
Mining	29.8
Transportation and other public utilities	23.1
Manufacturing	17.0

*Firms with fewer than 100 employees.
Source: U.S. Department of Commerce, Bureau of the Census, County Business Patterns, 1977:
Enterprise Statistics (Washington, D.C.: U.S. Government Printing Office, 1979), Table 2. Cited in H.
N. Broom, J. G. Longenecker, and C. W. Moore, *Small Business Management,* 6th ed. (South-
Western Publishing Company, 1983), p. 32.

and-development dollar than medium-sized firms and twenty-four times as
many as large companies.

Small business also contributes a great deal to values that are beyond
economics and employment. It encourages initiative, innovation, and risk-
taking. It provides self-esteem, social recognition, and a sense of independence from corporate employers. It enables individuals to serve their society through a variety of products and services. Above all, it allows one to
do one's "own thing," which, in turn, fosters free enterprise and democracy.

This zeal for self-expression, innovation, and community service has
enabled individuals and small establishments to make valuable contributions to society. Xerography, insulin, penicillin, the jet engine, the helicop-
ter, power steering, kodachrome, and the ball-point pen are some of such
contributions made in this century. The emergence of the entrepreneurial
economy is as much cultural and psychological as it is economic or technological.

FOR FURTHER DISCUSSION

1. What impact does the small size of a company—
say fewer than 100 employees—have (a) on the desirability of using standing plans, as described in
Chapter 6? (b) on the degree to which decentralization to first-level supervisors is wise? (c) on the internal communication practices executives should
use? and (d) on the frequency of using yes/no controls?

2. This chapter has focused on managing an *entrepreneurial* small business. Now consider managing
a less innovative small business, such as a retail
drug store or a residential construction company.
How would the managerial problems differ between
entrepreneurial firms and more stable firms?

3. Because of the innovative growth of some small
businesses, especially in the computer and electron-

ics industries, several very large corporations like Exxon and DuPont wish to encourage intrapreneurship. What advantages and disadvantages do such large corporations have in sponsoring new ventures within their organizations compared with entrepreneurs starting up new firms?

4. In your opinion, does an undergraduate business degree (or an MBA degree) best prepare a student for (a) a job in an entrepreneurial small business or (b) a staff job in a large company?

5. Currently there is much concern about foreign competition undercutting U.S. companies. Difficulties faced in the steel, television manufacturing, and garment industries are examples. Do you think small companies or large companies will be better able to withstand such foreign competition? Why?

6. Assume that after you graduate you wish to become an entrepreneur. Prepare a feasibility study that will help you get started in your own business right after you graduate. Cover the field that you would enter, your strategy for gaining differential advantage, your sources of capital, and the management design of your new company.

FOR FURTHER READING

Bhandari, N. C., "Flexible Budgeting For a Small Business," *Journal of General Management,* Summer 1982, pp. 40–41, 46–51. Tells how to prepare various types of budgets, including a weighted average flexible budget.

Broom, H. N., J. G. Longenecker, and C. W. Moore, *Small Business Management,* 6th ed. Cincinnati, Ohio: South-Western Publishing Company, 1983. An excellent comprehensive text on small business management.

Cohn, T. and R. A. Lundberg, *Practical Personnel Policies for Small Business,* New York: Van Nostrand Reinhold, 1984. A guide to personnel practices suitable for small firms.

Galbraith, J., "The Stages of Growth," *Journal of Business Strategy,* Summer 1982. Delineates the growth stages of a new venture from the business idea to the self-sufficient firm, and relates these to task, people, reward, process, structure, and leader.

Garland, J. W., F. Hoy, and J. C. Garland, "Differentiating Entrepreneurs From Small Business Owners," *Academy of Management Review,* vol. 9, no. 2, 1984, pp. 354–359. Offers a conceptual discussion of the distinction between a small business venture and an entrepreneurial venture, and between a small business owner and an entrepreneur.

Louis, A. M., "Doctor Wang's Toughest Case," *Fortune,* 3 February 1986, pp. 106–109. Provides insight into the inception, growth, and current problems of Wang Laboratories.

Pennings, J. M., "The Urban Quality of Life and Entrepreneurship," *The Academy of Management Journal,* vol. 25, no. 1, 1982, pp. 63–79. Offers a unique discussion of environmental role in the creation of new enterprises.

Scarborough, N. M. and T. W. Zimmerer, *Effective Small Business.* Columbus, Ohio: Chas. E. Merrill, 1984. An overall review of small business management concepts and tools.

MANAGEMENT IN ACTION CASE 23
The Post-it Innovation

Arthur L. Fry was a choir member in St. Paul who wanted a bookmark that wouldn't fall out of his hymn book but could be moved or removed when he didn't need it.

Fry was also a corporate scientist at 3M, and his solution to his hymnal dilemma became one of his company's most successful new office products—Post-it Note Pads, the sticky note pads that you can move or remove as you please.

Working in his basement and capitalizing on a company policy allowing employees to use 15 percent of their time to pursue their own ideas, Fry figured out a way to make Post-it Note Pads. He used an adhesive that had earlier been developed by 3M colleague Spencer Silver. Silver's glue had been a mistake of sorts; he hadn't made it sticky enough to suit his superiors.

Executives were sometimes impatient with Fry's persistent promotion of his invention, and marketing types were skeptical that it would sell, but 3M secretaries and other office workers got hooked on using the little sheets with the gentle adhesive.

In 1977, marketing tests of Post-it Note Pads in four cities were at first disappointing. But a second market test in Boise, Idaho—dubbed the "Boise Blitz" for the tremendous volume of Post-its that 3M dropped on the city—was much more encouraging.

The product was introduced nationally in 1979, complemented by heavy direct-mail and magazine advertising. Samples were hand-delivered to firms with 100 employees or more. In 1981, it was named 3M's Outstanding New Product. In 1984, it chalked up sales exceeding $100 million. By 1985, it was being called 3M's most successful product since Scotch Tape.

3M didn't forget that the pesky Fry had fathered this phenomenon. The company promoted him to senior scientist, allowed him more freedom to work on his own projects, and gave him the Carlton Society Award, 3M's top scientific honor.

Question

Which of the factors that contributed to Arthur Fry's success do you recommend for other companies wishing to foster intrapreneurship?

For more information, see *Time,* 4 February 1985.

APPLICATION CASES

For practice in applying concepts covered in this chapter to managerial situations, see the following managerial decision cases. The case questions particularly relevant to this chapter are listed by number after each case name.

Fyler International (p. 68) 1
Dayton Metal Works (p. 198) 17
GAIN Software (p. 303) 19
Norman Manufacturing Company (p. 538) 23

24

Managing Service Businesses

LEARNING OBJECTIVES

After completing this chapter, you should be able to

1. More quickly diagnose the unique problems service businesses face.
2. Explain how the distinctive characteristics of a service company are likely to affect planning, organizing, leading, and controlling by its managers.
3. Predict the general effect of the increasing importance of service businesses on management trends in the United States.
4. For any company, design a total management structure that is sensitive to its particular characteristics.

SERVICE BUSINESSES ARE DIFFERENT

Our ideas about how to manage a business have come largely from the world of manufacturing.[1] But do these ideas also apply to organizations that produce *services?* This chapter addresses that question. In responding to the question, we will emphasize again the "contingency" nature of management concepts: Effective management design must reflect the particular characteristics of the enterprise being managed.

Much of the discussion and many of the cases in this book have involved service businesses. Clearly, managers of nonmanufacturing firms can and do use basic management concepts. Nevertheless, a review of the problems of managing a service business will benefit all who wish to make a specific service company more effective.

Organizations that produce services, in contrast to organizations that produce goods, are rapidly increasing in importance. The overall employment picture in the United States evidences that service production has jumped from about 47 percent in 1930 to almost 70 percent of a much larger total in 1980. Figure 24.1 shows the fifty-year trends by major types of business. Twice as many managers today are concerned with services compared with goods, and the trend is continuing.

Actually, the term *service* comprises a wide range of activities. A service is any act, except for the production of tangible commodities, that creates a benefit for other persons. Parachute-jumping lessons, hospital

[1] Although Taylor's Scientific Management and early personnel management centered in manufacturing, there are significant exceptions. H. Fayol's *Administration Industriel et Generale* (1916) reflects experience mainly in mining. Early studies of organization in the United States were based on railroads and public utilities. See R. Robb, *Lectures on Organization,* privately printed in 1910, and R. Morris, *Railroad Administration* (New York: D. Appleton and Co., 1910).

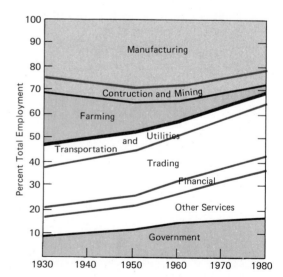

Figure 24.1 Shifts in Distribution of Employment, 1930–1980
Decline in percentage of total workers in the production of goods and increase in the production of services
Source: The Statistical Abstract of the United States.

Table 24.1 SOURCES OF EMPLOYMENT IN THE UNITED STATES—1980

	Millions of Employees
Services Production	
Financial services (banking, insurance, real estate)	5.7
Health care (hospitals,* doctors, other care)	6.7
Education†	6.6
Transportation (airlines, railroads, trucking, buses)	3.3
Communication (telephone, radio and television)	1.3
Public utilities (electricity, gas, water)	1.0
Trade (retail, wholesale)	22.5
Other (business, personal, household services)	15.1
Government, not included in above	10.4
Total services production	72.6
Goods production	
Manufacturing	20.7
Construction and mining	6.6
Agriculture‡	2.9
	102.8

* includes 1 million in government hospitals
† includes 4.8 million in government schools
‡ includes owners and managers

care, funerals, and insurance are all services—as is the production of a television program telling about them. A listing of the major kinds of services produced in the United States is shown in Table 24.1, along with 1980 employment in major divisions.[2]

Perhaps the differences among services—the contrast between, say, supplying electricity and presenting a Broadway musical—are more striking than the similarities. Certainly the management tasks entailed differ sharply. To explore these management implications, we will

1. identify characteristics of service businesses that may affect the way they need to be managed;
2. give examples of how these characteristics shape the planning, organizing, leading, and controlling in representative service companies.

[2]For a full analysis of the place of services in the U.S. economy, see T. M. Stanback et al., *Services: The New Economy* (Totowa, N.J.: Allanhead, Osmun & Co., 1981).

CRITICAL CHARACTERISTICS OF SERVICE COMPANIES

There is a bit of mystery or elusiveness about all service organizations. Their output can rarely be seen, smelled, heard, or felt. Because it is *intangible,* the output is typically harder to define and to measure than a physical product. Of course, we do measure services, especially such things as electricity or promptness of delivery; nevertheless, control of quality is a common hurdle for managers.

Another usual characteristic of services is that they must be consumed as soon as they are produced. For example, it is difficult to store airplane rides or education and take them off a shelf when a customer appears. We often do build and hold ready a capacity to produce a service, but the service itself tends to be *perishable* as well as intangible. Because of this perishability, one rarely sees an *inventory* of finished products listed on the balance sheet of a service company. In addition, the service producer usually deals directly with consumers of its service; you can't send a subordinate or other intermediary to the hospital for the operation you need. Of necessity, service companies must have fairly *close contact with their consumers.*

These typical characteristics of service businesses—intangible and perishable output, minimal finished inventory, and close consumer contact—sometimes do affect the way companies are managed, as we will note later. However, there are too many exceptions to build around them a set of universal guidelines for managing any and all service producers. Instead, as Figure 24.2 shows, we have to combine these features with other characteristics that are dominant in only some companies. Such combinations will enable us to suggest management practices that are likely to be effective—or necessary—when specified conditions prevail. In other words, to provide advice on how to manage service businesses, we fall back to the time-honored *contingency theory* of management.[3]

Many aspects of managing a service company are like those faced by manufacturing companies. For these aspects, managers in service firms can utilize well-developed practices, such as the basic-management devices illustrated throughout this book. However, the unusual and strategically vital characteristics of a service company call for special attention. These so-called critical characteristics may create a need for a distinct form of planning, a particular kind of organization, a special style of leading, or a specific sort of control.

To focus our discussion of critical characteristics, we shall deal with only six features that can have a strong impact on management design in some companies. Moreover, because these six characteristics vary in inten-

[3]See F. Kast and J. Rosenzweig, *Organization and Management: A Systems and Contingency Approach,* 3d ed. (New York: McGraw-Hill, 1979); and C. A. Snyder, J. F. Fox, and R. R. Jesse, "A Dependent Demand Approach to Service Organization Planning and Control," *Academy of Management Review,* July 1982.

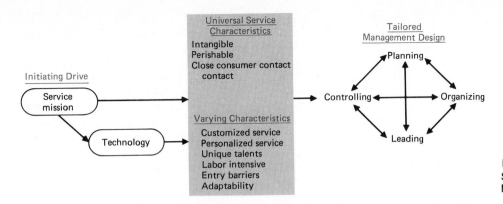

Figure 24.2 Linking
Service Goal to
Management Design

sity from high to low, we will treat each one as a continuum and contrast
its effect at each end of its range.

Customized Service

Some enterprises, such as law firms and advertising agencies, adjust their
services to the unique needs of each customer. What suits Coca-Cola obviously does not fit Chrysler. And it's likely that your tailor does not routinely give you a suit that is the same size as the one he made for the
person who just left his shop.

Customized   ⟵————————⟶   Standardized
service   service

At the opposite end of the scale are companies that give all their
customers one or more of a few standardized services. Commercial airlines,
for instance, fly on set schedules, and it is the customers who adjust their
travel plans. When you go to the opera, you watch what is playing and
hope that it fits your mood.

Clearly, if a company adjusts to the needs of each customer, it will
face special planning and other adjustment problems.

Personalized Service

In some settings, the particular person who creates the service is highly
important to the customer. When a friend takes you to the opera, for instance, you may care a lot whether Pavarotti is singing. And at the brokerage house there is often a particular individual in whom you have confidence because you believe she understands how you want to invest.

Personalized   ⟵————————⟶   Impersonal,
service   institutionalized service

In contrast, for many services we rely entirely on a company or institution, and don't know or care who does the work. The engineer of a train

is not even a name routinely posted in the front of the passenger car. The person who repairs your camera is similarly incognito. Confidence in the service, which may be great, rests on the reputation of the institution.

When an institution, rather than an individual, inspires customer confidence, managers face a different task of motivation and control.

Unique Talents

Occasionally, a service organization is highly dependent on the unusual capability of one or a few very talented members. A creative designer in an architectural firm, a great deal-maker in an investment bank specializing in mergers, a programming genius in a software house—all are examples. Typically, such people are highly paid.

Dependent on   ⟵————————⟶   People with necessary
unique talents   skills are widely available

More common is the opposite situation, in which people with the necessary skills to produce the company's service are widely available. A retail bank and a liberal arts college, for instance, do need highly competent and well-trained staff, and diligent effort is usually required to recruit a well-balanced team. However, the future of the enterprise does not depend on a few superstars.

The superstar situation is more likely to be found in a small company. When it does exist, the management structure must be adjusted to take full advantage of, and retain, the key individuals.

Labor Intensive

The ratio of labor costs to total costs of services sold indicates the extent to which a company is a "people business." (A ratio of labor costs to value added or to total revenue reflects the same labor-intensive characteristic.) For example, the growth and profitability of H&R Block, a nationwide income tax service, depends heavily on recruiting and training suitable personnel.

Labor   ⟵————————⟶   Capital
intensive   intensive

In contrast, while your local electric-utility company must have well-qualified employees, its profitability fluctuates more because of public-utility commission decisions on prices, efficiency of its generating plant, and interest rates on its debt. A low percentage of labor costs to total costs is an important indicator of these other factors. Also popular is the capital intensity ratio, measured either by total investment per employee or by the ratio of capital costs to total costs.

We often assume that all service companies are labor intensive, but this is not always so. Companies that are exceptions are likely to face quite different management problems than companies fitting the broad description.

Entry Barriers

Extreme differences prevail in the ease or difficulty with which service industries can be entered. Planned monopolies are normal in the public utility sector; and in banking, hospitals, and the arts (museums, opera, and so on), established prestige and size often make new entrance very difficult.

$$\text{High-entry barriers} \longleftrightarrow \text{Low-entry barriers}$$

On the other hand, opening up a new auto repair shop, real estate brokerage office, or beauty salon is relatively easy. Here the capital investment is low, licenses to operate can be obtained after only a short training period, and a convenient location can lure customers.

The nature of competition is greatly affected by such entry barriers. Easy entrance encourages strong competition. This forces managers to focus on short-run tactics and competitive costs. Where competition is restricted, managers can plan further ahead, and long-term investment may entail tolerable risks. Many other variations in the structure and imposed regulation of an industry will affect the tasks of managers in that industry.

Adaptability of Capacity

Service companies vary in their ability to expand or contract and, even more important in their ability to switch to new services. Many law firms and public relations firms, for instance, are adroit at moving into women's rights, environmental issues, or product liability as the fashions in litigation change. Similarly, investment bankers enlarge or trim their attention to new stock issues, hostile takeovers, or private placements.

$$\text{Adaptable} \longleftrightarrow \text{Change in services very difficult}$$

Such adaptability contrasts with the locked-in position of an electric utility, which is committed to one sort of service and can change its capacity only at high cost. Airlines, to cite another example, can change routes and schedules, but they face major difficulties with moving into other forms of transportation, let alone with moving into different industries. They have too many large, irreversible investments in equipment and standard practices. Managing the more fluid public relations firm calls for techniques not suitable to airlines, and vice versa.

Of course, service companies will differ from one another in many ways besides the six critical characteristics—customized services, personalized services, unique talents, labor intensity, entry barriers, and adaptability. Nevertheless, examination of a wide range of service organizations indicates that this list suggests distinguishing features that have a strong impact on management requirements. If we know how to fashion our management design in response to these characteristics, we will have gone a long way in achieving what Alfred Chandler calls a "strategy and structure" fit.[4]

IMPACT OF CRITICAL CHARACTERISTICS ON MANAGEMENT DESIGN

Identifying critical characteristics of a service company is only a first step. Managers must next translate the set of characteristics into an appropriate management design for that company.

Our analysis of planning, organizing, leading, and controlling—in Part II to Part V—has already laid the basis for such a translation. In the discussion of each management concept, we indicated the circumstances under which that concept would be most effective. This second step merely applies those insights. Two very different service companies will be used to illustrate the application process.

Characteristic Profile for Specific Companies

A diagnostic grid, such as the one shown in Figure 24.3, is a convenient way to position a service company in terms of the six critical characteristics. Comparison of a company with several others emphasizes the uniqueness of that company.

[4]See Chandler's classic study, *Strategy and Structure: Chapters in the History of Industrial Enterprise* (Cambridge: MIT Press, 1962).

Critical Characteristic	Company Illustrations					
	Management Consulting Firm	Local Telephone Company	Motel	County Seat Law Firm	Investment Bank	Retail Bank
Customized service	5	1	1	5	5	1
Personalized service	4	1	1	5	4	1
Unique talents	3	2	1	3–4	4	2
Labor intensity	5	2	3	5	4	4
Entry barriers	2	5	3	4	3	4
Adaptability	4	1	2	5	4	2
Strength of Characteristic	Hi Average Low 5 4 3 2 1					

Figure 24.3
Diagnostic Grid for
Service Companies

The businesses noted in Figure 24.3 are all different. Because of their divergent characteristics, we would expect their management practices to differ. For example, a motel and a law firm in, say, Tucson, Arizona, would have unlike organization and controls since their services, uniqueness of personnel, and adaptability are almost at opposite ends of the range.[5] Of course, differences in technology, size, and other factors would also affect their management practices.

To show the interrelationships between critical characteristics and management design in more detail, we will trace the major impacts of each characteristic for the first two illustrations in Figure 24.3—a management consulting firm and a local (statewide) telephone company.

Managing a Management Consulting Firm

Consulting firms are a variegated lot. Their services range from providing advice on executive salaries to conducting market research to carrying out time-and-motion studies.[6] Thus, we will use a specific firm for this example.

McKinsey & Company focuses on problems facing corporate executives or general managers of self-contained business units. Changing corporate strategy, integrating operations following a merger, reorganizing to meet global competition, and incentive planning for senior executives are typical subjects of McKinsey engagements. An overall viewpoint, rather than the interest of a single function, is the company's forte. Moreover, company policy states that each engagement must be treated as unique; there are no prepackaged solutions. Founded about sixty years ago by James O. McKinsey, the firm is now one of the most prestigious consultants to top managements in the United States. It also has offices in Europe and the Far East. The ratings in the first column of Figure 24.3 apply to this company.

Impact of customized service.   Because each engagement is considered to be significantly different from previous engagements, McKinsey & Company uses a matrix form of organization. Members of the staff have expertise in various disciplines—marketing, finance, production, human resources, and so on—and each person is loosely attached to one (or more) functional groups. Within each group are various specialists and a range of experience from junior staff to directors (partners).

For each engagement, or what we called a "project" in Chapter 11, a team is drawn from the various groups, and its membership is dictated by the specific situation under study. A senior member of the team is project manager. This is the team that serves the client. They may go to other

---

[5]For detailed studies of strategies and structures of British service industries, see D. F. Channon, *The Service Industries: Strategy, Structure and Financial Performance* (London: Macmillan Press, 1978).

[6]See D. H. Maister, "Balancing the Professional Service Firm," *Sloan Management Review,* Fall 1982.

members of the firm for information or suggestions, but it is the team that puts together the analysis and recommendation.

Incidentally, because of the uneven flow of work, a staff member may be on more than one team at any particular time. As each engagement unfolds, some people may be added to, and others dropped from, the team. Individuals play different roles on various teams, depending on need and availability.

A predetermined set of duties for each staff member is not practical because the work is customized. If the services provided were standardized—as is the case, for example, for some types of market research or for common operations in a hospital—then normal roles and relationships could be established. Actually, there will be some repetition and some variation in almost any task. When the variation becomes dominant, as in the McKinsey approach to consulting, the organization must be very adaptable. The matrix form provides this adaptability.

Customized service also poses difficulties in quality control. For services such as those that McKinsey provides, both the definition of good quality and the measurement of results in those terms are thorny. As the company grows and necessarily delegates to project managers the choice of advice to be given, quality control becomes more elusive. And each engagement has its own criteria for what constitutes good work.

In these circumstances McKinsey executives make limited use of postaction control over quality. They don't try to assess the correctness of the advice given, after the action, in situations in which they are unfamiliar with all the facts and issues. Instead, they rely primarily on *control of the process,* largely in a *steering-control* mode.

Control of the process starts with (1) having only highly competent individuals with strong professional values on the staff. The control points here are at selection, training, and promotion. Then, (2) engagements to be undertaken are carefully screened. The questions to be answered before an engagement is accepted are as follows: Does the company have the capability to do first-class work on this particular problem? Is there a good probability that the client will follow our advice? Are conflicts of interest involved? Is the nature of the work consistent with company strategy? Can we schedule the job with qualified staff in the required time frame? Incidentally, bringing in new business is highly rewarded in McKinsey, as it is in other consulting firms, so the application of the above standards may clash with the personal interest of the member who develops an opportunity that is being turned down.

The aim of staff-selection and engagement-selection controls is to create a situation in which quality work is likely to be done. A further process control lies in (3) the use of guidelines for working with clients and for programming the engagement. In this activity, a senior director of the firm does oversee the project manager, reviewing the initial program and the periodic revisions as the project unfolds. This is a steering control, as defined in Chapter 18. The underlying concept is that for highly customized work, the most effective controls are to have the right people assigned to a sound project following a well-designed program of action.

Some postaction evaluation of projects does take place in the performance reviews of individual staff members. Even here the viewpoint is future-oriented: What can be learned from past work that suggests ways to improve future effectiveness? This leads back to the first control listed—building a competent cadre of consultants.

Customized service has a third, related impact on the way McKinsey is managed. Staff members must exercise a high degree of self-control because of the delegation to project teams and the inability to measure and control output directly. Effective, low-key *leadership* is crucial to enabling such self-control. A wide array of attitudes and values are important—pride in work, confidence, integrity, dedication to serving the client, mutual help among the staff, and willingness—even eagerness—to work under pressure to meet deadlines while not sacrificing thorough analysis. McKinsey managers must be adroit in using the concepts outlined in Part IV to encourage widespread commitment of this sort. The people being led are themselves sophisticated, perceptive individuals; they will quickly detect whether the leading is respectful, sincere, and consistent. If it is not, the organization and control practices just described have too much opportunity for selfish maneuvering.

Impact of personalized service.   Personalized service, while not as pervasive as the customized character of the work, is nevertheless a prominent feature of McKinsey & Company activities. Many of the staff members are highly respected by clients, and the clients may request that particular people be assigned to their engagements.

One consequence of such personalization of services is a further pull for *decentralization*. Most clients, especially the sort served by McKinsey, will know whether the individual who inspires their confidence has a strong say in the recommendations. To take advantage of this valuable confidence link, the project team, which includes the confidence builder, perhaps as project manager, must be free to decide what will be proposed.

Such decentralization is quite compatible with the matrix organization that grows out of customized services. The addition of the personal tie to a client reinforces the key role of project teams. Of course, the personal tie does place a constraint on the composition of the project team, and to that extent it complicates the overall allocation of staff to projects.

Theoretically, the personal tie to a client should not affect the quality control process. In fact, there is a subtle shift in influence. The individual whose participation has been requested often feels a proprietary interest in the engagement and may be less responsive to progamming suggestions. Whenever one's personal reputation is directly involved in an event, he will push harder to run it his own way. To some extent, control by the formal structure is weakened.

Leadership takes on an additional dimension when clients want a particular staff person to work on their engagement. The possibility that a superstar will quit and the client will thus be lost lurks in the background. The leader's task of keeping such a person an enthusiastic member of the team may become more difficult and more important. Most people tend to have an exaggerated opinion of their own value, and the client may not be lost even if the superstar quits; nevertheless, that is an unknown that the leader would prefer not to test. Turnover of prestigious staff members is something to avoid, especially when dealing with an intangible, unmeasurable service.

Impact of unique talents. A company (or division) with unique *talents,* as we are using the term here, will have one or more members who are so gifted that company strategy centers around utilization of that skill. Instead of finding people who fit a strategy, the strategy is fitted to the person. During the early days of Disney Productions, for instance, its planning and organizing were designed to take advantage of Walt Disney's unusual ability to create animated cartoon movie films. Some law firms and research laboratories are similarly structured around exceptional individuals.

McKinsey & Company does not seek unique talents to this degree. Rather, its selected mission to serve top managers *as a firm* is the dominant theme. It prefers an image of being reliable and careful about progressive changes. Incidentally, Tom Peters, the imaginative senior author of *In Search of Excellence,*[7] resigned from McKinsey because he wanted to write and speak in his own way. Because McKinsey opts to stick to its central mission, it does not face the problem of designing a management system around unique personalities.

Impact of labor intensity. A high ratio of labor costs to total costs characterizes beauty shops and garbage collection as well as consulting firms. Thus, the emphasis on using people effectively may arise at various salary levels and in diverse technologies. Whatever the level, our specific management techniques for allocation and control of people do differ from the more formalized quantitative, and presumably exact, techniques used for capital.

In the broader planning, organizing, leading, and controlling, however, the same basic concepts apply to labor and capital alike. In this more comprehensive scope, the important issue is to be sure that managers focus on the major resource—be it labor *or* capital—and do not get trapped in a financial planning and control system that doesn't highlight the key variable.

Because labor is *the* major resource used by McKinsey, the availability of personnel is the primary factor in company *planning.* The issue of who is available when is the major constraint in accepting and programming specific engagements. Capacity for growth must be expressed in terms of the number of qualified staff members. Expansion into new areas depends to a considerable extent on availability of personnel. For example, the company does not have offices in Latin America largely because of the difficulty of attracting and retaining local people that fit into the McKinsey way of consulting. Clearly, then, in planning, availability of the

[7]New York: Harper and Row, 1982.

right people—not capital—severely limits the options that can be considered.

Motivation of people in a business such as McKinsey becomes unusually critical. No computer system or automated plant can relieve the pressure. As already noted, decentralization combined with only indirect quality control forces heavy reliance on the motivation of the consulting staff. And this motivation has to be fostered by company leaders. All companies need *leadership;* the degree of dependence on its skillful exercise is especially high in McKinsey & Company.

Impact of entry barriers.　McKinsey management is not very concerned about the entry of new competitors into its domain, and it does not change its management design because of competition. There are two explanations. First, entry is easy and, in fact, common. Little capital is required to start, and almost any unemployed executive or hungry professor can announce that he is a management consultant. Their personnel resources are limited, however, and they operate predominantly on the fringe of market, doing tasks that McKinsey would be unlikely to undertake. More serious are spin-offs from the big firms. For a variety of reasons, two or three partners who are already well known may decide to start a new company of their own. However, McKinsey simply accepts such competition as the normal state of affairs and concentrates on being a quality leader in its particular niche.

The second reason for minor attention to entry barriers is a belief that doing superior work today is the best defense for tomorrow. Much like a law firm, McKinsey relies on its reputation as a firm and on the reputations of its directors to surmount competition. In effect, a good reputation serves as a barrier that new consultants must overcome. The intangible, unmeasurable nature of consulting services does force potential new clients to rely heavily on reputations. From McKinsey's management viewpoint, then, resorting to competitive maneuvers to discourage new competitors is inappropriate. Instead, the focus should be on doing superior work with present clients. This has the double effect of serving today's clients professionally and at the same time making it a bit harder for those ever-present competitors to win engagements that McKinsey would like to have.

As in sports and the performing arts, there are numerous competitors. Nevertheless, a few recognized stars attract followers in spite of competition. The critical task is to perform in a way that maintains one's standing as a star.

Impact of adaptability.　The issues that McKinsey analyzes for its clients keep changing. How to manage a global business or clarify the corporate culture, for example, have become vital issues only in the last few years. If the company is to adequately serve its target market, it must be prepared to tackle such problems as they arise.

Since customized service is a central feature of McKinsey strategy, adapting to new issues is relatively easy. At least the company does not face resistance from whole departments that have specialized in a limited number of activities—as is often the case in other companies. Moreover, in-house training sessions on recent developments are held regularly as a part of staff development. Consequently, a pattern of adapting to change is already well established.

Even so, the company takes special steps to build understanding and enthusiasm within its staff for tackling the latest business challenge—be it downsizing or confrontation with an advocacy group. An important device for achieving such a shift in interest is frequent *participation* by individuals throughout the organization in studying changes in the business environment. When a significant change is identified, staff members anywhere are asked to describe relevant experience with comparable problems. Also, early company engagements dealing with the new problem are carefully evaluated, and a summary of the experience is circulated. In other words, there is no central planning unit that sends out bulletins on how to deal with fresh issues. Rather, members of the consulting staff itself do the internal planning.[8]

Summary comment. In the consulting firm just discussed, we note the following:

1. Some, but not all, of our six critical characteristics of service companies have a strong impact on the way the firm is managed. In other service companies, the particular mix of important characteristics will be different.

2. Management's response to one influence often eases adjustment to another influence. For instance, the matrix organization that fits customized service also lends itself to the decentralization needed for personalized service. Similarly, the flexibility needed for customized service helps to achieve the adaptability necessary to deal with the changing problems that confront top managements. In other companies, such convenient reinforcement may not exist. One aim in formulating any company strategy is to do things that are compatible and reinforcing. Such synergy, as we have found in the McKinsey example, is no accident.

3. A focus on service characteristics such as we are pursuing in this chapter does not tell the whole story. Other company features, like size and technology, also influence management design. They, too, are important, but they don't happen to be central to the service variable (the "contingency") that we are exploring here.

---

[8]Chris Argyris reports in *Strategy, Change and Defensive Routines* (New York: Pitman Publishing, 1985) that consultants, as well as business executives, may not be as open to new ideas as these paragraphs suggest. A serious hurdle arises when a change becomes threatening to an individual, and thus calls for additional learning skills. Fortunately, the kind of learning described here is usually not threatening to staff members of McKinsey & Company.

Managing a Telephone Company

Service companies vary widely in their technology and managment design. Management consulting firms typify highly professionalized, individually tailored services. On the other end of the scale are large bureaucratic companies that provide familiar, dependable services day after day. In terms of employment and contribution to the gross national product, the latter enterprises are much more important. We will use a typical statewide Bell Telephone Company to illustrate the management problems of such businesses.

As a first step toward understanding the management tasks of our Bell Company, we should note its profile on the six critical characteristics of service firms. The second column of Figure 23.3 shows that the telephone company appears toward the opposite end of the range for most critical characteristics when compared with McKinsey & Company. This immediately suggests that it will have to be managed differently.

Impact of standardized service. Both technology and government regulation require that the Bell Telephone Company offer identical services to all its customers in each category. This is in sharp contrast to the customized services of a management consulting firm.

The standardized services enable Bell Telephone to achieve the efficiencies of mass production. In the *planning* process, standard operating procedures lead to dependable, predictable, and efficient work patterns. In *organizing,* the large volume of repetitive activities permit a high degree of division of labor and the use of a functional organization. Indeed, most of the concentrated attention and skill that develops in such specialized units can be duplicated in each local region. Furthermore, standardization of repetitive operations makes close *quality control* feasible. (It was in the Bell System that the renowned statistical quality control techniques were developed.)

In the future, as new electronic communication systems are developed, it is possible that Bell will provide somewhat less standardized services in addition to the familiar telephone calls that we all make day after day. However, the millions of calls each day will be managed by a factory-like system for years to come.[9]

Standardized services, then, lead to a management design that is very different from the design that serves McKinsey so well.

Impact of impersonal service. The idea that the production and sale of services leads to a personalized relationship between the producer and consumer, and that we consumers develop confidence in the work of specific individuals whom we know personally, simply does not apply to Bell. Increasingly, we just push buttons, and when we do hear a human voice it

---

[9]See J. Browne, *Management and Analysis of Service Operations* (New York: Elsevier-North Holland, 1984); and J.A. Fitzsimmons and R.S. Sullivan, *Service Operations Management* (New York: McGraw-Hill, 1982).

is likely to be a recording. On the rare occasions when we do talk to some-one, that person is likely to be pleasant and helpful, but we don't know who it is nor do we expect ever to deal with that individual again.

An advantage of such impersonal service is Bell's unusual degree of dependability and speed—almost like the flow of electricity we expect from the flip of a light switch. But what kind of management is necessary to achieve such dependability? It is not the decentralized, permissive man-aging style we found in McKinsey. Instead, there is a tight set of instruc-tions each person must follow if the complex, highly interdependent sys-tem is to work. Indeed, a lot of effort is devoted to training, preventive maintenance, and back-up equipment to be sure that deviations do not occur. Changes come, not in adjustments to one-of-a-kind particular needs, but through thoughtfully designed refinements in the total system; and these refinements are typically made by centralized planning groups rather than by local performers.

Disinterest in unique talents.   Bell has limited need for employees with unique talents (as that term is being used here). Instead, the com-pany focuses on employing competent, reliable people who take continuing pride in producing good service. A Bell company by its very nature must be a bureaucratic institution, and it is not free to shape its activities around the unusual talents of particular individuals.

Although gifted mavericks do not fit in the Bell Telephone system, the company does occasionally need some prodding force for change. Con-centration on providing dependable, low-cost service tends to block out at-tention to basic shifts in the communication industry. Historically, though, Bell units relied on their corporate parents to employ mavericks to con-ceive of new forms of service.

Impact of capital intensity.   Bell Telephone companies have a very high capital investment per employee—in sharp contrast to McKinsey. As electronic technology improves and automation increases, the capital in-tensity will probably rise even more.

Because the choice of correct equipment is so important to the future of the company, and because engineering and other plans can be laid out in specific and quantitative terms, Bell plans its capital allocations in great detail. Each request for funds must be supported by a full description of what the money will be spent for, how this project will fit into the rest of the system, and the expected benefits and rate of return on the invest-ment. The preparation of such documents calls for an extensive planning system covering ten to twenty years!

Capital intensity at Bell also leads to detailed plans for maintenance, and to comprehensive controls over the use of capital. Even before comput-ers were available to spew out a glut of ratios, Bell calculated hundreds of financial control ratios—many dealing with the use of capital.

Impact of entry barriers.   For almost a century, Bell Telephone Com-pany held a monopoly on telephone service in its state. By law, competitors could not enter. Now, with deregulation—and new technology—several other companies are beginning to offer related or substitute services. For example, other firms with satellite connections hope to skim off the profitable segments of long-distance calls; some even use Bell lines to do so. Large customers are experimenting with their own transmission, especially of computer data; interactive cable television might bypass the telephone lines. Unless Bell meets at least part of this fringe competition, it will end up with only the unprofitable segments of the business.

The organization and planning practices just described are well suited to a stabilized business, which the regulated monopoly provided. However, this management design lacks flexibility in dealing with competition. It is engineering-oriented and ponderous. To survive when the entry barriers are down will call for more marketing orientation and fast response.

The high entry barriers of the past led to a way of managing that has been very effective in that setting. A change in the entry barriers poses new problems that this proven structure was never intended to confront.

Impact of stabilized structure.   The dilemma faced by the managers of Bell Telephone Company is that they need *both* the existing structure and an adaptive one. The large mass of their activities now, and in the foreseeable future, are well served by their stable management design, which has been refined over many years.

On the other hand, to deal with the new competition that has already appeared and new opportunities just around the corner, a more adaptable management design will be required. Tests are already being made of new ways to transmit computer data; transmission of facsimile copies of drawings, photos, and so on is possible but costly; checkless money transfer is common practice in Japan; mobile phone units are available in most big cities; remote reading of electric and gas meters seems likely soon. These are the kinds of services Bell should be able to offer to segments of its market.

To coooordinate both the marketing and production of such new services, the company needs "product" divisions in its organization. And because these new divisions will rely heavily on at least parts of the existing organization, a matrix design may have to be superimposed. Marketing of any new service will be an additional activity, probably independent of the prevailing "customer service" units. In other words, to secure the desired adaptability Bell will have to change its organization—and its planning—substantially.

Perhaps more difficult will be a shift in attitudes, values, and habits. Faster and riskier decisions will have to become acceptable in some, but not all, areas. More concessions to customers' preferences must be anticipated. Jockeying for competitive position will be a new consideration in programming. Employees will face more frequent modifications in their work and more uncertainty about their future. Such changes as these will call for new leadership styles.

By no means clear is how Bell Telephone Company can achieve the adaptability sketched in the three preceding paragraphs and at the same time retain its traditional strengths. Some semi-independent product divisions, akin to single-line competitors, will probably emerge. As soon as the technology and markets for any single service stabilize, however, there will be a strong push back toward functional planning and organizing. When this occurs, lower costs and dependable quality of service will again become more dominant than adaptability.

In the future, then, Bell Telephone will need *both* the traditional management system that works so well for its standardized services and, at the same time, more flexible systems to promote new services in very competitive markets. We have few examples of companies that have successfully maintained both kinds of management designs under the same roof. How well Bell overcomes this hurdle will affect the quality and convenience of services that are used almost daily by all of us.

Managing Other Sorts of Service Companies

The telephone company and consulting firm represent two very different kinds of service companies. And our review of the management design suitable for each one shows dramatically how diverse the planning, organizing, leading, and controlling may be. Many other configurations are possible, depending on the profile of critical characteristics of a specific company.[10]

As companies diversify their product lines or modify the scope of their services, the task of selecting an appropriate management design becomes more complicated. Three examples will illustrate the need for careful analysis.

Mixed service requirements.   The banking industry is in a state of flux. Traditional services provided by commercial banks for individuals are being mechanized. At the same time, the bigger banks are moving into "investment banking," which is largely a customized and often personalized service. As the analysis of standardized telephone service and customized consulting service suggest, banks need very different planning, organizing, leading, and controlling for these two types of business. And if the banks also move into insurance and stockbrokerage, their management design must become even more complex.

It is likely that banks (or insurance companies) seeking to provide a "department store" array of financial services will have to establish quite separate divisions, each with a compatible set of services *and* with an organization design fitted to those services. Whether a single central management will be capable of supervising such diverse groups remains to be seen.

---

[10]For examples of the diversity of service company characteristics, see the many cases in W.E. Sasser, R.P. Olsen, and D.D. Wyckoff, *Management of Service Operations* (Boston: Allyn and Bacon, 1978).

Goods and service mixtures. The distinction between goods-producing and service-producing companies is blurred. Many manufacturers now accompany their products with installation, advice on use, maintenance, and other services. Your neighborhood oil dealer will take care of your oil-burning furnace and decide when to refill your tank. And the provisions of such services call for a service-oriented management structure.

IBM is an intriguing example. You can either buy or lease most of their computer products. If you choose to lease, does this make IBM a "service" company? For large computers, regardless of whether you buy or lease, IBM will help design your information processing, train your workers, maintain the equipment, and provide software. If you take the full package, clearly you are buying a lot of services. One of the great achievements of IBM is its capability of producing and selling both products and services in an integrated way. And one of the reasons that IBM had trouble with personal computers is that providing both physical products and associated services at this level calls for a very different management design than the one for commercial computers.

Innovative service companies. A few companies have succeeded in providing on a large scale local services that include high social interaction. Friendly motel chains and McDonald's fast-food restaurants are examples. Such services traditionally have been provided by small, local enterprises. The key is to retain the local service on a decentralized basis, yet secure the benefits of large-scale mass production.[11]

The characteristics of such companies and the managerial structure that is essential to their success have been identified by Richard Normann in his penetrating analysis of ways to deliver consumer services.[12] A special blend of planning, controlling, and leading is vital. The potential for growth of companies that can achieve this sort of management is great.

These examples indicate that in the banking, computer, and personal service industries, our ability to find new syntheses of planning, organizing, leading, and controlling limits the kind of growth that will prosper. The need and the possibilities for *management* innovation in these and other service activities is a major challenge for the next decade.

CONCLUSION

Managing service businesses poses a diverse array of opportunities. Indeed, the concept of service embraces a wider variety of activities than does manufacturing. It is unrealistic to hope that some magic formula will

[11]See J.M. Carman and E. Langeard, "Growth Strategies for Service Firms," *Strategic Management Journal,* Jan. 1980.

[12]*Service Management: Strategy and Leadership in Service Businesses* (Chichester, England: John Wiley, 1984).

simplify the life of all service managers. Instead, even more resourceful-ness will be needed as we move further into a service economy.

Fortunately, most of the management concepts—the tool kit—that have been developed for the production of goods are equally appropriate for service enterprises. The processes of planning, organizing, leading, and controlling are as vital for one sector as the other. We don't need to scrap or shelve large blocks of what we have already learned. Nor have a set of ideas suitable only for services emerged. We can keep building on what we know.

One lesson does stand out in the analysis made in this chapter. Each service company needs a management design carefully tailored to fit its particular characteristics. The nature of the managerial task depends on the technology and strategy being followed, and corresponding adjust-ments should be made in the planning, organizing, leading, and control-ling of the company. This contingency view is not new, but it is particu-larly urgent in the service arena because of the diversity of work performed. A set of six "critical characteristics" was presented in the chap-ter to assist in diagnosing these managerial requirements of a service com-pany.

A second theme that keeps recurring in the chapter is the crucial importance of managing people. Because services are intangible, the man-aging of service companies tends to be "softer"—outcomes are more diffi-cult to measure and to manipulate than in manufacturing. Consequently, more reliance must be put on motivating people. The leadership style that is appropriate varies with the nature of the business, as we have just noted. Nonetheless, the human element looms large in most service pro-duction. It is here, rather than in physical engineering, that the greatest opportunities for improvement seem to lie.

Impact on Productivity

Economists say that productivity gains in the service sector are more dif-ficult to achieve than they are in the production of goods. This is partly a measurement problem; we have no adequate way to "count" the improve-ment in such areas as legal services, entertainment, government, even ed-ucation. What is more basic, major productivity increases in most services do not come from buying new equipment or better materials—as they do in agriculture, for example. Rather, we have to rely on *people working with other people,* and here there is rarely a high multiplier effect when we add more bodies. We may even get in each other's way and spend more time writing memos! All this means that managers in the service sector will have to be more skillful to secure the annual productivity increases that we have come to expect.

A related concept is the need to shift our focus from happy workers to productive workers. The difficulties of measuring output, and particu-larly quality, of services have made it easy for managers in service com-panies to accept the happiness push. The assumption was that contented workers would be more productive. Recent research suggests that the linkage is not so simple. The challenge is to combine both personal satisfaction and productivity. Managers in the service arena may have to induce cultural shifts about entitlements and about output if this worker source of productivity gains is to be realized.

FOR FURTHER DISCUSSION

1. Where would you place the following on the diagnostic grid shown in Figure 24.3: commercial airline, nursing home, beauty shop, advertising agency, opera company, real estate broker?

2. Midas Muffler & Brake Shops runs a national chain of small shops that feature automobile muffler replacement service "guaranteed for as long as you own your car." Service on brakes and shock absorbers is also provided. Compare the planning, organizing, leading, and controlling that you think would be optimum for this enterprise with that for a local garage/filling station. Why has Midas been successful even though it offers only a very limited range of auto repair services?

3. (a) Explain in your own words the *differences* in leadership style that you would recommend for McKinsey & Company versus a state's Bell Telephone Company (the two illustrations discussed in this chapter). How do these differences relate to the critical characteristics of the two companies that are listed in Figure 24.3? (b) How does your answer to (a) relate to the approach to leading discussed in Part IV of this book?

4. Two of the "Big Eight" public accounting firms have recently been prosecuted because a few of their employees made illegal certifications of company financial statements. There are many more instances of questionable advice given to clients regarding tax reports. While such occurrences are a very small part of the thousands of actions taken by employees, they do have a serious impact on the credibility and reputation of the firm. Assume that the CEO of one of these large accounting firms asks you how to *control* the actions of employees in its many local offices located throughout the country. What would you recommend?

5. Both commercial airlines and management consulting firms may operate in foreign countries as well as in the United States. How, if at all, does expansion from domestic to international operation affect the optimum management design (planning, organizing, leading, and controlling) for (a) a commercial airline? (b) a management consulting firm?

6. Television broadcasting involves several distinct activities, including (a) the production of shows to be broadcast; (b) the selection of shows by networks, the scheduling of the shows, and the sale of advertising time to accompany the shows; and (c) the direction by local stations and cable franchises of network programs to receiving sets in homes. For this question, set aside the production done by the networks (for example, news, sports broadcasts) and by local stations. Use the approach of this chapter—see Figure 24.2—to recommend a management design for a, b, and c. Do you see any conflict or coordination problems in uniting a, b, and c into a harmonious service?

7. Richard Normann reports that the Swedish health-care system, in its search for efficiency, took "big manufacturing industry" as its model and concentrated production into huge hospitals. Personnel policy, research and development, logistics—all became centrally managed and standardized. As a result, the system has become a monument to inefficiency. (a) Why do you think the Swedish moves have not worked well? (b) What activities in a hospital, if any, should be decentralized? Explain.

FOR FURTHER READING

MacMillan, I. C., M. L. McCaffrey, and G. Van Wyck, "Competitors' Responses in Easily Imitated New Products," *Strategic Management Journal,* Jan. 1985. Insightful study of unrecognized entry barrier in a service industry (commercial banking).

Mills, P. K. *Managing the Service Organization.* Cambridge, Mass.: Ballinger, 1986. Contrasts practices and procedures appropriate for service versus industrial companies.

Mills P. K., J. L. Hall, J. K. Leidecker, and N.

Margulies, "Flexiform: A Model for Professional Service Organizations," *Academy of Management Review,* Jan. 1983. Focuses on how "professionals"—physicians, lawyers, accountants, and so on—can organize their firms.

Normann, R., *Service Management: Strategy and Leadership in Service Business.* Chichester, England: John Wiley, 1984. The most penetrating and creative book available on managing service companies.

O'Neill, H. M., "Turnaround Strategies for Service Firms." A paper presented at the 1985 annual meeting of the Academy of Management. Explains how characteristics of service companies affect their choice of turnaround options.

Thomas, D. R. E., "Strategy Is Different in Service Industries," *Harvard Business Review,* July 1978. Briefly describes a range of actions that service companies might take to improve their growth or profits.

MANAGEMENT IN ACTION CASE 24
The Bell Breakup

On January 1, 1984, Ma Bell was forever changed. Under orders from a federal judge, American Telephone & Telegraph Company spun off its twenty-two operating subsidiaries. The world's most efficiently operated telephone system was suddenly thrown into turmoil.

For the operating companies, which had long enjoyed the monopolistic guiding hand of ATT, the breakup presented monumental management challenges—perhaps too monumental, at least in the short run. A year later, business and residential customers across the nation were complaining that basic phone service had become too complicated, confusing, and costly.

The troubles resulted in part because the federal government had not fully eliminated regulatory barriers obstructing the free competition that supposedly had been the objective of the breakup. But it was also clear that the Bell operating companies were having a tough time sorting out who was supposed to provide what products and services to whom.

Customers suffered. Jack Seitz, a Minneapolis restaurateur, complained, "ATT showed you basically what was best for your setup and you put it in. Now you have to call three or four people. You don't have the security of ATT. And when you're done, it doesn't seem any better or cheaper. We've got all this choice, but I'm not sure I wanted it."

Too, a year after the breakup, some benefits that proponents of divestiture had promised had still not appeared. Long-distance rates fell, but the declines did not offset local rate increases, as they were supposed to. Billing became puzzling to consumers, who were suddenly paying more than one source for a variety of phone services.

In waging the antitrust suit that resulted in the breakup, the U.S. Justice Department had argued that divestiture would spur competition and bring improved products and services to the market at lower prices. Certainly the breakup sparked competition in the long-distance market and prompted introduction of a bevy of new services. But customers seemed to prefer good, reliable, easy-to-get phone service to high-tech frills.

By late 1985, little had changed, at least in consumers' eyes. A *Wall Street Journal* survey found that 33 percent of those who had bought a phone or had one installed since the breakup thought service was worse than before divestiture; only 10 percent thought it was better.

Still, federal Judge Harold Greene, who presided over the AT&T breakup case, was sanguine about the future of phone service in America. "There's still a substantial amount of regulation, and it takes time to sort itself out. Competition has been the engine that has driven the American economy."

Question

Do you think Judge Greene was wise in insisting on a breakup of the long established AT&T system?

For more information, see *The Wall Street Journal,* 17 Dec. 1984.

APPLICATION CASES

For practice in applying concepts covered in this chapter to managerial situations, see the following managerial decision cases. The case questions particularly relevant to this chapter are listed by number after each case name.

Heartland Union Bank (HUB) (p. 183) 20
GAIN Software (p. 303) 19
Delphi Insurance (p. 316) 22
Graham, Smith, & Bendel, Inc. (p. 442) 3, 20

Index